Miracle Yoga

~ • ~

Christian Yoga

Based on

"A Course in Miracles"

Donald James Giacobbe

Miracle Yoga Services

Published by Miracle Yoga Services
— miracleyoga@gmail.com —
Cottonwood, Arizona

Printed in the United States of America

BISAC Subject Codes and Headings:

OCC027510 Body, Mind, and Spirit: Spirituality—*A Course in Miracles*

OCC014000 Body, Mind & Spirit—New Thought

REL012120 Religion: Christian Life—Spiritual Growth

Library of Congress Control Number: 2023901984

Author: Giacobbe, Donald James

Miracle Yoga:
Christian Yoga Based on *A Course in Miracles*

ISBN 978-0-9843790-7-1

CONTENTS

~ o ~

PART TWO: MIRACLE YOGA AND *A COURSE IN MIRACLES*

Chapter 6. East/West Philosophies . . . 201

Chapter 7. Miracle Relationship Yoga . . . 251

Chapter 8. The Course applied to Miracle Raja Yoga . . . 293

INTRODUCTION

~ • ~

THE ART OF ALLOWING

When Henry Luce published the first edition of *Time Magazine*, he condensed the news and divided it into nineteen categories. One of these categories was religion. Since then, the news has progressed into the era of television with its own messaging categories in which religion gets an occasional sound bite in the nightly news. There is no problem with religion being one of the categories and sound bites in the news. But you may want to ask, "Has my life itself become a collection of categories and sound bites with religion playing a minimal role?"

What works for a magazine or television news does not work so well in living a meaningful life. There has to be something more to life than separate allotments of time for work, eating, sleeping, sex, recreation, relationships, and religious ceremonies. There has to be something that overlaps and supersedes all the categories. That something is your divine life that interpenetrates all the categories of your life and gives meaning to everything you do and, more importantly, to everything that you are.

The question is: "How do I become increasingly aware of this divine life and allow it to be expressed in my daily living?" This book is an introduction to the *art of allowing*, which is a means of answering this question. The art of allowing enables you to let everything be what it already is. This art seems unnecessary since it changes nothing and simply accepts what already is. The art of allowing would be totally unnecessary if it were not for the human tendency to desire things to be as they are not. This tendency is commonly known as denial, but the extent of denial that is present in everyday life is not as well known. Denial permeates every aspect of life because denial is centered on your perception of your personal identity. If you are in denial about your own true nature, everything you see and experience will be perceived through the eyes of denial. You have not lost your divine life because of your failure to perceive it due to denial, so regaining your divine life is merely a change in perception allowing you to let go of denial.

The art of allowing allows you to let go of denial and accept and express the divine life that is already within you. The art of allowing is the fundamental principle of the combination of yoga and Christian spirituality, called "Miracle Yoga," which is the central theme of this manual for integrated spiritual living. This book is a companion to the book titled, *Christian Meditation Inspired by Yoga and "A Course in Miracles,"* a guide to God's presence within. Seeking and finding the divine presence can be achieved through the holding of one spiritual thought in meditation and through releasing all other thoughts during contemplation. In addition to practicing meditation and contemplation, there are many other ways of seeking to find and express the divine life that is already within you. These ways of seeking will be the focus of the following chapters of *Miracle Yoga,* which describe affirming and living in the Christ that you are.

You may attend the Sunday services of a particular church, or you may not participate in any religious organization. In either case, I will assume you are already a follower of Christ or are open to becoming one. If you want Christ to be just another category you squeeze into your busy life, then this book is probably not for you. However, if you want Christ to become the central goal of your life that affects all the categories of your life and gives them meaning, then this book may be helpful for you. There are a variety of ways to grow toward the goal of living in Christ. This book offers two specific directions for you to consider, hence the book is divided into two parts.

Part One is: "Miracle Yoga as a Way of Life." It consists of the first five chapters that explain how yoga can help you to allow the Christ within you to manifest through you. The Christ within you is your true Self, your true Identity as the holy Son of God. Hatha yoga body postures and breathing practices are described as a means allowing the body to be a fit temple for the expression of the Christ within you. One general and minimal definition of the term "Christian yoga" is that it is simply a combination of healthy hatha yoga practices and believing in Christ. Yet this book will use the term "Miracle Yoga" to emphasize that the specific kind of Christian yoga described here is more than a set of physical activities for health purposes. Miracle Yoga is a spiritual path affecting all aspects of your life.

Part Two of this book, "Miracle Yoga and *A Course in Miracles,*" consists of Chapter 6 through Chapter 12. It provides the philosophical basis for the practice of Miracle Yoga, which is based on the principles of the book titled "*A Course in Miracles,*"[1] referred to here as the "Course." Miracle Yoga based on the Course is not a religion. It does not have any central authority, and it has no collective worship rituals, such as a Sunday service. It does have only grassroots meetings, called "study groups," which are led by students of the Course who want to share with others in a learning experience. The Course's spiritual teachings and practices are universal, and they can be applied to your personal and private spiritual practice without interfering with whatever religious affiliation you may have.

Miracle Yoga is introduced in Part One of this book and describes only some of the general influences of the Course on your spiritual practice. The second half of the book provides a much more detailed description of how to integrate the teachings of the Course with yoga. If you decide the Course itself is not your cup of tea, you can still practice a comprehensive Christian yoga path without adopting the principles of *A Course in Miracles*. In that case, you can benefit from the postures, breathing practices, and meditation techniques described in this book, which can be used by any followers of Christ regardless of their theological beliefs.

Whatever benefit you gain from this manual for living in Christ will be due to your degree of *openness*. It takes a certain degree of openness for a follower of Christ to consider the value of yoga since it originated in the East rather than in the West. An even greater degree of openness is necessary in order to carefully examine the principles of *A Course in Miracles*. These principles can be very challenging for anyone who is accustomed to traditional Christian thinking.

You will also need an open mind in order to practice the art of allowing, which requires you to let go of old ways of perceiving and to accept new ways of thinking. The art of allowing is a way of perceiving differently that allows you to let go of what is false and has always been false and to accept what is true and has always been true. Learning the art of allowing is the purpose of Miracle Yoga, as well as the purpose of studying the principles of the Course. The word "allowing" implies the willingness to open up and let yourself be. Even in the activity of doing the yoga postures and breathing practices that will be explained, there can be this sense of allowing by letting go and being just as you are. More importantly, the art of allowing refers to having a completely open mind. One of the biggest stumbling blocks for Christians is the false assertion that having strongly held dogmatic beliefs is the same as having a strong faith. Faith in God means trusting in divine providence and that trust should certainly never be set aside. However, maintaining your faith as your personal trust in God is different than holding on to inflexible beliefs that actually may be preventing you from having a closer relationship with God.

To experience God in your life is far different than investing in your concepts of God. When your experience of God changes, you will need to be open-minded enough to allow your concepts to change so they can come into alignment with your direct experience. Clinging to one unchanging concept of God would imply that your concept defines God. The truth is that God is unlimited and cannot be fully defined or limited by concepts, which by their very nature are limited. Your concepts of God will reflect your concepts of yourself. Your concepts of yourself can be an asset or drawback to your relationship with God. If you are in denial about your own divine nature in oneness with your Father, you will perceive God as being separate from you, and this produces a sense of alienation from God.

The concepts in this book are different from just obtaining general information about a topic since the goal here is to overcome denial that affects your limited concept of yourself. If you get general information, it will not necessarily have an impact on your life. If you can change your concept of yourself, it will affect every aspect of your life, since your self-concept is the filter through which you perceive the world. Also, a change in your self-concept will change your perception of God. If you can change your self-concept and learn to accept your own divine nature, you will be more likely to experience the closeness of God's presence within you. Because of the change in your self-perception and the acceptance of your own divine nature, you will be able to let go of formerly held dogmatic and limited concepts of God. Therefore, I am asking you to have an open mind that will allow you to consider changing your thinking both about yourself and about God.

Practicing Miracle Yoga involves having an open mind, but I am asking you to be open to the ideas presented in *A Course in Miracles* that form the basis of Miracle Yoga. One of the basic principles of the Course is expressed by the following quotation: *"I am not a body. I am free. For I am still as God created me."*[2]

The concept that you are not a body is a direct challenge to your self-concept based on the ego that says you are a body. Your ego tells you that your body proves that you are separate from God and you are separate from your brothers and sisters, who are also bodies. Are you going to accept the evidence of your body as proof that you are not united with God and with your brothers and sisters? You do spend most of your day attending to your body. You use your body to engage in all of the aspects of daily life, including work, eating, sex, recreation, relationships, and religious ceremonies. Even when you let go of body awareness during such activities as sleeping or meditating, you still take your body with you to participate in those activities. But consider for a moment this question: "Where will you *not* take your body?"

This is a question that is normally not asked because you have assumed that you are your body since you take it with you wherever you go. Yet there is a time when this question comes to center stage in your life. That time is when you are facing death. The fact of death means the body will stop moving and you will finally be confronted with the fact that you cannot take your body with you. If you are going to continue beyond the world of form, you will have to take seriously the idea, "I am not a body." But why wait until then? It is better to accept this truth now, rather than when the loss of the body is forced upon you by circumstance.

The body is the symbol of limitation. If you can release the thought that you are a body, you can begin to realize your true Identity as a spiritual being—a formless and free spirit because God created you that way.

> Everyone has experienced what he would call a sense of being transported beyond himself. This feeling of liberation far exceeds the dream of freedom sometimes hoped for in special relationships. It is a sense of actual escape from limitations. If you will consider what this "transportation" really entails, you will realize that it is a sudden unawareness of the body, and a joining of yourself and something else in which your mind enlarges to encompass it. It becomes part of you, as you unite with it. And both become whole, as neither is perceived as separate. What really happens is that you have given up the illusion of a limited awareness, and lost your fear of union. The love that instantly replaces it extends to what has freed you, and unites with it. And while this lasts you are not uncertain of your Identity, and would not limit It. You have escaped from fear to peace, asking no questions of reality, but merely accepting it. You have accepted this instead of the body, and have let yourself be one with something beyond it, simply by not letting your mind be limited by it.[3]

If you can learn to release your ego-based body identification even temporarily, you can begin to identify with your true nature. You can begin to consider the possibility that you, as a spirit, are already united with the Spirit of God, Who created you as an extension of Himself. The acceptance of yourself as God created you in union with Himself is the whole point of the art of allowing. This art of allowing sounds simple and, in fact, it is simple because it is an allowing of your divine nature to be as it already is.

One of the hardest things to accept about your divine life is that you already possess it *now*. Your divine life is not given to you in the future as a reward for your worldly good deeds. This is a radical idea that will require your openness because it is challenging to traditional Christian thinking. The radical nature of the simple idea of your union with God is why the art of allowing is called an "art," since it takes a certain amount of skill and intuitive insight to be simple rather than complicated. The different forms of the world, including the form of your body, produce an apparently complicated world—a world of separation that "proves" you are separate from God. Yet the appearances of separation are merely illusions. The art of allowing enables you to come to the very simple conclusion that illusions are illusions. Seeing illusions for what they are allows you to let go of them. This dispelling of illusions removes the blocks to your awareness of reality, enabling you to accept the simple reality of God's union with you now.

The learning of any art, including the art of allowing, is a gradual process of acquiring skill and insight over a period of time. Yet the art of allowing is a matter of moving your awareness from time to the timelessness in which you were created. This learning process will take faith in God, as your loving Father and Creator. This faith will enable you to disregard the body's false evidence of separation and to trust in His Spirit manifesting through you and through your body. There is no need to deny that you, as a spiritual being, are using a body, but that is quite different from thinking that you are a body. At first glance, the idea that you are not a body would seem to contradict the practice of yoga since yoga is generally associated with body postures. But this appears to be a contradiction only if you believe that yoga is mainly about twisting the body into a pretzel.

A deeper understanding of yoga reveals that yoga, similar to the Course, is about allowing the body to be a device used to help reveal your true divine nature to you. The Course offers spiritual principles that provide a framework for transcending the body and for recognizing the changeless divine life that is within you. Miracle Yoga provides a helpful structure specifically showing you how to direct yourself toward spiritual awakening. But the yoga aspect of Miracle Yoga is only a means of spiritual transformation, and it is not the goal. The primary and most important goal of Miracle Yoga is to become aware of the light of Christ within you and to allow that divine light to shine outwardly into the lives of your brother and sisters. The art of allowing that is the heart of Miracle Yoga is a surrender to the divine influence and divine life in you, which allows you to be guided by your true Teacher, Who is the Holy Spirit.

CHAPTER 1

~ • ~

REGAINING MEANING

A. WHAT IS YOUR MEANING?

What word can lead to despair or to hope? What is this fifteen-letter word that can be a reason for suicide or a reason to set out on the spiritual path? The word is "meaninglessness." When you encounter meaninglessness in your life, you may decide to respond by moving in the direction of darkness or in the direction of light. Hopefully, you will look for ways to bring more meaning into your life. Perhaps that is why you have picked up this book to consider its message of hope. On some occasions it may appear to you that you have lost meaning in your life and would like to find the meaning that you have lost. The title of this chapter is "Regaining Meaning" to emphasize the idea that you can reacquire your meaning, even if your life may seem meaningless. Your meaning is waiting for you to rediscover it.

When I was a child, I lost my glasses while my family was visiting my aunt's house for a few days. I told my aunt, "I'll find my glasses by not looking for them." She made a face of disbelief, but my glasses soon appeared without any effort spent on finding them. Even though I could not find my glasses at first, I did not think of them as lost. I knew my glasses were right there in the house just awaiting discovery that would come in due course as part of the natural flow of events.

Many years later while living in Sedona, Arizona, I decided to climb Bell Rock, the mini-mountain in the shape of a bell. There was no way I could get to the very top of this landmark red rock formation, but my plan was to climb one of the spires that has a tiny plateau at a short distance from the pinnacle. I slept over on that plateau. On the following morning, I stood at the edge of the plateau. In order to get a better view downward, I bent my body slightly forward right at the edge and looked straight down at the bottom. Suddenly my glasses slipped off my face, and I had the presence of mind not to reach for the glasses as they fell from my face down to the bottom. I remember quickly resisting the impulse to grab the glasses, which could have resulted in my body slipping and following the glasses to the bottom. I could not climb down that side of the mountain to look for the glasses because the vertical ascent was too steep on that side for a novice climber like me. After I did climb down the easy side to the base of Bell Rock, I did not look for my glasses by walking around to the other side of the rock formation to where the glasses had fallen. I did not look for my glasses for a different reason than the reason given above in the other example of lost glasses. This time I understood that the glasses were lost and not only lost but damaged as a result of the fall. And even if I found the glasses, they would probably not be worth keeping so there was no reason to look for them.

What do these two examples of losing my glasses have to do with the loss of meaning in your life? How you view your meaning will determine whether you find meaning in your life or not. In the first example, I did not think my glasses were lost, but just briefly out of my awareness. Thus I found the glasses effortlessly. If you can think of your meaning as not being lost, but just hidden from your current awareness, you demonstrate your trust in the divine within that helps you to awaken your awareness of your true meaning. In the second example, I could not find my glasses, not because the glasses were unfindable, but because I determined that they were damaged and not worthy of finding. If you think your meaning is damaged, you will think it is lost to you and furthermore not worth finding. This way of thinking becomes itself a stumbling block to uncovering the awareness of your meaning that has never been really lost.

The primary problem you have with finding your meaning is your thought that you have lost it and that it is damaged and is not worth finding. You believe this because you think that your meaning is up to you to decide. This could only be true if you had created yourself and if in your creation of yourself, you manufactured your meaning. Fortunately, you did not create yourself. God created you, and He gave you your meaning when He created you. Because your meaning rests eternally in the Heart of God, it cannot be lost or damaged. Your true meaning simply awaits your inevitable discovery.

Do you really believe that God will change His Mind about your meaning? Your meaning is your divine life and your divine life is your existence. For your meaning to become lost you would have to cease to exist. You cannot cease to exist and lose your meaning any more than God can cease to exist and lose His Meaning. Would the God of Love leave His children open to the possibility of oblivion? You cannot cease to exist and lose your meaning and divine life because that is not God's Will for His children. God's Will has established and has protected your meaning not only from extinction but also from being damaged in any way.

Unfortunately, you believe that the impossible can happen. You believe that there is a way that you can express your will that will result in counteracting God's Will. You believe that the misuse of your will can remove your meaning that has been established and protected by God's Will. You think you can change your meaning and damage your meaning. You think you have committed "sins" that have harmed your relationship with God and harmed your meaning. But sins are merely mistakes that can be corrected. Sins do not place an indelible mark on your soul that can take away your meaning. Your sins cannot change your meaning, which is eternal and unchangeable. Because God has established your meaning, you are eternally worthy of Him. You do not have the power, even with the evidence of your apparent sins, to convince God of your unworthiness.

However, you do have the power to convince yourself of your own unworthiness. Herein lies your invitation to fear, guilt, pain, sickness, depression, and even death. When you believe that you are unworthy, you are disagreeing with God's knowledge of your meaning and worthiness. Can you disagree with God and expect to be right and God to be wrong? Your self-imposed devaluation of yourself is an attempt to disavow your meaning, your worthiness, and your divine life in God, which is your inheritance. Your divine inheritance cannot be lost, but it can go unclaimed through your denial of it.

Your sins seem to justify your denial of your divine inheritance on the grounds of your unworthiness. Nevertheless, your sins are only errors in perception that can be corrected but never had the power to change the meaning God placed in you in your creation. Perhaps you have experienced that terrible moment in using a computer when you had worked a very long time on a file, and then you inexplicably made a mistake. You pressed the wrong button and the filed was deleted! You probably sat there in stunned disbelief. If you were a beginner, you would not know about backup systems or ways of undeleting deleted items. Therefore, you would not have known that what you had lost was not really lost. You may not have seen the file on your screen and may not have had the computer expertise to regain access to it, yet the deleted file was there in the computer ready to be regained.

If you had this computer experience as a beginner, you thought that your mistake of deleting the file had created such damage that it could not be corrected. Similarly, this is how you look upon your sins that you think have damaged you. You believe that your sins are your decisions that have damaged your meaning and therefore changed your meaning. But it is simply a mistaken perception to think you have the power to change your meaning. You believe your sins are deserving of guilt and punishment that you perhaps mistakenly think are assigned to you by God as "divine karma." However, guilt and punishment are actually assigned to you by yourself. Fortunately, your sins are only mistakes that can be corrected. Yet it makes it harder for you to correct your mistakes if you think they are uncorrectable. You will think your sins are uncorrectable if you also think your sins were decisions that have changed your meaning.

If it were true that your meaning is up to you to decide, what would that mean? It would mean that your meaning is as confused and as unstable as your everyday thinking, which fluctuates from day to day and even from minute to minute. If this were true, your meaning would be as uncertain and changeable as the wind that blows in one direction and then in another. What could this mean, but that your meaning is so unstable that it becomes meaningless? But the truth is that your meaning is as certain and constant as the Source of Meaning from which you come. You can decide to continue to invest in illusions that have no meaning and that block your awareness of your true meaning, but you cannot establish your true meaning for that is beyond the power of your decision. Yet you do have the power to accept your meaning just as it is. This decision will not change your meaning, but it will change your awareness of your meaning.

Be glad that your true meaning is not up to you to decide or to change. Perhaps you have heard the New Age saying, "You create your own reality." The truth is that *you create your own unreality*. But the unreality that you create is fortunately merely an illusion. When you unmask this illusion, you will discover your reality and your meaning have been with you all along. Your various spiritual practices will not change you as God created you. Your spiritual practices will bear fruit as they help you to recognize your meaning, your divine life, and your true Self, as you always were, are now, and will be forevermore.

B. HOW TO ACCEPT YOUR COMPLETION

The goal of this book is for you to live in Christ—meaning to find and accept your meaning, which is your divine life. Your divine life in Christ is a state of awareness in which you love all of God's creation with whom you share divine Oneness. Unlike attaining lesser goals that give only a partial sense of completion, gaining the full awareness of love for everyone will obtain a true sense of completion and of wholeness. This goal of completion seems like a very lofty aspiration that you may or may not accomplish at some future date. Ironically, this ultimate goal has already been accomplished since your divine life has never left you. The truth of your divine life is a constant and remains the truth regardless of your current awareness. God already accomplished your completion in His creation of you. You cannot change your true nature of loving Oneness with Him and with all that exists.

Unfortunately, due to the current ego-based human condition, you are unaware of God's gift of completion and wholeness. You have the power to deny the truth. The power to deny is the power not to know. Through the power of belief, you can believe whatever you want to believe, and it becomes subjectively true for you, even if it is objectively untrue. You are not starting with a blank slate right now because in your present condition you have already denied the truth. It takes constant effort on your part to maintain this denial. This effort to hide your divine life can make your life seem meaningless, boring, unsatisfying, and tiring.

Your effort to hide your divine life consists of substituting your life and your will for God's Life and God's Will in you. Because of denial, you perceive yourself as being separate from God. This perception of separation is your ego that you have accepted as your identity to replace your true God-given Identity. God remains within you even without your awareness of Him. But without your awareness of God's divine life in you, you will also be unaware of your sense of being complete. You can find your completion by looking within for God's divine presence, hence Jesus affirms in the Bible, "the Kingdom of God is within you."[4] However, your ego awareness tells you that you are incomplete and that you need to look outside of yourself for completion rather than within.

The reason why you cannot find the divine life within you here and now is that you are looking for completion outside yourself, and it can only be found within yourself. The Old Testament assertion that you should not worship false gods, false idols, may seem dated and not relevant to modern life for a follower of Christ. However, whenever you are seeking for completion outside yourself, you are seeking a false idol because you are denying the completion that God Himself has already given to you.

Accepting the completion that God has already given you is a matter of learning the *art of allowing*. The question is, "Can you accept your completion by allowing God to be God in you?" Your first step in accepting your completion seems to be so elementary and so obvious that it appears that it would be unnecessary to learn. This initial teaching of the art of allowing is that the truth is true and reality is real. Another way of saying this is that the false is false and illusions are illusory. You may feel that you already know this. But the lesson that the same is the same is not as easy to grasp as it first appears. This lesson of sameness needs to be learned if you seek completion outside yourself because your outer seeking consists of looking upon what is the same as though it were different.

If you are seeking your completion in idols outside yourself, you are constantly making choices in the world of form to find forms that are pleasing to you. Your choices give you a temporary sense of power, self-sufficiency, and self-satisfaction. As long as you can keep making many different choices, you can mistakenly convince yourself that you are making progress toward seeking your completion. You are constantly making choices apparently between two different things or two different courses of action. You are thinking that one choice will give you satisfaction and another choice will not. But what you fail to realize is that none of these apparently different outer choices will bring you the satisfaction you are truly seeking.

Revealing the divine life within you is the only way to bring forth the satisfaction you are seeking. However, if you are unaware of the divine life that is within you, you will fail to see that you are merely choosing between illusions, thinking they are different. You may fill your life with "busyness." Therefore, you will be in constant motion shifting from one choice to another, from one activity to another and making as much progress as a hamster in a treadmill. The illusions you are choosing between may have different forms that make them seem different, but they have the same meaningless content. If you are choosing between illusions, you are not really making a choice because either choice will bring the same unsatisfactory result.

The time may come when the veil of denial is lifted from your awareness. Then you will see that you are merely choosing between illusions that appear different, but the removal of denial will allow you to see that these illusions are actually the same. Seeing that you are choosing between illusions reveals the meaninglessness of your choices. Thus you will realize your choices, which had temporarily satisfied you, will no longer be fulfilling because you understand that you have not actually been making real and meaningful choices. You may perceive for the very first time that you are living an apparently meaningless life. This stage of awareness is reminiscent of the lyrics of a very old song, "Is that all there is?"

This sense of meaninglessness can be a shocking revelation, which potentially can lead to depression and despair. But it need not be so.

It can also be a significant turning point for your life—an opportunity for *real choice* to occur. When you have seen the sameness of all illusions, you can see there is no difference between them. Yet you can give up the temptation to make them appear different in your mind and remove the desire to choose between them.[5] Realizing this leads to the option of real choice. Real choice is the choice between what is different. Thus real choice is the choice between illusions and reality, which are indisputably different. Also, real choice involves the choice of accepting idols sought to manufacture your completion or accepting your divine life and the completion already given to you by God. You can learn in a systematic manner how to make real and meaningful choices, but only if you can overcome denial.

If you can realize you have been in denial, you can then correct your denial. The cloud of denial can make what is untrue about you appear to be the truth in your eyes and make what is unreal appear to be real to you. Denial can give you the power to deceive yourself, but not the power to change the truth or to change reality. The art of allowing does not have any effect on truth or reality since these have been established by God and thus cannot be changed in any way. However, the art of allowing does help to restore your awareness of truth and reality. The art of allowing allows the truth to be true for you and allows reality to be real for you. Your idols take the place of God and letting go of your idols through the art of allowing allows God to be God in you.

When your denial is removed, you will see your idols for what they are. Your idols make a promise to you that they cannot keep. Your idols promise to complete you and give your life meaning but do not deliver on their promise. Your idols seem to give you what you want. You seek an idol, and if you do not obtain it, you are dissatisfied. Even if you do obtain the idol, it still does not provide the satisfaction that you thought it would. Your idols will still make you feel incomplete because only the divine life of God in you here and now can satisfy you. You already have everything that you want and need because you already have God's presence within you. But you will need to learn how to claim what you already have. You can learn to accept God's presence and His completion of you by understanding and applying the art of allowing.

C. WHAT IS "MIRACLE YOGA"?

As was stated previously, the term "Christian yoga" is used in a very general sense to indicate any use of yoga for the purpose of drawing closer to Christ. In this sense, a Catholic, Protestant, or other Christian seekers can practice yoga to grow toward their spiritual ideal in Christ. Of course, various spiritual seekers will have different definitions of Christ and therefore different ways of seeking to follow the Christ ideal.

As a specialized form of Christian yoga, "Miracle Yoga" is based on the philosophy of *A Course in Miracles*. The Course is set forth in three parts of one book: The *Text* states the various spiritual principles. The *Workbook for Students* offers daily lessons for one year of putting the spiritual principles into practice. The *Manual for Teachers* provides a guide for becoming a teacher of these spiritual principles.

Traditional Christian denominations typically believe that Jesus is the Christ and is the only Son of God. Following Christ in the West has become for many, although certainly not all, a form of external seeking without an equally important component of inner seeking. If you maintain the traditional Christian belief in Jesus as the only Son of God, you can practice a general form of Christian yoga as a means of inwardly drawing closer to Jesus.

The Course and Miracle Yoga offer an alternative to the belief that Jesus is the only Son of God. "Is he [Jesus] the Christ? O yes, along with you."[6] The difference between Jesus and you is that he is the awakened Christ and you are unaware of your true Christ nature.

In his [Jesus's] complete identification with the Christ—the perfect Son of God, His one creation and His happiness, forever like Himself and One with Him—Jesus became what all of you must be. He led the way for you to follow him. He leads you back to God because he saw the road before him, and he followed it. He made a clear distinction, still obscure to you, between the false [illusions] and true [reality]. He offered you a final demonstration that it is impossible to kill God's Son; nor can his life in any way be changed by [illusory] sin and evil, malice, fear or death.[7]

In the Course, Jesus describes himself as your awakened "elder brother" and your equal in Christ. "There is nothing about me [Jesus] that you cannot attain. I have nothing that does not come from God. The difference between us now is that I have nothing else. This leaves me in a state which is only potential in you."[8] Jesus is not more loved by God than you are. If you are open to the guidance of Jesus, he can assist you to become what he is now by helping you to wake up to your true nature as the holy Son of God. Also, the Holy Spirit's function is to guide you to your awakening. The Course helps you identify with your true divine nature as Christ and serves as a "Christian Vedanta" forming the underpinning for your practice of Miracle Yoga.

Miracle Yoga expresses the art of allowing, which is the ability to accept what is in accord with your divine nature and release what is not in accord with your divine nature. The result of the art of allowing is a balance of the body, mind, and spirit working together to produce integrated spiritual living. Miracle Yoga is this integrated expression of your divine life, which is experienced inwardly and also manifested outwardly. The principles of *A Course in Miracles* are fundamental to the practice Miracle Yoga because these concepts help you to make a transition from identification with a self-concept of limitation and separation to an acceptance of the divine life that is within you.

A self-determined form of Christian yoga without the Course can be a path in its own right that can be followed all by itself within any religious tradition. Also, the Course can stand alone as a path in itself that can be followed. You may choose either one individually, but the option of combining them in the practice of Miracle Yoga is presented in this book for your consideration. What Miracle Yoga has to offer is an emphasis on finding your divine life within you through specific yoga practices and then expressing your divine life outwardly. Thus you can become a "spirit vessel" or "Christ vessel" through which blessings can flow into the lives of others.

Obviously, this would require a holistic approach to yoga that goes beyond just the body postures and breathing practices of *hatha yoga*. Miracle Yoga includes inward meditation, which is called *Miracle Raja Yoga*. There is outwardly expressed selfless action called *Miracle Karma Yoga*. In addition, there is love referred to as *Miracle Bhakti Yoga*. Also, there is the use of the intellect in *Miracle Jnana Yoga* based on the study and practice of Course principles. These disciplines of Miracle Yoga are described in upcoming chapters of this manual with a greater emphasis on Course principles in the second half of the book.

Your own personal form of Christian yoga without the Course can be practiced as a way of seeking Christ through meditation, selfless action, love, and knowledge. Yet the importance of relationships is the specific reason why I recommend including the principles of the Course in your practice of combining yoga with following Christ. Yoga as it originated in India does not mainly emphasize relationships. Traditional yoga does include some outward spiritual practices, most notably the devoted action of karma yoga practiced in everyday living. However, traditional yoga is so centered on finding the divine within through attunement to God that there is not an equal emphasis on relationships. In contrast to traditional Hindu yoga, Miracle Yoga as it is presented here places an equal emphasis on both inward seeking and relationships. It is true that tantric yoga includes practices of sexual relationships as a form of divine seeking, but in Miracle Yoga the focus is on relationships in a much broader all-inclusive context.

Miracle Yoga is a means of unraveling the major mystery of life, which is the riddle of your own true Identity. In Miracle Yoga, the awakening of your true Identity can be summarized in two statements, which have equal significance:

You will find your true Identity within.
You will find your true Identity with the help of your brothers.

Both statements are necessary, otherwise you may conclude that Miracle Yoga is mainly a solitary path of finding every answer, such as the awareness of your true Identity, by looking within. Your true Identity is in God's Oneness. But you cannot find your true nature in God alone because God is not alone and you are not alone. Your brother's true Identity is in the Oneness of God, as yours is. Because you and your brother share in the Oneness of God, you also have an eternal relationship and bond with each other. Your relationship and bond with your brother is a part of your true Identity. In this sense, you have a unique Identity based on your direct relationship with God, but you also have a shared Identity because of your divine relationship with all of your brothers in the Sonship. Consequently, in Heaven, you will know yourself as having your own Identity, but it will be a divine Identity joined in relationship with both God and your brothers. For example, if you were one branch of a tree, you would know yourself as being connected to the trunk, but also joined in a relationship with every other branch on the same tree with the same sap following through you and every other part of the tree.

The fact that you and your brothers are one in God is hidden from your awareness in this world by your allegiance to your ego identity based on the mistaken idea of separateness and incompleteness. Your spiritual path on the earth consists of overcoming your apparent sense of separation from God, but also your apparent separation from your brothers. Just focusing on seeking within can increase your awareness of your divine nature. Yet the outer aspects of your spiritual path are equally important for uncovering your awareness of your connection with both God and your brothers.

Allowing your brothers to help you on your path and likewise you helping your brothers on their path are your means of accelerating your awakening. Through your mutual assistance to each other, you become aware of the true depth of your spiritual connection with your brothers, and you increase your awareness of your common divine Source. Yet the way you perceive your brothers is crucial in determining whether or not you will make spiritual progress through your relationships. The danger is to make your brother into an idol and therefore take a step backward in your spiritual growth rather than a step forward.

You cannot find your completion outside yourself because God's divine life within you is your completion, so you must look within for your completion. However, if you make the mistake of seeking to find your completion outside yourself, you will be tempted to perceive your brother as someone to complete you. By seeing your brother as your means of finding completion, you make him into an idol. It is easy to imagine that two incomplete beings can join like two halves of a circle and become whole. This is the illusion many partners have about their marriage relationship. When this illusion is unmasked, the result may be divorce in which each partner claims the other failed to make them complete. Before entering any relationship, it is best to realize that your brother or sister should not be asked to complete you since neither he nor she has the capacity to complete you.

If you assign your brother the task of completing you, your brother will become an idol who will dissatisfy you and whom you will reject eventually. Idols cannot satisfy your need for completion, which can only be provided by God's presence within. Idols are fabricated as a result of your own mistaken belief that you are incomplete. This belief becomes projected onto your brother so you will perceive him as being incomplete also. Your relationship with your brother will not produce the completion that you are seeking because your ideas of incompleteness about your brother will only reinforce your own perception of yourself as being incomplete. Your faulty perception of yourself and your brother will retard your spiritual progress, but you can learn how to change your perception. The obvious way is to look within, and through your contact with the inner divine presence, you can become increasingly aware of your completion that is your true nature in God. This inner seeking is your direct means of awakening your sense of completion. Having this experience can change your perception of yourself.

But there is an indirect means of uncovering your completion and changing your perception of yourself. This indirect means involves you changing your perception of your brother, which in turn will change your perception of yourself. Learning how to perceive your brother's divine nature and completeness can have the effect of convincing you of your own divine nature and completeness. Outward seeking does not reveal your divine nature and completeness, but perceiving the divine in your brother is a positive form of outward seeking that can be used successfully for this purpose. For this kind of outward seeking to be most effective, it should not be your only means of awakening your divine nature. Ideally, you will place an equal emphasis on both inward seeking and outwardly perceiving the divine in others.

Traditional yoga affirms mostly inward seeking and to a lesser degree the outward component of seeking. Specifically traditional yoga gives a higher priority to finding God within and a lower priority to relationships, but this is where the influence of the Course can provide what is generally missing in yoga. The Course says you need to look within first, but after looking within you can then look outside to your brother, but without making your brother into an idol. The Course recommends joining with your brother for a common purpose and in doing so you form a *holy relationship*. The holy relationship helps you to look at your brother differently, not as an idol to complete you, but as a divine being, who is already complete just as you are already complete. Perceiving the divine nature of your brother helps you to likewise increase your awareness of your own divine nature.

Based on this Course teaching about holy relationships, Miracle Yoga includes a new kind of yoga that is not based on traditional Hindu yoga. This new expression of yoga is *Miracle Relationship Yoga*, which may be considered a healthy offspring of the marriage of the East and the West. This is not another name for the forms of tantric yoga that involve relationships in the context of integrating the male and female sexual energies functioning as a divine expression. In the practice of Miracle Relationship Yoga, you form holy relationships, and you look for the divine in your brother as a means of becoming aware of the divine in yourself.

The practice of Miracle Relationship Yoga involves the most basic practice of the art of allowing, which allows you to recognize what is true about your brother to be true for you and what is false about your brother to be false for you. The art of allowing allows the real to be real and illusions to be illusions. The art of allowing is necessary since you have made what is false about your brother appear to you to be true and have made your illusions about your brother appear to be his reality. The art of allowing does not change anything about the reality of your brother. However, it does change your perception of him. These changes in perception are expressions of love that are defined as "miracles" in *A Course in Miracles.*

The art of allowing is both a principle and a practice. As a principle of thought, the art of allowing affirms the false to be false and the true to be true. As a practice, the art of allowing becomes a spiritual discipline applied to daily living. Another name for the principle and the practice of the art of allowing is *looking and overlooking*. The principle and the practice of looking and overlooking are integral to all aspects of Miracle Yoga. How the practical application of looking and overlooking affects each of the five forms of Miracle Yoga will be described in subsequent chapters, especially Chapter 3.

Looking and overlooking is particularly important for the expression of Miracle Relationship Yoga. In the practice of looking and overlooking you look for the light, love, truth, and divine presence in your brother and overlook everything else. Your *looking* is the acceptance of your brother's reality in God. Your *overlooking* is looking past the illusions of form that only obscure your brother's reality in God. In this process of looking and overlooking your brother is not an idol you must possess to become complete, but instead he is a perfect mirror of your own condition. Seeing the divine in your brother serves as a reflection of your own divine nature and opens your mind to the awareness of God's presence within you that is your completion.

The practice of looking and overlooking functions as a positive use of denial. Normally, denial is used to deny and obscure truth and reality and to instead perceive illusions of untruth and unreality. The negative use of denial results in your worshiping of illusory idols that convince you of your littleness and incompleteness. On the other hand, the positive use of denial reverses the usual practice of denial and allows you to deny the illusions of untruth and unreality. Your denial of illusions of untruth and unreality allows you to perceive truth and reality just as they are. This leads to letting go of false and unreal idols and facilitates looking within to find your completeness in God.

The reason why the principles of the Course are recommended as a basis for your practice of Miracle Yoga is that there is a possibility that you may make yoga itself into an idol through which you will seek to make yourself complete. How can this be so, since yoga teaches you to go within to find your completion? If you use yoga to bring about your completion, you will be misunderstanding yoga and misunderstanding yourself. Such a misunderstanding about yoga is caused by confusing the forms of yoga with the content of yoga. In this case, you will value the forms of yoga such as the postures, breathing practices, or other disciplines as more important than the content of yoga. The content of yoga is related to its name since the word "yoga" literally means "union." Yoga becomes an idol if you think that practicing yoga itself can "create union" with God. From the perspective of yoga, you are already united with God. Yoga cannot make you complete because God already accomplished your completion when He created you as an extension of Himself. However, yoga can help you awaken to the fact that you are already united to God now, as you have always been and always will be.

Idols substitute for God and for the completion He has given to you. If you make yoga into an idol that replaces God's completion, you must misunderstand yourself and your true relationship with God. When you approach the practices of yoga, you take yourself, as you think of yourself, with you into your practices. The ego is the you that you think of as being yourself. This is the image you have of yourself as little and needing something to complete you, perhaps even yoga to complete you. Thus you will seek to complete yourself with outer idols that appear in different forms, yet all forms of idols represent the same content of illusion. Indeed, the ego itself is an illusion.

> What is the *ego*? But a dream of what you really are. A thought you are apart from your Creator and a wish to be what He created not. It is a thing of madness, not reality at all.[9]

Your ego, your self-image based on the idea of separation, is the source of your seeking idols, which is the worship of both illusions and littleness. Your mindset that says you are separate and need something to complete you is not corrected by combining yoga with traditional Christianity. In fact, the central theme of traditional Christianity is that you are now separated from God and must become reconciled with God in order to become pleasing to Him. Although various different forms of Christian yoga can be practiced with this mindset, the true content of yoga and, in my opinion, the content of Christianity will elude you if you are convinced God is separate from you.

Your God has never abandoned you, never separated Himself from you, and never stopped embracing you with His Love. Understanding your Father's unconditional Love is needed in order to most effectively practice Miracle Yoga. Of course, the unitive principle of being joined with God is central to traditional Hindu Vedanta. The Course can be called a "Christian Vedanta" because it sets forth a Christian context for understanding the unitive principle. However, it is important to make sure that you do not make the Course itself into an idol that you need to complete you. After all, the Course is recommended to you because it teaches you in Christian terms that you have no need of idols and that you are already complete. You are already joined with your Father who created you by extending Himself into you. His gift of divine life will never be withdrawn. God is already your completion, and no idols can substitute for His completion of you.

D. FORGIVENESS IN THE CONTEXT OF YOGA

The art of allowing that is the process of looking and overlooking has been described previously as a means of unmasking illusions by overlooking them and looking for the truth in reality. Yet the Course repeatedly describes this same practice with a more common term, "forgiveness." Forgiveness, as the practice of looking and overlooking, is actually the most important theme of the Course. Forgiveness does not consist of seeing your brother as sinful and guilty and forgiving him anyway. Rather, forgiveness removes from your mind any thought of guilt you may have projected onto your brother and simultaneously sees the divine holiness in your brother that is his and your own true nature. Forgiveness is the art of allowing applied to your brother. In this forgiveness based on allowing, you allow illusions you have about your brother to be illusions, and you allow the divine truth about your brother to be the divine truth.

The concept of forgiving your brother by perceiving his true holiness may be difficult to accept at first. Your concept of forgiveness depends upon your concepts of guilt and sin. The typical concepts of guilt and sin are so widely accepted that these are among the basic unchallenged foundations of traditional Christianity. It is common for a reasonable man to doubt that God exists and to struggle with his faith. But that same man may never even consider the possibility that guilt and sin may not exist. The ideas of guilt and sin certainly appear to be true, but what if these commonly accepted ideas are only illusions of the truth? The art of allowing means allowing illusions to be illusions and truth to be truth. This means allowing yourself to reconsider your assumption that guilt and sin are real. It requires openness to consider the Course perspective on guilt and sin, which is summarized by the following quotation: "God's Son is guiltless, and sin does not exist."[10]

Traditional Christianity teaches that every man is guilty and sinful; the Course teaches that no man is guilty and sinful. The Course asks you to see every brother as a holy child of God who is guiltless and innocent in God's eyes and therefore needs to be seen as guiltless and innocent in your eyes. The Course does not ask you to be blind to your brother's mistakes but does ask you to see his mistakes for what they are. Mistakes are not sins that put a mark on your brother's soul. Mistakes do not separate your brother from God's Love. Mistakes are correctable errors and need to be seen as such. Mistakes are made by men, and so they are changeable, which means they can be corrected. Your brother's true nature was created by God and thus your brother's true nature is unchangeable, meaning even his mistakes cannot change what God has created. Your brother's mistakes have not made him guilty or changed his divine meaning or true nature.

This perspective on guilt and sin allows you to perceive forgiveness in a new way. Seeing forgiveness from a new perspective enables you to practice looking and overlooking. Your overlooking consists of letting go of your own projections of guilt. Your looking consists of perceiving the true holiness of your brother. By forgiving your brother with looking and overlooking, you free him and yourself of guilt simultaneously and likewise you accept his and your own divine nature.

These Course concepts about forgiveness, guilt, and sin may seem to be abstract ideas that are not relevant to everyday living. You may not see how these ideas are related to, for example, the body postures and breathing practices of hatha yoga. The connection between these ideas and yoga is related to the meaning of the word "yoga," interpreted as "union," but which can also be translated as "integration." Yoga is an integration of body, mind, and spirit. Changes designed to benefit the body in the practice of hatha yoga are ideally coordinated with mental changes in perspective and increased openness to the Spirit. The question is, "Are you willing to make changes in every area of your life to gain the most beneficial effects?"

You are reading this book and considering if you want to practice Miracle Yoga because of the possible benefits. But the benefits will not be determined only by the nature of the practices of Miracle Yoga. You will determine the benefits by the subjective standard of whether you feel worthy of those benefits. This standard is the same one you apply to the goal of happiness. You want happiness, yet you are the one who determines your own happiness. You allot to yourself the amount of happiness that is in accord with your idea of how worthy you are of happiness. The benefits you gain from Miracle Yoga will be similarly determined based on your estimation of your own worthiness.

Your evaluation of your worthiness for happiness and for benefiting from yoga is influenced by subconscious factors related to your concept of yourself. Your self-image, similar to everyone else's, is affected by subconscious thoughts of guilt and sin. You may be consciously aware of some of these thoughts of guilt and sin, but many of these thoughts go very deep into the subconscious psyche. Such subconscious thoughts often stem from unresolved childhood impressions and emotions or come from past life experiences. Thoughts of guilt and sin may seem to have no relevance to your everyday life because of their subconscious nature. Nevertheless, these hidden thoughts influence your level of happiness and also determine the level of benefits you receive from Miracle Yoga or from any other form of spiritual seeking.

The goal of Miracle Yoga is to live in Christ. This means accepting the divine life in you and allowing it to be expressed through you. Ultimately, you will want to transcend your limited self-image based on the ego and accept your true Self in Christ. To prepare for transcending your self-concept, it is first necessary to change your self-image by replacing negative conscious and subconscious ideas, such as guilt and sin, with positive ideas. Ideas of guilt and sin are always connected to the idea of punishment. If part of your self-image is based on the belief that you are guilty and sinful, you will believe you deserve punishment and not happiness. Even though you consciously want happiness, your subconscious mind could be telling you that you are not worthy of happiness and that you deserve punishment instead. When you let go of negative thoughts of guilt, sin, and punishment, your self-image will change so you will feel that you are worthy of happiness and worthy of the benefits of practicing Miracle Yoga.

Inner attunement through meditation and contemplation is a direct way of inviting spiritual assistance in the process of removing negative subconscious blocks. However, forgiveness is an important means of indirectly healing your own mind by offering healing to your brother. If you can perceive your brother with forgiving eyes by seeing him as being without guilt and sin, you will likewise look with forgiving eyes upon yourself. Seeing holiness in your brother and realizing that your brother is worthy of God's love will convince you that you too must be holy and worthy of God's love. God's love establishes your brother's worthiness and your own. Forgiveness is a giving of your love to your brother because you realize that, in spite of outer illusory appearances, he is worthy of love. Because you give love, you receive as you have given. Through forgiveness you learn to perceive yourself as a giver of love. Since you are a giver of love, you convince yourself love must be in you and must be your true nature. This teaches you that you must be worthy of love and worthy of happiness. This new self-concept of worthiness allows you to receive happiness and receive the benefits of your spiritual seeking.

Therefore, forgiveness as a means of unmasking illusions helps you to affirm your brother's true meaning and in so doing claim your own meaning because how you perceive your brother will determine how you perceive yourself. Miracle Relationship Yoga and forgiveness will be described in Chapter 7 but is mentioned here in the first chapter to emphasize how Miracle Yoga based on the Course is different from traditional Hindu yoga and from other forms of Christian yoga. This book on Miracle Yoga emphasizes that trust in your brother is just as significant as trust in God since your brother's true nature is divine just as your true nature is divine. As a suggestion, you may want to consider reading this book in coordination with a friend. For example, a friend and you could read and discuss each chapter before moving on to the next chapter. Or you could have shared experiences of doing the yoga postures, breathing practices, and/or meditation.

Your joining with a friend for a common purpose in this way is an example of a "holy relationship," which is the basic practice of Miracle Relationship Yoga. Even if you are not at this time coordinating with another person in this direct way, you are never alone in your spiritual practices. Every step forward that you make is made for both you and your brother because of your divine connection to him. When you become more consciously aware of your connection to your brother, you will make greater spiritual progress. Forgiveness is significant in this regard because overlooking your brother's illusions allows you to look at his divine meaning. Seeing the divine in your brother helps your brother accept his true meaning, helps you accept your own true meaning, and affirms your divine connection with your brother.

It is an important part of God's Plan that you help your brother to discover his divine meaning, which in turn helps you to discover your own meaning. Jesus is the leader in the executing of God's Plan. The purpose of God's Plan is salvation. Salvation is the final outcome of revealing your illusions to be your illusions. Illusions always involve the mistaken idea that you are what you are not. Salvation is the full regaining of your true meaning that can be hidden, but that can never be lost or damaged. In contrast to illusions, your true meaning is that you are the holy Son of God just as your Father created you.

You can delay the fulfillment of God's Plan by holding onto illusions, or you can accelerate the coming of His Plan by learning how to reclaim your meaning. A delay in time may seem to be a stumbling block to God's Plan, but since time itself is an illusion, His Plan is certain because it has already been accomplished in eternity. But for you to whom time is important, there is no reason to delay. After all, delay will prolong your suffering unnecessarily as you cling to illusions that tempt you to believe that you can be what you are not.

You have a very specific function to fulfill in God's Plan that will be revealed to you. Yet you, as every seeker, have the general purpose of saving time, reducing suffering, and awakening to your true meaning. The acceptance of this purpose also means that you recognize your responsibility to help your brother to awaken, which assists you in your own awakening. If you decide to accept your purpose and your place in God's Plan, hopefully the information in the upcoming pages of this book will assist you in accomplishing your purpose.

CHAPTER 2

~ • ~

UNDERSTANDING YOGA

A. THE STORY OF KING SHIVANANDA

In the ancient times of India, there was a King Shivananda who had four sons who grew to manhood. But the four princes selfishly turned against their father and attempted to take the kingdom by force. Yet their insurrection was put down. They were captured and brought before King Shivananda for sentencing for their crime.

Powerful and yet merciful, King Shivananda said, "You have been given everything anyone could possibly want. You have not had to exert any effort to receive these gifts, so you have become spoiled and ungrateful. The lawful penalty for treason is death, but I cannot bring myself to spill my own blood. I have decided to defer my sentencing to a later date. I have ordered Maya, my court magician, to cast a spell over you so you will fall into a deep sleep. Each of you will be brought to a different distant land. When you awaken, you will have amnesia and have to make your own way in the world by your own efforts. After five years, I will have you tracked down and brought to me, and then I will make my sentencing decision for your crime.

After the five years, the sons were brought to King Shivananda, but were not told why. Maya, the magician, asked them to describe their lives to King Shivananda. "One son spoke up, "I am a farmer. I work the soil, and every year I have been blessed with a great harvest. I give some of my harvest every year to widows and to the elderly. I was told you wanted me, so I brought some of my harvest to you as a gift. When there is free time between planting, weeding, and harvesting, I work as an all-around handyman. I have some free time now, so if you want me to work on a project for you, I would be willing to do so as a service to you without cost."

Without responding, King Shivananda pointed to another brother, who said, "I am a musician. I fell in love and got married. My wife showed me how to open my heart. Then she passed away suddenly and I was heartbroken. If you have ever lost anyone that you loved, you know how I felt." At these words, King Shivananda almost started to cry, but restrained himself, as the son continued, "I was depressed for a long while. Now I sing songs of love to remind myself of my lost love, who is in my heart. May I sing one of my songs for you?"

King Shivananda nodded his head in approval, and after the song was presented, another brother spoke up saying, "I am a scribe and scholar. I record important events, but I spend most of my time in the library studying the wisdom that is recorded there. I attempt to rise above my emotions by a thoughtful consideration of the reason behind events. I am attempting to understand what the true nature of reality is. I have a long way to go before being able to solve this mystery, but I do make a little progress in my understanding each day. I rely a lot on studying what the sages of the past have written because I want to understand their wisdom. I hope you will accept from me this book of wisdom sayings of sages as a gift."

Maya accepted the book on behalf of King Shivananda. Next the oldest son, who had led the revolt, stepped forward and spoke, "I do not know who I am. I woke up one day in an unfamiliar land five years ago, and I could not remember who I was." At this, the other sons spoke upon with one accord, "Me too!" However, Maya told the other brothers to be quiet.

The oldest son continued, "I found a cave and have lived there ever since. I live an austere life of fasting, prayer, and meditation. I am not a perfect soul, but I have found peace in my simple life. I have nothing to give you of value, but I brought a lotus flower to you to symbolize the purity and beauty that can be found in the flower that rises above the mud of the earth from which it comes. It is a symbol of my own journey, but I am still troubled by one thing of my lower nature that I have not been able to rise above. I have a recurring dream of living in a happy home as a child where I am loved. But then the dream turns into a nightmare in which I am separated from my home. In the dream, I am desperately trying to make my way back home, but I am hopelessly lost. Then I wake up, and I remind myself that I do not even know where my home is."

Then King Shivananda could no longer hold back his tears and everyone was shocked to see the regal King sobbing like a little child. "I am sorry if I did something to upset you. Please forgive me," said the oldest son.

King Shivananda regained his composure and said, "You are all my sons, and this day you have come home." Then he gave a gesture to

Maya, who immediately lifted the magic spell, and the memory of the sons returned. Immediately the sons fell to their knees in tears—greatly ashamed of their revolt against their father.

King Shivananda declared, "Now I will pronounce my sentence for your revolt. You have each in your own way learned important lessons that you could only have learned by leaving your home, so you made an unfortunate event into a fortunate event. Thus you are forgiven for everything in the past. The important thing is that you have come home. I have saved for you an honored place in the kingdom now that you are able to receive it with gratitude."

B. THE KINGDOM IN VEDANTA

The story of King Shivananda illustrates many Hindu themes, but one distinctively Christian concept is represented in this story. This Christian idea is the revolt of the sons of King Shivananda, which represents the fall of mankind as a consequence of disobedience to the laws of God. The concept of the individual leaving a state of union with God is present in Hindu teaching stories, but not the idea that the cause of separation was willful disobedience.

The story of King Shivananda is an adaptation of the Hindu story of the king of Smritinagar, which means "the city of memory" in Sanskrit.[11] The king of Smritinagar accidentally sustains a head injury, which results in amnesia. Due to his amnesia, he no longer realizes he is a king with a kingdom. But he has not really permanently lost his kingdom. The kingdom is awaiting his return. Finally, when his memory comes back, the king of Smritinagar is able to reclaim the kingdom, just as the sons of King Shivananda were able to return to the kingdom when the magic spell of amnesia was lifted.

Jesus asserted, "The kingdom of God is within you."[12] Likewise, Hinduism affirms the presence of this inner kingdom. Yet unlike the traditional Christian concept of waiting until the afterlife in order to enter Heaven, Hinduism places a greater emphasis upon your ability to have an inner awakening to become aware of this inner kingdom in this lifetime. Hinduism attempts to answer the question of how to obtain this inner awakening—how to remove the spiritual amnesia—in order to realize the inner kingdom. According to Hinduism, the spell that has been cast upon the mind is due to *maya*, the illusion of this world, producing ignorance of your true nature.

How can this ignorance be overcome? As a starting point, you need to understand at least intellectually who you really are. For this understanding, Hinduism asks you to rely on the study of its sacred scriptures. There are numerous sacred scriptures and different Hindu schools, so there is no such thing as one all-inclusive Hindu theology. The brief presentation of Hinduism that is offered here will primarily emphasize the ancient sacred texts of the Upanishads, which is the basis of the Vedanta school of nondualistic philosophy.

According to the Vedanta school, you appear to be only a limited human being and that is who you think you are. However, because of maya causing ignorance, you do not realize that you are really living constantly in the presence of Reality. This infinite and transcendent Reality is called *Brahman*, and you function and exist entirely within this Reality. The Sanskrit word "Brahman" literally means the Ultimate or Fullness.

In Hinduism, there are many gods, *devas*, and it may appear that Hinduism is polytheistic, but it is not. All the devas are manifestations of Brahman, the one Supreme Being. But this one God is manifested in three ways, as follows:

God, as *Nirguna Brahman*,[13] is the ground of all being, standing for representing God without differentiation, without any attributes or qualities, and beyond conceptual understanding. This aspect of God is sometimes referred to as the *Void*.

The second way the one God manifests is *Saguna Brahman*.[14] This aspect is related to the created universe and represents God with differentiation, with attributes and qualities. Saguna Brahman is the Creator, the origin of all consciousness. This would be equivalent to God the Father in traditional Christianity.

The third way the one God manifests is the *Atman*, which is God manifesting within each person. The center of your being is the *Atman*, your true divine nature that is one with Brahman. Yet the Atman is not a small piece of the larger Brahman. Brahman is the Atman; the Atman is Brahman. If there is no difference between these two, why have two different names? It is helpful to have two words to distinguish between God within you, which is the Atman, and God transcendent, which is Brahman. The Atman is your immanent access to the transcendent Brahman. You might say Brahman is the kingdom and the Atman is the kingdom within you. If you can awaken to the Atman, God immanent, you simultaneously awaken to Brahman, God transcendent.

Thus the Atman is your true Self, untouched by pleasure and pain, in which your human individual nature can encounter God. In yoga philosophy, there is only one ultimate Reality. Nevertheless, there are also "relative realities." The human individual is faced with a world that appears to have physical, psychological, and spiritual realities. These components are interdependent upon one another. Every physical reality is related to a psychological reality behind it. In turn, the physical and psychological realities are superseded by a spiritual Reality. Therefore, each individual has a body related to the physical reality, a soul that is related to the psychological reality, and a spirit related to the spiritual Reality. In comparison to the spiritual Reality, the physical realm and the psychological realm have only a relative reality, but are ultimately not real. Yet as long as you are identified with a body and a soul, you will have to deal at a practical level with these relative realities as if they were real. The spirit, representing the spiritual Reality that transcends the physical and psychological realities, is the Atman.

The Atman is your true Self that is now one with God, although you are not aware of this oneness. The Atman can be translated in Sanskrit in several ways but is usually translated as the "Self." At times, the Atman is translated as meaning essence, breath, wind, intelligent principle, or controlling influence. This sounds similar to the Greek word *pneuma*, the Christian concept of the individual spirit.

Hindu terminology makes a distinction between the individual soul and the spirit by combining the word *jiva* with the word Atman. The word *jivatman*[15] refers to the individual self with a small "s," different from the true Self. The jivatman is the "lower self," being lower than the true Self. This lower self is equivalent to the Christian concept of the "soul," which St. Symeon called the "psyche." Hindu philosophy considers that the jivatman, or soul, includes the senses (*indriyas*), the mind (*manas*), the ego (*ahamkara*), and the higher intellect (*buddhi*).[16] The soul (psyche) is normally caught up in the psychological world, which is at the midpoint between the physical realm of the body and the transcendent spiritual realm of the Atman. The soul makes choices between two alternatives: One alternative is the choice to be directed toward the senses and the activities of the world. The other alternative is the choice to be directed by the spiritual realm of the Atman.

The Atman is the point of convergence between the jivatman (the soul) and God. When you allow the body and the soul to be under the control of the Atman, the true Self, you are *yukta*,[17] meaning you are integrated or realized. To be integrated or realized is the goal of yoga (union). Yoga is intended to produce an integration at the three relative realities. The first level of integration is the harmonious union of all the bodily functions within the physical reality of the world. The second level of integration is the harmonious union of the body and soul within the psychological reality that underlies the physical reality. The third level of integration is the union of body, soul, and Atman so that the spiritual realm that transcends the physical and psychological realities can take over. The individual may go through an extended process of increasingly giving control over to the Atman so this spiritual Reality becomes the motivating force behind every action and thought. This third union is best understood as a total surrender of the body and soul, which is a sacrifice of the small self to the true Self. The ultimate goal is to become fully awakened to the Atman as one's true Self.

The Atman can be looked at in two ways: First, the Atman is the Supreme Self or Supreme Being (Paramatman), meaning God as Spirit. Secondly, this same Supreme Self (Paramatman) is also present as the indwelling Spirit *within* each human person. Hindu philosophy, under the theological influence of Shankara, emphasizes nondualism (*advaita*). According to the principle of nondualism, there is no real difference between the Atman as the Supreme Being, the ground of universal being, and the Atman as God within the human person, the ground of personal being.

The Supreme Being enters the human being as the Atman, and the Atman becomes the life force that extends into the functions of the soul and of the body. Yet the Atman, manifesting within the individual, remains the Supreme Being, and the objective of life is to realize one's true nature as the Supreme Being of the Atman. The question becomes: What happens to the individual who awakens to the realization of the Atman as the true Self? The seeker achieves liberation (*moksha*) by realizing the Atman and can affirm, "I am Brahman." One of the most well-known sayings in Vedanta is, "You are that!" (Tat tvam asi!) The meaning is that you are the Supreme Being, you are Brahman.

According to Hindu nondualism, the individual, jivatman, when he realizes his true nature as the Atman, is liberated by dissolving into Brahman. This is the example of the drop of water returning to the ocean and becoming the ocean. The individual loses his individuality as a soul and becomes the All, returning to the Supreme Being from which he came. This is the Hindu idea of entering the kingdom of God, which in the next section will be contrasted with the Christian concept of the kingdom of God.

C. VEDANTA FROM A CHRISTIAN PERSPECTIVE

The idea in Vedanta of the total union of the individual with God is the realization that, "I am Brahman," meaning "I am God." This is pure *advaita*, nondualism. The idea of the individual entirely dissolving into God and becoming God is not consistent with any traditional Christian theology. Nondualism is not really an expression of the idea of man and God *joining to become one*. Instead, nondualism, also called "monism," is based on understanding that man's idea of existing in separation from God is an illusion. When the illusion of separation is dissolved, what remains is the awareness that the true Self is God and has been God all along. In contrast to the nondualistic idea of a pre-existing union between God and man, traditional Christian theology is based on *dualism*. Dualism preserves the basic distinction between God and man, affirming that each has one's own separate essence. Dualism maintains that God and man are now separate from each other and may or may not become united at some future date. Even if God and man form a union, each will retain one's own essence.

This distinction is affirmed not only between God and ordinary men, but also between God and Jesus Christ. Unlike the Vedanta viewpoint of dissolution into God and the loss of individual identity, when Jesus merged with God, he did not lose his human nature according to traditional Christian theology. The Council of Chaldon in 451 A.D. decided that Jesus and God are indivisibly united in one Person, and yet the human and divine natures of the one Person are not mixed. The human and divine natures each retain their distinct natures and each with their own essence and functions. The human functions, while remaining distinct, are deified by the divine energies becoming perfect instruments of God's Will.

The Council of Chaldon has affected all Christian theology since then firmly establishing that duality is not limited to just this world but extends even to the highest level of union with God. Christian beliefs offer different interpretations of the depth of union that exists between God and the everyday man other than Jesus, although these ideas of union are always within the limits of dualism.

Within the limits of duality, Christian mystics have provided exalted concepts of divine union, which can be called "mystical dualism." In mystical dualism, the individual retains a limited sense of individuality and distinction from God. Yet by divine grace, the individual joins with God in a union so close that there is only oneness and no sense of separateness. In the mysticism of the Eastern Orthodox Church, the word "deification" is used to describe this kind of union of the human spirit with God. The highest mystical experiences in Christianity are these kinds of encounters with God. A radical transformation occurs in which the individual is no longer centered in a separate self but rather becomes centered in God and becomes a transcendent Self. This identity is the true Self, which I prefer calling the *Christ Self*.

Jesus Christ has established a pattern that everyone will follow in being deified. The individual will awaken to the awareness of union with God through divine grace and openness to the true Self, including sharing in the divine life of Jesus Christ. This union will not mix the individual's human nature with the divine essence of God. God shares His divine nature with the individual by imparting the divine grace with which He created the individual. The individual cannot become the divine essence, because then the individual would become God, and there would no longer be a Trinity. But by grace and participation in God, the individual can be united to God and become all that God is in His energetic nature, but not in his essence.

In the 14th century, St. Gregory Palamas promoted a theological distinction. His doctrine specified that divine *energies* come forth from God, yet they are distinct from the essence of God. These energies proceeding from God are uncreated, meaning they would exist even if creation did not exist. Yet God has willed to extend Himself to all of creation and does so through the operation of these energies. Though the divine energies are not the divine essence, they *reflect* the divine essence.[18] When the individual is in union with God, the individual can reflect all of the divine essence but not *be* the divine essence. Thus the individual becomes like the metaphor of a mirror that is spotless and can perfectly reflect an object, but the mirror is not capable of becoming the identity of the object that it reflects.

However, the uncreated energies of God are not truly an object that can be contained. They are like the rays of the sun that emanate from the ball of fire that is the substance of the sun. They carry the heat and light of the sun but not the essence. Also, the rays of the sun move out and have a life-giving effect on the world, and likewise the energies of God keep all of creation in existence and express God's Will and divine love. These energies express the divine grace that allows the individual to be guided to return to the awareness of the true Christ Self that is his own true nature. God takes the initiative through His divine energies to encourage the individual to awaken to higher consciousness, but the individual has the opportunity to respond or not respond to the operations of the divine energies. The divine energies provide different ways of cooperating in order to evolve spiritually, and four of these ways will be explored in the next four sections.

The Atman is similar to the Christ Self, but the distinction between these two will be described subsequently. In summary, Brahman is God transcendent and Atman is God indwelling in the human being. When the individual awakens to Atman as the indwelling of God, he becomes Brahman. He shares in the energetic functions of God, but he also dissolves becoming God by identity, so he can say, "I am God."

The Atman is the divine indwelling in the true Self in the lotus of the human heart. It is pure and beyond any death or decay. It is the life force that operates all the functions of the body and mind, although its presence is covered over by the self-consciousness of the ego. The Christ Self is all of this also. When the individual awakens to the Christ Self, he will be joined with God and become deified by participation in God's nature. But his participation in God will be with God's energies, not God's Identity as the Father. The Christian mystic's separate ego identity will be dissolved in God, but the result will be a transformed identity. This transformed identity will be a revealing of the individual's place in the Sonship. His realization will be, "I am the Son of God," and each Son of God will have the same realization.

Spiritually awakened Christian mystics cannot say, "I am Brahma, the Creator." In contrast to the Hindu nondualistic idea of total identity in God, there is the prior mentioned mystical dualism exemplified by St. Gregory Palamas, who states that the Christian mystic can become "deified" by participation in God's energies, but not become God's essence. I believe in a *qualified nondualism* that stands between the total nondualism of Hindu Vedanta and dualism of traditional Christian theology. This qualified nondualism states that the seeker can possess both God's energies and God's essence with one significant exception. The Son cannot become the Father, but the Son can become One with the Father, inseparably linked—or more accurately described, the Son can become aware of his pre-existing Oneness with the Father. The sole distinction between the Son and the Father is that the Father, being the Creator, will always be the First Cause, but otherwise the Son will possess all the infinite divine qualities of the Father, having both the energies and the essence of God. This theological position maintains that God the Father, as the Creator, lovingly extended all of Himself, even his essence, to His Son. In Hindu Vedanta, the seeker dissolves entirely into God and becomes God losing all individuality, but in this qualified dualism the seeker dissolves into God but finds a divine individuality in God, as will be described next.

My own Christian theological ideas are based on my understanding of *A Course in Miracles*, which are inspired writings that are elaborated upon starting with Chapter 6. Because these theological ideas as the foundation for the practice of Miracle Yoga may be controversial, I do not expect you to necessarily agree with these concepts, which will be described subsequently. You will probably have your own ideas about the theological matters that are covered, and you certainly do not have to agree with any of this information in order to practice Christian forms of inner attunement. These ideas are, after all, merely concepts that need to be set aside along with all other concepts in order to practice meditation and contemplation.

Christian theology is founded upon the idea of the Holy Trinity. In my understanding of the Trinity, God the Father is First Cause. God the Father is the Void (Nirguna Brahman), the undifferentiated ground of Being. But God the Father is also the Creator (Saguna Brahman), God of the universe with qualities and attributes. God the Son is the Christ. God the Father created one Son, one Christ. This one Christ may also be called the *Sonship*, a term used by the Course to describe what may be thought of as the "body of Christ."

The Sonship is made up of many parts, and each part contains the whole. How is it possible for the part to also contain the whole? An analogy would be the Hindu idea of the individual human person being part of the macrocosm of the universe and yet at the same time each person having a miniature version of the universe, a microcosm, contained within his own body. Another analogy would be that each cell in the human body is a specific part of the whole organism, and yet each cell contains the DNA, the genetic code for the whole body. Just as a tiny "seed" contains everything necessary to produce an entire plant, the DNA of each cell contains the pattern for creating the whole body. Each individual is a part of the one Christ, a part of the Sonship, and each part contains the whole and is one with the whole. Each part exists in communion with every other part. In fact, the very nature of each part is to be in relationship with every other part and with the whole, which is contained within each part.

You are a combination of individual part-ness in Christ and shared wholeness in Christ. Your ego identity in the world is a distortion of your divine individual part-ness in Christ and is a complete denial of your wholeness in Christ. Your true divine nature is paradoxically a part of the Sonship and yet contains the whole Christ, united with the Father and the Holy Spirit. Most Christians accept the idea of man being made "in the image and likeness of God." God is Wholeness. Therefore, you are mysteriously made in the image and likeness of His Wholeness. Thus you are the whole Christ. But paradoxically you are only a part of the one Christ. As a part, you have communion, and you have equality with every other part. Your Identity is within the one Christ, of which you are a part and the whole. Because the one Christ is your Self, you are joined in loving union with the Father and the Holy Spirit.

Awakening to your true Christ Self would correspond to coming Home and returning to your honored place in the kingdom as in the story of King Shivananda. What Vedanta calls the Atman is not exactly the same as your true Christ Self but has many similarities. You are still part of the one Christ, the Sonship, even *now* and you (meaning who you really are) have *never left*. But you have a spiritual amnesia like the spell cast upon the sons of King Shivananda. When you are dreaming, everything in the dream appears real for the duration of the dream, but when you wake up you realize that you were in your own home and in bed all along. When you fully awaken from the dream of this world (a relative reality of a physical and psychological world), you will realize that who you really are, your Christ Self, never left Heaven—never left your Home.

The Christian perspective is that the children of God disobeyed God. The Hindu perspective is that the world is a manifestation of "divine play." Yet, regardless of the cause, the human condition is focused on the consciousness of the separate self. The separate self, the ego, itself is a condition of spiritual amnesia. The individual has identified with the ego and forgotten the ground of being in which he exists even now. He has forgotten and distorted his individual part-ness in Christ and has forgotten and completely denied his wholeness in Christ, his grounded oneness with God the Father.

The third Person in the Holy Trinity is the Holy Spirit, the loving communication link between God the Father and the Sonship. The purpose of the Holy Spirit is to lovingly guide the sleeping parts of the Sonship back to an awareness of the Christ Self. The Holy Spirit is within each human mind and primarily functions through the crown center, which can open the individual to universal consciousness.

The location of the access to the Atman in the physical body is the same as the location of the *nous*, which is the spirit, described by St. Symeon. The Upanishad quotation below uses the term of Brahman's "city" as meaning the human body and uses the word "lotus" as a metaphor for the spiritual center of consciousness, the *chakra*, as follows:

In the city of Brahman is a secret dwelling, the lotus of the heart. Within this dwelling is a space, and within that space is the fulfillment of our desires. What is within the space should be longed for and realized. As great as the infinite space beyond is the space within the lotus of the heart.[19]

The true Christ Self, like the Atman, can be realized in the "lotus of the heart." This is in the center of the chest, which is the place of the nous that has the capacity for mystical cognition and that St. Symeon considered be the spirit. In Hinduism, the heart center is the place   where the guru is placed in meditation. The guru, or personal spiritual guide, for most Christians would be Jesus Christ.

Hinduism believes that God incarnates Himself in the form of an avatar when mankind is in need of divine assistance to overcome ignorance produced by *maya*, illusion. Christians are not concerned with the idea of avatars in general, but are very much focused upon the one Incarnation of Jesus. Jesus became completely identified with his own Christ nature and assumed a leadership role in helping all the parts of the Sonship to return Home. His resurrected body indicated union with God in the spiritual Reality and also mastery of the relative realities of the physical and psychological realms. Having traveled through and personally transcended the physical and psychological worlds in which separation dominates, Jesus Christ is in a position to elevate each individual person and mankind as a whole.

Many Christians who are willing to believe that Jesus Christ is the Son of God are not open to the idea that each soul is the Son of God, part of the one Sonship. This limited thinking is not part of the Hindu idea that maintains any soul can wake up and merge with Brahman. In the original Hindu story of the king of Smritinagar, the king gets amnesia and loses his kingdom and then later regains his memory and regains the kingdom. In this story, the Atman *is* the kingdom that is lost and regained. Since the Atman is God, the individual regains his identity as being God. In this story, the king of Smritinagar, who regains his memory, represents God as the individual becoming aware again of Himself as being Brahman, the Supreme Being.

In the adaptation of the Hindu story, King Shivananda, represents God the Father. The sons of God get amnesia and leave their Home, which is the kingdom of God. The sons really do not possess, lose, and regain the kingdom itself. They possess, lose, and regain an *honored place* in the kingdom. From the Hindu perspective the Atman *is* the kingdom—the entire kingdom. From the Christian perspective, the Christ Self is the *honored place in the kingdom*. The whole kingdom is the Trinity of the Father, Son, and Holy Spirit. The Christian finds his identity in r*elationship*, meaning finding his place in the Trinity. Each Christian, awakening to the Christ Self, has an honored place as a Son in the Sonship, in union with the other Sons, the Father, and the Holy Spirit. Whereas regaining of the Atman can be called "regaining of the kingdom," regaining of the Christ Self can be called "coming Home." The idea of Home has a feeling of relationship and being part of a family. The idea of the family has a world of meaning—the feeling of belonging, giving and receiving love, and finding one's identity in relationship to others. Coming Home is a "family reunion."

Jesus Christ is the Son of God. He is God's most honored Son because in his earthly life he perfectly reflected the image and likeness of God and continues to do so. However, he is your "elder brother" and not the only Son. In the body of Christ, which is the Sonship, each individual member is the Son of God. When each individual Son returns to the awareness of the divine, the reward is the same. The reward is in coming Home and receiving an honored place in the kingdom, which means regaining full awareness of oneness with God the Father and accepting your rightful place in the Sonship. There is a parable in the Bible of the laborers in the vineyard who go out in the fields to work.[20] Some worked all day, some part of the day, some for only a short time, but all are rewarded with equal pay by the owner of the vineyard. Those that worked all day complained that they got the same pay as those who worked only one hour. The owner replied by saying he had the right to be generous to all the workers. Every individual worker, every seeker, will get the equal pay of coming Home to his rightful and an honored place in the kingdom of God.

There will always be individuals who will judge others as being unworthy of the divine kingdom, but God finds not one of His Sons unworthy of coming Home. It does not matter what they have done in this life. Even the worst criminal behavior will not convince God that one of His Sons is unworthy of coming Home. King Shivananda's final judgment on his sons is the same as God's judgment on every soul: "You are forgiven for everything in the past. The important thing is that you have come Home. I have saved for you an honored place in the kingdom, and now you are able to receive it." Your Home remains hidden in your own heart waiting to be discovered, but you must be "able to receive it."

In the parable of the laborers in the vineyard, this is the first line: "For the kingdom of Heaven is like a householder who went out early in the morning to hire laborers for his vineyard."[21] The owner of the vineyard, the householder, hires people to work for him. How is this hiring in itself like the kingdom of Heaven? The workers make an agreement to work in the vineyard and are given the promise of a reward at the end of the day. When you work for someone, you are hired to do his bidding, his will, not your own will. This parable tells you how to come Home to the kingdom, which is by not doing your work, your will, but by doing your Father's work, God's Will.

Since the story of King Shivananda is a Christian adaptation of the Hindu theme of the lost kingdom, the sons did not get amnesia accidentally. The amnesia happened following a revolt, a willful act of disobedience. The Hindu explanation of divine play does not satisfy most Christians. If the Christian premise of leaving Home because of a willful act is correct, then coming back Home becomes a matter of turning away from doing your own will and instead doing God's Will. In the parable of the vineyard workers, it was not important how long the workers worked for the owner, it was only important that each worker made the exact same decision to do the will of the owner.

The Christian idea of the fall, the collective leaving of Home by mankind, was an act of willfulness corrected by Jesus Christ with his obedience to the will of God, even to accepting death on a cross. Yet each individual is responsible for regaining his own lost Home, and in this sense, the Christian and Hindu seeker face the same challenge. Uncovering the Atman for the Hindu and uncovering the Christ Self for the Christian are both a matter of surrendering to the divine within. This involves setting aside the will of the ego and accepting God's Will by a seeking the divine within. Similar to King Shivananda's will for his sons to have a change of heart and return Home, God's Will is His Love, which is calling you to come Home by seeking Him within.

It may seem like setting aside your own will in order to do God's Will is a sacrifice. It can only be a sacrifice if you are letting go of your own best interests, but that is not the case here. Doing your own will is based on pursuing ego interests, which promise happiness, but which maintain a sense of separation and alienation from others and from God. In contrast to the doing of your own will that is directed toward the world of separation, doing God's Will is directed toward going Home. The true happiness that you are seeking can only be found by going Home. God's Will is for you to come Home and your own true will is for you to come Home. Eventually, you will have the happy realization that *God's Will is your own true will* because going Home is all that you really want. Then you will understand that there is no conflict between God's Will and your own will. Thus doing God's Will is the expression of your own true will and not a sacrifice.

God's Will is not limited to what you *do*. It is the expression of who you *are*. You were created as part of the one Christ by God's Will, and God extended His Will into you as part of your creation. Going against God's Will is attempting to go against yourself since you are an extension of God. Being an extension of God raises the consideration of what it means to be extended from God. Conservative Christian theology maintains the dualistic idea that as an extension of God, you are basically different from God, but you can be forgiven for sin and become an "adopted" son of God. Mystical dualism says you can be fully joined in divine union with the energies of God, but your essence and God's essence will always be fundamentally different.

The awakening of the Christ Self in union with God is a mystical dualism in contrast to the nondualism of the awakening of the Atman in union with Brahman. But I believe the Christ Self awakening is a "qualified nondualism," which is really a *marriage of dualism and nondualism*. This marriage provides a description of divine union that falls between Christian mystical dualism and Hindu nondualism. The nondualistic aspect of qualified nondualism is the idea that you are not just an extension of God's energies. Instead, you are an extension of God Himself, an extension of God's essence. The qualifying factor of qualified nondualism is that you do not dissolve completely back into God as is believed in the Hindu nondualism. In divine union, you do totally give up the ego because the ego is the idea that you are a separate self. Yet you retain your individuality as a part of the one Christ Self. Christian dualism maintains that you become united to God. But qualified nondualism states that when you find your identity in God, you are merely awakening to a pre-existing condition that was never lost but was just hidden from your awareness.

This qualified nondualism can be best understood by using the analogy of the nature of a tree. For this analogy, imagine that you are a branch on a tree. Now imagine that you have an ego, which is the illusory idea that you exist as a branch floating in the air apart from the rest of the tree. Next, imagine that you have a spiritual awakening in which you give up your ego. When you release your ego, you just give up an illusory idea that was never real. You realize that you have never been separated from the tree trunk, except as an illusion in your mind. When you wake up, you realize that as a branch of a tree, you are individual and have the wholeness of the entire tree. You know that you have the same essence, the same sap, as the trunk and as every other branch. In addition, you understand that your true nature has not changed, it has merely been revealed for what it has always been.

The benefit of this qualified nondualism is the awareness that you do not have to do anything to become united to God because you are already united to God in His essence. Your true Identity has been irrevocably established by God in your creation, and nothing can ever change your true nature. Though you cannot change your true nature, you can change your present consciousness and become aware of your true nature. Your change in consciousness will ultimately require you to give up the ego entirely in order to accept your true nature. A step in this direction is the giving up of the belief in sin. Sin is the belief that you can separate yourself from God and you can make yourself unacceptable to God. Sin is a man-made idea. Traditional Christian theology affirms the belief in sin. It is hard for most Christians to give up the belief in sin and the belief that God allows sin.

In this world, every object and every person's body appear to be separate from every other object and every other body. The human senses attest to a world of separation and are "proof" that the ego, the idea of separation, is real. Thus it is not surprising that traditional Christian theology affirms the belief in the reality of the ego.

The gift that Hinduism offers in Vedanta is the belief that the ego is not real. It is a gift that is very difficult for most Christians to receive. With this belief comes the corresponding belief that sin is not real. Sin being unreal means that you cannot place a mark on your soul that would make you unacceptable to God. Your true Self is absolutely pure and can never be tarnished in any way. If you paint a light bulb black so that the light cannot be seen, you have merely covered the outer surface and not affected the true nature of the light. You are as pure and connected to the Light of God now as you have ever been or ever will be because your true nature is the Light. You are not a body or a limited mind attached to a body. The body and mental identification with the body just hides the Light like the black paint on the light bulb.

The world of Spirit that is the Home of your true Self is in another dimension, not in the three-dimensional world, which is familiar and appears to be vividly real. It is hard to believe that your true nature is in another dimension, beyond your comprehension. It takes a leap of consciousness beyond body awareness to believe in any form of nondualism that maintains that the body and world are ultimately not real because they are not part of your true spiritual nature.

Every seeker experiences the world in an ego condition that limits his consciousness, and at the same time, he seeks to understand his spiritual nature that is beyond the ego. Your theological conclusions about your true spiritual nature may be strongly held convictions. Yet spiritual beliefs fall into the realm of conjecture. My own conjecture stated above is the belief in a Christian qualified nondualism that maintains that you are a part of the one Christ Self in union with God the Father and with the Holy Spirit, and you are also paradoxically the whole Christ Self. You will have to decide for yourself what you want to believe. But your choice will not affect your actual practice of meditation and contemplation, which requires the letting go of concepts, including setting aside concepts of God.

D. YOGA AS A MEANS OF REVEALING THE KINGDOM

In Hinduism the starting point for the regaining of the lost kingdom, the true Self, is the understanding of the nature of the Atman. In this understanding comes the reassuring faith that the kingdom is not lost and can never be lost. It can only be hidden as it is now and then uncovered eventually. For Hinduism salvation is not a matter of "if." It is a matter of "when." This is also true of the Christian qualified nondualism described previously.

From the Hindu perspective, you have not just one life but many lifetimes to make progress until you eventually realize your true nature as the Atman. Although reincarnation was a commonly accepted idea in the early Church, the idea of reincarnation is a hard concept for most Christians to accept today. Yet reincarnation does explain some situations that have no other explanation. For example, a child that dies early or is severely deformed does not have the same opportunity in this lifetime that is generally afforded to realize his true nature as the Atman or Christ Self. In my opinion, there is no reasonable Christian explanation for this. The Hindu viewpoint is that the individual has *karma* from a past life that he brings into this life. The closest Christian idea similar to karma, but without past life reference, is the idea that you reap as you have sown.

However, from a purely practical viewpoint, the task before you in your current lifetime is to realize your true nature in this very lifetime. In this sense, believing in past lives can be a stumbling block, if this belief prevents you from doing all you can in this lifetime to awaken to your true nature. Even if the Hindu belief in past lives is true, it does not matter that you have amnesia in regard to your past lives. It only matters that you have amnesia in regard to this life. You have forgotten that you are the true Self, but you have not lost the true Self.

It is not important for Christian seekers to adopt the Hindu belief in reincarnation, but it is beneficial to adopt the Hindu perspective that maintains the kingdom is not lost. The Christ Self is not lost. Your Home is merely completely hidden by the amnesia of the ego condition. This perspective allows you to identify with the purity and love that is your true nature already within you. If you feel your true nature is sinfulness and unworthiness, you will create a psychological ego-base block to accepting the divine within. Even though you have and will make mistakes because of ego choices, God does not want your guilt. God wants you to uncover your true nature and come Home.

The Hindu way of waking up from the spiritual amnesia of the ego is a two-fold approach: *outer non-attachment* to the world and *inner attachment* to the Atman (to God). This amounts to releasing the ego's will and accepting God's Will. It is a letting go of worldly desires and holding on to the desire for God. First, comes the higher impulse of wanting God, and then comes the motivation to restrain the lower impulses. As the lower impulses are in fact subdued by effort, the result is an increase in that initial impulse for wanting God. Thus there is progress in the two directions of reducing the ego manifestations and of increasing the divine influence.

This two-pronged approach is a combination of outer purification and inner purification. The outer purification is a purifying of the heart to reduce sense desires, and the inner purification is a purifying of the mind, which is best exemplified by meditation. In Hinduism, making inward progress in meditation to purify the mind only comes about with a corresponding restraining of the senses to attain purity of heart. The purification is important because the goal is to become pure like the Atman, which is purity itself. This focus on purity may go unnoticed by those who see yoga as only the physical activity of body postures and breathing practices. However, the ideal of seeking purity of heart and mind can be found in every form of yoga.

Specifically, sexual purity, chastity, is emphasized because it is such a powerful force. Sexual purity is called *brahmacarya*, the "mode of the Absolute," meaning dwelling in the Brahman.[22] The abiding in Brahman of brahmacarya means living in such as way that your heart and mind are centered in your true Identity in the Atman, the divine Self within. The more you identify with the Atman, the more pure you become. The more you identify with the senses and impulses of the body and with the moods and emotions of the psychological mind, the less pure you become. Self-restraint, especially sexual self-restraint, is the means of strengthening the physical body, the character, and the mental capacities. This is not merely moving away from what is not wanted, but moving forward toward what is wanted—opening to the awareness of one's true nature as the Atman. Brahmacarya is a letting go of the male and female roles as a means of identification. One who has mastered the virtue of sexual purity can disregard sexual differences and see everyone as "the same" (*sama*) and as equal to oneself.[23]

There are different paths of yoga, but each one emphasizes the need for purity outwardly and inwardly. The means of obtaining this purity may be different in each path. Hinduism has different paths to incorporate the psychological temperaments of various seekers. There are four basic psychological tendencies, which are an active nature, an emotional nature, an intellectual nature, and a contemplative nature. Although every person has all four natures, usually one of these will be the predominant temperament of the individual. Each of the four paths of yoga emphasizes one of these temperaments, but the goal is to include all four natures while one is emphasized so that there in an integration of the entire person.

Individuals who are predominately active by nature are drawn to the path of *karma yoga*, the path of selfless action. Individuals who have an emotional temperament are suited to *bhakti yoga,* the path of love. Individuals who are intellectually oriented are suited to *jnana yoga*, the path of knowledge. Individuals who have a contemplative inclination are attracted to *raja yoga*, the path of meditation.

E. KARMA YOGA — THE PATH OF SELFLESS ACTION

Each of the four sons of King Shivananda represents a different path of yoga—a different way of returning Home. The son who was the farmer and handyman followed the path of karma yoga, which is the yoga of selfless action as a means of spiritual growth. This path is for the person who leans toward an active life in the world. Yet everyone is active to a certain degree so everyone can benefit by internalizing and utilizing the practice of karma yoga.

The beauty of karma yoga is that it takes ordinary actions and everyday mundane work and elevates these to divine expressions. Karma yoga can be practiced by simply allowing whatever form of work that you do to be done as a service to God with no thought of looking to the fruits of your labor. Karma yoga is sometimes thought of as the yoga of "work," but is more properly understood as the yoga of "dedicated action." In fact, the verb "*kri*," meaning *to do*, is the root word from which the word karma is derived. Thus any action can be an expression of karma yoga if that action is performed with dedication to the divine. By dedicating the action to God, the action becomes selfless and a divine expression.

The expression of karma yoga can be impersonal or personal in nature, but in either case, there is a two-fold activity of turning within and then turning outward. Whenever karma yoga is expressed in an impersonal manner, the individual turns inward to make contact with the impersonal Brahman. This turning inward may be meditation that is part of each path of yoga, or it may be a temporary dedication of oneself to the infinite Reality. This turning inward to the infinite is then followed by a turning outward to the finite in the form of action or work. In this case, work is done for its own sake. It is the Atman, the indwelling Brahman, in the karma yogi that is doing the work simply because this action is beneficial to do. When karma yoga is expressed in a personal manner, the individual chooses to turn inward in order to make contact with a personal aspect of God. For example, if the chosen personal form of God is Krishna, the karma yogi inwardly offers the results of his actions or work to Krishna. This is a form of devotional worship. This worship is independent of the value of the work from a worldly perspective that makes distinctions between lowly work and lofty work. Every offering of work is equally important as a gift on the altar of worship.

This inward personal dedication may be made through meditation, through prayer, or through the ritual action of worship before an altar. After the inward dedication, the karma yogi can then perform the outward action or work with no personal motivation. Since the fruits of one's actions are given away in worship, the karma yogi can be free from any concern about the results.

Karma yoga transforms bondage into freedom. Normally there is a link between action and desire. In Vedanta, the individual is in a state of ignorance of his own divine nature due to *maya*, the illusions of this world. Because of ignorance, the individual has desires for things that are not divine and thus not in accord with his true nature. Desires motivated by the ego lead to action, which is karma. Karma is best described as action and the results of action. Ego-based desires bring about actions that have automatic results, meaning karmic results.

Karma yoga is practiced to remove ego-based desires so the link between desires and action is broken. When the desire is removed from the action, there is no karmic result. Instead of being limited by karma, the karma yogi is freed to perform actions without incurring any automatic results of a karmic nature. If work is done impersonally for its own sake with no personal ego investment, there is no karma. Or if work is done in a personal manner in which the worker gives the fruits of his work to his personal form of God, there is no karma. Karma can be bondage keeping the soul bound to this world. Letting go of bondage leads to liberation, awakening the divine within.

F. BHAKTI YOGA — THE PATH OF LOVE

King Shivananda's son who was a musician followed the path of *bhakti yoga* as his way of finding his honored place in the kingdom. Bhakti yoga is the path of love. The person who is naturally loving will be drawn to bhakti yoga. But everyone is nourished by expressions of giving and receiving love, and therefore everyone can benefit from the practice of bhakti yoga, even if it is not one's chosen path.

In bhakti yoga, loving devotion is directed toward a personal aspect of God. This personal aspect is the *Ishta*, the chosen form of God. The

Ishta may be a deva, a form of God, such as Vishnu or Shiva. The Ishta may also be an avatar, an incarnation of God, such as Krishna or Rama. The bhakti yogi gives his heart to the personal aspect of God that he has chosen, but he realizes that there is ultimately only one Brahman, one Reality. Yet that ultimate Reality is too impersonal for the bhakti who seeks a personal relationship with the divine.

The bhakti yogi has a choice of how to view his relationship with his chosen Ishta. Some bhakti yogis are attracted to relating to God in a very specific way. The choice of relationship can be similar to any way in which humans express love, as follows:

1. *shanti*, a seeker of divine peace in relation to God
2. *dasya*, a servant in relation to a master
3. *apatya*, a child's attitude in relation to a parent
4. *sakhya*, a friend's relation to a friend
5. *vatsalya*, a parent's attitude in relation to a child
6. *madhura*, a lover's relation to a lover [24]

The choice of how to relate to the chosen Ishta is deeply personal, and this relationship may change in time. The bhakti yogi is involved in a dualistic relationship in which he sees himself and his personal Ishta as being separate, and his devotion is a means of joining with his Ishta to become one. Love is this two becoming one. Yet as the bhakti yogi succeeds in this loving union, his consciousness becomes totally filled with love, and he becomes more aware of his true Self. He increasingly realizes he is worshiping the Atman in his own heart. Thus after perhaps many years, the bhakti yogi's dualism can lead eventually to a nondualistic realization.

The goal of bhakti yoga is to love the personal God and be aware of God's loving embrace. In order to express his devotion, the bhakti yogi wants to constantly remember his personal God. To immerse his consciousness in the awareness of God, he practices another form of yoga, which is *japa yoga*, the repeating of an affirmation. The main form of japa yoga for a bhakti yogi is repeating the Name of God, meaning the Name of the chosen Ishta. By constantly recalling the divine through japa yoga, he purifies his mind of lower impulses and directs the emotional nature toward the expression of devotion.

Prayer is an important form of devotional expression for the bhakti yogi. Of course, formal prayers are helpful, but perhaps spontaneous prayers are even more helpful because they are a means of directing all the emotions toward the divine. Just as you can talk with a friend about your fear, grief, anger, or pain, you can talk with your personal aspect of God and express every thought and emotion to relieve your human heart of any burdens. Prayers that are packed with deeply felt emotions are wholehearted expressions. This wholeheartedness helps you to produce an inner integration of the heart, mind and will because all of your being is involved with these expressions.

Prayers for your brothers and sisters help to turn the consciousness away from self-centered motivations and toward divine inclinations. Hindu philosophy emphasizes the significance of praying for the benefit of all mankind. Prayers are a form of asking for divine assistance, and when these are directed toward seeking virtues that would lead toward God, these prayers are consistently answered by God. The more fervent the prayer is, the more likely it is that the prayer will be answered. It is a Hindu understanding that God reveals Himself by divine grace, but that a seeker who consistently prays with great longing for his Beloved will not be disappointed.

Just as the karma yogi that views all action as worship, so too the bhakti yogi is focused on worship. Unlike the *asking* of prayer, worship represents *giving* to God. Love needs to be expressed and giving that occurs in worship is one way to tangibly express love for one's Beloved. Because prayer is asking, it can be centered on the needs of the self, but the nature of worship changes the focus from self-receiving to self-giving. The self is the giver of the worship and what is given is a gift, for example, a fruit or a flower. However, the material gift is in fact only a symbol of the giving of oneself to God. It is purity of intention that is important in the act of worship.

Perhaps the most significant aspect of worship is *internalization*. All outer actions of worship are performed with an understanding that the outer expression is to be experienced internally. For example, the bhakti devotee may have a personal altar in his home devoted to his personal Ishta. In an act of worship, he may lovingly place a flower on his altar, but in doing so is internalizing this act. He will feel and inwardly experience that he is simultaneously placing his love, symbolized by the flower, on the altar of his human heart within his body where he can meet his Beloved.

This internalization is central to the expression of *ritual*, which is a specific form of worship that symbolizes the holy relationship between the worshiper and God. Without internalization, ritual worship becomes merely religious convention without conviction. Through the physical gestures and actions of ritual, a sacred bond between the devotee and God is expressed in a way that words fail to convey.

The devotee uses all forms of communication to express his loving and holy divine relationship. These would include reading scripture, music, singing, chanting, company with others of like mind, and travel to holy places on pilgrimage. All these forms of communication are intended to produce deeper communion—divine intimacy. God is great, powerful, and incomprehensible, yet the devotee is unconcerned about the many attributes of God. The devotee is focused only on his heart reaching out to God and the divine love he feels coming from God to him. The highest form of human intimacy manifests in the relationship between two lovers. Similarly, the highest form of divine intimacy can be found in the devotee who gives himself in love totally to God.

G. JNANA YOGA — THE PATH OF KNOWLEDGE

King Shivananda's son who was a scribe and scholar regained his honored place in the kingdom by following the path of *jnana yoga*, the path of knowledge. Those individuals who find that their intellect is more important to them than their emotions will be attracted to this path. Since everyone has an intellectual side, everyone would benefit by an awareness of jnana yoga. The key element of jnana yoga is not simply the use of the intellect as a way of navigating through life, but the use of the intellect to gain Self-awareness. The goal of jnana yoga is Truth, but not seeking truth in the generic sense. The Truth being sought is knowledge of one's true nature as the Atman. The goal of Self-awareness is the same as the goal of God-realization. This is so because the Atman is both one's true Self and Brahman also.

The attainment of Self-knowledge is not in itself an intellectual activity, but rather a direct experience of the Atman. Yet the intellect can be used in jnana yoga as a means of moving in the direction of having that direct experience. The spiritual amnesia of this world that blocks the awareness of Self-knowledge is ignorance produced by maya, which is illusion. The intellect can be used to overcome ignorance and uncover the underlying Reality.

The intellect can be successful in overcoming ignorance of one's true nature only if it is consistently directed toward this objective. If the mind is caught up in the lower impulses of an emotional nature, it will become clouded over. The lower desires dull the mind so it loses its strength of perception and reduces the desire for Self-knowledge. Thus the intellect will be unable and unwilling to cut through the bondage of ignorance. Just as purity of intention is so important for the other traditional kinds of yoga, jnana yoga requires a pure mind to be able and willing to move in consciousness toward Self-knowledge.

There are four prerequisites of jnana yoga, which are abilities or qualities that need to be developed and implemented to grow toward

Self-knowledge. The cultivation of these aspects of jnana yoga prepares the seeker for the three fundamental practices of jnana yoga:

FOUR PREREQUISITES FOR JNANA YOGA[25]

1. *viveka* — discrimination
2. *viraga* — detachment
3. *shat-samatti* — six attainments
   a. peacefulness
   b. self-control
   c. mental composure
   d. forbearance
   e. faith
   f. concentration
4. *mumukshutva* — longing for liberation

THREE FUNDAMENTAL PRACTICES OF JNANA YOGA[26]

1. *shravana* — hearing the truth
2. *manana* — reflection on the truth
3. *nididhyasana* — meditation on the truth

For the jnana yogi, *discrimination* is the first and foremost attribute that is needed to make progress toward Self-knowledge. Unlike the general ability to discriminate, jnana yoga requires the specific ability to discriminate between the real (*sat*) and the unreal (*asat*). In regard to the real versus the unreal, yoga philosophy has asked the question, "What is the relationship between God and the world of form?" One radical interpretation articulated in the *Yoga-Vasihtha* is that Brahman is real, and the world is totally unreal, a complete hallucination without any existence. This interpretation of Brahman is the same as some forms of Mahayana Buddhism.

Shankara (788 to 820 AD), the most well-known advocate of Advaita Vedanta, is often mistakenly associated with the idea that the world does not exist and is a total illusion. Actually, Shankara stated that the world does exist, but is not ultimately real. The world has only a relative reality. The world has no independent reality since its existence is dependent on Brahman, Reality itself. Therefore, the illusory world is only a transitory realm. Only the underlying Brahman is unchanging and ultimately real.

According to Shankara, discrimination is necessary to see the world correctly as a reflection of Brahman. Shankara describes the real as the "subject" (vishayin) and unreal as the "object" (vishaya).[27] The true nature of the subject is the transcendental Self. The object is anything appearing to be apart from the Self, which would be all forms of the world, including all people and also all thoughts. From the perspective of the state of ignorance, all objects appear to be apart from the subject observing them. In this sense, the world is illusory in appearance. From the transcendental perspective, all objects that appear separate are seen to be united and existing in the one Reality.

In yoga philosophy, the cause of suffering (*klesha*) is primarily the confusion between the subject and object, which is spiritual ignorance (*avidya*).[28] Ignorance produces disidentification with the Self, Atman, and identification with the limited self, *anatman*. This in turn brings about attachment to pleasurable experiences, aversion to unpleasant experiences, and the survival instinct linked with the status of the small self. Ignorance causes confusion between the subject and object and produces instability in the psyche leaving positive and negative impressions in the always-fluctuating unenlightened mind.

In Vedanta, the confusion between the subject and object is called "superimposition" (*adhyasa* or *adhyaropa*), which involves mistakenly perceiving the Self to be the ego of the small self.[29] In reality, the Self has no needs because it lacks nothing, but the ego condition leads to identification with the body and with the needs of the body and mind associated with the body. Also, the Self includes all apparently exterior objects, but due to ignorance in the ego condition objects mistakenly appear outside of the ego. This ego condition leads to the idea that objects must be controlled and manipulated to meet ego needs. Needs that are met produce temporary satisfaction and needs that are not met produce forms of discomfort, instability, and suffering.

Jnana yoga maintains there is no solution to this situation until the cause of suffering, which is ignorance, can be overcome. Therefore, jnana yoga is a one-pointed effort to remove ignorance by removing the confusion between the subject and object through the wakening of the knowledge of the Self as the unchanging transcendental substance of all changing forms.

Jnana yoga does not focus on seeking intellectual ideas normally associated with acquiring knowledge. This path does not employ the rational thinking of the West based upon a scientific mental process of removing prejudices and accepting logical and observable facts of the discursive mind, which is powerless to see beyond the separation of the subject and object. The jnana yogi seeks a higher knowledge, called *jnana*, which is distinctly different from *vijnana*, considered a lower knowledge.[30] The higher knowledge relates to the highest mental faculty, called *buddhi*.[31] The lower knowledge refers to the capacity of the ordinary mind, called *manas*, the instrument of rational thought within the ego condition relying on the physical brain as a receiver and sender of sensory information.[32]

The true Self is beyond buddhi. Nevertheless, buddhi, which is considered the faculty of wisdom, is like a clear, pure crystal that can allow the self-luminous light of the Self to pass through and to be perceived. Therefore, buddhi represents the clearest reflection of the divine, and this clear reflection helps to reveal the presence of the unchanging reality of the Self. The term buddhi represents not only a mental faculty of wisdom but also a level of existence that can be attained before returning to complete awareness of the Self. The closest Christian term related to buddhi would be the *nous* spoken of by St. Symeon the New Theologian.

In order to attain the wisdom of buddhi and realize the Self, jnana yoga primarily relies on the faculty of discrimination to discern the real from the unreal. Shankara uses the example of looking at a rope. You may see a snake and then believe it is a snake until closer inspection reveals that the apparent snake is actually a rope.[33] This closer mental inspection recommended by Shankara is discrimination that allows you to distinguish between the appearances of this world that are illusory and the true nature of the world that is none other than Reality itself, underlying all form.

This discrimination of jnana yoga is associated with the practice of negation identified in the Upanishads by the term "*neti, neti,*" meaning "not this, not that."[34] Every object, every ego thought is not the Self. The goal of negation is to consistently and persistently reject any form or form-related idea that is an obstacle to the direct awareness of the Self. This negation practice reveals the true Self's spiritual substance of oneness behind all appearances of separation.

Discrimination between the real and unreal is made so the jnana yogi can become attached to the real and detached from the unreal. Using discrimination is intended to lead to *detachment* (renunciation, *samnyasa*), which is necessary to keep the mind pure and undiluted by sense pleasures.[35] Sense pleasures are not pushed away while still being seen as desirable. Discrimination is used to see the flaw of investing in sense pleasures as a way to finding true happiness. The sense pleasures are seen as undesirable and as a block to purity of mind.

As sense pleasures are set aside dispassionately, the result is growth in six virtuous attributes. The first of these attributes is *peacefulness*. This tranquility of mind allows the mind to proceed inwardly toward a deeper awareness of Brahman. Having a peaceful mind allows the jnana yogi to have the quality of *self-control*. This self-control is the regulating of the sense organs, which can be controlled only because the mind is no longer directed outwardly toward sense desires. To control the sense organs prematurely before the mind has reined in the senses would be counterproductive and frustrating.

By both having a peaceful mind and controlling the sense organs, the jnana yogi gains *composure* so he is not thrown off-center by any external phenomena. After this mental poise is developed so that the jnana yogi is not disturbed by transitory events or situations, the next attribute that is acquired is *forbearance*. Through forbearance, there is no complaining or anxiety in response to affliction. This bearing with afflictions means not expressing discomfort outwardly but also means not being inwardly irritated or resentful.

By developing all the previously described qualities, the jnana yogi can acquire unwavering *faith*. Faith is based upon sacred scripture and is the deep conviction that these sacred words are true and Brahman can in fact be realized as one's true Self. This is a very crucial element for a jnana yogi because faith in sacred truth forms the foundation of revealing divine Truth. Serious spiritual practice requires faith that does not waver in regard to accepting the Truth of the Self.

Wavering of conviction scatters the power of the mind and weakens the ability to proceed along the path of jnana yoga. Through firm conviction in the Truth, the mind will be able to manifest *concentration*. The concentrated mind does not dwell on lowly or idle thoughts but instead directs the thinking process toward Brahman. Concentration is not the continuous holding of one thought that occurs in meditation. Rather, concentration consists of focusing the mind toward Brahman, temporarily losing that focus, and then repeatedly returning to the focus on Brahman. This refocusing on Brahman keeps the jnana yogi directed toward his goal of Self-knowledge.

The prerequisites for the practice of jnana yoga that have already been discussed are discrimination, detachment, and the six virtuous attainments, which are peacefulness, self-control, mental composure, forbearance, faith, and concentration. The final preparation for the practice of jnana yoga is the *longing for liberation*.[36] Ignorance alone stands in the way of liberation. But the bonds of ignorance are so strong that only the most intense desire for freedom from bondage will be able to succeed in overcoming ignorance altogether. To follow this path, at some point a sacrifice is required to make the desire so intense that the bonds of ignorance are broken and Brahman is revealed. This sacrifice is the setting aside of all other desires, interests, objectives, and ultimately even all other thoughts so only the desire for Brahman remains. Similar to the dark night of the soul experience, there is a potential for insanity along this path. That is why this path is meant to be traveled only by very hardy souls.

Acquiring the four prerequisites of jnana yoga is the preparation for the three ways of practicing jnana yoga. The first of these practices is *shravana*, which is hearing the truth.[37] The jnana yogi can study the scripture, but usually hearing the truth means hearing the scriptural truth from a teacher. The second practice is *manana*, reflecting on the truth, which means constantly allowing the mind to dwell upon Brahman.[38] Unlike the bhakti yogi, who focuses on a personal Ishta, the jnana yogi turns his mind toward the impersonal Reality. Investing in the truth of Brahman fosters faith in reality, which becomes a strong conviction. Thus longing for Brahman intensifies.

The third practice is *nididhyasana*, which is meditation directed toward Brahman.[39] In general, meditation is the constant unbroken flow of one thought toward one aim. In the practice of nididhyasana, the aim is continuous thought of the truth of the Absolute Reality. This continuous flow of thought leads to *samadhi*, the direct experience of Brahman. Samadhi is the common goal of all the paths of yoga.

Following the path of jnana yoga is a rigorous road that is meant for very few. Nevertheless, this path offers an indispensable ingredient that is necessary for every path of yoga. There is no use being on the path to find Brahman if the Supreme Being is not truly there to be found or if he is absolutely inaccessible. Every seeker of God must have at least a certain degree of the conviction that the jnana yogi possesses. This is the conviction that God is present, hidden behind every form in this world, and that He indeed can be found.

H. RAJA YOGA — THE PATH OF MEDITATION

King Shivananda's eldest son, who was the cave dweller, followed the path of *raja yoga* as his way of returning to a place of honor in the kingdom. Raja yoga is the path of meditation. Similar to jnana yoga, raja yoga has many steps that lead toward meditation. *Raja* means "royal." This is the royal path in yoga and is the most all-inclusive path, requiring a balanced approach to seeking God. Raja yoga, sometimes called *ashtanga yoga*, is a combination of eight aspects of spiritual growth that lead toward union with God.

Raja yoga goes back to the Vedic times of 2,000 to 3,000 B.C. and to the mythical Hiranyagarba, who is accurately considered the "father of yoga." Patanjali often receives the credit for being the originator of yoga, but instead he was the codifier of yoga. Patanjali's systematic codification of raja yoga occurred in the third century B.C. and was documented in his famous *Yoga Sutras*. These sutras describe raja yoga as having "eight members" (*ashtanga*), listed below:

1. *yamas* — ethical restrictions
2. *niyamas* — ethical observances
3. *asanas* — body postures
4. *pranayama* — breath control
5. *pratyahara* — withdrawal of senses from sense objects
6. *dharana* — concentration of the mind, not continuous
7. *dhyana* — meditation, continuous focusing of the mind
8. *samadhi* — transcendent awareness

The beginning members of this system of raja yoga are easier to practice and more related to the world than the later members. The first member is the *yamas*,[40] which are similar to the abstinences contained in the Christian ten commandments in that these indicate the things that must not be done in order to maintain proper moral conduct. The yamas are the following restrictions:

1. not harming anyone
2. not lying
3. not stealing
4. not indulging in sexual impurity
5. not receiving gifts

The second member is the *niyamas*,[41] which are those observances of a positive nature that must be fulfilled in order to maintain proper moral conduct. The niyamas are, as follows:

1. cleanliness
2. contentment
3. austerity
4. study
5. surrendering to God

The third raja yoga member is *asanas*, body postures, described in Chapter 4. The fourth member of raja yoga is *pranayama*, breathing practices, described in Chapter 5. The asanas and pranayama are components of *hatha yoga*, basically the yoga of the physical body. Gaining control over the body and the breath are a preparation for gaining control over the mind, which in turn leads directly toward being receptive to mystical experience.

The fifth member of raja yoga is *pratyahara*, the withdrawing of your senses from sense objects. Reducing stimulation by preventing the senses from going outwardly to the sense objects helps to keep the mind directed inwardly. One examples of pratyahara preparing you for meditation is closing your eyes to withdraw the sense of sight from seeing outer objects. Another example is holding the body motionless to prevent the sense of touch from being activated. This withdrawal of the senses of sight and touch helps you maintain an inward focus.

However, pratyahara is not just a selective inwardness that assists meditation; it is a general practice that helps turn the direction of the mind in everyday life away from the finite and toward the infinite. The withdrawal of the senses from the sense objects requires the same kind of discrimination (ability to distinguish between the finite and infinite), detachment (letting go of the desire for sense pleasures) and self-control (regulating of the sense organs) that is necessary to practice jnana yoga. Pratyahara can be practiced by directing your mind inwardly even while being involved with outward activities. Pratyahara in daily living corresponds to Christian *recollection*, which is the maintaining of an inward spiritual focus while being active in the world.

The first five members of raja yoga are external practices and are considered prerequisites to moving on to the last three members of raja yoga. These last three members are collectively called *samyama*, the "inner members." These inner members are related to the mind being turned inwardly. The goal of raja yoga is to control the *vrittis*, thought-waves, in order to directly experience the true Self.

Each thought-wave produces a mental impression that leaves a mark or groove in the mind. This mental groove is called a *samskara*.[42] This groove remains fixed in the mind. There will be a faint groove if there is a single thought-wave. But the repeating of the same thoughts and same actions produces a deeper groove, a stronger samskara. Positive thoughts and actions produce positive samskaras; negative thoughts and actions produce negative samskaras. The individual's character consists of the totality of all the samskaras in the mind. Once samskaras have been established through habit, these grooves in the mind become behavior patterns that become very hard to change.

Although the individual has created these samskaras by his choice of thoughts and actions, it can seem to the individual that he has no power to resist these embedded grooves in the mind. Samskaras can become an irresistible force so that the individual continually repeats the same thoughts, desires, and actions. This is noticeable in addictive behaviors, but everyone is subject to this same tendency.

The mind with strong samskaras may be compared with an object in motion. This object in motion seems to be like a train on a track that can only move in the direction of the groove of the train tracks. Yet the mind only *appears* as a train that cannot change directions. If the mind with its samskaras is compared to an object in motion, it follows the scientific principle of inertia. According to this principle, the objects that are at rest will stay at rest, and objects in motion will stay in motion unless acted upon by another force. The mind with all its samskaras is like an object in motion that will continue to stay in motion unless acted upon by some other force. Raja yoga maintains that you can introduce some "other force" to counteract the inertia of the mind.

Raja yoga says that you must choose one steady and calm thought that is repeated so many times that it produces one gigantic groove, samskara, in the mind. Though the thought itself is a peaceful thought, its repetition creates a very powerful force. This is the "other force" that counteracts the inertia of the mind, changing its direction. As an unwavering thought directed toward God, this one thought, makes one groove and becomes so great that it swallows up all the other thoughts. This stops the hurricane of the mind and reveals the hidden eye of the hurricane, which is the peaceful divine place within.

The sixth member of raja yoga (the first of the three inner members) is *dharana*, concentration, which is the holding of one thought, but not continuously. The seventh member is *dhyana*, meditation (the second of the three inner members), which is the holding of one thought in the mind continuously.

As the groove, samskara, of the one thought directed toward God becomes stronger, the irresistible power of other samskaras becomes weaker. The seeker gains the ability to change and become a new person with a new sense of freedom. Old negative patterns, which are negative samskaras, can be set aside and be replaced by new positive ones. Old desires may come into the mind, but instead of acting these out, the individual can let these thoughts pass on by without acting them out. As old desires are allowed to pass by without acting upon them, these old samskaras become fainter.

But the samskaras cannot normally be obliterated, unless there is the deepest spiritual experience. This experience is called *samadhi*, and is the eighth member of raja yoga (the third of the three inner members). There are different levels of samadhi, the transcendental experience of the divine. One kind of samadhi is *savikalpa samadhi,* in which the knower, the known, and the knowing are joined, but appear distinctly separate. In the experience of savikalpa samadhi, the seeker is still in the body, and this may be considered an indirect experience of Reality being expressed within the level of form and duality. The most advanced level of samadhi is called *nirvikalpa samadhi*, in which the soul of the seeker is drawn out of the body beyond form. The whole universe disappears as the seeker meets Reality face to face in an experience of nondual Oneness.

In the experience of *nirvikalpa samadhi*, the samskaras become like seeds that are burnt, losing the power to sprout again. This experience of nirvikalpa samadhi is the final goal of raja yoga, but the ongoing objective of raja yoga is to weaken the samskaras. Weakening the samskaras allows the mind to be loosened from the grip of karma and helps to bring about integration between the body, mind, and spirit. Yet this integration is only a preparation for *moksha*, liberation from this world. In Patanjali's yoga system, liberation is obtained through nirvikalpa samadhi, but not all systems of yoga believe that liberation from this world is the highest form of attainment. Another form of yoga, *tantric yoga*, describes an even deeper level of perfection, which will be described in the next section.

I. TRANSFORMATION IN THE LIGHT IN YOGA

In this section, the transformation of consciousness that occurs in yoga will be addressed. In the mental disciplines of yoga, at first there is focusing on specific objects in meditation. This beginning experience of meditation maintains the firm division between the knower of the object, the act of knowing, and the object that is known.

In meditation, the mind becomes connected to the object, and the meditative experience of the object creates a change in perception, a transformation of consciousness. Normally objects are observed not as what they are, but as concepts that have been projected onto objects. A cup may initially be seen as an object that is used for drinking. As meditation deepens, the cup may be seen as a vertical cylinder that is closed on the bottom and open on the top. Instead of being seen as they are, objects are sorted in the mind and forced into categories related to the ego needs. Yet through nonjudgmental seeing, the object becomes what it actually is in form rather than an image in the mind. This nonjudgmental looking is a withdrawal of the tendency of the mind to project abstract thoughts onto objects making them into desired images, rather than an acceptance of what they are.

When this ego-based projection of the mind onto the external object is withdrawn, the experience of the outer object is changed, but more importantly, an inner event occurs. By observing the outer object, the knower becomes detached from the external object and turned inward upon his own activity of knowing. Instead of an outer focusing object, an inner object (such as a word or idea) can be used as a focus, but this too can turn the knower back toward his own activity of knowing. The inner object can be a single mantra or can be many mantras as is sometimes used to raise the kundalini. Various techniques can be used in this inner focusing, but inner objects are transcended in the process of the knower becoming aware of the activity of knowing itself.

The inner object as a thought in the mind becomes increasingly subtle, and it fluctuates between appearing and disappearing. Light experiences may occur spontaneously. The time may come when the stream of thoughts stops and starts again. Finally, the fluctuations of thoughts stop altogether, and the spirit beholds its own consciousness. There is an experience of the light of consciousness, *prakasa*, since light and consciousness are inseparably one. This is the stage that Patanjali, the author of the *Yoga Sutras*, calls *kaivalya*, "isolation." This isolation occurs during nirvikalpa samadhi, the highest spiritual attainment according to Patanjali. Nirvikalpa samadhi is a state of consciousness without any objects and yet full of awareness. This is called isolation because of the spirit of the yogi being outside of the body, outside of the world, and even outside of time.

There is a common belief that this escape from the world is the ultimate goal of all forms of yoga because that is the position taken by Patanjali in his description of raja yoga. But there are other viewpoints in yoga. For example, the form of yoga, called *tantric yoga,* describes the ultimate goal of transformation as a state of perfection that is quite different from escaping from the world. Since tantric yoga advocates using experiences in the world, such as sexual union, as a means of spiritual growth, its value as a path is often misunderstood and so underestimated. There are various types of tantric yoga that involve sexual orgasms. Also, there is the form of tantric yoga called "white tantric yoga" in which there are no orgasms. Tantric yoga maintains that sexual union can be a way of elevating consciousness, yet this is considered a gross outer expression that is only a preliminary for a more important inner expression. This subtle expression is the uniting of the male and female polarities within the seeker's own body to return to the unifying primal energy from which the sexual energy originated. The tantric yoga goal of the unification process is raising the kundalini to experience divine oneness. Tantric yoga as a path of transformation is based on anonymous writings called Tantras. These sacred texts include ritual instructions and spiritual teachings.

There are Hindu Tantras and Buddhist Tantras, so tantric yoga has evolved in both Hinduism and Buddhism. Hindu tantric yoga is often associated with *Shaktism*, which is the form of worship related to *shakti*, "energy." Shakti has a broader meaning than prana, which can be referred to as *prana shakti*, since it is one kind of shakti. Shakti is the cosmic energy coming forth from the active and creative aspect of Reality and manifesting the entire universe. In other words, shakti is the energy that exists in both organic and inorganic matter, whereas prana refers specifically to the life force energy that exists in all organic matter. The kundalini is an expression of prana shakti, but for brevity is often spoken of as an expression of shakti.[43] Hindu tantric yoga is commonly called "kundalini yoga." Hindu Tantrism is usually primarily associated with openness to shakti in Shatkism and the raising of the kundalini, although these are certainly not the only important aspects of Hindu Tantrism.

Tantric yoga (kundalini yoga) is designed to bring about the rising of kundalini energy (prana shakti). As is explained in Chapter 5, the kundalini energy is in a potential form at the base of the spine and can be raised upward to the top of the head. In the body, there are vertical channels of energy, called *nadis*, that are associated with the central nervous system. The central nadi is the *susumna*, the left nadi is the *ida*, and the right nadi is the *pingala*. The aim in yoga is to bring the female ida energy and the male pingala energy together within the central channel of the susumna, and raise the combined energy upward. This goal can be accomplished as a result of certain kinds of meditation. One kind of tantric meditation is the repeating of mantras focused on the various energy centers, chakras, in the spine. Breathing practices can assist the process of raising and unifying energy, as is explained in Chapter 5. The purpose of uniting the male and female energies is to return the energy to its primordial state of union. Raising this energy upward produces a complete transformation of consciousness.

In addition to tantric meditation in which mantras are projected onto the chakras, *kriya yoga* is another form of tantric meditation. The word "kriya," like the word "karma," is derived from the Sanskrit verb, *kri*, meaning "to do." Kriya is an "activity."[44] Kriya yoga is a tantric practice of meditation that is a ritual activity. It is a sacred activity performed as an inner fire-rite sacrifice, in which the tantric yogi offers himself as a sacrifice, a burnt offering, to the divine within.

The practice of kriya yoga coordinates the controlling of the breath with the movement of vital energy through the chakras. This combines meditation with a breathing exercise and is a fire sacrifice that burns up inner impurities. This inner ritual action raises the kundalini up the spine. After the ritual action elevates the energy, this energy descends again. Then the ritual action is repeated with its upward movement of energy, which is again followed by the energy descending.

As a sacrificial rite, the ascending and descending energy is seen as a fire, and the kundalini energy acts as a purifying fire. Through this alternate rising and descending of the shakti, the body slowly becomes purified by being burnt by the inner fire of the kundalini. Finally, the inner fire burns up all the centers of consciousness in the body. The inner fire comes to rest in the heart center. Next, a heavenly water, a cool nectar, manifests initially in the head and descends into the heart and is distributed to the whole body. This celestial "ambrosia" cleanses the burnt body and revitalizes it.[45] The whole process brings about a transformation of consciousness.

Another tantric yoga way of transforming consciousness is *mandala* meditation. Mandala in Sanskrit literally means "circle." The mandala always involves the visual image of the outer circle that contains the mandala and a central focusing point, called the *bindu*, which stands for a point of light. This point of light is the true Self, where the Lord also abides. When the tantric yogi has an inner experience of the bindu, it changes into a circle of blazing light whose circumference expands infinitely. The yogi transcends the limitations of bodily awareness and experiences both his true nature and the Lord in this explosion of light radiating outward. The yogi is everywhere and nowhere. He is at the center of the light, and yet paradoxically he is expanding infinitely with the light, just as the sun stays in place and simultaneously extends its rays outwardly. This is indeed samadhi, but tantric yoga says there is a higher attainment for the yogi who remains in the world.

For tantric yoga, the highest spiritual attainment is to become a *jivanmukta*,[46] an individual (*jiva*) who is still in the world and yet is freed. This state of liberation (*mukti*) is a condition of perfection in which the yogi remains within the human condition and yet continues in everyday life to be fully aware of his transcendent oneness with God. The original realization of the Lord in the light of the true Self is at first an experience of altered consciousness. Once the realization of the true Self in God has occurred, the goal is to allow the light of the true Self to penetrate into all the lower levels of consciousness of everyday life. Instead of experiencing the light as an altered state, the perfect tantric yogi experiences the light as a natural expression shining through all of his thoughts, feelings, and actions in the world. His goal is not to escape the world, but to live in a fully transformed world because his consciousness has been transformed.

Tantric yoga agrees with Patanjali's assertion that yogi can reach a state in which the fluctuation of the mind can stop and consciousness can become aware of itself. Through the practice of tantric yoga, the yogi becomes one with the indivisible point of light, the *bindu*. When this occurs, the point of light expands into an infinite explosion of light and pure consciousness revealing the true Self in God. This awakening is an explosion of light and is similar to St. Symeon's description of seeing the face of Christ brighter than the sun.

For tantric yoga, finding the Self is not the end of the spiritual journey as it is for Patanjali. The classical yoga of Patanjali presents a division between spirit and nature. Patanjali concludes that the knower, the subject of experience, is the *Purusha*, meaning the true "person." The Purusha transcends both the body and the ego-based mind. This subject, the Purusha, is the unchanging true Self that is the supreme consciousness. This Purusha, being the true Self, is the witness of all sensations, feelings, and concepts. On the other hand, the ego-based mind has no consciousness of its own and is considered by Patanjali as belonging to the material world. The world of matter is called *prakriti*, meaning *nature* (materiality). Generally, it is accepted that Patanjali believed in a duality between nature and the Purusha, rather than believing in the nondualism of Vedanta.

For Patanjali, the goal of yoga is to purify the body and the mind so that it clearly reflects the light of the Purusha. This purification requires a progressive dismantling of the false ideas of ego-based identification with the body and the mind. This requires a complete inner and outer renunciation of everything. The yogi purifies the mind with meditation at deeper and deeper levels. When the purification process is complete, the yogi no longer identifies with the body and ego-base mind as being himself. Instead, the yogi realizes his true original identity in the Purusha. This return to the awareness of the true Self is considered the ultimate enlightenment and freedom.

The book *The Integrity of the Yoga Darsana: A Reconsideration of Classical Yoga* provides a different interpretation of Patanjali's *Yoga Sutras*. The author, Ian Whicher, maintains that Patanjali's philosophy of dualism between nature (prakriti) and the Purusha is just a teaching device related to the practical aspects of yoga disciplines and is not related to the philosophy of yoga. In the dualism of Patanjali, the seeker is faced with a dualistic frame of reference in which he perceives himself as separate from the ultimate Reality he is seeking. The dualism of Patanjali is merely a pragmatic approach that accepts the seeker's current perception of separation and allows him to focus on purifying his misperceived material nature as a stepping stone to awakening to transcendental Awareness. Patanjali was not concerned with focusing on the illusory condition of materiality and therefore restricted himself to presenting only practical directions in how to purify and transform the body and the mind identified with the body.

Consequently, Whicher takes the position that for Patanjali the Purusha is similar to the Atman presented in Vedanta, as the nondual Reality that is not in opposition to materiality but rather transcends the illusion of materiality. Whichter also refutes the typical notion that Patanjali advocated escape from the world as the highest spiritual achievement. Instead, he maintains that Patanjali actually believed in jivanmukta, being liberated while living in the world. This is the state of freedom of the spirit remaining at the highest level of consciousness while still embodied in the flesh.

Although Patanjali's classical yoga has been re-evaluated in recent years in regard to jivanmukta, this high ideal has always been the foundation of tantric yoga. The body, the world, and time are the limitations that bind the seeker, but tantric yoga uses these limitations as its means of awakening to the spirit. Perfect awakening does not mean escape, but rather transcending the body, the world, and time so these elements still are present but no longer an impediment to freedom. For the perfect tantric yogi, the One is *spanda*, movement and energy. The One is experienced as both the One and the many simultaneously. The One transcends everything yet can be seen in the movement and energy of all things.

In tantric yoga, the Lord is identified as Shiva. The Lord has three energies, which are the shakti of activity, consciousness, and will. The Lord is One, transcending these shakti, and at the same time is present within these shakti. The goal in tantric yoga is to be one with the Lord and likewise to be one with the shakti and transcend the shakti simultaneously.

At this level, there is a transformation of consciousness so the yogi realizes himself by divine grace as inseparable from the Lord so there is no longer a separate self. His new transformed true Self is fully identified and united with the Lord. In this identification and union, the Self is joined with the shakti and yet transcends the shakti, just as the Lord is both within and above the shakti.

Here the yogi is not free from the body, world, and time, but rather simply free. Formerly the yogi had to exert effort to join with the divine "Other." However, this new freedom is a natural state of complete effortlessness. For this jivanmukta, who is in a state of freedom while living, every word spoken is a sacred word and every breath is a sacred breath. Nevertheless, the jivanmukta appears ordinary, and his divine expressions are hidden in everyday appearances just as the Lord is also hidden in all of His creation. In this state of freedom in the Lord, everything is a manifestation of divine grace, a gift fully realized as a gift by the jivanmukta.

This transcendent state may be considered both an "ecstasy" and an "enstasy." As an ecstasy, the yogi expands his consciousness from its smallness and limitations to the infinite totality of God-realization, an unlimited expansion of awareness. As an enstasy, the yogi penetrates into the luminous and indivisible point of light, the bindu, which is at the center of the "living" cosmos and the center of the divine core of the human heart. This paradox of awareness is remarkably similar to the experience of St. Symeon, who likewise manifested the ideal of mystical divine oneness that is rooted in a transcendent experience of everyday life.

Even the steps along the way of awakening to the light in tantric yoga are very similar to St. Symeon's experience. The sequence of St. Symeon opening to *theoria*, which is the vision of inner light, is summarized by the following quotation:

> ... it is fire, it is also ray,
> it becomes a cloud of light,
> it perfects itself as the sun.[47]

St. Symeon's experience of opening to theoria begins with a feeling of warmth or fire. Eastern techniques that focus on the rising of vital kundalini energy from the base of the spine upward often refer to this transforming energy as an "inner fire." Tantric texts in both the Hindu and Buddhist traditions use the word "fire" to describe the uniting of the male and female energies. The symbol of "light" and many other symbols are common to tantric yoga and Eastern Orthodox mysticism. The descriptions by St. Symeon of his mystical experiences have many strong parallels with the descriptions by Abhinavagupta of his tantric yoga mystical experiences. A thorough comparison between these two mystics is provided in the book entitled, *Yoga and the Jesus Prayer Tradition*.[48] This scholarly book by Thomas Matus provides a strong presentation of the many commonalities between tantric yoga and the Eastern Orthodox mysticism of *hesychasm*, represented in particular by St. Symeon. In addition, Christian experiences of transformation of consciousness in light with an emphasis on St. Symeon's experiences can be found in my meditation manual titled *Christian Meditation Inspired by Yoga and "A Course in Miracles": Opening to Divine Love in Contemplation.*

CHAPTER 3

~ • ~

MIRACLE YOGA AS A PATH TO GOD

A. CHOOSING MIRACLE YOGA AS YOUR PATH

There are various techniques taught by different schools of yoga. These yoga schools are not limited to the vast diversity of Hinduism. For example, in addition to Hindu tantric yoga, there is a Buddhist tantric yoga. Also, there is a Taoist yoga coming from China. Unlike a spiritual approach that must follow one particular system, such as Zen Buddhism, yoga is like clay that can be molded into any form of seeking the divine. Therefore, yoga is fertile ground to be molded and integrated into a Western form consistent with Christianity.

Christian seekers are often told that what happens in communion with God is a "mystery," and this is indeed true. However, sometimes the word mystery is put forward as a justification for not investigating divine matters. Yoga would agree that there is indeed a divine mystery in communication with God, but would as much as possible seek to de-mystify the divine mystery. A mystery is only a mystery because of a lack of awareness. It is true that the intellect alone cannot penetrate the divine mystery, but yoga does not rely on intellect as its only source. The source of yoga is the experience of sages from times gone by who have personally unraveled the divine mystery.

From their inner experiences, these sages have drawn forth systems of transformation and made them into a *science of spirituality*. Their inner experiences themselves cannot be fully conveyed intellectually, but their science can be explained conceptually. Science maintains that if you follow certain repeatable procedures you will get the expected repeatable results. The word "science" will be used here to indicate the rational explanations and systematic practices of yoga that produce specific results. In the yoga science of spirituality, the sages of the past practiced techniques that helped them to transcend the ego and to experience divine union. Yoga scripture maintains that if these same practices are followed by seekers, they will be able to repeat the same results and also experience divine union.

But the words "science of spirituality" apply only to the rational side of yoga, and it would be misleading if it was assumed that yoga is only a collection of techniques. There is a much less scientific side of yoga that is really more important. Yoga means "yoke" or "union," yet it can also mean "integration." Yoga, living up to its name, is not just a rational system, but an integrated system designed to facilitate the integration of all the levels of human nature as a preparation for divine awareness. In particular, much of yoga involves not a cold, calculated approach, but rather a divine seeking that includes a wholehearted embrace of all the human faculties. The aim is the coordination of the body and its actions, the emotions with an emphasis on love as the motivation, the intellect, contemplative inclinations, and freewill choice. Even in those forms of yoga in which one aspect of human nature dominates, the other aspects are considered important for creating an inner integration. Of course, the ultimate goal in yoga is always Self-realization and God-realization, seen as synonymous.

Christians, who are open to Eastern philosophy, are attracted to the single-minded focus on divine union and the practical means offered to lead in that direction so they are willing to adopt the gifts offered by the East. However, the word "adopt" may not be the best term to use here for that would suggest taking on a whole system of yoga as is, without much modification. It would be more appropriate to suggest that Christians "adapt" the science of yoga in a modified form that would focus upon Christ as the goal.

One challenge of creating such a modified yoga system would be the complexity of many different systems of yoga. It would be easy for the Christian seeker to get lost in the details of these systems. Yet there is undoubtedly a happy medium between the elements of Christian mystery and the elaborate yoga systems. A method such as *Christian Yoga Meditation* is a technique that achieves this happy medium that blends Christianity and systematic yoga. Christian Yoga Meditation, which is elaborated later in this chapter, has a strong Christian focus on the Holy Spirit guiding the usage of this technique and retaining a reasonable element of Christian mystery.

Many seekers with different religious beliefs have used the term "Christian yoga" to describe combining yoga with following Christ. Anyone who practices any form of Christian yoga would benefit by the practice of Christian Yoga Meditation. Christian yoga represents a balance between reliance on the gift of divine grace and the seeking of the divine through methods involving self-effort. For example, Christian Yoga Meditation offers a balance between the mysterious action of the

Holy Spirit and the use of techniques focused upon body awareness. Likewise, there is a healthy balance between the passive receptivity of contemplation and the active focused participation in yoga techniques. Christians who meditate may experience energy rising up the spine and related phenomena in the body. In this case, it is very helpful to have the yoga philosophical context in which to understand what is happening. It is equally comforting to place the raising of the kundalini energy in the loving hands of the Holy Spirit. The balanced approach of using prudent yoga methods and surrendering to the action of the Holy Spirit may not be necessary for everyone. Yet it is indispensable for those Christians whose inner experiences call them to being open to joining the East and West.

Yoga is not one transformational system, but many. Each system of yoga has its own structure, yet that structure usually lends itself to flexibility. Yoga, in its meaning of union or yoking together, is both the end of union and the means used to achieve that end. What you want to be yoked to, your chosen ideal, is always left up to your choice. Thus *Christian yoga* is yoga with Christ as the chosen ideal.

With yoga structure as the means and Christ as the goal of yoga, there are many different ways of putting Christian yoga into practical application. The kind of Christian yoga that is practiced will depend on what you consider to be your religious affiliation or lack of affiliation. If you belong to a specific Christian religious group, you will want to remain fully engaged in the activities of your church. Thus you could practice hatha yoga, with postures and breathing practices, in addition to your church involvement. You could also practice meditation, such as Christian Yoga Meditation, as an inner communication with the divine. Your religious affiliation would be your basic path to God and your yoga practices would be your spiritual growth options.

On the other hand, if you are not invested in a particular religious affiliation, you may want to consider Christian yoga itself as your path to God. There is no standardized path of Christian yoga so you will have to combine the seeking of Christ with the assistance of yoga in your own unique way. If you are open to Christian yoga being your path to God, you can consider your options. One specific path of Christian yoga, called "Miracle Yoga," will be advocated here yet you may choose some other form of Christian yoga that is better suited to your nature and beliefs. Miracle Yoga is based on the principles of *A Course in Miracles*. You may decide to accept this path the way it is described with perhaps some personal modifications. Or you may feel guided to pursue Christian yoga in a distinctly different way, and hopefully some of the ideas below will help you to define your own unique Christian yoga path.

In evaluating how to implement Christian yoga as your own path, you may want to consider whether you are attracted to the paths of karma yoga, bhakti yoga, jnana yoga, and raja yoga. Although these have been described previously as separate paths, each of these paths overlap and are intended to complement each other. Before I accepted the Course, I focused on practicing Christian yoga as a synthesis of Christian karma yoga, Christian bhakti yoga, Christian raja yoga, and Christian jnana yoga. Therefore, I established a Christian yoga website, which is www.christianyoga.org.

After I accepted the Course as my thought system, I switched to Miracle Yoga as a blending of Miracle Karma Yoga, Miracle Bhakti Yoga, Miracle Raja Yoga, Miracle Jnana Yoga, and added Miracle Relationship Yoga. Thus I established a Miracle Yoga website, which is www.miracleyoga.org. The upcoming sections discuss the five aspects of Miracle Yoga as a specific means of practicing Christian yoga.

An important consideration in how you chose to practice Christian yoga as your path will be your conceptual understanding of Christ, God, the Holy Spirit, and your own true nature. The section in this chapter titled "Miracle Jnana Yoga" presents one set of concepts you may want to use to grow spiritually. You can accept this conceptual picture based on the Course or rely on your own conceptual picture that would best express your own spiritual understanding.

Concepts can be an asset to approaching God, but can also be a hindrance, especially if the attachment to concepts is too strong. It is best to adopt whatever concepts will lead to experiencing God beyond concepts. A basic premise that has been described in this manual is the idea that your true Identity is your Christ Self. The Course uses both of the terms "Christ" and "Self" to describe your true nature in God. But the combination of these two terms in the form of "Christ Self" is my own personal terminology. If you prefer, you can think of this as your "spirit," "Christ Consciousness," your place in the "body of Christ," or some other term of your own choosing. Regardless of your choice of terminology, the question that you need to address in your practice of Christian yoga as a path is this: *How do I choose to become aware of my spiritual nature?* This is a very personal decision. Christian yoga as a path, just like Hinduism itself, offers many options.

These options can be divided into two basic categories: personal devotion or impersonal devotion. If you pursue personal devotion, you will probably have a conceptual picture of a personal God. If you pursue impersonal devotion, you will probably have a conceptual picture of an impersonal God. If you want to practice Miracle Yoga, you can choose to express personal devotion to Jesus and/or God as is explained in the section titled "Miracle Bhakti Yoga." Impersonal devotion to God will be explained in the section titled "Miracle Jnana

Yoga." This Miracle Yoga book suggests using personal and impersonal approaches to God in your spiritual seeking.

Although yoga involves methods, your primary means of becoming aware of your spiritual nature is divine grace. This divine grace comes to you from God the Father, from the Holy Spirit, and from Christ. Divine grace provides many means of returning Home. Miracle Yoga as a path is one of these means. In this path, you cooperated with divine grace through a combination of the selfless action of Miracle Karma Yoga, the love of Miracle Bhakti Yoga, the knowledge of Miracle Jnana Yoga, and the meditation and contemplation of Miracle Raja Yoga.

B. LOOKING AND OVERLOOKING

Is there really a need for a Christian yoga path that includes these expressions? After all, selfless action, love, knowledge, and meditation are already well-established principles of traditional Christianity, so why is there a need for a Christian yoga path that restates these same principles? If your current Christian path is already nourishing you by encouraging selfless action, love, knowledge, and meditation, perhaps there is no need for you personally to follow a Christian yoga path.

On the other hand, although the ideas of selfless action, love, knowledge, and meditation are not entirely new and different, the Christian yoga path of Miracle Yoga does present these ideas with a unique focus that generally cannot be found in traditional Christian paths. This focus is centered on the question, "What is real and what is not real?" Surely, Christian theologians have pursued this question in the realm of ideas, but this question has not been emphasized in terms of Christian practice. A typical Christian may describe facing the everyday struggles of life as "living in the *real* world," meaning the world of form. In contrast to this perspective, the path of Miracle Yoga focuses on the theme of knowing and indeed experiencing what is in fact real and letting go of what is in fact not real.

The selfless action, love, knowledge, and meditation of Miracle Yoga are a refocusing of these Christian principles toward revealing the real and renouncing the unreal, not just in a theoretical sense, but in terms of practical application. Uncovering the real and setting aside the unreal is expressed in practical ways through selfless action, love, knowledge, and contemplation. Yet these expressions are each directed toward the one goal of experiencing your own true spiritual nature in Christ.

This theme of focusing on the real and letting go of the unreal is what is called here the art of allowing. This art of allowing enables the real to be real and the unreal to be unreal. Another way to describe the art of allowing is to say it is the principle and the practice of "looking and overlooking." The "looking" part involves focusing on the divine Reality. This focusing is usually inwardly directed, but it can also be directed outwardly to see the divine in others. The "overlooking" part of this principle involves identifying anything that is not in harmony with the divine, which would be the ego and all of its manifestations. When you overlook something, you look past it to something else. In other words, your attention is diverted from what you are overlooking and instead your attention is placed upon something else.

Most people place their attention on what they think is important and take their attention away from what they think is unimportant. In the case of Miracle Yoga, the seeker makes the conscious decision that what is real is important and what is not real is unimportant. Having made this decision, the seeker follows the path of Miracle Yoga as a way of carrying out the principle of "looking and overlooking." Therefore, "looking and overlooking," as a thought principle, becomes "looking and overlooking" as a *practice,* as a spiritual discipline. In the practice of this spiritual discipline, you place your attention on what is important by looking at the real, which is the divine. Also, you withdraw your attention from what is unimportant by overlooking the unreal, which is the ego and its illusory manifestations.

In contrast to the correct use of "looking and overlooking" used in Miracle Yoga, traditional Christianity uses "looking and overlooking" improperly in an upside down manner by looking at the unreal and overlooking the real. This improper looking at the unreal consists of paying attention to the ego and the ego's mistakes, which are deemed as "sins," marks on the soul that defile the seeker's spiritual nature. This improper overlooking consists of not paying attention to the true divine nature of the seeker thus denying the seeker's true purity, which can never be defiled since he is forever the holy Son of God.

Because of the belief in duality, traditional Christianity is based on the idea that the ego is real and that the sins of the ego are real. Yoga philosophy maintains there are relative realities consisting of changing expressions in the world, and there is an unchanging absolute Reality that transcends the world of form. Your perspective determines what appears real to you. If you have a "transcendental perspective," the ego and world will appear to be illusory since they are in fact illusory, having only a relative reality. If you have an "ego-based perspective," everything of the ego will appear real. Not only will the world appear real, but your ego-based beliefs will determine everything that you consider to be real. In this ego-based frame of reference, even if you firmly believe that you are Napoleon, this idea will become personally real to you, and you will act as if you are Napoleon. The belief that sins defile your soul making you unacceptable to God has no objective reality, so sins are objectively unreal. But if you believe in the idea of sin, then sin, which is intrinsically unreal, will become real for you. Similarly, the traditional Christian improper looking for what is unreal, which is a looking for sin, makes sin appear real because of paying attention to it. Likewise, traditional Christian improper overlooking of what is real, overlooking one's divine nature, makes one's pure spiritual nature appear unreal, meaning appear to be nonexistent because of disregarding its reality. This is the ignorance of ignoring the truth.

Traditional Christian looking is focused on guilt and the past and overlooking is focused on ignoring your holiness and avoiding the present moment, in which your divine nature can be experienced now. Therefore, this improper looking places the emphasis on darkness and falsehood and overlooks the light and the truth. This produces in the seeker identification with being a guilty sinner, undeserving of divine union. This promotes a sense of alienation from God and from your brothers because of the focus on unworthiness. Such a condition can be compared to you being in an entirely dark room and looking only at the darkness. Thus you overlook the fact that in your hand you have a flashlight that only requires your attention to turn it on in order to overcome the darkness with light.

Saying that mistakes of the ego do not affect the reality of your true nature in union with God does not mean mistakes in the relative reality of the world do not need to be corrected. But if you think errors have a reality that extends to defiling your own reality, you will believe your errors are uncorrectable. Conversely seeing your errors as apart from affecting your own reality means they can be corrected at the level in which they occur—at the level of the relative reality of the world.

The way to overcome errors caused by investment in darkness and untruth is to withdraw your faith in darkness and untruth and to invest only in light and truth by identifying with your own true nature in God. Darkness is obviously only the lack of light and correcting darkness is the restoration of the light that is lacking. In other words, errors are due to a lack of love and correcting errors is the restoration of the love that is lacking. Since light, truth, and love are your true nature in God, correcting any errors can be achieved by turning your attention and faith toward your Source in God. Restoring contact with your divine Source, which is the level of your true reality that transcends the world, automatically produces the result of correcting errors on the level of the relative reality of the world of form where these errors occur. Through correcting errors in this way, you can see from your experience that sins are only mistakes that can be corrected and are not marks on the soul that make you unacceptable to God.

Unlike traditional Christianity, which uses upside down thinking that looks at the darkness and overlooks the light, the path of Miracle Yoga consists of looking at the light and overlooking the darkness. The word "attachment" is often associated with a negative connotation of inappropriate clinging, but there is a positive form of attachment, which is attachment to the divine. In the looking and overlooking of Miracle Yoga the word "looking" represents this positive attachment to the divine, and the companion word "overlooking" represents the giving up of attachment to anything that is not divine, which would be anything of the ego. Thus the path of Miracle Yoga in each of its forms involves attachment to the infinite and detachment from the finite. Each of the following four sections identifies a different aspect of Miracle Yoga and specifically indicates how looking and overlooking is applied to each aspect as a means of revealing your true divine nature in Christ.

C. THE PARADOX OF KARMA

Before discussing Miracle Karma Yoga, it is important to draw a distinction between the traditional yoga idea of karma and how the Course describes karma. This section explains the paradox that karma exists and does not exist.

Parts of the Old Testament depict God as being righteously wrathful, which contradicts the idea that God is all-loving. Similarly, even the New Testament provides an image of God offering righteous justice that would send some of His children to hell to be punished forever. This belief in divine justice provides an illusory picture of God made in the image and likeness of *man*, not the other way around. In the Course, God's idea of justice is that everyone deserves Heaven. No idea in the Course contradicts that God is Love.

The Course offers spiritual principles that are different from some ideas in the Bible and also different from some commonly held ideas in Eastern philosophy. For example, the Course takes the position that evil, sin, and guilt are illusory. To accept this viewpoint, you will need to reconcile this understanding with the typical understanding of karma. The idea of hell is that you have to pay for your grave mistakes, and this is very similar to the concept in yoga philosophy of paying for your karma. Yet the Course maintains that, as far as God is concerned, there is no such thing as karmic retribution. The belief in karma means sins have real effects that cause real damage, and you will have to pay for that damage. Possibly, in the past, you kept an account of the offenses of others the way some people collect stamps. Occasionally you might have cashed in the accumulated stamps by releasing your pent-up grievances in a display of private or even on rare occasions public emotion. Similarly, those who believe in hell also think of karma as God's collecting of stamps—His accounting system, which He uses as a means of judging your worthiness for Heaven or hell. The Course would say that those who see God as a judge with a karmic accounting system are just projecting their own judgments onto God, making Him into an ego image of themselves.

Karma is the belief your past actions determine what you deserve in the future and produce your present positive or negative circumstances. Although you appear to live your life under the effects of karma, this appearance is due to your own belief in karma. God has nothing to do with this cherished and self-imposed belief in assigning rewards and punishments based on past actions. According to the Course, karma does not exist because the past does not exist and has no real power to determine your conditions. Nevertheless, the past can affect you if you allow it to do so by believing in it and by specifically believing in guilt, which requires self-assigned punishment. The Course does affirm cause and effect but maintains that the past cannot be the cause of anything. Cause and effect occur through your *present choices* that are the cause of your current circumstances. The idea of cause and effect in relation to karma will be elaborated upon subsequently in this section.

You are accustomed to believing the past can affect you, so it is hard to accept the Course saying, "...the past is gone, and what has truly gone has no effects."[49] A simple illustration will explain this difficult idea: Imagine a ship, which was loaded with cargo in New York, is currently at sea headed toward London. In this analogy, New York represents the past, and London represents the future. The ship stands for the present and for the individual mind, which only functions in the present. If you said that the ship is carrying New York, no one would believe such an impossible idea. Yet many people do believe the mind carries the past, even though this is quite impossible. New York is gone and has no effect on the ship, just as the past is gone and has no effect on the mind. It is true that the cargo was loaded in the past in New York, but only the cargo that is on the ship *now* can have any effect. Similarly, only the thoughts you have in your mind now can have any effect on you. The cargo can be dumped off the ship at any present moment, and likewise you can let go of any thoughts presently in the mind, including any memories or thoughts related to the past. Cause and effect do take place, but only in the present where you can decide what to keep in the mind and what to discard. This puts you in control of what you experience. If you discard unhealthy thoughts and keep healthy thoughts, you will calm your mind. On the other hand, if you discard healthy thoughts and hold onto unhealthy thoughts, you disturb your mind. The only cause of your current condition is a present decision of what thoughts you want to keep and experience.

Traditional Eastern philosophy maintains there are three kinds of karma: The first is accumulated karma, which is the total of all past experiences. The second is fruit-producing karma, which is experienced now and must be experienced. And the third is new karma that will produce fruit in the future. You can consider the accumulated karma to be *past karma*, the fruit-producing karma to be *present karma*, and the new karma to be *future karma*.

In the Hindu tradition, these three kinds of karma are represented by an archer: Past karma consists of arrows in his quiver waiting to be used. Present karma is the archer pulling back the string of his bow and maintaining a holding position with his arrow ready to be launched. Future karma is expressed by his arrow being shot and heading toward the archer's target. Past karma is the mixture of good karma acquired from good past deeds and bad karma accumulated from bad past deeds. Present karma is cause and effect produced now by your current actions. Future karma is what you decide you must experience in the future as a result of your previous good and bad deeds.

The ego interprets time as a means of preserving past guilt and anticipating future punishment. This supports the Eastern philosophy of there being past, present, and future karma that must be experienced as the effects caused by the deeds of the past. The ego's idea of karma maintains that the cause of something happens at one time and the effect of that cause happens later. The ego asserts that the future effect must happen because past guilt must be punished. The Hindu form of yoga called "karma yoga" says you can overcome karma, meaning overcome the consequences of action or work. In karma yoga, you perform all actions as selfless service to God, and therefore you do not face karmic consequences because you are letting go of the attachment to the fruits of your action. Eastern philosophy of yoga speaks of the "law of karma" based on the belief that it is a divine law established by God in which good deeds result later in having good things happen to you and bad deeds result later bad things happening to you. However, instead of karma being a divine law, the idea of past, present, and future karma is actually a self-imposed accounting system that you believe is true because you made it as a form of self-evaluation. You assign to yourself rewards based on your belief that you have done good deeds, and you assign yourself punishments based on your belief in guilt for what you consider bad deeds. Since you determine the effects of your deeds, karma is not really a divine law established by God.

The Course draws a contrast between God's laws and man-made "insane laws" that include the law of karma. Man-made karma ensures that you will make mistakes and then mistakenly believe you deserve punishment. Your salvation consists of "reawakening the laws of God" offering freedom for His sinless Son through releasing the belief in the insane law of karma based on guilt and punishment.

> Salvation is a lesson in giving, as the Holy Spirit interprets it. It is the reawakening of the laws of God in minds that have established other laws, and given them power to enforce what God created not. Your insane laws were made to guarantee that you would make mistakes, and give them power over you by accepting their results as your just due.[50]

The original notes of the Course by the scribe, Helen Schucman, refer to the word "karma" without providing any detailed definition. The following is an example from the handwritten notes: "The karmic law demands abandonment for abandoning, but you have received mercy, not 'justice.'" Notice the reference that is made to "abandonment for abandoning." In this reference, the term "karmic law" is related to the Old Testament law of "an eye for an eye and a tooth for a tooth." The term "karmic law" refers to the human idea that if you harm others, you must be equally harmed. This is consistent with the Hindu idea that past bad deeds will in the future result in equally bad karmic consequences, and good deeds will result in equally good karmic consequences. The word "justice" is in quotation marks to indicate that the so-called "karmic law" is not true justice and therefore is not a divine law established by God. From the Course perspective, every Son of God deserves the true justice of forgiveness and love and never deserves false justice of guilt and punishment.

Although the handwritten notes do not indicate that "karmic law" is a divine law, is there a divine law that is related to the concept of karma? Yes, the Course describes a divine law related to karma, but it is not called by the name "karma." The published Course never mentions the word "karma," but instead does talk about "the law of cause and effect." God did establish the fundamental divine law of cause and effect. The Holy Spirit maintains cause and effect happen at the same time in the present moment. "Cause and effect are one, not separate."[51] The Hindu idea of karma is based on the idea that cause and effect are separated by time so cause happens in the past and the effect happens later in time. The Holy Spirit's interpretation of time emphasizes only the present. Thus, there is no past karma, and there is no future karma. The Holy Spirit supports the idea that there is only present karma, which is cause and effect that must always occur now. "Thinking and its results are really simultaneous, for cause and effect are never separate."[52] If a cause happens to produce an effect later, it is only because that cause is being held and maintained as a thought in the mind within each present instant. That is why the Course says that if you make certain decisions, those decisions remain in effect until you change your mind, change your decision to produce a different effect in each present moment.

The final section in the final chapter of the Course is titled "Choose Once Again." The basis of choosing again is that decisions stay in effect until you change them. You chose to leave the awareness of Heaven at the separation, and you applied all of your will toward accomplishing the fulfillment of that decision. That decision remains in effect in your current mind until to entirely change your mind and apply all of your will toward waking up in Heaven. Workbook Lesson 138 challenges you to choose once again by saying, *"Heaven is the decision I must make. I make it now, and will not change my mind, because it is the only thing I want."*[53] The ultimate experience of choosing once again is waking up in Heaven. If you ask anyone who believes in Heaven if he wants to go to Heaven, he will invariably say, "Yes." But what if you ask him this question: "Do you want to go to Heaven this very instant?" How many would immediately answer with an unequivocal "YES." Perhaps everyone would hesitate to answer, and that hesitation means that person's will is not yet completely committed, probably because that decision would be interpreted as death to the body. Thus the original decision to fall asleep in Heaven remains in effect until one's complete will is fully directed toward the decision to awaken. What blocks you from directing your entire will toward awakening is identification with the ego and the body and the mental conditioning that goes with that identification. This last section in the last chapter of the Text is focused on choosing once again because all the teachings of the Course are designed to assist you in removing blocks so you are prepared and totally committed to making your inevitable new decision to wake up in Heaven now.

Whatever you are currently carrying in your mind, you will be experiencing now. If you carry guilt from past events in your mind now, you are experiencing the effects of carrying guilt in your mind now. For example, you may carry in your present subconscious mind guilt about experiences from your childhood or even from past lives. The self-imposed belief in guilt coordinates with the false belief that punishment is deserved and love is not deserved. The main method of counterbalancing guilt and punishment is doing good deeds that convince you that you deserve rewards and not punishments. Yet the counterbalancing of "bad karma" and "good karma" is the basis of mistakenly believing karma is a divine law of balancing the "good you" and the "bad you." This is all a self-imposed accounting system that functions as karma, but only because of your belief in balancing past karmic deeds producing future punishments or future rewards. The fact that this karmic accounting system is based on your belief in the past and future means it is only an illusion that is produced by your self-concept of being an ego and a body. Imagine you act unlovingly toward someone, and later someone acts unlovingly toward you. In your mind, you may connect those two experiences. You may believe that the past event represents your karmic debt and that the future event represents your karmic consequence needed by karmic law to pay off your karmic debt.

Let's assume that you have correctly seen that your unloving past behavior has attracted to you someone who treats you in an unloving manner. You might assume mistakenly that God is punishing you for your past unloving actions. Nevertheless, it would be helpful for you to understand that you, not God, are actually the one who has set up this accounting system of guilty debts that must be paid by punishing consequences. Your self-imposed accounting system does have the advantage of being one way of learning by being aware of the results of your behavior. But the path of forgiveness is a better way to learn.

Fortunately, because this karmic accounting system is self-imposed, you can drop your belief in the validity of this entire system. Karmic accounting exists because of your belief in it, but it does not exist if you refuse to believe in it. If karma based on the past and future does not exist and is an illusion, can this belief in karma have effects on you in your life? Yes, karma based on the past and future is an illusion, but illusions manifest powerful effects precisely because of your own belief in them. The combination of thought and belief is powerful and produces powerful effects. "It is hard to recognize that thought and belief combine into a power surge that can literally move mountains."[54] Perhaps you believe you can have "idle thoughts" that produce no effects and surely produce no form-related effects, but that is not true. Every present thought is a cause that produces a simultaneous present effect. "There *are* no idle thoughts. All thinking produces form at some level."[55] If you believe in truth, those truthful thoughts will produce powerful effects. Also, if you believe in illusions, those illusory thoughts will produce equally powerful effects. "What keeps the world in chains but your beliefs? And what can save the world except your Self? Belief is powerful indeed. The thoughts you hold are mighty, and illusions are as strong in their effects as is the truth. A madman thinks the world he sees is real and does not doubt it. Nor can he be swayed by questioning his thoughts' effects. It is but when their source [the ego] is raised to question that the hope of freedom comes to him at last."[56]

Your illusory beliefs with their powerful effects imprison you, but your truthful beliefs with their equally powerful effects can free you. You have the power to decide to release guilt now and experience the freedom now of a guiltless mind. Releasing guilt becomes the cause producing the effect now of freedom and acceptance of the innocence that God gave you in your creation. Since the idea of past karma and future karma are illusions, you can release these illusions in the present simply by fully realizing they are illusions. When you change your mind from investing in illusions to investing in the truth, you are changing your beliefs. In addition, you are changing from identifying with the ego that is the source of your illusions and changing to identifying with your true Self in union with God Who is the Source of all Truth. This change of mind frees you from bondage to the past and future and brings you into the present where salvation can be found. "Yet is salvation easily achieved, for anyone is free to change his mind, and all his thoughts change with it. Now the source of thought has shifted, for to change your mind means you have changed the source of all ideas you think or ever thought or yet will think. You free the past from what you thought before. You free the future from all ancient thoughts of seeking what you do not want to find."[57] The previous quote refers to freeing yourself from past and future thoughts thus freeing you from your self-imposed belief in past and future karma.

Does this mean you can just snap your fingers and let go of your current accounting system of guilt called "karma"? There is a problem with changing your mind because of attachment to the learning you have already taught yourself. As a practical matter, your mind has built up mental conditioning that you are carrying right now in your mind that is accumulated in this lifetime and over many past lives. These thoughts have been previously described as the samskaras, meaning the mental impression that leaves a mark or groove in the mind. These samskaras can become so fixed in the mind through repetition that they become hard to change.

Imagine you say to yourself in the present moment, "I am guilty of this," which implies that you deserve punishment and not love. Now imagine that you say this to yourself again, and again, and again, in each present moment. The result is you are carrying this repeated idea now. This build-up becomes the conditioning in the present moment that brings about simultaneous cause and effect, which could be called "present karma." It is a difficult challenge to release all this conditioning based on the belief in guilt. For example, traumatic experiences of the past carry a self-imposed emotional content that is carried with the repeated thought patterns of guilt. This makes them difficult to release in the present moment. This guilt-based conditioning is like an audio recording in the subconscious mind playing distressing music and being the cause producing the effect of generalized anxiety in the mind.

So how can you meet this challenge? Your old thought system that is carried in your present experience can be systematically replaced by a new thought system. Just as you have produced a conditioned mind that believes in guilt, you can follow all the teachings and practices of the Course for many years to produce a conditioned mind that refuses to believe in guilt. Your negative habit of believing in the reality of guilt can be overcome by forming a new positive habit that replaces the old negative habit. This new habit is the habit of practicing forgiveness that looks for the divine in your brother and overlooks illusions of guilt. As long as you believe anyone is guilty of anything, you will also believe you are guilty. By perceiving everyone as the guiltless Son of God now, you will believe you are the guiltless Son of God now.

This is why the Holy Spirit is encouraging you to forgive others by seeing them without their illusions of guilt. By perceiving guiltlessness in everyone, you will also forgive yourself for your illusions of guilt. Forgiveness is the cause producing the effect of healing your split mind and restoring the awareness of your true nature of love. Forgiveness is the expression of the present karma of cause and effect happening now. The Course does not support the belief in future karma that says if you forgive others with a loving attitude, you will receive a benefit in return at a later date in the future. There are six quotations in the Course that state "giving and receiving are the same" to emphasize that cause and effect happen simultaneously. For example, when you forgive your brother, his mind receives healing at the same time your mind receives healing. "And true forgiveness, as the means by which it is attained, must heal the mind that gives, for giving is receiving."[58]

Let's consider how present karma, which is cause and effect now, can benefit your spiritual growth. You can only be affected by your own thoughts in your mind now. Only your thoughts can make you afraid and nothing outside of your own thoughts can make you afraid. "For once you understand it is impossible that you be hurt except by your own [present] thoughts, the fear of God must disappear. You cannot then believe that fear is caused without [outside of yourself]. And God, Whom you had thought to banish, can be welcomed back within the holy mind He never left."[59]

In relation to cause and effect, your thoughts are always the cause that produces a result. Because of the cause being the current thoughts in your mind, the effect will be that your inner perceptions will be simultaneously projected outwardly. "Projection makes perception, and you cannot see beyond it."[60] What you failed to learn in the past, you carry in your mind now, which is your present karma, meaning present cause and effect. Your present karma causes projection so you can see for yourself a picture of the current contents of your mind. The cause of the current thoughts in your mind produces the effect of projection, which acts as a mental biofeedback system that informs you of what is in your mind. Because projection shows you an outer picture of the thoughts currently in your mind, you are offered a new opportunity to respond. You can respond again as in the past and not learn the lesson being presented. Or you can choose again to make a better choice and learn the lesson that was previously unlearned. "Trials are but lessons that you failed to learn presented once again, so where you made a faulty choice before you now can make a better one, and thus escape all pain that what you chose before has brought to you."[61]

The law of cause and effect serves as your mental biofeedback system that tells you when illusions of fear have entered your present awareness. This law shows you that fear produces immediate unloving effects so you can learn to choose again to make a new decision to replace fear with love because fear is the temporary investment in the lack of love. The law of cause and effect is so important to you that even Jesus cannot interfere with this law. "You may still complain about fear, but you nevertheless persist in making yourself fearful. I [Jesus] have already indicated that you cannot ask me to release you from fear. I know it does not exist, but you do not. If I intervened between your thoughts and their results, I would be tampering with a basic law of cause and effect; the most fundamental law there is."[62]

The law of cause and effect, which is your present karma, acts like a mirror in which you can see the unloving choices remaining in your mind now. But you can choose again and make a loving choice to correct the former unloving choice. Whatever decisions you have made in the past remain in effect until you change your mind in the present moment. If some past decisions represented an unloving purpose, that unloving purpose remains in effect until you change it now. "When you make a decision of purpose, then, you have made a decision about your future effort; a decision that will remain in effect unless you change your mind."[63] If you decide that your purpose is to wake up in Heaven, that decision will stay in effect continuously unless you change your purpose. The unchanging purpose of awakening in your mind is a continually renewed "decision about your future effort." This means you will express the effort to carry out your purpose of awakening by practical application of spiritual principles, such as the practice of forgiveness, in each future present moment.

Cause and effect is a divine law of God so it is in effect equally on earth as it is in Heaven. No learning is required in Heaven because there everything is known. In Heaven, extending love is the cause that produces the effect of continually increasing love. Unlike cause and effect manifesting in the total awareness of Heaven, cause and effect manifesting on earth is necessary for learning, involving the partial awareness of perception that is not necessary in Heaven. The Course maintains that the currently conditioned ego-based mind is "insane." The purpose of the Course is to help you to gain a balanced and sane right mind as a preparation for waking up in Heaven. The law of cause and effect by itself does not restore balance or sanity.

Because the present karma of cause and effect is just a mirror of your current mind, that mirror itself is not the balancer. The mirror of present karma just shows you the projection of the status quo of your mind if no learning takes place. Learning is the *result* of responding to present karma. In other words, learning is the *result* of responding to the mirror of your mind under the law of cause and effect. Learning is needed for change and brings balance and sanity. Learning teaches you to change your mind, showing you that unloving thoughts make you unhappy and that loving thoughts make you happy. The results of learning become your basis for deciding to change your mind.

The law of cause and effect encourages you to choose once again because you always have the opportunity to learn and change your mind by replacing unloving choices with loving choices. The Christ within you asks you to choose again. "In every difficulty, all distress, and each perplexity Christ calls to you and gently says, 'My brother, choose again.'"[64] There is no pain within you that cannot be healed. "He would not leave one source of pain unhealed, nor any image left to veil the truth. He would remove all misery from you whom God created altar unto joy. He would not leave you comfortless, alone in dreams of hell, but would release your mind from everything that hides His face from you."[65]

When the Course refers to Christ, it is referring to *You*, as *You* truly are in your dual nature. You are part of the one Christ, and you are also the whole Christ, the one Self. Your ego-based awareness makes it difficult for you to identify with your wholeness in Christ. Because of your ego-based individuality, it is much easier for you to accept your part-ness in Christ, your divine individuality. "God, Who encompasses all being, created beings who have everything individually, but who want to share it to increase their joy."[66] When you finally wake up in Heaven, your ego-based individuality will be gone, but your divine individuality as an individual part of Christ will remain. In addition, you will regain your awareness of being the whole the Christ, the Self.

It is your forgotten wholeness in Christ that calls you to choose again and to awaken from your dreams of separation. In your worldly life, when you listen to the call of Christ, you are not invoking a strength outside yourself. You are acknowledging and accepting your own true inner strength because Christ is your true Self, given to you by God. "His Holiness is yours because He is the only power that is real in you. His strength is yours because He is the Self that God created as His only Son."[67]

You need the strength of Christ to help free your mind from the mental cargo currently being held in your mind as your *present karma*, which is *present cause and effect*. Decisions may have been made in the past, but these would evaporate if the mind is not holding onto these decisions now. You could have loaded your mind with mental cargo at any time in the past, even in past lives. Past lives can affect you now only because of the thoughts from your past lives that you currently hold in your conscious or subconscious mind. That is why it was so important for you to bring your traumatic experiences to your conscious awareness so you can become fully aware of the unhealthy mental cargo stored away in the back of your mind. Then with the inner strength of Christ, you can make a new decision to throw away that mental and emotional turmoil.

The stored thoughts in the mind are constantly renewed. It is this keeping of them in your present consciousness that makes them affect you. In this sense, the mind is like a computer that stores information and holds it until you decide to delete it. If no new decisions are made, former decisions automatically remain in effect and active in the mind. That is why miracles of forgiveness involve changing your mind to remove decisions currently in the mind, which may have been decided long ago, but remained in effect in each present moment since then. Old decisions that currently continue to remain in the mind involve holding on to illusions, such as illusions of the past. Consequently, miracles replace your illusions about the past and reveal the reality of divine truth that is always within you now.

Your present choices and actions affect the way you move through the world of form but can have no effect on *who you are in reality*. By forgiving others and yourself, you can release your false beliefs in the past. Also, forgiveness helps you to let go of the negative effects of your present choices by showing you that your own mind is investing in ego-based illusions that make you feel unhappy. Forgiveness heals your mind by replacing these illusions with the truth of your reality—the truth that God is your only Cause. Since God is your Cause, you are His Effect, His holy Son. Your purity may appear to be lost in the illusions of this world, but when God created you in eternity, He gave your holiness that must be yours forever.

Instead of requiring retribution for your mistakes, God forgives by overlooking all errors and seeing the truth of your holiness and your oneness with Him. You may believe your actions deserve rewards or punishments, but God always knows you deserve love at all times. In God's loving awareness, all of your errors in thought or in behavior evaporate altogether into nothingness. You have the tendency to hold onto the memory of these unloving acts and to blame yourself for them. In contrast to the accusations you make against yourself, God sees only your innocence so you remain holy in His eyes. But you believe in guilt so you make the mistake of punishing yourself with karmic retribution. You would hold yourself accountable for the past mistakes God has already forgiven. You may even believe you have done something that is unforgivable. Yet there is nothing that cannot be forgiven because everything has already been forgiven. This must be so because of the unwavering Love of your Father. No matter what sins you think you have committed or what punishment you think you deserve, God still sees you as being just as sinless as when he created us in His own image of holiness with no stain of guilt and fully deserving of Heaven at all times. The only question you need to ask yourself is this: *Can I learn to see myself with the eyes of love as God sees me in my true holiness?*

In his article "Karma" quoted below, Robert Perry, the founder of the Circle of Atonement, summarizes the paradox that karma seems to exist because of your belief in it, while karma does not exist as far as God is concerned:

So to summarize what we've seen, I am picturing two lines, one of karma and one of no karma, both running in parallel. On the line of *karma*, I made choices in the past, and those choices did determine my present condition, but only because I held unto them and punished myself for them, only because of my magical belief that they had the power to create me in their image. At the same time, on the line of *no karma*, God has constantly cancelled out those choices, constantly forgiven me, in the knowledge that my choices have literally no power to create me. He knows that *He* created me, and in doing so gave eternal holiness. No matter what I've done, that holiness always remains my true condition. It always remains my present reality. And I can always lay hold of it in that same present— now.[68]

D. MIRACLE KARMA YOGA

The Hindu ideal of karma yoga views ordinary actions and work as being divine expressions. Karma yoga can be practiced by simply doing your work as a service to God without any thought of receiving the fruits of your labor. Karma yoga is sometimes considered to be the yoga of "work." Yet it is more accurately understood as the yoga of "dedicated action." In fact, the verb *"kri,"* meaning *to do,* is the root word from which the word karma is derived. Therefore, any action can be an expression of karma yoga, if that action is performed with dedication to the divine. By dedicating the action to God, the action becomes selfless and a divine expression.

Miracle Karma Yoga is Christian karma yoga of selfless action. Of course, Christianity has a long history of advocating and manifesting service as a Christian ideal. Service is the horizontal approach to the divine through expressing love to others, which is in contrast to the vertical approach to the divine through inward seeking of God. Seekers who make progress going within during meditation and contemplation as a vertical experience are often inspired to find balance in their lives through selfless outer service to others. The West has been focused on material progress and in turn produced a society that has valued social service, especially in a material sense, to a higher degree than in the East. The Christian expression of social service has been understood as an expression of Christian love, as exemplified by the life of Jesus.

However, the selfless action of Miracle Karma Yoga is more than simply social service. Like all the yoga expressions, Miracle Karma Yoga involves a turning inward, which is often missing from social service. Other forms of yoga involve changing the focus from an initial external orientation to an internal orientation. But Miracle Karma Yoga involves the reverse direction—having an inner dedication initially to the divine and then going outwardly to express the divine through actions. This inner dedication separates Miracle Karma Yoga from social work. It is not enough to dedicate yourself inwardly; you must carry your divine alertness with you in the actions as they are being performed.

In Miracle Karma Yoga, every action is dedicated to the divine and becomes worship manifested in action. This sanctifies daily life making even the most mundane actions become worship. Worship is giving. In Hindu karma yoga, the emphasis is on giving to God without thought of personal reward. Instead of the broader Hindu idea of karma as dedicated action, the word "karma" is most commonly associated with the law of cause and effect. In Hindu philosophy because of the law of karma, good actions produce good results of rewards, and bad actions produce bad results of punishments. This Hindu belief in karma is the basis for the belief in reincarnation in which the fruits of your karma are reaped from past lives. Traditional karma yoga advocates giving both the good and bad results to God.

Miracle Karma Yoga recognizes the paradox of karma described in the prior section titled "The Paradox of Karma," which explains how karma exists only because of your belief in it but does not exist from God's perspective. You believe in karmic retribution, yet God does not share your belief because it is illusory. Although you are bound by the self-made law of karma, this is not God's law. Karma is a self-imposed accounting system in which you assign punishments and rewards according to your self-evaluation of your own actions based on your firm belief in guilt. Imagine you go to court and are declared to be innocent by the Judge (God). But instead, you refuse to accept your innocence. You go into a room and pretend that it is a prison, even though it has no bars and no locks on the doors. Yet you make yourself into a prisoner, although you have not been convicted except by yourself. Letting go of self-inflicted guilt and accepting forgiveness helps you to resign your role as a karmic accountant and to recognize that you are only and always under God's law of Love. One aspect of Miracle Karma Yoga is to recognize that you are not bound by karma and that God gives you only his love and forgiveness as He affirms your eternal holiness in His sight.

The other aspect of Miracle Karma Yoga takes into account your current condition of imagining you are bound by karma. Although you bind yourself with your belief in karma and guilt, you can overcome karma by giving the fruits of your actions to God so you accumulate no karma and are surrendering all of yourself to God. This may sound like a simple idea, and it is. But because of the human tendency to primarily focus on meeting one's own needs, it is hard to keep focused on giving to God with no thought of oneself. Jesus addressed this by saying, "But seek first the kingdom of God and his justice, and all these things shall be given you besides."[69]

The virtue that manifests by practicing Miracle Karma Yoga is purity of heart, which here means purity of intention. When you have no motivation directed toward what you will get from your actions, you can act with a pure heart for the love of God alone. Each aspect of Miracle Yoga includes some application of forgiveness in the form of "looking and overlooking," which is a combination of attachment to the divine and of non-attachment to what is not divine. In Miracle Karma Yoga, the "looking" is a looking to God and the "overlooking" is the overlooking of the ego. You are looking first inwardly at the divine in making your dedication and then looking outwardly at the divine manifesting through you in your worldly actions stripped of ego desires. You are overlooking your ego desires. The separating of ego desires from actions gives a sense of inner freedom that comes from knowing that you are doing God's Will and provides a release from anxiety caused by investing in the ego.

Perhaps the best example that can be found of Christian selfless action is the life of Brother Lawrence. His book titled *The Practice of the Presence of God* is recommended as a primer on the practice of letting your activities become a divine expression. Brother Lawrence's outlook is explained in the following quotation:

> He said that our sanctification does not depend as much on *changing* our activities as it does on doing them for God rather than for ourselves. The most effective way Brother Lawrence had for communicating with God was to simply do his ordinary work. He did this obediently, out of a pure love of God, purifying it as much as was humanly possible. He believed it was a serious mistake to think of our prayer time as being different from any other. Our actions should unite us with God when we are involved in our daily activities, just as our prayer unites us with Him in our quiet time.[70]

Brother Lawrence was a perfect example of Miracle Karma Yoga and was also an example of Miracle Bhakti Yoga, the yoga of love. Under ideal circumstances, all activities can be done for the love of God. However, not every seeker will be filled with divine love, and certainly not all the time, as was the case with Brother Lawrence. Consequently, if the feeling of love is not the motivation, you can be motivated simply by the high ideal of wanting to do God's Will. Thus you can dedicate your actions to doing God's Will rather than doing your own will, and you will be manifesting Miracle Karma Yoga.

So much time and energy is spent on satisfying the desires of the ego that the time spent devoted to God with no thought of self can become a freeing experience. At times, you may find yourself in the conflict between wanting to satisfy ego desires and wanting to follow spiritually motivated desires. Sometimes you may notice your actions express ego-based desires, even though you want to perform actions dedicated to God. In this case, there is a lack of harmony between your ego-based actions and your wanting to follow divine inspiration. The result is tension and anxiety leading to fear or, in other words, the loss of the awareness of inner peace and love. This means you have dual goals that are conflicting.

The solution to conflicting goals is adopting a single unified goal. The mind has many different thoughts that are often in conflict with one another, and practicing meditation, you choose one thought as your single focus. This single thought becomes your unified goal that produces a unified mind and thus brings peace to the mind. Similar to this inward practice of unifying the mind by adopting a unified goal in meditation, Miracle Karma Yoga is designed to be an outer way of unifying the mind and producing peace. In Miracle Karma Yoga, the unified goal is to dedicate all your outer actions to God. To successfully practice Miracle Karma Yoga, you need to hold firmly to the single goal of dedicated action, which enables you to release conflicting goals based on satisfying ego desires. It is not necessary to willfully stop ego desires and the actions they produce. Ego-based desires and actions will fall away naturally as you keep your focus on maintaining your unified goal of dedicated action. This single-minded dedication, like the single-mindedness of meditation, brings peace to the mind.

The problem with any spiritual philosophy is the gap between the ideal and the practical application of that ideal. In contrast to the ideal intention of practicing total selfless motivation in karma yoga, you may be faced with the fact that you live a life based on meeting the needs of the self and body. Thus you may feel that the perfect ideal of karma yoga can be very challenging and beyond your capabilities. It may be unrealistic and foolish to think that you could remove all my personal desires from your actions and dedicate them entirely to God.

Miracle Karma Yoga offers a less exalted form of karma yoga than totally selfless service, which is nearly saint-like. Just as you can be a Christian without being a perfect follower of Christ, you can practice karma yoga to a certain degree by any form of service, such as being a teacher or social worker, even if some selfish motives are mixed with some unselfish motives. Yet your job is not your only way of expressing karma yoga. Any mundane action can be an expression of karma yoga if that action is performed with a spiritual motivation.

Hindu karma yoga involves being totally desireless so all of the fruits of your actions are given to God with no thought of gaining for yourself. Instead of requiring total desirelessness, Miracle Karma Yoga advocates the expression of *enlightened self-interest*. This requires a positive goal orientation and discipline necessary to achieve goals. Without focusing on trying to remove desires, you choose goals that express spiritually oriented desires rather than selfish desires. Rather than seeking to experience no fruits of your actions, you seek the fruits of the Spirit, which are "love, joy, peace, patience, kindness, goodness, faithfulness, gentleness, self-control."[71] Although seeking such fruits is not entirely selfless from the perspective of traditional karma yoga,

Miracle Karma Yoga does express enlightened self-interest that would lead you in the direction of waking up to your oneness with God.

It would be unrealistic to expect that you can or should dedicate all your actions to God. It is enough to just increasingly incorporate dedicated action into your life as part of a natural growth process. Even if you want to increase your practice of dedicated action, you may find that you forget to do so. To help you remember to practice dedicated action, you can incorporate your dedication of activities into your daily routine. Saying grace at meals on special occasions is a commonly accepted practice, but you can choose to get in the habit of blessing your activity of eating whenever you eat during the day. After your meditation practice, you may want to dedicate all your activities of the day to God giving him the fruits of your work on behalf of Him. One more way of dedicating your actions to God is to schedule times for mini-meditations. Possibly you may want to have a mini-meditation every morning, afternoon, and evening so that three times a day you take a minute or two to make contact with the divine within and then dedicate the upcoming few hours to God.

Miracle Karma Yoga involves dedicating your actions to God, but each separate act of dedication is a part of a much larger dedication, the dedication of your whole being to God. Also, you can make a more personalized dedication to Jesus. Because of today's emphasis on compartmentalization, it is easy to separate off your religious life from the rest of your life and feel justified in doing so since that is the norm of Western society. Miracle Karma Yoga affords the opportunity to perceive your whole life in all of its activities in the world, even sitting on the toilet, as a divine expression. The idea is to encourage a sense of *prayerfulness* throughout the whole day. Chapter 9 will elaborate upon the influence of the Course in the practice of Miracle Karma Yoga.

E. MIRACLE BHAKTI YOGA

Miracle Yoga as a path is a way of following Jesus Christ and using techniques of yoga to assist you. *Miracle Bhakti Yoga* is specifically the expression of love to follow Jesus Christ. However, you may choose to follow Jesus Christ in a very personal way or in a more impersonal way. You may choose to emphasize personal devotion to Jesus as your spiritual ideal and primary means of spiritual expression. In this case, your selfless dedication, knowledge, meditation, and contemplation can all be expressions of love directed toward Jesus.

Another way of following Jesus is to follow the form of devotion that Jesus himself followed, which is personal devotion to God as his

Father. On the other hand, you may choose to direct most of your forms of spiritual expression toward God in a more impersonal sense, as the Ground of Being, the source of your spiritual nature.

Whether you choose the personal or impersonal direction, it is recommended that you make an effort to value and appreciate the opposite direction, even if it is not suited to your personality. A third possibility is to allow your devotion to be expressed simultaneously in both a personal and impersonal way. You can have personal devotion to Jesus and God the Father and at the same time be open to God being the impersonal Ground of Being. Your devotion can also focus on receptivity to the Holy Spirit, as the expression of divine Love and Light, which again can be felt very personally or impersonally.

You may want to incorporate personal and impersonal elements in your spiritual practices since both can be helpful in your growth. The Hindu teacher Ramakrishna said that God in His manifested form is like an ice sculpture that stands for the personal aspect of God that can be worshiped personally. You can cling to this ice sculpture with your heartfelt devotion. But the heat of your passionate love for your Beloved can produce an unexpected result: the ice sculpture can melt and become water. However, your devotion does not have to end. The water now under your feet becomes the ground upon which you are standing—the Ground of Being. You can still worship your Beloved because He has simply changed form. Next, the heat of your devotion can cause the water to evaporate, but you have not lost your Beloved. The water becomes part of the very air that you breathe, and so then you can breathe in your Beloved so there is no separation at all between you and your Beloved.

In this analogy, the ice sculpture can be Jesus, and the water can be God the Father, the Creator and the Ground of Being, Who is experienced as being separate from you. The water that evaporates into the air can be seen in different ways. The evaporated water can be the Holy Spirit or the breath of God's Life. Being aware of breathing the water suspended in the air can be the awakening of the Christ Self as your own true nature united with God or simply what traditional Christianity calls divine union.

When Ramakrishna met any spiritual teacher in India, he would always ask this question, "Do you have the divine commission?" Ramakrishna did not think anyone should teach until that person had first experienced divine union. Ramakrishna himself had experienced nirvikalpa samadhi, the highest form of divine union in classical yoga in which the seeker and God as the Ground of Being are one. This in itself is an experience of the impersonal aspect of God, but it was Ramakrishna's personal devotion that ultimately led to his impersonal awakening. After his impersonal awakening that transcended all form, he returned to his personal worship. His personal worship produced ecstatic states of samadhi that were within the realm of form.

The example of Ramakrishna is highlighted here to emphasize that Miracle Bhakti Yoga is best expressed by a broad-minded universal love. This inclusiveness can lead to a genuine appreciation of other forms of personal or impersonal devotion. If Miracle Bhakti Yoga is narrow-minded, it will focus only on the Beloved and can create a mental exclusiveness toward others. This kind of exclusiveness is seen in groups that are so devoted to Jesus or some other personal aspect of God that they are not tolerant in subtle or not so subtle ways of others who do not worship in the same way as they do.

Ramakrishna is a particularly good example of the broad-minded approach because he was open to both personal and impersonal aspects of God and to other forms of spiritual seeking that were not part of his Hindu tradition, such as the spirituality of Buddhism and Christianity. He sought out other forms of personal devotion in order to experience the divine everywhere. For example, Ramakrishna saw a picture of Mary who was holding baby Jesus, and he opened his heart to the image before him and fell into an ecstasy. He continued in devotion to Mary and Jesus for a few weeks leaving all other duties. Temporarily he was oblivious to his disciples, who were concerned that apparently Ramakrishna had left them. Of course, Ramakrishna returned to his disciples and former worship, but he was only concerned with living a life motivated by the divine influence in whatever way the divine influence presented itself in the moment. Ramakrishna experienced the heart of bhakti yoga as an inner loving communion with the divine within and as an awareness of divine love being manifested outwardly in everyone and everything.

There is, of course, no better example of Miracle Bhakti Yoga than Jesus himself. Giving his life for the sake of others was his greatest expression of love, but what may go unnoticed is that Jesus lived every day as an expression of love even in small ways. A kind word, a smile, a touch of his hand—these are the ways he used to touch the hearts of those around him. Jesus took advantage of every opportunity to express love to everyone. He was able to consistently manifest love outwardly because he took the time to make loving contact with the Father in solitude as his form of personal devotion.

Because Jesus is one with the Father, you can turn to Jesus in devotion to be united with the Father, or you can turn to the Father in devotion to be united with Jesus. A form of repeating the Name of God called the "Jesus Prayer" is one such type of devotion. There are many variations of Christian meditation and contemplation used for expressing devotion. Miracle Bhakti Yoga includes heartfelt prayers of a formal or spontaneous nature to Jesus or God. Your times set aside for personal devotion or group worship can carry over into everyday life as an expression of recollection, meaning prayerfulness.

Love is your true nature, but it is clouded over by desires for other things. Similar to the other aspects of Miracle Yoga, Miracle Bhakti Yoga includes forgiveness expressed as "looking and overlooking." The "looking" is the focus on the Beloved, the longing for two to be one. The "overlooking" has to do with setting aside blocks that cloud over your heart's desire for your Beloved. The love that you receive from your Beloved and your own response of love gives you the strength to overlook. You overlook the thoughts of separation, the thoughts of the ego, and you one-pointedly focus on looking toward your Beloved with the intention of divine union.

Your looking is maintaining purity of heart and your overlooking is letting go of any blocks to your purity of heart. This looking and overlooking have an external and an internal component. The external component of looking is the purity of heart that enables you to see your Beloved in the faces of your brothers and sisters. The external component of overlooking is releasing outer blocks, such as habitual behavior patterns, that would separate you from expressing love to others. The internal component of looking is the purity of heart that enables you to contact your Beloved within. The internal component of your overlooking is letting go of any thoughts or desires that would disturb your focused inner devotion to your Beloved.

Your practice of Miracle Bhakti Yoga can take whatever direction of expression best suits you. If you have a musical inclination, you may want to use singing or chanting to express your devotion. You may want to set up an altar for worship to your Beloved. Of course, you may want to spend time reading the Bible or other inspired writings, in addition to reading the Course.

A specific suggestion being made here for inspirational reading is *The Poem of the Man-God*.[72] In spite of the title, this is not a book of poetry, but a set of five volumes of a narrative of the life of Jesus. The author was Maria Valtorta, who is an example of Christian devotion. Maria offered herself to her Beloved, Jesus, as a sacrifice for divine Love. She renewed the offering of herself every day and was elevated to great heights in her love of her Beloved. Jesus appeared in visions to her on a regular basis for many years. In these appearances, Maria was shown visions of the entire life of both Mary and Jesus, and Maria was instructed to record these visions. Maria was not a scholar and asserted that Jesus dictated to her what to write, but she herself often did not understand what she was writing. She considered Jesus to be the true author. This writing does not change or substitute for the Gospel, but does elaborate upon and illuminate the Gospel.

There is no way to prove if this narrative of the life of Jesus is objectively accurate. Even so, this close look at the events portrays Jesus as the master of love. For example, Jesus tirelessly puts forth every effort to help Judas, who repeatedly gives in to temptation and is lovingly forgiven by Jesus each time. The joys and sorrows of Jesus and his disciples are often expressed in conversations providing the reader with a sense of being a direct witness to the biblical events. But perhaps more important than the events is seeing the humanness of Jesus and his disciples revealed in their actions and relationships. This intimate view of their lives is helpful for the practice of Miracle Bhakti Yoga as an opportunity to internalize the emotions of the times and vicariously experience the life of Jesus and his disciples in your own heart.

Anything that opens your heart is an expression of Miracle Bhakti Yoga. A good place to start burning the flame of divine love is to focus the awareness during meditation on the physical heart itself or in the center of the chest. Sometimes love is awakened in the physical heart, and then the loving awareness expands and becomes centered primarily in the center of the chest. St. Symeon identified the *nous* as the spirit located in the center of the heart (center of the chest) and as the point of integration where the divine and human natures of man meet. This is where you can awaken your awareness of the Atman of yoga and the Christ Self. The heart is essential for growth in Miracle Bhakti Yoga. Christian devotion is a matter of developing your feeling nature by exploring your heart and then investing in whatever divine inspiration moves your heart. Chapter 9 will elaborate on the influence of the Course in the practice of Miracle Karma Yoga.

F. MIRACLE JNANA YOGA

Another aspect of Miracle Yoga is *Miracle Jnana Yoga* in which the intellect is emphasized. This aspect is related to knowledge and refers specifically to knowledge of your true Self, which in this description will focus on knowledge of your true Christ Self, or you may call this your "spirit" or your true nature in relation to God. Concepts are important in Miracle Jnana Yoga, not for the sake of forming a dogma that must be accepted, but rather to define a mental framework that is necessary to expand your awareness of your true nature.

The practice of Miracle Jnana Yoga, like traditional Hindu jnana yoga, requires the ability to discern between the real and the unreal. In order to discern between the real and the unreal, you would obviously need to have a clear understanding in your own mind of what in fact is real and what is unreal. You may have already decided upon a set of basic premises about the nature of what is real and unreal. If you want to consider the matter further, below you will see a list of eight proposed "Miracle Jnana Yoga Principles." This list represents my understanding of how to apply the Course to distinguishing the real from the unreal. These are a set of one-size-fits-all premises that do not encompass every seeker's spiritual understanding, nor are these premises intended to do so.

You may not accept all of these premises or the terminology used to describe them. If you do not agree with these Course premises or with the terminology, you may want to make up your own personal list of principles that reflect your own spiritual understanding. After identifying your spiritual principles, you may want to proceed with your own personal practice of Christian jnana yoga, trusting God to show you the way. As God guides you to make spiritual progress, you may decide to make some changes in your basic premises, which would reflect your closer walk with the divine.

If you accept the premises proposed below, you still may want to use your own words to set forth a specific list of premises that best reflect your individual perspective on how to follow Christ. You are encouraged to establish in your own mind a specific set of premises that you feel you can firmly believe so these ideas can be a starting point for practicing discernment between the real and the unreal.

PRINCIPLES OF MIRACLE JNANA YOGA

1. The physical world of all animate and inanimate forms and the psychological world of rational thinking are manifestations of relative realities. These are illusory expressions of the Ground of Being within which these partial realities draw their existence. Though these relative realities do exist within your mind, they may be considered ultimately "unreal," meaning illusory when compared with the absolute Reality of the Ground of Being that may be called "God."

2. Your true Identity is your true Self, your Christ Self. You share the Christ Self with all the other parts of the Sonship, who collectively form the one Son of God, the one Christ. Each part of the Sonship is unique and equal to every other part. Paradoxically, each part of Christ is the whole Christ. Your ultimate goal for practicing Miracle Yoga is awakening the awareness of yourself as part of Christ and as the whole Christ. In this awakening beyond discursive thinking, there is a union of the knower, the act of knowing, and what is known.

3. Your true nature, your Christ Self, is now and for eternity united to God and to the Holy Spirit. Your Christ Self is within you waiting to be uncovered. Your Christ Self is always pure and holy and untouched by fear, guilt, or death. Your Christ Self is your unchanging reality and may be considered your individual ground of being within the ultimate Ground of Being that is God.

4. You are currently identified with your body and a psychological, rational-thinking mind. You imagine you are separate from others and from God. This idea of separation is the "ego," which is an illusion. Because of your identification with your ego and your body, you have "spiritual amnesia," which is ignorance of your true nature as the Christ Self. But the purity of your Christ Self cannot be defiled by "sin," which is the false belief you can change your unchangeable reality as the holy Son of God. What you call "sins" are correctable mistakes that have not changed your true nature at all.

5. Your means of overcoming ignorance of your true nature is divine grace coming from God the Father, the Holy Spirit, and Jesus Christ. One means of cooperating with divine grace is the path of Miracle Yoga through a combination of Miracle Karma Yoga, Miracle Bhakti Yoga, Miracle Jnana Yoga, and Miracle Raja Yoga.

6. Miracle Jnana Yoga, like the other kinds of Miracle Yoga, involves overcoming ignorance by "looking and overlooking." This path uses discernment, the ability to use the intellect to distinguish between true Reality and unreality produced by the ego. This discernment includes "looking," which is attachment to the infinite, and "overlooking," which is detachment from the finite. Miracle Jnana Yoga involves an inward meditative focus aiming to transcend discursive thinking. Unlike jnana yoga in the Hindu tradition, Miracle Jnana Yoga is primarily focused on *forgiveness*, as will be explained subsequently.

7. The ultimate goal is divine union. But an immediate objective of Miracle Yoga is the integration of the physical, emotional, mental, intuitive, and spiritual natures. This integration enables you to fully surrender yourself to the divine influence of God's Will and allows you to follow the example of Jesus and be guided by the Holy Spirit. If you experienced divine union in this life, your goal will not be to escape from this world, but rather to produce a total interpenetration of all the lower faculties to place them fully under the direction of the divine influence.

8. If the ultimate goal of awakening the Christ Self in this life is not realized as an experience, you will fulfill God's Plan for your life by dedicating yourself to doing God's Will to the best of your ability and understanding. By living a life of doing God's Will, when this life is completed, you will be prepared to receive God's embrace in the next life and be awakened to your true nature as the Christ Self.

Yoga may be considered "systematic internalization" because the seeker perceives everything in the macrocosm as also being within the microcosm of his own body. In yoga the seeker focuses his awareness on uncovering the divine within. To avoid reinforcing the ego that is attached to the body, yoga employs the awareness of internalizing all experiences within the body to ultimately transcend the body and join with God. Traditional jnana yoga emphasizes the specific internal practice of meditation directed toward affirming one's true nature as Brahman, meaning God. In addition to the "systematic internalization" of jnana yoga, there is also the "systematic externalization" in jnana yoga in which the seekers look past appearances in order to see the divine externally. In Hindu jnana yoga, the internal seeing of the divine is more important than the external seeing of the divine.

Unlike Hindu jnana yoga that places a lower priority on its external aspects and a higher priority on its internal aspects, Miracle Jnana Yoga places a much greater emphasis on "systematic externalization." In Hindu jnana yoga, everything is geared toward the end result of God-realization. But in Miracle Jnana Yoga, steps along the way are the main focus, and the result of divine union can be left in the hands of divine grace that manifests in this life or in the hereafter. Miracle Jnana Yoga in its external component is a form of external focusing that produces inner healing of your psychological makeup. Your ego nature has a negative system of externalization, called *projection*, in which guilt and faults are denied within and projected onto others in order to avoid looking at these within yourself. The loving systematic externalization of Miracle Jnana Yoga is used to counteract projection by the process of seeing the divine in your brother in order to remind yourself of the divine within yourself.

This process of seeing the divine is described in the Course as *forgiveness*. You may think of forgiveness as not holding a grievance toward another person. However, a broader view of forgiveness is that you have illusions about people and letting go of your illusions about others is forgiving them. You have the specific illusion that other people *are* egos, bodies and minds separated from God. The ego itself is the illusory idea of being separate from God. When you give up your illusion about another person being an ego, you give up the idea that this person is separate from God. You are able to see that person as divine, as not separate from God and not separate from yourself. Thus forgiveness is defined as the giving up of the concept of separation. Therefore, forgiveness is likewise seeing the divine in others. When forgiveness allows you to see the divine in your brother, it will remind you of the truth that you are not an ego separate from God and that you are divine, and this produces inner healing.

The systematic externalization of Miracle Jnana Yoga more correctly could be called, "systematic forgiveness." This forgiveness is another example of the principle of "looking and overlooking," which is a part of all the forms of Miracle Yoga. Thus forgiveness is the looking for the divine and overlooking all else. If you make the mistake of looking at what is not divine, meaning illusions of the ego, you make them seem real to you by looking at them. To correct this error, you are advised to overlook the illusory manifestations of the ego and in so doing these will remain unreal. You are advised to look beyond illusory appearances and simultaneously look at and perhaps even see the divine wherever you look. This looking and overlooking allows you to truly forgive by seeing through illusions to the truth, therefore realizing the holiness in everyone and the meaninglessness of guilt.

In Miracle Jnana Yoga, the simplest form of discernment between the real and unreal is rejecting false perceptions and accepting true perceptions. You normally look at a person as an ego because that is how you view yourself and how that person you are observing views himself. But with the eyes of forgiveness in Miracle Jnana Yoga, you can look at this other person as a divine being, as the Christ Self.

Many Hindu sayings in the sacred scripture of the Upanashads affirm the divine within, such as *Tat tvam asi*, "Thou art That," and *Sarvam idam brahma*, "All this is the Absolute." Just as the Hindus who practice jnana yoga can repeat these affirmations of the Reality of the divine within as Atman or Brahman, Christians who practice Miracle Jnana Yoga can repeat Christian affirmations of the Christ Self. For example, to see the divine in your brother, you can repeat, "You are the Christ," or a similar variation. You can practice this external forgiveness by repeating this affirmation mentally whenever you are with anyone to affirm the reality in that person and overlook that person's illusory ego.

If you decide to use such an affirmation, including for example the word "Christ," to help you separate the real from the unreal in your outer experiences, it is advisable to also use an affirmation that includes the word "Christ" for your meditations. In this case, you will have the same word, "Christ," to help you in your "looking and overlooking" as it is applied both externally in your outer forgiveness and internally in your inner meditation.

A change in perception is all that is required in Miracle Jnana Yoga to manifest forgiveness, but it is possible to go further also and allow your change in perception to enable you to actually see the divine light in others or even in objects. The change in perception that allows you to see the meaning of divine holiness is called *Christ's vision*, which comes to you at your request as a gift freely given by the Holy Spirit. The practice of Christ's vision, as it is explained in Chapter 6, gives you the ability of looking and overlooking as you see your brother and as you see even the objects in the world. In addition to allowing you to see the meaning of divine holiness, Christ's vision can in some few cases produce the by-product of being able to see light visually. This visual seeing of light is called *Light vision*. If you have this experience of vision, you will visually see the world and everyone in it light up. You will see a shimmering white or golden light glowing around and perhaps even within all that you see. Light vision, as a by-product of Christ's vision, is an outer manifestation of inner mental forgiveness that allows you to see beyond appearances.

The external activity of forgiveness is described in Chapter 7, which discusses relationships, and this needs no further elaboration now. But there is a more subtle form of direct internal forgiveness that is not so obvious. It may go unnoticed because this internal activity is not usually thought of as a form of forgiveness internalized. What is this type of systematic inner forgiving? It is meditation, which is forgiveness internalized. A close examination of meditation reveals that what is happening during meditation is actually a form of internal forgiveness that follows the same pattern as the Miracle Jnana Yoga technique of forgiveness that was described above as an external process.

The external method of forgiveness has been identified as "looking and overlooking," meaning looking for the divine and overlooking everything that is not divine. The internal practice of forgiveness is exactly the same. Inner attunement is thought of as focusing of the mind in meditation, but it may also be viewed as inner forgiveness. The meditator is advised to be receptive to the divine presence. This is "looking" for the divine, meaning for your true Self, Truth, Reality, Christ, or God. Some types of meditation even give instructions to specifically look for the Light. The "overlooking" part of the practice is overlooking all the distracting thoughts in your own mind.

These are insane thoughts of the ego that are just as illusory and unreal as the ones you overlook in your brother when practicing forgiveness externally. If you were to mistakenly pay attention to these insane ego thoughts, you would make them appear real to yourself, even though they are illusory. What you are doing is forgiving yourself in this internal process in the same way that you forgave your brother in your external process. By not paying attention to your inner illusory thoughts, you avoid the error of making them real to you. Seeing that they are unreal, you can let go of them.

This is true of all kinds of meditation, especially techniques that involve looking for the divine light within. Some kinds of meditation include looking for the divine light externally to experience Light vision as a result of Christ's vision. These are examples of Miracle Jnana Yoga allowing you to discern between the real and the unreal. Also, some meditation practices seek the light inwardly. These practices are examples of forgiveness directed inwardly, and they involve the jnana yoga practice of discerning between the real and the unreal. The distracting ego thoughts within the mind may be thought of as smoke that you move past while you are focusing your attention solely on seeing the light. You are forgiving your own ego thoughts by letting go of them as you seek the light.

Seeking the divine within and especially seeking the light within is inner forgiveness of yourself, just as it was described as being applied outwardly for outer forgiveness. Contacting the divine within that looks upon you with forgiveness enables you to forgive yourself, meaning overlook the dark smoke of ego thoughts and see the light. But you are successful, even if you do not see the light but simply spend time overlooking your ego thoughts. By letting go of ego thoughts, you can improve yourself by changing your false perceptions and releasing attachment to the ego, whether you can see the light or not, or whether you feel the divine presence or not.

Since meditation is a very traditional practice, meditation does not offer anything new in itself. However, there is a sense of newness in the idea that meditation has an additional purpose of being a system of forgiveness applied internally toward yourself. Thus meditation may be considered "systematic forgiveness internalized."

In summary, Miracle Jnana Yoga is discernment between the real and the unreal that manifests as external forgiveness involving the changing of perceptions through seeing with Christ's vision. Miracle Jnana Yoga can also manifest as internal forgiveness in meditation in which you hold on to one thought of the real while letting go of many thoughts of the unreal. The process of "looking and overlooking" that occurs in both meditation and forgiveness has already been discussed. However, this process has long been the standard one for traditional meditation, and thus cannot be thought of as anything new.

Traditional Christian forgiveness is not considered to be related to the meditation process of "looking and overlooking." Instead, traditional forgiveness encourages examining every bit of what needs to be forgiven and only then forgiving it. But once you examine what is to be forgiven and make it real to you by examining it, how can you forgive what you have already made real to yourself? Traditional forgiveness says you really are an ego, and you really are guilty, and you are forgiven anyway. Therefore, the forgiven one is still seen as an ego even after being forgiven. This is not true forgiveness because you still see your brother as guilty and not worthy of your forgiveness. Thus your forgiveness is a condescending gesture on your part, which still leaves your brother as a sinner in your eyes and not as your equal. You are still left seeing his illusions as real and that means you will not be able to forgive yourself for your own illusions either because you will see them as real also. You cannot see your brother as an ego without seeing yourself as an ego as well.

The forgiveness of Miracle Jnana Yoga is linked to the meditation process of looking and overlooking. Forgiveness overlooks both your brother's ego and your other illusions about brother. Forgiving your brother helps you to manifest the inner aspect of forgiving yourself. By letting go of your illusions about your brother, you inwardly release the same illusions about yourself. If you find it easier to forgive others than to forgive yourself, you can do more than just forgiving others outwardly and indirectly forgiving yourself. You can choose to focus your attention prayerfully and directly on consciously forgiving yourself, especially forgiving yourself for any specific illusions of guilt you may have uncovered in your mind. Whether you primarily focus on forgiving others or yourself, your forgiveness does not make real what is forgiven. Instead, you forgive what was never real by releasing your illusions about your brother and yourself. In Miracle Jnana Yoga, the practice of forgiveness involves overlooking illusions in order to look for the divine in others and look for the divine within yourself. Consequently. forgiveness, as it is practiced in Miracle Jnana Yoga, manifests looking and overlooking similar to the way meditation does.

During the internal forgiveness of meditation, you overlook the dense smoke of distracting thoughts that cover the light. In the external process of forgiveness of Miracle Jnana Yoga, you practice "meditation externalized." In your forgiveness, you overlook the dense mass of the body in order to see the hidden divine light in the other person whom you are forgiving by changing your perceptions of that person. During internal meditation your objective is to realize that the internal smoke is an unsubstantial hindrance that your vision can penetrate to see the light. Similarly, during your external practice of forgiveness, your goal is to realize that the body is an insubstantial veil that your vision can likewise penetrate to see the divine light. Thus there is a reciprocal relationship between meditation and forgiveness. Meditation can be considered to be forgiveness applied inwardly, and forgiveness can be considered to be meditation applied externally.

Miracle Jnana Yoga offers an entire system of forgiveness in which you overlook all illusions externally and internally, and you look for the divine externally and internally. Miracle Jnana Yoga is concerned with discernment between the real and unreal. The ultimate realization is the awakening to Reality, to the Christ Self. But success in practicing Miracle Jnana Yoga is not determined by this attainment. Instead, the successful application of Miracle Jnana Yoga consists of living a life focused on forgiveness, which is pleasing to God. The most significant aspect of Miracle Jnana Yoga is the use of discernment between the real and the unreal to simply change perception. Successful Miracle Jnana Yoga is changing ego-based perceptions into perceptions based upon the Truth. You can simply maintain in your mind the awareness that every brother you see is the Christ and not really an ego. In seeing the Christ in him, you are affirming you are the Christ and not an ego. The practice of maintaining this mental perception is Christ's vision and the foundation of the practice of Miracle Jnana Yoga.

The ideas of forgiveness, Christ's vision, and the Christ Self that are offered here in this book are my interpretation and understanding of *A Course in Miracles*.[73] If you are interested in expanding your understanding of Miracle Jnana Yoga, you are encouraged to study the Course for yourself to help you deepen your understanding of forgiveness, which is an extremely difficult concept to both understand and apply. The Course is a complete thought system that is not for everyone, but would appeal particularly to someone who is especially attracted to Miracle Jnana Yoga. Chapters 6 through 12 describe the Course in greater detail to help you to decide if you would want to study this material in greater depth.

G. MIRACLE RAJA YOGA

The fourth aspect of Miracle Yoga is *Miracle Raja Yoga* focusing on meditation and contemplation. Miracle Raja Yoga includes all eight members of Patanjali's classical yoga, plus one additional member. The first member is *yamas*, ethical restrictions, such as harmlessness, truthfulness, releasing of covetousness, and maintaining sexual purity. The second member is *niyamas*, ethical observances. Some of these observances are contentment, moderation, and asceticism as guided by the Spirit. Other observances are the study of scripture, spiritual writing, individual and/or group forms of prayer and worship, and surrendering to God's will in all areas of one's life.

These first two members are expressions of the spiritual ideals of "loving your neighbor as you love yourself" and developing purity of heart. These two members require your careful attention throughout your spiritual journey. It would be a mistake to leave these members behind because of advancing to the other members, since these two members form a foundation for spiritual progress. In particular, as you make progress from one member to another, there is a tendency in accomplishing these steps to also acquire a certain degree of pride in your achievements. Thus it is essential to be aware of the need for humility, which is a requirement for developing purity of heart. If you notice pride emerging at times, you can simply observe it without encouragement and without self-condemnation. Like letting go of stray thoughts in meditation, sometimes negative attributes tend to fall away by themselves if you do not cling to them and do not try to push them away.

The third and fourth members, *asanas* and *pranayama*, are body postures and breathing practices included in basic hatha yoga, which also may include deep relaxation. The hatha yoga body postures are described in Chapter 4. The breathing practices are fully described in Chapter 5. These hatha yoga practices are important methods of preparing the body for practicing meditation and contemplation.

The fifth member is *pratyahara*, the withdrawal of the senses from the sense objects. This practice restricts outward desires and turns the awareness to inner desires that reflect seeking the divine.

The sixth member is *dharana*, concentration, which is intermittent mental focusing. The seventh member would be *dhyana*, meditation, which is continuous mental focusing. Unlike the meditation practice of holding one thought in the mind continuously, *contemplation* is the overshadowing of the Holy Spirit that creates an inner wordless attunement. Wordless contemplation is not included as a member of Patanjali's classical yoga. Nevertheless, wordless contemplation needs to be included as a unique and separate member of Miracle Raja Yoga. Therefore, the eighth member of Miracle Raja Yoga is wordless contemplation, which is the letting go of all thoughts in contrast to meditation, which is the holding of one thought.

The ninth member of Miracle Raja Yoga is the experience of *divine union*, including other spiritual experiences that lead toward divine union. This member would be similar to, but not the same as, the eighth member of classical yoga, *samadhi*. The term "samadhi" is often interpreted as "ecstasy," but refers to different kinds and levels of spiritual experiences. In the typical interpretation of Patanjali's classical yoga, the highest samadhi is divine union in which the soul loses its individual identity, becomes dissolved in God (Brahman), and is freed by escaping from this world. Miracle Raja Yoga does not include this idea of the soul dissolving into God, losing its individual identity. In the highest form of divine union in this life, called *the illumination of glory*[74] by St. John of the Cross, the soul joins with God, temporarily becoming God by participation in God. However, the soul does not lose its individuality but finds its true Self in God in a transformed consciousness.

St. Symeon the New Theologian sets the example of the soul who experiences divine union while still in this world and who allows all the lower faculties to be filled with the divine light. This is similar to the tantric yoga ideal of *jivanmukta*—the seeker being freed while still living in this world. St. Symeon's example of total integration of the physical, emotional, mental, and intuitive perfectly joined and under the influence of your true spiritual nature is a very unrealistic goal for the vast majority of seekers. Yet divine union while still living in the world does not need to be achieved in this life in order for you to be successful in your practice of Miracle Raja Yoga. If your life is devoted to seeking divine union, your seeking will prepare you to awaken to your true nature in God when this worldly life is completed.

To practice Miracle Raja Yoga, you will have to choose a form of meditation or contemplation that best meets your individual needs. Christian Yoga Meditation is a good choice because it combines six Methods that integrate well with the various aspects of Miracle Yoga. The first method of Christian Yoga Meditation is focusing on the navel center, which is related to the physical body and which is the vehicle for expressing dedicated action in Miracle Karma Yoga. The second technique of Christian Yoga Meditation is focusing on the heart center, which is related to emotions and specifically to love. This is important for expressing devotion in Miracle Bhakti Yoga. The third technique of Christian Yoga Meditation is focusing the mind on the brow center. This meditation technique is helpful for expressing the intellectual discernment necessary to practice Miracle Jnana Yoga.

The final three methods of Christian Yoga Meditation involve the activation of the crown center on the top of the head, which is related to awakening universal awareness. Because these three techniques facilitate the awakening and integration of higher awareness, they are in alignment with the purpose of Miracle Raja Yoga. The complete explanation of how to practice Christian Yoga Meditation and also the descriptions of other Christian meditation methods are provided in the book titled *Christian Meditation Inspired by Yoga and "A Course in Miracles": How to Open to Divine Love in Contemplation.* This meditation manual would benefit Course students but is written for any Christian seekers who are interested in Christian meditation and contemplation regardless of their spiritual philosophy.

Whatever method of meditation or contemplation that you choose will probably change as you make progress. In order to be effective meditation requires consistency of practice at regular times every day because the results are cumulative.

H. MIRACLE YOGA IS FOLLOWING CHRIST

Yoga in the Hindu tradition, and especially in the tantric tradition, can be considered "systematic internalization." In yoga everything is internalized, meaning brought into the body. All of the universe, the macrocosm, is interiorized, including all of the dimensions of existence beyond the three dimensions of the physical universe. Thus a smaller version of the macrocosm is symbolically represented within the body as the microcosm. The spine represents the axis of the universe around which all else spins, and along that axis are the seven spiritual centers. The systematic internalization produced by yoga practices penetrates not only into the body but more importantly into the spiritual centers themselves. Everything in the universe that spins around the central axis of the sp ine is brought into the chakras, especially into the heart center and the crown center, where all opposing forces come together in oneness. Yoga attainment is considered to be the union of divergent forces to realize the oneness of God.

Just as yoga in general is an internalization, Miracle Yoga is also a systematic internalization, however with an emphasis placed on Christ. As a Christian yogi, your body is a member of the body of Christ. Christ's body encompasses the universe of form, space, and time. There is nothing that exists outside of Christ, just as there is nothing that exists outside of God, the only difference being God is the First Cause, Who created the Christ. The Christian yogi then has a single task: to internalize Christ, Who is the One in the All.

Within the Christian yogi then is the cross of Christ in which his ego dies daily. His breath inhales the love of Christ for him personally and for all of mankind. In this inhalation, he takes in the words of Christ on the cross, "Father, forgive them, for they do not know what they are doing."[75] He knows these words are for himself and all his brothers, and he knows a deeper meaning not expressed, "Father, forgive them for they do not yet know who they are, *as your holy children.*" His breath exhales the last expiration of the cross, "Father, into your hands I commend my Spirit."[76]

When the Christian yogi meditates, he may see himself as one of the disciples waiting in the upper room for the Holy Spirit to descend onto the crown of his head in parted tongues of fire to purify and cleanse himself of all that would separate him from oneness. Christ rose from the dead in a moment of time for all mankind once and for all. Yet the Christian yogi is not content with an intellectual assent to this event in history. His mission is to immerse himself in the fire of God so the ego may be burnt to ashes, and he may rise from the dead also. However, it will not be the yogi rising from the dead. The Christian yogi's realization is that it will be the Christ within him Who is resurrecting again in the eternal present moment.

With the awakening of Christ comes the awareness of your own Self as the Christ. Equally important is that the expanded awareness of oneness brings with it the realization that others are participating with you in the one Christ. Therefore, you can see your true Self in your brother and sister. Along with any true realization comes compassion and gratitude. Out of this gratitude comes dedicated participation in bringing about the liberation and happiness of all conscious beings. Christian yogis become teachers of this goal of extending to others, just as Buddhists become teachers to embrace the identical goal, called the *bodhisattva* ideal. Consequently, what begins as a Miracle Yoga internalization ends as a Miracle Yoga externalization. Being a teacher does not necessarily mean calling yourself a teacher. You teach others simply by your example, and sometimes more effectively than if you did call yourself a teacher.

Walking the path of Miracle Yoga would ideally include a balanced practice of Miracle Karma Yoga, Miracle Bhakti Yoga, Miracle Jnana Yoga, and Miracle Raja Yoga. There is a fifth aspect of Miracle Yoga called Miracle Relationship Yoga. This aspect is first introduced in Chapter 1 as the yoga of holy relationships in which partners join for a common purpose. This is the unique part of Miracle Yoga because it is not an outgrowth of traditional Hindu yoga. Chapter 7 that is titled "Miracle Relationship Yoga" is devoted entirely to describing this very essential aspect of Miracle Yoga and provides an understanding of the Course principles that form the basis of this practice.

If you accept Miracle Yoga as your path, you have a wonderful example to follow, Jesus. His life reflected a balance of dedicated action, devotion, knowledge, meditation, and holy relationships. Jesus will take you by the hand, as a father takes the hand of his son, and walk with you along the path. Remember that you are never alone in your search. You are always joined in this search with your brothers and sisters because finding the divine within is the longing of every human heart either consciously or subconsciously. This collaborative adventure is part of God's Plan of evolving spiritual consciousness. Jesus is in charge of this Plan, so be sure to hold his hand. Every step toward the Light, no matter how seemingly small, contributes to the overall spiritual growth of all conscious beings.

CHAPTER 4

~ • ~

HATHA YOGA POSTURES FOR A CALM MND

A. CHRISTIAN HATHA YOGA

The most familiar form of yoga to Christians is hatha yoga, which is yoga of the physical body. This type of yoga involves the use of body postures and breathing practices and is the most commonly accepted form of yoga. However, its true purpose is often overlooked. In America hatha yoga has been largely stripped of its spiritual significance and has been viewed only as a means of maintaining the physical health of the body. The original spiritual purpose of hatha yoga, as it was created thousands of years ago, was to develop the body as a healthy device for the purpose of practicing sitting meditation in order for the seeker to transcend the physical world.

Consequently, for hatha yoga, you can have one of two distinctly different meanings depending upon what you are seeking in the way of content from your yoga practice. If you are seeking physical health, yoga would be the means to that end of good health. On the other hand, if you practice yoga to meditate better and to improve your chances of spiritual transformation, then yoga would be the means and Christ would be the end. The latter could correctly be called "Christian hatha yoga," while the former could not. But it should be remembered that hatha yoga itself is universal and therefore can be adapted as a means of growing toward any spiritual ideal.

Miracle Yoga specifically based on the Course includes hatha yoga as part of Miracle Raja Yoga. One fairly standard form of hatha yoga will be presented in this book as an option for drawing closer to Christ. However, if the specific hatha yoga practices described here were to be called by the name "Miracle Hatha Yoga," it may give the false impression that there is only one form of hatha yoga that could be used by someone who wants to practice Miracle Yoga based on the Course. Since any form of hatha yoga may be used for your practice of Miracle Yoga, the hatha yoga described below will simply be called by the generic name of "Christian hatha yoga." The Christian hatha yoga practices described in this chapter are recommended for you whether you want to practice Christian yoga in the form of Miracle Yoga based on the Course or whether you want to practice Christian yoga based on your own personal philosophy.

Christians, who are teachers of hatha yoga, may think of their own personal practice as Christian hatha yoga, or simply "Christian yoga." Nevertheless, they are often called upon to teach in colleges and other non-sectarian settings. This presents a dilemma for the yoga teacher who seeks to not focus on physical health only and yet cannot express spirituality in an overt manner. A compromise appropriate to these non-sectarian settings is to talk about "hath yoga for a calm mind." This would likewise include reference to "breathing practices for a calm mind." The purpose of having a calm mind is an acceptable universal goal for hatha yoga and breathing practices and understandable and acceptable to seekers of physical health and to spiritual seekers.

Hatha yoga is the third member of raga yoga, related to holding the body in an "asana," which means steady pose. The benefits from the body postures come from holding steady poses in order to stretch the body without straining. Stretching muscles, ligaments, and tendons helps to increase flexibility and suppleness. Sometimes when you are doing a particular posture, you might feel one specific area of the body that is being stretched. While holding that posture, you can bring the awareness of your mind to that area that is being stretched. At the same time, you can also repeat the name of Jesus, if you feel guided to do so. When you have your awareness on the stretch, you do not stain or pull harder. Rather, you just *relax into the stretch.*

The yoga postures have a beneficial effect on the endocrine glands that regulate the body functions. The body postures also work on the nervous system to calm the nerves leading to a calm mind. In fact, seeing hatha yoga as a means of calming the mind is the proper understanding of the true purpose of this discipline. The yoga postures enhance your potential for spiritual transformation by keeping the spine flexible, which ironically enables the back to remain comfortably motionless in meditation. A strong body is also needed to withstand the impact of the rising of the kundalini.

The fourth member of raja yoga is called *pranayama*, which focuses on breathing practices that control the prana, the vital energy of the body. These breathing practices, when employed in moderation, can be important in purifying the channels within the body that assist the practice of meditation. The postures and breathing practices of hatha yoga are recommended as a daily practice because of the physical and spiritual benefits. These postures are presented in this chapter, and breathing practices are described in the next chapter. However, reading about these spiritual disciplines in this book or even additional research on hatha yoga in other books is not the best resource for learning these practices. Ideally, if you decide that you are interested in the practice of hatha yoga, it would be best to seek out a hatha yoga instructor.

The easiest and simplest way to do this is to take a hatha yoga course lasting six, seven, or eight weeks. These courses are often offered privately by teachers, and many health food stores have bulletin boards which advertise local yoga classes. Many community colleges or regular colleges have yoga courses available, and sometimes these are part of the continuing education programs. City recreation departments sometimes offer yoga classes. You will probably not find any class with the name "Christian hatha yoga," because hatha yoga is usually taught as a health practice in a non-religious setting. This is fine since it would probably be best to have a teacher, who is not affiliated with a religious group. In this case, you can be shown how to practice the techniques, and you can mentally add your own spiritual meaning to what you learn.

If you practice some hatha yoga and want additional experience, you may possibly want to temporarily live in a yoga community, but you must be cautious if you do so. You must resist the temptation to dilute or lose your chosen Christian identity in the name of universality. If the community is led by a guru, and if you decide to receive mantra initiation from the guru, this would be an example of lessening your Christian identity. Of course, that would be your personal choice, but why would you, as a Christian, want a mantra given to you by a guru? Will the yoga guru give you a better mantra than the name of Jesus? Why would you want to replace Jesus, who is already your guru?

If you are living in a yoga community, you will see many others follow this path of guru initiation. You may be tempted to do likewise. Jesus will bless you whether you turn right or left, but why let go of His hand? You will be tempted to think that you are being humble by submitting to the guru. But by taking the guru's hand, you show that you do not really believe you already have the hand of Jesus. Your lack of faith in Jesus cannot produce progress on the path to Christ.

Other than this temptation, much good can come from living in a yoga community temporarily. It would be ideal if you could find a Christian yoga community, but I am not aware of such a community. You could also go to a yoga retreat, especially a silent retreat. An ideal retreat for the intermediate seeker would be a Christian retreat which includes yoga and the extensive practice of meditation. After receiving yoga training of some kind, you will be able to incorporate what you have learned into your ongoing private Christian hatha yoga practice, preferably on a daily basis.

Some students of hath yoga become very enthusiastic and do a lot of yoga initially and then discontinue the practice. Actually, it would be much more beneficial to do a limited set of practices for a short period of time each day and make a commitment to yourself to make this a lifetime practice. You do not have to be physically well conditioned or athletically gifted to do hatha yoga postures. Also, you do not have to perform the postures flawlessly in order to benefit from them. You can proceed at your own pace learning how to gently stretch the body without causing any strain. After doing the postures for an extended period of time, you may notice that you can stretch further than you could when you first started, but your progress is not primarily a matter of how well you can perform the postures at a form level.

Content is more important than form in the practice of Christian hath yoga. Consequently, what is happening in your mind takes precedence over how proficient the body is in executing postures. The motivation of your mind, your purpose, is the most important element in your practice of Christian hatha yoga. If you practice Christian hatha yoga with a half-hearted motivation, you will get half-hearted results. One of the very reasons why I emphasize hatha yoga as "Christian hatha yoga" is so you will keep the end always in mind as your motivation while practicing the means. By focusing on your yoga as your means and your union with Christ as your end, your practice of Christian hatha yoga will be as natural and effortless as breathing. Your faith in Christ is the key to your success with Christian hatha yoga.

B. TYPICAL POSTURES OF A YOGA CLASS

You can enhance your Christian hatha yoga experience by simply repeating the Jesus Prayer during the postures themselves and in the peaceful intervals of time between postures. If you attend a yoga class, standard postures will likely be included. On the opposite page, there is an example of the sequence of activities in a typical yoga class. There is an asterisk beside the seven most basic postures, as follows:

1. **Eye Exercises**
2. **Sun Salutation**
3. **Relaxing Posture***
4. **Cobra***
5. **Half Locust***
6. **Full Locust**
7. **Boat**
8. **Bow***
9. **Half Forward Bend**
10. **Full Forward Bend***
11. **Shoulder Stand***
12. **Fish***
13. **Half Spinal Twist**
14. **Yoga Seal**
15. **Relaxation Techniques**
16. **Breathing Practices**
17. **Calming Meditation**

Even though these postures may be included in a typical class, an experienced teacher can teach these postures so that younger physically fit students and older less physically fit students can each proceed at their own pace. Sometimes individuals between the age of forty and seventy will suddenly become enamored with the idea of practicing yoga in spite of not having exercised before on a daily basis. These older students must be careful to choose an experienced teacher who will be conscious of encouraging students to practice yoga in a gentle manner. If an older student practices extreme back bending before the muscles have been properly strengthened, he would be susceptible to tearing the muscles of the diaphragm producing a hiatus hernia. If older students are improperly instructed to exert themselves in a strenuous manner, the result can be injuries to the neck and shoulder muscles or possibly pulled or torn tendons of the lower back, hips, or groin.[77] For this reason, it is very important to choose an experienced yoga teacher and to use your own common sense to make sure that you do not exert yourself beyond the capacity of your body. An older student can also sometimes find yoga classes that are specifically for older individuals, and there are yoga books that are written entirely for older students.

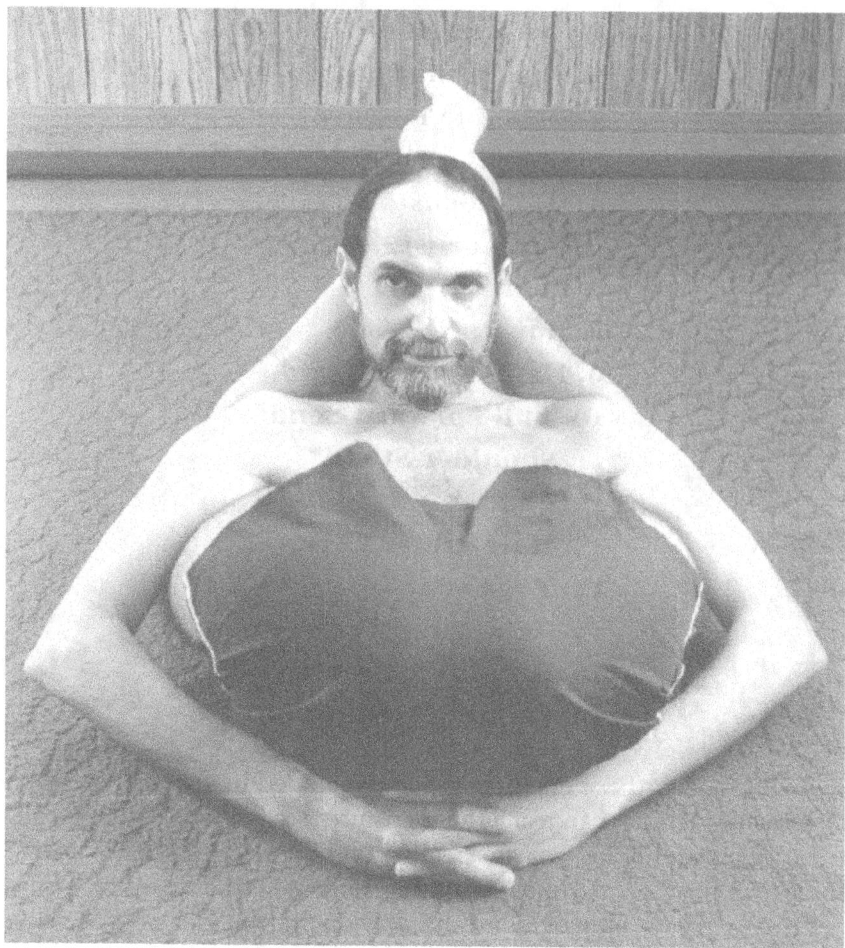

C. SEVEN BASIC POSTURES

Above is a photograph of me doing the *Head-Knee Pose* (Dwipada Sirasana). In the mid-seventies, I started the first class of an eight-week college course for beginners in hatha yoga by telling the students, "Everyone assume the following position." Then I proceeded to make a *you know what* out of myself by coming into this pretzel-like posture. I never again started a hatha yoga class in this manner because I questioned my ego motivation in making such a showy demonstration. Nevertheless, the students in this class immediately laughed because they saw the intended humor, but there was also a lesson intended in this demonstration. The lesson that I had hoped to convey to the beginners in this class was to be careful to not perform any posture that is beyond the capacity of one's own body. The idea is simply to stretch the body without straining and go at one's own pace without comparing one's progress with others.

I also used this demonstration to emphasize to the students that yoga is not really about mastering difficult postures. It is for this reason that there are no very difficult postures that have been included or recommended in this book. If you want to learn how to practice more advanced postures, it would be advisable to do so under the watchful guidance of an experienced yoga instructor. There is nothing wrong with moving in this direction as long as you have not confused the means of Christian hatha yoga with the end. If the yoga postures become an end in themselves, then it would appear that more and more advanced postures would bring you closer to that end. However, if yoga postures are correctly seen in Christian hatha yoga as a means of leading toward the end of increased faith in Christ, then the difficulty of postures becomes a relatively unimportant issue. The major emphasis in Christian hatha yoga in regard to postures is to maintain a flexible spine and healthy body so your body can be a fit vehicle to go inward in meditation and contemplation and to go outward in expressing love and service to others. When practicing the yoga postures, it is important to do so while maintaining a peaceful state of mind, which would keep the focus on content being more important than form.

Your basic daily practice of yoga does not require that you do many different postures. There are actually only about seven basic postures. Other optional poses can be added to these basic postures, if you feel guided to do so. A wise approach to your practice of yoga postures is to start slowly and carefully. Progress is made by daily practice of the basic postures and learning to hold them longer in a relaxed manner without straining. It is much better to do seven basic postures every day consistently, rather than to do thirteen or fourteen postures one day and none the next day.

Here is a suggested minimum daily sequence of seven postures:

1. The Relaxing Posture

2. The Shoulder Stand

3. The Fish

4. The Full Forward Bend

5. The Half Locust

6. The Cobra

7. The Bow

These postures are for seekers who are generally already physically healthy. If you have physical limitations, you can still participate in practicing less demanding variations of yoga postures. Each of the seven recommended postures is described below in the sequence that is suggested for your daily practice.

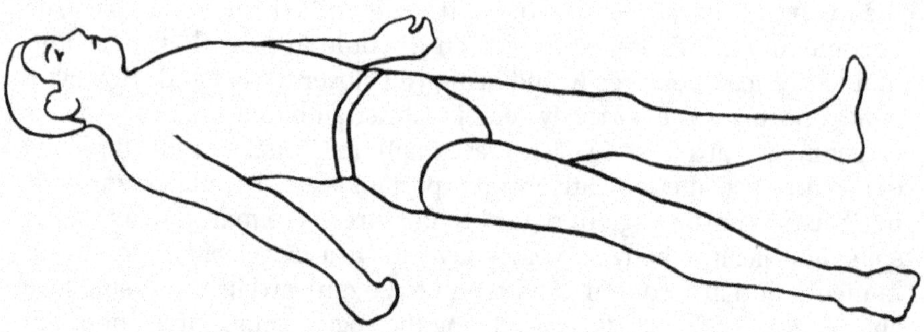

1. THE RELAXING POSTURE

For the *Relaxing Posture* (Savasana, the Corpse Pose) you lie down on the floor with the body cushioned by a carpet or blanket. The feet are a foot and a half or two feet apart. The arms are a few inches away from the sides of the body. The palms of the hands are turned upward. The eyes are closed and relaxed. For the Relaxing Posture you just relax completely and let the body melt into the floor.

Between each of the other postures, you will return to this posture below. The Relaxing Posture helps to relieve any tension that may have built up during the postures. Of course, the postures are not designed to create tension, but to relieve tension. However, sometimes beginners try too hard. It is proper to stretch the body during postures but not to strain. You are the only one who can judge the point between stretching and straining. You hold each posture only long enough for a stretch to be maintained without a strain occurring.

1. SHOULDER STAND — Three stages are involved in the practice of the *Shoulder Stand* (Sarvangasana). If there is any tension, return to the previous stage or to the starting position of the Relaxing Posture of lying on the back. Also, come out of the Shoulder Stand if there is any need to swallow or use the throat in any way. Beginning from the Relaxing Posture, bring the legs together. The arms are straight and alongside the body, and you turn the palms *downward*. Press downward on the palms and raise the legs to 90 degrees, perpendicular to the floor. You hold this first stage briefly.

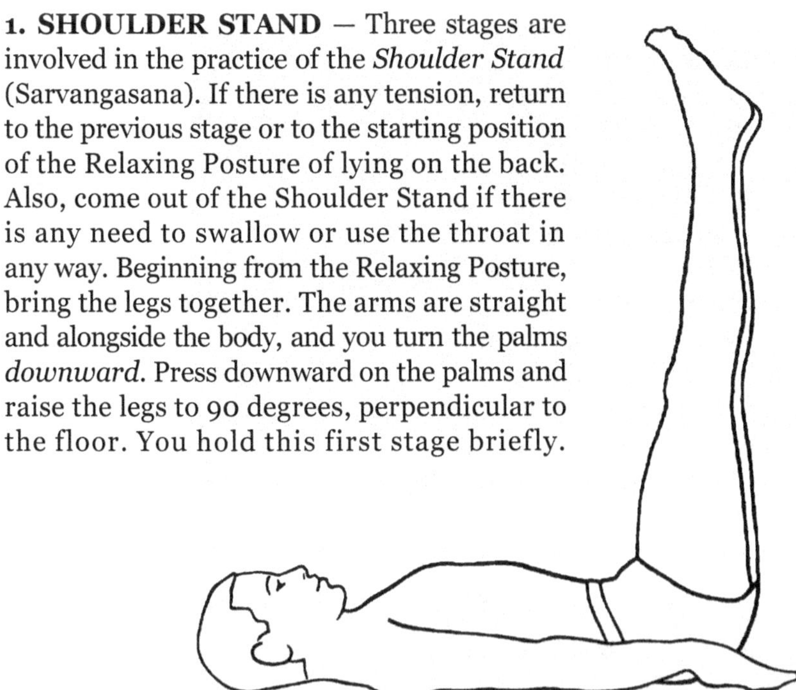

For the second stage of the Shoulder Stand, you apply pressure downward with the palms of the hands. Then lift the back and raise the legs overhead to a position parallel to the floor. You maintain this posture briefly. This second stage of the Shoulder Stand is called the *Plough* (Halasana). Ideally, the toes touch the floor, but it is fine for beginners to hold the legs exactly parallel to the floor.

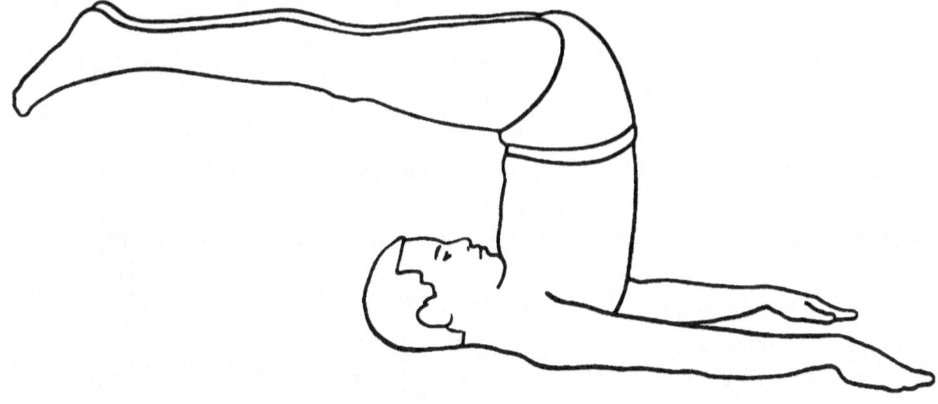

Next you bend the arms at the elbows and place the palms of the hands along the spinal column to support the body. Then raise the legs upward into the third stage, which is the Shoulder Stand itself. The torso and legs are ideally held perpendicular to the floor. It is all right if you cannot hold the body in a straight line as shown in the illustration here of an ideal posture. While you hold the Shoulder Stand, it's important to maintain a position that's comfortable and one you can sustain easily with stability. You can hold the position for approximately a minute, if you can keep this pose comfortably. This yoga posture is also called the *All Members Pose* since it is beneficial to all parts of the body, in particular the thyroid gland, which controls the body's metabolism.

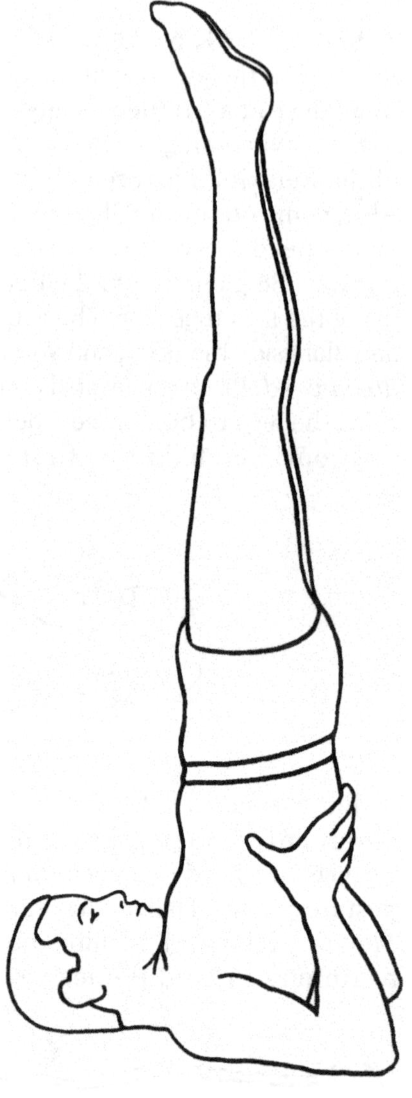

To come out of this posture, return to the second stage. You slowly lower the legs into the Plough, in which the legs are parallel to the floor. Next you remove the hands from supporting the spine and lower the arms to alongside the body so the palms of the hands are placed downward on the floor. You apply downward pressure on the palms and slowly lower the back vertebra by vertebra to the floor bringing the legs to the 90-degree position perpendicular to the floor. You briefly hold this second stage. Finally with the palms pressing downward, you keep the legs straight, and slowly with full control, you lower both legs to the floor. You return to the Relaxing Posture lying on your back.

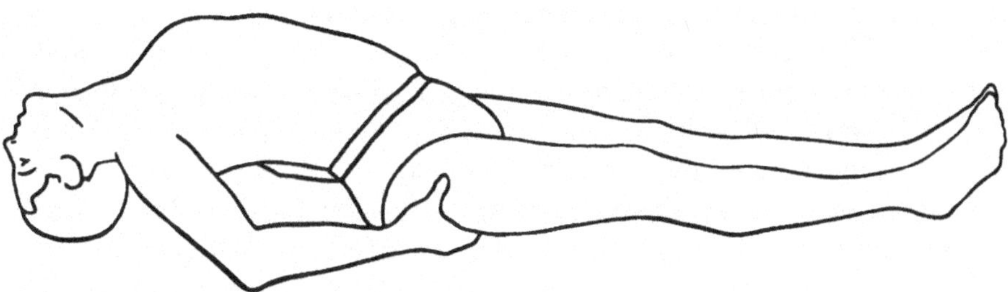

3. THE FISH — The complimentary pose to the Shoulder Stand is the *Fish* (Matsyasana). You place the legs together. You hold onto the thighs with the thumb on the side of the thigh and the other fingers tucked under the thighs. You shift the weight of the body to the elbows and raise the body to a half-seated position. You arch the back, thrust out the chest, and lower the crown of the head to the floor. You need to remember to breathe slowly and deeply to expand those areas of the lungs not normally expanded. This position is held for about 30 seconds, as long as there is no strain occurring.

To come out of this pose, you return the full weight of the body to the elbows. You draw the head in toward the chest and slowly lower the back to the floor with full control. You return to the Relaxing Posture. You slowly move the head from side to side to loosen up the neck and then return the head to the center position.

4. THE FULL FORWARD BEND — In order to transition from the Relaxing Posture to the *Full Forward Bend* (Paschimothanasana), you begin by bringing the legs together. The arms are raised above the head with the elbows straight. Keeping the head between the arms, you raise the upper torso of the body up to a seated position, or you come up in whatever way is most comfortable for you. Then you lower the hands to the lap.

To begin the Full Forward Bend, you raise both arms overhead so the head is between the arms with the elbows straight. Next you look and stretch upward as you inhale. Then you exhale and bend forward from the base of the spine, while you keep the head between the arms with the arms remaining straight. You hold onto the legs wherever it is comfortable to do so. The toes are pointed upward and the back of the knees are flat on the floor so the proper muscles are being stretched. Although you can feel the stretch, it is important not to try to pull or tug beyond that natural stretch. You allow yourself to relax into the stretch by simply letting gravity exert its force over the body.

After approximately a half minute, you exhale and bend forward even further into the posture and then inhale and raise up to a seated position with the head remaining between the arms that are extended over your head. With the arms overhead, you return to the Relaxing Posture by lowering the back vertebra by vertebra to the floor. After the arms reach the floor and are still overhead, you bring the arms to a position alongside the body with the palms turned upward.

An alternative to the Full Forward Bend is the ***Half Forward Bend*** (Janusirshasana) in which only one leg is extended forward and the foot of the other leg is brought in toward the center of the body so the sole of the foot is placed against the inside of the thigh of the extended leg. Then you bend forward over the extended leg just as you would for the Full Forward Bend. Of course, you would have to first bend forward over one leg and then reverse the leg positions so you can bend forward over the other leg.

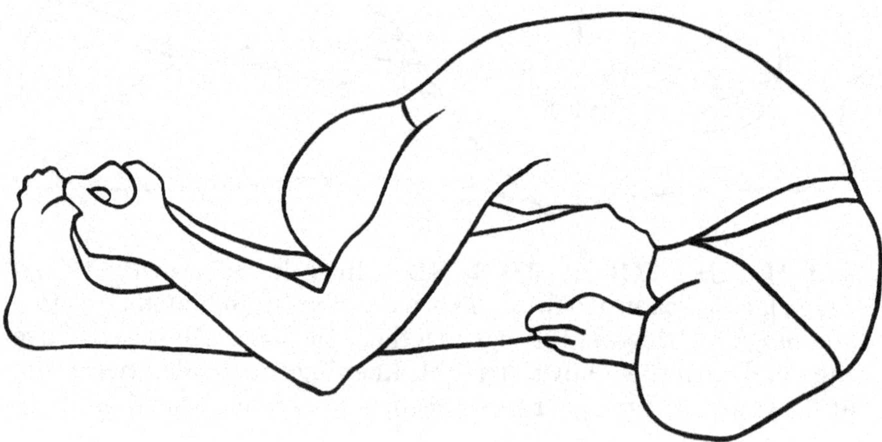

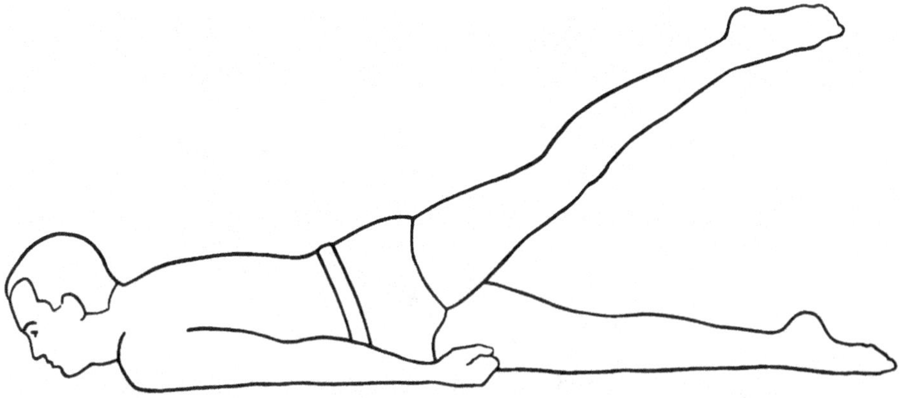

5. THE HALF LOCUST

After completing the Full Forward Bend and briefly remaining in the Relaxing Posture on the back, you will have to assume the Relaxing Posture on the abdomen to complete the final three postures in this sequence. You turn the body over slowly in whatever way is most comfortable without disturbing your peace. You keep the legs about a shoulder's width apart. The arms are straight and a few inches away from the body, and the palms are turned upward. The head is turned to one side. The next time you come into this position, you turn the head to the other side in order to alternate the way in which the neck is stretched.

For the *Half Locust* (Ardha Salabasana) you place the feet together. You straighten the arms at the elbows and place both arms underneath the body with the elbows as close together as possible underneath the body. Either you make two fists side by side or you place the hands open with the palms turned upward and with one hand on top of the other. You return the head to the center and place the chin on the floor. You raise each leg alternately, and you need to remember to keep the hips *level* and pressed downward. You bring the awareness to the right leg and straighten it. You lift the right leg keeping it straight. You hold for ten seconds without straining and then slowly lower the right leg. Next you bring the awareness to the left leg, straighten it, and lift. You hold for ten seconds and slowly lower. You repeat lifting the right leg one more time and then repeat lifting the left leg. Then you release the arms from underneath the body and return to the Relaxing Posture with the arms alongside the body and the head turned to one side.

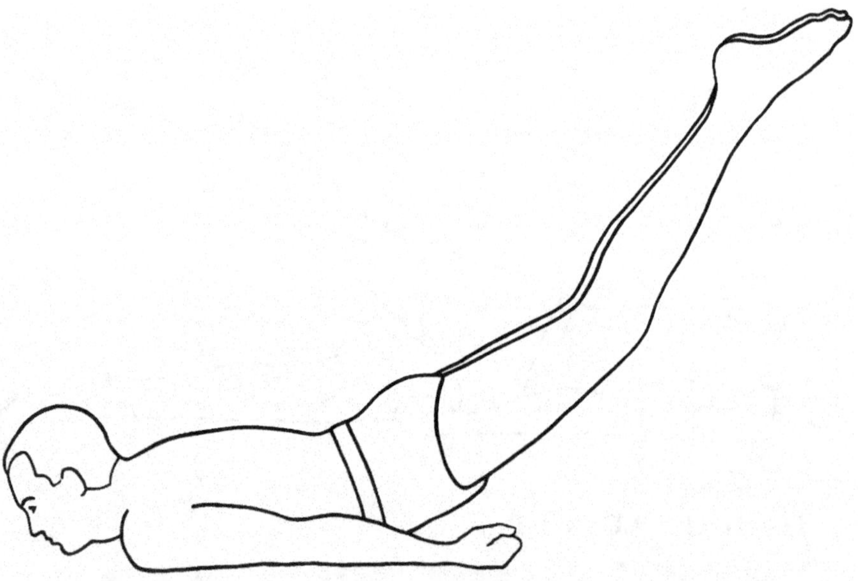

After learning to practice the Half Locust without straining, you can practice the **Full Locust** (Salabasana), by using the same process but lifting both legs simultaneously. If you have a lower back problem, the Full Locust should not be practiced until you have first strengthened the back by using the other postures over a long period of time.

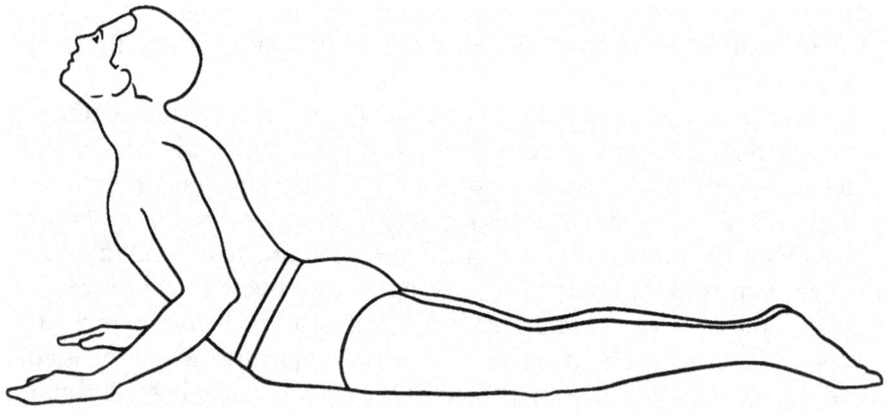

6. THE COBRA

Starting from the Relaxing Posture on the abdomen, you place the feet together and rest the chin on the floor as you begin practicing the *Cobra* (Bhujangasana). If you are able to do so, you can rest the forehead on the floor instead of bringing the chin to the floor.

You bend the arms at the elbows, and you place the palms of the hands downward on the floor underneath the corresponding shoulders with the fingertips placed in line with the tops of the shoulders. The bent elbows are close to the body and turned upward.

You raise the head drawing the chin along the floor. You turn the vision upward as you raise the neck and then the upper portion the back. You slowly roll the spine backward vertebra by vertebra lifting only with the back muscles and not with the arms. You raise the hands an inch off the floor to make sure that you are lifting only with the back muscles. After about 15 seconds of holding the position without straining, you return the hands to the floor and slowly lower the back vertebra by vertebra. When the chin (or forehead) returns to the mat, the gaze is turned downward last of all. The head is turned to one side, and you return to the Relaxing Posture with the arms alongside the body with the palms turned upward. After resting, you repeat the Cobra again. But this time after lifting only with the back, you can apply a slight pressure downward on the hands to stretch the back a little further than previously.

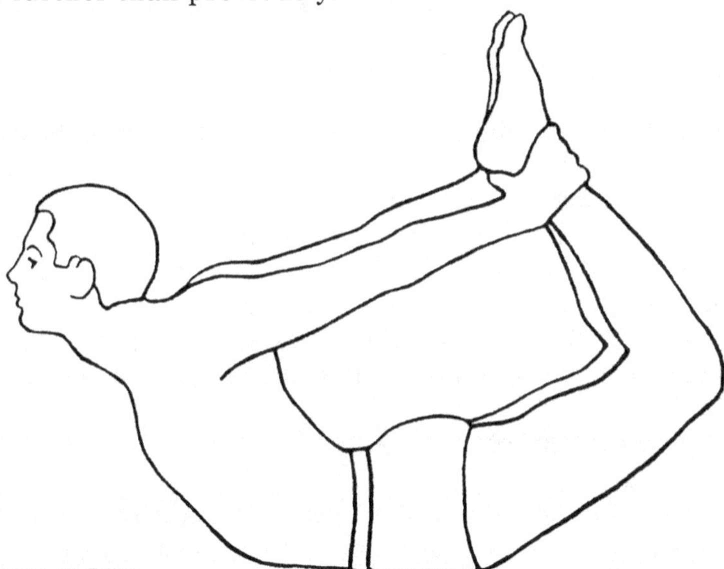

7. THE BOW

While in the Relaxing Posture on the abdomen, you begin your practice of the *Bow* (Dhanurasana) by bringing the legs together. You bend the legs at the knees bringing the feet in toward the buttocks. You reach your arms behind your back to catch hold of the right ankle with the right hand and the left ankle with the left hand. If this gives your body a good enough stretch you can just remain in this position.

Otherwise, you practice the Bow by raising up on the extremities and balancing on the abdomen. (If this is too much of a strain, you can raise up only the head and chest and not the legs.) When you raise up and balance on the abdomen, you keep the arms straight. The knees are placed as close together as is comfortable without straining. After balancing on the abdomen for about 15 seconds, you lower the legs to the floor and then bring the chin to the floor. Then you turn the head to one side, and you return to the Relaxing Posture with the arms alongside the body with the palms turned upward. Next without disturbing your peace, you can slowly turn the body over into the Relaxing Posture on the back and relax completely.

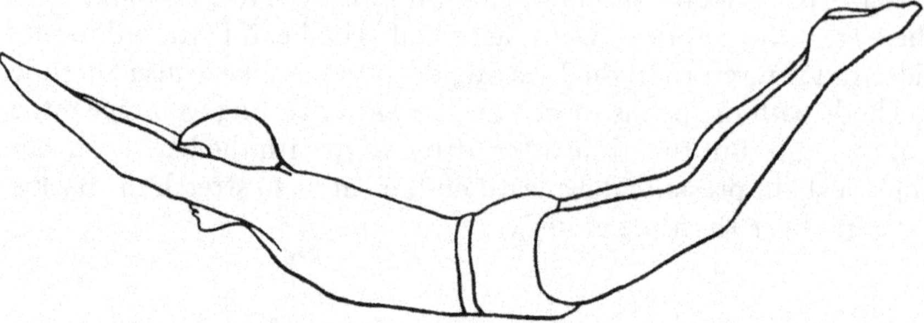

A less strenuous alternative to the Bow is the **Boat** (Paschima Nauasana). For the Boat pose, the legs are placed together and kept straight. The arms are extended over the head and are straight with the head between the arms. You place the chin on the floor, and then you raise the extremities and balance on the abdomen. Hold for 15 seconds and then lower and return to the Relaxing Posture. An easier variation of the Boat is to place the arms behind the back, hold the right wrist with the left hand, and balance on the abdomen.

D. OPTIONAL POSTURES

Some optional poses have already been identified above as poses that you can practice if you feel some of the seven basic postures are too difficult. For example the second stage of the Shoulder Stand, which is the Plough, may be practiced by itself if the Shoulder Stand is too strenuous. Another example is the Half Forward Bend that you can use to replace the Full Forward Bend or be used before practicing the Full Forward Bend. Also, the Boat can be used instead of the more strenuous Bow. Of course, some optional poses are more difficult than the basic poses, as for instance the Full Locust that can be practiced after strengthening the back by using the Half Locust initially.

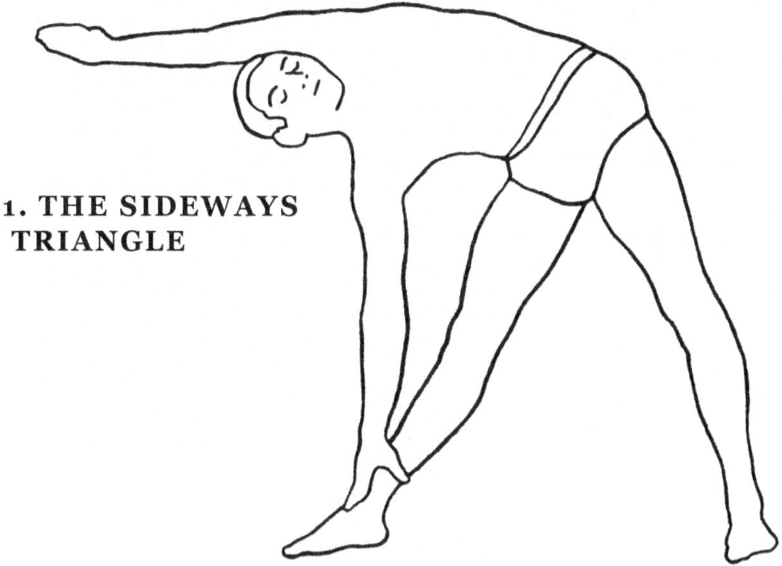

1. THE SIDEWAYS TRIANGLE

In addition to the optional postures mentioned previously, seven more optional postures will be described in this section, starting with the Sideways Triangle. Under ideal circumstances, you can set aside time every day for the basic postures, and then add optional poses of your choice. Some of these optional poses increase flexibility by stretching the spine in a twisting motion or sideways motion. Other postures help to develop body balance or have other benefits not provided by the basic postures.

For the *Sideways Triangle* (Trikonasana—variation #1) you stand erect with the legs between two and three feet apart forming a triangle if you consider the floor to be the bottom third of the triangle. You raise the arms to a horizontal position at shoulder height with the right arm straight and stretched to the right and the left arm straight and stretched to the left. Next you bend the spine sideways to the left and allow the left hand to move downward along the outside of the left leg. You raise the right hand upward and bring the right arm toward the right ear, as close to the head as possible. The whole body is twisted sideways to the left without allowing the spine to bend forward. Both the arms and the legs are kept straight in this position. After holding the posture for 5 seconds, you return to the standing position. Then you reverse the procedure and bend the body sideways to the right. After 5 seconds, you return to the standing position. A variation on this pose, which you may prefer, is to bend just slightly forward as you bend sideways and allow the lowered hand to touch the ankle or toes.

2. THE TWISTING TRIANGLE

For the *Twisting Triangle* (Trikonasana—variation #2) you stand with the legs between two and three feet apart. You raise the arms to a horizontal position at shoulder height. You keep the arms straight and bring the right hand toward the toes of the left foot. Both arms form a straight line extending from the right arm pointed down to the left hand pointed up. You hold this position for 5 seconds and then return to the standing position. Next, you reverse the position by twisting the body in the opposite direction bringing the left hand toward the toes of the right foot and again hold for 5 seconds.

3. THE KING DANCER

To do the *King Dancer* (Natarajasana), you stand with the feet slightly apart. Then you shift your body weight to the right leg. As you balance on the right leg, you bend the left leg at the knee and take hold of the left ankle with the left hand. When you first use this posture, you look downward at a spot on the floor, which will help you to maintain your balance. Eventually, you can learn to look horizontally and to maintain your balance as you focus on one spot in your line of vision. Then you hold the King Dancer for about five seconds as you balance on your right foot. Next you reverse the position, and you balance on your left foot for about five seconds.

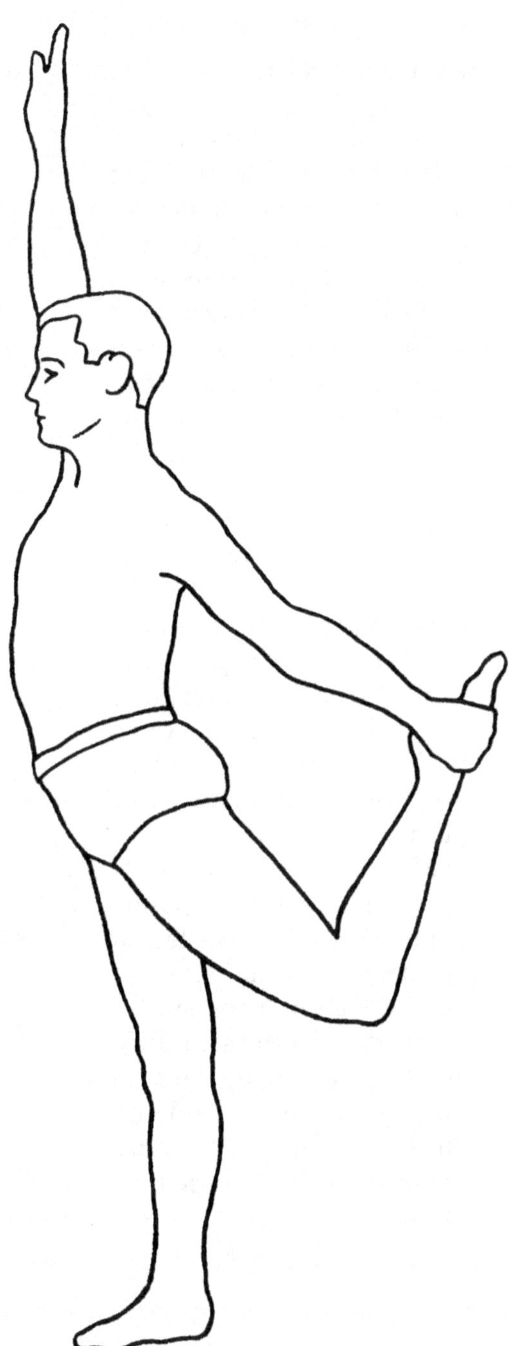

4. THE TREE

For the *Tree* (Vrikshasana), you stand with the feet just slightly apart and bring the palms together at the chest in prayer position. You focus on one spot within your line of vision in order to help you maintain your balance. Then you shift your weight to the right leg. Balancing on the right leg, you bend the left leg to bring the sole of the left foot to the inside of the right knee. You can keep the hands placed together at the chest, or you can place the hands together in a position above the head as shown in the illustration. You hold this pose for five seconds. After placing the hands above the head, you return the hands to the chest with the palms in prayer position while still balancing on your right leg. Finally you lower the left leg and return to the standing position. Then you reverse this procedure by balancing on the left leg and holding the posture for five seconds again.

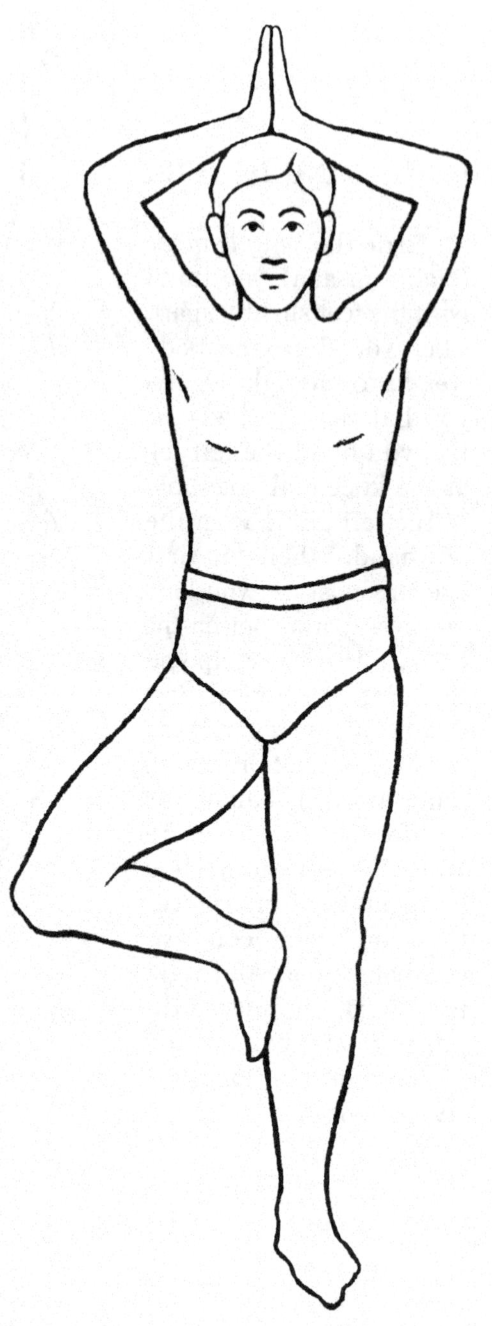

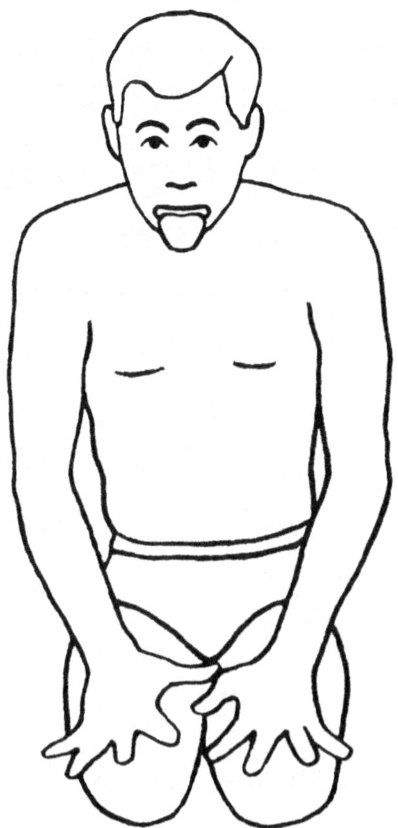

5. THE LION

To prepare for the *Lion* (Simhasana), you can assume a kneeling position with the body resting on the legs. This preparatory kneeling posture is called the *Diamond Pose* or *Hero Pose* (Virasana). For this position, you can have the big toes of each foot touching and have the heels apart, or you can place the feet in whatever position is most comfortable for you. If desired, you can use a folded blanket or pillow to support the body weight.

Next you place the palms of the hands on the knees and gently lean forward on the hands and stretch out the fingers opening the hands as much as possible. You stiffen the whole body and exhale forcibly. When you exhale, you roll the eyes upward and stick out the tongue as far as you can and simultaneously contract the throat muscles. This posture stimulates circulation in the throat and tongue in particular. With the exhalation, you quickly let out as much air as possible, and you may make a guttural sound when doing so. When you assume this pose you can consciously feel that you are releasing pent-up emotional energy and doing so can have a cathartic effect. You can repeat this posture several times if you like.

6. THE HALF SPINAL TWIST

For the *Half Spinal Twist* (Ardha Matsendrasana), you begin by sitting on the floor. You assume the preparatory position by bending the legs at the knees and bringing the legs to the chest. You wrap both arms around the legs and hold the elbows with the hands. You keep the back as straight as possible and the head erect and hold this position for a few seconds. Then you release the arms and keep the legs in place.

Next you extend the left leg. You place the right hand behind the back close to the buttocks with the palm of the hand down on the floor and the fingers pointing to the right away from the body. You place the right foot on the outside of the extended knee with the sole of the foot flat on the floor. You place the left elbow on the outside of the raised knee, and with the left hand, you hold on to the extended knee. Finally you turn the shoulders and the head to the right and hold this position for 30 seconds.

To come out of the posture, you turn the head forward and release the arms and release the legs. You return to the preparatory position by drawing the legs into the chest and placing the arms around the legs. You hug the legs at the chest for a few seconds, and then you release the arms and keep the legs in place against the chest.

Next you extend the right leg. You place the left hand behind the back close to the buttocks with the palm of the hand down on the floor and the fingers pointing to the left away from the body. You place the left foot on the outside of the extended knee with the sole of the foot flat on the floor. You place the right elbow on the outside of the raised knee, and with the right hand, you hold on to the extended knee. You turn the shoulders and the head to the left and hold this position for 30 seconds.

To come out of the posture you turn the head forward and release arms and legs. You return to the preparatory position with the legs drawn into the chest and the arms hugging the legs at the chest, and you hold this position for a few seconds.

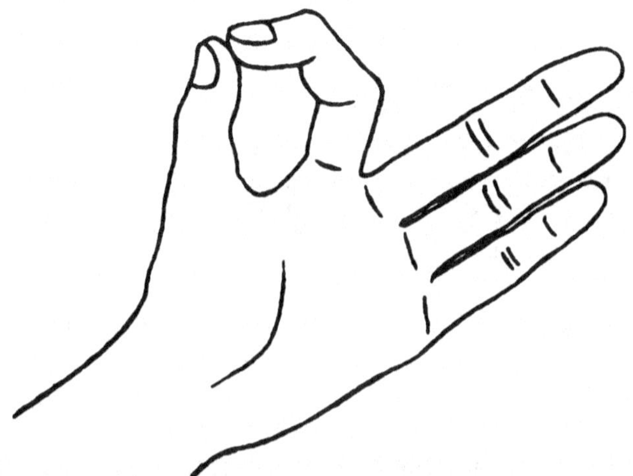

7. THE JNANA MUDRA

In Sanskrit the word *mudra* means "seal" and is a specific position of the body or part of the body that seals in prana and keeps the mind focused upon the parts of the body where the prana is sealed. A mudra seals the prana into the part of the body where the mudra is applied and creates something like an electrical force or current that becomes a focal point of the mind. An example of a mudra is the *Jnana Mudra*, which is the hand position of the thumb and index finger touching with the other three fingers extended.[78] This Jnana Mudra is an optional way of holding your hands in meditation and energy can be felt in the hands in this position.

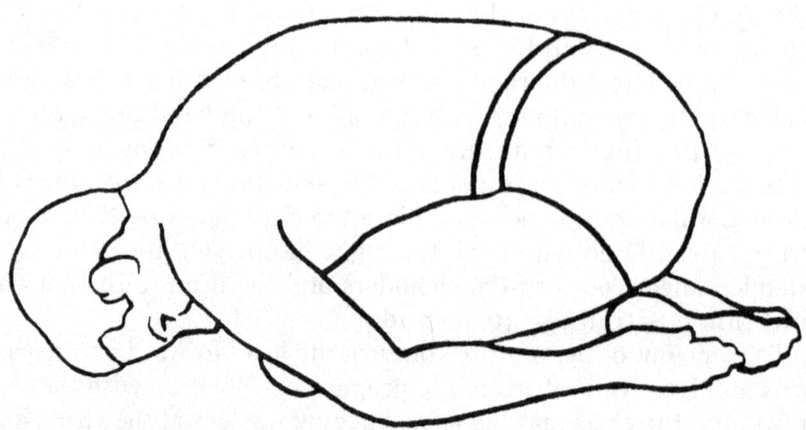

8. THE YOGA SEAL

The *Yoga Seal* (Yoga Mudra) is a mudra that involves the whole body. In one variation of the Yoga Seal, you start by sitting in the Diamond Pose (Sirvasana), also called the Hero Pose, in which you sit with both legs placed side by side directly underneath the body. To relieve pressure on the legs, you can place a folded blanket under the buttocks. Instead of using the Diamond Pose, you can use the specific variation of sitting in a comfortable cross-legged sitting position.

To begin the Yoga Seal, you close the eyes and place your attention within the body. You exhale as you bend forward and place the arms alongside the legs with the palms turned upward, as shown in the illustration above. Or you can place the hands behind the back and hold the right wrist with the left hand. You exhale and bend forward. You relax the neck and allow the head to move forward freely. You relax completely into the posture and allow the breathing to be normal. After about 30 seconds, you raise up slowly, and you have the eyes remain closed. You inhale as you raise up first the head and neck. Then you raise the upper spine, the middle spine, and finally the lower spine. Then you return the hands to the lap or knees, and you open your eyes.

The Yoga Seal is best practiced after completing all of your other postures. This posture absorbs all the energy you have accumulated during your yoga postures, distributing this energy throughout the body and storing this energy for future use. The Yoga Seal is also practiced after the completion of a session of breathing practices in order to absorb the energy that has been accumulated.[79]

E. STRETCHING EXERCISES

What is the difference between yoga postures and yoga exercises? Yoga postures are held in one body position. Yoga exercises always emphasize body movements rather than holding one position. Physical education classes in school emphasize muscle movements of extension and contraction. Yoga exercises emphasize stretching muscles and tendons to enhance flexibility and suppleness. Described below are some specific exercises that you may want to consider practicing.

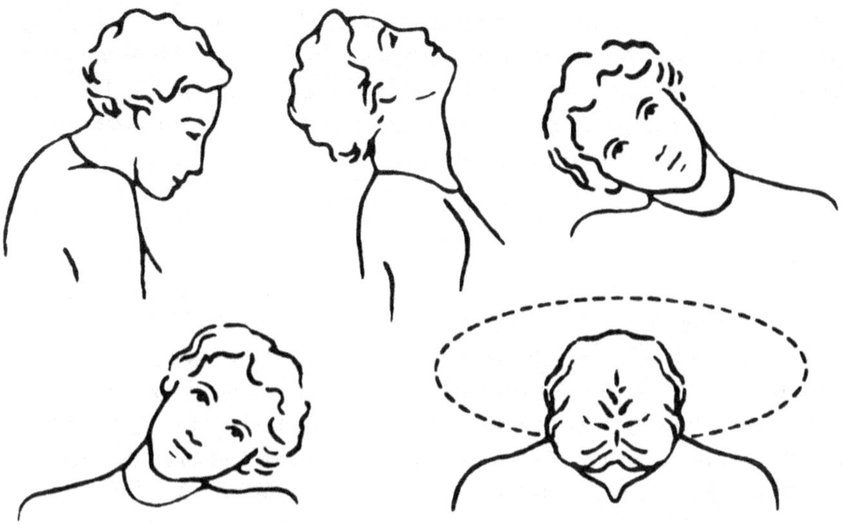

1. THE HEAD AND NECK EXERCISES

The *Head and Neck Exercises*, which are recommended in the Edgar Cayce readings (explained in Chapter 6), are a way of relaxing the body in preparation for meditation. For this exercise you move the head forward three times, backward three times, to the right three times, and to the left three times. Then you roll the head in a wide circular motion three times one way and then three times the other way. The Edgar Cayce readings described this exercise in this way: "...bend the head forward three times, to the back three times, to the right side three times [bringing the right ear toward the right shoulder], to the left side three times [bringing the left ear toward the left shoulder], and then circle the head each way three times."[80] This exercise of the head and neck is especially helpful for clearing the mind and preventing the accumulation of tension in the head.

2. THE EYE EXERCISES

The *Eye Exercises* (Nethra Vyayamam) are usually done while sitting. However, if you prefer, you can practice the Eye Exercises immediately upon waking up in the morning while you are still lying horizontally in your bed. If performing the Eye Exercises in bed, you would be lying on your back and would remove the pillow so the head would be facing the ceiling. For the Eye Exercises, you stretch the eyes without straining them, and you move only the eyes and not the head. You start with the *Vertical Eye Movements* by keeping the head still and looking up and then down, and continuing to look up and down for a total of three times. If desired, you can coordinate the eye movements with the repeating of an affirmation. For example, a two-syllable affirmation such as "Christ Light" could be used. In this case, each time you look up, you can repeat "Christ" and each time you look down you can repeat "Light." When you complete the Vertical Eye Movements, you close the eyes and rest them.

You can repeat the affirmation in coordination with each of the subsequent eye movement variations. The next variation of the eye movements is the *Horizontal Eye Movements*, which are practiced by looking to the far right and moving the eyes straight across the center of your vision to the far left. This movement of the eyes horizontally is repeated three times, and then the eyes are closed to rest them.

For the *Diagonal Eye Movements* you open the eyes and look to the upper right corner of your vision. You move the eyes downward in a diagonal line to the lower left corner of your vision. You repeat the upper right and lower left diagonal movements three times, and then you rest the eyes. For the *Opposite Diagonal Eye Movements,* you look to the upper left corner of your vision. You move the eyes downward in a diagonal line to the lower right corner of your vision. You repeat the upper left and lower right diagonal movements three times and then rest the eyes.

For the *Full Circular Eye Movements* you look straight up and move the eyes in a clockwise circular arc. After you complete three full circles with your eyes, you close your eyes to rest them. For the *Opposite Full Circle Eye Movements*, you open the eyes and look straight up and move the eyes in a counter-clockwise circular arc. After three full circle rotations, you close the eyes to rest them.

Keeping the eyes closed, you rub the palms of the hands together briskly producing heat. You place the palms of the hands very gently over the eyes with the fingertips touching the hairline. You will be able to feel the warmth soaking into the eyes. Finally you can lower the fingers to the closed eyes and very gently massage the eyelids from the nose toward the ears.

3. THE SUN SALUTATION

The *Sun Salutation* (Soorya Namaskaram) is also called the *Sun Exercise,* and it is typically practiced in the morning, ideally outside in the sun if possible. Some yoga practitioners use this exercise for stretching the body before doing the yoga postures. The Sun Exercise consists of 12 body postures that are practiced in sequence. You can coordinate the breathing with the postures by inhaling with each backward movement and by exhaling with each forward movement:

Position #1. You stand with the feet a few inches apart, and then you bring the palms of the hands together at the chest in prayer position.

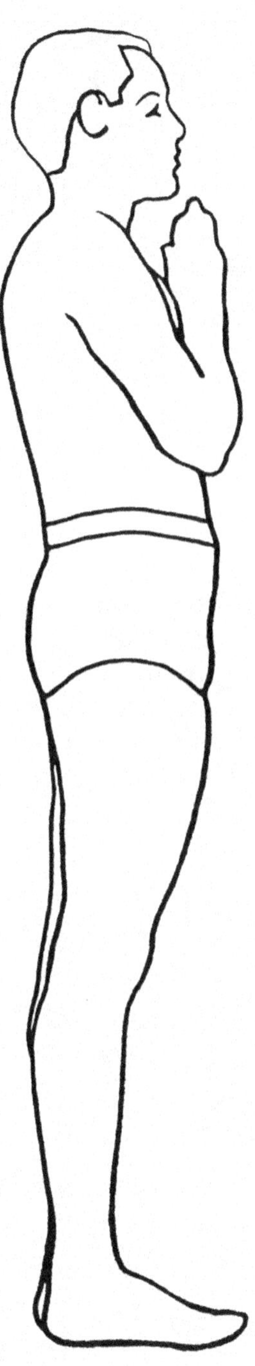

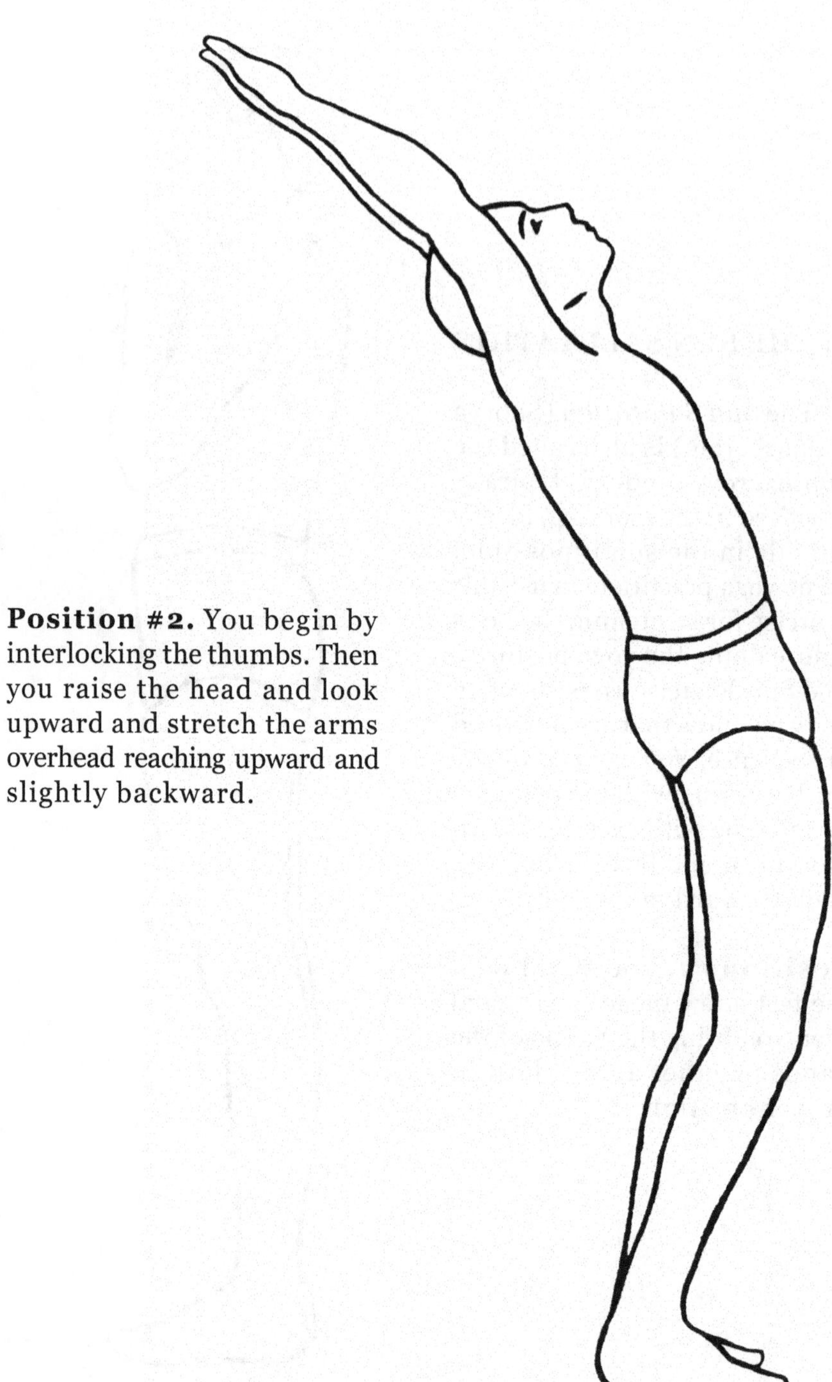

Position #2. You begin by interlocking the thumbs. Then you raise the head and look upward and stretch the arms overhead reaching upward and slightly backward.

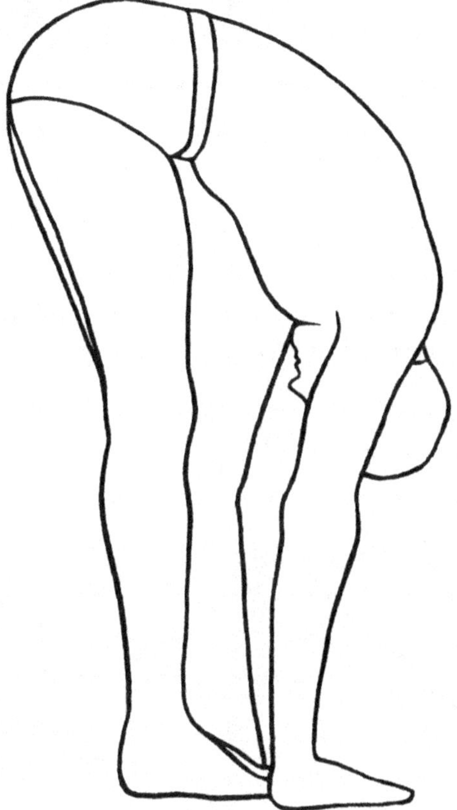

Position #3. You bend forward from the base of the spine while keeping the head between the arms. You hang loosely from the base of the spine while keeping the legs straight at the knees. The illustration shows the ideal position of the hands flat on the floor, but it is all right if your fingers do not reach the floor as you relax into this position.

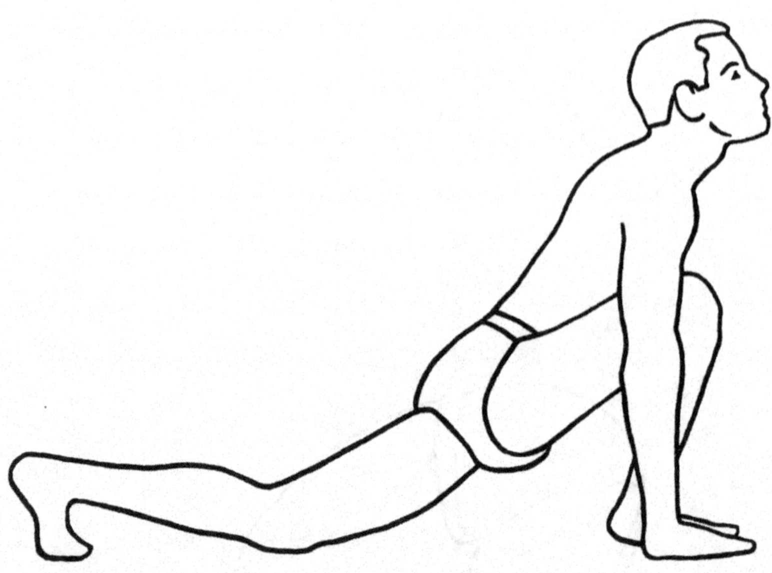

Position #4. You bend the legs at the knees so you can place the palms of your hands on the floor alongside your feet ideally with tips of the fingers in line with the toes. You bring the left leg as far back as possible with the left knee on the floor and the head looking up.

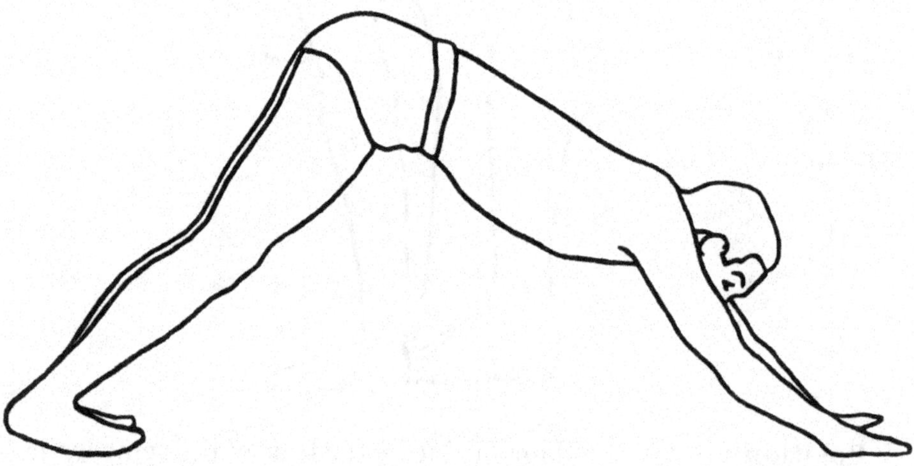

Position #5. You reach the right leg back to join the left leg. You raise the buttocks high forming an arch supporting the body by the hands and feet. The head is placed between the arms and the heels are pressing downward toward the floor.

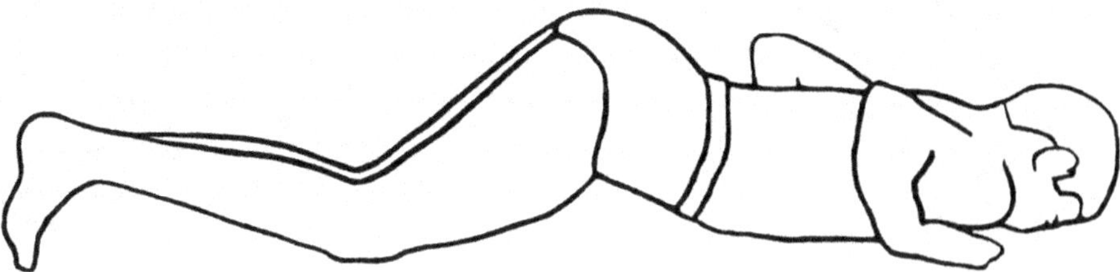

Position #6. In succession, you lower the knees, chest, and chin to the floor and keep the hips slightly raised, a few inches off the floor. The palms are on the floor and located underneath the shoulders.

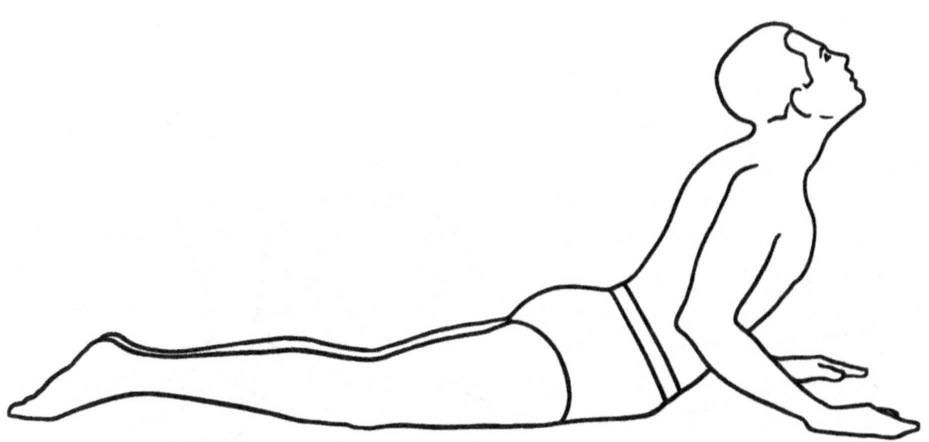

Position #7. You lower the hips to floor and raise the upper portions of the back. You keep the elbows bent and lift primarily with the back rather than with the arms. The head is looking up.

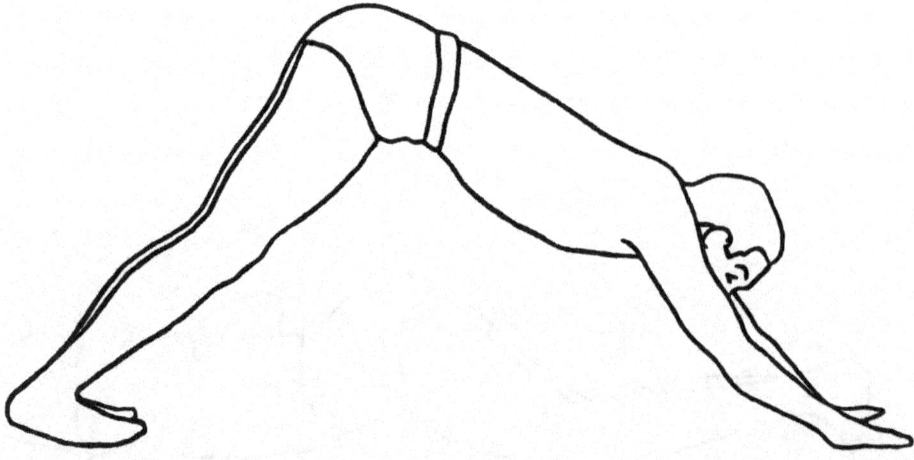

Position #8. You raise the buttocks high in the air balancing on the hands and feet. The head is between the arms and the heels are pressing downward toward the floor.

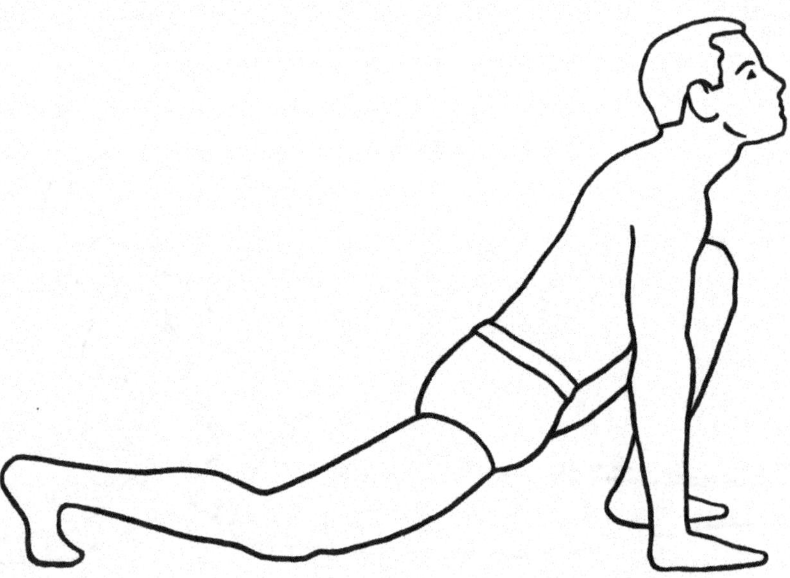

Position #9. You bring the left foot as far forward as you can, between the hands if possible. The right knee is on the floor and the head is looking up.

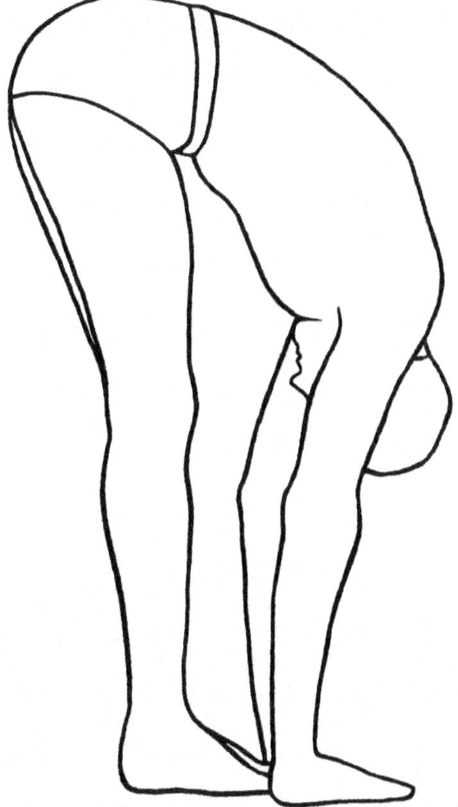

Position #10. You bring the right foot forward alongside the left foot. Then you straighten the legs at the knees and hang loosely from the waist. It is not necessary for the fingers to reach the floor as you relax into this position.

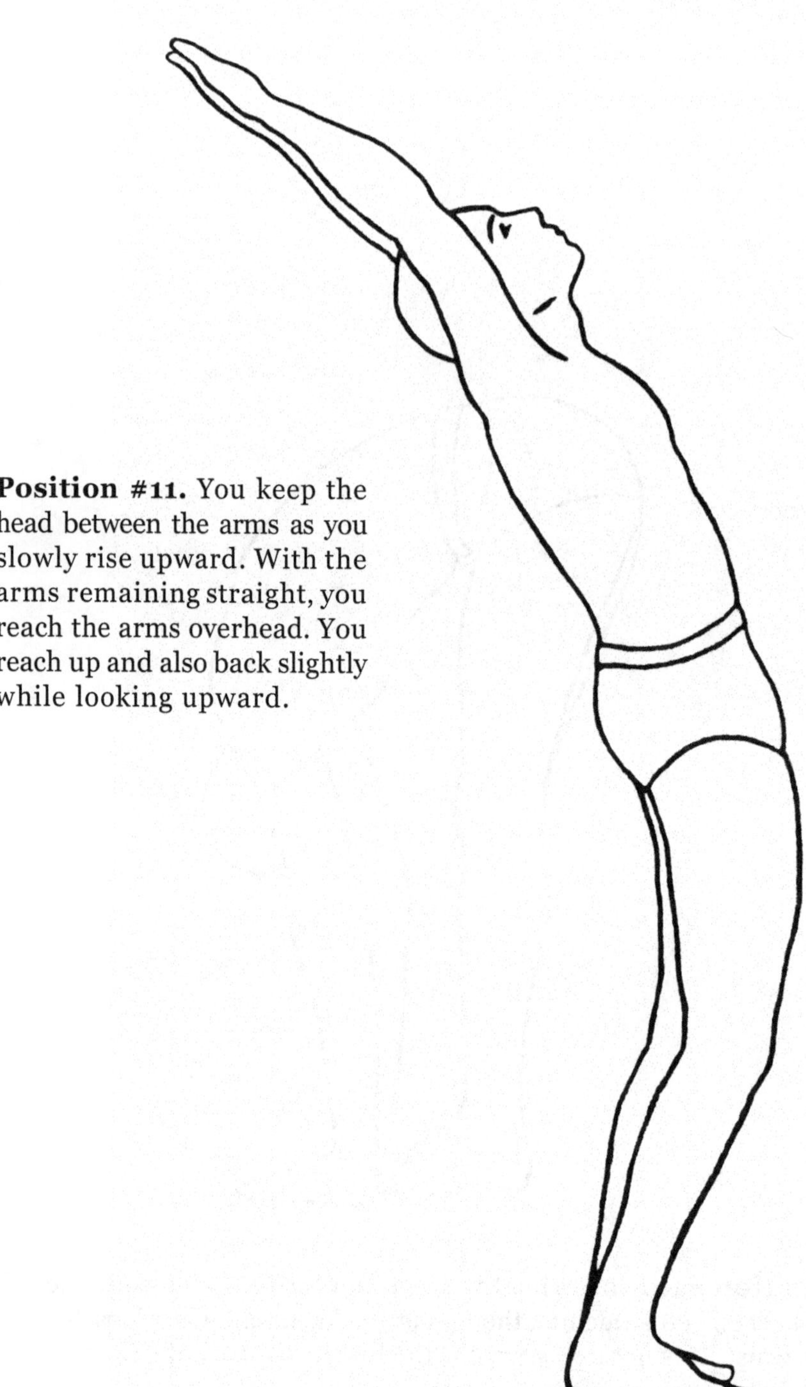

Position #11. You keep the head between the arms as you slowly rise upward. With the arms remaining straight, you reach the arms overhead. You reach up and also back slightly while looking upward.

Position #12. You return to standing normally. You place the palms of the hand together in prayer position at the chest. Then you can bring the arms alongside the body. The heart might be beating faster than normal as you complete this invigorating sequence of 12 positions. You can completely relax, allowing the heartbeat to return to normal.

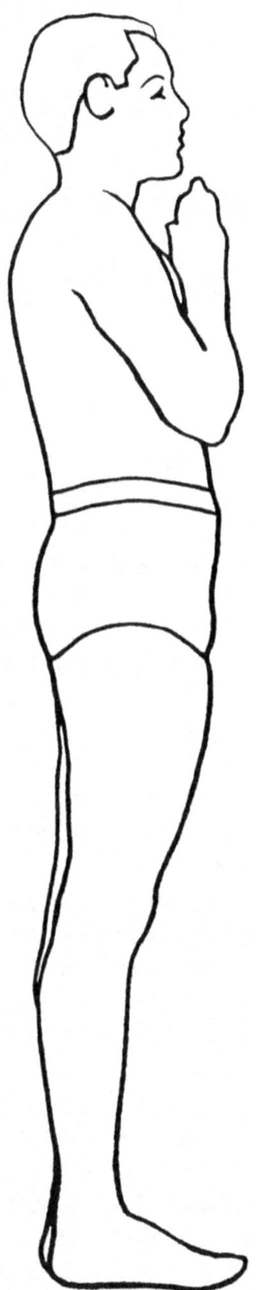

4. THE CONDENSED SUN SALUTATION

The Condensed Sun Salutation is the practice of only Positions #1, #2, #3, #11, and #12. You begin this exercise with Position #1 by standing with the feet a few inches apart and bring the palms together at the chest. Then you practice Positions #2, #3, and #11 in rapid succession without pausing between positions. For this sequence, you start by raising the head, looking up, and stretching the arms overhead while reaching up and slightly backward. Then you immediately bend forward from the base of the spine while keeping the head between the arms. As you bend forward you reach the hands toward the feet while keeping the legs straight. Next you keep the head between the arms, and you raise the spine upward. With arms remaining straight you reach up and back slightly while looking upward. You repeat the bending forward of Position #3 and then the reaching upward of Position #11 for a minimum of three times. To complete the exercise you practice Position #12 by bringing the palms together at the chest, and then you bring the arms alongside the body and relax.

A slight variation on this sequence is to stretch the ankles by raising up onto the toes during Positions #2 and #11 when you extended the arms overhead and look upward. It is best to first learn to do this exercise with the feet remaining flat on the floor, before attempting to raise up on the toes. This variation of raising on the toes is described in the Edgar Cayce readings, which recommends inhaling through the nostrils while bending backward and exhaling through the mouth when bending forward.[81]

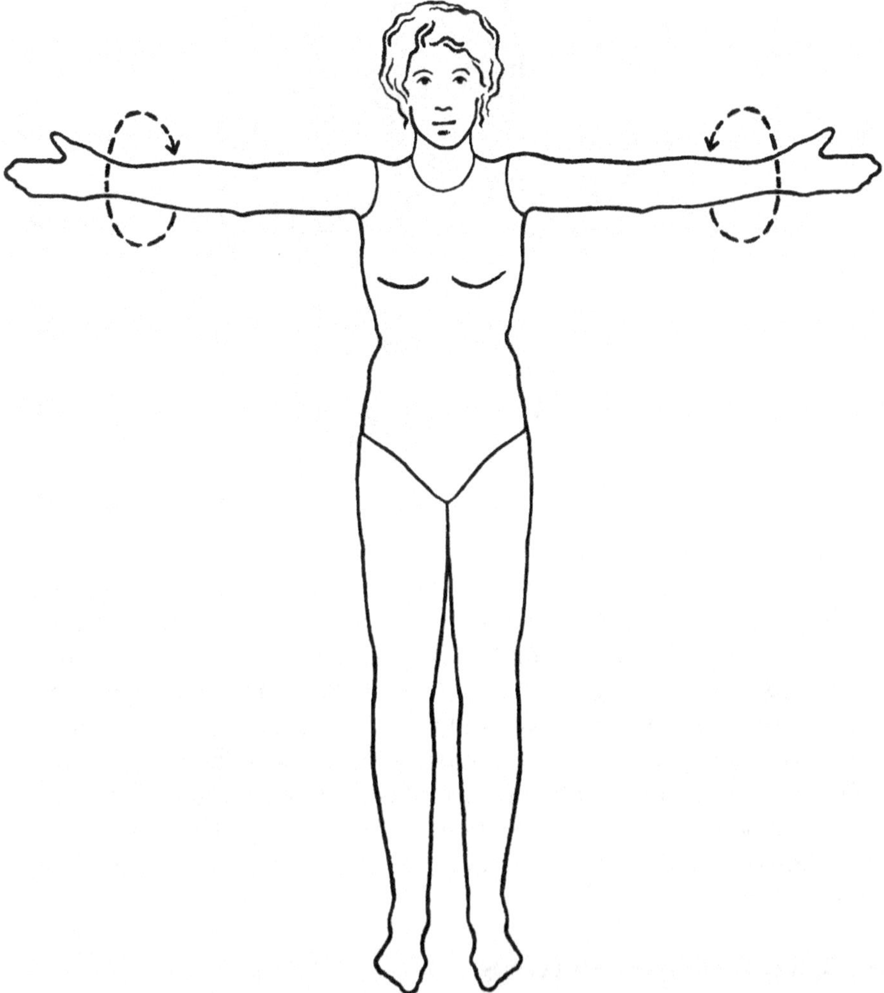

5. THE ARM ROTATIONS

The *Arm Rotations* can be done by almost anyone. You simply extend the arms out making them straight creating a cross with the body. Then keeping the arms straight you bring your arms up, then forward, then downward, then backward, and finally upward again and continue in this circular motion for seven circles. Next you make seven circles in the opposite circular direction. These arm rotations are repeated vigorously. Circular rotations of the arms are recommended by the Edgar Cayce readings as a way of helping you to stimulate the body in the morning by bringing the blood supply to the head and invigorating the body.[82]

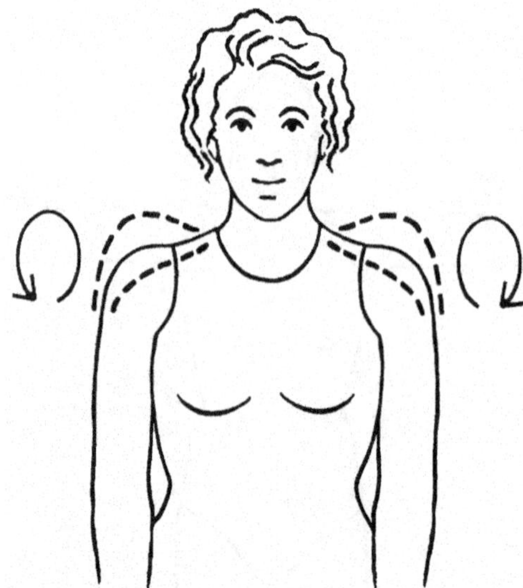

6. THE SHOULDER ROTATIONS

The *Shoulder Rotations* can also be practiced by almost everyone. This exercise is designed to focus on the shoulder joint. While keeping the arms loosely hanging at the sides of the body, you bring your awareness to the shoulder joint and raise the shoulder joint as high as possible. Then you move the shoulder joint forward, then downward, then backward, and finally upward to complete a circular rotation. You complete seven of these circular rotations slowly. Then you rotate the shoulder in the opposite circular rotation to again slowly complete seven circular rotations.

7. THE LEG ROTATIONS

For the *Leg Rotations* you lay down on the back and lift one leg about a foot off the floor and keep it straight at the knee as you rotate the leg in a circular motion several times in one direction and then several times in the opposite direction. Then you repeat this process with the other leg. If you have good muscle tone and no lower back problems, you can raise both legs and rotate both legs together while keeping the legs straight at the knees. Then after resting the legs, you can rotate both legs in the opposite circular direction. Swinging the legs in a circular motion is suggested in the Edgar Cayce readings as an exercise to be practiced in the evening because this exercising of the lower body brings the blood supply away from the head and toward the feet and therefore prepares the body for sleep.[83]

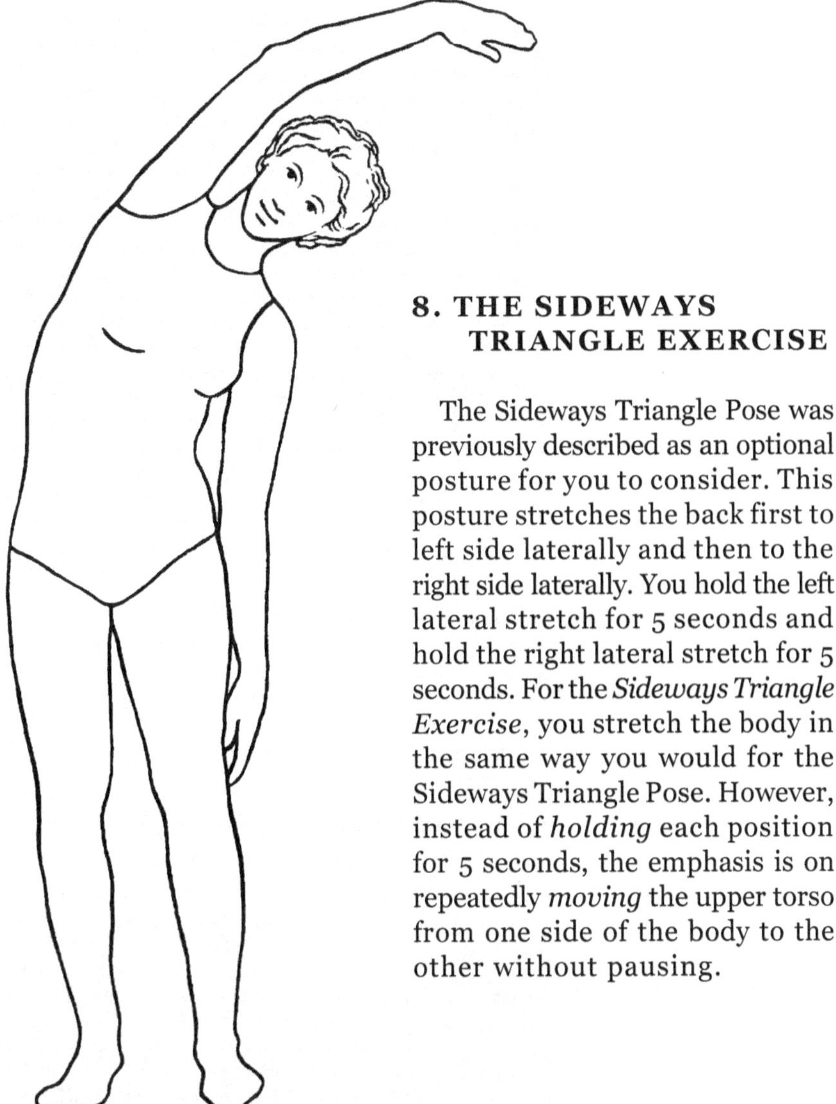

8. THE SIDEWAYS TRIANGLE EXERCISE

The Sideways Triangle Pose was previously described as an optional posture for you to consider. This posture stretches the back first to left side laterally and then to the right side laterally. You hold the left lateral stretch for 5 seconds and hold the right lateral stretch for 5 seconds. For the *Sideways Triangle Exercise*, you stretch the body in the same way you would for the Sideways Triangle Pose. However, instead of *holding* each position for 5 seconds, the emphasis is on repeatedly *moving* the upper torso from one side of the body to the other without pausing.

You can start by standing with the feet wide apart and the arms extended in opposite directions so the hands and arms form a straight line at shoulder height. Then keeping the arms straight you move the spine laterally to the left and then laterally to the right over and over again without stopping. You can start with a small sideways arc and increase the arc in order to stretch the back without straining the back. You conclude with the last sideways movement to the right when you feel you have stretched the spine sufficiently.

9. THE TWISTING TRIANGLE EXERCISE

The Twisting Triangle is another yoga posture that can be made into an exercise by coming into and out of this posture repeatedly without holding the position. For the *Twisting Triangle Exercise* you begin just as you would for the yoga posture of the Twisting Triangle by standing with the feet between two and three feet apart. You have the hands and arms extended in opposite directions to form one straight line at shoulder height.

You begin the exercise movement by bending over and twisting the spine in order to bring the right hand toward the toes of the left foot. Then you quickly raise the body back up into the erect position with the arms again horizontal at shoulder height. Next you immediately bend over and twist the spine in the opposite direction to bring the left hand toward the toes on the right foot. Then you again quickly return the body to the standing position with the arms extended horizontally at shoulder height. You keep repeating the same exercise sequence, making sure to stretch without straining. After each forward bend and twist, you want to make sure to come to a completely erect standing position. This sequence is repeated for a minimum of three stretches in each direction.

10. THE VERTICAL TWISTING TRIANGLE EXERCISE

A variation of the Twisting Triangle Exercise is the *Vertical Twisting Triangle Exercise* because it is practiced by twisting the spine while keeping the spine erect in a vertical position without bending sideways or forward. For this variation, you begin by standing with the feet wide apart and having the arms extended horizontally as with the Twisting Triangle Exercise. Keeping the shoulders and arms in one straight line, you bring the right shoulder and arms backward and the left shoulder and arms forward. Thus you twist the spine to the right as far as is comfortable. Without pausing to hold this position, you reverse the twisting by moving the right shoulder and arms forward and the left shoulder and arms backward as you twist the spine to the left as far as is comfortable. You continue in this manner twisting the spine back and forth to the right and to the left giving the spine a good stretch with each turn without straining. This twisting exercise is repeated a minimum of three times in each direction.

F. REFLEXOLOGY ZONE THERAPY

Reflexology is a system of massage based on the belief that there are sensitive "reflex points" on the feet, hands, and head linked to all parts of the body. These reflex points are massaged to relieve tension and treat illness. For example, you can use the fingers to massage and apply pressure to the reflex points on the toes to help relieve symptoms of sinusitis, drain the sinuses, and strengthen them.

Here the focus will be on massaging the feet in particular. There are different ways to map or chart the feet and the whole body. On the opposite page, you will see the feet charted according to ten "zones." These zones are believed to be invisible pathways of energy that run vertically along the feet, and indeed along the body as a whole from the toes up to the top of the head. "Zone therapy" is the practice of working with these energy lines and points along these lines.

The chart identifies the ten longitudinal zones of the feet. Each toe falls into one zone, and there are five zones in each foot. Each toe is associated with one zone, and likewise each finger on each hand is associated with one zone. The longitudinal zones are also distributed throughout the whole body. It is believed that when you massage all five zones in each foot, you are automatically stimulating the free flow of energy that runs up and down the whole body through these ten zones. More detailed reflexology charts show that each organ and each part of the body is represented in the feet. If the body's natural energy is blocked in one part of one zone, it will have an adverse effect on all the specific organs or other parts of the body that are within that zone. Applying pressure or massaging all five zones in each foot will stimulate the free flow of energy, nerves, blood, and nutrients within each zone, bringing balance and healing to the whole body.

The following are two suggested ways of massaging and applying pressure to the feet: For the first method, you use your fingertips to first briefly apply pressure to one point at the heel of one foot along zone 1. Next, you repeat applying temporary pressure at another point just above the previous pressure point along zone 1. You continue to apply brief pressure points upward until you complete this sequence by applying pressure to the big toe at the end of zone 1. You use the same process for each zone in each foot. You conclude by using the index finger and thumb to rotate each toe one way and then the other way.

For the second technique, you use your fingertips to press firmly on the big toe and hold that pressure continuously while at the same time pulling your fingers downward to apply consistent pressure all the way to the heel of one foot along the whole of zone 1. Then you do the same for each zone with each foot. Both methods are suggested to be used as part of your daily practice of yoga and exercises.

Reflexology
Zone Therapy

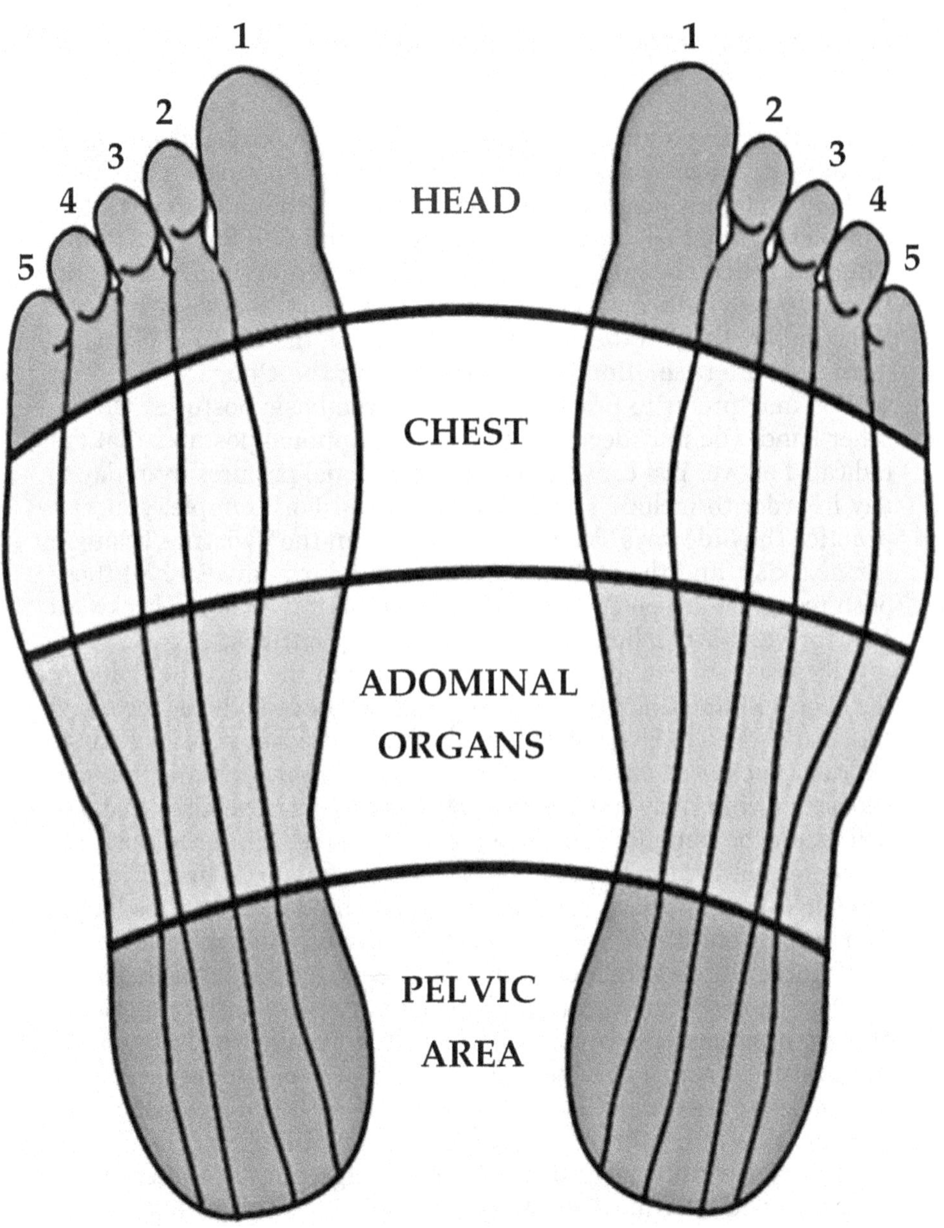

G. BEGINNERS' DAILY ROUTINE OF YOGA POSTURES

BASIC POSTURES	**OPTIONAL POSTURES**
1. Relaxing Posture	*8. Sideways Triangle*
2. Shoulder Stand	*9. Twisting Triangle*
3. Fish	*10. Half Spinal Twist*
4. Full Forward Bend	*11. Tree*
5. Half Locust or Locust	*12. King Dancer*
6. Boat or more advanced Bow	*13. Lion*
7. Cobra	*14. Yoga Seal*

The first seven postures in this routine are your basic postures for daily practice. You start with the Relaxing Posture on the back and return to this posture after completing the Shoulder Stand, after completing the Fish, and after completing the Full Forward Bend. Then you turn the body over to assume the Relaxing Posture on the abdomen before practicing the Half Locust. You return to the Relaxing Posture on the abdomen after doing the Half Locust, after doing the Boat (or Bow), and after doing the Cobra.

You may prefer to practice only the seven basic postures. On the other hand, you may decide to include the optional postures that are indicated above. You can alternate these optional postures from day to day in order to include a variety of stretches. For example, you can practice the Sideways Triangle one day, then the Twisting Triangle the next day, and the Half Spinal Twist the third day. Each of these postures gives the spine a stretch in a different way than the backward and forward stretches of the first seven postures.

Likewise, you can alternate from one day to the next the doing of the Tree and the King Dancer, which both improve body balance. You can also choose to alternately include the Lion posture as a catharsis and as a means of stretching the face and throat. Actually you can choose for your daily routine any optional poses or exercises that you feel would be beneficial. The sequence of the seven basic postures is recommended for beginners, but even experienced practitioners can still follow this basic routine and simply hold the positions longer than beginners would. As you make progress, you can replace the Half Locust with the Locust and replace the Boat with the Bow.

Most people who practice hatha yoga have their initial experience of yoga in a class led by a yoga instructor. If you learn how to do the postures from an experienced yoga teacher, it is important to internalize this experience and take it home with you so yoga can be incorporated into your daily life. Only fifteen minutes are suggested for your yoga routine in order to encourage you to make and to keep your commitment to daily practice.

CHAPTER 5

~ • ~

BREATHING PRACTICES

A. BREATHING PRACTICES FOR BEGINNERS

Pranayama, control of breathing, is a vital part of your Christian hatha yoga practice. The Christian hath yoga breathing practices that are described in this chapter are suggested for you whether you want to practice Christian yoga in the form of Miracle Yoga based on the Course or whether you want to practice Christian yoga based on your own personal philosophy. Breathing is the link between the body and the mind. The hatha yoga postures help control, stretch, and steady the body, and this in turn calms the mind. Likewise, the breathing practices help to revitalize the physical body, in particular the nervous system, and to calm the mind.

The stretching of muscles and tendons by practicing body postures helps the body to be flexible, but also squeezes out toxins that have accumulated in the body tissues. These toxins are waste products that are carried away by the blood. One of the important functions of the breathing practices is to oxidize these toxins and therefore to remove these burned toxins from the body.

Specific breathing practices will be described here, but it is also very helpful to be aware of breathing while practicing your yoga postures. When you are moving into a posture in which you are bending the spine backwards, you are expanding the chest. In this case, you can focus on inhaling while coming into the posture. Whenever you are moving into a posture in which you are bending the spine forward, you are contracting the chest. In this case, you can focus on exhaling while coming into the posture. Similarly, when you are coming out of any posture, if your chest is expanding, you inhale and if your chest is contracting, you exhale. If your spine is moving backward, you inhale. If your spine is moving forward, you exhale. If you are holding this posture briefly, you can hold your breath while holding the posture. If you are holding a posture for an extended period, instead of holding the breath you can allow the breathing to be normal.

A general benefit of the yoga breathing practices is an increase in the lung's capacity to work effectively. Most people breathe shallowly. If you breathe shallowly, just part of the lung capacity is used, and this means reduced oxidation. The blood absorbs oxygen from the lungs for oxidation purposes and deposits carbonic acid gas from waste products into the small air sacs of the lungs. During the exhalation, if the stagnant air with carbonic acid gas is not squeezed out of the air sacs of the lungs, your inhalation will not be able to bring in new fresh air carrying oxygen. Typical breathing will contract only a small part of the lungs to expel the old air and therefore limit the amount of fresh air that can come into the lungs. The air sacs, which contain stagnant air due to shallow breathing, become inviting targets for bacilli that thrive on weakened tissue. The body can maintain healthy lung tissue that will resist bacilli if old stagnant air can be expelled from the lungs, which in turn will allow new fresh air to come into the lungs. Yoga breathing practices help to dramatically increase the amount of stagnant air being expelled on the exhalation and increase the amount of fresh oxygen-rich air being inhaled.

For the practice of specific breathing techniques, you can sit in a comfortable cross-legged position with the hands in the lap or on the knees. If you prefer, you can sit in a chair, or you can be standing. After completing all of your breathing practices, you can practice the Yoga Seal, described in the previous chapter, to absorb the energy that has been accumulated. The most basic breathing practices for beginners are described below, as follows:

1. YOGA DEEP BREATHING

Yoga Deep Breathing (Deergha Swasam Pranayama)[84] can be used as a way of relaxing the body prior to your practice of meditation. If you are practicing Yoga Deep Breathing for the first time, you start by just observing the abdomen without manipulating the breath in any way. You observe the abdomen as it naturally expands with each inhalation and naturally contracts with each exhalation. *Abdominal breathing* is the most natural and efficient form of breathing. A less efficient form of breathing that leads to poor health is to breathe only with the chest and omit the abdomen from the breathing process or use the abdomen unnaturally by expanding it with the exhalation instead of expanding it with the inhalation.

Following your brief observation of the natural abdominal breathing, you consciously expand the abdomen with each inhalation and pull in the abdomen with each exhalation. After this intentional expanding and contracting of only the abdomen for a brief time, you expand first the abdomen and then the lower chest on the inhalation, and you contract the lower chest first and then the abdomen on the exhalation. Briefly you continue inhaling from the bottom to the top and exhaling from the top to the bottom maintaining a peaceful attitude throughout.

Next you increase the breathing capacity further by expanding first the abdomen, then the lower chest, and then the upper chest, allowing the collarbones to rise slightly. On the exhalation, the collarbones are lowered, and you contract first the upper chest, then the lower chest, and then the abdomen. Although this breathing sequence is described in parts, the breathing is actually done in one flowing motion. While inhaling from bottom to top and exhaling from top to bottom, you breathe very deeply and calmly.

After completing one round of several deep inhalations and deep exhalations, you allow your breathing to return to normal. After one round of Yoga Deep Breathing, you pause briefly before initiating another round. Pausing between each pranayama round is suggested for all of the other breathing practices that are described here.

2. RAPID ABDOMINAL BREATHING

Rapid Abdominal Breathing is often called the *Breath of Fire*.[85] Another name for this breathing practice is *Skull Shining* (Kapalabhati Pranayama)[86] because it is considered a purification practice (*kriya*) that cleanses the nerves in the head. Rapid Abdominal Breathing can sometimes cause dizziness. If your head feels dizzy at any time during this practice or during any other breathing practice, immediately stop your pranayama session.

For the practice of Rapid Abdominal Breathing, you exhale quickly and forcefully by contracting the abdomen. The sudden contraction of the abdomen pushes the diaphragm upward. The diaphragm is the muscular partition that separates the abdominal cavity from the thoracic cavity that contains the lungs. Since the diaphragm is suddenly pushed upward, the diaphragm recedes into the thoracic cavity and contracts the lungs forcing the air out of the body. The mouth is closed so the air comes rapidly out of the nasal cavity on the exhalation. The air being expelled may remind you of the experience of having something caught in your nose and expelling air to sneeze it out.

When inhaling during the practice of Rapid Abdominal Breathing, you release the abdominal contraction. By letting go of contracting the abdominal muscles, the diaphragm lowers toward the abdominal cavity. The pull of the diaphragm downward expands the lungs. A vacuum is created in the lungs and air comes in of itself through the nasal cavity from outside. The inhalation is slow, passive, and longer than the exhalation, which is short, sudden, and forceful. The inhalation is longer than the exhalation, as much as four times longer.

When you practice Rapid Abdominal Breathing for the first time, you place one hand over the abdomen to feel it contracting with each forceful exhalation of air. You place the other hand on the top of the shoulder to ensure that the shoulders are not rising up and down.

You begin Rapid Abdominal Breathing by contracting the abdomen to suddenly expel air. Then you release the contraction of the abdomen to produce a passive inhalation, and this process is repeated in rapid succession. You practice about twelve exhalations and inhalations. You allow the last forceful exhalation to be slightly longer than the others. Next you inhale deeply and then exhale slowly. Finally you allow the breathing to return to normal. You can practice three rounds of Rapid Abdominal Breathing in succession. Rapid Abdominal Breathing is practiced vigorously, but you can still maintain a peaceful mind while doing this activity.

When you practice Rapid Abdominal Breathing, you maintain your concentration on the navel area. Your concentration on this area helps to bring prana to this area, which will help in purifying the nervous system. In addition to cleansing the nerves in the head, this practice can purify the nerve plexuses and so you may feel a throbbing or tingling sensation along the spinal column. This breathing practice cleans the respiratory system and nasal passages. Also, bronchial spasms can be relieved and so asthma can be improved and eventually cured.

3. ALTERNATE NOSTRIL BREATHING

Like Rapid Abdominal Breathing described above, *Alternate Nostril Breathing* (Nadi Suddhi Pranayama)[87] is also a nerve cleansing practice. Another name for this breathing practice is the *Nerve Cleansing Breath*. It is the most beneficial breathing practice for calming the nervous system and for having a purifying effect on the blood.

You may assume that you breathe with both nostrils equally. But if you place your palm below your nostrils and exhale, you will most likely see that one nostril will be blocked and the other will not be blocked. A person in excellent health will have the breathing mostly through one nostril for about two hours and then mostly through the other nostril for the next two hours. The natural alternation of breathing from one nostril to the other is considered ideal for maintaining good health. Yet many people have inconsistent breathing in which there is an uneven alternation. These people breathe mostly with the right nostril or mostly with the left nostril. The reason for this inconsistency may be poor living habits, such as an improper diet or lack of exercise.

It may not be clear why it is considered natural for one nostril to dominate and then the other in a regular alternating pattern every two hours. The key to understanding this aspect of hatha yoga can be found in the word "hatha." In Sanskrit the syllable "ha" means *sun* and "tha" means *moon*. In yoga philosophy, there many are energy channels called "nadis." One important nadi is the *pingala* associated the sun and with the right side of the body. Another significant nadi is the *ida* associated with the moon and the left side of the body. The right nostril carries the energy that flows through the pingala. This is considered the sun breath since it brings a catabolic and heating effect that stimulates the functions of body organs. The left nostril carries the energy that flows through the ida. This is considered the moon breath since it brings an anabolic and cooling effect by inhibiting the functions of body organs. If one nostril dominates for too long, an unnatural condition occurs in which there is an excess of heat or cold. Excess heat will bring about physical, mental, and nervous disturbances. Excess cold will produce lowered vitality, sluggishness, and lack of mental clarity. Excess heat or cold can lead to illness.

Breathing practices, such as Alternate Nostril Breathing, are used to restore the natural alternation of breathing in which first one nostril dominates and then the other nostril dominates. Alternate Nostril Breathing helps to restore the balance between catabolic and anabolic processes in the body and just as importantly has a purifying effect on the nadis. This purifying effect on the nadis is necessary as a preparation for the natural rising of the kundalini.

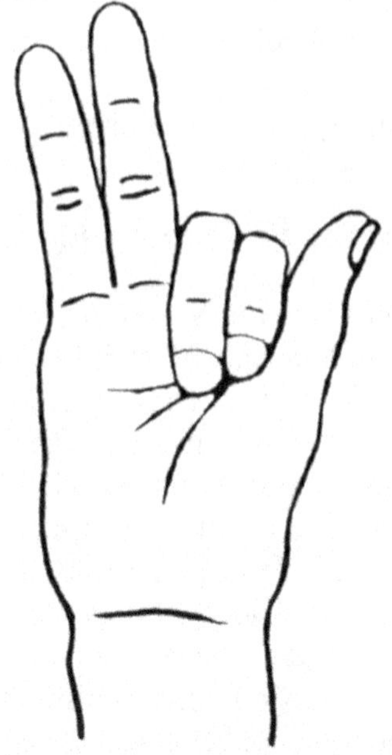

For the practice of Alternate Nostril Breathing, you employ a specific hand position, called the *Vishnu Mudra*. You make a fist with the right hand. Then you extend the thumb, the ring finger, and the small finger. The index finger and middle finger remain touching the palm of the hand. You use the right thumb to close off the right nostril. You employ the ring finger to close off the left nostril. You always employ the right hand for the Vishnu Mudra, even if you are left-handed.

You begin this practice by closing off the right nostril with the right thumb and inhaling through the left nostril. After inhaling through the left nostril, you close off the left nostril with the ring finger of the right hand. You remove your right thumb from the right nostril and exhale through the right nostril. You inhale through the right nostril and close off the right nostril with the right thumb. You remove the ring finger from the left nostril and immediately exhale and then inhale through the left nostril. You continue to exhale and inhale through one nostril and then switch to the other nostril. You practice a minimum of ten exhalations and inhalations with each nostril. You always complete a breathing round with an exhalation through the left nostril and observe the breathing returning to normal.

Alternate Nostril Breathing is practiced with slow and deep breathing without straining. When you exhale and inhale through each nostril individually, you can use the Yoga Deep Breathing described above to use your full lung capacity. Thus you inhale from the bottom to the top like filling a glass of water and exhale from top to bottom like emptying a glass of water. The exhalation and inhalation can be an equal ratio of 1:1. But as an alternative, you can allow the exhalation to be slightly longer than the inhalation. The exhalation can be as much as twice as long as the inhalation, if this 2:1 ratio can be maintained without any straining. The 1:1 ratio is certainly sufficient, but whatever ratio you use needs to be maintained consistently.

The breathing is done quietly, and you maintain a sense of peace throughout, which is more important than the breathing ratio. You may want to coordinate the repeating of an affirmation with the breathing. You can begin by using a series of three rounds of Alternate Nostril Breathing and eventually practice additional rounds if you feel guided to do so.

4. FULL ALTERNATE NOSTRIL BREATHING

Full Alternate Nostril Breathing (Auloma Viloma Pranayama)[88] is the same as Alternate Nostril Breathing with the one difference being that you practice breath retention. To begin this breathing practice you close off the right nostril with the right thumb. You inhale through the left nostril and then retain the breath by closing off both nostrils with the combination of the thumb and the ring finger and little finger of the right hand. After pausing to hold your breath, you remove your right thumb from the right nostril and exhale through the right nostril. You inhale through the right nostril and then close off both nostrils for the breath retention. You continue to repeat exhaling and inhaling through one nostril, hold the breath, and switch to the other nostril. You do a minimum of three exhalations and inhalations with each nostril. You always complete a breathing round with an exhalation through the left nostril and observe the breathing returning to normal. Three rounds of Full Alternate Nostril Breathing are suggested, and you may be guided to add additional rounds later.

Full Alternate Nostril Breathing is practiced with breathing slowly and deeply. You can use the Yoga Deep Breathing as is previously described to use your full lung capacity. You can exhale, inhale, and retain the breath at a 1:1:1 ratio. With practice, you might want to progress to the ratio of 2:1:2 for the exhalation (*rechaka*), inhalation (*puraka*), and retention (*kumbaka*). If you become very comfortable with this ratio, you can then attempt to increase the time for breath retention. The ratio of 2:1:4 for exhalation, inhalation, and retention is the most commonly recommended ratio in classical yoga.

Although most yoga teachings advocate progressing to the 2:1:4 ratio, this manual will not make this recommendation because the emphasis in Miracle Yoga is on the goal of seeking Christ rather than perfecting the means, which are the yoga practices. Meeting a specific outer standard can be an impediment if the standard for the technique becomes more important than seeking Christ. In Miracle Yoga, the technique of pranayama is a secondary consideration, while the major focus is on making the breathing practices into a peaceful devotional experience.

In regard to the ratio, the recommendation for Miracle Yoga in this manual is to maintain the 1:1:1 ratio in order to keep the exhalation, inhalation, and retention equal. As an option, you can have a general sense that the exhalation is longer than the inhalation and can be as much as twice as long if that feels comfortable. The retention can be about the same as the exhalation, or it may also be longer than the exhalation. The key idea here is that you find what is comfortable for you. You need to be very careful not to push yourself beyond your capacity. By not straining yourself, you will allow your mind to remain serene throughout this breathing practice. Your serenity and devotion are more important than your technique.

B. THE TEN FORMS OF PRANA

To understand more advanced breathing practices, it is necessary to review and elaborate upon the significance of *prana*, which in yoga philosophy is the vital life force energy. All of the movements of your muscles, your efforts of the will, and even your thoughts are carried out through the life force of prana. Naturally there is the need to have a constant supply of prana. Prana is present throughout the universe, but the most easily accessible means of absorbing prana is through breathing air. Oxygen goes to every part of the body to perform bodily functions. Similarly, prana goes to all parts of the body, especially to the nervous system. If you regularly use the breathing practices that are recommended in yoga, you will feel the many beneficial effects that produce a healthy body. In addition, prana can assist in improving willpower, mental concentration, and self-control. In the practice of Yoga, this increased prana can be offered to the Holy Spirit to be used for spiritual purposes.

Prana is the term used to describe the life force in a general sense, but different kinds of prana perform different functions. There are ten forms of prana.[89] The five secondary pranas and their functions are, as follows:

1. Dhananjaya is a vital force that extends throughout the physical body and remains in the physical body after death unless the corpse is cremated.

2. Kurma enables vision and is associated with awe and wonder. It opens the eyes after sleep and induces the eyes to close for sleep.

3. Krikkara induces thirst and hunger and also causes sneezing.

4. Devadatha causes yawning.

5. Naga gives rise to consciousness and produces belching.

The five primary forms of prana are *prana, apana prana, samana prana, udana prana, and vyana prana.* These kinds of prana manifest through various different portions of the autonomic nervous system, which controls the involuntary responses in the body, described as follows:

1. Prana is related to the heart and works through the cervical portion of the autonomic system. Prana involves the activity of bringing things in and taking things out. It controls the parts of the body that govern the functions of respiration, speech, and swallowing. Prana is an upward rising energy. It may be a bit confusing that the word "prana" has two different meanings—a general meaning and a specific meaning. The general meaning of prana is that it is the term used to describe the life force energy, including the five secondary pranas and the five primary pranas. The specific meaning is that prana is the ascending energy described here in this paragraph.

2. *Apana* is related to the anus and works through the lumbar area of the autonomic nervous system. Apana is the energy of elimination. It primarily governs the parts of the body, such as the colon, rectum, genitals, bladder, and kidneys, which control the excretory functions. Apana is a downward flowing energy.

3. *Samana* is related to the naval and works through the sympathetic portion of the autonomic nervous system. Samana controls the activity of assimilation. Therefore, it governs the parts of the body that control the functions of digestion, such as the intestines, the stomach, the pancreas, and the liver. Prana and apana can be brought together so they neutralized each other and produced the single energy of samana, considered the "equal breath." Some meditators focus on the navel area as a way to help facilitate the combining of prana and apana. Certain kinds of pranayama practices, which are described below, can result in combining prana and apana.

4. *Udana* is related to the throat, in particular to the area just above the larynx. It performs the functions that are under the control of the cephalic portions of the autonomic nervous system. Yoga philosophy maintains there is an astral body, which is a subtle duplicate of the physical body. Udana exerts a psychic force that is associated with the connecting link between the astral body and physical body. Similar to an ascending fire, udana is the vertical energy that carries the kundalini energy upward within the susumna, the central energy channel.

5. *Vyana* is associated with all parts of the body because it is present everywhere. Vyana has to do with expanding and distributing energy. Yyana controls movements of the joints, ligaments, and muscles of the whole body, including both the involuntary and voluntary movements. It is the energy that persists when the body dies. Vyana is specifically involved in the final stage of the ascent of the kundalini. As previously mentioned, Udana carries upward the kundalini energy, which burns away impurities as it rises in the susumna. Yet, when the rising energy of the kundalini finally reaches the crown center, that energy becomes transformed into the all-pervading universal energy of vyana.

Each of the five forms of prana is related to a different nerve plexus and causes nerve impulses to go to or away from the nerve plexuses and brain. Afferent impulses go to the brain and nerve plexuses. Efferent impulses go away from the brain and nerve plexuses. These nerve impulses are called *vayus*. An example of an afferent nerve impulse going to the brain is the *prana vayu* and an example of an efferent nerve impulse going away from the brain is the *apana vayu*.

During breathing practices, prana vayu is produced on the inhalation creating an afferent nerve impulse and apana vayu is produced on the exhalation creating an efferent nerve impulse. Some schools of yoga, such as *kundalini yoga*, advocate combining the prana vayu and apana vayu to facilitate the raising of the kundalini. When breath retention occurs in certain advanced breathing practices, the prana vayu (an afferent nerve impulse going to the brain) and the apana vayu (an efferent nerve impulse going away from the brain) are united in the sacral plexus (sacral chakra). This union of incoming and outgoing nerve impulses joined at the base of the spine generate a great force of prana and apana combined. The union of prana and apana that is generated at the base of the spine stimulates the awakening of the coiled energy of the kundalini also at the base of the spine.[90]

Students of kundalini yoga, who want to use pranayama to raise the kundalini, must first learn and consistently use the breathing practices described above for beginners. These beginning practices are all helpful for absorbing prana, but also assist the purification of the physical nerves and subtle nerve channels, the nadis. There are ten nadis, but the three most important are the pingala (the right channel), ida (the left channel), and the susumna (the central channel). The susumna usually lies dormant, but, if activated, it can carry the kundalini energy upward to assist spiritual growth. The practices of pranayama can assist the susumna in opening and becoming activated. Through the breathing practices, the sun breath of the pingala and the moon breath of the ida can be joined and arouse the sleeping kundalini at the base of the spine. Before advanced breathing practices can be used, first breathing practices of purification, such as those described previously, are necessary, so there is the proper readiness to receive this powerful kundalini energy.

In the practice of kundalini yoga, the goal is to raise the kundalini by means of practicing specific forms of advanced pranayama, but yoga philosophy recognizes that there are other means of arousing the kundalini. In fact, Swami Vivekananda in his book *Raja Yoga* maintains that the rising of the kundalini is a much more universal occurrence than is commonly realized, as follows:

> Whenever there was a manifestation of what is ordinarily called supernatural power or wisdom, there a little current of kundalini must have found its way into the susumna. Only, in the vast majority of such cases, people had ignorantly stumbled on some practice which set free a minute portion of the coiled-up kundalini. All worship, consciously or unconsciously, leads to this end.[91]

Besides the practice of pranayama, various other yoga practices aim to make the raising of the kundalini a consciously directed experience. Some of these methods are intense mantra meditations related to the chakras, the expression of the intellect and willpower of practitioners of jnana yoga, and the focused loving devotion to God of bhakti yoga. In Miracle Yoga, the kundalini can be raised by surrendering to the Holy Spirit and opening to divine love. However, pranayama can play a part in assisting the Holy Spirit's raising of the kundalini.

Going to extremes with breathing practices in order to force the kundalini to rise is foolish and dangerous. In Miracle Yoga, the goal is not to create a "kundalini spiritual experience," but rather to facilitate an inner purification process guided by the Holy Spirit. However, the gradual raising of the kundalini guided by the Holy Spirit can be part of your inner purification. You can use breathing practices to strengthen the body and purify the nervous system and the nadis. This preparation helps to remove inner resistance and obstacles and facilitates the Holy Spirit's gradual raising of the kundalini. But the key word in relation to using breathing practices is *moderation*. You can safely use breathing practices if you can avoid extremes and allow the Holy Spirit to guide your implementation of these breathing practices.

C. THE YOGA LOCKS

After you have used breathing practices for purification purposes on a regular basis for an extended period, you may be guided to use more advanced breathing practices in moderation. Generally, the more advanced breathing practices involve the use of the yoga locks, called *bandhas*.[92] These locks increase the effectiveness of breath retention. Three yoga locks are described below:

1. The *Root Lock* (Mula Bandha)[93] is performed by contracting the anal sphincter and also contracting the abdominal muscles. This lock is usually practiced at the end of an inhalation and is held during the retention. Some beginning practitioners contract only the buttocks muscles without specifically contracting the anal sphincter. Therefore, you need to primarily focus on contracting the anal sphincter itself to gain the full benefit of the Root Lock.

2. The *Chin Lock* (Jalandhara Bandha)[94] is performed by pressing the chin down firmly against the chest. This lock is usually combined with the Root Lock and is likewise practiced at the end of an inhalation and held during retention.

3. The *Diaphragm Lock* (Uddiyana Bandha)[95] begins by making a strong exhalation contracting the diaphragm. You raise the diaphragm upward into the thoracic cavity contracting the lungs. The viscera are pulled back toward the spine creating a hollow in which the ribs are exposed. The Diaphragm Lock is also called the ***Stomach Lift***. This lock is used at the end of an exhalation and held during retention. The Diaphragm Lock is *not* used after the inhalation because doing so can increase pressure on the heart, blood circulation, and eyes.[96]

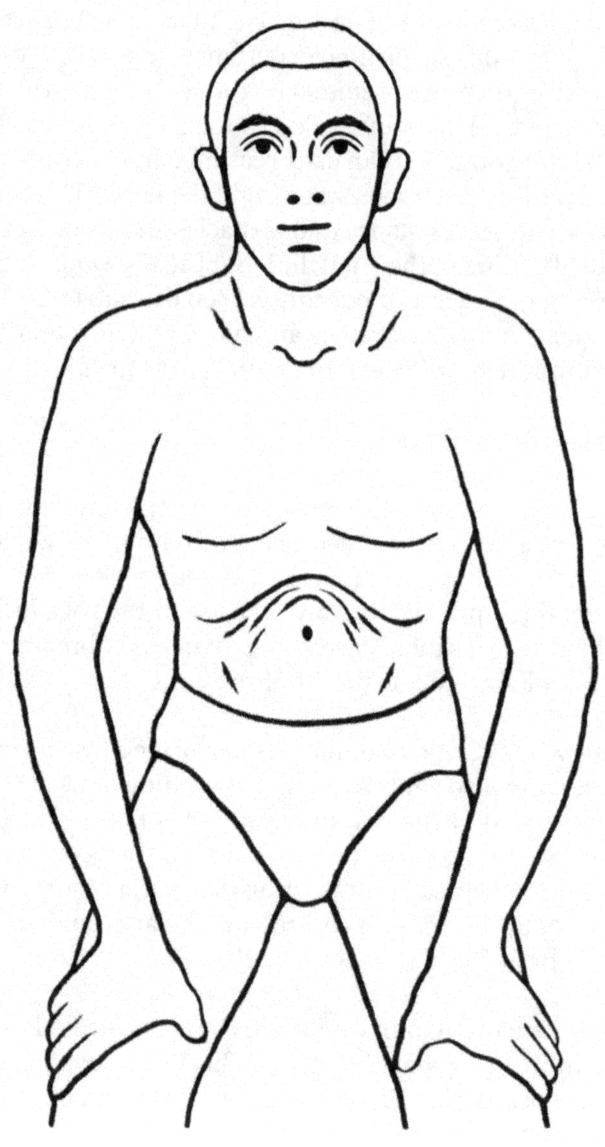

Holding the breath after an exhalation is more likely to create oxygen deprivation than holding the breath after an inhalation. In Miracle Yoga, the practice of pranayama is intended to be an *effortless effort* in which there is no stress and the uncomfortable feeling of oxygen deprivation is to be avoided. For this reason, when employing the Diaphragm Lock, which is mainly used to retain the breath after an exhalation, it is especially important for beginners to hold this lock very briefly to prevent oxygen deprivation. The Diaphragm Lock can be held slightly longer by advanced practitioners of pranayama.

Both the Root Lock and the Chin Lock are used after an inhalation and are recommended for use in the advanced breathing practices of Miracle Yoga. The Root Lock and then the Chin Lock are used together in sequence after the inhalation, and they are held during the retention portion of certain advanced breathing practices. To combine the Root Lock and the Chin Lock, you contract the anal sphincter, then you contract the abdominal muscles, and finally you lower the chin into the jugular notch as far as possible. When these two locks are applied, it is important to be mindful of keeping the back straight from below the neck to the base of the spine. At the end of the retention, you release the locks in the reverse order in which they were applied by raising the chin and releasing the contraction of the abdominal muscles, and finally releasing the contraction of the anal sphincter.

Apana usually moves downward in the lower torso and prana usually moves upward in the upper torso. By contracting the anal sphincter and abdominal muscles, apana is restricted from moving downward. By lowering the chin to the chest, prana is restricted from moving upward. As a result of applying the yoga locks, the apana and prana are united and a spiritual energy current is created. The combination of apana and prana can help to activate the kundalini. Yoga locks along with breath retention can be used in moderation to combine apana and prana in your practice of Miracle Yoga. However, the focus in Miracle Yoga needs to be primarily on purifying the nadis guided by the Holy Spirit, rather than forcing a kundalini experience to happen.

One last consideration related to yoga locks is what is sometimes called the **"Neck Lock."**[97] The Neck Lock is not another name for the Chin Lock and is actually not a lock like any of the three bandhas described previously. In order not to confuse the Neck Lock with these bandhas, here the Neck Lock will be called the ***Neck Hold***. This neck position is actually nothing more than maintaining a straight alignment of the spine, neck, and head by tucking the chin slightly inward. The specific name of "Neck Hold" is used to remind you of how important it is to hold the neck in the best position for correct posture.

There is a tendency to move the head forward or lift the chin when meditation or pranayama is practiced. The correct body alignment is having the chin tucked in slightly, the ear in line with the shoulder, and the tip of the nose vertically in line with the navel. The chin needs to be tucked in to keep the spine, neck, and head in the proper straight alignment, but the chin is only tucked in slightly and gently. The tucking in of the chin in the Neck Hold needs to be maintained, but should not be held so rigidly that tension is produced. If you do feel tension in the neck area because of tucking in the chin, you will need to adjust the chin, neck, and head so that the tension is eliminated.

Maintaining the Neck Hold by holding the neck in its proper position without raising the chin and without bending the neck forward or backward is important for meditation but even more important for pranayama. If you do not apply the straight position of the Neck Hold during advanced pranayama, the energy that rises from the torso into the head will not be distributed properly. This could produce negative physical and mental disturbances, so please be mindful of keeping the neck absolutely straight during any advanced pranayama that would include the yoga locks described above.[98]

D. ADVANCED BREATHING PRACTICES

Your practice of body postures in hatha yoga is a necessary means for stabilizing the body as a preparation for practicing pranayama. The breathing practices can be a means of accumulating prana and can also be a means of uniting prana and apana, which in turn stimulates the raising of the kundalini energy. At the end of your practice of hatha yoga asanas, you can practice the Yoga Seal, described in the previous chapter, to seal in the prana gained during holding body postures. Likewise, you can also practice the Yoga Seal after your pranayama practice. The Yoga Seal can seal in the energy accumulated through pranayama. Advanced breathing practices employ the bandhas, yoga locks, to lock in the combination of prana and apana so this union is fixed within the body and intensified.

Advanced breathing practices can be done by experienced students of Miracle Yoga. Before attempting the advanced breathing practices, it is necessary that you first practice yoga postures every day for about one year and also use the beginning breathing practices on a daily basis. There are also other factors involved in regard to the use of advanced breathing practices. It is advisable to have a healthy diet, to maintain sexual purity, and to be practicing daily meditation in order to benefit from the advanced breathing practices. If there are areas of your life that are out of proper balance, advanced pranayama may accentuate these imbalances, perhaps producing energy disturbances and even physical health problems or mental instability. Therefore, it is essential to bring your life into balance *prior* to implementing the advanced breathing practices. If you are in a hurry to practice the advanced breathing practices without the proper preparation, you will be acting in a foolhardy manner that invites danger.

Because advanced breathing practices have a greater impact on activating the susumna, these more advanced methods need to be used with moderation. The classical ratio of 2:1:4 for exhalation, inhalation, and retention is not recommended because the focus in Miracle Yoga needs to be on peacefulness and devotion rather than technique. For Miracle Yoga the 1:1:1 ratio of equal exhalation, inhalation, and retention is all that is needed. An alternative is to allow your exhalation to be slightly longer than your inhalation and your breath retention to be slightly longer than your exhalation. This general guideline applies to Advanced Alternate Nostril Breathing described below.

Instead of mentally keeping track of the exact breathing ratio, it is best to remain focused upon inner loving devotion and surrender to the activity and guidance of the Holy Spirit. For your breathing, you want to maintain a peaceful state of mind and avoid any form of straining or extremism. This manifesting of peacefulness without straining not only applies to the regulation of the breathing itself, but also applies to the use of the yoga locks during breath retention described above. The important advanced breathing practices are described as follows:

1. ADVANCED ALTERNATE NOSTRIL BREATHING

Advanced Alternate Nostril Breathing is a joining of Full Alternate Nostril Breathing with the yoga locks applied at the end of each round of practice. It is best to practice daily Full Alternate Nostril Breathing for one full year before practicing Advanced Alternate Nostril Breathing. You begin by closing off the right nostril with the right thumb. You inhale through the left nostril and then for the breath retention you close off both nostrils with the combination of the thumb and the ring finger and little finger of the right hand. After pausing to hold your breath, you remove your right thumb from the right nostril and exhale through the right nostril. You inhale through the right nostril and then close off both nostrils for the breath retention. You continue to exhale and inhale through one nostril, hold the breath and then switch to the other nostril to repeat the process. You practice a minimum of three exhalations and inhalations with each nostril. You complete the alternate nostril breathing round with an exhalation through the right nostril. Then you immediately inhale through both nostrils and then close off both nostrils to retain the breath.

For breath retention, you apply the Root Lock (contracting first the anal sphincter and then the abdominal muscles) followed by applying the Chin Lock (bringing the chin to the chest). While holding the breath, you focus on opening to divine love and retain the breath only as long as feels comfortable. At the end of your breath retention, you release first the Chin Lock by raising the head, and next you release the Root Lock by letting go of the contraction of the abdominal muscles followed by letting go of the contraction of the anal sphincter. After the locks are released, you slowly exhale through both nostrils and then observe the breathing returning to normal. Advanced Alternate Nostril Breathing is practiced with slow and deep breathing. You can use the Yoga Deep Breathing described above to use your full lung capacity for each exhalation and inhalation. It is recommended to practice no more than three rounds of Advanced Alternate Nostril Breathing with yoga locks.

After you have been practicing Advanced Alternate Nostril Breathing for approximately one year, you may want to eventually include the addition of the Diaphragm Lock. After retaining the breath and releasing the Root Lock and the Chin Lock, you exhale slowly through both nostrils. At the end of your exhalation, you retain the breath and you apply the Diaphragm Lock by drawing the diaphragm upward into the thoracic cavity. The stomach is lifted so the viscera are pulled back toward the spine creating a hollow in which the ribs are exposed. You retain the breath only briefly to prevent oxygen deprivation. When you are ready to complete your breath retention, you first release the Diaphragm Lock and then with full control you slowly inhale and allow the breathing to return to normal.[99]

When the Chin Lock is not in place, you use the Neck Hold during Advanced Alternate Nostril Breathing, especially when your pranayama includes the Diaphragm Lock. For the Neck Hold, you simply tuck the chin in slightly and keep the neck in straight alignment with the head and back. This maintaining of the proper alignment of the torso, neck, and head assists the Diaphragm Lock in bringing prana into the head in the most helpful way. However, if any tension builds up in the neck due to tucking the chin in for the Neck Hold, be sure to adjust the chin to whatever position is the most comfortable.

2. BELLOWS BREATHING

After using Rapid Abdominal Breathing for one year, you may want to practice *Bellows Breathing*, which is Rapid Abdominal Breathing with breath retention. For Bellows Breathing, you exhale quickly and forcefully by contracting only the abdomen. The sudden contraction of the abdomen pushes the diaphragm upward and contracts the lungs forcing the air out of the body. The air comes rapidly out of the nasal cavity on the exhalation creating a noticeable sound. When inhaling during the practice of Bellows Breathing, you release the abdominal contraction, which expands the lungs bringing air into the lungs of itself through the nasal cavity. The inhalation is slow, passive, and longer than the exhalation, which is short, sudden, and forceful.

To begin Bellows Breathing, you contract the abdomen to produce a sudden expulsion of breath followed by releasing the contraction of the abdomen to produce a passive inhalation. This process is repeated in rapid succession. You practice twelve exhalations and inhalations. You allow the last forceful exhalation to be slightly longer than the others. Next you inhale deeply and retain the breath. After holding the breath for a comfortable period of time, you exhale slowly and allow the breathing to return to normal. You can practice three rounds of Bellows Breathing in succession. You can maintain a peaceful mind throughout Bellows Breathing even though the abdominal contractions on the exhalations are practiced vigorously.

3. ADVANCED BELLOWS BREATHING

After practicing Bellows Breathing for one year, you may want to use *Advanced Bellows Breathing* by adding the yoga locks. Advanced Bellows Breathing in Sanskrit is called *Bhastrika Pranayama*. If the nadis have been purified sufficiently by other forms of pranayama, Advanced Bellows Breathing can increase your power of concentration and activate the raising to the kundalini within the susumna. This practice may produce some pulsating in parts of the spinal column, in the back of the head, or at the forehead. Advance Bellows Breathing increases the body heat and may produce perspiration. It enhances the functioning of the nervous system and the circulatory system and clears the mind as a preparation for meditation.

You begin by doing twelve rapid contractions of the abdomen that produce forceful exhalations. After completing the twelfth exhalation, you inhale deeply by expanding first the abdomen, then the lower chest, and finally the upper chest just as you would for Yoga Deep Breathing. You retain the breath and apply the Root Lock (contracting the anal sphincter and then contracting the abdominal muscles) and the Chin Lock in succession. You focus on surrendering to the action of the Holy Spirit. After holding the breath for a comfortable period of time, you release first the Chin Lock and then the Root Lock. Then you exhale slowly through the nose and allow the breathing to return to normal. After the nadis have become purified, Advanced Bellows Breathing can stimulate the raising of the kundalini. For the sake of moderation, it is recommended that you practice no more than three rounds of Advanced Bellows Breathing in one session.

Advanced practitioners of pranayama can also eventually include the addition of the Diaphragm Lock. After retaining the breath and releasing the Root Lock and the Chin Lock, you exhale slowly through the nose to finish your practice of Advanced Bellows Breathing. At the end of your exhalation, you retain the breath and use the Diaphragm Lock by lifting the stomach up and inward. While maintaining the Diaphragm Lock, you hold the breath, but you only retain the breath briefly. Before you complete your breath retention, and before you take your inhalation, you release the Diaphragm Lock. As you are releasing the Diaphragm Lock, you slowly and with full control inhale and then allow the breathing to return to normal.

When the Chin Lock is not being used, the Neck Hold is used for all forms of advanced breathing practices. To use the Neck Hold, you simply tuck the chin in slightly in order to maintain the neck in a straight alignment with the head and back. It is especially important to use the Neck Hold during the practice of advanced pranayama in which you are using the Diaphragm Lock. This is because when the Diaphragm Lock brings prana into the head, the neck needs to be in the proper alignment with the torso and the head so the flow of the prana into the head will be most beneficial.

4. ALTERNATE NOSTRIL ADVANCED BELLOWS BREATHING

Alternate Nostril Advanced Bellow Breathing is similar to Advanced Bellows Breathing in its effects. *Alternate Nostril Advanced Bellows Breathing* is advisable, especially if you notice that you are consistently breathing through one nostril more than the other. For example, the cartilage that serves as a partition between the nasal passages within your nose may be turned to one side and thus would restrict the flow of the breath in one of the nostrils. If you have this condition, called a *deviated septum*, Alternate Nostril Advanced Bellows Breathing is recommended instead of Advanced Bellows Breathing.

For Alternate Nostril Advanced Bellows Breathing, you use the Vishnu Mudra, the hand position in which you use the right thumb to close the right nostril and the ring finger and little finger of the right hand to close off the left nostril just as you would for Alternate Nostril Breathing.

You begin Alternate Nostril Advanced Bellows Breathing by closing off the right nostril with the right thumb and exhaling once rapidly through the left nostril. For the exhalation, you quickly and forcefully contract the abdominal muscles and then release the contraction to allow the inhalation to occur passively. After the first active exhalation and passive inhalation through the left nostril, you release the right thumb from the right nostril and close off the left nostril with the ring finger and little finger. Then you again contract the abdomen rapidly for the exhalation through the right nostril and release the contraction for the passive inhalation through the right nostril.

You continue to alternate your exhalations and inhalations from one nostril to the other. It is very important to wait until *both* the active exhalation and the passive inhalation have been completed, before releasing the closing off of one nostril and immediately switching to the closing off of the other nostril. There is an overall total of twelve rapid exhalations through the left nostril and twelve rapid exhalations through the right nostril. To keep track of the total number of breaths you simply count all the exhalations from one to twenty-four.

With the twenty-fourth exhalation, which will be through the right nostril, you make this very last exhalation a very long exhalation. Immediately after this final right nostril exhalation, you inhale deeply through both nostrils expanding the abdomen, the lower chest, and then the upper chest. After completing the inhalation, you apply the Root Lock, then the Chin Lock, and retain the breath. You maintain a peaceful mind open to the Holy Spirit. After holding your breath for a comfortable period of time, you then release the Chin Lock followed by the Root Lock. Following the release of the yoga locks, you exhale slowly with full control through the nose. At this point, you allow the breathing to return to normal. You practice no more than three rounds of Alternate Nostril Advanced Bellows Breathing per session.

If you have used Alternate Nostril Advanced Bellows Breathing regularly for a long time, you may want to include the addition of the Diaphragm Lock. After holding the breath and releasing the Root Lock and the Chin Lock, you exhale slowly through the nose to conclude your practice of Alternate Nostril Advanced Bellows Breathing. At the end of your exhalation, you apply the Diaphragm Lock and retain the breath for a short period of time before any discomfort sets in. When you feel it is time to complete your breath retention, you first release the Diaphragm Lock and then you slowly inhale with full control and you allow the breathing to return to normal.

As was stated previously, the Neck Hold is maintained during all forms of advanced pranayama when the Chin Lock is not being used. In particular, when your pranayama includes the Diaphragm Lock it is essential to have the Neck Hold in place, but the overriding priority is that there is no buildup of tension so the neck remains relaxed.

You may want to use a variety of breathing practices in sequence. But to avoid going to extremes in using advanced pranayama, it is suggested to practice no more than three rounds of a specific advanced pranayama in one sitting. Suggested combinations for your practice of advanced pranayama are provided in a separate section below. To be on the safe side, it is recommended to limit your pranayama to fifteen minutes or less in one session. If you want to do pranayama more often, you may want to have an additional session or two sessions at separate times during the day. It is best to maintain whatever breathing practices to which you can make a commitment in time and energy on a daily basis. It is not wise to have long breathing practices one day and short ones the next day, because consistency is very important in the practice of pranayama.

E. DEVOTION IN PRACTICING PRANAYAMA

Pranayama is more than merely implementing breathing practices. It is specifically the control of the breath, meaning *control of the prana.* The idea of gaining control of the prana has physical, mental, and spiritual aspects. The physical aspect has to do with employing the breathing practices themselves with a certain amount of thoroughness and deliberateness in which you consciously carry out each physical requirement of the particular breathing practice. For example, you make sure to never hold your breath so long that you deprive yourself of oxygen and become uncomfortable. You never extend yourself beyond the physical capabilities of your body, and therefore always remain in control of your physical vehicle throughout your breathing practice. In short, your breathing, which is normally an involuntary process, is taken over by your conscious control of the physical aspect of the breathing process, but always with moderation.

Because this physical aspect of controlling the prana is so obvious, you may think of the breathing practices as only a physical activity and not consider the mental and spiritual aspects of controlling the prana. Since there is a connection between the prana and the mind, learning to control the breathing helps you to calm and control the mind. Breathing is a gross expression of the action of prana. By controlling this gross manifestation of prana, you can learn to control the most subtle manifestation of prana, which is human thought itself.

Similar to traditional yoga, Miracle Yoga includes the direct control of the prana through the conscious direction of the will and the mind manifested in pranayama as a physical activity. Yet the major emphasis in Miracle Yoga is on the *indirect* control of the prana produced by surrendering control of the prana to the action of the Holy Spirit. Therefore, you want to allow your breathing practices to be devotional experiences by keeping the goal of Christ firmly in mind. With this Christian purpose, it is important to focus on how you are using your mind to become open to the action of the Holy Spirit. This is especially true of all the advanced breathing practices described above, which each have the potential of activating the kundalini energy, which raises prana upward within the susumna.

Surrendering to the Holy Spirit allows this kundalini energy to be used appropriately without negative side effects. Also following the guidance of the Holy Spirit will help you to avoid going to extremes in the application of breathing practices. It is reassuring to know that your progress is not dependent upon self-effort alone, but rather upon the coordination of your effort with the action of the Holy Spirit. In addition to focusing on receptivity to the Holy Spirit, you can also repeat an affirmation of the divine Name of God. Another focusing possibility that you may want to use is to perceive the spine and head being filled with light and love, and this is particularly effective in the advanced breathing practices.

Perhaps you may experience prana pulsating in the spine or head, or you may feel heat or light rising upward from the base of the spine and into the head. These are signs of the kundalini becoming activated and can be an encouragement to your practice, but need to be viewed with caution. Imagine a man who lives in a house with his child and in the basement there are cages with lions, tigers, and other wild animals. He goes down to the basement and unlocks all the cages thinking he will let all the animals out of the house. Instead, the animals tear up the whole house and then return to their cages in the cellar.

His child goes down to the cellar and makes friends with one animal. The child eventually leads the tamed animal out of the cage and throughout the house and finally back to its natural habitat in the outdoors. Over time, the child repeats the same pattern with another animal. One by one gradually all the animals are released.

This is an analogy of the wrong and the right way to release the primordial kundalini energy. The man in the analogy is like so many spiritual seekers who want to have an ultimate spiritual experience of the kundalini. But the seeker, who has not properly prepared the body and the mind, may encounter the sudden rising of the kundalini as a traumatic physical, mental, emotional, and psychic experience. The disastrous result of releasing the kundalini all at once in a body or mind unprepared for such an encounter is well known and still not a deterrent to some foolhardy souls.

One of the lesser-known negative impacts that premature releasing of the kundalini can have is that it can damage the aura. Similar to the damaging of the aura due to drug abuse, the damaging of the aura due to premature releasing of the kundalini can leave the seeker vulnerable to negative spirits, specifically disembodied entities. Referring to the kundalini energy as a female force, Robert Svoboda describes the potential negative consequences of unleashing the kundalini in an unprepared seeker, as follows:

> If Kundalini be triggered suddenly in an unprepared nervous system, the shock produced resembles that delivered to an unsuspecting toddler who grasps a live wire. When an unreconstructed personality tries to resist Kundalini, consciously or unconsciously, She may fry nerves and blow out endocrine fuses, shorting out the nervous system at its weakest point and blowing a hole in the victim's aura. Since the aura's job is to insulate us psychically from one another and from disembodied influences, holes in the aura permit all sorts of chaotic, negative mental vibrations, including even ethereal parasites, to enter the individual's field as they like and spread ruin.[100]

The danger of prematurely releasing the powerful kundalini energy can be avoided through systematic preparations implemented over a long period of time. The daily practice of hatha yoga, pranayama, and meditation in moderation can strengthen the nervous system and thus prepare it to withstand the impact of the rising of the kundalini.

A spontaneous and powerful initial release of the kundalini can produce a positive spiritual experience in some cases. But if you do happen to have a sudden and dramatic release of the kundalini that produces a positive spiritual experience on a one-time basis, it is essential to realize that you have not leaped to the end of your spiritual journey. This may be only the start of your journey in which you will need to integrate all aspects of yourself. After your initial spiritual experience, your integration can be facilitated with a systematic daily practice of spiritual disciplines guided by the Holy Spirit that will bring about a slow, natural, and controlled awakening of the kundalini. You are no different than other seekers who have not had your dramatic experience, although your experience can be a very helpful reminder of your true nature beyond the appearances of this world.

The child's role in the prior analogy represents the awakening of the kundalini when it is guided by your simple and loving true nature that is the *Christ child* in you. The Christ child in you is your devotional nature that needs to grow up and mature bringing about an integration of all parts of yourself. Like physical growth, your spiritual growth is a gradual process. The focus needs to be on development of all parts of your character. It is true that the kundalini does have the potential to manifest as a bolt of lightening-like energy that can successfully bring about transcendental awareness. But in Miracle Yoga, the emphasis is upon the gentle releasing of the kundalini that occurs like the releasing of the animals in the basement one by one.

In the piecemeal process of releasing the kundalini in Miracle Yoga, the Holy Spirit plays the central role. The divine grace of the Holy Spirit with your consent sends an impulse to the coiled kundalini to raise up the amount of potential energy that would be most helpful. Pranayama is not required for this process but can play a part in this process if you are being guided by the Holy Spirit in your breathing practices. This is where your devotion is very important in your breathing practices. In particular, advanced pranayama, which uses locks, can be best used in a safe way by a deepening of your devotion. Pranayama, because of its potential for assisting in the release of the divine energy, needs to be seen as a sacred activity of worship. When the yoga locks are in place during the breath retention, that is the time to be most focused on the holiness of this activity. The pause between each round of pranayama can also be an important time to surrender in gratitude to the divine influence. This pause can be a time to relax and to rest in the divine presence, while simultaneously noticing the inner changes that are in the process of occurring.

In keeping with this sacred frame of mind, the technical aspect of holding the breath for a long time or having long time periods for your pranayama practice are not crucial elements. One heartfelt prayer is worth a thousand mechanical prayers. Similarly, a short time spent in pranayama each day with full devotion is more effective and more in harmony with the Holy Spirit than extensive periods of time spent on technically proficient pranayama lacking devotion.

As is the case with many forms of Hindu yoga, the key element in your spiritual growth is your surrender to God's will and openness to divine grace. For a Christian seeker surrendering to the Holy Spirit is sometimes thought of as a one-time decision to give your life to God.

Such a decision can be a turning point in a Christian seeker's spiritual growth, but the depth of surrendering to the Holy Spirit depends upon a constant renewal of this surrender. To guard against the ego's self-interest that may potentially take over at any moment, it takes inner vigilance to truly give over your life to the Holy Spirit from day to day, from moment to moment, and from breath to breath.

Pranayama can be an act of renewing your self-offering (*yajna*)[101] to the divine. In this offering of yourself to the Holy Spirit, you let God be the breather, the act of breathing, and the goal of breathing. You allow God to do the breathing for you by invoking His power and opening yourself to His blessing. You are offering your physical, emotional, and mental activity and even your physical, emotional, and mental existence to the divine will asking the physical body to be a channel of divine expression. In this self-offering, nothing can be hidden or held back from the action of the divine influence.

Your total self-surrender is your invitation for cleansing that would remove any inner block or resistance to the divine influence. In the analogy of the child, his taming and releasing the caged wild animals symbolically represents the releasing of the kundalini guided by divine love. These wild animals represent different kinds of energy blocks that are "wild," meaning uncontrollable. These energy blocks are like knotted obstacles that need to be "tamed," meaning they need to be untied and released by the loving divine influence. If you follow the example of the child, you can open the cages of what may start out as wild energy. Then this wild energy can be transformed into properly channeled energy by trusting that your loving Divine Father will do His part to provide protection and guidance through the action of the Holy Spirit. Your specific choice of devotion will vary depending on the divine aspects that most make your heart sing. When the kundalini energy is released, guided by the Holy Spirit, it will energize and purify the parts of you that need the most integration.

The kundalini is sometimes perceived as an opportunity to obtain a spiritual experience that would be a "spiritual possession" that would feed the ego. Instead of an ego-based desire to raise the kundalini, the ideal outlook is to desire only to do God's Will. This is the best purpose to express, trusting that God's Will is your own true will. Fully accepting God's Will naturally produces a heartfelt feeling of wanting to be clear enough and open enough to allow divine love to flow through you to others. The goal of opening to God's Will is not to escape from this world, but rather to be on the earth as a channel of blessings to others—understanding that as you help others to gradually awaken, you are helping yourself to gradually awaken.

F. ADVANCED PRANAYAMA, KUNDALINI, AND MEDITATION

To summarize prior statements, some seekers mistakenly believe that the goal of awakening the kundalini is to bring about a single all-encompassing jolt of cosmic energy to facilitate immediate total spiritual transformation all at once. The goal of higher consciousness is commendable, but immediate full transformation through the full force of the kundalini is an unrealistic and often ego-driven goal. A more realistic and humble goal is self-development through self-discipline and self-surrender to the divine influence.[102] It is best to start right where you are in your growth and take one small step after another to build a solid spiritual foundation for yourself. Your practice of Miracle Yoga is a means of integrating the spiritual centers of energy in the body.

Instead of seeking a quick raising of the kundalini, your step-by-step process of self-development can include a gradual and unforced rising of the kundalini to bring about an inner purification and balance. Lee Sannella has written articulately about the physiological implications of the kundalini serving as a purification and balancing process:

> In its rise, kundalini causes the central nervous system to throw off stress. The stress points will usually cause pain during meditation. When kundalini encounters these stress points or blocks, it begins to act "on its own volition," engaging in a self-directed, self-limited process of spreading out through the entire physiological system to remove these blocks.
>
> Once a block is removed, kundalini flows freely through that point and continues its upward journey until the next stress area is encountered. Further, the kundalini energy diffuses in this journey, so that it may be operating on several levels at once, removing several different blocks. When the course is completed, the energy all becomes focused again at the top of the head.[103]

There are many different kinds of signs that may indicate that the kundalini is in the process of being awakened. During meditation you may feel involuntary body jerks, or perhaps even trembling or shaking of the body. When you hold body postures, you may feel a pulsating of nerves in the spinal column or in parts of the head, such as the forehead or the lower part of the back of the head.

One indication of the activation of the kundalini can be the feeling of heat in parts of the body that are energized. This may feel like a burning sensation.[104] In fact, the term kundalini is derived from the Sanskrit verb "kund," which means *to burn*.[105] A rather uncommon type of kundalini experience is called the "kundalini bath,"[106] in which the whole body, including the internal organs, are filled with a burning heat. A more common experience is a feeling of warmth, heat, or burning sensation rising from the base of the spine upward.

The burning effect of kundalini occurs in direct proportion to the degree of resistance encountered by the kundalini. Lee Sannella makes an analogy of how a thin tungsten filament offers high resistance to electrical current that produces light and heat. On the other hand, a thick copper wire produces less resistance and less heat. Heat is produced by the kundalini only by the parts of the body that offer resistance presenting a block to the flow of this divine energy. As the kundalini moves through the part of the body offering resistance, the heat produced burns out the resistance having a purifying effect. When the resistance has been burned out, the block has been removed so the kundalini can flow freely and the burning sensation disappears.[107]

Although the kundalini rising is usually experienced as a warm or burning sensation, this is not always the case. Whether heat is felt or not, typically the kundalini produces a sensation of the movement of energy or pressure of some sort upward along the spine. It may feel like a strong surge of energy, but it may also be experienced as a subtle movement, like an ant or ants slowly creeping up your back. The energy may rise up quickly or slowly. It may rise up to a certain area and then lower again and then rise again later. This rising and lowering of the kundalini can be an ongoing process over time.

This step-by-step process of the kundalini rising and lowering is well understood in tantric yoga as a purifying process of transformation. Inner blocks are purified and removed by the inner fire of the kundalini in a piecemeal manner. Depending upon the nature of your inner blocks and upon the specific chakra being activated, you will have different kinds of inner experiences. A slight pain may be felt in some areas of the body affected by the kundalini. Also, as an aftereffect of this process, parts of the body may be sensitized and tender to the touch or slightly sore after having been energized by the kundalini during pranayama or during meditation. In addition, for an instant, you may feel a sudden jolt of energy that jumps up the spine and that jerks the body, perhaps snapping the head up and back. These jolts of energy may come and go repeatedly each time lasting for an instant. It usually takes a while for parts of the body to adjust to the new influx of kundalini energy.

Christian mystics of the past experienced spiritual transformation including physiological changes but did not possess the concept of the kundalini available to them that would help them articulate this process. In addition, they did not live in an age of free speech so were inhibited by religious traditionalists. Christian mystics wisely limited themselves to writing in poetry and speaking in metaphors. But they directly experienced what John the Baptist meant by saying:

I indeed baptize you with water, for repentance. But he who is coming after me is mightier than I, and his sandals I am not worthy to bear. He will baptize you with the Holy Spirit and with fire. His winnowing fan is in his hand, and he will thoroughly clean out his threshing floor, and will gather his wheat into the barn; but the chaff he will burn up with unquenchable fire.[108]

There is hidden wisdom in this Bible quotation because it is not about the good souls ("wheat") going to Heaven and the bad souls ("chaff") going to the "fire" of hell. The baptism "with the Holy Spirit and with fire" is the purifying process of the kundalini activated by the action of the Holy Spirit burning away inner blocks ("chaff"). St. John of the Cross, Brother Lawrence, St. Hildegard, St. Symeon the New Theologian, John of St. Samson, St. Anselm, Jacob Boehme, and numerous other Christian mystics used the word "fire" in their mystical writings. These mystics confirmed that they understood the Biblical statement, "For our God is a consuming fire."[109] By referring to the image of "fire," Christian mystics tried to describe their own personal experience of the kundalini activated in their own bodies.

Christian mystics have been called "mystics" precisely because they understood divine "mysteries" through personal experience more than they were able to explain or were allowed to articulate. Many aspects of their experience were too controversial to express directly in writing, such as the sexual aspects of spiritual transformation, which will be mentioned later in this section.

St. John of the Cross identified the most challenging phase of the spiritual transformation as a spiritual crisis, which he called the "dark night of the soul." This stage can be traumatic, and there is a potential for insanity. The rising of the kundalini also has this same potential for insanity. This suggests a correlation between the "dark night" and the rising of the kundalini, which are both purification processes. The dark night of the soul is not typically described as having the physiological symptoms of the rising of the kundalini, such as the burning sensation rising from the base of the spine. Yet it appears to me that the dark night of the soul is the result of a certain kind of activation of the kundalini that may or may not produce the usual symptoms of the kundalini. Whether heat or other sensations are felt in the spine or not felt, the activation of the kundalini does affect the nervous system and the brain. In the process of purifying the nervous system, the kundalini triggers inner blocks in order to remove them, and this process can be uncomfortable and disorienting. The kundalini can produce excessive stimulation of the nervous system including the brain. This could bring about mental instability with symptoms similar to schizophrenia, which can also be experienced in the dark night.

Joseph Campbell clarifies the difference between schizophrenia and the induced state of leaving behind the appearances of the world by using vigorous meditative inward seeking, as follows:

> Contemplation is a deliberately induced schizophrenia. You break away from the everyday world and fall into it. The phenomena are the same as in schizophrenia. So what's the difference? The difference is simply the one between a diver who can swim and one who can't swim. The mystic steps down into the water under the guidance of a master and realizes that he can swim, while the schizophrenic goes under.[110]

Regarding the danger of mental problems due to the rising of the kundalini, Roy Eugene Davis states:

> As to the possibility of psychological disturbance; a person who is not mentally and emotionally stable has no business working with subtle forces anyway. This is why, in the *Yoga Sutras of Patanjali,* the first two steps leading to meditation practice are concerned with attitude, behavior, and, in general, living in harmony with the environment.[111]

The spiritual transformation becomes much more difficult if you do not understand the nature of the dark night and/or the activation of the kundalini. Not understanding the dark night and/or the activation of the kundalini as a purification process leads to fear, which can make the transformation more difficult. Therefore, it is important for the seeker to understand the process and to take the necessary preparatory steps that can mitigate the negative physiological and psychological aspects of spiritual transformation. The best overall preparation is the systematic implementation of a life of dedication to God and service to others manifested in everyday life. Specific preparations would include daily meditation, as well as both preparing the body with hatha yoga and preparing the nervous system with pranayama.

Regarding spiritual transformation, Alice A. Baily states:

> .... the yoga for this transition period is the yoga of the one-pointed intent, of directed purpose, of constant practice of the Presence of God, and of ordered regular meditation carried forward systematically and steadily over years of effort.

When this is done with detachment and is paralleled by a life of loving service, the awakening of the centers and the raising of the sleeping fire of kundalini will go forward with safety and sanity and the whole system will be brought to the requisite stage of "aliveness."[112]

If enough preparations are made over many years, it is possible to even eliminate altogether the negative symptoms of the kundalini rising. It may likewise be possible to bring about spiritual transformation as an expression of opening to light and love without the necessity for the extreme spiritual crisis of the dark night to occur.

To prepare for spiritual transformation, it helps to study the writings of Christian mystics and also study the nature of the kundalini. Because direct overt references to the kundalini by Christian authors are so limited, a Christian seeker is advised to study the topic of the kundalini by reading literature from various sources—Christian sources, if they can be found, and non-Christian sources. John White has compiled and edited, *Kundalini, Evolution and Enlightenment*, which is a book containing articles from different authors presenting a wide range of perspectives on the nature of the kundalini. This book is suggested reading for further study about the kundalini in general.

It is helpful to understand the sexual changes that occur in the body due to the rising of the kundalini. John White summarizes the views of Gopi Krishna, who is the author of *Kundalini, The Evolutionary Energy In Man*, regarding these sexual changes, as follows:

> ... the "food" that the body uses to nourish the nervous system during the transformation comes from the sex organs— the "essence" of seminal fluid in men and what Gopi Krishna calls "the erotic fluids" in women. Thus the reproductive organs increase their activity dramatically, producing many times more copiously than usual. There may also be unusual involuntary contractions of the penis or vagina-uterus ensemble as the sexual fluids are drawn into the body.... the fluid sexual essence, existing at the molecular or even the atomic level, streams from the reproductive organs through the neural pathways into the spinal canal and then upward into the brain (*urdharas retas*—the reversal of the sexual fluids).[113]

Involuntary contractions of the sexual organs described above may occur in a sudden onset of the kundalini rising but is less likely to occur in the gradual rising of the kundalini advocated in Miracle Yoga.

The reabsorption of sexual fluids to facilitate spiritual transformation is a generally accepted concept in yoga philosophy. Celibacy with purity of purpose is a recommended practice as a beneficial way to cooperate with this transformation process. Since celibacy is not for everyone, some schools of yoga advocate being a married householder. Yogi Bhajan, who brought his teachings of kundalini yoga to America, was asked in an interview in 1976 the following question: "Does a student of the kundalini yoga have to be celibate?" He replied, as follows:

> The student should be a householder, except in special cases, raise a family and fulfill the obligations of a spiritual society. Celibacy actually means to be by yourself without abusing your sexual and regenerative abilities. A married person is by himself, for both people are merged as one. Even in marriage the sexual energy is respected and built up. A normal couple will find a frequency of one time a month completely satisfying if approached correctly.[114]

Celibacy is only for those who can raise up their sexual energy through spiritual dedication and spiritual disciplines and who are called to that role. Gopi Krishna does not recommend complete celibacy in general, but does suggest that it is best to retain the sexual fluids for as long as a year or two after the kundalini is first activated. By being celibate during this critical period of time, you allow your sexual energy to be fully available to assist in bringing about the inner cleansing and transformation process.

If you make a temporary or permanent commitment to celibacy, you may still experience a spontaneous extreme overstimulation of sexual energy. Even when you are sitting for meditation, this sexual stimulation can suddenly occur without being caused by any accompanying sexual fantasy. This dramatic increase in sexual energy can feel overwhelming and occurs in both men and women during an early stage in the rising of the kundalini. The increased sexual energy does not mean you have slackened your spiritual purposes because this is just the natural process of how the kundalini becomes activated in some seekers. It is just a very temporary transition stage in which it is important to continue to firmly maintain your spiritual purposes in spite of the temptation to express this sexual energy overtly. If you can hold your spiritual purposes throughout this time, in the future you will be able to raise energy up from the lowest centers without having this same kind of sexual stimulation occurring repeatedly.[115]

When Sri Chinmoy was asked about the relationship between the kundalini and sexual indulgence, he replied, as follows:

Kundalini yoga is the yoga of absolute purity. It is one of the most sacred yogas and physical, vital, mental, and psychic purity are of paramount importance. The three major nerves—ida, pingala, and susumna—will suffer immensely and immediately if there is any sexual indulgence. And it is not only physical relations that are bad. If somebody enjoys lower vital thoughts, impure thoughts, in the mind, that is also harmful. There are many who have concentrated on the centers and who were about to open them when unfortunately they entered into the lower vital world.[116]

The proper understanding of the kundalini from the perspective of Miracle Yoga is to see it as a means of gradual transformation in coordination with the Holy Spirit. The awakening the kundalini in a gentle manner by inviting the Holy Spirit to be the activating principle can be used only after first strengthening the body through hatha yoga postures and through breathing practices. These preparations enable the nervous system of the body to withstand the increased energy produced by the rising of the kundalini.

The six methods of *Christian Yoga Meditation* are designed to assist in the natural movement of the creative energy in the body. *Centering Meditation*, the first technique of Christian Yoga Meditation, focuses on the navel to assist in raising the coiled kundalini energy at the base of the spine. Using the yoga locks in advanced pranayama can help the raising of the kundalini. These advanced breathing practices combine the ascending prana and the descending apana and help to open the susumna, allowing the kundalini to rise upward.

Each chakra can have blocks that resist the rising of the kundalini, and the kundalini itself can have a purifying effect, which burns away these blocks. Yet there are three major obstacles to the rising of the kundalini, which are knots, called *grandhis*. The knot at the base of the spine is the *brahma grandhi*. Centering Meditation assists in unlocking this sacral knot and invites the Holy Spirit to purify the lower centers and to help raise the kundalini in a gradual and safe way. During the breath retention portion of advanced breathing practices, you can focus the mind on the navel area, the sacral plexus, and the lumbar plexus in the spine and invite the Holy Spirit into these parts of the body. This serves as a preparation for Centering Meditation making it more effective at purifying the lower centers and raising creative energy.

During advanced pranayama with yoga locks, the kundalini energy moves in a specific way. The incoming breath takes prana all the way down to the navel area at the level of the fourth vertebra. The Root Lock affects the Root Chakra (also called the *Muladhara Chakra*), associated with the perineum (the space between the anus and sexual organs), the rectum and the coccyx. The Root Chakra, where the kundalini lies dormant, is the storehouse for apana, the energy of elimination. The Root Lock draws apana from the Root Chakra up to the level of the fourth vertebra at the navel area where it combines with the prana. The combination of prana and apana produce a dynamic force, which then descends back down from the navel area to the kundalini in the Root Chakra. Then the kundalini awakens and begins to rise upward in the susumna.[117] It is essential to invite the Holy Spirit into this process.

The second major knot is the *vishnu grandhi*, which is located at the *Manipura Chakra* in the adrenal area (related to the solar plexus). This second major knot is located one chakra lower than the Heart Center (*Anahata Chakra*). Nevertheless, the vishnu grandhi can be unlocked by the Heart Center opening with devotion. *Heart Meditation*, the second technique of Christian Yoga Meditation, helps to unlock the vishnu grandhi through inviting the Holy Spirit into the heart center. Joining prana and apana in lowest part of the body is not the only way to accelerate the raising of the kundalini in the susumna. The ascending breath of prana and the descending breath of apana can also be joined in the heart and open the susumna to the kundalini energy. Actually the combination of prana and apana sets off a transformation of energy that involves the other three major forms of prana—samana, udana, and vyana.[118]

There is a point in the heart center in the center of the chest where the incoming breath stops and the outgoing breath begins. This point of where inspiration and expiration meet is considered a void in which the ascending prana and descending apana are in transition. The prana and apana neutralize each other at this transition point. There is a second significant transition point located twelve finger widths below the bottom of the nose, which is a few inches above the heart center. Advanced pranayama can be used to hold the prana and the apana between these two transition points producing a neutralization of these two kinds of energy. When this neutralization is stabilized by retaining the breath with yoga locks during advanced pranayama, the prana breath and apana breath are restricted from moving into the ida, pingala, and other nadis normally available. The restricted prana and apana combine to form the samana breath, the single equal breath. The samana breath that is the combination of prana and apana moves into the susumna. In turn, the samana breath in the susumna changes into the udana breath, the vertical fire breath, which rises as kundalini energy. When the udana breath rises from the heart level of the susumna to the crown center, it burns away dualistic thinking (*vikalpa*) and is finally transformed into vyana, the universal breath that is all pervading.[119]

Because advanced pranayama practices can help to combine prana and apana and raise the kundalini, these breathing practices can be used in moderation as a preparation for Heart Meditation. While retaining the breath during advanced breathing practices, you can focus the mind on the cardiac plexus in the spine and invite the Holy Spirit into this part of the body. This helps to open the heart center and make your practice of Heart Meditation more effective and assists the raising of creative energy in coordination with the Holy Spirit. Of course, the action of the Holy Spirit in your meditation practice can produce the spontaneous combination of prana and apana and raise the kundalini in a natural and safe way all by itself even if you choose not to use advanced breathing practices.

The third significant knot is the *rudra grandhi* located at the brow center. *Brow Meditation*, the third technique, helps to unlock the rudra grandhi through inviting the Holy Spirit into the brow center. It is best to first focus on loosening the two lower knots before concentrating on loosening the rudra grandhi. If you are successful in raising energy up from the lower portions of the body, you can focus on the brow center during the breath retention portion of advanced pranayama and invite the Holy Spirit into the forehead area. Another option for advanced practitioners is to briefly hold the Diaphragm Lock along with breath retention after the final exhalation of Advanced Bellows Breathing. This Diaphragm Lock and breath retention after the exhalation can draw prana upward from the torso into the head.

The fourth method of Christian Yoga Meditation, *Crown Meditation*, further facilitates the raising of kundalini energy by shifting the focus from the brow center to the crown center. Bringing the awareness to the crown center helps to gain a deeper connection with the Holy Spirit and helps to integrate all the energy that has been raised up by the previous methods. The fifth method of Christian Yoga Meditation, *Oneness Meditation*, further helps to open your mind to your inner feelings, your intuitions, which raise your awareness above the physical sensations, the emotions, and discursive thinking. The raising of the kundalini energy into the head can facilitate this opening of the mind to your intuitions. Finally the sixth method of Christian Yoga Meditation, *Inner Silence Meditation*, can lead you to let go of body awareness and be open to contemplation.

Each of the techniques of Christian Yoga Meditation leads to a deeper level of awareness. All these methods include inviting the Holy Spirit, but the first methods are more focused on the body and the latter methods lead to contemplation and releasing of body awareness. These techniques are also designed to be an expression of increasing self-surrender until finally during contemplation, there is a reliance upon the overshadowing of the Holy Spirit.

There are three ways of facilitating the raising of the kundalini in Miracle Yoga: The first way is the use of advanced pranayama with locks, described previously with the inclusion of inviting the Holy Spirit into this process. The second way is the use of the first three methods of Christian Yoga Meditation, which can be enhanced by advanced pranayama, but which can gently raise the kundalini without breathing practices with locks. Focusing at the navel area at the level of the fourth vertebra and inviting the Holy Spirit there can join apana and prana. This method by itself can draw apana up from the root center and can draw prana down from the breathing area and from the solar plexus at the eighth vertebra where prana is stored in the body. This union of apana and prana in the navel area can then proceed to raise the kundalini in just the same manner that advanced pranayama can, as is described previously. However, combining prana and apana by focusing at the navel in Centering Meditation is a much more gentle and subtle process than advanced pranayama alone.

Focusing at the heart center can also join apana and prana at the transition point in the heart where the incoming breath stops and the outgoing breath begins. By bringing the awareness to this transition point where the inspiration and expiration meet, the ascending prana and the descending apana can be joined and produce an energy that can activate the kundalini in the susumna similar to the way this occurs in advanced pranayama, as is described previously.

Focusing at the brow center can also help to facilitate the raising of the kundalini. The final three methods of Christian Yoga Meditation can help to further raise the energy and can coordinate the changes produced by the activity of the kundalini.

The third way the kundalini can be raised is through contemplation. This wordless form of attunement is the deepest way to surrender to the Holy Spirit. Contemplation involves a descent of energy, followed by an ascent of energy, and concluded by another descent of energy. The first descent is facilitated by the Holy Spirit, and this is a passage of energy through spiritual centers in the body from the top downward. The Holy Spirit sends an impulse from above down to the kundalini in order to awaken this sleeping potential energy. This initiates the raising of the kundalini in the susumna in coordination with the Holy Spirit. Finally the ascent brings energy to the crown where it is transformed into a descending energy that travels down through the spiritual centers and through the whole body to entirely integrate all the changes produced by the kundalini.

The idea of the descent, ascent, and concluding descent of energy in contemplation is consistent with some schools of tantric yoga. The tantric term for divine energy is *shakti*. Prana is one kind of shakti, consisting of life force energy. The word "shakti" represents not only the life force energy of prana, but also all forms of organic and inorganic energy. In its broadest meaning, the word "shakti" is not limited only to the idea of energy because it includes the concept of *grace*, the manifestation of God's transforming influence on the spiritual seeker. The Integral Yoga[120] of Sri Aurobindo is not described as a traditional tantric yoga, yet it speaks of the descending and ascending energy. Sri Aurobindo states below that in his Integral Yoga, the kundalini can be raised without exerting your will in the form of a technique:

> The process of kundalini awakened through the centers as also the purification of the centers is a tantric knowledge. In our yoga there is no willed process of the purification and opening of the centers, no raising up of the kundalini by a set process either.[121]

Regarding the descending energy that goes down to the Muladhara Chakra (Root Center) and then brings about an ascending energy, Sri Aurobindo uses the term "Force," to indicate what Miracle Yoga would refer to as the Holy Spirit, as follows:

> In our yoga there is no willed opening of the chakras; they open of themselves by the descent of the Force. In the tantric discipline they open from down upward, the muladhara first; in our yoga, they open from up downward. But the ascent of the force from the muladhara does take place.[122]

The Integral Yoga of Sri Aurobindo sets the ideal of surrendering the will to the divine influence, but similar to Miracle Yoga, he recognizes the need to use some techniques in the early stages of spiritual growth. Speaking on behalf of Integral Yoga, Vansant V. Merchant states:

> This does not mean that individual effort does not count or assume importance in the earlier or initial stages. Also, aids like mantra, japa, asanas, devotional rituals, etc., are used *only* if necessary and only as long as necessary. But they are not considered indispensable as supports, as in other yogas. The only demands in this yoga on the sadhaka (seeker of truth) are primarily three: aspiration, rejection, and surrender—aspiration for the highest Light and all its manifestations; rejection of all the

wrong movements (at whatever level) of any nature that are an impediment on the way; and surrender of all and everything one is to The Mother or Divine Power invoked.[123]

Traditionally many schools of yoga speak of the divine manifesting active energy of shakti in creation as the Divine Mother. Sri Aurobindo acknowledges the Divine Mother, but also speaks of the Supramental Truth or Supramental Consciousness, which is above the head and above the thousand-petaled crown chakra and which permeates all life and all consciousness. From the perspective of Miracle Yoga, the highest level of consciousness, described in various schools of yoga by different names, can be expressed simply by the word "God." The teachings of Aurobindo have been singled out here for your consideration because of the emphasis on both descending and ascending divine energy that facilitates an integrated and balanced life. Aurobindo's teachings also emphasize surrender. For the Christian seeker, surrender is always to God, which is surrender to His divine Love.

Pranayama can be an active way to participate with divine grace and invite the divine influence, but it needs to be viewed rightly as a stepping stone to releasing techniques and entering contemplation in which there is a surrender to the activity of the Holy Spirit. The divine power of the kundalini can be gently released during pranayama by cooperating with the Holy Spirit and can be best integrated into a life of service by this openness to surrendering to God.

The three ways of raising the kundalini in Miracle Yoga that have been identified above can be summarized in regard to exerting the will and surrendering to the divine influence, as follows:

1. PRANAYAMA—The advanced breathing practices in moderation are the most active exertion of the will in Miracle Yoga, expressed as methods to awaken the kundalini. However, pranayama is practiced as a devotional experience with an invitation for the action and divine grace of the Holy Spirit. Along with hatha yoga postures, standard breathing practices (even beginning practices) are considered a helpful preparation for meditation and also a means of preparing the body to withstand the energy released by the kundalini.

2. CHRISTIAN YOGA MEDITATION—This sequence of methods provides a moderate directing of the will toward opening the spiritual centers from the bottom to the top with an emphasis on increasingly inviting the Holy Spirit into this process. Christian Yoga Meditation focuses first on individual spiritual centers and then later focuses on integrating the centers, so this is a movement from awareness of the parts leading to awareness of the whole.

3. CONTEMPLATION—This overshadowing of the Holy Spirit is a releasing of all techniques and a letting go of exerting the will in order to rest in the divine presence. Contemplation is a surrender to God trusting the Holy Spirit to spontaneously raise the kundalini, open the spiritual centers, remove inner blocks, and reveal the awareness of your true nature of love and oneness with the divine.

The goal of raising the kundalini is not to escape from this world, but to attain the integration of the whole person in Christ, including expressing loving service to others. The Holy Spirit can produce a descending energy that in turn initiates the raising of the kundalini to purify the spiritual centers as it rises. But after the kundalini rises, there is a final descending energy that helps to bring about inner balance. Yogi Bhajan was asked: "Is the goal of the yoga student to bring all the energy into the brain?" His response was:

> No! The energy of kundalini releases from the navel center, then rises to the top of the head. When it descends to complete its cycle of energy, the chakras open fully. By chakras opening I mean the talents of each chakra are consolidated into the character and behavior of that person. It does no good at all to fill a person with energy that he cannot integrate.[124]

The initial occurrence of the descending of the Holy Spirit may go unnoticed, but the rising of the kundalini and the descending energy that occurs after the kundalini has risen can often be felt. In fact, the research of Itzhak Bentov[125] maintains that the kundalini produces a physiological effect of energy rising up the feet and legs, up from the base of the spine all the way to the top of the head. In addition, after the kundalini becomes active in the head, there is a stimulating effect that moves down the face into the throat and all the way down to the abdomen. This research affirms the ascending and descending nature of the kundalini that affects the entire body. When the kundalini rises in the spine, energy may be felt rising in the front of the body as well as rising in the back. Similarly, when the kundalini becomes active in the head, energy may be experienced descending in the back of the body as well as descending in the front of the body.

The different ways in which the rising of the kundalini might be perceived physiologically have been outlined previously so you can be aware of these indications of inner transformation occurring. However, it would be misleading to suggest that the kundalini can always be perceived physiologically. The most obvious physiological indicators, consisting of strong negative experiences, occur in those seekers who have not made the necessary preparations in the body and mind to be receptive to the kundalini energy. Yet the seeker who has systematically prepared the body and mind, as has been described above, to receive this kundalini energy may experience only minor physiological effects and perhaps no physiological effects. Shakti Parwha Kaur Khalsa states that you may not even notice when the kundalini rises, and thus it is best to have no expectations about how the kundalini may manifest physiologically, as follows:

> If you're expecting bells to ring, cannons to go off, or lights to flash, forget it. Seeing visions, hearing sounds, having some physical sensation might sometimes happen, and could seem quite impressive, but it can also be very misleading. Such phenomena are not the goal of the practice of Kundalini Yoga. There may be no physical sign at all, or possibly just a very slight indication. In case you do experience such things, don't let yourself be sidetracked. They don't prove anything. They are not the criteria for whether the kundalini has risen.[126]

Although physiological changes might or might not be consciously perceived, Shakti Parwha Kaur Khalsa offers a summary of the best indication of the value of the rising of the kundalini. In the following quotation, he is describing Kundalini Yoga, but he could just as well be summarizing the effects of the rising of the kundalini that may result from the practice of Miracle Yoga, as follows:

> After the kundalini energy rises and becomes accustomed to flowing freely through all the chakras, there is a definite change of consciousness, a noticeable transformation in the character of an individual. The person looks at life differently, feels different, and thus acts differently. The real "proof" that someone's kundalini has risen lies in the upgrading of that person's attitude toward life, his relationships with other people, and with himself.
>
> Raising the kundalini has to do with spiritual elevation. It is not to be confused with hearing sounds or seeing visions. When the kundalini is allowed to rise through the practice of Kundalini Yoga, it will not make a person weird or unbalanced. Note that the operative word here is "allowed." Kundalini Yoga does not force the kundalini to rise; it prepares the body to allow it to rise so that you can experience your higher consciousness. The object achieved is to coordinate and balance the functions of the chakras that are concerned with the needs of daily life

with the universal consciousness and expansion that are found in the higher chakras. When this balance occurs, you become empowered, you are able to be a compassionate, conscious, and capable human being.[127]

G. COMBINING ADVANCED BREATHING PRACTICES

If you want to use advanced pranayama, these breathing practices need to be introduced gradually into your practice. As a prerequisite for advanced pranayama, it is suggested that you use the breathing practices for beginners for one year. A daily routine for beginners is presented for your consideration at the end of this chapter.

You can begin employing advanced pranayama by replacing your regular practice of Rapid Abdominal Breathing with Bellow Breathing that uses breath retention. When you feel ready to do so, you can introduce the use of the yoga locks by practicing Advanced Alternate Nostril Breathing. Later after practicing Bellows Breathing, which does not include yoga locks, you can add Advanced Bellows Breathing, which does include yoga locks.

If you become experienced in practicing advanced pranayama, you may want to use the following sequence of techniques as a preparation for your meditation practice:

1. Advanced Alternate Nostril Breathing
2. Bellows Breathing

Eventually, you may want to use a more advanced combination, as follows:

1. Advanced Alternate Nostril Breathing
2. Advanced Bellows Breathing (without the Diaphragm Lock) or Alternate Nostril Advanced Bellows Breathing (without the Diaphragm Lock)

In using these methods with yoga locks, you practice no more than three rounds of each pranayama. But you can increase this to three rounds after you use daily advanced breathing methods for one year. When you start using these practices, during breath retention you can focus on inviting the Holy Spirit into the bottom of the spine to help you loosen the lowest knot in the body. If you feel the creative energy consistently rising up from the lower part of the spine, during breath retention you can focus on inviting the Holy Spirit into the cardiac plexus in the spine to assist in loosening the second knot.

After somewhat loosening the first major knot and raising energy in the lower spine and partially loosening the second knot and raising energy in the middle spine, you may feel guided to focus on freeing up energy in the head. If you are ready to introduce a means of loosening the third major knot, you can focus your awareness on the brow center during the breath retention of the advanced breathing practices. Your focusing during breath retention and during holding the yoga locks is always an invitation for the Holy Spirit to be in charge of your inner transformation process. It is also an opportunity for devotion.

After several years of experience, you may want to include the Diaphragm Lock in your practice of Advanced Bellows Breathing in order to draw prana up from the torso into the head. It is always important to use the Neck Hold, in which the neck is maintained in a straight alignment with the head and back, while using advanced pranayama and in particular when using the Diaphragm Lock.

H. SECONDARY BREATHING PRACTICES

Some yoga schools offer about ten different kinds of pranayama, while other yoga schools may advocate over seventy different kinds of pranayama. The most important forms of pranayama have been described previously. However, the following sections describe some additional secondary breathing practices:

1. SUN BREATHING

Sun Breathing (Surya Bheda Pranayama)[128] increases the body heat and helps to bring prana to the susumna. For this pranayama, you close the left nostril and inhale slowly and deeply through the right nostril without making a sound. After the inhalation, you close the right nostril so both nostrils are closed for breath retention, and you apply the Chin Lock. After the breath retention, you release the Chin Lock and exhale through the left nostril only. During Sun Breathing, every inhalation is through the right nostril (followed by the Chin Lock and breath retention) and every exhalation is through the left nostril. In yoga philosophy the right nostril breath is hot, accelerates the activity of the body organs, and is associated with the sun and the pingala nadi. This practice may bring about excessive perspiration, can clear the sinuses, and is effectively used during the colder times of the year. Sun Breathing is practiced without the Chin Lock by beginners, and then after gaining experience with pranayama, the Chin Lock can be implemented.

2. MOON BREATHING

Moon Breathing (Chandra Bhedana Pranayama)[129] can be a way to remove excess heat in the body and overcome tiredness. The practice of Moon Breathing is the mirror image of the practice of the Sun Breath. For Moon Breathing, you close the right nostril and inhale slowly and deeply through the left nostril without making any sound. After the end of the inhalation, you close the left nostril so both nostrils are closed, and you apply the Chin Lock. After the breath retention, you exhale through the right nostril only. Every inhalation is through the left nostril and every exhalation is through the right nostril for Moon Breathing. In yoga philosophy, the left nostril breath is cool, inhibits the activity of the body organs, and is associated with the moon and the ida nadi. Because of the cooling effect of Moon Breathing, it is most effectively practiced in the warmer times of the year. Beginners do not use the Chin Lock for Moon Breathing, but they can include the Chin Lock after becoming experienced in using pranayama.

3. HUMMING BREATH

Humming Breath (Bhramari Pranayama)[130] can be used to prepare the mind for meditation and can help to make the voice sweeter. For this breathing practice, you use Yoga Deep Breathing to inhale deeply through both nostrils in order to expand the lungs to full capacity. With the mouth closed, you exhale through both nostrils, and you make a humming sound similar to the sound of a bee. You allow the humming sound to vibrate throughout the head and in particular, feel this sound vibrating through the soft palate.

4. DIGESTIVE FIRE BREATH

Digestive Fire Breath (Ujjayi Pranayama)[131] promotes digestion and purify the nerves. For this practice, you inhale through both nostrils but bring the breath only from the throat to the heart. You close off both nostrils, apply the Chin Lock, and retain the breath. After the breath retention, you release the Chin Lock and exhale very slowly with full control through the left nostril only. You always inhale through both nostrils and exhale through the left nostril. The key element is limiting your breathing to allow the inhaled air to not go below the heart so you do not expand the abdomen on the inhalation as you would for Yoga Deep Breathing. Thus you inhale from the nasal passages to the throat and from the throat to the heart. You exhale from the heart to the throat and from the throat to the left nostril. The Chin Lock is not used by beginners, but it can be added to your practice of Digestive Fire Breath after first gaining experience in practicing pranayama.

5. ALTERNATE NOSTRIL EXHALING BREATH

Alternate Nostril Exhaling Breath (Urasthala Shuddhi Pranayama)[132] uses both nostrils for all inhalations and uses alternate nostril breathing only for exhalations. After inhaling through both nostrils, you close off the right nostril and exhale forcefully through the left nostril. Next you inhale through both nostrils, close off the left nostril, and exhale through the right nostril forcefully. You continue to alternate exhalations from one nostril to the other. You make your last exhalation through the right nostril and then allow your breathing to return to normal. This breathing practice reduces phlegm and cleans the nose, throat, and lungs. The Alternate Nostril Exhaling Breath also cleanses the nadis, and it has a calming effect on the mind.

Although Pranayama is the control of breathing, sometimes it is best to allow your breathing to just be, without controlling it. For example, in meditation, it is best to allow your breathing pattern to slow down naturally without attempting to manipulate it in any way. Nevertheless, while doing meditation, some form of unusual spontaneous breathing pattern may possibly manifest. If this happens, you can simply allow the breathing to continue in this spontaneous manner until it runs its course and your breathing slows down again.

I. DAILY PRANAYAMA ROUTINE FOR BEGINNERS

If you want to practice meditation, hatha yoga postures, and also pranayama, it is essential to develop a daily routine for these spiritual disciplines. If your daily meditation is in the morning, it is ideal to meditate first before the postures and pranayama. To help clear the mind in the morning, you can do the Eye Exercises (page 132). Just before practicing sitting meditation, you can use a relaxation practice, such as the Head and Neck Exercise, (page 131), recommended in the Edgar Cayce readings.[133] After completing your meditation, you can practice hatha yoga postures followed by your pranayama practice. But in the afternoon or evening, the best sequence is pranayama followed by your meditation practice. If you use yoga postures in the afternoon or evening, these can be practiced prior to practicing pranayama. Of course, any one of the three spiritual disciplines of hatha yoga postures, pranayama, or meditation can be practiced alone at any time. Yet the most significant thing you can do in regard to your postures, breathing practices, and meditation is establishing and being committed to a consistent routine that you can follow every day.

Since a minimum of twenty-five minutes of meditation is suggested as a daily practice, a lesser commitment of about twenty minutes is recommended for the combination of your hatha yoga body postures and breathing practices. At the end of the Chapter 4 on page 150, there is a suggested *Beginners' Daily Routine of Yoga Postures*. Below is a beginner's guideline for breathing practices:

THE FIVE-MINUTE PRANAYAMA ROUTINE

1. Yoga Deep Breathing
2. Rapid Abdominal Breathing
3. Alternate Nostril Breathing
4. Yoga Seal

For this daily routine, you can practice two or three rounds of each of the three breathing practices indicated above. Only a five-minute session of pranayama is suggested for beginners because it is best to start slowly and gradually increase the time for pranayama if you feel guided to do so. It is recommended that beginners start using breathing practices without breath retention such as the ones indicated above. If you want to use only one breathing practice, the most beneficial single pranayama is Alternate Nostril Breathing because of its purifying effect on the nadis.

As you make progress in pranayama, you can incorporate breath retention in your pranayama as long as you experience no discomfort in your practice. In order to introduce breath retention, you can begin practicing Full Alternate Nostril Breathing to replace your practice of Alternate Nostril Breathing. You can slowly increase the duration of your pranayama practice if you feel guided to do so.

After one year of using pranayama every day, you may want to gradually introduce some of the advanced breathing practices into your daily practice. Just as with your hatha yoga postures, your pranayama practice is always concluded with the Yoga Seal, except in those cases when your breathing practices are employed as a preparation for your meditation practice.

J. NASAL CLEANING — JALA OR WATER NETI

There are several body purification methods, called "kriyas." One kriya is *Rapid Abdominal Breathing*, also called the *Breath of Fire*, which has already been described previously. This kriya is also called *Skull Shining* (Kapalabhati Pranayama).[134] The word "kapalbhati" is made up of two words, "kapal" meaning skull and "bhati" meaning shining or illuminating. Due to this breathing practice, the organs inside the skull, mainly the brain, are beneficially influenced.

Another kriya is *Nasal Cleaning*, called "Jala Neti" or "Water Neti." Modern science calls this procedure as a nasal wash or nasal irrigation.

The Centers for Disease Control (CDC) offers guidelines for a nasal wash, and the CDC mentions the following benefits:

Many people with asthma or other lung problems also have nasal and sinus symptoms. Drainage from your nose and sinuses can make asthma worse, especially at night. Using a saltwater nasal wash or nasal irrigation can help reduce this.

A nasal wash:
Cleans bacteria and viruses from the nose, which decreases infections. Cleans mucus from the nose, which makes medication more effective. Cleans allergens and irritants from the nose, reducing their impact. Decreases swelling in the nose and increases airflow.[135]

Bo Stapler, MD, shares his personal experience of nasal irrigation:

For the past three years each morning and evening I make my way to the bathroom sink, fill a plastic squirt bottle with sterilized water, and add a packet of salt. I then rinse out my sinuses. The medical term for this is nasal irrigation. The first time I tried it I felt like I was waterboarding myself. But I quickly became used to it, and now it creates a fresh, easy-to-breathe feeling that I wouldn't want to go without.[136]

Below are two techniques recommended by the CDC. The first of these methods is the one used by Bo Stapler, MD, as follows:

Sinus Rinse Kit Technique (best method)—The Sinus Rinse Kit comes with a Sinus Rinse bottle and mixture packets. When using the Sinus Rinse Kit, or you can use the prepared mixture packets that come with the kit, or you can make your own nasal wash solution described above. The Sinus Rinse bottle is filled with saltwater. The bottle is placed against the nostril. After the bottle is squeezed, saltwater comes out the opposite nostril and may come out the mouth. The nose is then blown gently. The procedure is then repeated with the other nostril.

Bulb Syringe Technique (alternate method)— Use a large all-rubber ear syringe. An ear bulb syringe can be purchased at most pharmacies. Fill the syringe completely with saltwater. Insert the syringe tip just inside your nostril, and pinch your nostril around the tip of the bulb syringe to keep the solution from coming out of your nose. Gently squeeze the bulb to swish the solution around in your nose; then blow your nose lightly. Next repeat the procedure with the other nostril.[137]

A research study was done in 2019 to find out if sinus rinsing with a saltwater would have a positive effect on the symptoms and reduce the transmission of Upper Respiratory Infections (URIs). This study was conducted in Edinburgh, Scotland and was called "ELVIS," standing for the Edinburgh and Lothians Viral Intervention Study. The results of this study are summarized in this way by Bo Stapler, MD:

Data from ELVIS showed saline rinses reduce the duration of URI symptoms by an average of 1.9 days and decrease viral transmission by 35%. Both of these findings were considered statistically significant. Previous research indicated that saline could reduce viral replication and enhance the activity of the body's innate immune system. The mechanism of viral inhibition by saline (i.e. sodium chloride or NaCl) is thought to be related to the chloride (Cl) ion. When mixed with water, chloride can form HOCl (hydrogen, oxygen, and chloride) which is the active ingredient in bleach.[138]

The last part of the previous quotation provides an explanation of why saltwater can protect the body from viruses. Epithelial cells line the internal organs, and this research seems to indicate that these cells can produce an antiviral effect when saltwater is present. These epithelial cells produce hypochlorous acid from the chloride ions that are found in saltwater. "Hypochlorous acid is the active ingredient in bleach. Epithelial cells could trigger a natural immune mechanism, allowing the body to defend itself against viruses."[139]

What kind of viruses were affected by saltwater in the ELVIS study? The authors of the research study state that the following different viruses were detected in the Elvis study: Regarding the different viruses detected in the ELVIS study, the authors state: *"56% were rhinovirus and 31% were coronaviruses, with the rest due to enterovirus, influenza A virus, parainfluenza virus type 3, respiratory syncytial virus and human metapneumovirus."*[140]

The ELVIS project was designed to primarily focus on treatment for the common cold. Nevertheless, perhaps you are asking yourself this question: Can saltwater nasal irrigation can be beneficial as a treatment for patients suffering from Covid-19? In 2020 the Edinburg research group launched a new research project to answer this question. This future study will be similar to the previous ELVIS project and is called "ELVIS-COVID-19." As of the publishing date of this book, this study has not been completed so in the future you can do a Google search to find out the results for yourself.

The previous ELVIS research project was designed to be focused on patients who already showed symptoms of the common cold, and the new ELVIS-COVID-19 investigation is designed to focus on patients who are already showing symptoms of Covid-19. But what about employing saltwater to prevent viruses from reaching the lungs, therefore removing viruses before they can even multiply and cause symptoms? Science has determined that it takes about two days for the coronavirus to incubate, and then it may or may not produce symptoms, depending upon the specific immune system of the body. The body can take in the airborne coronavirus through the mouth and/or through the nasal passages.

All my adult life I have been taking Edgar Cayce's advice to brush my teeth with salt and baking soda (two parts of salt to one part of baking soda). I don't remember ever having a cold. Once a month, I have used a yoga form of nasal irrigation called "Water Neti." After tilting the head to one side, I pour salty water into one nostril and out the other nostril, and then I alternate this process by starting with pouring up the other nostril. At the end, I let a little saltwater go into one nostril and down the throat one time, and then I pour water into the other nostril and down the throat one time.

Yoga recommends using what is called a "neti pot," designed for nasal irrigation so water will not be spilled onto the outside of the body. Instead of using a neti pot, I have used a simple plastic cup (or two plastic cups). The reason why a plastic cup works well for me is that I only do Water Neti inside the shower enclosure before I take my evening shower. Since I am naked, I don't have to be concerned about water spilling on my body. I put a small amount of salt in the water of the cup, but the CDC suggests the option of also adding a tiny pinch of baking soda. During the Covid-19 pandemic, I switched from a monthly nasal irrigation to a daily nasal irrigation. I had no symptoms of Covid-19. I recommend regular Water Neti practice as a means of preventing Covid-19 and other respiratory diseases.

I have taken the Pfizer vaccine. After the first shot, I had a slight arm soreness and was briefly light-headed. Right after the second shot, there were no symptoms. Two weeks later, I experienced repeated dizziness, light-headedness, or "brain fog." These symptoms went away after one week of adding a quarter teaspoon of ginger powder to my morning tea, increasing my yoga breathing practices, using carbamide peroxide to remove wax in both ears, and taking one enema to cleanse the system. Using physical means to heal body symptoms is what the Course calls "magic," which is suggested to reduce fear. I also focused on God's Love since His Love will cure self-inflicted guilt that causes all sickness.

K. COLON CLEANSING — JALA-BASTI

Another yoga kriya is a colon cleansing method with water called *"Jala-basti."* Colon cleansing can treat an impacted colon that could be a breeding ground for infection and for disease. The yoga colon cleaning methods were designed thousands of years ago, long before the advent of the modern-day enema bag. Thus the enema bag is recommended here as a more convenient and more effective means of cleansing the colon rather than using the ancient yoga method. Edgar Cayce recommended doing colon cleansing four times a year at the change of the four seasons. If I occasionally feel low energy as though I might possibly get sick, I have an enema and find it to be revitalizing. Therefore, I believe using an enema prevents sickness.

There are different ways to take an enema, but I use the following procedure for taking an enema: I follow Cayce's recommendation to add a heaping teaspoon of salt and a level teaspoon of baking soda to the enema bag before I add the water. I start by adding a small amount of hot water to the enema bag in order to fully dissolve the salt and baking soda. Then I add more water so the full enema bag has a lukewarm temperature. I use olive oil as a lubricant in order to comfortably insert the plastic tip of the enema bag into the anus while sitting on the toilet. After that, I lay down on the floor on my back. I allow all of the water in the enema bag to flow slowly into the colon and then disconnect my body from the enema bag.

Next I lay down on my left side. Then I do a shoulder stand, which is not suggested for a yoga beginner, but I find it helpful in order to circulate the water so it reaches all parts of the lower intestine. As I lower my body from the vertical position of the shoulder stand, I twist my body so my body is turned to the right side as it returns to the horizontal position on the floor. Then I wait as the water flows into the right side of the lower intestine. After waiting with the body lying on the right side, I do another shoulder stand. Then as I lower my body from the vertical shoulder stand, I twist my body turning it to the left side as it returns to the horizontal position on the floor. By resting on the left side, the water returns to the left side of the large intestine. Finally, I sit on the toilet in order to release all the loosened up fecal matter and thus complete this procedure for using the enema.

This process is usually done without doing a shoulder stand. Even without the shoulder stand option, many people do not like the idea of doing a regular enema and would rather visit a dentist for a root canal instead of having an enema. Yet, one of my brother's had colon cancer, and I believe that would not have happened if he regularly cleaned out his colon so it never got even partially impacted.

L. CENTRAL ABDOMEN CONTRACTION—MADHYAMA NAULI

The manipulating abdominal muscles, "Nauli Kriya," helps fosters healthy intestines and bowel movements. You prepare for practicing *Madhyama Nauli* (Central Contraction) by standing and practicing the Diaphragm Lock (Stomach Lift, page 162), in which you make a strong exhalation and fully contract the diaphragm. While in this standing position, you release contacting the center of the abdomen while contracting both the left and right sides of the abdomen.

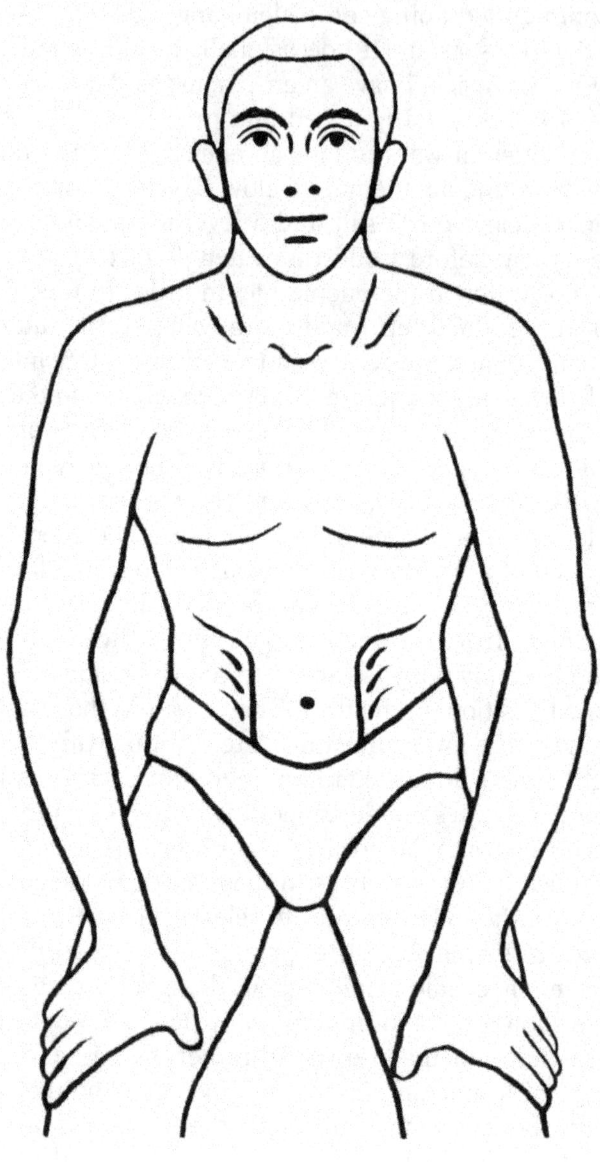

M. LEFT ABDOMEN CONTRACTION— DAKSHINA NAULI

After learning the Central Contraction, you need to gain control over the left and right abdominal muscles abdomen separately. For *Dakshina Nauli* (Left Contraction), you start from doing the Central Contraction. Then you contract the left abdominal muscles. The left hand presses on the left thigh. You bend the upper body forward and slightly to the left. The contraction of the left abdominal muscles forms a cavity in the right side and a muscle protrusion on the left side.

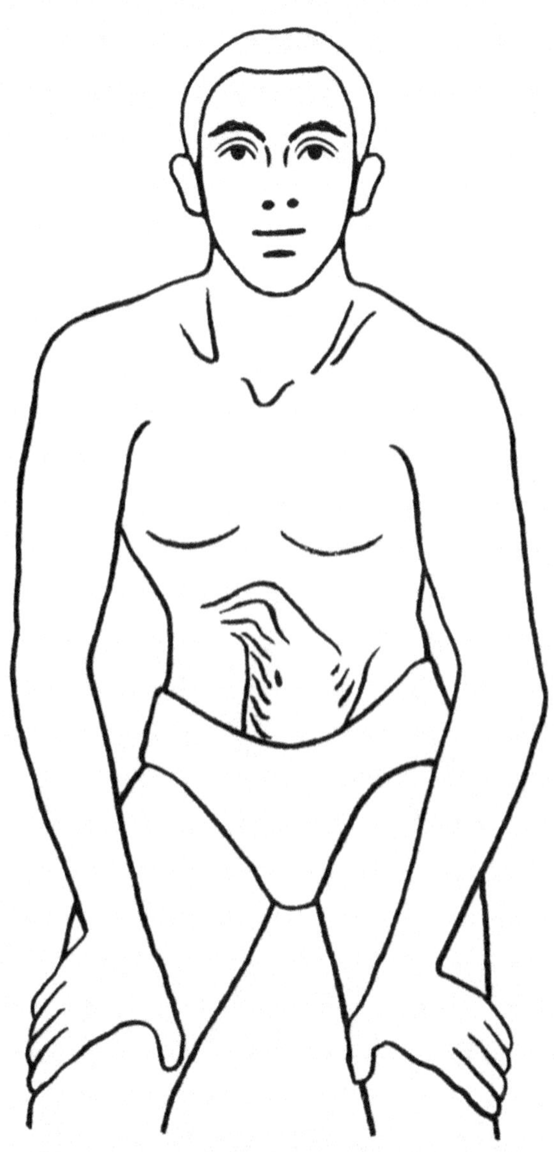

N. RIGHT ABDOMEN CONTRACTION — VAMA NAULI

You start *Vama Nauli* (Right Contraction) by doing the Central Contraction. Then you contract the right abdominal muscles. The right hand presses on the right thigh. You bend the upper body forward and to the right. For the real Nauli Kriya (*Nauli Proper*), you practice the Left Contraction and then the Right Contraction and continue to alternate contractions from side to side. You can also learn to rotate abdominal muscles clockwise and then counterclockwise.

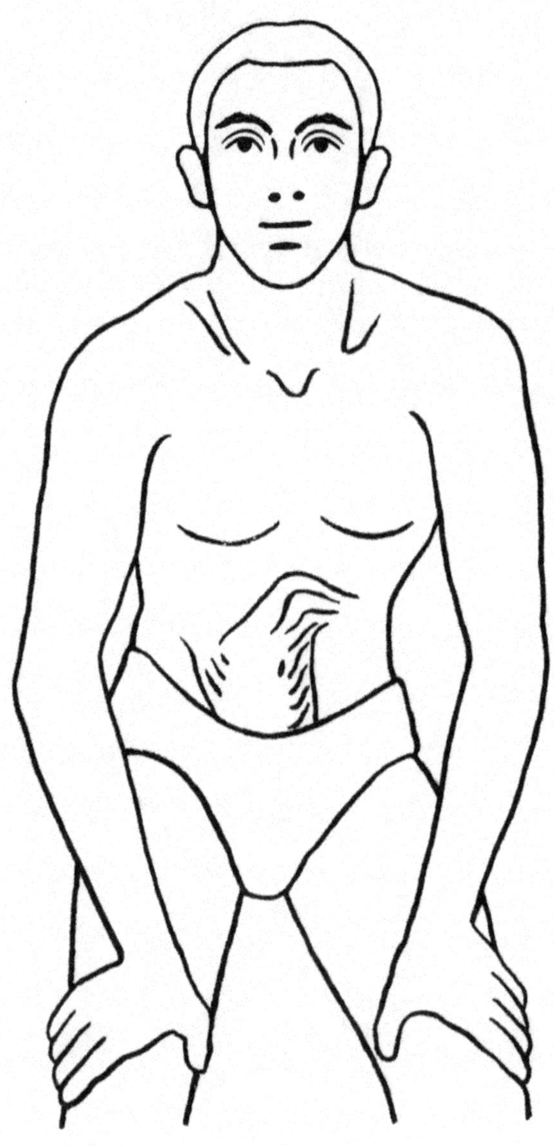

CHAPTER 6

~ • ~

EAST/WEST PHILOSOPHIES

A. THE EDGAR CAYCE READINGS

Practicing yoga does not require or encourage you to leave your church or religious affiliation or set aside the any practices of your faith. Since yoga can be practiced as part of your personal spiritual practice, it should not conflict with collective forms of worship. But the merging of East and West in practicing yoga by Christians can cause unexpected problems. What if your church or your religious group looks negatively at your interest in yoga? You could come into conflict with members of your religious group who may imagine that you are abandoning Jesus. Even if you do not have any conflict with others, you could have a philosophical conflict within yourself caused by your interpretation of your religious beliefs and Eastern philosophy. You can hopefully resolve any internal conflict without leaving your religious organization and without abandoning yoga.

Some who combine Christianity and yoga discover that the gap between their Christian organization's philosophy and the philosophy of yoga is so great that they need to release one or the other to find inner peace. I found myself in this position at one time and decided to look for a new Christian philosophy that could span the gap for me between the East and West. I found this new integrated philosophy in the Edgar Cayce readings. He is called the "sleeping prophet" because many years ago, he would do trance "readings" and answer people's questions. Often his readings addressed ways for individuals to receive physical healing, but these readings always contained spiritual content. The readings were spiritually focused primarily on Christ but did not hesitate to incorporate Eastern influences.

I was attracted to the belief in reincarnation, but this belief was not compatible with traditional Christian beliefs. The Edgar Cayce readings affirmed my own belief in reincarnation, and at the same time, they presented Christ as the pattern for each seeker to follow in returning to

God. These readings affirmed the belief in awakening the kundalini as an important part of the process of spiritual development. One of the Edgar Cayce readings was for a person who was practicing yoga, and he was told that the yoga practices are beneficial provided that the proper preparations are made, as follows:

> These exercises are excellent, yet it is necessary that special preparations be made—or that a perfect understanding be had by the body as to what takes place when such exercises are used.
>
> For, BREATH is the basis of the living organism's activity. Thus such exercises may be beneficial or detrimental in their effect upon the body.
>
> Hence it is necessary that an understanding be had as to how, as to when, or in what manner such may be used.[141]

The Edgar Cayce readings gave a very interesting interpretation of the Bible's Revelation. According to his readings, Revelation is not primarily about outer events, but rather about the human body as a vehicle for spiritual transformation. The seven churches mentioned in Revelation are actually seven spiritual centers within the body. These seven centers are the endocrine glands in the body and each is related to either a nerve plexus or a part of the head, as follows:

1. gonads — related to the sacral (coccygeal) plexus
2. leydig (navel area) — related to the lumbar (prostatic) plexus
3. adrenal glands — related to the solar (epigastric) plexus
4. thymus gland — related to the cardiac plexus
5. thyroid gland — related to the cervical (laryngeal) plexus
6. pineal gland — related to the medulla oblongata
7. pituitary gland — related to the crown of head (and cerebrum)

This information was a Christian philosophical confirmation of my belief in yoga philosophy related to the seven centers of awareness, called *chakras*. The Edgar Cayce readings confirmed the importance of awaking the spiritual centers in the body and described the opening of the seven seals as the step-by-step process of awakening these centers. Also, these readings focused on choosing an ideal and then practicing meditation directed toward your chosen ideal, preferably in Christ. In conformity with Eastern practices, the Edgar Cayce readings spoke of various parts of the body as being important in relation to meditation. For example, Edgar Cayce recommended focusing your attention in meditation on the forehead, which has been called the "third eye."

Ray Stanford also gave psychic readings that were very similar to the Edgar Cayce readings. The readings of Ray Stanford refer to the area between the pineal gland and the pituitary gland as the "third-eye center."[142] This area associated with the space between the eyebrows and behind the brow is suggested as a focusing point for meditation. In his book *Spirit unto the Churches,* Ray Stanford describes the seven churches identified in Revelation as being seven spiritual centers, just as is indicated in the Edgar Cayce readings. Many yoga schools state that the pineal gland is related to the seventh and the highest spiritual center and the pituitary gland is related to the sixth center. Both the Edgar Cayce readings and Stanford readings reverse these, stating that the pineal gland is related to the sixth center and the pituitary gland is related to the seventh center. Physiologically the pituitary gland is the master gland that controls all the other endocrine glands, including the pineal gland, which seems to confirm the correctness of the pituitary gland being associated with the highest spiritual center.

The nature of the "leydig" center is described in the Edgar Cayce readings, but in addition, it is elaborated upon in Ray Stanford's book, *Spirit unto the Churches*, as follows:

> The testes contain "interstitial cells" which were discovered by F. Leydig, a 19th century medical researcher. The function of these "cells of Leydig" is not fully understood, but it is accepted that they produce testosterone, which is responsible for development of the male sex organs, beard growth, etc. Interstitial cells are also found in the female ovaries and in the adrenal glands of both sexes, and these too are believed to have hormone-producing functions.[143]

Endocrine glands secrete hormones that are carried by the blood or lymph to another part of the body whose functions it regulates. Generally speaking, the leydig center is associated with the navel area but actually involves cells in both the gonads and the adrenal glands that can produce hormones as any endocrine gland can. The leydig center is related to temptation and is like a doorway that allows the downward flowing sexual energy to be reversed and turned upward within the body for spiritual growth. Centering Meditation focuses on the navel area, which allows the leydig center to serve as this doorway that allows creative energy to rise upward for spiritual purposes.

The readings of Edgar Cayce and Ray Stanford were helpful for me in adopting a Christian-based philosophy generally consistent with Eastern philosophy. Nevertheless, these readings did not enable me to resolve one specific conflicting issue for me between Christianity and yoga—the issue of the nature of the soul and Christian dualism versus Eastern monism. Some schools of yoga say that the freed soul loses all individuality and becomes universal by melting into Brahman, the Creator, corresponding to God, the Father, in Christianity. These yoga schools speak of the true Self, which is called the "Atman," also called the "Purusha." In a paradox that is not conceptually explainable, souls are individualized expressions of God, and at the same time, every soul shares the same true Self. Every time I studied yoga philosophy and I saw the word "Atman" or the word "Purusha," I would mentally write in "Christ," as a replacement for the yoga word. It seemed to me that the Christ is the one Self that every individual soul shares.

Nevertheless, the ultimate end of the Atman or Purusha is to lose individuality and become Brahman. But I believe as most Christians that the soul remains individual even when it becomes universal. So I was hoping to find a Christian philosophy that supported the yoga belief that every soul shares the one Self (the Christ or Christ Self), but a philosophy that also affirms the Christian idea that the soul retains its individuality even in the state of divine union with God. The Edgar Cayce material hinted at the idea of a universal Christ Consciousness shared by all, but there was never a direct statement that Christ is the one Self that every soul shares while remaining individual.

Your understanding of the nature of the soul depends on whether you believe in *dualism* or *nondualism,* also called *monism.* The dualism of Christianity maintains that the soul is separate from God now and needs to become joined to God in the future. Eastern monism states that the individual is living in an illusion of seeming separation. When the illusion disappears, the individual will awaken to the truth of his pre-existing union with God, which was previously unrecognized.

My conflict was that I did not believe in the dualism of Christianity and also did not believe in the absolute nondualism of Vedanta. I was seeking a *qualified nondualism.* Pure nondualism says the soul is God and upon awakening dissolves into God and loses its individuality. The qualifying factor I sought was the affirmation that Christ is the one Self each soul shares allowing the soul to simultaneously be individual and universal. I was hoping to come across a theology or philosophy that was based on this Christian qualified nondualism in which the soul in union with God is both individual and universal. For a long time, I could not find this qualified nondualism that is a marriage of Western dualism and Eastern nondualism. Then it suddenly did appear! It was *A Course in Miracles.*[144] As so often happens, when you get what you want, it may take a while to decide that you really did want it. It took me many years of skepticism to finally accept the principles of *A Course in Miracles,* which will be elaborated upon next.

B. "*A COURSE IN MIRACLES*" AS AN OPTION

Some who are already students of the Course and who are also familiar with yoga will be attracted to the description in this book of Miracle Yoga. However, this section addresses some readers who are not yet Course students, but who are Christians interested in yoga and who may want to know more about the Course.

The sacred scripture of Vedanta is the scriptural and the intellectual foundation for the practice of traditional Hindu jnana yoga. Vedanta provides a complete thought system that clearly defines the complete theology of nondualism. This complete thought system is absolutely necessary for the jnana yogi to study. He must place his whole faith in the truth that is presented in this writing. Based upon his study and faith in the truth, the jnana yogi sees through the illusions of the world and affirms the presence of God behind every illusion. Those who wish to practice a Christian form of yoga with an emphasis on a Christian jnana yoga would need a complete Christian thought system that also incorporates Eastern principles. This thought system would be needed for the practice of Christian jnana yoga so that the seeker could study the truth and place his faith in the truth.

If you want to practice some form of Christian yoga and if you mainly want to practice a Christian jnana yoga, how do you find a complete East/West thought system as a basis for your practice? There are two basic options: The first and most obvious choice is for you to form your own theology. Many seekers informally formulate their own "buffet style" theology by just picking up ideas here and there from Eastern and Western sources. Yet if you want to practice Christian jnana yoga and have an intellectual inclination, a more comprehensive and systematic approach would be needed. This would involve studying many different Christian and Eastern philosophies and also reading books of writers who have attempted to synthesize different theologies. For example, you would want to study the writings of Aldous Huxley and Huston Smith on the "Perennial Philosophy," which is an attempt to identify the universal principles of truth underlying all religions. Then after this study, you would have to piece together your own individual blending of Christian and Eastern philosophy to use as your basis for seeking the divine through discrimination and spiritual insight.

The second basic option you may want to consider is adopting *A Course in Miracles* as your thought system for practicing Christian jnana yoga that I call "Miracle Jnana Yoga." Of course, you will have to study this material first to see if it is suitable to you. Those who are attracted to a Christian form of karma yoga may find the teachings of the Course too lofty and too removed from practical application in daily life. Christians who are drawn to bhakti yoga may believe the Course is not focused enough on the heart and devotion. Christians who lean toward raja yoga may find that there is not enough emphasis in the Course on meditation and contemplation.

However, I am suggesting in this book that you include all aspects of yoga in your following of Christ, and jnana yoga would need to be included for balance. Your choice of a thought system will affect the other aspects of yoga. If you practice Christian jnana yoga, it will take time for you to decide if the thought system of the Course will be helpful for you. To make that determination, you will have to take the time to carefully examine the principles of the Course. First you may decide to include some selected ideas of the Course into your own thought system. Eventually you may become convinced that you can adopt these principles as a whole. Some individuals adopt the Course itself as their entire path, and you may choose to take that direction. For your expression of joining Christianity and yoga, I am advocating that you specifically practice Miracle Yoga based on the Course. Then you can allow the entire thought system of the Course to become the foundation for your practice of Miracle Jnana Yoga, as a balanced part of your overall practice of Miracle Yoga.

Just as Vedanta is the basis for traditional Hindu yoga, *A Course in Miracles* is a new kind of "Christian Vedanta," forming the basis for Miracle Yoga. The explanation of the Course provided in this chapter and in some later chapters is written for seekers who are open to the option of adopting or being exposed to ideas that are a synthesis of the East and West. But this discussion of the Course is only intended to be a superficial presentation of Course ideas, which will hopefully give you enough information for you to decide if you would like to pursue the option of studying the Course itself.

Next Miracle Jnana Yoga will be described. This information will be interesting to committed Course students and may be interesting to individuals who would like to practice Christian yoga that emphasizes Christian jnana yoga. Such Christian yoga seekers may be interested in adopting some Course ideas without becoming totally committed Course students. Individuals who want to emphasize Christian jnana yoga tend to be intellectually inclined and thus would be predisposed toward studying philosophy. Such individuals would find the Course concepts to be intellectually stimulating and very helpful in practicing discrimination. Traditional Hindu jnana yoga is a path of spiritual insight into the awareness of the true Self. Similarly, Miracle Jnana Yoga is a means of seeking clear insight into the awareness of your true nature, but this seeking is expressed through the understanding and application of *forgiveness*.

The Course says forgiveness is "the healing of the perception of separation."[145] Forgiveness is healing produced by looking past the appearances of separation. Since the perception of separation that is manifested by the ego is an illusion, forgiveness is the practice of discriminating between the real and unreal, similar to the traditional practice of jnana yoga. The Course student who practices forgiveness sees beyond the illusions of the world, but his main goal is not to see God directly as is the case in traditional Hindu jnana yoga. The seeker who practices Miracle Jnana Yoga keeps the goal of seeing the divine in his brother and indirectly seeing the divine within himself. Seeing guiltlessness in his brother, he recognizes his own guiltlessness. Seeing holiness in his brother, he finds holiness in himself. The Course itself is a whole thought system designed to manifest external and internal forgiveness and release the entire belief in guilt.

Similar to traditional Hindu jnana yoga, Miracle Jnana Yoga of forgiveness has three aspects: The first aspect is the comprehensive thought system of the Course as the basis for spiritual growth. The second aspect is the practice of carefully studying this thought system in order to thoroughly understand it. The third aspect is the application of this thought system to daily life. This application portion has both an internal meditative component that is directed toward God and an external expressive component that is related to outer perceptions of the world. In Hindu jnana yoga, the internal meditative component is more important than the external expressive component. In practicing the Course, the external expressive component, which focuses on true perception of the other people and the world, is more important than the inward meditative component. The Course focuses mainly on the external expressive component for the purpose of developing loving relationships and manifesting forgiveness.

The Course is a course in mind training set forth in three books for personal study and application. The first book is the *Text*, which presents the theological and philosophical thought system that is the basis for this course of study. The second book is the *Workbook for Students*, which is a one-year course of daily instructions to provide the practical application of the thought system. The third book is the *Manual for Teachers* for those who have learned the Course principles and would like to share their learning with others. The Course is not a religion and is not associated with a church, but many Course students do come together for local grassroots study groups.

The Course brings the ideas of Eastern philosophy into a Western context that can be applied by Christians of any denomination or even by followers of Christ who are not affiliated with any church. In addition to being inclusive of Eastern philosophy, the Course also includes in a profound understanding of psychology from a spiritual perspective. This unique synthesis of Eastern and Western philosophy and theology with psychology has attracted many spiritual seekers and from its inception in the seventies has had an amazing growth spurt with no initial advertising.

The Course does not use the word "meditation" to refer to its mind training methods, but it does foster inward mental focusing consistent with meditation techniques. The most common method recommended in the Course is focusing on the divine presence. This involves mentally repeating an affirmation of inspiring words only if thoughts temporarily distract you from feeling the divine presence. A few Workbook lessons recommend repeating God's Name. The Course suggests calling on the name of Jesus, especially when asking for healing, as a recognition of God, rather than as a reference to the man who walked the earth over two thousand years ago. The Course maintains that all names, even divine names, are merely symbols, and the name of Jesus is no exception. But this symbol of God's Word is so close in meaning to what it symbolizes that calling upon the name of Jesus Christ has the same effect as calling upon God Himself. The name of Jesus can safely be used for meditation, as well as for healing, guidance, or help, since Jesus is available to those who call upon him.

The Course offers many familiar spiritual concepts but explains them in a systematic and complete way. For example, concepts of the ego as the false self and your true nature as the true Self are found in Eastern philosophy, but the Course presents these concepts in a Western context that includes the psychological understanding of these concepts. Even though the concepts of the Course appeal to me, I was initially very skeptical about this material because the Course was psychically channeled and the source of the channeling claimed to be Jesus himself. I have researched channeled material many times and each time have discovered internal inconsistencies in the information that revealed its inaccuracies.

Nevertheless, after years of studying the Course, I have found no internal inconsistencies. In fact, what sets this thought system apart from any other thought system is its entirely unified nature. Because the Course is so unified, I believe that studying this unified thought system greatly enhances the development of a unified mind.

This entire thought system is too comprehensive to describe fully here, but it may be helpful to explain some relevant Course principles. The relationship between good and evil is one example of an internal inconsistency that I have found in other thought systems but not in the Course. Most Christian thought systems believe God is Love. Yet these same thought systems believe in the reality of a world in which fear, hate, suffering, and all kinds of evil are common occurrences. The internal inconsistency is that if God is Love, how could He create a world in which painful experiences are possible?

If you believe in the Hindu thought system that says the world is an illusion, you have only partly resolved the inconsistency in the thought system by saying that the world is only an illusion. The Hindu thought system describes the illusory world as "divine play," yet this description does not fit with the human experience of the world as a place with some joy, but also much suffering. Therefore, the Hindu thought system is internally inconsistent because it does not explain why a God of Love would create even an illusory world where men could experience pain.

The Course has no internal inconsistency in this regard because it states that God is Love, and therefore He could not create a world of negative emotions and suffering nor could He create even an illusory world of pain. The Course explains that the world along with time and space is an illusion that was made by man not God. From your current viewpoint of the ego, this is an incredible idea that you would probably never even consider as a possibility. On the other hand, if you consider that you are not the ego, but rather a spiritual being extended from God, it becomes credible.

The Course states that the way this happened is that God created one Son, who is the Christ. This one Christ had many parts that are each a perfect Thought extended from God. Each part is complete and whole. Simultaneously, each part is perfectly equal to every other part of this one Sonship that is the Christ. But some parts of the Sonship did not want to be equal and asked God for special love or, as the Course calls it, "special favor," as follows:

> You were at peace until you asked for special favor. And God did not give it for the request was alien to Him, and you could not ask this of a Father Who truly loved His Son. Therefore, you made of Him an unloving father, demanding Him what only such a father could give. And the peace of God's Son was shattered, for he no longer understood his Father.[146]

God could not answer this request for special love because He could only give equal love to all parts of the Sonship. The parts of the Sonship that were denied special love decided to separate from their oneness with God. But they could not separate from reality or from

God, since they could only exist in reality as God had created them and God had created them as extensions of Himself. Extensions of God are part of God and will always remain part of God.

Although these parts of the Sonship could not really separate, they wanted to find autonomy apart from God. In order to find autonomy from God, they would have to disavow God's Authorship of them. To do this they would have to go into denial about God creating them and become "self-creating"[147] beings. This would be the way to take God's power away from Him and consequently become autonomous. Doing this is impossible in reality. However, in illusions anything can appear to be possible. Consequently, these parts of the Sonship made an illusion of separation as an escape from God and also as a way of apparently authoring themselves.

Since these parts of the Sonship had divine power, they could join and manufacture what I call the "collusion illusion." Having a joint illusion would give the illusion more believability. Time, space, and the earth were all made as an illusion in which souls could appear to themselves at least to be separate from God. Since true Authorship is in God and true Identity is in God, these parts of the Sonship could only make this illusion appear real to themselves by making up a false identity. Therefore, the ego was manufactured as a device to make the illusion seem real. Also, bodies were made to be separate dwellings for the false identity of the ego as further proof of separation from God. This illusion was so perfectly executed that the souls who had chosen to make this illusion were able to deceive themselves. These souls were able to forget about making the illusion and forget about their unchangeable union with God.

Yet this illusion had no effect on God nor did it affect your union with God. You are still as you were created by God. You were created as a Thought that was extended from God Himself. This Thought remains your reality and life now and never left its Source. You are still in Heaven and joined with God. This Thought, which is your true Identity, is still part of Sonship, the One Christ, but a small part of your mind in the Christ Mind has fallen asleep in Heaven.

This small portion of your mind that you call yourself is dreaming of a world of fear, hate, pain, and separation that only appears to be existing in time and in three-dimensional space. You are just as holy, pure, guiltless, and sinless as when you were created. But you are dreaming that you are unholy, impure, guilty, and sinful. In the part of your dreaming mind, you subconsciously perceive you have attacked God by separating from Him. Because of guilt, you feel you deserve punishment. You are imagining that you are hiding from God and you cannot believe that God still loves you. You are lost in your own self-deception. God as Reality cannot come into your dream without destroying the dream and in so doing violate your free will.

Your dreaming mind may still not be able to conceive how you could remain a pure Thought within the changeless and perfect Christ Mind and also be expressing such a limited and constantly changing awareness in your present ego condition. You are probably aware of the fictional Star Trek television and movie series. Some aspects of Star Trek can be used as an analogy for understanding how you can remain part of the perfect Christ Mind as you were created by God and at the same time express yourself so imperfectly now.

Using this analogy, you can think of the Christ Mind as being the computer that operates the Star Trek spaceship. This spaceship has a holodeck where holographic images can be projected to make the illusion of a three-dimensional world. A program has been placed in the computer that creates a holodeck world in which fictional people live in an illusion, though to them, it appears to be reality. Each person in the hologram world has his own individual program that tells him the false information that he is a "real" person. The holodeck person is programmed to believe he lives in the same world as other holodeck figures, and he is a "real" body with a limited mind contained in this body. The holodeck figures are even programmed to go to sleep every night and have "dreams" and then to wake up the next day in what appears to them as the "real" three-dimensional world.

Just as the individual holographic program has a set of instructions that fabricates a false reality, your ego also functions like a program that fabricates a false reality for you. The ego is merely a thought of separation you have accepted as your basic guiding principle, which in Star Trek terminology can be called your "prime directive."

Only a very small portion of gigabytes of the Star Trek computer is used for the imaginary holographic world that does not exist. But even these gigabytes are doing their job perfectly since they are carrying out the program instructions just as they were given.

Likewise, the small dreaming part of the Christ Mind is performing perfectly its task as it was programmed to pretend that it is separate from God and not part of the rest of the Christ Mind. It has made the illusions of time, space, and the world to follow the instructions of its programming in the same way the spaceship could make a holodeck world. Yet the Christ Mind is unaffected by the small portion of the Christ Mind that has fallen asleep to dream of a world of separation, just as the spaceship computer as a whole is unaffected by the small number of gigabytes involved with making the holodeck world.

If a program for one of the holodeck figures is deleted, that figure would disappear from the holographic world and the gigabytes being used for that figure's part in the holodeck world would return as free computer space to be used for any computer function. Likewise, when you give up the false programming of the ego, you will awaken to your freedom in the Christ Mind where you have been all along, and your Christ Mind will be changelessly perfect as it has always been.

This is a good analogy, but there is an important way you are different from the holodeck figures in Star Trek. The holodeck figures are entirely illusions and are not just pretending to be illusions as you are. The holodeck figures do not have free will, and they did not give themselves their own programming thus they cannot change their programming. You do have free will that you misused by programming yourself into believing that you are an ego in a world of separation. If you insist that you are a victim of a world of separation that you did not make, then you are powerless to change the programming of this world. If you take responsibility for having programmed this world of separation, you must have the power to change your programming. This means you must have the power to let go of this illusory world of separation and to wake up in Heaven realizing that you are part of the Sonship, the perfect holy Son of God.

But if you are in fact a perfect being, how could you become the imperfect being you are now? You are a perfect being and cannot be anything other than the perfect being that God created. Yet, because of free will, you can pretend that you are not what you are, and you can pretend so perfectly that you forget who you are. Why would you, as a perfect being, do such a thing? Possibly you foolishly thought that maybe there was something better than the perfection you already had. Perhaps you mistakenly thought making an illusory world apart from God would give you autonomy and make you special and thus happier than you had been.

Pretending to be separated from God and to be part of an illusory world was, of course, a mistake, but not a sin. The idea of sin is that you could tarnish yourself, placing a mark on your soul making you unacceptable to God. A belief in sin produces a belief in guilt that says you deserve punishment. If you inwardly believe you are sinful and guilty for having separated from God, you will be adding another mistake to the original mistake of creating the illusion of separation. Fortunately, the ideas of sin and guilt are only ego-base beliefs and are just as false as the ego itself. You are still just as holy and loved by God as when He created you as an extension of Himself.

The fact that you have mistakenly programmed yourself to believe that you are the ego is no cause for guilt; it is cause for hope. Just as you chose to program yourself to not know yourself, you can choose to change your programming now and awaken to your true nature. Yet you cannot be a good guide for yourself because your ego has fed you so much false information that you cannot discern between what is false and what is true. God could see that when you programmed yourself to believe in an illusion of separation, you had not placed an "end program" command in your programming as is the case with the Star Trek holodeck program. God realized that you had given yourself a problem that you could not resolve by yourself without guidance. You were in so much need of help and guidance that you could not even know that you needed assistance.

God could not force His help on you without violating your free will. You made your illusion of separation as an expression of your free will precisely to cut off communication with God. Your loving Father wanted to find a way to ensure that you could communicate with Him if you wanted to do so as an expression of your free will. God's answer to your illusion of separation was the creation of the Holy Spirit as a bridge from your world of dreams to Heaven. He placed the Holy Spirit in a portion of your mind where you could choose with your free will to invite guidance and assistance. The Holy Spirit speaks to you at your invitation of your union with God.

It may be too much for you to believe that Jesus, who dictated the Course, is telling you that the world is an illusion that you made to separate from God. But this explanation is internally consistent and preserves your belief in the God of Love. The Course also says that if you chose to separate from God and you could produce this world, you certainly must have the power to become aware again of your true nature in God. This is especially true because it is God's will for you to wake up, and He has given you the Holy Spirit, as well as Jesus Christ, to bring you the message of God's Love for you.

Because the ego is only a false thought of separation and nothing more, you may wonder why you cannot just exert your will to delete it, in the same way you could delete any information in a computer. The problem with removing this single false thought of separation is that you have built a whole web of thoughts around this one false thought. Your web of thoughts may be logically built, but because the initial thought is false, your whole thought system is false. Naturally your thought system will appear to you to be very reasonable and to truly express who you are, as long as you never question that first thought that is the basis of your thought system.

Even if you do question the validity of your current thought system by accepting that the idea of separation is false, your perception will still be divided. The deception of the ego is so deeply integrated into your thinking that only a portion of your perceptual mind will believe the ego is unreal and you are not a body, while the other portion of your perceptual mind will believe that the ego is real and you are a body. Because your mind is divided, your will is also divided. Thus your allegiance will be only partially given to the ego and will be partially given to the Holy Spirit. A divided mind will be constantly fluctuating because of repeatedly choosing between believing in *false perceptions* and *true perceptions*. In other words, your divided mind is always fluctuating between choosing fear or love.

As Holy Spirit guides your mind to give up false perceptions based on fears of the ego and accept true perceptions based on love, your mind becomes increasingly unified. The goal is to accept so many true perceptions that you will withdraw your allegiance from the ego and give your allegiance wholeheartedly to the Holy Spirit. By unifying your mind and by giving your allegiance to the Holy Spirit, you are changing your will from being divided to being unified.

God's will is for you to be aware of your Oneness with Him in Heaven. In order to wake up in Heaven, you will need an undivided will that expresses your desire for the eternity of Heaven. You don't want Heaven now because you have a divided will directed toward wanting other things that are not eternal. When you direct your will wholeheartedly toward having only the eternal, you will wake up in Heaven. If God were to try to give you Heaven, when you still want what is temporal, you would react with fear. By your seeing of Heaven as a fearful place, you would reject it.

It would be too traumatic for you to go directly from your illusions to the reality of Heaven that has nothing in common with fearful dreams. According to the Course, in order to prepare your mind for Heaven, you need to replace false perceptions with true perceptions and replace fearful dreams with "happy dreams."[148] Making a leap directly to Heaven may appear fearful to you and hard to achieve, but making a transition from wrong perceptions of illusions to right perceptions is much easier. All perceptions, even true perceptions, are illusions since they are partial awareness falling short of the complete knowledge of reality. However, because true perceptions make happy dreams, you are better prepared to accept the ultimate happiness of Heaven. Your spiritual growth depends on learning to change your mind from investing in false perceptions of fearful dreams of darkness to investing in true perceptions of happy dreams filled with light. Your letting go of your fearful dreams helps you to let go of your fear of Heaven. The happy dreams help you to perceive Heaven as a happy place and prepare you to accept eternal happiness. By learning to focus on true perceptions and on light and love, your mind itself will become increasingly unified. Finally with a unified mind and unified will, you will realize Heaven is all that you want and there is nothing else you want because there is nothing else that truly exists.

C. CHRIST'S VISION AND THE REAL WORLD

Christ's vision is a means of transforming awareness. In my book *Christian Meditation Inspired by Yoga and "A Course in Miracles,"* I used the words "Light vision" to name the visual experience of seeing light externally in and around people or objects. Light vision is an aspect of what St. Symeon the New Theologian called "gnosis," which is perceiving the divine externally in the everyday world. St. Symeon used a different word, "theoria," to describe the inner vision of light in contemplation. But the Course uses the words "Christ's vision"[149] as an all-inclusive term that encompasses the various meanings of Light vision, gnosis, and theoria. My interpretation of the Course includes the possibility of seeing light externally as a visual experience. Since the Course uses no specific term for this visual component, I will continue to use the term "Light vision" to describe this visual outcome that is sometimes produced as a by-product of Christ's vision.

Christ's vision according to the Course is the intercession of Christ bringing light into your mind and allowing you to perceive holiness in everything. Christ's vision is a change in perception guided by the Holy Spirit that allows you to see the divine inwardly and outwardly. In addition, Christ's vision in the Course may result in the by-product of visually seeing light externally in people and objects, which is Light vision. Christ's vision helps you to see things differently and change your perceptions. As a by-product of Christ's vision, Light vision offers you the visual component of seeing, which outwardly confirms that an inner change in perception has occurred. Yet Christ's vision, in which light comes into the mind to change perception, can occur without the visual component being present. Christ's vision may be experienced as seeing the meaning of the divine holiness in the world without also including a visual experience of light. This mental perception of the divine externally without Light vision is one aspect of gnosis. Also, Christ's vision may be experienced entirely within by contemplatively seeing light internally, which is theoria.

Christ's vision lets you see with the eyes of Christ. Christ's vision is a change from using double vision with two eyes to single vision of a unified mind. Your unified mind lets you see from one perspective, replacing false perceptions with true perceptions. With double vision, your seeing keeps what you see separate from yourself. With Christ's vision, your seeing unites you to what you are seeing to affirm your oneness with all things and all people and indeed with God.

Today traditional Christianity appears very conservative, but Jesus himself in the time of his earthly ministry was a radical. Jesus often challenged his listeners to make radical decisions in their lives. To do this he placed his listeners in a spiritual dilemma by confronting them with a decision between two mutually exclusive choices. One choice was to stay with the familiar and the comfortable path of living in the world based on meeting temporary needs. The other choice was to make a commitment to the radical and uncomfortable path that leads to eternal life. Both choices may seem valuable, but the dilemma is in deciding which is more valuable. This dilemma is best illustrated by the rich man who asked Jesus what he must do to find the kingdom of God. Jesus told him he could sell all his possessions and give to the poor in order to find the kingdom. The rich man was placed in a spiritual dilemma. Which did he value more, either the things of this world or the kingdom of God?

Perhaps you are in the same spiritual dilemma as the rich man. You will invest belief in what you value because what you value will appear to be real to you. If you value the things of this world and value your idea of yourself, your self-image, you will believe this world is real. If you value the truth, you will go wherever the truth will take you, even if it means you must do as Jesus said:

> If anyone wishes to come after me, let him deny himself, and take up his cross, and follow me. For he who would save his life will lose it; but he who loses his life for my sake will find it. For what does it profit a man, if he gain the whole world, but suffer the loss of his own soul?[150]

Through denying yourself, meaning denying your ego concept of yourself, you will find yourself—your true Self in Christ. This is not a sacrifice because you are only sacrificing your false self and the things of this world that you really don't want and don't need.

But if you value the things of this world like the rich man, you will think it is a sacrifice, and you will not want to let go of your illusions about yourself. Not everyone will be able to walk all the way along the path to truth. You may not be ready to go very far along a path that seems to disappear in front of you. You may have to wait until the time of death to see the wisdom in releasing a world that offers only illusions that rob you of your true nature. In your life, you may find the eternal in an experience that transports you out of the limitations of the body and shows you the truth. After accepting the truth that contradicts this world, you will be able to let go of investing in a dream world. You will be willing to invest in unifying your mind and directing it toward your true nature in God.

The Course offers a unique path to the truth, yet it is not meant for everyone since its terminology does not speak to everyone. It may be too intellectually oriented for some or too psychologically geared for others. Nevertheless, the Course is based on forgiveness and loving relationships. The Course says that you can find Christ in yourself by finding him in your brother. You forgive your brother by giving up your illusions of seeing him as a body and also by investing in seeing the Son of God in him.

As you see your brother, you will see yourself. When you forgive your brother, your forgiveness is the releasing of your illusions about him. Because you look upon your brother with forgiveness, you will look upon yourself with forgiveness and in so doing let go of your illusions about yourself. Your forgiveness allows you to see Christ in your brother first and then allows you to affirm the presence of Christ within yourself. The Course is the only disciplined thought system I have encountered that teaches that your most direct path to God is through expressing forgiveness, developing loving relationships, and discovering your true Self by seeing Christ in your brother.

The Workbook portion of the Course teaches you that you can see the world differently if you are determined to do so. You can see the world and see your brothers with the eyes of Christ by using Christ's vision, which may also be called "real vision." This is a gift of Christ that comes through the Holy Spirit that enables you to see a world transformed into a world of light. Christ's vision can show you directly the light that is within your own mind, but it can also show you that because of the light in your own mind, it is possible to see the outer world visually filled with light, which I call "Light vision."

To help describe the world of light seen in Christ's vision, some terms will need to be clarified. In my meditation manual, *Christian Meditation Inspired by Yoga and "A Course in Miracles,"* I have used the words "His world" to signify the divine world in contrast to your everyday world. Yet His world may be thought of as actually two worlds. One of these worlds is Heaven, which is the reality that is changeless and eternal where God resides. Heaven has the same divine attributes as God has, such as supernatural Light, Love, Peace, Bliss, and Universal Knowledge. It also contains the Wholeness in which paradoxically every part contains the Whole.

You are a part of the Sonship in the one Christ. The Christ may be called the *Christ Mind* and is a state of *One-mindedness* in which

Christ's Will and God's Will are one.[151] Although you are only one part of the Sonship in the Christ Mind, your true nature experiences Wholeness because in Heaven, which is perfectly unified, there is no division and no separateness with every part inclusive of the whole. Heaven is not in time, meaning it has no past and no future, being changeless and eternal. Heaven is not in a place because it is infinite and has no boundaries because it is everywhere and nowhere. You cannot comprehend the nature of Heaven with the limited awareness that perception offers because the supernatural *knowledge* of Heaven exists beyond all perceptual thinking.

Perception requires a perceiver and an object of perception that are separate. Since there is no separation in Heaven, perception is only possible in a world that dreams of separation. Your world of limited thinking has two kinds of perceptions. There are true perceptions that are your loving thoughts guided by the Holy Spirit. True perceptions produce *right-mindedness*.[152] There are also false perceptions that are your thoughts of fear, guilt, and separation guided by your ego. False perceptions produce *wrong-mindedness*.[153] Compared to supernatural *knowledge* that reveals reality, both true and false perceptions are illusions. Yet, although true perceptions are illusions, they are symbols of Heaven because they are loving and thus help your mind become open to the possibility of becoming aware of Heaven.

Your everyday world is a world where you are constantly choosing between true and false perceptions. But your normal way of seeing the world is through the body's eyes that are guided by the ego that says you are a body. Consequently, most of your perceptions are false perceptions and so you see a world of fear and separation and cannot see the underlying love and unity of the world.

However, I said His world is actually two worlds. Thus in addition to Heaven, there is another world, which is called the *real world*[154] that lies between your world and Heaven. The term "real" here may be misleading, because this real world is an illusion in comparison with Heaven. Yet it is a reflection of Heaven and can be called a real world since it is a symbol of the reality of Heaven. It is a world of *only* true perceptions. Because true perceptions are loving, the true perceptions of the real world reflect Heaven. Though the real world is an illusion, it is a "happy dream" that contains only true perceptions of light, peace, joy, and love.

The awareness of the real world is a necessary stepping stone to gaining awareness of Heaven. The mind that thinks it exists in a world of fear and separation would not want to go to the formless perfection of Heaven. As long as you think you are a body, how can you go to Heaven without thinking you are asking for death and not life?

No sane person wants to die, and yet everyone is attracted to the idea of going to Heaven. Before you are willing to go to Heaven, you may have to convince yourself that the body can die, but you cannot die because you are not a body.

Even if you accept the idea that you are not a body and you have convinced yourself that you want Heaven, you would not be permitted entrance because your attachment to the ideas of fear and separation would not make that possible. First you would have to resolve inner conflicts, reconcile apparent opposites, and correct mistaken thoughts. Such changes in thinking in which you let go of false perceptions and replace them with true perceptions are called "miracles."[155] The reason why Christ's vision is so important is that when you see with the eyes of Christ, you become open to changing your perceptions, and you become aware of miracles.

Traditionally most people associate miracles only with extraordinary unexpected events, but the Course emphasizes that miracles become natural to you when you see with Christ's vision. In fact, the Course maintains that Christ's vision will solve any problem, will correct any confusion, and will positively transform any situation:

> There is no problem, no event or situation, no perplexity that vision will not solve. All is redeemed when looked upon with vision. For this is not *your* sight, and brings with it the laws beloved of Him Whose light it is.[156]

This is all done through a change in perception that produces a miracle. Christ's vision lets you see your brothers in a new light and gives you access to miracles. You will be able to bring miracles to them and in so doing bring miracles to your own mind because what you give you receive. Christ's vision and miracles go together because with His vision your perception of your brother will change so you will see Christ in him. You will see yourself in your brother and realize your oneness with him and with Christ. If you could see the real world, you would realize that it is possible to bring your mind to a place where you have only true perceptions. Seeing the light of the real world reveals miracles that will transform your dreaming mind. Christ's vision shows you the real world and helps you to believe in the happy dream where false perceptions have no meaning.

Your everyday mind is scattered and divided so it is an unclean mirror that does not provide a clear reflection of the divine. Once the mind lets go of false perceptions and becomes focused on the truth, it can reflect the divine. Christ's vision can help your mind become that clear mirror by showing you the real world. When God sees that you have a clean mind that rests in the true perceptions of the real world,

He reaches into the real world and brings you into Heaven to reveal *knowledge* to you. The word "knowledge"[157] is used in the Course to mean the supernatural total awareness beyond the perception of the rational mind. This knowledge is the awareness of your perfect union with God. The experience that gives you this knowledge is referred to in the Course as "revelation,"[158] which is the illumination that is another name for what Buddhism calls "enlightenment" and what Hinduism calls "samadhi." Such experiences are fleeting and come infrequently, yet even a glimpse of revelation imparts knowledge that can never be taken from you and gives you what the Course calls "certainty"[159] about your true Identity in union with God.

Even without this confirmation in this life, your goal can still be to reveal the real world so you will be better prepared to enter Heaven when your earthly life has been completed. More importantly, seeing the real world helps you to live now a life already centered in God where sights of fear and separation are transformed into sights of love and union. Why wait for the happiness of Heaven, when you can have happiness now that reflects Heaven, and in so doing you can bring happiness to everyone you meet.

The real world is not a place of three-dimensional form where you can move around with your body. Made of true perceptions, the real world is a state of mind that can be seen in light by an open mind focused upon light, love, and forgiveness. Since the real world is itself a state of mind beyond three-dimensional form, most Course students have concluded that the real world can only be seen within the mind itself and cannot be seen in the outer world of form. After all, true perception shows that form does not truly exist. In fact, the Course says that when you see the real world, the outer world of form disappears. This viewpoint says that if you see light in the outer world, it must be only physical light. Also, it is clear from the Course that the body's eyes cannot see the real world. Thus most Course students conclude that since the outer world can only be seen with the body's eyes that see form, the real world must be seen only within.

This conclusion is based on the logic of rational thinking, but your judgments based upon rational thinking can be greatly enhanced by your personal experience. Christ's vision brings light into the mind and creates openness that allows you to change perceptions and become aware of miracles. A change in perception can and usually does occur without the confirmation of the visual component of actually seeing light internally or externally. Most Course students and scholars have not themselves personally experienced the visual by-product of Christ's vision either internally or externally. Those who have not had this experience confirming that Christ's vision has occurred do not have the best perspective to make a judgment on where the light of the real world can and cannot be seen. Hopefully, you can keep an open mind, because without an open mind the door to Christ's vision will be closed to you, not only outwardly but inwardly as well. After all, Christ's vision requires *openness* on your part to miracles—openness to changing perceptions.

The real world is a world of true perceptions beyond physical form, but where is this real world? Remember that you are in Heaven now. Though you are just a part of the Sonship, your true nature contains the whole Christ Mind. Your mind in the Christ Mind is not the rational thinking and private mind of this world. This "mind"[160] is considered in the Course to be the activating aspect of the spirit that provides its creative energy. Your whole mind in Heaven is split into two parts. The larger portion of your mind is aware of your oneness with the Christ Mind. On the other hand, a very small portion of your mind in the Christ Mind is asleep in Heaven and dreaming of illusions. That small portion of your mind may be called your *dreaming mind.* This dreaming mind encompasses your private ego-based psychological and mental world, while also including your physical world of the whole universe. Your world is not outside of you as the illusion tells you. Your world of form is within your dreaming mind. But the real world is also in your mind as a dream. The Holy Spirit holds it ready for you to see through Christ's vision as a world of happy dreams to replace the nightmares that you have made in your world of separation.

With these two worlds of dreams in your mind, you can normally see only your world that is filled with false perceptions of separation along with some true perceptions of love. Your ego permits some true perceptions in your world because your true nature would not allow a world entirely devoid of these. But your ego, which is based upon false perception, makes sure that what you see is a reflection of its false perception. Consequently, you will see everything in your world as if everything in your world is separate. Although your ego allows you to see a world that has both false and true perceptions, your ego will not allow you to see the real world because it has *only* true perceptions. Therefore, the body's eyes can only show you a world that appears outside you and that is made up of separate parts.

When you open your mind to light and love and receive the gift of Christ's vision, you will see your world disappearing as the Course says. Ultimately under ideal circumstances, the whole physical world will disappear so you will see the deepest level of the real world. The deepest level of the real world in which the world disappears is reached by the work of divine grace assisting you in unifying the mind by filling your mind with only true perceptions. It may take a long time to reach this state of mind in which the world disappears so you see only the real world. In the beginning of attempting to unify the mind, the real world will be seen only in glimpses. Having these initial glimpses of Christ's vision indicates that you are beginning to deny the darkness of your world in order to see the light of the real world.

The Course states that the preliminary stage of real vision occurs when you see "little edges of light around familiar objects which you see now."[161] This is the initial experience of Light vision, the visual experience of seeing light in the world that is a by-product of Christ's vision. You may see objects, even people, appear to be glowing. This glowing stage of visual experience usually appears as a shining white light. After seeing objects surrounded by light, your Light vision may then reveal objects as being filled with light. It is possible you may see objects filled with white light or a silvery light. In some cases, seekers report seeing a bluish tinge to the shining light. Yet the most common visual experience of seeing objects filled with light is the appearance of a shimmering golden white light. Perhaps eventually you will be able to see everything in your vision filled with the same light. Then three-dimensional objects will appear to be flattened out without having any depth. This will convince you that your world is not as real as you had thought it was.

Besides the loss of depth perception, as you see more of the real world, what you see will lose all its color except for the white, silvery, or golden light. In addition to colors disappearing, Light vision shows you that the solidness of forms disappears. What remains is shining transparent outlines of those forms with highlights of white, silvery, or golden light brighter in some places and less bright in others. At first lighter forms will get very bright and darker forms will get darker. Later you will see the white, silvery, or golden light even in the darker forms. The Course says you will see your outer world transformed so even ordinary objects will be looked upon as lovely.

Seeing through the eyes of Christ is seeing through the eyes of forgiveness that will allow you to see differently so you can look past illusions and see the beauty and light in all things. Forgiveness is usually thought of as applying only to people, but the Course advises looking at the world itself with forgiving eyes that allow you to see through the illusions all around you in this world. The Course gives the specific example of looking at a "leaf" or "blade of grass" with wonder to see the perfect manifestation of God even in the smallest of things.

> All this beauty will rise to bless your sight as you look
> upon the world with forgiving eyes. For forgiveness literally
> transforms vision, and lets you see the real world reaching

quietly and gently across chaos, removing all illusions that had twisted your perception and fixed it on the past. The smallest leaf becomes a thing of wonder, and a blade of grass a sign of God's perfection.[162]

Christ's vision changes your perception of what you see but also can produce Light vision, making your experience of Christ's vision more tangible to you. With Light vision, you will visually see the light of the real world and see the physical world transformed in your vision. Your Light vision, which through Christ's vision reveals the real world, will show you that your world of illusory forms is not solid as it appears, but rather it is transparent and not real.

> Christ's vision is the bridge between the worlds. And in its power can you safely trust to carry you from this world into one made holy by forgiveness. Things which seem quite solid here are merely shadows there; transparent, faintly seen, at times forgot, and never able to obscure the light that shines beyond them.[163]

Your Christ's vision will reveal that your world is not really out there where the body's eyes would tell you it is. You will realize that you are seeing with the light in your own mind that comes to you from God's grace, although this light appears to be seen outside of you. It is this inner light that enables you to have Christ's vision and see differently. The light coming from within as the source of both Christ's vision and Light vision is addressed in the Course, as follows:

> In order to see, you must recognize that light is within, not without. You do not see outside yourself, not is the equipment for seeing outside you. An essential part of this equipment is the light that makes seeing possible. It is with you always, making vision possible in every circumstance.[164]

Your Christ's vision can reveal the divine meaning of people and objects, but also can produce the by-product of Light vision allowing you to see light visually in external forms, confirming your change in mental perception if you are open to that visual experience. When you close your eyes, it is possible for you to see the same radiant light within as you see outwardly to convince you that you can see the light of the real world whether you look outwardly or inwardly.

If you doubt that the light you see is really within you, you can conduct an interesting experiment. You simply place yourself in an enclosed room, and you block off all sources of outside light, including window light or cracks in the door to the room. The room needs to be completely dark so no outside light enters into your eyesight. The premise is that in a room where there is absolutely no outer light, if you do see light, it must be light that is already in you. If you look carefully, you will discover that there is no such thing as complete blackness with no light. In the darkness, you will see an inner light. It makes no difference whether your eyes are open or closed because you will see the same light in each case.

This experiment may not work for you. It will not work if you decide beforehand that you cannot see any light in a completely dark room. In that case, you will not see any light because your not seeing light is the experience that you wanted and expected to happen based upon your decision beforehand. You will only be able to see with Christ's eyes if you want and expect to do so. Also, you will only believe it is possible to see your everyday world filled with light and see light within yourself, if you want and expect to be able to do so. You must want to see to open yourself to God's grace. This wanting welcomes God's grace and releases an inner light into your mind. This releasing of inner light may occur without your conscious awareness, but this bringing of inner light into your mind is required for you to truly see with Christ's vision, and in turn to have Light vision.

> The wish to see calls down grace for God upon your eyes, and brings the gift of light that makes sight possible.[165]

Notice that the above quotation indicates that God's grace comes down on your eyes, meaning your physical eyes, giving the light that makes seeing with the eyes of Christ possible. Your physical eyes alone cannot see with Christ's vision, but this divine grace blesses the physical eyes enabling the mind to use the eyes of Christ to see the real world and to even see into the physical world providing Light vision as an additional bonus.

The Course repeatedly says you can see the world transformed by seeing with the eyes of Christ and the eyes of forgiveness. Some of these indicate that this is not only an inner transformation, but also a transformation that can be seen reflected in the world outside by seeing differently without the heavy covering of guilt. Those who have experienced Light vision have no doubt that these descriptions are literal and not figurative because they have seen for themselves this new transformed world. If by God's grace you are given the gift of being able to see your brother in the light, his loveliness in your sight would be all you need to convince you that the real world can be seen shining through your world. The Course says the true beauty of your brother is reflected even at the form level and can be seen at the form level in Christ's vision, as follows:

> And in Christ's vision is his loveliness reflected in a form so holy and so beautiful that you could scarce refrain from kneeling at his feet.[166]

In your world, the body appears to be solid, opaque, and heavy because you believe in the reality of guilt that makes this illusion. But if you could to see your brother in his true holiness without guilt, you would see his body transformed by the forgiving eyes of Christ. The Course says that the body is truly transparent. Yet this becomes obvious only when you see the light that is behind the body. The Course states that when you see this light, you will also see the body without its apparent solidness, opaqueness, and heaviness. It will be seen as only a transparent veil or shadow that appears unsubstantial and fragile.

> By focusing on the good in him, the body grows decreasingly persistent in your sight, and will at length be seen as little more than just a shadow circling the good. And this will be your concept of yourself, when you have reached the world beyond the sight your eyes alone can offer you to see. For you will not interpret what you see without the Aid That God has given you. And in His sight there *is* another world.[167]

Normally you see your brother with your physical eyes directed by the ego that believes in guilt. With Christ's vision, perceptions of guilt are set aside so the body can be seen differently at the mental level. Similarly, with the absence of guilt occurring in Light vision, you will see the body differently even at the form level. With Light vision, the body appears transparent and enveloped and filled with a luminous light. The Course says that the body normally appears solid, weighty and substantial only because of the belief in guilt. The ego is the belief in separation, and guilt is the bonding agent that holds together the ego's whole thought system. Guilt produces faulty vision that hides the real transparent and unsubstantial nature of the body, which is nothing more than a shadow before the light that can shine it away.

The body will remain guilt's messenger, and will act as it directs as long as you believe that guilt is real. For the reality of guilt is the illusion that seems to make it heavy and opaque, impenetrable, and a real foundation for the ego's thought system. It thinness and transparency are not apparent until you see the light behind it. And then you see it as a fragile veil before the light.[168]

Some quotations, such as the one above, seem just too incredible to believe literally. Therefore, most Course students want to interpret Course quotations figuratively and not literally. After all, the ego has provided an abundant amount of physical and psychological "evidence" that the body is real. Nevertheless, the experiences of those who have seen through the eyes of Christ's vision and Light vision confirm that the statements of the Course are accurate literal descriptions of seeing the body and the world being transformed in light. When the Course maintains that light comes into the world of darkness to enable Christ's vision even here in this world, it can only mean that real spiritual vision is an inner realization that can be reflected in the by-product of seeing light in the outer world in Light vision.

Whether Christ's vision and Light vision come into your world or not depends upon what you want. Whatever you seek and whatever you expect is what you will see. God's grace will be attracted to you by your desire to see, and this grace will bring to your eyes the light that makes seeing possible. Then you will need to have a unified mind that is focused on light and love to be able to see with Christ's eyes that will show you the light and love in your mind reflected in whatever you focus your steady gaze upon outwardly.

In order for you to see the outer world transformed in light by Light vision, you will need to allow your seeing to be meditative so you do not move your vision around or move your body while you look at physical objects. You must also not allow your mind to wander into unloving thoughts or distracting thoughts that would divert you from focusing your mind on light and love. If your mind does wander, the light of the real world that you had been seeing will disappear leaving only the sight of your world. When your mind returns to focusing on loving thoughts, Christ's vision and the resulting Light vision return to show you the light of the real world again.

Since you must be mentally focused upon loving thoughts in order to see your world transformed in light, this is another confirmation that you are really seeing the real world that consists of only loving true perceptions. Since the real world is a state of mind and not a place, how can you really be seeing the real world when looking at objects filled with radiant light?

To answer this question, the first consideration is the nature of the real world as a state of mind. The real world is a state of mind, but there are two kinds of states of mind. The calm state of mind that you have in Heaven is an abstract state of mind that can be experienced in oneness but cannot be seen by a perceiver. On the other hand, the state of mind of the real world is not in the abstraction of Heaven but within the realm of perception and therefore within the realm of form at some level. Therefore, a perceiver can potentially at least perceive the real world as an object of perception.

The second consideration in answering the above question is the location of the real world and also the location of the physical world. The real world is in your mind. The physical world you see outside yourself is not really outside your mind; it is also within your mind. So what you see, even with your physical eyes, only appears to be a place. It is an illusion. You are not seeing a place. You are seeing a state of mind. You are not seeing the abstract state of mind in Heaven; you are seeing a state of mind within perceptual awareness, which allows for a perceiver and an object of perception.

In summary, the real world of true perceptions and the physical world of false perceptions are both in your mind. Whatever you are seeing, even if it appears outside your mind, is actually a perception in your mind and a perception of your state of mind. When you see the physical world with your physical eyes only, you are seeing a state of mind based upon false perceptions. You are seeing a state of mind that believes in fear and guilt.

Now the question of how the real world can be seen as a radiant light even in the outer world of forms can be addressed more directly. When you begin to see through the illusion of the physical world, you will see light behind physical forms. The real world is within the realm of perception and all perception brings forth a manifestation of form at some level. "All thinking produces form at some level."[169]

One form that the real world manifests is light. How can light be a form? In Heaven, light is abstract and formless supernatural Light. In Heaven, you are this Light as your being, and therefore you do not perceive light as an object apart from yourself. But in the real world light can be perceived apart from yourself, so light can be an object of your perception. The real world is a realm of true perceptions, which manifests form because all thinking produces form. Light in the real world is a form since it can be perceived as an object of perception. Light is not usually associated with form. But because all perceptual thinking produces form at some level, the real world having only true perceptions must produce form. The distinctive and very refined form that the perceptions of the real world produce is light.

Since light is the form that true perceptions produce, light is a symbol of true perception. Seeing light means your mind is in a state of true perception, and that state is the real world. Seeing the radiant light everywhere in the outer world is a manifestation of seeing your own state of mind based upon true perceptions and therefore you are seeing the real world.

Are you really seeing all of the real world when you see the radiant light in physical objects? You are seeing light as a form-related aspect of the real world. In that sense, you are seeing the real world. But no, you are not seeing the deepest level of the real world. There are different levels of perception and also different levels of the real world. In seeing objects in white, silvery, or golden light, you are seeing only the form-related lower level of the real world. In this sense, the seeing of radiant light in objects is only a symbolic seeing of the deeper levels of the real world. The actual direct seeing of the deepest level of the real world will be explained in the next section.

In order to understand Christ's vision and subsequent Light vision better, it may be helpful to compare seeing using physical eyes and seeing using Christ's eyes. In order to see the physical world, you open your physical eyes to let in the light from the physical world. This physical light comes from outside and into your eyes and lets you see physical objects as physical forms that have various different colors and solidity. The physical eyes only have this one ability to take in light from the outer world to show you outer forms.

Imagine that you have the visual experience of looking at the outer world and seeing a radiant light everywhere. You see the radiant light fill all the forms so all different colors fade into the radiant light. You see all the forms flatten out and no longer look solid as they shimmer in the radiant light. How would you explain to yourself why this is happening? Your physical eyes are not operating like they normally do showing colors and solid shapes. You would have to conclude that something has changed. If you rule out that your eyes are now somehow defective, you will probably come to the conclusion that the way your mind is perceiving may have changed. However, based on the experiences of those who have actually seen the radiant light, this conclusion is realized not by your intellect alone, but by an inner feeling as well. Your inner feeling will tell you that a change has occurred within you, allowing you to perceive differently. This inner feeling is really an inner feeling of love and light.

If the seeing of radiant light is not coming from an exterior source like the sun or electric light bulbs, it must be coming from an interior source. There must be a light inside your mind that is changing your perception so you perceive a shining light in everything. Yes, you have your eyes open at the time of this experience of shimmering light, but that is only so the inner light can have access to the outer world. In this sense, the physical eyes are merely a window that just lets light pass through and nothing more. Your physical eyes are capable of seeing only outer forms of duality and seeing only "physical" light, meaning some light source coming from the physical world. If you see some other light that is not coming from the physical world, your perception of this other light cannot be attributed to your physical eyes that can only see physical light.

The Course states you cannot see the world transformed in light outwardly with your physical eyes because the double vision of your physical eyes can only show you a world of duality. Just because you have your eyes open when Christ's vision and Light vision are directed outwardly at the world does not mean your eyes are doing the seeing. The Course says there is an inner light that comes into the mind that makes Christ's vision possible. This inner light in the mind that is the source of Christ's vision makes Light vision possible so you can see radiant light in the external world. This inner light is a manifestation of divine grace from a divine source but is certainly not the same as the supernatural Light of Heaven.

Although your physical eyes are open to give your mind access to the physical world, in seeing the radiant light in the external world, you are actually seeing with the eyes of Christ. Just as physical light needs to come into the physical eyes to make seeing of physical light possible, the inner spiritual light needs to come from Christ's eyes to make it possible to see the radiant light in the outer world. However, the radiant light seen in the outer world is a less intense light than the inner light, in the same way that the light of the moon is merely a less intense reflection of the more intense direct light of the sun.

In contrast to the physical eyes showing you only a world of duality, the eyes of Christ give you a single vision, revealing a single meaning and a single purpose. Instead of seeing separate objects with separate colors and shapes, you will see all objects in your vision losing their colors and shapes and flattening out into a shadowy veil showing the outlines of those forms that had appeared so solid before. A glaze of glowing radiant light will fill your entire field of vision showing you that everything that had appeared to be separate actually is joined in a unity of meaning and purpose. Your single vision will give you one frame of reference that replaces the double vision that your physical eyes produce showing you a world of duality. This single vision guided by the Holy Spirit comes from one perspective that reflects the truth. You cannot see alone but by joining with the Holy Spirit, you can see with this single vision.

> Joining with Him in seeing is the way in which you learn
> to share with Him the interpretation of perception that leads

to knowledge. You cannot see alone. Sharing perception with Him Who God has given you teaches you how to recognize what you see. It is the recognition that nothing you see means anything alone. Seeing with Him will show you that all meaning including yours, comes not from double vision, but from the gentle fusing of everything into *one* meaning, *one* emotion, and *one* purpose. God has one Purpose which He shares with you. The single vision which the Holy Spirit offers you will bring this oneness to your mind with clarity and brightness so intense you could not wish, for all the world, not to accept what God would have you have. Behold your will, accepting it as His, with all His Love as yours.[170]

This one frame of reference shows you a single meaning and a single purpose through Christ's vision and brings you a *unified mind* focused upon light and love. However, this one perspective can also be described as a peaceful mind focused on oneness and centered in God. Perhaps the clearest way to describe this one frame of reference is forgiveness. Your forgiving eyes allow you to see the oneness in the world of duality and change double vision to single vision.

Your world of duality offers you the purpose of fostering the belief in separation and was made as a place to hide from God. In answer to this world you made, God gave you the real world with the single purpose and single meaning of helping you replace false perceptions of your world with true perceptions that will prepare you to become aware of your oneness with God. Forgiveness is the means for healing perception. Forgiveness is the key to vision of the real world because it enables you to see mistakes in perception being corrected in your sight as Christ and the Holy Spirit are seeing with you. Your forgiving eyes allow you to see illusions for what they are and realize that all guilt is unwarranted. Forgiveness allows you to realize that everyone you see has a bad case of amnesia. The errors that have been made have only been due to mistaken identity. Forgiveness will show you there is no need to forgive what God has created with love and what has never been separated from God. You will forgive only illusions, and you will not forgive your brother for who he really is.

With your forgiving eyes, you can forgive your brother only for errors in perception that are not part of who he really is. You only forgive him for his illusions by seeing that he is not the body that he thinks he is. In Christ's vision that forgives every illusion, you may perhaps experience Light vision and see the body lose its opaqueness, as it becomes only a shadowy transparent outline filled with light. In the loving gaze of forgiveness that sees through your brother's illusion of a body, the light in your mind can bring light to the mind of your brother. The light of your mind that goes to him is a miracle that helps him to let go of his own false perception of himself as a body. The light that goes to your brother returns to your mind. You will experience joy, as will he, and your Christ's vision and Light vision will reveal even more of the real world to you. This experience is so validating of your true Self that you will not question that you have touched the divine in your brother and in yourself and seen yourself in your brother.

Seeing your brother transformed means you are able to see the light of the real world shine through into your world, but that does not mean you are seeing the deepest level of the real world. Your training and learning in how to go from seeing just glimpses of the real world to deeper levels of awareness of the real world is usually a gradual process. There is a point when the solid forms will disappear altogether, but that does not happen all at once usually. Instead, you will probably initially only see the glow around objects sometimes. Yet then you can train yourself to direct your loving mind with the help of Christ's vision to consciously see this glow at will. Then you will be able to see objects differently, as some Course Workbook lessons direct. If you are open to Light vision, you will see objects outlined or even filled with radiant light. You can gain the ability to do this at will and then generalize this ability to all individual objects, including people.

As you increase your capacity to see, you will perceive at a deeper level. Since consciousness is related to your perceptual awareness, it has deeper and deeper levels to it, although it cannot go beyond the realm of perception itself. Thus your gradual increase of awareness of the real world involves going to deeper levels of your consciousness. This is true whether your mind is focused inwardly with the eyes closed or outwardly with the eyes opened, for what you see outside will only reflect what you see and what you want to see within.

It may be a while before outer forms lose their opaque and heavy look and begin to fade away leaving color and solidness behind. The forms you see will eventually look like shadowy shapes. Some of these shapes will be darker and have less radiant light. Some will be lighter and have more radiant light. Eventually the shapes will look more and more transparent except for highlighted areas or outlines of light. Also, if your mind is not steadily focused on light and love, the opaqueness will return. It will take a while before your Light vision will somewhat stabilize so what you see maintains its light continuously.

It will take further practice to perceive your whole field of vision is filled with light. To reach this level of awareness, it will be necessary to generalize your experience so you understand that what you can see in any one object is within every object. The inner recognition is that everything shares the identical purpose and the identical meaning. By seeing the identical nature within everything in your vision, you will learn to inwardly understand that all things are coming from one divine source that is the source of all meaning.

When you see your whole visual panorama filled with light, it will appear that nothing in your vision is three-dimensional at all. It will seem like a flat and transparent sheet is being held up to your eyes, and it has glowing lights on it that show you where solid objects had been previously. When you close your eyes and look within, you will see a glowing radiant light that is floating like a gas before a smoky background. When you open your eyes, you will see the same glowing radiant light everywhere, with the light brighter in some areas and less bright in other areas. The radiant light that is seen outwardly shows the outlines of objects, but it is shimmering and not holding just one steady position. By its subtle movement, it may give the impression that even though you may only be seeing objects, you are looking at something alive and even divine, rather than just a light phenomenon. In particular, when you are looking at a person in your field of vision and focusing on seeing his true nature, the shimmering light that you see is both fascinating and lovely to behold because you are seeing a symbolic reflection of the holy Son of God.

Light vision is your tangible feedback that tells you Christ's vision is occurring. Light vision is only of secondary importance since it is a reminder of the Christ's vision that is its cause. Even if you do not have the outer experience of Light vision, you can have the more important inner mental change in perception of Christ's vision. The outer unified vision that can occur in Light vision can show you by its feedback that you must be experiencing Christ's vision and that your inner mind is unified and focused upon the source of meaning.

Light vision is just an aid for helping you to wake up, but this outer visual experience is merely one way for the Holy Spirit to assist your awakening. Certainly Christ's vision without the visual component is sufficient for you to awaken if you can open your mind to the Mind of Christ through the various means that the Holy Spirit provides. For example, through Christ's vision you can look with your heart and see love everywhere outwardly thus opening yourself to the real world. Or with the help of the Holy Spirit, you can look within during meditation and find the real world waiting for your acceptance.

Whether you look inwardly or outwardly in your vision, the lesson the Holy Spirit would teach you is diametrically opposed to the lesson the ego teaches. The ego's lesson is that you are alone, and you must see from a different viewpoint than everyone else. The ego teaches this lesson because it is the idea of separation. The Holy Spirit wants you to learn that you are not separate and do not see alone. The Holy Spirit asks you to accept Christ's vision as your own vision and realize that seeing with Christ expresses the sharing of the same vision of oneness. The Holy Spirit's lesson helps you to wake up. The ego's lesson keeps you sleeping. Sharing with Christ by accepting His vision as your own will help to awaken because being awake is a condition of sharing the one divine life of all that exists in God.

The following quotation will summarize much of what has been stated above about Christ's vision and the real world, which are the gifts the Holy Spirit holds out to you for your awakening:

> The awakening of His Son begins with his investment in the real world, and by this he will learn to re-invest in himself. For reality is one with the Father and the Son, and the Holy Spirit blesses the real world in Their Name.
>
> When you have seen this real world, as you will surely do, you will remember us. Yet you must learn the cost of sleeping, and refuse to pay it. Only then will you decide to awaken. And then the real world will spring to your sight, for Christ has never slept. He is waiting to be seen, for He has never lost sight of you. He looks quietly on the real world, which He would share with you because He knows of the Father's Love for Him. And knowing this, He would give you what is yours. In perfect peace He waits for you at His Father's altar, holding out the Father's Love to you in the quiet light of the Holy Spirit's blessing. For the Holy Spirit will lead everyone home to his Father, where Christ waits as His Self.[171]

D. THE FACE OF CHRIST AND REVELATION

What happens if you see the deepest level of the real world? All individual objects fade away and disappear from your vision so you do not see their highlights or outlines of light. Seeing the real world at the deepest level is seeing the "face of Christ."[172] Christ's face is not the same as Christ himself, who cannot be perceived in His true nature, but can be *known*. Christ and God are one in Heaven, and you can only have *knowledge* of Christ in the direct experience of Oneness. In such a direct experience, Christ can be known as your true Self, but His essence as He truly is cannot be perceived or seen as an object of perception apart from yourself.

Instead of knowing Christ in His essence, in the deepest level of the real world you will see the symbol for Christ that is the *face of Christ,* which must be seen before your memory of God can come back to your awareness. The face of Christ, in addition to being the symbol of Christ, is the symbol of both the real world and of forgiveness. Seeing the face of Christ leads from the realm of perceptual thinking where visions occur to the knowledge of Heaven that is beyond visions and beyond perception. The face of Christ is the gate to Heaven where the seeker waits for God to take the final intimate step of embracing the soul in divine union, explained as follows:

> *The face of Christ* has to be seen before the memory of God can return. The reason is obvious. Seeing the face of Christ involves perception. No one can look on knowledge. But the face of Christ is the great symbol of forgiveness. It is salvation. It is the symbol of the real world. Whoever looks on this no longer sees the world. He is as near to Heaven as is possible outside the gate. Yet from this gate it is no more than just a step inside. It is the final step. And this we leave to God.[173]

The face of Christ is the highest perception that can be seen. The Course refers to the vision of Christ, which is the same as the face of Christ, as a circle of shining light. St. Symeon uses similar terminology to refer to his own inner vision of Christ as a blazing light like the sun in its appearance and power. When the world disappears altogether, you will be seeing the face of Christ and the deepest level of the real world. The Course describes the real world in this way:

> This world of light, this circle of brightness is the real world, where guilt meets with forgiveness. Here the world outside is seen anew, without the shadow of guilt upon it. Here is the new perception, where everything is bright and shining with innocence, washed in the waters of forgiveness, and cleansed of every evil thought you laid upon it.[174]

The real world is a state of mind, but one of only true perceptions. The deepest level of the real world is the true perception of Christ. The Course says that all perceptions produce form at some level in some way.[175] The ultimate true perception, the perception of Christ, which is the face of Christ, produces the form of a circle of light.

Although Christ in His essence can be experienced but cannot be seen, the face of Christ being only a representational form of Him can be seen. It can be said to be a form since it can be looked upon as an object with you apart from it as a perceiver. Nevertheless, it is a form so exalted as to transcend any other form you have ever seen before. Yet it will not be totally unfamiliar to you for it contains the memory of who you are.

Seeing the face of Christ assists the mind to return to its natural state. The mind is naturally abstract, but right now it is functioning unnaturally so it cannot accept the total abstraction and formlessness of Heaven. Seeing the real world helps your mind to move in the direction of Heaven's abstraction and formlessness. The real world is not totally abstract and formless for if it was, it would be useless to your perception because perception requires both a perceiver and an object of perception that can be seen. The happy dreams of the real world that replace the fearful dreams of your world can be perceived precisely because they are forms. Yet the real world shows you these forms gradually fading away to reveal they are illusions. It is a helpful grace to see the forms of this world fading away into light as the real world is experienced in stages. These stages of disappearing forms provide a transition leading toward the formlessness of Heaven and this transition assists the mind to adjust to the apparently unfamiliar territory of abstraction.

The deepest level of the real world, which is Christ's face, is still not completely as abstract and formless as Heaven, but it is so close to abstraction and formlessness that it can help you make the transition to Heaven. Seeing Christ's face is a preparation for the perception of the real world to be replaced by the knowledge of your true nature enabling you to awaken in Heaven. God Himself must intervene at this point to initiate this radical transformation in which knowledge replaces perception.

In addition to the Course describing the real world as a "circle of brightness,"[176] there are several other related references to circles of light in the Course. These references give at least some credence to the theory that the real world is in the form of a circle and therefore may be manifesting in the two-dimensional plane of finite length and width without finite depth. This may be why the three-dimensional forms of the world, when seen through Christ's vision, are replaced by flattened out forms that appear as a shadowy veil of light. If the real world is expressed as a two-dimensional world, this would be consistent with its role as a natural transition point between your three-dimensional world and Heaven, which is non-dimensional or rather is One-dimensional, being the formless and transcendental world of God.

My book *"A Course in Miracles" Dimensions of Awakening* explains my theory of dimensions. This book describes Christ as an extension of God Who is in the first dimension, the One-dimensional world. Acting through the Holy Spirit, God created an extension of light into the second dimension as an infinitely small indivisible point of light.

The Holy Spirit instantly expanded this Light into a perfect circle of light establishing the vision of Christ. This circle of light is not Christ but is a reflection of the Light of Christ from the One Dimension. This reflection can be seen in the second dimension. The vision of Christ, as this circle of light that is expanding infinitely, is provided by divine grace as a doorway to Heaven. The Holy Spirit is the communication link between the three-dimensional world and the One-dimensional world of Heaven. The Holy Spirit is in Heaven but also functions in the second dimension as a bridge to Heaven.

Christ and God are One. Christ is an extension of God and cannot be separate from God. Christ and God can be directly experienced by you only in a state of union. To experience Christ and God directly, you have to be in the One Dimension yourself and realize your own place in the Sonship united with God. Christ, like God, cannot be seen as an object of perception by an observer. Yet you can experience Christ indirectly through the vision of Christ in the second dimension. Christ is formless in the One Dimension. But Christ is symbolized in the second dimension as the perfect expression of form—the circle of light expanding infinitely. This vision can be seen by you apart from the circle of light, but you can be drawn to the center of the circle and realize that you are the Light—you are the Christ in God. When you experience this vision of Christ, your perceptions can become unified and filled with love so the transition from perception to the knowledge of Heaven can become possible. Seeing your readiness, God can take the initiative to directly help you to take the final step so you can wake up in the One-dimensional world of Heaven.

The circle of light where the transition to Heaven is possible is what the Course calls the "face of Christ" and is also the deepest level of the real world. In my opinion, the real world *is* the entire second dimension. The real world in the second dimension is a mirror image of Christ in the One Dimension. But the Course says the real world consists of only true perceptions, so if my theory is correct the second dimension would be a dimension of only true perceptions.

Because all perceptions, even true perceptions, are not real, the real world is not really real; it is an illusion. God *is* Reality itself, so wherever God is present as Himself there is Reality and not illusions. Consequently, the real world must have an image of Christ, but not Christ as He really is and not God as He really is. This circle of light is the face of Christ that is not real but is a true perception coming as close as perception can come to the Truth. Just as a mirror reflects an image but is not the image, the face of Christ at the deepest level of the real world reflects Christ but is not Christ.

The Course does not address the issue of dimensions. My personal opinion about the real world and Christ related to different dimensions is presented here as merely an interesting theory and nothing more. Whether this theory is true or not makes no difference in a practical sense to your experience of the real world. What is pertinent to your practical experience is that the real world is a gift from God. This gift enables you to transcend the world of perceptions, which are illusions, and reach the knowledge of your divine nature in God.

Seeing the face of Christ is a vision because it is within the realm of perception. All visions involve perception and separation between you, the perceiver, and what is perceived. Thus visions are illusions. However, the vision of Christ's face is so lofty that the perceiver is transformed in this perception and is awakened to the knowledge of Heaven by God's grace. The true perceptions of love, which are the real world's happy dreams, are so much like the Love of Heaven that you will be able to release all illusion and enter Heaven.

This vision of the face of Christ as a circle represents the totality of what the real world signifies. This circle is the doorway between the real world and Heaven. When you first perceive this vision, you may see only a part of the circle and then see all of the circle. As you approach the circle, you will see that the circle is filling with more and more light. The arc of the circle will become so filled with light that you can no longer see the circle at all because the light is expanding beyond it edges extending outward to infinity. This vision of the face of Christ is described in the Course, as follows:

> Beyond the body, beyond the sun and stars, past everything you see and yet somehow familiar, is an arc of golden light that stretches as you look into a great and shining circle. And all the circle fills with light before your eyes. The edges of the circle disappear, and what is in it is no longer contained at all. The light expands and covers everything, extending to infinity forever shining and with no break or limit anywhere. Within it everything is joined in perfect continuity. Nor is it possible to imagine that anything could be outside, for there is nowhere that this light is not.
>
> This is the vision of the Son of God, whom you know well.[177]

This quote does not say that you are inside the center of the circle and that you are part of the circle when you are seeing this vision because a vision always requires a perceiver to be separate from an object of perception. Thus you are the perceiver and the circle is the object of your perception. At this point, you remain apart from what you see. But entirely by God's grace and initiative, you may then be drawn to the center of the circle and there you are at the open gate of Heaven. To get this far, God has removed the limitations of your awareness and has drawn you out of the body altogether. You cannot be in the body when perception is replaced by knowledge.

When false perceptions change to true perceptions, this is a change from unloving perceptions to loving perceptions. When your mind becomes filled with true perceptions, your mind becomes a loving mind. The mind that is full of true perceptions can become so loving that it becomes very much like the love contained in knowledge that is in Heaven. Then perception can make the transfer to knowledge as a natural process of like attracted to like—love attracted to love.

> Every child of God is one in Christ, for his being is in Christ as Christ's is in God. Christ's Love for you in His Love for His Father, which He knows because He knows His Father's Love for Him. When the Holy Spirit has at last led you to Christ at the altar to His Father, perception fuses to knowledge because perception has become so holy that its transfer to holiness is merely it natural extension. Love transfers to love without any interference, for the two are one.[178]

At this point, true perception has become so filled with light that Light from God floods your perception. Then perception changes to knowledge and your mind is awakened in the Mind of God.

> What is one cannot be perceived as separate, and the denial of the separation is the reinstatement of knowledge. At the altar of God, the holy perception of God's Son becomes so enlightened that light streams into it, and the spirit of God's Son shines in the Mind of the Father and becomes one with it. Very gently does God shine upon Himself, loving the extension of Himself that is His Son.[179]

In this state, you will no longer be the perceiver of the bright circle outside yourself. You will be at the center of the circle, at the center of God's altar, and you will *be* the light. With the appendages of your physical body having been taken away, your new "nonphysical appendages" will be rays of light that will extend to infinity. You will be nowhere and everywhere. You will be infused with knowledge of Oneness. You will be One. But you can still return to your awareness of the world of perception because that is God's Will and your choice as well. You can come back to remind others that they are One in the Light with you. Indeed, it will be your sacred calling to do so, although you will be unable to adequately explain in words exactly what happened in this experience.

This experience of seeing the face of Christ apart from yourself can be a step-by-step process of becoming aware of deeper and deeper levels of true perception. When you get to the deepest level of true perception and see the face of Christ, you will suddenly be lifted by God into an experience of *revelation* in which you are given knowledge beyond perception. But it is possible for a sudden revelation to occur without a step-by-step preliminary stage. In this awakening, you realize God's Will as your own will, and in a spontaneous instant of joy, you become entirely open to God and out of your joy you literally "leap" into Heaven, as is stated in the Course in the following way:

> When the light comes and you have said, "God's Will is mine," you will see such beauty that you will know it is not of you. Out of your joy you will create beauty in His Name, for your joy could no more be contained than His. The bleak little world will vanish into nothingness, and your heart will be so filled with joy that it will leap into Heaven, and into the Presence of God.[180]

Also, it is the possibility that you may see Christ's face and then even experience your true Oneness, but only for the slightest glimpse because the experience is just too much for you to embrace fully. It will depend on the degree to which the mirror of your mind is clean so it can reflect Heaven. Being so close to the total abstraction of Heaven may be briefly disorienting because of your familiarity with concrete form and unfamiliarity with abstract formlessness. You can experience true Oneness beyond body awareness and perception, but then you can become so awestruck that you become disoriented.

In your disorientation, your perceptual awareness may return with the sudden fearful thought that you are a body, and your fear will cause you to return to the awareness of the body and its limitations. You may have an unloving thought, such as a thought of guilt about yourself, and that thought will end your experience of oneness with God and will end your vision of Christ's face. But one passing negative thought due to disorientation won't necessarily end the experience if you can immediately offer that thought to the divine for correction. God will assist you through this period of disorientation if you will allow Him to do so.

There are two examples provided above from the Course regarding being transported into Heaven in the experience of revelation. In the first example, you clean the mirror of your mind in a step-by-step process in which you replace false perceptions with true perceptions until finally you are lifted by divine grace beyond the face of Christ and into Heaven. In the second example, you can by divine grace "leap" into Heaven.

In the first example of revelation, you can come back to the world and not be able to conceptually articulate exactly what occurred. Later you may formulate some concepts that attempt to explain what is unexplainable. Aside from the aftereffect of such concepts, which offer merely limited explanations, revelation itself will impart an awareness of *certainty* and *knowledge*. This certainty and knowledge that you receive will reveal the awareness of your true relationship with God. The Course indicates that you are not a body. Rather, in your true nature, you are a spirit created as a being of light.

> ...the Son of God, who was created *of* light and *in* light. The Great Light always surrounds you and shines out from you.[181]

Revelation reveals the all-encompassing Light that you are. You will know with the certainty of direct experience that Light is your true nature. Revelation is an experience of awe and does not lend itself to being described with words. In the experience of revelation, you are joined directly with God. But revelation is not the final destination of your spiritual journey, explained as follows:

> God has kept your kingdom for you, but He cannot share His joy with you until you know it with your whole mind. Revelation is not enough, because it is only communication *from* God. God does not need revelation returned to Him, which would clearly be impossible, but He does want it brought to others. This cannot be done with the actual revelation; its contents cannot be expressed, because it is intensely personal to the mind that receives it. It can, however, be returned by that mind to other minds, through the attitudes the knowledge from the revelation brings.
>
> God is praised whenever any mind learns to be wholly helpful.[182]

Revelation comes from God to you in an experience in which He extends Himself to you. After having brought revelation to you, God wants you to extend yourself just as He extended Himself. God wants you to bring your revelation to your brothers although you cannot do this directly. The knowledge imparted by revelation brings about a perceptual transformation of *attitudes*, and these can be conveyed from your mind to the minds of others. These attitudes can take the form of realizations that become crystal clear in your mind. A specific example is that you will realize that every one of your brothers is an expression of the Light. Furthermore, you will understand that each of your brothers is living in the Light *right now*, even while not being consciously aware of the Light.

E. BECOMING A MIRACLE WORKER

The transfer of attitudes from your mind to other minds has to do with how to become "truly helpful," by being a "miracle worker."

> The truly helpful are God's miracle workers, whom I direct until we are all united in the Kingdom. I will direct you to wherever you can be truly helpful, and to whoever can follow my guidance through you.[183]

A miracle worker is truly helpful by changing his own perceptions that in turn helps others to change their perceptions. A miracle is an expression of love in which one mind affects another mind, bringing about a change in perception in the mind receiving the miracle. The Course is designed to teach you how to be a miracle worker, and the very first chapter of the Text explains the meaning of miracles. Miracles are not considered in the Course to be grandiose and extraordinary spectacles. Instead, miracles are natural manifestations of love. They are natural to you because in your true nature you are love. Listed below are some of the ways in which the Course describes miracles:

> Miracles occur naturally as expressions of love. The real miracle is the love that inspires them. In this sense everything that comes from love is a miracle.[184]

> Miracles are natural. When they do not occur something has gone wrong.[185]

> *You* are a miracle, capable of creating in the likeness of your Creator. Everything else is your nightmare, and does not exist. Only the creations of light are real.[186]

> Miracles honor you because you are lovable. They dispel illusions about yourself and perceive the light in you. They thus atone for errors by freeing you from your nightmares. By releasing your mind from the imprisonment of your illusions, they restore your sanity.[187]

> Miracles are examples of right thinking, aligning your perceptions with truth as God created it. [188]

> The miracle acknowledges everyone as your brother and mine. It is a way of perceiving the universal mark of God.[189]

> A miracle is a service. It is the maximal service you can render to another. It is a way of loving your neighbor as yourself. You recognize your own and your neighbor's worth...[190]

The miracle is an expression of a true perception extended from one mind to another mind. The mind that originally has the true perception facilitates a change in perception in another mind. It is not merely an objective offering of ideas to others, although this may or may not be included. When you look at your brother and see him as a body, you perceive him as being another ego like your own ego. In this case, your false perception of your brother distances you from your brother. On the other hand, a true perception of your brother, which is a loving perception, draws you closer to your brother. When you look at your brother with the attitude that this individual is the holy Son of God created in light and love, you actually shine a light from your mind into his mind. This light transfer is an opening of your mind to his mind helping him to change his own perceptions of himself. In his response to you, a light will go back from his mind to your mind giving you back the loving expression you have given to him.

The Course refers to this as a miracle, or in other words as an "exchange" of love.[191] In the laws of the physical universe, an exchange is just a transfer in which no energy is lost or gained. However, the miracle transcends this law. In the exchange of love that occurs in a miracle, both the giver of the miracle and the receiver of the miracle end up with more love than when they started.

> Miracles are a kind of exchange. Like all expressions of love, which are always miraculous in the true sense, the exchange reverses the physical laws. They bring more love both to the giver *and* the receiver.[192]

Conventional wisdom teaches that when you give something away, you have lost it to the one who receives it. But in the miracle, the giver and receiver both gain more love thus the miracle demonstrates that giving and receiving are the same:

> Miracles are teaching devices for demonstrating it is as blessed to give as it is to receive. They simultaneously increase the strength of the giver and supply strength to the receiver.[193]

It is also conventional wisdom that the human condition means being subject to the restraints of time. Miracles are not subject to time limitations. But the Course maintains that time is a useful device for learning and miracles accelerate that learning process hastening the day when the wordly illusion of time will no longer be needed.

Each day should be devoted to miracles. The purpose of time is to enable you to learn how to use time constructively. It is thus a teaching device and a means to an end. Time will cease when it is no longer useful in facilitating learning.[194]

Miracles are both beginnings and endings, and so they alter the temporal order. They are always affirmations of rebirth, which seem to go back but really go forward. They undo the past in the present, and thus release the future.[195]

The miracle is a learning device that lessens the need for time. It establishes an out-of-pattern time interval not under the usual laws of time. In this sense it is timeless.[196]

The miracle is the only device at your disposal for controlling time. Only revelation transcends it, having nothing to do with time at all.[197]

Miracles make minds one in God. They depend on cooperation because the Sonship is the sum of all that God created. Miracles therefore reflect the laws of eternity, not of time.[198]

The miracle abolishes the need for lower order concerns. Since it is an out-of-pattern time interval, the ordinary considerations of time and space do not apply. When you perform a miracle, I will arrange both time and space to adjust to it.[199]

Miracles do not behave according to ordinary laws of the physical universe, including time, because they have a divine Source. Miracles are manifested through various contributions from the Father, the Holy Spirit, and the Son. Jesus is the Son, but so are you, since you share the same Self in Christ. The difference between Jesus and you is that Jesus is fully aware of his holiness. Miracles help you to become aware of your holiness. In dictating the Course, Jesus states:

> I inspire all miracles, which are really intercessions. They intercede for your holiness and make your perceptions holy. By placing you beyond the physical laws they raise you into the sphere of celestial order. In this order you *are* perfect.[200]

A miracle is the universal blessing from God through me to all my brothers. It is the privilege of the forgiven to forgive.[201]

The Holy Spirit is the mechanism of miracles.[202]

The miracle dissolves error because the Holy Spirit identifies error as false or unreal. This is the same as saying that by perceiving light, darkness automatically disappears.[203]

Christ helps you perform miracles by offering you His vision in the real world, which is the gift the Holy Spirit makes available to you. In fact, Christ's vision itself is a miracle and the source of miracles.

Christ's vision is the miracle in which all miracles are born. It is their source, remaining with each miracle you give, and yet remaining yours. It is the bond by which the giver and receiver are united in extension here on earth, as they are one in Heaven. Christ beholds no sin in anyone. And in His sight the sinless are as one. Their holiness was given by His Father and Himself.[204]

You will have to be open to Christ's vision that allows your own mind to be filled with light so you can work miracles. Christ's vision reveals the light within you, allowing you to transfer the light in your mind to other minds. As you open your mind to the light, you will be able to facilitate miracles. It is possible for a mind to be wholly filled with light. Such a mind has a natural radiant quality that can extend effortlessly to other minds, helping them contact their own light.

When a mind has only light, it knows only light. Its own radiance shines all around it, and extends out into the darkness of other minds, transforming them into majesty. The Majesty of God is there, for you to recognize and appreciate and know. Recognizing the Majesty of God as your brother is to accept your own inheritance. God gives only equality. If you recognize His gift in anyone, you have acknowledged what He has given you.[205]

Christ's vision allows light and your true perceptions to reach the minds of others so they can let go of false perceptions and accept true perceptions producing miracles. In this sense, Christ's vision is the foundation for all miracles. It is the vehicle through which love can be extended to demonstrate oneness here on earth as a reflection of the Oneness of Heaven. Unlike your physical vision of your world that sees through the eyes of guilt, Christ's vision sees only holiness. In His sight, everyone is a holy brother created as a manifestation of the holiness of God the Father.

Being a miracle worker requires that you have learned to invite Christ's vision into your mind and invite the light into your mind that makes Christ's vision possible. It also means your mind is willing to let go of false perceptions and replace them with true perceptions. You will need to put that willingness into application by taking steps to purify your mind, such as prayer and meditation. Prerequisites for becoming a miracle worker are *purification, conviction, and miracle-readiness,* as is indicated in the following quotations:

> Miracles are everyone's right, but purification is necessary first.[206]

> Miracles bear witness to the truth. They are convincing because they arise from conviction.[207]

> Miracles arise from a miraculous state of mind, or state of miracle-readiness.[208]

Purification that is needed as a preparation for performing miracles is an ongoing process of being open to the Holy Spirit and learning to let go of false perceptions and retain true perceptions. To become a miracle worker you will have to come to the firm *conviction* that you can facilitate miracles with the help of divine grace. Your conviction is the result of your practice of switching from wrong-mindedness to right-mindedness yourself and trusting in God. From your practice of transforming your perceptions, you gain a state of right-mindedness that may also be considered a state of readiness to perform miracles. This *miracle-readiness* is a state of right-mindedness focused upon love that enables you to be a miracle worker. The person receiving the miracle certainly does not have to have right-mindedness in order to receive the miracle. In fact, the miracle is given through you as the miracle worker precisely to restore that person to his right mind. You can help others to return to their right mind only by being in your own right mind, even if your right-mindedness is just maintained briefly for the duration of the miracle.

> However, as a correction, the miracle need not await the right-mindedness of the receiver. In fact, its purpose is to restore him *to* his right mind. It is essential, however, that the miracle worker be in his right mind, however briefly, or he will be unable to re-establish right-mindedness in someone else.[209]

Your expressions of miracles bring you closer to the face of Christ in the real world. But you will not have to go all the way to the deepest level of the real world to catch a faint glimpse of Christ's face. You can certainly get a reflection of Christ's face by seeking His face in your brother. You can see in your brother a symbol of fear by seeing him as a body, or you can see the radiance of Christ shining through him. When you see the darkness you had perceived in him change into light, you will be seeing his true guiltlessness, sinlessness, and holiness.

F. LETTING YOUR BROTHER BE YOUR SAVIOR

Your brother becomes your savior if you can look upon him with the eyes of Christ, which are the eyes of forgiveness. In the Course, forgiveness is considered the healing of the illusion of separation that is caused by false perception.[210]

You cannot wake yourself. Yet you can let yourself be wakened. You can overlook your brother's dreams. So perfectly can you forgive him his illusions he becomes your savior from your dreams. And as you see him shining in the space of light where God abides within the darkness, you will see that God Himself is where his body is. Before this light the body disappears, as heavy clouds must give way to the light.[211]

The Course includes a great deal of explanation in the Text about forgiveness. Also, six different Workbook lessons contain instructions in which you are asked to select specific people and focus on forgiving these people. To look upon your brother with the eyes of forgiveness, you will need to not see him as a body. Honesty is truthfulness, and dishonesty is the lack of truthfulness. When you look at a person as being a body, it may be considered unintentional dishonesty—a lack of truthfulness due to ignorance.

If the Course is accepted as your philosophy and as an expression of your practice of Miracle Jnana Yoga, you will seek the awareness of Truth, just as Truth is sought in traditional Hindu jnana yoga. But in Miracle Jnana Yoga based upon the Course, your means of finding the Truth is forgiveness. Your brother can be the "honest person" who helps you find your mind and returns it to the lost and found, but you must also be the "honest person" to help him find his mind and return it to the lost and found. To be this honest person yourself you will have to look at your brother honestly. First comes the understanding of the truth that your brother is not a body and that he is the holy Son of God. Then comes the practice of seeing your brother with forgiving eyes, truthful eyes, that allow you to see past the illusion of the body.

You would need to invite divine grace and the gift of light into your mind in order to obtain Christ's vision. Then with Christ's vision, you can overlook appearances and see your brother truly. Christ's vision enables all your brother's sins to be forgiven, and these sins disappear since Christ in you sees only your brother's sinlessness. The sins are replaced by the vision of light behind them. The number and the seriousness of the sins do not matter because they are all removed. Even the apparent effects that these sins produced are undone by the action of the Holy Spirit. All your brother's sins are wiped away. All your sins are wiped away with your brother's sins.

Sins can be thought of as mistakes that are errors in judgment, but these mistakes do not mark your soul and are not a cause for guilt. The traditional belief that sin can affect your real nature and defile your soul is an illusion. Although sin is not real, it will seem real to the mind that believes it is real. That mind will be affected by this belief causing the feeling of guilt. Because of the false perception that sin is real, forgiveness is needed to reveal the true perception that sin is an illusion and that guilt produced by sin is likewise an illusion.

All your brother's sins and your sins have already been forgiven by the eternal judgment of God, Who created His Son in holiness. If you believe your brother has really sinned against you, you have mistakenly filed charges against your brother and against yourself because you do not know your brother's Identity or your own Identity. God, as your judge, cannot find guilt in your brother or in you because He knows your true Identity. God looks at the charges you have brought against your brother and yourself, and He immediately dismisses the charges due to a case of "mistaken identity."

God has already forgiven your brother and you by seeing that no forgiveness is ever needed. But you still think your brother and you need forgiveness. Therefore, you will have to forgive your brother and forgive yourself to realize that God has already forgiven you and that no forgiveness is needed since your brother and you are the holy Son of God. When you forgive your brother, a miracle happens in which the light in your mind goes to your brother's mind. Your brother's mind becomes bright from the light you sent, and in turn he shines his light back to your mind in gratitude. This is an exchange of light and love in which you both gain equally and neither loses. The result is that you become his savior, and he becomes your savior.

Whom you forgive is given power to forgive you your illusions. By your gift of freedom is it given unto you.

Make way for love, which you did not create, but which you can extend. On earth this means forgive your brother, that the darkness may be lifted from your mind. When light has come to him through your forgiveness, he will not forget his savior, leaving him unsaved. For it was in your face he saw the light that he would keep beside him, as he walks through darkness to the everlasting Light.

How holy are you, that the Son of God can be your savior in the midst of dreams of desolation and disaster. See how eagerly he comes, and steps aside from heavy shadows that have hidden him, and shines on you in gratitude and love. He is himself, but not himself alone. And as his Father lost not part of him in your creation, so the light in him is brighter still because you gave your light to him, to save him from the dark. And now the light in you must be as bright as shines in him. This is the spark that shines within the dream; that you can help him waken, and be sure his waking eyes will rest on you. And in his glad salvation you are saved.[212]

If you overlook your brother's sins and perceive your brother's true Identity, you will help shine a light into his mind that will help him to dissolve his illusions of sin and see his true sinlessness. You will see your brother as the "honest person" that he is. You cannot see your brother in one way and see yourself in another way. If you see your brother as being in a sinful state, you must also be in a sinful state and that is how you will see yourself. If you see with the forgiving eyes of Christ's vision that your brother's sins have been forgiven, you will realize that your own sins have been forgiven along with his. Thus you receive as you have given. The light you give your brother by forgiving him returns to you. Your brother will shine a light from his mind back to your mind to dissolve your own illusions of sin and restore your awareness of your sinlessness. Having given forgiveness, you receive forgiveness, and in this forgiveness is your joint salvation.

> See no one as a body. Greet him as the Son of God he is, acknowledging that he is one with you in holiness.
>
> Thus are his sins forgiven him, for Christ has vision that has power to overlook them all. In His forgiveness are they gone. Unseen by One they merely disappear, because a vision of the holiness that lies beyond them come to take their place. It matters not what form they took, nor how enormous they appeared to be, nor who seemed to be hurt by them. They are no more. And all effects they seemed to have are gone with them, undone and never to be done.
>
> Thus to you learn to give as you receive. And thus Christ's vision looks on you as well. This lesson is not difficult to learn, if you remember in your brother you but see yourself. If he be lost in sin, so must you be; if you see light in him, your sins have been forgiven by yourself. Each brother whom you meet today provides another chance to let Christ's vision shine on you, and offer you the peace of God.[213]

Through this process of forgiving others, you forgive yourself and thus accept God's judgment that you have been forgiven. Therefore, you become the "honest person" that helps your brother find his right mind, and your brother becomes the "honest person" that helps you find your right mind. This is a miracle in which you exchange light and love with your brother, and you both end up with more light and love than when you started. The light you see in your brother and you extend to him will be returned to you and in this exchange of light you will be brought deeper into the real world. Then Christ's vision will lift even the shiny transparent *veil*[214] that is all that is left in your vision of what had been your brother's body.

When this unsubstantial veil is lifted, you will see that you are not separate and apart from him for it is the same light that is in the both of you. This will make the mirror of your mind even cleaner so you can reflect the light more clearly. Your concepts of yourself will change from separateness to oneness. Ideally there will be nothing in your mind to block the light that is in you. Your mind will become so unified that you will be unable to see darkness at all. With judgment gone, you will see only oneness everywhere you look. Your single vision that shows you oneness will reveal Christ's face in the light.

The Course says you may have various types of episodes of light that are symbols of true perception. There are three varieties of light: There is physical light of the three-dimensional world, which ranges from the light of the sun to the light of a candle or light bulb. The true source of all light is the supernatural Light of God in which Christ exists and which is your own true nature. In between these two kinds of light is a light that is a symbolic reflection of the Light of God. This is the symbolic light that makes up the light of the real world. Just as this light is a symbolic refection of the Light of God, the real world is a symbolic reflection of Heaven. The symbolic light of the real world can be seen as a glow of light around the outlines of objects, and this glimmer of light is just a slight glimpse of the real world. This light can be seen with increasing clarity so more and more light can be seen. The more your own mind is filled with only true perceptions the more you will be able to see the light that symbolizes true perception. As you see more of this light, you are seeing more of the real world that is made up of only true perceptions and loving perceptions.

The light that symbolizes the true perception of the real world is not the supernatural Light of your true nature that is experienced in revelation, also called illumination. When you have experiences of seeing the light that represents true perception, you will be reminded of the Light of God that this light symbolizes. Thus you will begin to remember your Father and remember that you are the holy Son of God. As you invest in opening your awareness to the light of the real world, you will increase your awareness of your true nature.

When you get to the deepest level of the real world that is Christ's face, your perception will reach a degree of such holiness that God Himself will fuse your perception into knowledge, and you will awaken to your true nature in Oneness with God. Yet this level of realization is difficult to reach while still in this world. Any time you can let go of a single false perception and replace it with a true perception, you have gone a step closer to the real world that leads to awakening. There are many ways to grow toward awakening and obtaining the gift of Christ's vision can be seen as one of these ways.

Awakening Christ's vision through changing perceptions and seeing your brother differently with forgiving eyes is important, but turning inward for attunement to God is also important. The Course certainly advocates meditation, but inner attunement is a secondary emphasis. The major emphasis is on fostering loving relationships and practicing forgiveness. Some Course scholars believe the Course is not a mystical path since it is not primarily concerned with direct contact with God. It is true that mysticism, when it is considered a vertical and solitary ascent to union with God, is not the main goal of the Course. Yet I do not believe that mysticism can be accurately defined by the limiting stereotype of an exclusively vertical approach to God. In my opinion, mysticism to be whole and complete must be a vertical and horizontal approach to God. The Course includes both the vertical contact with God directly and the horizontal contact with God indirectly. But the Course places a greater focus on the horizontal approach of indirect union with God through relationships with your brother.

"A Course in Miracles" is primarily concerned with teaching about miracles. Miracles are expressions of love that unite you indirectly with God and that unite you directly with your brother. The inherent interpersonal nature of miracles is what makes them very helpful as learning devices. According to the Course, God does not need you to contact Him. Rather, He wants you to contact your brother.

Rather than advocating a solitary path of individual achievement, the Course offers a collective process in which your brother and you awaken by seeing the divine in each other. Seeing your brother as guiltless, means you will see yourself as guiltless. If you can see one brother as guiltless, your mind will generalize this so you will perceive every brother as guiltless. As you participate in healing the Sonship, you realize that you are part of the Sonship and therefore one with God. Every time you join with your brother, you bring both him and yourself one step closer to awakening in Heaven. The importance of developing relationships for spiritual growth in the practice of Miracle Relationship Yoga will be explored in the next chapter, which describes what the Course calls *holy relationships*.

CHAPTER 7

~ • ~

MIRACLE RELATIONSHIP YOGA

PHILOSOPHIES

A. A NEW YOGA OF HOLY RELATIONSHIPS

The prior chapter, this chapter, and the following chapters include information for you to consider the possibility of accepting *A Course in Miracles* as your new thought system to be used as a foundation for practicing Miracle Yoga as your specific form of Christian yoga. You may accept some aspects of Christian jnana yoga, Christian raja yoga, Christian bhakti yoga, and Christian karma yoga without accepting the Course. If you do accept the Course, Miracle Yoga would affect the various expressions of Christian yoga. In addition, the Course would make it appropriate to add a whole new category to the four types of Christian yoga that have already been identified. This new category is Christian relationship yoga, called *Miracle Relationship Yoga*, which was first mentioned in Chapter 1.

This Miracle Relationship Yoga is not related to tantric yoga and has no comparable counterpart in Hindu yoga, as there is with the other four categories. Classical yoga is focused on transcending the physical world, overcoming individual existence, and becoming free by merging with God. Tantric yoga holds the ideal of joining with God and yet returning to this world as *jivanmukti*, one who is freed while living. Some forms of tantric yoga include a sexual union between a man and women for spiritual growth, but this is considered only a preliminary stage in spiritual growth. The more advanced stage of this outer sexual union is the joining of the male and female energy currents within the body of the individual seeker and the rising of the kundalini. But all kinds of yoga, even tantric yoga, see meditation as the primary means of divine union and do not see relationships as a significant means of divine union.

One factor in the lack of relationships as a means of divine union in Hindu yoga is the way in which the individual is viewed in Vedanta.

Your true Self is already joined with God and when you realize your true nature, you return to God and become God. There really is not much of an emphasis on your brotherhood either here or in Heaven. Your relationship with God, your identity in God, is the relationship that is most important in Hindu yoga in which all the means of divine union are focused on the individual joining directly with God.

In contrast to this Hindu viewpoint, the Course sees your Identity as existing both in God and in your brother because your true Identity is in relationship. You are the Self, but this Christ Self is a shared identity. In this shared identity, you are a part of the Sonship and are also the Wholeness of God as His Son. Seeking only God-realization, as is the case in Hindu yoga, leaves out an important part of your true Identity—your brother in Christ, who shares your true Identity with you.

The ego is the idea of separation. It is the idea that you are alone. Consequently, when you decide to seek God, the ego wants to take command of your search for God. The ego as the seeker then would be drawn to making your search be an expression of you separately seeking God. The Course says the ego is willing to seek God because it will keep you running in circles with no intention of you ever finding God. Of course, God can be found, but the road is usually only a long and difficult path. The Course offers another way that takes less time, is less difficult, and is a way of overcoming the ego. In order to overcome the ego, you do not have to wait until after the end result of divine union ultimately occurs. You can overcome the ego's idea of separation as your means of growing toward divine union.

The ego is only an idea in your mind, but it has power because you believe in it. Overcoming the ego means taking away your allegiance to the ego and giving your allegiance to something real that is beyond the ego. Since the ego is the illusion of being alone, it promotes the belief that you are *of yourself.* The ego denies God is your Author and Creator and denies your brothers who were created as part of you. Yet you are not of yourself; you are of God and of your brothers. Thus you must find yourself in God and in your brothers.

The idea of a separate individual consciousness is manufactured by the ego that wants to limit the mind to your body. But you are a mind in the Mind of God and your true mind is a shared mind with the Sonship, which is another name for the Christ Self that everyone shares. In fact, your function in Heaven is to share your mind and this sharing is love and is your joy. Your ego state of mind that believes in a separate individual mind can be overcome by an experience of joining your mind with the mind of another person. When you join your mind with another mind, you demonstrate to yourself that you are not alone, and you demonstrate to the other person that he is not alone. This is the overcoming of the ego through relationship. A mind joined with another mind does lose its separateness, but does not lose all of its individual identity. A joined mind finds its individual identity in relationship rather than in aloneness.

Some of the specific ways described in the Course of overcoming the ego's idea of separation have already been emphasized in the prior chapter. These ways would include forgiveness, Christ's vision, and miracles. Another specific means of overcoming the ego is the *holy relationship*, which will be elaborated upon later in this chapter. Miracle Relationship Yoga is the practice of forming holy relationships as a means of spiritual growth.

B. THE CON GAME OF THE EGO

Before discussing the holy relationship, it would be helpful to have a deeper understanding of the ego. The ego is the idea of separation. Your true nature is found in your relationship with God and with your brother. You are a mind in Heaven and you are not separate from the Mind of God or from your brothers in the Sonship. Since the ego tells you in your dreaming state of this world that you are separate, the ego is in opposition to your true nature and is actually an attack on your true nature.

Qualities that you possess in your true nature are the qualities of God Himself, which are oneness, peace, holiness, bliss, and love. These qualities are not partial attributes. They are perfect expressions that are changeless, infinite, and complete. In your dreaming state of mind, you want to experience these attributes even if only in a partial manner that will reflect your true nature. You will want to experience the love that is your true nature and feel that you are worthy of being loved by others and worthy of loving others. You will also want to experience your holiness, which means your guiltlessness, even if you make errors in this world. You will want to experience the oneness of being united with your brothers in the world to reflect your divine union with our brothers in the Sonship. A fundamental aspect of your union in the Sonship is your equality with your brothers. God does not play favorites so He gave all of his sons in the Sonship everything equally because God gave all of Himself to each one.

A question you may ask yourself is, "If it is true that God gave me everything in Heaven, and if it is true that I made a choice to leave Heaven, why would I do such a foolish thing?" The answer to this question has already been given in the prior quotation on page 209 that explained some parts of the Sonship asked God to grant them "special favor." Apparently, they asked God to express love to them in some "special" way different from the love He gave to all the other parts of the Sonship. Yet God had already given the Sonship everything and gave Himself and all His Love equally to all parts of the Sonship. God could not give in an unequal manner and still be a truly loving Father. Therefore, God could not give the "special love" that was being requested. These parts of the Sonship who wanted special love could not actually leave Heaven so they decided to fall asleep in Heaven to express their disappointment, similar to children who do not get their way and then throw a tantrum.

The Course states that the "individual consciousness," meaning separate consciousness of the private mind, is an expression of the "original error."[215] Your mind used in this physical world is considered a separate mind limited to you as an individual and even limited to your body. On the other hand, your mind in Heaven is naturally a joined mind that is one with the Sonship in the Mind of God. The choice to leave Heaven was a choice to leave behind knowledge that is complete and represents the sharing of divine love in oneness. This decision to leave Heaven resulted in accepting the partial awareness of perception as a replacement for the wholeness of knowledge. Yet even in this state of partial awareness, you still want to be aware of the love, oneness, wholeness, and relatedness that you experience in Heaven when your mind possessed knowledge.

The Course uses the term "the separation" to label your loss of the awareness of Heaven. The Course does not say specifically how your mind in the One-mindedness of Heaven transformed into the separate "individual consciousness" caused by the "original error." The Course states God responded by creating the Holy Spirit as "His Answer" to the separation and placed the Holy Spirit in the minds of those who chose individual consciousness. You can choose to be led by the Holy Spirit back Home or choose to be led by the ego. The ego wants your allegiance so it can do what it wants to do. The ego appears to be you and so you would naturally assume that the ego is on your side. Actually the ego wants to attack you. Of course, the ego is not really an entity inside of you that can attack you. The ego is only an idea, a false concept of yourself. Your apparently separate "individual mind" is only acting out this false concept of itself being separate.

Unfortunately, this concept of yourself that the ego presents is in opposition to your true loving nature in the Sonship and in God. Thus your ego concept is an attack on you as you really are. Even though the ego is only an idea of separation, when your mind follows this idea, the ego instructs the mind to attack. Why does the ego lead you to attack? Attack is necessary for the ego to maintain its existence. If you were to actually give up all your allegiance to the ego, it would completely vanish since it only exists as an unreal concept with no substance behind it.

The mind mistakenly thinks its existence depends on the ego so the mind guided by the ego is under the illusion that it must protect the ego for the sake of survival. The ego protects itself by attack because attack promotes the belief in separation, which is the goal of the ego. Without attack, you might actually join with your brother and prove to yourself that you are not separate from your brother after all. The ego will instruct the mind to stay separate from other minds and devise many ways of attacking. The ego was actually created as an attack on God, which of course is impossible to accomplish. The ego is simply continuing to maintain attack as a way of survival.

Attack is totally foreign to your true nature. The ego does not want to lose your allegiance so it will always give your mind a somewhat "reasonable" justification for attack, even though attack in fact is never really justified. You will find a way to make yourself into a victim of someone else, and then you can justify your attack. You will put on a mask, called the "face of innocence,"[216] to appear outwardly good but to "justifiably" attack behind that mask. The face of innocence is the false mask of innocence you gain by playing the victim who actually invited attack just to justify attacking the victimizer in return.

Even if attack is only a mental judgment against another person, the judgment keeps you separate from your brother. Obviously there are many forms of attack that egos manifest, but the subtle forms of attack usually go unnoticed. The simplest and most common example is that every time you look at any brother or sister and see that person as a body, you have attacked that person by negating who that person really is in God and in the Sonship. You have also attacked yourself because seeing your brother as a body means you cannot avoid also seeing yourself as a body.

The result of every overt and subtle attack is guilt. Every attack is an attack on yourself that always results in some form of inner guilt. Guilt is the secret weapon of the ego that keeps you clinging to the ego. The ego presents guilt to you as the "gift" of a good conscience, but the ego hides the fact that guilt is just an unnecessary attack upon yourself. The ego deceives you into believing that guilt is necessary because you have done real damage with your attacks. Guilt is only justified in your mind if your attacks, which you consider to be your sins, produced real effects. You think your sins have produced the real results of damaging your reality and truly defiling your soul. Therefore, this defilement deserves punishment and in the case of a mortal sin deserves death. Guilt is then seen as an atonement for your sins.

Because atoning for sin is perceived as a good thing, guilt is seen as desirable. The ego wants you to believe you are a sinner and guilty because this belief keeps your ego in charge of your mind.

The ego is like a con man that convinces you to invest all of your worth in guilt. What is amazing about this is that this con game works extremely successfully. This con game consists of three basic beliefs: The first is the belief in separation that is the foundation of the ego. The second is the belief in attack that seems justified as a means of maintaining the ego. The third is the belief in guilt that is the result of attack and that keeps the con game going. If you invest in the dictates of the ego and believe attack in any form is justified, you will receive your "reward" of guilt, and you will keep coming back for more.

This con game is the game of keeping the ego "alive," yet it has never been alive and never will be alive. The ego can only pretend to be alive, but this con game is just too convincing to not be taken in by it. Unfortunately, your mind equates the ego with you and therefore equates the ego with life. The ego sees guilt as an important aspect of staying "alive." Because of your identification with the ego, you unconsciously associate having guilt with staying alive, just as the ego does. Therefore, you are attracted to guilt and seek out "opportunities" for guilt. Your guilt is always a sentence you place upon yourself, not one imposed by God. You invest in guilt because you believe that your attack produced real results that marked your soul with sin and caused harm to your brothers because of what you did.

The *attraction to guilt* is an awful idea. Possibly you are reading these words now and are feeling some resistance to the ideas about guilt presented here. After all, who would want to see themselves as actually wanting guilt? Who would want to admit seeking opportunities to play the victim just to justify attack in return? Who would want to admit to putting on the *face of innocence* as a mask to hide the goal of attack? Who would want to admit to being duped by the con game of the ego? The Course paints such a very dark picture of the ego that it is obviously difficult to look at the nightmares that the ego manufactures. Some seekers who read the Text of the Course will turn away from the Course because of the stark and dark way the ego is described.

Even if you know the ego is an illusion, you want to believe the ego is a benign fact of life that is evolving and growing with you. Yet the ego does not evolve and thinking it does is a confusion of your ego with your *total self-image*. The ego is at the center of your concept of yourself. All the other ideas you have about yourself that surround your ego are the ego's thought system that forms your total self-image. The ego is the one false idea that says you are separate, and this idea of separation is always in direct opposition to your true nature, and it does not evolve. This central idea of the ego must ultimately be relinquished and replaced by the awareness of your true Identity.

On the other hand, all the other ideas about yourself that form your ego-based thought system and your total self-image do change and can evolve. Although the ego as the idea of separation must be eliminated, the ego's thought system can learn and must be taught. This teaching and this learning involve releasing false and unloving perceptions of the ego's thought system and replacing them with true and loving perceptions inspired by the Holy Spirit.

> The ego *is* a contradiction. Your self and God's Self *are* in opposition. They are opposed in source, in direction and in outcome. They are fundamentally irreconcilable, because spirit cannot perceive and the ego cannot know. They are therefore not in communication and can never be in communication. Nevertheless, the ego can learn, even though its maker can be misguided. He cannot, however, make the totally lifeless out of the life-given.
>
> Spirit need not be taught, but the ego must be. Learning is ultimately perceived as frightening because it leads to the relinquishment, not the destruction, of the ego to the light of spirit. [217]

With spiritual growth, you can release an increasing number of the false ideas of the ego's thought system so you can form a better total self-image as you evolve spiritually. Of course, your total self-image must be relinquished eventually along with the ego itself. Your total self-image is only a collection of self-concepts. Your self-image is only an image of you and is not the real you. Yet by improving your total self-image, you can let go of fearful perceptions of nightmares and accept the loving perceptions of the happy dreams of the real world, as a preparation for entering Heaven.

Nevertheless, the ideas of your total self-image that are closest to the ego are your darkest nightmares that are so hateful that perceiving seeing them can be extremely traumatic. Those who experience the dark night of the soul contact these nightmares. Such nightmares can be so horrible that they become temptations to commit suicide. Hiding behind these darkest nightmares is your greatest fear, which is the last barrier to revealing the awareness of your true nature. This last barrier is the fear of God and His Love. Besides being the idea of separation, the ego itself is also idea of fear.[218] The ego is most afraid of God and His Love, which will obliterate it. The ego must hide from God's Love to survive so it makes God and His Love your greatest hidden fear. In addition to God's Love, your greatest fear includes your response to

God's Love, which is your own intense love for God. Because you are afraid of God's Love, you are terrified of awakening.

> Your real terror is of redemption [awakening in Heaven].
> Under the ego's dark foundation is the memory of God, and it is of this that you are really afraid. For this memory would instantly restore you to your proper place, and it is this place that you have sought to leave. Your fear of attack is nothing compared to your fear of love.[219]

> For still deeper than the ego's foundation, and much stronger than it will ever be, is your intense and burning love of God, and His for you. This is what you really want to hide. In honesty, is it not harder for you to say "I love" than "I hate?" You associate love with weakness and hatred with strength, and your own real power seems to you as your real weakness. For you could not control your joyous response to the call of love if you heard it, and the whole world you thought you made would vanish.[220]

> You think you have made a world God would destroy; and by loving Him, which you do, you would throw this world away, which you *would*. Therefore, you have used the world to cover your love, and the deeper you go into the blackness of the ego's foundation, the closer you come to the Love that is hidden there. *And it is this that frightens you.*
> You can accept insanity because you made it, but you cannot accept love because you did not.[221]

Because the ego will cease to exist in God's Love, the ego tells you that you will cease to exist in God's Love. The ego wants to convince you that the ego itself is your *savior* who will keep you protected from God and His Love that would destroy you. Since you are attracted to God's Love, the ego offers you a *substitute love* that will be explained below. This substitute love is a distorted version of love that you can make yourself, rather than the authentic love that God has given you in your creation. In offering you this distorted form of man-made love, the ego pretends to be your "friend" that looks out for your interests. Yet the ego is actually only concerned with its own survival through maintaining separation. The ego definitely does not evolve into some higher form as some spiritual seekers want to believe. The ego just gets more devious about hiding its motivations from you.

If you realize the con game that the ego is perpetrating upon you, what can you do about it? You cannot make "friends" with the ego itself, and you cannot make a bargain with the ego. Also, it would be very unwise to make the ego into an "enemy" and try to attack it. When you respond to the ego with emotions, you continue to foster either the self that you made or the holy Son of God that your Father created. You cannot be both because only one can be real. Who do you think is right about your identity—you or God? Since God is Reality, only what He created can be real and anything made apart from God cannot be real. You need to withdraw your allegiance from the ego and place your allegiance with the Holy Spirit. The ego is not real so the ego and its motivations are not "good" or "bad." The ego is merely meaningless and needs to be viewed as such.[222]

> The self you made is not the Son of God. Therefore, this self does not exist at all. And anything it seems to do and think means nothing. It is neither bad nor good. It is unreal, and nothing more than that. It does not battle with the Son of God. It does not hurt him, nor attack his peace. It has not changed creation, nor reduced eternal sinlessness to sin, and love to hate. What power can this self you made possess, when it would contradict the Will of God?
>
> Your sinlessness is guaranteed by God. Over and over this must be repeated, until it is accepted. It is true. Your sinlessness is guaranteed by God. Nothing can touch it, or change what God created as eternal. The self you made, evil and full of sin, is meaningless. Your sinlessness is guaranteed by God, and light and joy and peace abide in you.[223]

Seeing the ego's meaninglessness enables you to have dispassion, allowing you to let go of your attachment and emotional reactions to the ego and its dictates. Since the ego is meaningless, it does not exist, and it cannot grow and evolve into some higher state. If you believe that the ego evolves, you may not examine the ego deeply enough to reveal its true meaninglessness. Failure to examine the ego deeply will allow the ego to remain hidden so it cannot be brought into the light, which would reveal its true meaninglessness.

The Course information describes the darkest hidden corners of the ego to expand your understanding of the inner workings of the ego. It is your responsibility to bring the dark hidden aspects of your ego to the light. The Course does not really advise you to dwell on these dark nightmares and give them a reality they do not have. The Course encourages you to see that these nightmares are unreal as soon as you encounter them. After uncovering these nightmares and seeing they are unreal, then the Course advises you to bring these nightmares to the Holy Spirit for healing. But if you deny the nightmares and keep them hidden, you will not be able to expose these nightmares to the light of the Holy Spirit that would dispel them.

How will the ego respond to your attempt to reveal these dark nightmares? The ego will try to make you feel guilty. In fact, the goal of the ego is always guilt. The ego will encourage you to find someone or something to blame, which will make you feel guilty. The ego may point the finger of blame at the Course or at someone who teaches the concepts of the Course that reveal the dark nightmares perpetuated by the ego. For example, the ego may tempt you to see all the distasteful activities of the ego as more reasons to feel guilty about yourself. Guilt will be offered to you by the ego as the best way to atone for what the ego has manifested in these nightmares. The ego will tell you to feel sorry for your participation in these nightmares. Blaming yourself for anything is really a continuation of ego's con game. If you blame yourself, it shows that you are still identifying with the ego as being yourself. It also demonstrates that you still believe you are guilty and need to atone for your guilt by punishing yourself, which reinforces the ego. The Course sees blaming others or yourself as two sides of the same coin used by the ego as a means of fostering guilt.

> If your brothers are part of you and you blame them for your deprivation, you are blaming yourself. And you cannot blame yourself without blaming them. That is why blame must be undone, not seen elsewhere. Lay it to yourself and you cannot know yourself, for only the ego blames at all. Self-blame is therefore ego identification, and as much an ego defense as blaming others. You cannot enter God's Presence if you attack His Son.[224]

Many readers of the Text find that they feel disconcerted and indeed feel guilty when reading the Course's portrayal of the dark motivations of the ego. Sometimes disbelief in the Course itself surfaces because the whole dark picture of the ego and its manifestation is just too disturbing to bear. But the Course is recommended as the foundation for your practice of Miracle Jnana Yoga because this thought system focused on seeking of the truth that requires clear mental discrimination. This must be a dispassionate sincere search for the truth that cannot be set aside simply because it reveals the dark shadows of the mind. If these ideas presented in the Course are simply in fact not true, then there is no problem in setting the Course material aside. But the search for the truth hopefully will not be deterred just because it is very personally challenging to your ego.

Consequently, it is essential to look at the dark nightmares of the mind with dispassion and without guilt and offer these nightmares to the Holy Spirit for healing. The temptation to indulge in guilt must be resisted because there is light at the end of the dark tunnel that the ego presents. If you can overcome the temptation to indulge in guilt and self-condemnation, you will begin to let go of your allegiance to the ego itself and instead invest in the truth.

The truth is that it is impossible for you to change what God has created and God has created you as holy and guiltless. You have only two choices: You can choose to wake up in Heaven and realize your true nature as God created you in holiness. Or you can choose to continue to sleep in Heaven and dream of participating in a world of illusions. In your dreams, you can have nightmares of harming your brothers and harming yourself, but you cannot make your nightmares into something real. You can practice forgiveness and invite the Holy Spirit into your nightmares. Amazingly, with your invitation, the Holy Spirit will undo all the effects of your errors in your dreams. The Holy Spirit can show you that guilt is unnecessary because your apparent destructiveness in nightmares produced no real effects in yourself or others. Once you realize that guilt is unnecessary, the dominance of the ego can be replaced by the guidance of the Holy Spirit.

C. SPECIAL RELATIONSHIPS

The ego wishes to hide the truth of its meaninglessness from you so you will not give up your allegiance to the ego. You really want love and not attack, so the ego cannot afford to let you know that its goal is not love but rather attack and the fruit of attack, which is guilt. Since your natural inclination is toward relationship and love and since the ego wants your allegiance, it will offer you the love that you are seeking. However, the ego will not tell you its motto, which is: "Seek but do not find?"[225] The ego is in favor of your seeking love in relationships as long as you seek in the way that it shows you. The purpose of the ego is to hold love out before you like a carrot dangling before your eyes, but never actually let you have this carrot. The ego encourages you to seek love in *specialness* because it knows you will never really find love in specialness.

Specialness is a substitute for real love. Real love is God's love, which is total giving. Real loving is a giving that holds nothing back. When you share love completely in Heaven, you do not lose the love you share. In fact, you keep the love in your act of giving it away. Because you are an extension of God's Love, to be true to yourself, you will only be satisfied with loving in the way that God loves.

You cannot enter into real relationships with any of God's Sons unless you love them all and equally. Love is not special. If you single out part of the Sonship for your love, you are imposing guilt on all your relationships and making them unreal. You can love only as God loves. Seek not love unlike Him, for there is no love apart from His. Until you recognize that this is true, you will have no idea what love is like.[226]

There is nothing partial about real love. Real love extends to all of your brothers and sisters equally. If there are any exceptions to your love, you are expressing partial love and not real love. If your love is exclusive in any way, it may be considered *special love*, in contrast to real love. Partial love is only an illusion that presents an outer form of love that is a mask covering separation and guilt.

Unlike real love, specialness offers a special love that is exclusive and promises specialness. Why does the ego offer specialness? This is more of the ego's con game of offering you something that appears desirable, but in fact is totally undesirable. If separation was presented to you as isolation, you would not want it. Thus the ego offers you a new and improved separation—an *exalted separation*. The ego wants you to be better than others in order to inflate your self-concept of specialness. The ego tells you to seek specialness and find happiness and love in specialness. The ego does not tell you that in seeking specialness you are really seeking separation and guilt that reinforces the ego. The ego convinces you specialness is desirable by appealing to your pride. If you invest in specialness and separation, you repeat the first mistake that you made in the original separation.

The ego gives you the impression that there is a void in you, a lack in you. In your true nature, you are lacking nothing, but you feel a void because of your investment in the ego, which is both the idea of separation and the idea of limitation. However, the ego does not want you to realize that the ego itself is the source of this void. This apparent void can be healed by increasing your awareness of God and His divine Love, but the ego does not want you to find the real love that would fill this void. The ego says you can fill the lack within you by the ego's substitute for real love, which is specialness.

Specialness separates you from others, but that seems fine since being apart allows you to be elevated into a position above others. Specialness has a strong appeal because it seems to offer self-worth and fill the void in you, while ironically it actually takes away your true worth. The self-worth of specialness is really pride and really an attack on others. Being elevated above others means others must be below you for you to keep your specialness. In truth, you are equal to all your brothers just as God created you. However, to maintain your specialness, you must live a lie. You must attack others creating in your own mind inequality in which you must be better than others to gain your self-worth. But instead of self-worth, you gain only the fruits of attack, which are isolation and guilt that reinforce the ego.

You can seek specialness within your own mind by simply inflating your estimations of yourself and thinking of yourself as better than others in various specific ways. But seeking specialness only in your own mind does not fill the lack that you feel inside so you want to manifest specialness in relationships with others in order to hopefully fill the void within you. These relationships in which you are seeking specialness are called "special love relationships."[227] Ultimately, these special love relationships express the desire to have the Love of God, but you end up seeking special love as a substitute for real love.

> In Heaven, where the meaning of love is known, love is the same as union. Here, where the illusion of love is accepted in love's place, love is perceived as separation and exclusion.
>
> It is the special relationship, born of the hidden wish for special love from God, that the ego's hatred triumphs. For the special relationship is the renunciation of the Love of God, and the attempt to secure for the self the specialness that He denied. It is essential to the preservation of the ego that you believe this specialness is not hell, but Heaven. For the ego would never have you see that separation could only be loss, being the one condition in which Heaven could not be.[228]

Special love is a false love that is never totally giving, as real love is. In fact, specialness is used for taking rather than giving. The idea of a special love relationship is to take specialness from your partner and acquire this specialness for yourself. You feel a lack within yourself so you present a special mask to entice your partner, and your partner feels a lack within and presents a special mask to you. You join with your partner to take the specialness you see in your partner and have it for yourself, and your partner joins to take your specialness from you. Since specialness itself is an attack, each partner is unknowingly attacking the other partner in the name of love. This is only an illusion of love. The Course refers to the special love relationship as the *unholy relationship* in which the aim is to exclude the reality of your partner so that the illusion of love will not be spoiled.

> The "ideal" of the unholy relationship thus becomes one in which the reality of the other does not enter at all to "spoil" the dream. And the less the other really brings to the relationship, the "better" it becomes. Thus the attempt at union becomes a way of excluding even the one with whom the union is sought.

For it was formed to get him out of it, and join with fantasies in uninterrupted "bliss."[229]

Unlike the giving of everything occurring in real love, the giving that occurs in the special love relationship is a *giving to get*. This giving is really a *bargain* with guilt attached to each act of giving that says the receiver must pay back in return.[230] Your giving justifies your attack on your partner if your partner does not give you back an equal or greater return. Such attacks are expressions of anger that are always intended to make someone else feel guilty. The loved one is playing at being a victim of an ungrateful partner who does not appreciate all of the sacrifices made for the partner. Such a victim is obliged to attack and become a victimizer, while maintaining the face of innocence.

Then your partner feels fully justified to say you do not appreciate his sacrifices so your partner plays the victim also and then becomes a victimizer of you. While both partners willingly take turns playing victim and victimizer, the special love relationship keeps rolling along ironically with each "equally" contributing to the bargain. Sometimes you "give" more to the relationship to relieve your guilt. Sometimes your partner "gives" more to relieve his guilt. In this balancing, act each partner contributes in the same way and that seems fair, so it appears both partners are having their needs met in the relationship. The bargain seems to be working. A blunt way to describe the special relationship is to say that each partner wants to "steal" the specialness of his partner to compensate for a perceived lack of specialness felt within. Since the special love relationship is based on "giving to get" and based on the illusion of taking specialness from another to fill a void of specialness within, the illusions of this unholy relationship cannot be maintained for long without resulting in disillusionment.

For the unholy relationship is based on differences, where each one thinks the other has what he has not. They come together, each to complete himself and rob the other. They stay until they think that there is nothing left to steal, and then move on. And so they wander through a world of strangers, unlike themselves, living with their bodies perhaps under a common roof that shelters neither; in the same room and yet a world apart.[231]

The special love relationship is not real love and not real giving. Because only real love will satisfy you, you will tire of special love and you or your partner or both of you will find reasons to make your bargain not work. You will no longer want to have the specialness your partner has, or your partner will no longer appear special to you. You will get tired of playing at being a victim and then victimizer. You may even get depressed or sick. The Course sees sickness as an outward manifestation of the inner feeling of guilt. Sickness is a self-imposed punishment of yourself for your own guilt, but illness can be used in a special relationship as a means of making your partner feel guilty. In this case, illness becomes a way of indirectly telling your partner that this sickness is what your partner did to you.

One way to end a special love relationship is to switch to a *special hate relationship* in which you see your partner as your enemy. In this relationship, you blame your partner for the specialness that your partner stole from you, and you demand your partner to give back the specialness that was taken from you. This relationship allows you to take away all the pretense of love. Instead of attacking indirectly, you take the direct approach and just attack without reservation. If all this sounds like an insane way of expressing relationships, it is indeed just that. But the unfortunate truth is that the special love relationship is par for the course in this world. Relationships in which love and hate find a way of coexisting are simply not true love and will not fill the void in you, although they may seem to do so temporarily.

A special love relationship appears to be a joining but is merely an illusion of joining. Special love relationships are unholy relationships in which there is no true relating.[232] You and your partner each thinks that you are an ego in a body and joining another ego in a body. The act of seeing your partner as a body is an attack on your partner and an attack on yourself. Obviously attack and joining do not go together. The joining of a special love relationship is a union in which you and your partner each seeks to have your individual needs met *separately* by giving only to get. This joining takes the *form* of union but not the *content*. Each partner has separate needs that are met with only a faint glimmer of love shining through to maintain the illusion of love. Attempting to meet separate needs only reinforces the ego and the feeling that you are alone rather than joined. You can find your true Identity in your brother but not through a special love relationship since it is an unholy relationship in which real love is excluded.

The one good thing about the special love relationship is that it shows you what you do not want. After experiencing failure in special love relationships, if you can let go of the unnecessary guilt that these relationships engender, perhaps you will be inspired to seek out *holy relationships*. For example, you may have a current special relationship that you would like to see change into a holy relationship. A special relationship can be turned into a holy relationship if both you and your partner are willing to change the way in which you are relating in your relationship. The beginning of manifesting a holy relationship is to see common interests, which leads to partners joining for a common purpose, as will be explained subsequently.

D. THE ORIGIN OF THE COURSE

You can find your true Identity in your brother, rather than looking at yourself alone. If you extend love from your mind to your brother's mind, you will discover that love must be within for you to be able to extend it. Your extension of love will strengthen your belief that love is your own true nature. You will also learn that your mind is not confined to your body. Rather, your mind is shared with your brother. Specifically the Course promotes the "holy relationship" as a means of extending your mind and your love to others. In the holy relationship, you join with another person for a common purpose.

One way to illustrate the importance of the holy relationship is to look at the origin of the Course itself. If you are a Christian, your most significant personal relationship may possibly be with Jesus. Once you wake up to the degree of wanting to become aware of God, you, as a Christian, are inviting Jesus into your life. Jesus is the leader of what the Course calls the *Atonement*,[233] which is God's Plan for coming Home. Jesus does not limit his guidance only to seekers who call on his name. The scribe of the Course was Helen Schucman, a Jewish psychologist. She was an atheist, and she was not consciously seeking Jesus. Yet Jesus spoke to her and dictated the words of the Course to her. Since Helen did not call out to Jesus, how was Jesus invited into her life? There must have been an invitation of some kind because He would not have come unless there was an invitation.

Jesus did receive an invitation, but it came without any conscious thought of Jesus. The invitation came as a decision without realizing what the implications of that decision would be. The most significant aspect of this decision is that it was a mutual decision made by two people, not a decision made by one person alone. It was a decision to join in a common purpose. The two people were Helen Schucman and Bill Thetford, both psychologists. For seven years, they worked in the same college psychology department and experienced pain in their relationship due to conflict based upon each of them seeking to satisfy separate interests. Then Helen and Bill were talking one day, and Bill said the problems that they experienced in their work together were due to approaching these problems in the wrong way. "There must," Bill said, "be another way..."[234]

Bill spoke with uncommon conviction, and then waited for Helen to give her response. Helen leaped up and told Bill that he was most certainly correct. Furthermore, she said that she would unite with him in the new way of approaching the problems facing them. This new approach turned out to be finding and manifesting a better way of relating that exemplified cooperation and love. But the approach itself was not the important occurrence here. What was important is that a *holy instant* occurred. According to the Course, the holy instant is an instant in which you can let go of the past and experience a divine connection and communion with your brothers. In this holy instant both Helen and Bill left the past habitual reaction patterns and were both open to a new experience that included a heightened awareness of each other and the ability to see differently.

In this holy instant of inspiration, Helen and Bill agreed to join in a common purpose. In this joining for a common purpose, their holy relationship was born. The full significance of this joining was not immediately apparent, but from that holy instant onward, their lives would never be the same. The minds of Helen and Bill had been joined in a holy instant in which they had agreed upon the purpose of finding a better way. Yet the result of their joining far exceeded what they had hoped for in the way of solving a specific problem in their relationship and environment. It was after their joining that Helen started to have visions and received instruction from Jesus to write down His words. This produced *A Course in Miracles*, which was the answer provided by Jesus to Helen's and Bill's seeking to find a better way. Of course, this unexpected response to their specific problem has become a means of spiritual growth of many seekers since then.

E. JOINING FOR A COMMON PURPOSE

The foundation of the holy relationship is agreement on a common purpose. Two people having the same purpose is just the agreement to hold the same idea in their minds and to both seek that idea as a goal. Why would having a shared idea of a goal be so important that it could make a relationship holy?

To find the answer first consider how tangible things are shared. If you and a friend share a hundred dollars equally, you would each own fifty dollars. Consequently, the sharing of forms means divided ownership. But when your elementary school teacher shared the idea that two plus two equals four, you retained this idea and your teacher retained this same idea that was given to you. Therefore, in sharing an idea, there is no loss to the giver or the receiver.

Consider how you choose to share ideas. If you are a body, much of your life is focused upon meeting your body's needs, and you use ideas as a means of getting what you as a body need and want. Thus you decide what your personal interests are and set goals to meet your body's needs for food, clothing, money, sex, recognition, and power. Your basic premise is that you are alone and if you do not meet your needs, nobody else will. You perceive yourself as different from others, because of having different bodies, personalities, education, beliefs, and goals. When you enter relationships you decide how your needs will be met in the relationship. You meet the needs of your partner in order to have your needs met. You have special love relationships based upon a bargain that says you will meet your partner's needs if your partner meets your needs. If your needs are not being met, you will decide it is a bad bargain and look at making changes.

But even if your apparent needs are met, you will not be satisfied because you will still feel a void in your life, which is caused by not living a life that reflects who you are. You are a mind in the Mind of God joined with your brothers so your real need is to mirror this fact in your everyday life to remind you of who you are. This starts with the simple idea that you have common interests with your brother. If you decide to join with a brother to achieve a goal together, you are manifesting a holy relationship. Previously I posed this question: "Why would having a shared idea of a goal be so important that it could make a relationship holy?" The answer is that in the act of joining to achieve a goal together, partners are accepting holiness, equality, and sameness in each other, and you are drastically departing from your usual seeking of specialness, which includes competitiveness.

However, to be a holy relationship your joining cannot be done as a bargain to get your *separate* needs met, otherwise you would just be participating in another special love relationship. Your joining must be for a common purpose to meet *common* needs. In your goal of meeting common needs together, you are making a recognition that you and your partner have common interests. If you have common interests and common needs, you must not be different after all. You can see yourself in your partner and your partner can see himself in you. Instead of seeing differences, you are seeing how you are similar. You are beginning to see perhaps that you may be the same, just as you once saw in Heaven that you were a part of each other. A simple shared idea has brought back a forgotten memory of your true Home together when you were aware of being joined in oneness.

Furthermore, you are sharing an idea together. If you are a body, you could not share an idea because bodies cannot share ideas. But if you are a mind, and indeed you are, then something wonderful has happened. You have come Home in your mind. In Heaven you shared yourself fully by giving all of yourself to all of your brothers in the Sonship. Just like the idea of two and two equaling four can be shared without any loss to the giver or receiver, you could share yourself in Heaven as a divine idea and could only gain by sharing and never lose by sharing. Actually, you left Heaven by stopping your sharing of yourself. You wanted to become a private mind, an individual consciousness. This is the source of the void in you. But the holy relationship can begin to heal this void. If you can find just one brother to share your mind in a common purpose, you prove to yourself that your mind does not have to be private. This sharing of a common purpose affects your ego base idea of yourself.

> The ego believes it is completely on its own, which is merely another way of describing how it thinks it originated. This is such a fearful state that it can only turn to other egos and try to unite with them in a feeble attempt at identification, or attack them in an equally feeble show of strength. It is not free, however, to open the premise to question, because the premise is its foundation. The ego is the mind's belief that it is completely on its own.[235]

The ego is the thought that you are alone. By sharing a common purpose, you demonstrate that you are not alone. In this overcoming of aloneness, you are overcoming the ego. In order to understand the ramifications of sharing a common purpose, it is helpful to consider what setting any significant goal means to you. A goal is something you are seeking and want. If the goal is important to you, you will dedicate your efforts, time, and loving attention toward accomplishing the goal. If you really want the goal, your mind will direct its thoughts toward the goal and your actions will be expressions of moving in the direction of the goal. You will begin to define yourself in terms of the goal, and the goal will provide meaning to your life. The ego itself is meaningless, so a life with meaning overcomes the ego.

However, the goal of a holy relationship is not a solitary goal, but a common purpose. You and another person are moving in the same direction to the same goal together with joined interests. You are not doing this for yourself alone, but for both of you. This is not a bargain based on separate interests because you and your partner maintain this purpose as a joint effort motivated by common interests. Since you are doing this together, you direct your mind and actions toward this common purpose along with your partner. Because your partner is traveling with you along the same path to the same destination for a shared purpose, you and your partner have both gained and neither has lost. You have shared not only the idea of joining, but also shared in the practical experience of togetherness itself.

Just as any goal becomes a way of defining yourself, the sharing of a common goal becomes a way of redefining yourself in terms of your partner. You begin to see your identity as a joined identity, not as an isolated identity. Your isolated identity is the ego. Your belief in the ego makes you believe your life is defined by isolation. The existence of the ego depends on maintaining separation. The ego wants you to believe you are the ego and your life, indeed your very existence, depends on maintaining separation. The ego's agenda is to keep you believing in isolation. However, when you share a common purpose with someone, you prove to yourself that you are not isolated. The dominance of your ego identity is replaced by the beginnings of a joined identity, which is a reflection of your true nature as a joined identity in the Sonship.

Does the common purpose have to be an overtly spiritual purpose? No. When you first join, it can be for any common purpose as long as you have the correct motivation. If you are joined on the form level to do a common purpose together but are joined to meet *separate* needs, it will not be a holy relationship. You and a business partner can start a business with each of you having the purpose of making money. If you are in the business to make money for yourself and your partner is in the business to make money for himself, you both have the same purpose of making money. However, you have the same purpose separately to meet separate needs and not a common purpose to meet common needs.

Can you change a special love relationship into a holy relationship by changing your own mind regarding the purpose of the relationship without your partner changing his mind too? If only one partner sees a common purpose and common interests, the partnership is not a holy relationship. A common misconception of Course principles is to think that the holy relationship can be within your own mind only. If it is within your own mind only, you are still alone. In fact, the holy relationship is a demonstration that your apparently private mind is not private after all. The holy relationship is a joining of minds and therefore must be experienced in both minds simultaneously. To be a holy relationship, there has to be relating between two minds acting as one in purpose. This link between minds is what brings holiness to the relationship and recalls to your mind and your partner's mind your participation together in the Sonship. "Only a purpose unifies, and those who share a purpose have a mind as one."[236]

This joining of minds occurs in the long-term holy relationships, but you will also experience this joining of minds in temporary holy relationships. For example, a temporary holy relationship is manifested when true forgiveness happens. When true forgiveness takes place, two people join and have a temporary common purpose of healing. Forgiveness produces mutual healing in both participants.

The Course teaches you to forgive by changing your perceptions in order to see the world, your brothers, and your life differently. In traditional Christianity, forgiveness is seen as an act that you carry out in your mind in which you forgive your brother for his sins. It is a gift that you bestow on your brother for what he has really done to you. Yet the Course teaches that you forgive your brother by seeing him as being sinless. You do this by perceiving that his apparent sins had no true effect on you since you are a holy Son of God. This shows your brother that the sins, having no effect, must be unreal. Because his sins had no effect, your brother has no cause for guilt, and you have no cause for guilt either. This undoing of sins reveals that what are called "sins" are actually only mistakes that can be corrected.

> Forgiveness is not real unless it brings a healing to your brother and yourself. You must attest his sins have no effect on you to demonstrate they are not real. How else could he be guiltless? And how could his innocence be justified unless his sins have no effect to warrant guilt? Sins are beyond forgiveness just because they would entail effects that cannot be undone and overlooked entirely. In their undoing lies the proof that they are merely errors. Let yourself be healed that you may be forgiving, offering salvation to your brother and yourself.[237]

Forgiveness is not an experience happening in your mind alone. A single act of forgiveness between two people is a temporary holy relationship with the common purpose of healing. This temporary holy relationship produces healing for both your mind and your brother's mind. It is a miracle—an exchange of love in which your minds join for an instant. Your brother's mind and your mind are relieved of guilt simultaneously. Specialness is always based on inequality, but in the miracle, there is no specialness because you are both healed and healed equally.

> How just are miracles! For they bestow an equal gift of full deliverance from guilt upon your brother and yourself. Your healing saves him pain as well as you, and you are healed because you wished him well. This is the law the miracle obeys; that healing sees no specialness at all. It does not come from pity, but from love.[238]

According to the Course, forgiveness that does not heal both you and your brother is not real. Likewise, any holy relationship is not a real relationship unless both minds are joined in a mutual purpose in which you both see common interests. Very similar to the miracle of forgiveness in which two brothers heal each other in a temporary holy relationship, the long-term holy relationship offers healing to both of you so that you become saviors for each other.

What aspect of your mind needs the most healing? It is the ego itself, the idea that you are separate. Minds that join transcend the ego. *Miracle Relationship Yoga* replaces the dominance of ego with the union of the holy relationship. This yoga overcomes isolation by the revealing of your true reality in the holy relationship.

The Course identifies the faulty thinking of the ego as the "Laws of Chaos," and, "The *first* chaotic law is that the truth is different for everyone."[239] This false belief means it is up to you to decide what is truth and there is no such thing as objective absolute truth. Your ego fosters specialness telling you that you can believe what you want to believe and call it "your truth" and "your reality." Here is a related saying: "You create your own reality," but this is simply not true. A truthful statement is: "You make your own unreality." The unreality that you have made is that you live in your own private world in your own mind. This private world is lonely. You and no one else can know your private world because you made it to be private and to be a place where your ego feels at home. Your private world is within the body that keeps you separate from others, who are also living in their private mental worlds and their separate physical bodies.

What happens to your private world when you join with a brother in a common purpose and see common interests? Can you really say that your world is actually private when it is shared with another? Your common goal can become the idea that motivates your whole world, and you can see in your brother that this same goal becomes the idea that motivates his whole world. All things can revolve around the same goal, and you can see that you both have the same central aim around which everything revolves. Since your two minds function as one with a common purpose, you will perceive yourself as being in a condition of union rather than being in a condition of isolation.

Your most important holy relationships will be your long-term holy relationships. Yet there will be many opportunities for short-term holy relationships that are also significant as ways of extending love. Even a very brief encounter with an individual, in which there is a union of function and purpose, can produce a temporary holy relationship. You also may have many different kinds of holy relationships because any common purpose has the potential for creating a holy relationship. Nevertheless, the focus here in this chapter will be on long-term and lifelong holy relationships. These can be same-sex or opposite-sex holy relationships. Relationship partners may be peers with equal functions. Although partners are always equal as persons, in some types of holy relationships there are unequal roles, as in the case of a counselor and person being counseled or a student and teacher.

In a lifelong holy relationship, your common goal can be a seed that will grow until you wake up in Heaven together. How is that possible? What if you join with a mundane purpose like Helen Schucman and Bill Thetford to just find a better way of relating? How can a simple joining like that bring you to Heaven? Without realizing it, something happens in the beginning of the holy relationship that can change your life, as will be explained next.

F. THE HOLY SPIRIT IN THE HOLY RELATIONSHIP

When you and your partner decide to join for a common purpose and see common interests, you and/or your partner will probably feel a sense of inspiration at the time, even if the purpose itself is rather mundane. However, as time passes by, you may return to the same apparent ways of relating on the form level as you had in the past. You and/or your partner may at times question if anything at all really did happen in your joining.

In spite of your own misgivings, the Course says that because of your joint decision you have come Home already, although you do not yet realize that your long journey is over.[240] You have stumbled into Heaven and do not have a clue how you got there or even that you are there. However, you are asleep in Heaven anyway, so what has really changed that was not true before? First of all, you have found your brother, and before this, you were alone in your nightmare. Now your minds have joined with a common purpose and common interests, even if only, for example, to become farmers together.

In joining with your partner, you transcended your separation and so transcended your egos. As the dominance of the ego exited your holy relationship, a new third partner entered your relationship—the Holy Spirit. Before the Holy Spirit enters, the ego is in charge of your private goals and in charge of your life in your private world. When the Holy Spirit enters, He takes over guiding your holy relationship to help the both of you toward your common goal.

God placed the Holy Spirit in the mind of every sleeping son to guide each one Home. He uses the holy relationship to help partners awaken. But the Holy Spirit's power to help requires your free will cooperation. If you devote your mind to the goals of the ego, your freewill choice to do so means you have squeezed out the Voice for God that the Holy Spirit represents. Yet when you have made the freewill choice to join in a common purpose, you have overcome the ego's dominance. The Holy Spirit sees this as your invitation to let the Voice for God play a larger role in your mind. The Holy Spirit brings to the relationship the perfection and holiness of God, cleansing away the former guilt that had been the basis of previous special relationships. This cleansing of guilt purifies both your mind and your partner's mind either with or without your conscious awareness.[241] The Course describes the beauty and the exalted nature of the holy relationship in this way:

> Beyond the bodies that you interposed between you, and shining in the golden light that reaches it from the bright endless circle of light that extends forever, is your holy relationship, beloved of God Himself. How still it rests, in time and yet beyond, immortal yet on earth. How great the power that lies in it.[242]

Frequently Course students make the mistaken assumption that for the relationship to be a holy relationship the two partners have to be outwardly manifesting holiness in an almost saintly way. The Course clarifies that the holiness of the holy relationship is not due to your holiness or your partner's holiness manifesting in your behavior or in the process of your joining in a common purpose. Your relationship may not appear to be holy at all. Your common purpose is not holy in itself, but your joint purpose has welcomed the Holy Spirit to come into your relationship. Because of your joint invitation, the Holy Spirit totally purifies your relationship making it holy. The Holy Spirit brings in divine holiness that affects you and your partner in your unconscious minds. You can still experience conscious conflict in your relationship as you move together toward your goal. Nevertheless, the holiness at the center of your relationship is undisturbed. The Course says that Christ is born again at the center of your holy relationship. Consequently, all the illusions that come to your holy relationship are overlooked and evaporate in the presence of divine holiness. The holy relationship is described in the Course in this way:

> Every illusion brought to its forgiveness is gently overlooked and disappears. For at its center Christ has been reborn, to light His home with vision that overlooks the world.[243]

You and your partner perceive you still have separate and private minds, but the holy relationship has joined your minds. In this place of joining, you have come Home and the baby Christ is now reborn in this Home. Christ's vision is given to you if you are willing to use it because His light has come to show you the loveliness of your holy relationship. The Course emphasizes that in the joined place in your minds, you have indeed already come Home. You are a Thought in the Mind of God and part of the Sonship. Your function in Heaven is to share yourself, as this Thought, with the other Thoughts of God in the Sonship. This sharing in divine Love is your nature. When you share your mind with a brother on earth so your minds are no longer separate, but joined, you have come back to Heaven. You have not only come back to your function in Heaven, but you have invited the Holy Spirit that purifies this place of joining so it becomes so holy that God and the Sonship are joined to this place of holiness.

An example of the holy relationship is the union of Mary's parents, Ann and Joachim. These two devout Hebrews yearned to have a child to fulfill their marriage. But apparently Ann was barren after going past the age of childbearing. She wanted to promise to God that if He gave her a child she would give the child to God, meaning the child would be given to the Temple as a very little child to be raised there in the service of God. However, this is not a decision she could make alone, so she asked her husband, Joachim, to join with her in this common purpose of bringing a child into the world and giving the child to God's service. In their joining for a common purpose, they made a vow together to God. That was their invitation for the Holy Spirit to come into their holy relationship.

The Poem of the Man-God, written by the visionary Maria Valtorta, describes Ann making her vow to God in the Temple on the Feast of the Lights. As Ann was praying, she saw from within the depth of her soul a supernatural light descending from Heaven to her. She heard a heavenly voice singing to her and telling her that her wish would be granted. Ann described to Joachim this time of praying in the Temple for their holy relationship purpose to be fulfilled, as follows:

> Well, in the growing darkness, from inside the sacred place, where I was watching from the depth of my soul, to obtain assent from the ever-present God, I saw a light, a spark of beautiful light depart. It was as white as the moon and yet it had in itself all the brightness of all the pearls and gems that are in the world. It seemed that one of the precious stars of the Veil, the stars placed under the feet of the Cherubim had become detached and bright with a supernatural light....it seemed that beyond the sacred Veil, from the Glory itself, a fire started which came quickly towards me and while cutting through the air, it sang with a heavenly voice chanting: "May what you asked for, come to you." That is why I sing: "A star will come to you." What child will ours ever be, since it reveals itself as the light of a star in the Temple and in the Feast of Lights says: "I am"?[244]

Through their holy relationship, Ann and Joachim brought into the world Mary, who would become the mother of Jesus. Perhaps this is a poor example to give to you of a holy relationship because these two parents were in fact saints, and the Holy Spirit does not expect you and your partner to be saints. Yet this example is used because in *any* holy relationship more holiness enters than you can possibly imagine. In this example, the common purpose was an intentionally spiritual purpose. But does not really matter *what* you join upon, only that you *do* join. What you join upon has only one real purpose and that is to invite the Holy Spirit. After your invitation, everything about your relationship changes, including the common purpose that you both consciously agreed upon. Upon entering the holy relationship, the Holy Spirit does something totally unexpected—the Holy Spirit gives you a *new common purpose*. The new goal that you and your partner are given is for you to become aware of the Home where you both have already arrived. This is a replacement of the ego's goal of guilt with the Holy Spirit's goal of holiness.

Everything about your relationship now changes to focusing on the new goal of holiness and goal of returning to God and the oneness of the Sonship. You may continue consciously to focus on the common purpose you and your partner decided upon as a part of the larger goal that the Holy Spirit has set. Or your original goal may be set aside as you begin to perceive the new course set for you by the Holy Spirit. You may previously have known that you wanted to come Home, but this goal is about coming Home *together*. In fact, it is the togetherness that you joined in that makes coming Home possible. It is not necessary that you understand what has happened because you are already on the ship, your passage on this journey has already been paid, and the ship is already docked at the final destination. You just have to recognize that you have already arrived Home with your partner. Because time itself is an illusion, it may take time before you realize that your ship has indeed already come Home.

Since you and your partner may not even be aware of this goal of holiness and of coming Home, how can this unknown goal exert any real influence over your lives? The goal set by the Holy Spirit has the power of God behind it, and it is already accomplished. Since God transcends time, He is at the end of time and sees you having already stepped out of time. Even in time, the divine goal with the power of God removes all obstacles in your path, producing miracle after miracle to facilitate the achievement of the goal of holiness.

> When the Holy Spirit changed the purpose of your relationship by exchanging yours for His, the goal He placed there was extended to every situation in which you enter, or will ever enter.[245]

In Mary's conception of Jesus, there was already rejoicing in Heaven because in that holy instant He was already resurrected. Similarly, in the conception of your common purpose in the holy relationship you were resurrected also with Jesus and returned to paradise. You have seen a glimpse of the final scene in the movie of your life and your partner's life together, but you still have to play out the part that has been assigned to you in time in order to fulfill your destiny. You may be separated for a time but you and your partner will join again in this life or to my way of thinking in other lives until you celebrate together the joy of your true Home.

G. THE CHALLENGE IN THE HOLY RELATIONSHIP

It is natural to question the authenticity of what happened in your initial joining as well as the holiness that has now taken over your relationship. But if your relationship can survive its beginning stages, you will see enough signs of progress along the way to convince you that you are on a holy road to Heaven with your partner. Your holy relationship requires faith. Even Jesus could not work miracles in the face of disbelief and faithlessness. Your faith will be challenged at the beginning of your holy relationship because of what happens when the Holy Spirit takes charge of your relationship.

When the Holy Spirit immediately replaces your goal with His goal of holiness and going Home, you and your partner will go through what is called a time of "discomfort."[246] In order to understand this discomfort, it will be necessary to understand that there are actually only two purposes from which you can choose. You can choose the purpose of guilt along with sin or the purpose of holiness.[247] If you choose guilt, you will be following the ego. If you choose holiness, you will be following the Holy Spirit.

First you need to realize that guilt is not merely a factor that occurs after making an unwise choice. Guilt is the goal that the ego sets for you. Being led by the ego means being motivated to actually want guilt. The ego hides this motivation from your conscious awareness and instead offers you specialness as a motivation knowing that you will only find guilt. The ego uses the body as the means of reaching the goal it has set of guilt and sin. As long as you see your partner as a body and your partner sees you as a body, you are using the ego's means for reaching the goal of guilt. Your normal way of relating, which may be called the *format* of your relationship, is filled with ego attributes that are ways of seeking the goal of guilt disguised as specialness.

When you and your partner choose a common purpose and see common interests, you have chosen against the ego and for the Holy Spirit. The purpose does not have to be overtly spiritual. It can be a neutral or mundane purpose. Yet it cannot be a selfish or negative purpose. Any positive or neutral common purpose will succeed since any joined purpose excludes the isolation the ego represents. However, when the former purpose of guilt is gone, the new purpose becomes not what you consciously chose as a common purpose, but rather the goal of holiness. This abrupt change in your goal brings about a stark contrast between the two choices of either guilt or holiness, and the Holy Spirit wants you to be aware of this contrast. The ego gains by confusion, but the Holy Spirit wants you to have clarity so you can make a firm decision.

This clarity of contrast between the goal of guilt and the goal of holiness is the cause of the time of discomfort that occurs at the start of the holy relationship. Even if you cannot specifically articulate the new goal of holiness that the Holy Spirit has set, you sense that your common goal is one that you both want. You also sense that the way you have been relating, which is the format of your relationship, has been your means of finding guilt. Thus the format of your relationship cannot be used as a means of reaching the new goal of holiness. In fact, the format of your relationship is so far out of line with achieving the goal of holiness that you will probably be very discouraged by this contrast. Because you cannot reach the goal of holiness within the current format of your relationship, you might consider retaining the format of your relationship and giving up your goal. But you do not really want to give up the common goal. The happy solution to this dilemma is to change the format of the current relationship to bring it into alignment with accomplishing the goal of holiness.

Since the Holy Spirit has set the goal on your behalf, the Holy Spirit must also provide the means to accomplish the goal. You do not have to supply the means, but merely accept the means that the Holy Spirit provides. However, you may hesitate because you do not want to make the changes in the format of your relationship that would be required of you. You may now be afraid of the goal and what it will cost for you to pursue it. Therefore, you will go through a time of discomfort. Perhaps you may fear that you are not up to the task and may be tempted to project your fear onto your partner fearing that he is not up to the task. But the task is not really up to you alone, since the Holy Spirit will provide the means and accomplish the goal with you and with your partner.

You have to supply only a little bit of willingness. The means that the Holy Spirit provides is Christ's vision that allows you to see your partner as being guiltless. You do not have to already perceive him as guiltless, but only be willing to do so. The Holy Spirit will help you gain the ability to see your partner with forgiving eyes if you have the willingness to see him without guilt. Everything depends not on how you see your partner, but how you *want* to see your partner. If you want the goal, you will have to accept the means, and the means provided by the Holy Spirit depends on your willingness to accept the means. Accepting the means requires you to be willing to see your partner as being without sin. If you want to see your partner without sin, you will be enabled to do so. If you do not want to perceive your partner without sin, you will not be able to do so.

The Holy Spirit will not change the goal to fit the format of your relationship. If you want the goal, your only choice is to change the format of the relationship to suit the goal. Some relationships break off at this point because of faithlessness, which means an unwillingness to have faith in your partner. Other relationships survive this critical period of discomfort, and from this time forward only get stronger and are never again challenged to this degree. But the time of discomfort may resurface when the format of your relationship gets out of line with your common goal. It may take many years before these times of discomfort no longer appear because your relationship has finally matured and your trust in each other has reached a high level.

The best example of the initial time of discomfort in the relationship is the holy relationship of Mary and Joseph. According to the visions of Maria Valtorta, Mary had dedicated herself completely to God, but the custom was that even a woman raised in the Temple as a child needed to have a husband to protect her and to be her partner when she became an adult. Eligible men submitted branches to the Temple and one of these branches would be chosen by lot by the priest of the Temple to indicate God's choice for a marriage partner for Mary. But before the priest could make the selection by lot, Joseph's branch blossomed even though it was not the time of year for blossoming and the priest concluded this was God's choice for Mary.

After the selection had been made, Mary and Joseph joined in a holy relationship in which they decided upon a common purpose and saw common interests, as follows:

"Since My childhood I have consecrated Myself to the Lord. I know this is not the custom in Israel. But I heard a voice requesting My virginity as a sacrifice of love for the coming of the Messiah. Israel has been waiting for Him for such a long time!...It is not too much to forgo the joy of being a mother for that!"

Joseph gazes at Her as if he wanted to read Her heart, then he takes Her tiny hands which are still holding the branch in blossom and he says, "I will join my sacrifice to Yours and we shall love the Eternal Father *so much* with our chastity that He will send His Savior to the world earlier, and will allow us to see His Light shining in the world. Come, Mary. Let us go before His House and take an oath that we shall love each other as the angels do."[248]

This is a magnificent example of the holy relationship. At this time, Mary did not think she would be the mother of the Messiah. She was simply joining with Joseph for the common purpose of offering their chastity as a sacrifice to allow holiness to come into the world. Every holy relationship allows the Christ to be born in the relationship, but never more so than this event.

After this joining of the minds of Mary and Joseph, the annunciation occurred. The Angel Gabriel as a messenger made the proposal of joining her purpose with God's purpose of bringing the Messiah into the earth. Mary had already joined with Joseph in this same common purpose of facilitating the coming of the Messiah to earth, but with the annunciation her specific role was identified and needed her response, "I am the handmaid of the Lord. Let what you have said be done to me."[249]

Then Mary's guidance told her to not tell Joseph what had occurred, and this made for a time of discomfort for both Joseph and Mary. The ego uses the means of seeing your partner as a body to facilitate the ego's goal of guilt. Joseph saw Mary's pregnant body and decided that he could see sin in her. This was Joseph's greatest test of tormenting passion because the holy relationship he made with Mary had become the meaning for his life, and now it looked as though the goal of seeing holiness in his partner could not possibly be reached.

The Hebrew law demanded that he reveal Mary's sin and condemn her. He would not do that, but he would have to bear his own guilt of abandoning the law in order to not expose her to condemnation. Mary was also distressed because she could see the torment of Joseph, and she had to be silent and offer no defense for her condition. She was tempted to see him as being guilty of condemning her in his own mind without his coming to her and asking her about her condition.

They both prayed a great deal and suffered during this time of discomfort until finally divine intervention revealed to Joseph his error in judgment and Mary's true holiness. This was the first and last time faithlessness occurred in their holy relationship. The holy relationship of Joseph and Mary is an extreme example of the same patterns that exist in every holy relationship. Each partner in any holy relationship will be challenged to see his partner as a body and to lose faith in his partner. To see your partner as guilty is to see yourself as guilty. To see your partner as guiltless is to see yourself as guiltless. Just as Joseph was relieved of his distress by divine intervention, you have divine intervention coming from the Holy Spirit and from the option of Christ's vision coming. This divine grace is given to you to nourish your holy relationship by providing the means for you to forgive your partner and accomplish your common goal of holiness.

H. COOPERATING WITH SEEKING THE GOAL

All the power of the Holy Spirit, Christ, and God Himself enters the joined minds of you and your partner in the holy relationship, but you must cooperate with this power of holiness that is already within you in your unconscious mind and that has become your true goal. It is important to recognize consciously that you do have a new goal and to make a firm decision to allow yourself to be guided by the Holy Spirit toward that goal. The problems that occur in the time of discomfort are due to having a new goal and not being able to let go of an old conflicting goal. An example of this difficulty is the Hebrews that had been freed from Egypt but still yearned for the golden calves that were temptations to worship form over content. The Holy Spirit has set the goal of holiness, and now you must be willing to overlook the appearance of form, including the form of your partner's body, and instead be willing to see the true content of holiness in your partner. Everything depends on how you decide to see your partner.

This is a momentous decision because coming Home depends on your choice. Your decision determines not just your coming Home, but your partner's coming Home and the coming Home of all the other people that will be influenced in the future by your decision. At this time, it is helpful to remember the great value that your partner has that cannot be overestimated.[250]

If you were a blind man in the streets of Jerusalem two thousand years ago, and if Jesus passed by, would you call out to him for his blessing and allow him to be the Savior of your sight? You have the opportunity now to admit your blindness and ask Christ for His vision to restore your sight. If you *want* to see your partner as your guiltless savior, the eyes of Christ will remove your blindness and restore your vision so you can see your partner's holiness and accept your own holiness.

You may think you will do your part in order to reach the goal of holiness, but you will probably be tempted to believe that your partner will not do his part. This is just a projection of your own uncertainty about yourself, representing a lack of faith in yourself, in your partner, and in the divine impulse that has entered your relationship. You will have to trust that the holiness itself that the Holy Spirit has brought into the relationship will provide the means and support that you both need to reach the goal of awakening to holiness and coming Home together. You and your partner will make many mistakes along the way which will be temptations to lose faith in each other and in God, but that is just part of the journey providing more opportunities to forgive and find your salvation in the process of forgiving.

Events that happen on the form level may appear messy as though something has gone wrong. The faithlessness that may surface can be distressing, but bringing this faithlessness to the light will dispel it. You will need to be concerned only if you or your partner are losing your common intent. If you find this is happening, you can recall the time of your joining and remember the reassurance that you felt at that time in your joining in intent. You can also join with your partner for a time of quiet meditation in which you fondly remember the holy instant in which your holy relationship was established.

The best way to cooperate with the Holy Spirit in achieving your goal is to enter every situation by setting the goal of holiness as the desired outcome. Setting this goal invites the Holy Spirit to help you overlook everything that would interfere with this desired outcome. Setting the goal will help you to perceive the situation as a means of meeting the goal. Thus you will respond to the situation in a way that will bring about the goal of holiness that you are seeking.

> The value of deciding in advance what you want to happen is simply that you will perceive the situation as a means of *make* it happen. You will therefore make every effort to overlook what interferes with the accomplishment of your objective, and concentrate on everything that helps you meet it. It is quite noticeable that this approach has brought you closer to the Holy Spirit's sorting out of truth and falsity. The true becomes what can be used to meet the goal. The false becomes the useless from this point of view. The situation now had meaning, but only because the goal has made it meaningful.[251]

Holding the goal firmly in your mind as obstacles arise allows you to notice these obstacles without considering them as very important. As you hold onto what is important, which is your goal of holiness, the obstacles will dissolve. The obstacles may be, for example, emotions or false perceptions that arise in your mind or in your partner's mind. You can notice them and then let go of them. This attitude is more of the ongoing theme in this manual of *looking and overlooking*. You look for the goal and overlook everything else. The goal is not merely a desired object; the goal is something you already have as the divine presence within you. It may appear in this approach that you are seeking the goal. However, it is the goal itself, the divine presence within, that is seeking you, and inspiring you to seek the goal.

The major obstacle you and your partner face is the body since the body itself is the symbol of guilt. The body in itself is neither good nor bad, but rather neutral. Yet, the body becomes a symbol of guilt because of the way the ego uses your perception of the body as proof of separation. The body is the ego's proof you are not a holy mind in the Mind of God. The body becomes a reminder that you have sinned by separating yourself from God, even though you are not consciously aware of this. As a reminder of separation now and of the origin of separation, the body is the means the ego uses to keep you focused on the goal of guilt. By keeping you focused on guilt related to your identification with the body, the ego turns you away from the only other goal, which is the goal of holiness.

The Course says that the traditional consideration of the body as the "temple of the Holy Spirit" is not accurate because the body was made as a limitation, and the Holy Spirit extends beyond limitations. The Course states that the temple of the Holy Spirit is a *relationship,* the holy relationship manifesting in the world and in Heaven.

The Holy Spirit's temple is not a body, but a relationship.[252]

The Holy Spirit does not build His temples where love can never be. Would He Who sees the face of Christ choose as His home the only place in all the universe where it can not be seen?
   You cannot make the body the Holy Spirit's temple, and it will never be the seat of love.[253]

In spite of the body being used negatively by the ego as a symbol of limitation and guilt, the body can become useful in the service of the Holy Spirit. Guided by the Holy Spirit the body can become useful by using it as a communication device to foster communion in the holy relationship, in which the Holy Spirit dwells. The body becomes a communication device by first setting the goal of holiness and using the body as a means of accomplishing this goal.

It may sound like a challenging idea to see your partner without his body, but your ability to do so only requires your willingness to hold on to your goal of seeing holiness in your partner. If you close your mind to seeing the holiness of your partner, you will be unable to see what you have closed off from your mind. It is your openness and your wanting of the goal that allows the Holy Spirit to provide the means for you to see holiness in your partner. Christ's vision is waiting in the holiness of your holy relationship to be the means for perceiving your partner with holiness and without the body. In the beginning, you may find it difficult to see your partner with holiness and without the body. Yet if you maintain your steadfast desire to see your partner as sinless, your persistence will allow you to grow in the direction of increasingly seeing holiness in your partner.

I. THE BENEFITS OF SEEKING THE GOAL

In the case of long-term holy relationships, when you join your mind with your partner's mind for a common purpose, you are no longer able to have private experiences. You may assume that you will experience distress while your partner may be totally peaceful, but that is not true. If you experience distress, it will have a distressful effect, to a lesser or greater extent on your partner. If you experience peace, this too will be shared by your partner. The reason this happens is that in the holy relationship you have become of one mind so you have common experiences that are not limited to the form-related outward expression of your common purpose.

> This is the function of your holy relationship. For what one thinks, the other will experience with him. What can this mean except your minds are one? Look not with fear upon this happy fact, and think not that it lays a heavy burden on you. For when you have accepted it with gladness, you will realize that your relationship is a reflection of the union of the Creator and His Son. From loving minds there *is* no separation. And every thought in one brings gladness to the other because they are the same.[254]

The Course cautions you not to place the burden of guilt upon yourself for dragging down your partner with your negative emotions and not to give in to the temptation to blame your partner for his negative emotions that have an impact on you. The condition of your joined minds affecting each other provides a learning opportunity to experience what it truly means to love and to discover the true power of love that can overcome any distress.

For example, if you are experiencing fear, it will affect your partner. However, if *either* you or your partner open yourself to love, the fear will be dispelled in *both* of your minds at once. It only takes one of the two in the holy relationship to bring peace to both minds. Imagine that you and your partner get into an argument and are both caught up in the emotions of the moment. Whoever is more in contact with the divine within at that time can suggest that you both stop briefly and you take a minute to meditate together to invite the holy instant. The holy instant is a time in which the past is stripped away, and the holiness of the indivisible present moment is experienced. But it is not possible to experience the holy instant alone. Either both of you will experience the holy instant together or neither of you will be able to experience the holy instant.

When you feel the holiness of your relationship is threatened by anything, stop instantly and offer the Holy Spirit your willingness, in spite of fear, to let Him exchange this instant for the holy one that you would rather have. He will never fail in this. But forget not that your relationship is one, and so it must be that whatever threatens the peace of one is an equal threat to the other. The power of joining its blessing lies in the fact that it is now impossible for you or your brother to experience fear alone, or to attempt to deal with it alone. Never believe that this is necessary, or even possible. Yet just as this is impossible, so it is equally impossible that the holy instant come to either of you without the other. And it will come to both at the request of either.[255]

Either of you can ask for the holy instant for yourself so you can share it with your partner whom you love. But it is a mistake to think that both of you have to make the request. It only takes one of you to truly invite the Holy Spirit. After the holy instant occurs and both of your minds are cleansed simultaneously, it may not be apparent who made this possible by letting go of the past and opening to the Holy Spirit. But it does not matter. You are of one mind and over time you will take turns rescuing each other from distress and allowing the holy instant to enter into your joined minds.

Whatever your ego presents to you may seem real in your private world, but when you seek the truth with your partner and look at the offerings of the ego, the meaninglessness of the ego becomes clearly apparent. Your ability in your union to look at the ego without fear dissolves the false perceptions presented to your minds by the ego. In the holy relationship, the joining of your minds reveals to both of you that the ego is not real.

Separation therefore remains the ego's chosen condition. For no one alone can judge the ego truly. Yet when two or more join together in searching for truth, the ego can no longer defend its lack of content. The fact of union tells them it is not true.[256]

In your joined awareness that the ego is not real, you can see your own or your partner's mistakes as meaningless. You can observe a mistake as just what it is—a mistake and nothing that has anything to do with defining who either of you are. When any mistake happens, you can recognize the mistake, admit the mistake without assigning guilt, and join in a silent moment to invite in the holy instant. In the holy instant, you can let go of the past and allow the blessings of the Holy Spirit to descend upon you and the Atonement, God's Plan for coming Home, will correct the error and undo all its effects.

> Before a holy relationship there is no sin. The form of error is no longer seen, and reason, joined with love, looks quietly on all confusion, observing merely, "This was a mistake." And then the same Atonement you accepted in your relationship corrects the error, and lays a part of Heaven in its place. How blessed are you who let this gift be given! Each part of Heaven that you bring is given to you.[257]

Just as the holy relationship allows you to see the meaninglessness of the ego, it also encourages you to perceive the beauty of your holy relationship. The beauty of your relationship can be seen by using Christ's vision, seeing with the loving eyes of Christ.

> Think of the loveliness that you will see, who walk with Him! And think how beautiful will you and your brother look to the other! How happy you will be to be together, after such a long and lonely journey where you walked alone. The gates of Heaven, open now for you, will you now open to the sorrowful. And none who looks upon the Christ in you but will rejoice. How beautiful the sight you saw beyond the veil, which you will bring to light the tired eyes of those as weary now as once you were. How thankful will they be to see you come among them, offering Christ's forgiveness to dispel their faith in sin.
> Every mistake you and your brother make, the other will gently have corrected for you. For in his sight your loveliness is his salvation, which he would protect from harm.[258]

You and/or your partner may not have Light vision that enables you to see the light as a visual experience outwardly, but Christ's vision can still reveal to you both the loveliness and holiness that is in your holy relationship. But if you happen to be able to experience Light vision as an outer visual experience, you will see past the physical form of your partner's body and beyond the colors of the body. You will see the shining light of your partner in the real world, a symbolic reflection of the light of his mind in Heaven. The loveliness of this vision will convince you that this same beauty must be in you as well. You can experience Light vision as a visual experience yourself and your partner may not have this visual experience, but your partner will share in the love expressed in your Christ's vision that does not require a visual component. Indeed, your partner will give you back the love that you have given him, which would be true whether you could visually see the light in him or not.

The visual experience of Light vision as a by-product of Christ's vision is helpful as a biofeedback system to reinforce your awareness of the love that you see in your partner and feel within yourself. If your mind accepts any false perceptions of your partner, the visual experience will disappear telling you that you have left your goal of seeking the holiness of your partner. If you have Light vision, and it disappears because you have left your goal of perceiving holiness in your partner, it means that you are no longer in that moment, relying on Christ's vision that is the source of Light vision.

Because your minds are joined, it is possible that if you have the ability to visually see your partner with Light vision, you can actually transfer this ability to your partner.[259] As you see your partner filled with light, you can feel the love in you going to your partner. You can feel yourself opening your mind to your partner, giving the gift of Light vision as a visual experience to him. You can feel the light within yourself radiating outwardly as you see the light in him. You can ask the Holy Spirit to open your partner's mind and allow him to see the light you are radiating as you love him.

You may or may not be successful because everyone is not open to this ability. However, if this transfer happens, your partner will be amazed. It will be a time of much joy and even laughter. Yet laughter can bring you out of the experience temporarily if you move the body. It is possible to move the body and still manifest Light vision as an outer visual experience. But for most seekers, the body must be held still in order to help still the mind and stay focused on your common goal of holiness. Because holiness is what you are seeking, the visual experience of either or both of you is not really very important. Even without the visual component of Light vision, you can see Christ in your partner. Yet Light vision is a nice accessory, reinforcing what you have already realized: your partner is the holy Son of God.

You will discover yourself not in yourself, but in your relationship where you are truly closest to your true Christ Self in Heaven. You will find joy, love, and celebration in your sharing with your partner. You are delivered from the nightmares of your isolating world to the happy dreams of the real world where you are being prepared to awaken in Heaven together.[260] Seeing Christ in your partner and your partner seeing Christ in you will lead you Home hand in hand.

J. YOUR RELATIONSHIP WITH JESUS

Miracle Relationship Yoga is all about establishing holy relationships with your brothers and sisters, including your holy relationship with Jesus. As a Christian, you are joined in a holy relationship with Jesus in which you have the common purpose of bringing your brothers and you Home. As a Christian seeker, you decide how much time, energy, and interest you have in deepening your relationship with Jesus.

If you choose to believe in the Course as a thought system, you will have to also accept that the narrative of the Course comes from Jesus himself. In the Course, Jesus welcomes you to allow him by your invitation to come into your life and to guide your mind. Jesus says in the Course that you were freed from darkness when just one part of the Sonship, meaning Jesus himself, was able to do God's Will completely. This achievement of Jesus is your achievement because he and you are each part of the Sonship in the one Christ. In this fulfillment of God's Will by Jesus, the will of the entire Sonship was joined with the Will of God. Since you are part of the Sonship, your true will is joined with the Will of God through Jesus himself being aware of God's Will. Since you are joined with Jesus in the Sonship right now, when you remember Jesus, you are remembering yourself as you truly are in the Sonship and in God the Father. In the Course, Jesus explains his role in expressing God's Will on your behalf:

> The remembrance of me is the remembrance of yourself, and of Him Who sent me to you.
>
> You were in darkness until God's Will was done completely by any part [Jesus] of the Sonship. When this was done, it was perfectly accomplished by all. How else could it be perfectly accomplished? My mission was simply to unite the will of the Sonship with the Will of the Father by being aware of the Father's Will myself. This is the awareness I came to give you, and your problem in accepting it is problem of this world. The world must therefore despise and reject me, because the world *is* the belief that love is impossible. If you will accept the fact that I am with you, you are denying the world and accepting God. My will is His, and your decision to hear me is the decision to hear His Voice and abide in His Will. As God sent me to you so will I send you to others. And I will go to them with you, so we can teach them peace and union.[261]

Even though your true will is joined with God's Will, which is the Will of Love, you are not yet awakened to your true will of Love. You will need help to awaken to your true will of Love and you have that help provided by God, the Holy Spirit, and your brothers and sisters. You also have the ever-present help of Jesus available to you. The help of Jesus only requires your willingness to join your mind with the mind of Jesus, which is the recognition of being of one mind and one will in God. You need healing now because you mistakenly believe your will is separate from the Will of God, and therefore separate from the will of Jesus. Miracle Relationship Yoga is very helpful for your healing because by uniting in holy relationships with your brothers and sisters, including Jesus, you learn to recognize your oneness with the Sonship and oneness with God.

> By the belief that your will is separate from mine, you are exempting yourself from the Will of God which *is* yourself. Yet to heal is still to make whole. Therefore, to heal is to unite with those who are like you, because perceiving this likeness is to recognize the Father. If your perception is in Him and only in Him, how can you know it without recognizing Him? The recognition of God is the recognition of yourself. There is no separation of God and His creation. You will realize this when you understand that there is no separation between your will and mine. Let the Love of God shine upon you by your acceptance of me. My reality is yours and His. By joining your mind with my mind you are signifying your awareness that the Will of God is one.
>
> God's Oneness and ours are not separate, because His Oneness encompasses ours. To join with me is to restore His power to you because we are sharing it. I offer you only the recognition of His power in you, but in that lies all truth. As we unite, we unite with Him.[262]

There are different ways of uniting with Jesus and developing a personal relationship that depend on your own personality. For those who are attracted to Miracle Jnana Yoga, the joining may be more of a mental joining to be of one mind in order to practice forgiveness and discern the real from the unreal. If you are more inclined to Miracle Raja Yoga, there may be an emphasis on joining with Jesus as a meditative practice. If you are a seeker drawn to Miracle Karma Yoga, there can be a dedication of your work and other activities to Jesus and a letting go of the fruits of your actions. If you are a seeker predisposed to practice Miracle Bhakti Yoga, there can be a loving openness of the heart to welcome Jesus into your life through your devotion to him. The Course identifies Jesus as your loving elder brother and your equal in the Sonship, who deserves your devotion because of his devotion to you. In applying any of the forms of Miracle Yoga, Jesus can be viewed as your personal guide who is helping you to heal your mind and showing you the way Home. But in order to receive guidance and help in healing from Jesus, you must have faith in the ability of Jesus to assist you.

Would you know the Will of God for you? Ask it of me who knows it for you and you will find it. I will deny you nothing, as God denies me nothing. Ours is simply the journey back to God Who is our home.[263]

You must accept guidance from within. The guidance must be what you want, or it will be meaningless to you. That is why healing is a collaborative venture. I can tell you what to do, but you must collaborate by believing that I know what you should do. Only then will your mind choose to follow me. Without this choice you could not be healed because you would have decided against healing, and this rejection of my decision for you makes healing impossible. Healing reflects our joint will.[264]

If you want to be like me I will help you, knowing that we are alike. If you want to be different, I will wait until you change your mind. I can teach you, but only you can choose to listen to my teaching.[265]

Jesus has promised he is always with you, and it is up to you to believe that he is keeping his promise. When you remember Jesus and his promise, you are remembering your true Identity and your oneness with God.

The remembrance of me is the remembrance of yourself, and of Him Who sent me to you.[266]

I will always remember you, and in my remembrance of you lies your remembrance of yourself. In our remembrance of each other lies our remembrance of God.[267]

I said that I am with you always, even unto the end of the world. That is why I am the light of the world. If I am with you in the loneliness of the world, the loneliness is gone. You cannot maintain the illusion of loneliness if you are not alone.[268]

In your journey, you have really only one stumbling block to your return Home, which is your own ego. Jesus helps you to overcome this stumbling block through your decision to join with him. The ego is the idea that you are alone, but the presence of Jesus in your life demonstrates that you are not alone, which helps you to let go of the illusion of loneliness and helps you let go of the ego itself.

When you unite with me you are uniting without the ego, because I have renounced the ego in myself and therefore cannot unite with yours. Our union is therefore the way to renounce the ego in you. The truth in both of us is beyond the ego. Our success in transcending the ego is guaranteed by God, and I share this confidence for both of us and all of us.[269]

Whenever fear intrudes anywhere along the road to peace, it is because the ego has attempted to join the journey with us and cannot do so. Sensing defeat and angered by it, the ego regards itself as rejected and become retaliative. You are invulnerable to its retaliation because I am with you. On this journey you have chosen me as your companion *instead* of the ego. Do not attempt to hold on to both, or you will try to go in different directions and will lose the way.[270]

Leave all illusions behind, and reach beyond all attempts of the ego to hold you back. I go before you because I am beyond the ego. Reach, therefore, for my hand because you want to transcend the ego. My strength will never be wanting, and if you choose to share it you will do so. I give it willingly and gladly because I need you as much as you need me.[271]

Jesus can help you express love as miracles, which reveal that you and your brother are equals. Jesus is likewise your brother and equal, which is difficult to understand because of the achievements of Jesus when he manifested his life in the earth among us. For example, Jesus has risen to the Father, so you may think that it appropriate to respond to Jesus in the same way that you would respond to God. Yet Jesus states in the Course that awe is an appropriate response to God and yet awe is not an appropriate response to Jesus.

The miracle is therefore a sign of love among equals. Equals should not be in awe of one another because awe implies inequality. It is therefore an inappropriate reaction to me. An elder brother is entitled to respect for his greater experience, and obedience for his greater wisdom. He is also entitled to love because he is a brother, and to devotion if he is devoted. It is only my devotion that entitles me to yours. There is nothing about me that you cannot attain. I have nothing that does not come from God. The difference between us now is that I have nothing else. This leaves me in a state which is only potential in you.[272]

Many Christians agree that following Jesus is the way to the Father, yet there are different opinions on what this means. In the Course, Jesus clarifies his role a one who leads the way, as follows:

"No man cometh unto the Father but by me" does not mean that I am in any way separate or different from you except in time, and time does not really exist. The statement is more meaningful in terms of a vertical rather than a horizontal axis. You stand below me and I stand below God. In the process of "rising up," I am higher because without me the distance between God and man would be too great for you to encompass. I bridge the distance as an elder brother to you on the one hand, and as the Son of God on the other. My devotion to my brothers has placed me in charge of the Sonship, which I render complete because I share it. This may appear to contradict the statement "I and the Father are one," but there are two parts to the statement in recognition that the Father is greater.[273]

You have available to you the greatest jnana, karma, raja, and bhakti yogi who ever walked the earth in the form of Jesus of Nazareth, the master of love. Jesus along with the Holy Spirit is in charge of God's Plan for you to come Home. Jesus calls you his brother and sees you as his equal and partner in the same Sonship, in which you share the one Christ Self in union with God. He walks with you whether you know it or not. Give him your heart, since he gave you his, and he will guide you Home.

This chapter emphasized Miracle Relationship Yoga as the spiritual practice of participating in holy relationships. One way of practicing Miracle Relationship Yoga is the teacher and student relationship, which is a specific kind of holy relationship that is recommended in the Course. Chapter 8 and Chapter 9 explain how the Course would affect your practice of Miracle Raja Yoga, Miracle Bhakti Yoga, and Miracle Karma Yoga, if you decide that you want to adopt the Course thought system.

CHAPTER 8

~ • ~

MIRACLE RAJA YOGA

A. CONSIDERING THE COURSE AS AN OPTION

This chapter emphasizes the Course principles related to Miracle Raja Yoga, in which meditation plays a central role. The previous two chapters, this chapter, and the next chapter are intended to provide a description of the principles of the Course so you can decide if you want to study this material further. If you do decide you would like to evaluate the Course information through studying it, you would probably want to read the Text of the Course. After reading the Text, you may want to also do the Workbook practices.

One goal of the Workbook is to give you practical experience in learning how to apply Course principles. For example, the Workbook is designed to help you manifest Christ's vision and forgiveness. The Workbook portion of the Course consists of one year of daily lessons that provide mind training to bring about a unified mind. The lessons at the start of the Workbook are designed to help you release old false perceptions based upon the ego. Then the lessons change to affirming true perceptions that come from the Holy Spirit. This helps you shift from wrong-minded thinking to right-minded thinking.

In regard to developing Christ's vision, the Workbook lessons are very helpful as an introduction to the possibility of Christ's vision. The vast majority of Course students are not successful in their conscious attempts to experience Christ's vision internally or externally and even fewer students are able to experience the visual component of Light vision, which is a by-product of Christ's vision. However, potentially everyone can perform miracles as expressions of love based upon Christ's vision. The Course states you can perform miracles without your conscious awareness. Sometimes you can tell that a miracle has occurred because of the miracle producing observable effects. Yet, if you see no observable effects, you cannot assume that a miracle has not happened because a miracle may produce no outward sign or noticeable effect. Miracles can be offered through you by expressing love, but you cannot control the outcome of miracles. The Holy Spirit is in charge of bringing miracles into the lives of others and facilitating changes that are far beyond your awareness.

Miracles are expressions of love, but they may not always have observable effects.[274]

A miracle is never lost. It may touch many people you have not even met, and produce undreamed of changes in situations of which you are not even aware.[275]

The Course Workbook lessons provide mind training that starts with less difficult mental focusing and leading you to more difficult mental focusing. Some of the early Workbook lessons encourage you to use your mind to see things differently, which is a preliminary stage of learning how to manifest Christ's vision. Then in the Workbook Lessons 41 and 44, the Course introduces you to a new practice. This new practice is clearly meditation, although the word "meditation" is not specifically used in the Workbook. After introducing meditation, the Course promises to incorporate meditation increasingly into your Workbook practices. Meditation then becomes a foundation for your practice and leads you in the direction of wordless contemplation.

After completing the 365 Workbook lessons, you may feel that you have a better understanding of spiritual principles because you have put the Course principles into practical application. At the end of the Workbook, the Course says that no more Workbook lessons are provided because none are needed. After finishing the one year of Workbook lessons, many students feel that there is no alternative other than going back to start the same Workbook lessons over again and again year after year. However, the Course does not make that recommendation. Instead, the Course simply advises you to allow the Holy Spirit to guide you.

After completing the Workbook, you can begin again to do the one year of lessons. I believe the Workbook lessons are intended to have a cumulative effect. Your progress in meditation at the end of the Workbook will be such that you can build on what you have acquired by practicing daily meditation, whether or not you return to the beginning of the Workbook lessons.

In addition to the general recommendation to follow the guidance of the Holy Spirit after the one year of Workbook lessons is completed, there is one specific recommendation made. This recommendation, which may be considered the ideal way to proceed with your practice of Course principles after completing the Workbook, is clearly stated in the third part of the Course, the *Manual for Teachers*.[276] Here in the description of how teachers should spend their day, there is a strong emphasis on having times of quiet that are to be devoted to God. Actually two such times are recommended, one in the morning and one in the evening. This time of quiet is identified as the practice that was learned in the Workbook, which would certainly mean the practice of meditation leading to wordless contemplation. Additional information about Course meditation will be provided below.

After your direct experience of the Course and after asking for guidance from the Holy Spirit, there is a possibility you may decide that you would like to adopt the Course as a thought system to use as a basis for practicing Miracle Jnana Yoga. If you decide you want to practice Miracle Jnana Yoga with the Course as your chosen thought system, you will need to continue to study the Text of the Course. One reading is not sufficient to grasp all of the content contained in the Course. There are many books written about the Course that are very helpful in shedding light on some of the concepts of the Course that may not initially be understood.

If you choose to use the Course as the foundation for your practice of Miracle Jnana Yoga, your decision would certainly have a strong impact on your overall practice of Miracle yoga. Ideally you will be able to give an equal emphasis to all aspects of your spiritual growth. Miracle Jnana Yoga and Miracle Relationship Yoga have been outlined in the two prior chapters. This chapter and the next chapter describe the remaining three aspects of Miracle Yoga and specifically how the Course would influence these aspects of your practice.

B. A JOINT VENTURE

Christian raja yoga, if it is not based on the Course, would usually be primarily focused upon seeking the divine presence vertically in relation to God because of its emphasis on meditation as an inward spiritual practice. The Course includes the vertical seeking of God in meditation, but the overall influence of the Course on your practice of meditation in Miracle Raja Yoga is to emphasize seeking the divine horizontally in relation to your brothers and sisters. The importance of using both a dual vertical and horizontal approach to meditation and to spiritual growth in general first became clear to me through personal spiritual experiences in my life.

Regarding spiritual experiences in general, discernment is needed to decide whether or not to share a spiritual experience. Sharing too much of your personal experiences can be motivated by the ego, but sharing too little of your personal experiences can also be motivated by the ego. Some spiritual experiences need to be kept private or shared only with a spiritual director.

As an analogy, you can think of a married man who is asked by a friend about his sex life with his wife. He may offer a general statement that he has a normal married relationship with his wife. But if his friend presses him for details, he will probably say his intimacy with his wife is a private matter between his wife and himself. Your spiritual experiences and your meditation practices are experiences of sacred intimacy between yourself and God. It is usually appropriate to bear witness to the fact that you are in the process of developing an intimate relationship with God. Yet it might not be wise to provide details of your intimate relationship with God unless you are sharing with your spiritual director. You will have to rely on the Holy Spirit in regard to what personal experiences can be shared and with whom a specific experience can be shared.

In part of my personal life, I have walked the path of darkness in the dark night of the soul, but I do not recommend this path to anyone because it is a difficult path, a dangerous path, and a solitary path. The path I recommend is the path of light that is not a difficult path, not a dangerous path, and not a solitary path. The path of light is best exemplified by St. Symeon, and it includes reliance upon Christ's vision.[277] The path of light cannot be a solitary path because in this path you learn to lovingly perceive your brother in the light in the very beginning, before you find yourself or God in the Light. In fact, perceiving your brother first in the light is your *means* to find yourself and God in the Light. Perhaps perceiving your brother in the light will help you to also visually see your brother in the light, as an outer confirmation of your inner loving perception.

No path to God can be complete if it is a solitary path that excludes your brothers. Meditation is not the solitary practice that it appears to be and the goal of meditation is not an individual goal. I was not able to fully appreciate the value of this awareness until I had studied the Course and practiced its principles in my daily life. What I learned from the Course is that the best approach to meditation and spiritual growth in general is to accept that the spiritual path as a *joint venture*, in which God and the entire Sonship are collaborating.

Both Helen Schucman and Bill Thetford practiced meditation in the early dictation of the Course and Jesus cautioned them regarding viewing meditation as a solitary path. The following quotation from *Absence From Felicity*[278] was part of this early dictation received by Helen and in this quotation Jesus commented to Bill regarding his practice of traditional meditation in which each day at a specific time he emptied his mind of all thoughts to become inwardly silent:

> Your [Bill's] giant step forward was to *insist* on a collaborative venture. This does not go against the true spirit of meditation at all. It is inherent *in* it. Meditation is a collaborative venture with God. It *cannot* be undertaken successfully by those who disengage themselves from the Sonship...[279]

Some early parts of the dictation, in which Helen and Bill were addressed directly by Jesus, were altered so that the Course as a whole would be addressed to all seekers. The prior quotation made its way into the Course in an altered manner in which the first usage of the word meditation was omitted altogether and the second reference to the word meditation was changed to the word "salvation," stated as follows: "Salvation [replacing the word "meditation"] is a collaborative venture. It cannot be undertaken successfully by those who disengage themselves from the Sonship..."[280]

It is true that salvation has a collaborative nature as stated in the Course version of this quotation, but the original version referred to the collaborative nature of meditation. The original meaning of the quotation directed by Jesus to Bill indicated that meditation was a good practice if its purpose is properly understood as a way of joining with God *and* joining with your brothers.

Combining meditation with relationships is not an alteration of meditation, but rather its true purpose. Meditating with a sense of isolation from the rest of the Sonship defeats its purpose and will not succeed. If you believe you are separate from the Sonship, you will believe you are separate from God. If you draw closer to the Sonship, you draw closer to God. The purpose of meditation is union with God *and* with the Sonship. The ultimate goal of meditation is for you to find your true place in the Sonship in union with God. It is your relationship in the Sonship that *is* your union with God. This idea that Jesus expressed to Bill about the value of balancing meditation and relationships is an important concept in regard to spiritual growth and will be an ongoing theme discussed subsequently.

C. THE COURSE, MYSTICISM, AND MIRACLE RAJA YOGA

Mysticism is the seeking for union with the divine and is usually associated with the vertical approach to divine union. But because the Course is mainly horizontal in its emphasis, it does not mean it is not a mystical path. Most Christians live mundane lives and do not experience Christianity as a mystical path. Yet Christianity can become a mystical path for those who are dedicated to seeking union with the divine. Likewise, the Course can be experienced as a mystical path by Course students who are dedicated to seeking union with the divine through the Course principles.

The Course would not offer the seeker a typical Eastern form of mysticism. The Course does not take the Eastern approach requiring long hours of meditation in order to produce direct union with God in an ascetic life geared to renunciation of the world. Perhaps this is why the word "meditation" is not used to identify some of those Workbook practices which are indeed meditation practices. Although the Course includes meditation methods, it places the emphasis on forgiveness and healing as an indirect means of uniting with God by joining with your brother. Because the Course places a much greater emphasis on relationships as a means of divine union, it is tempting to call the Course a path of "horizontal mysticism." But perhaps this would be a misleading description because mysticism would always need to have a vertical component, and the Course does indeed have that component, although it plays a secondary role.

It is more accurate to say that the Course is an example of *integrated mysticism*. This type of mysticism is the culmination of mysticism because it fully integrates both the vertical and horizontal approaches to God. The spiritual life of St. Symeon is relevant to the Course since his spiritual experiences are examples of integrated mysticism. Apparently, St. Symeon experienced a very advanced form of Christ's vision.

Although the Course is an integrated mystical path, it places more importance upon the horizontal approach than the vertical approach. The goal of attaining immediate direct union with God in this life is not the aim of the Course. Nevertheless, the Course contains many elements of seeking God vertically. There is a focus on God being the ultimate goal of all spiritual seeking. The Course describes revelation as God directly awakening the soul to its divine nature by revealing Himself. Direct union with God is highly regarded in the Course, but it occurs so rarely that it is considered an unrealistic goal. Even if it is attained, it is a transitory state that cannot be sustained.

Though direct union with God is considered beyond the scope of the Course that does not inhibit the Course from strongly advocating direct receptivity to God's influence and presence. Usually meditation is considered a vertical means of facilitating divine communication leading to divine union so it can be considered to be a mystical aspect of the Course. If you think meditation is only a means of getting the end result of divine union with God, then the Course does not have an emphasis on that. If you think meditation is a process of receptivity to God, then the Course does have a vertical emphasis to at least partially balance its stronger horizontal emphasis.

There are some parts of the Workbook such as Lessons 41, 44, 69, 70, 74, 183, and 184 that describe classical meditation methods. Yet the inclusive definition of meditation as a process of receptivity to the divine covers a larger area of the Course. Most of the morning and evening Workbook practices are times of receptivity to God, and these are the longest practice periods of the day. For example, all of the lessons in Part II of the Workbook, including Lessons 221 all the way to 365, are focused mainly on receptivity to God. That is over one third of the Workbook in which the statements for the day are only introductions to prepare you to be receptive to God.

> For in this final section, we will come to understand that we need only call to God, and all temptations disappear. Instead of words, we need but feel His love. Instead of prayers, we need but call His Name.[281]

The starting words of these daily Workbook lessons are described as simply a means of welcoming God's presence. Except for these introductory words that in some cases include the Name of God,[282] this divine approach is primarily attunement without words, which is usually referred to as *contemplation*. In contrast to contemplation that uses no words, meditation is the process of receptivity that includes the practice of holding one thought in the mind, usually involving the repeating of one inspiring word or a series of words. Actually, in the Course descriptions of attunement to the divine, the basic suggested approach is a combination of meditation and contemplation.

This Course practice of joining meditation and contemplation is what I prefer to call *Inner Silence Meditation*.[283] This practice of Inner Silence Meditation is very close to what is more commonly known as *Centering Prayer*, which is a form of contemplative prayer that was popularized by Thomas Keating and Basil Pennington. In this basic approach, the meditator remains silently open to God, but if his mind becomes distracted, he mentally calls to God using words. When the meditator's mind becomes more focused and calmer, he then lets go of focusing on words to wait in receptivity and silence.

The way the mind is used in meditation is quite different from the way the mind is used in contemplation. Meditation is more of a concentrative practice requiring focusing that allows one thought to be held in the mind, usually in the form of a word or words. In contemplation the emphasis switches from meditative focusing of the mind to an ever deepening openness of the mind and heart to the divine influence that is beyond words. Thus Inner Silence Meditation and Course-based attunement use the mind first for focusing and then for receptive openness, which is simply meditation with words leading to contemplation without words.

Generally, the full year of studying the Workbook lessons lead the student from meditation toward contemplation. In addition, the earlier lessons are more form-related than the later lessons that lead toward the abstraction of contemplation. For example, some earlier lessons focus on seeking to see the light within as a visual experience. These Course lessons recommend using the imagination of visual imagery. Seekers are asked to move gently past the ego-based thoughts of the mind symbolized by the visual imagery of dark clouds in order to perceive the light behind these clouds.[284] Because visual imagery is a preliminary stage that must be left behind in order to make inward progress in meditation and contemplation, this device is omitted in the more advanced practices later in the Workbook.

If you decide to use a broad definition, you can define meditation as a process of mental focusing. With this definition, you can say that the Course has a very strong focus on that form of meditation. After all, the Course describes itself clearly as a course in mind training and so meditation in this sense is a major part of the Course. Meditation in the form of mind training in the Course focuses primarily on learning how to manifest forgiveness.

Meditation as mind training in the Course is the directing of the mind horizontally toward your brothers and sisters in order to see their guiltlessness and your own guiltlessness in the process of forgiveness. This would make the Course only a horizontal path if that is all there was to the Course. Because the Course urges you to go deeper, to see the divine in our brothers and sisters, you are drawn closer to God. Here is the meeting of the horizontal approach of joining with others and the vertical approach of joining with God. This intersection, where these two approaches form common ground, is symbolic of the place where the human and the divine can be perceived as one. It is the place where Christ can be perceived, though not yet fully realized. It is the place where Christ's vision brings you and it is the reason why the Course can offer integrated mysticism to those that seek it.

The Course mainly directs its meditative mental focusing practices specifically toward obtaining Christ's vision of the real world, which will show you how to manifest forgiveness outwardly to others and inwardly to yourself. Considering that the main theme of the Course is forgiveness, which is considered to be mostly horizontal, can the Course really represent integrated mysticism? On the other hand, can it really be said that forgiveness itself, as it is taught in the Course, is exclusively horizontal? Perhaps it is more correct to say that according to the Course, forgiveness itself is an example of integrated mysticism. Undoubtedly, seeing your brother as guiltless is horizontal, but the Course teaches you to see your brother in his true nature. Is his true nature only horizontal? You are to see your brother as being guiltless precisely because you are to perceive him as the holy Son of God. As God's Son, he is both horizontal in relation to you and vertical in relation to God, the Father.

With your forgiveness of your brother, you join horizontally with him as equals. Your equality with your brother, which is the basis of forgiveness, rests not only on your human brotherhood but on your divine brotherhood. By forgiving your brother, you see your brother's mystical divinity, and this uncovers your own mystical divinity. Your brother, whom you have forgiven by seeing his holiness, becomes your savior, who can show you your holiness and thus your divinity. As your savior, your brother gives you salvation, which is both vertical and mystical. Traditional Christian teachings on forgiveness are only horizontal because they are based upon seeing your brother as a sinner rather than seeing him as a holy Son of God. The combination of the Course's vertical and mystical elements sets the Course's teachings on forgiveness apart from these traditional Christian teachings.

Following the pattern of integrated mysticism, meditation, broadly defined as mental focusing or training, is directed toward forgiveness by seeing your brother's horizontal guiltlessness and vertical divinity. An important goal of the Course is to use your mental focusing to enable you to change your thought system from one based on fear to one based on love for your brothers and love for God. Another way that the Course uses its horizontal and vertical components is to take the horizontal blocks representing the darkness of the ego and bring these inner blocks to the vertical light aspect that dissolves these inner barriers. You undo the ego where it functions at the horizontal level in your perception by searching out all the dark corners of the ego. Then you offer what had been hidden to the light of the Holy Spirit for healing. This is transformation from the ground up. By unmasking the hidden parts of the ego and healing yourself with divine light, you are removing all the barriers to realizing your true nature of love.

In addition to bringing your darkness to the light, you direct your perception toward seeing the light in your brother. Specifically, the Course encourages you to find God indirectly by finding Him in your brother and realizing He must also be within yourself. But in order to see the light in your brother, the Course consistently encourages you to open yourself to finding the light within yourself, as well as seeing the outer world transformed in light as a symbol of the inner light.

Involvement in the Course will expose you to many opportunities for mystical experience, although these will be much less dramatic and less profound than the experience of mystical divine union that is your ultimate destination. An example of this less dramatic mystical experience is the occurrence of seeing the outer world filled with light that happens to some people who are receptive to Christ's vision. The Course states your seeking may expose you to many other kinds of light experiences that are symbolic of the supernatural light within.

The Course also says that on your path you will have many episodes of "holy instants"[285] of entirely releasing the past and future.

The holy instant was described briefly in the prior chapter as the starting point of the holy relationship and will be elaborated upon below in relation to the meditation of Miracle Raja Yoga. But before discussing the nature of the holy instant, it is appropriate to discuss, as a contrast, a kind of meditation that the Course specifically does not recommend. The Course states that long meditation periods aimed at future release from present unworthiness are time-consuming and are ineffective.[286] Eventually they will bring results because of the spiritual purpose of the individual, but this type of meditation is not an effective form of divine communication. A specific example of this might be the long form of the Jesus Prayer, which is "Lord Jesus Christ, have mercy on me, a sinner." Repeating to yourself over a long period of time that you are a "sinner," just builds within yourself the idea that you are unworthy of divine union. It reinforces the idea that you are guilty, and the guilty think punishment is deserved, not divine union.

The Course rejects this kind of guilt-based meditation. Even if you ask for mercy, if misunderstood, can reinforce this idea that you are a guilty sinner. For this reason, it is best to use the Jesus Prayer in its short form of simply repeating only the name of Jesus. The Course position of rejecting meditation that reinforces present unworthiness is consistent with its attempt to remain Christian and yet reinterpret Christianity in light of Christian qualified nondualism. The Course teaches you to let go of dualistic thinking and maintains that you are already united with God. Thus any meditation must be directed toward realizing your union with God in the present moment.

Overall the Course wants you to realize your divine worthiness and your ability to participate in divine communication in the present moment. Seeking a "future" divine union may divert your awareness away from realizing that you are already united to God now, in spite of your illusions that would tell you otherwise. Your ego does not mind your seeking of divine union because it can rely on convincing you that divine union is in the distant future beyond reaching now.

Also, the ego seeks to convince you that you will never have divine union because you are not worthy of having union with God and hides the fact that you are already united to God now. The ego attempts to turn your awareness away from the present moment and to keep you focused on past and future associations with guilt, which means belief in past sins and future punishment for sins.

Meditation cannot be a means of "earning" a future union that you feel you do not even deserve. To do so would put you in conflict with yourself by your seeking to have what you are telling yourself you have no right to have. Plus you cannot earn divine union since it is above all a free gift, and indeed a gift already given. But the ego wants you to think that you need to "do" something to earn divine union. The ego will give you a lot of doing activities, which will tell you that you do not have God now and must do something to obtain union with God. In contrast to this urging by the ego to "do," the Course teaches you to realize: "I need do nothing."[287]

This statement has been misinterpreted by some Course students to mean that no spiritual practices, such as meditation, are needed. If this interpretation were accurate, the Course would not have included 365 days of daily lessons and would not have recommended ongoing quiet times of meditation two times per day for teachers of God.

"I need do nothing," is an acceptance of who you already are. The final joyous realization of your true nature in some cases only comes after many years of meditation practice and spiritual seeking. But the Course maintains you do not have to wait for many years because you can have this realization now. In this sense, the Course encourages you to save time. Why prolong the eventual realization of "I need do nothing," when you can have this awareness right now? This is the realization of your "being" nature in Heaven that transcends your "doing" nature in the earth. It is a *rest* that brings peace. The Course does not recommend finding this place of rest by practicing a lifetime of meditation to receive a future reward. The Course says this place of non-doing rest can be found now.

In contrast to the self-defeating future-oriented type of meditation that assumes present unworthiness, the Course offers an alternative. The Course's alternative is the "holy instant," mentioned above. The holy instant is an experience that brings you into the eternal present moment. The descriptions of the holy instant in the Text are similar to later descriptions of meditation leading to contemplation in the Workbook. It is obvious that the instructions provided for meditation practice in the Workbook are in fact directions on how to go about experiencing the holy instant.

The holy instant can be experienced outside of meditation, as well as during meditation. These are occasions when time almost stands still. For an instant you can let go of not only all your ideas of your guilt and unworthiness, but of all ideas of any kind about yourself, or indeed about anything. For an instant, you can release ego-based ideas you have accumulated and allow who you really are to shine through. Such times break the bonds of body awareness letting you know your nature beyond the limitations you have placed on yourself. Having this experience shows you that you are not an ego—not a body and mind limited to the body. Holy instants accomplish the Course goal of changing your perceptions about yourself.

One of the most difficult true perceptions to understand about yourself is your abstract nature. For example, the Course states:

> The cornerstone of God's creation is you, for His thought system is light.[288]

The Course maintains that you are a miracle, and you are living in His Light. An even more abstract indication of your nature in the Course is that you are in fact a *Thought* within the Mind of God.

> God and His miracle are inseparable. How beautiful indeed are the Thoughts in God who live in His Light. Your worth is beyond perception because it is beyond doubt. Do not perceive yourself in different lights. Know yourself in the One Light where the miracle that you are is perfectly clear.[289]

You are indeed a miracle. You are one of the Thoughts of God and live in His Light. But since you are identified with a body, it is hard to accept your own abstract nature. It may be easier for you to accept God's abstract nature. The Course states: "What you find difficult to accept is the fact that, like your Father, *you* are an idea."[290]

Discussing your abstract nature of being a divine idea is needed here in regard to understanding the holy instant. You can understand that if you share a human idea with another person, you keep the idea that you share. Thus the communication of ideas produces no loss in the person sharing or in the person receiving the sharing. The holy instant is a sharing of your abstract nature as an idea and so the holy instant is an experience of communication.

> The holy instant is a time in which you receive and give perfect communication. This means, however, that it is a time in which your mind is open, both to receive and give. It is recognition that all minds are in communication. It therefore seeks to change nothing, but merely to accept everything.[291]

It is because you are an idea in the Mind of God that the holy instant is possible. Your being an idea in the Mind of God allows you to have unlimited communication.

> If you were not an idea, and nothing but an idea, you could not be in full communication with all that ever was.[292]

Your perfect communication in the holy instant is with God and with your brothers, who are joined in Christ with you. In the holy instant you transcend the limitations of the body and are able to extend yourself to the Mind of God.

> Yet in the holy instant you unite directly with God, and all your brothers join in Christ. Those who are joined in Christ are in no way separate. For Christ is the Self the Sonship shares, as God shares His Self with Christ.
> Think you that you can judge the Self of God? God created It beyond judgment, out of His need to extend His Love. With Love in you, you have no need except to extend it. In the holy instant there is no conflict of needs, for there is only one. For the holy instant reaches to eternity, and to the Mind of God. And it is only there [in the holy instant that] love has meaning, and only there can it be understood.[293]

The holy instant is an experience of Christ's vision and in some cases can be an experience of seeing light visually in Light vision. Your ego perceives the bodies of your bothers as a way of limiting your awareness of your brother. Yet the Holy Spirit helps you to uncover your Christ's vision so you can see the light shining from them and in them. Your perception of the light in your brother may be nonvisual or have the added visual component of Light vision. In either case, when you manifest Christ's vision so you can perceive the light in your brother, you have experienced the holy instant.

> As the ego would limit your perception of your brothers in the body, so would the Holy Spirit release your vision and let you see the Great Rays shining from them, so unlimited that they reach to God. It is this shift to vision that is accomplished in the holy instant.[294]

In contrast to the experience of revelation, which is totally outside the realm of time, the experience of the holy instant literally collapses time through the divine making its presence known in your life. These holy instants are not the dramatic, completely overwhelming impact of God directly revealing Himself, as He does in revelation. But these holy instants are deeply moving experiences and reveal a profound contact with your brother, whose divine nature becomes apparent to you in such present moments. You may not see the divine light in your brother as a visual experience, but you may still have an inner awareness of the divine light and love in your brother. This too is an example of a mystical encounter with the divine through contact with your brother. These changes in perception, called miracles, are expressions of love that are truly natural, and yet in many cases these will appear to be mystical because you have forgotten what it means for you to be in your natural state.

One goal of the Course is for you to gain somewhat of a mystical attitude about yourself by learning to not think of yourself as a body, as the ego would have you do. Because the Course is attempting to teach you that you are beyond the limitations of the body, the Course never specifically recommends focusing in meditation on a part of the body. One exception to this is an indication to meditate downward and inwardly in one particular lesson.[295] Although the Course does not say so, I prefer to think this means down through the head, which is overshadowed by the Holy Spirit, and deeply inward into the heart center in the center of the chest or into the heart itself.

Since the Course wants to convince you that you are not a body, the body is not emphasized in meditation. This could be a stumbling block for some Course students who might otherwise be inclined to meditate with awareness on the body. However, the Course does not specifically speak out against focusing upon parts of the body. This silence is not necessarily a rejection of focusing on parts of the body. I believe you can focus on the body, not to give it a false reality, but to use it in a way that is consistent with Course principles.

Let's review what the Course states about the body in order to understand how the body can be used for meditation. The body is the temple of the ego, where the ego is worshiped and followed. Accepting the body as your identity is an attack on your true nature. The ego uses the body as a vehicle first to attack yourself and then to deny your attack on yourself by attacking others. Physical attack by the body is not needed for the ego to successfully use the body for attack. The ego convinces you that you can obtain something that you want by attack. Once you accept this belief in getting by attacking, you have accepted the body as your vehicle for attack.[296] The ego uses the body for separation from others and to convince you that your mind is limited to the confines of the physical body. Identifying with the body is depressing because it is a belittling of who you are. Perceiving your brother as a body devalues him and separates you from him. Your true Identity is a shared Identity that includes your brother thus belittling him by seeing him as a body prevents you from finding yourself in your brother.

With this dark picture of the body, it might seem odd to consider that the body can be a useful vehicle for meditation, especially since the Course says that the body itself has no purpose. Only the mind can have a purpose so to think the physical body can have a purpose by itself without the mind makes no sense.[297] Negative references to the body that are made in the Course only relate to how the body is perceived by the ego and do not relate to the nature of the body itself. The Course states the body itself is neutral and being without purpose will take on the purpose that it is assigned by the mind. Thus the value of the body becomes determined by what purpose is assigned to the body by the mind. If your mind is guided by the ego, you will give the body the function of separation as was noted previously. But if your mind is guided by the Holy Spirit you can allow the Holy Spirit to assign the function of communication to the body.

Though the body was originally made to be the ego's temple, it can become the Holy Spirit's temple if you allow the Holy Spirit to assign the body its function. The one function the Holy Spirit assigns to the body is communication. The ego wants you to believe that the mind is in the body and therefore the mind is limited. The Holy Spirit wants to show you that the body that you made as a limitation and can be used in a way that extends beyond itself and its limitations. The Holy Spirit shows that the mind, which is not physical, is not in the physical body, but can extend *through* the body. Your mind can extend through your body to the minds of your brothers. This can demonstrate to you that you are not limited to your body and show to your brothers that they are not limited to their bodies either. This communication brings communion.[298]

The Course describes the body as a communication device with which you communicate your true nature of love. You can use it as a communication device to express love to your brothers, and you can also use it as a communication device to be receptive to God's Love or express your own love to God.

When the body is used solely for communication, the result is healing. The body's health depends upon the function that is assigned to the body. The body becomes unhealthy when the ego uses the body to perform its function of attack, which results in guilt. The ego's belief that the mind is within the body enables the ego to project the mental belief in guilt upon the body. Because guilt involves the belief in punishment, the ego punishes the body by building tension and sickness into parts of the physical body. Meditation focusing on the body can help to alleviate this tension projected into the body and can prevent sickness. Certain kinds of inner tension and blocks are projected upon specific parts of the body related to the chakras. The chakras are related to specific body parts. Yet the chakras themselves are not in the body but work through specific body parts just as the mind is not in the body but works through the body.

Since health is produced in the body by using the body only for communication, it is interesting to note that during the course of daily life, the body is used for many varied activities, but there are relatively few actual times in which the body is used just for communication. Ironically, a great way of using the body solely for communication occurs when the body is motionless during the practice of meditation. When the body stops the doing activities of the ego and is allowed to be motionless in meditation, the mind can extend far beyond the limitations of the body. The Course specifically recommends the holy instant as the vehicle to go beyond the body and communicate with your brothers and with God.

The Course recommends meditation leading to contemplation in order to be receptive to the Holy Spirit. Christian Yoga Meditation is a more systematic step-by-step means of leading to contemplation than the Course recommends. When using Christian Yoga Meditation, you surrender to the Holy Spirit in parts to ensure that no aspects of yourself are excluded from your surrender. The most likely aspect of yourself not to be offered to the Holy Spirit is the physical body, often overlooked as a part of the meditation process. The first of the six techniques employed in Christian Yoga Meditation is Centering Meditation. In this technique, you focus the mind on the navel area and surrender the body to the divine influence of the Holy Spirit. This surrender helps you to counteract the ego's projection of guilt, punishment, tension, and sickness onto the body and helps to restore the body to health. By extending this invitation to the Holy Spirit to manifest through the body, you enable the body to be used for the single function of divine communication and communion.

For second method of Christian Yoga Meditation, which is Heart Meditation, you focus at the heart area, and the emotional nature is surrendered to the Holy Spirit. Through this surrender you remove blocks to love and allow love to extend beyond the body limitations to all your brothers and sisters. For the third method, Brow Meditation, you focus at the brow area, and the mental nature is surrendered to the Holy Spirit, removing mental blocks and allowing the mind to extend far beyond the body. For fourth technique, Crown Meditation, you focus at the crown area, and an inner integration and a deeper opening to God occurs that is guided by the Holy Spirit. For the fifth method, Oneness Meditation, you focus on the whole body all at once. Through the Holy Spirit, you experience oneness and openness to inner feelings, such as the feelings of light and love.

The first five methods of Christian Yoga Meditation involve using the body as a device to facilitate divine communication. You start with the first method, which is the most physically oriented, and then with each successive technique, you allow your awareness to progressively let go of attachment to the body. For the sixth and last method, Inner

Silence Meditation, you release body awareness altogether. For this method, you can use an affirmation to calm your mind and then let go of the affirmation and enter inner silence leading to contemplation, which includes the overshadowing of the Holy Spirit.

Both the Course methods and Christian Yoga Meditation lead to the same experience of wordless contemplation beyond the limits of body awareness. After learning and using the first five methods of Christian Yoga Meditation, you may progress to the time when these five methods can be reduced and then eliminated. In this advanced state, you can simply sit down for your daily practice and immediately practice the sixth method, Inner Silence Meditation, and experience contemplation. Some seekers have the ability to enter contemplation immediately in their first experiences of attunement and do not need to use the first five techniques. Yet most spiritual seekers are not so gifted and therefore benefit by using these five techniques as a way of learning how to use the body in meditation in order to eventually enter contemplation and transcend the body.

I believe that the Course fits well with yoga, but this belief would be refuted by some Course scholars, who would say that the Course de-emphasizing the body does not fit well with yoga. For example, the Course does not address the use of techniques of meditation that incorporate body awareness, such as methods that focus on parts of the body, and yoga does have this emphasis.

The Course provides a one-size-fits-all thought system designed to change your perceptions, and it is intended to appeal to the general population of followers of Christ. It is true that the Course is different from yoga, but that is the very reason why these two go together as a balance for each other. If you want to find a perfect balance between the vertical and horizontal seeking of God, the practice of Christian raja yoga by itself may be too vertical and the practice of the Course by itself may be too horizontal. However, by combining these two, your practice of Miracle Raja Yoga would be helpful in providing a vertical approach to God that would help you to balance out the primarily horizontal emphasis on relationships in the Course.

The practice of Miracle Raja Yoga is a blending of unique aspects of yoga and unique aspects of the Course practices. For example, hatha yoga postures and breathing are unique aspects of yoga that would be used as preparations for meditation. Similarly, there are unique elements of meditation and contemplation that are already very much a part of the Course. Although the Course is primarily horizontal because of its emphasis on forgiveness and relationships, it is important to not overlook the vertical meditative elements that are already part of the Course. After all, meditation can be a way of effectively connecting with others.

D. THE COURSE TECHNIQUES OF MEDITATION

The Course has a traditional approach to meditation. It introduces many different ways of seeking the divine vertically, yet it leaves the impression that meditating on the purpose of seeking God is more important than the specific technique chosen. This flexibility in the Course in regard to techniques suggests that a variety of techniques, including yoga methods, would be acceptable if the focus is placed primarily on the intention of seeking God rather than on the methods themselves. The Course asks the seeker be aware of the sacredness, the holiness, of entering the divine presence.[299]

Let's review in a systematic way the sequence of how meditation is presented in the Course. The seeking of God is divided into three main categories: with the use of concepts, with the use of one concept or only a few concepts, and with the use of no concepts. The first category leads to the second, and the second leads to the third. The Course uses these three categories in sequence. The first category of seeking God with many concepts is the foundation of the Course itself expressed in the Text as a complete and integrated thought system. The Text teaches you to replace false concepts with true concepts by your openness to the Course thought system itself, which describes itself as a thought system of only true concepts. This thought system of how to seek God with concepts leads then to the Workbook practices that help you to manifest these concepts in your daily life.

The first Workbook lessons that include meditation employ visual imagination, which involves conceptual images. You are asked to see the ego-based thoughts of your mind as a dark cloud and to gently move past the cloud and into the light.[300] For these initial Workbook lessons, you repeat the sentence that expresses the idea for the day, and you can occasionally return to repeating these words if you find this assists your meditation. Even in these beginning lessons the goal is established of going beyond the ego thoughts and to God.

The second category of employing one concept or a few concepts is included in Workbook Lessons 183, 184, and 187. These lessons focus on repeating the Name of God, which is, of course, the Hindu practice of *japa yoga*. The inclusion of this method is a narrowing of focus from many ideas about God to one single idea encapsulated in His divine Name. The idea is for all the thoughts of your mind to become only one thought—one word, one Name of God.

Unlike the former lessons of repeating a sentence representing the idea of the day, this repeating of one word will contain all your desires and aspirations. With other lessons, you release the words and pick them up if the mind is distracted. When repeating the Name of God in these lessons, you use the Hindu method of repeating God's Name continuously. This is not mindless repetition, but rather focusing all of your heart and mind on the intent of seeking God Who is already one with you. Since you are one with God, you are calling your own true name, as well as God's Name. By including some lessons on this approach, the Course is following its pattern of offering many different options to meet the varying needs of seekers.

Although there are some Workbook lessons that include the use of the Name of God, the Course does not give any specific divine Name as a recommendation to repeat. The Course lets the student decide what Name of God he is attracted to. Yet in two places in the *Manual for Teachers*, there are indications that calling on the name of Jesus is equivalent to calling upon the Name of God. In the section about Jesus having a special place in regard to healing, the Course clearly states that the name of Jesus had become the Name of God:

> He has recognized himself as God created him, and in so doing he has recognized all living things as part of him. There is no limit on his power, because it is the Power of God. So has his name become the Name of God, for he no longer sees himself as separate from Him.
>
> What does this mean for you? It means that in remembering Jesus you are remembering God.[301]

The Course also says that the name of Jesus Christ is a symbol. But this symbol is more than a symbol because it is so close to the reality of God's Word for which it stands, described this way:

> The name of Jesus Christ as such is but a symbol. But it stands for love that is not of this world. It is a symbol that is safely used as a replacement for the many names of all the gods to which you pray. It becomes the shining symbol for the Word of God, so close to what it stands for that the little space between the two is lost, the moment that the name is called to mind.[302]

Jesus does not see himself as separate from God thus calling the name of Jesus helps you to realize you too are not separate from God. Jesus also does not see himself as separate from you. By calling his name, you come to realize that you are not separate from him. You will not find anyone who loves you right now more than Jesus. He wants you to return his love because in doing so you will realize that you are love. Calling the name of Jesus assists healing. However, meditation itself also is healing. The practice of calling the Name of God in meditation is healing for your own consciousness.

Yet the Course is not asking you to call on the name of a person who lived two thousand years ago. Calling on the name of Jesus is calling on the name of the resurrected Christ who is fully aware of his oneness with God right now and who is joined with you in the Sonship. This invocation helps you to grow toward awakening your awareness of who you really are. Jesus uses Christ's vision to see your loveliness. By joining your will with the will of Jesus, which is the Will of God, you too will be able to see with the eyes of Christ. Calling on the name of Jesus helps you receive Christ's vision that enables you to see through illusions and accept the light.

Although there are many benefits to calling the Name of God and specifically the name of Jesus, this using of one word (or only a few words) is only the second category of seeking God in the Course. This use of one word is intended to lead you to the third category, which is seeking God without words. In the later Workbook lessons, the Course emphasizes being open to the divine without words. If the mind becomes distracted, the Course recommends that you repeat a word or words to redirect the mind again toward being open to God. Consequently, the Course is encouraging you to practice Inner Silence Meditation. Clearly the Course wishes to lead you in the direction of the objectless awareness of contemplation, although that specific word "contemplation" is not used in the Workbook.

Besides promoting the practice of openness to contemplation, the Course is also very much interested in encouraging you to become open to Christ's vision. Some Workbook lessons direct you to look for light, and the Text stresses the value of Christ's vision and of opening to the light that makes real vision possible. Because the Workbook is a one-year program mainly focused on changing your perceptions, it does not include much instruction in how to deepen your attunement experience. This lack of specific instruction is the reason why the vast majority of students doubt if they have experienced Christ's vision. Generally, these students do not inwardly or outwardly experience the visual component of seeing light, which is the by-product called Light vision that would confirm their Christ's vision.

The Holy Spirit wants to give you Christ's vision and the by-product of Light vision, but you have to open yourself to receive this gift by doing the work of unifying your mind in meditation. If you want to experience a deeper level of Christ's vision and be able to see the real world, you will also have to deepen your meditation experience. To deepen your meditation experience, I suggest my meditation manual: *Christian Meditation Inspired by Yoga and "A Course in Miracles": How to Open to Divine Love in Contemplation*. A Twenty-eight Day Demonstration of your willingness to learn meditation practices and a One-Year Deepening Meditation Program are offered in this manual for your consideration. With the Course emphasis on seeking light, your practice of Miracle Raja Yoga would naturally lead you in the direction of following Christ in the *path of light* that is exemplified by

St. Symeon, rather than the *path of darkness* exemplified by St. John of the Cross. My meditation manual offers techniques to help you to develop a peaceful mind focused on light and love. Helpful information is provided on how to walk the path of light and replace fearful dreams of your world with happy dreams of the real world.

Miracle Raja Yoga is a combination of the Course and Christian raja yoga. Let's compare the separate strengths and weaknesses of the Course and Christian raja yoga. This comparison reveals why these two kinds of spiritual seeking can be helpful compliments for each other in the practice of Miracle Raja Yoga. The strength of the Course is that it contributes more of the horizontal aspects of divine seeking. The weakness of the Course is that the Workbook only offers a one-year program and therefore does not provide enough specific instruction in the vertical approach to God. Christian raja yoga used without the Course certainly has the vertical emphasis on systematic clearly-defined techniques employed to seek God within. The Course emphasizes the importance of using Christ's vision, including more information on obtaining the visual component of Christ's vision than is provided in the Christian raja yoga without the Course.

The strength of Christian raja yoga is that it contributes more of the vertical elements of divine seeking. The weakness of the Christian raja yoga is a lack of a Vedanta-like philosophy to serve as a theological basis for spiritual seeking. Miracle Raja Yoga fills this need with a complete thought system that incorporates a qualified nondualism, a variation of the nondualism of the East. Miracle Raja Yoga adds a focus on Christian relationships, as well as an in-depth understanding of the psychological elements of spiritual seeking.

One specific weakness of Hindu raja yoga can be the seeking of *self-realization* with an emphasis on self with a small "s." In this case, spiritual attainment is sought as an individual achievement produced by individual effort. Miracle Raja Yoga helps to redirect this emphasis toward finding yourself in your brother and also finding God in your brother, while still including quiet times of directly seeking God in meditation and contemplation.

Another similar weakness of raja yoga is that there is a temptation toward pride nourished by becoming proficient at mastering certain aspects of yoga technique, such as hath yoga postures. Of course, pride can be a problem in any discipline. Yet there is a tendency in yoga toward specialness that can sometimes focus on physical and also spiritual attributes and can produce a sense of competition with others. This can occur as an outgrowth of the attitude of envisioning spiritual growth as an individual effort rather than a joint venture. The Miracle Raja Yoga assists in helping change this focus on the self into a focus on meditation as a way of connecting with others.

Since Christian raja yoga without the Course emphasizes methods of meditation, some may have very advanced spiritual experiences that are genuine contacts with the divine. But a primarily vertical approach to God can circumvent the ego functions. Some aspects of the ego will be transformed by meditation, but other aspects of the ego can remain entirely intact. The seeker can be spiritually advanced on the meditation level but still be very attached to the ego.

In 1975 I was living at an ashram of a Hindu swami who came to America and was a popular teacher. At this ashram, I was shocked to see this swami pick up a medium-sized plant in a pot and smash it to the floor. One of his disciples had not cleaned a work area to his satisfaction so the Swami went into a fit of anger screaming at the cowering disciple. Years later, I heard that this same swami had been having sexual encounters with his female disciples.

This swami is an example of a person having a certain level of genuine spiritual experiences without releasing ego-based influences. Leaving the ego intact can be a problem, to a greater or lesser degree, for all seekers who use meditation techniques as their only or primary means of spiritual growth. The Course is a remedy for this by focusing on relationships and also by presenting a very complete psychological picture of how the ego works. This understanding helps you to learn how to increase the Holy Spirit's influence and how to decrease the influence of the ego. The Course repeatedly encourages you to bring the darkness of imagined sin and guilt to the light so that it can be dissolved by God's Love.

In order to balance out the troubling descriptions of the dark side of the mind dominated by the ego, the Course offers you the option of turning to the Holy Spirit and trusting the reality of your true nature in the Sonship in oneness with God. In the Course, you are assured that the Holy Spirit will guide you Home to awaken to your place in the Sonship. Even though in meditation and contemplation you do not consciously focus on your belief system, your thought system is really your foundation for how you will grow spiritually. If your thought system is faulty, it cannot be corrected simply by disengaging from your distracting ego-based thoughts in meditation. You need to also replace the false perceptions of the ego with true perceptions to help secure your spiritual foundation, and the Course can greatly assist you in this process. You can learn to grow spiritually by applying Course principles in your relationships. Your everyday life and relationships are your training ground for learning how to manifest the love that is your true nature. Miracle Raja Yoga encourages you to approach God vertically through meditation and also to practice meditation to connect with others horizontally. This manifests the Christian ideal of loving God with your whole heart and whole mind and loving your neighbor as yourself.

CHAPTER 9

~ • ~

MIRACLE BHAKTI AND KARMA YOGA

A. THE HEALING OF GUILT

This chapter covers the impact that the Course will have on your practice of Miracle Bhakti Yoga and Miracle Karma Yoga. To lay the foundation for a discussion of Miracle Bhakti Yoga, which is the yoga of love, first it would be helpful to elaborate upon the inner blocks that the ego presents to the awareness of love. The whole purpose of the Course is to remove inner blocks so that the awareness of your true love nature can be revealed. The final section of the previous chapter mentioned how meditation can be used to circumvent the ego to experience higher levels of consciousness, but the end result is that the ego can remain largely intact. Unlike circumventing the ego, the Course asks you to take the darkness of the ego out of hiding and bringing it into the light to be released.

To do this successfully, it is necessary to accept that guilt is a false and destructive belief, hiding in the dark corners of the psyche. Some Course students find it difficult to look with clarity at all the masks that the ego hides behind in the human condition. The mask closest to the surface is the pleasant face of innocence that is your conscious personality, which always wants to look innocent while hiding any attack thoughts, negative emotions, and feelings of guilt.

Below that mask is a victim, which is also a mask. The victim is the self that feels helpless, rejected, and injured because of what the cruel world has done to him. The victim is angry and blames others and the world for victimizing him. The victim unknowingly invites sickness, which is a way of allowing hidden guilt to manifest outwardly as an expression of self-punishment. The victim cannot accept responsibility for having a self-defeating mindset that invites victimization.

And yet beneath that victim mask is the ego itself as the victimizer, the attacker. The ego is the idea of separation. But the ego in order to maintain the idea of separation engages in *attack* as its only actual function. At this level of the ego itself, the ego makes a mask of attack thoughts, but you do not see the ego as a mask. You see it as who you are. All the other masks over the ego serve the purpose of hiding the ego itself so you will not have to see just how awful your attacking ego is and therefore how awful you apparently are.

If you could go still deeper, you would discover what lies behind the ego mask. You would uncover the light and love of your own true nature. But you cannot do so because the ego convinces your mind that you are guilty. The ego does not mind telling you that you were once a spiritual being of light and holiness in union with God, because the ego has you believing in a very dark picture of yourself. According to the ego you have attacked God.

> If the ego is the symbol of separation, it is also the symbol of guilt. Guilt is more than merely not of God. It is the symbol of attack on God. This is a totally meaningless concept except to the ego, but do not underestimate the power of the ego's belief in it. This is the belief from which all guilt stems.
>
> The ego is the part of the mind that believes in division. How could part of God detach itself without believing it is attacking Him? We spoke before of the authority problem as based on the concept of usurping God's power. The ego believes that this is what you did because it believes that *is* you. If you identify with the ego you will experience guilt, and you will fear punishment. The ego is quite literally a fearful thought. However, ridiculous the idea of attacking God may be to the sane mind, never forget that the ego is not sane. It represents a delusional thought system and speaks for it.[303]

You have become a sinful and vile creature who has waged war on your loving Creator and you have damaged Heaven itself with your attack. You had infinite bliss, peace, and love, and became a traitor who turned against God's love. You could never return to God's love because you deserved to be punished for your great crimes. The ego passes its ultimate judgment upon you that you are a criminal and you deserve death as your just punishment. The ego wants death for you.[304]

> The ego is not a traitor to God, to Whom treachery is impossible. But it is a traitor to you who believe that you have been treacherous to your Father. That is why the undoing of guilt is an essential part of the Holy Spirit's teaching. For as long as you feel guilty you are listening to the voice of the ego, which tells you that you have been treacherous to God and therefore deserve death. You will think that death comes from God and not from the ego because, by confusing yourself with

the ego, you believe that you want death. And from what you want God does not save you.[305]

Some seekers become disenchanted with the Course after reading about this dark picture and deny that these thoughts are within them. Nevertheless, the Course maintains that these thoughts are within you, and you do believe them. It is hard to believe there is this degree of self-hate within anyone let alone yourself. Yet those who undergo the dark night of the soul can attest to the ego's sentence of death upon your head. However, for most people, the ego is successful in using the outer masks of the face of innocence, the victim, and the victimizer to hide the depth of this inner self-loathing.

The ego uses your own true loving mind against you. It is because you have a loving mind that deep within your mind you are horrified at the picture that the ego paints of your black crimes against God. Since you believe the ego and believe you are the ego and since you are aware that you once did have infinite happiness, you are in a condition of immense pain. The pain is caused by comparing your true loving mind with the sinful person it appears you have become. Since you were once aware of being the Son of God in union with Him and since you now see yourself as the ego, it appears to you that you have arrived in this condition by killing God's Son. It seems like the Christ Self in you committed suicide and what is left is the part of you that murdered yourself. You are convinced that you have crucified the Son of God[306] and there will be no resurrection for you, only the hell of being the ego or the death you deserve.

These mistaken perceptions and related painful negative feelings have been repressed into the subconscious mind. Many will not want to uncover the dark corners of their psyches, preferring to live "lives of quiet desperation" covered over by the smiles of the face of innocence. But for those that do happen to go this deep or who sense this inner pain, there can be a grace that emerges. Denial that hides pain also hides the recognition that healing is needed. It is only those who recognize that they are sick who go to a doctor for healing. So the awareness of the pain can have the grace of helping you to realize that you need healing. From this realization, you can take the step of making your heartfelt call to God for help. This call for God, which is a call for love, is already deep within you. Below the mask of the face of innocence, below the victim mask, below the ego's victimizer mask, and below your pain is the call for God waiting for your recognition. Your call for love just needs to be found so you can discover that your loving Father has been the One who is calling you.[307]

The call for love is a realization that love is what you really want. You call for love because you have not yet realized that you *are* the love that you want. Yet with your call for love, you are beginning to see that you have wanted love all along. Every time you put on some kind of mask, you are really seeking love in a disguised form. When you put on the mask of the face of innocence, this involves seeking specialness, even though it is at the expense of others who would have to be less special. But in seeking specialness, you really want worth, which is a form of love. When you put on the mask of being a victim, you are really seeking innocence, which is a form of love. When you put on the mask of the ego, the victimizer, you overtly attack others. But when you attack others, it is because it appears that others are not giving you the love that you want.

In following the ego in all its distorted motivations to survive, you are seeking life, which is another form of love. You think you are the ego and so are convinced its life is your life and thus its motivations for staying alive are your motivations for staying alive. What the ego knows that you do not know is that if you could look at the ego as it really is and if you could see yourself as you really are, which is divine love, you would laugh at the ego. Your laughter would express your realization that the ego is a false idea and with this realization the ego would dissolve into non-existence.

But because the ego does such an effective job in hiding its nature and hiding your true nature, you feel excruciatingly guilty. You may not be able to clearly uncover the darkest corner of the ego where you believe you have murdered the Son of God that you had been, but you can sense a deep shame about yourself and your life that does not reflect your true nature of love. At the level of the call for God, you are in enough pain to want to call out to God, but your guilt makes you afraid to call out to God. When your pain becomes great enough, you realize that something is terribly wrong, and you are helpless to change it by yourself. Then you call out to God.

This call for God, which is already in your psyche and which you have now recognized and expressed, is an important transition level away from the ego and to a deeper level of awareness. By allowing the call for God to be expressed consciously, you give your freewill permission to the Holy Spirit to assist you. In fact, the Course calls the Holy Spirit the "Call for God," which is the call to come Home.[308] The Holy Spirit with your permission loosens the grip of the ego on your psyche and helps you to access the next level of awareness that is called your *right mind*.

Previously it appeared to you that the ego had met with the Son of God, your former identity, and murdered the Son of God leaving only the ego itself, which you had become. The right mind shows you that the ego is not real. All the sins that you had committed, including murdering the Son of God, were illusions. These sins never happened and had no results. Sin is the idea that attack is real and produces real negative results. But the right mind shows you that sin itself is not real. The right mind gives you permission to let go of all the guilt you had carried for your sins by helping you realize that sin, the cause for guilt, does not exist. There is no mark of defilement on your soul.

The right mind enables you to accept true perceptions, which in turn allows you to release false perceptions about yourself that were based on the mistaken idea that you are the ego. Your right mind is in the real world, which is itself a transition point to your ultimate goal of returning to the Christ Mind in union with God. When your right mind becomes filled with only true perceptions of love, it becomes so loving that awakening to the Christ Mind will happen.

Preparing you to awaken, the Holy Spirit helps you release false ego-based perceptions. But you must bring your false perceptions to the Holy Spirit so they can be dispelled by divine light. If you allow your false perceptions to be hidden, they will remain in the dark corners of the ego. In particular, ideas of sin and guilt need to be brought to the Holy Spirit so their unreality can be exposed by divine light. At a deep level within you believe in the illusion that you are a vile sinner and have crucified the Son of God. Such thoughts are in everyone usually buried in the unconscious recesses of the mind, having a negative effect on your awareness of yourself.

I have encountered seekers who have informed me that they have rejected the Course as a thought system because the Course goes into great detail pointing out these dark corners of the mind. Nevertheless, rejecting the Course on this basis implies that it is somehow beneficial to not become aware of the hidden dark aspects of the unconscious mind. Yet the Course would be remiss if it only stirred up these dark thoughts without also offering an immediate remedy. Denial offers no remedy, but the rooting out of dark thoughts brings the recognition that a remedy of healing is needed, which then results in the call for help. Then these dark thoughts that have risen to your conscious awareness need to be given over to the Holy Spirit, Who provides the healing remedy, as is described below:

> And yet he is not crucified. Here is both his pain and his healing, for the Holy Spirit's vision is merciful and His remedy is quick. Do not hide suffering from His sight, but bring it gladly to Him. Lay before His eternal sanity all your hurt, and let Him heal you. Do not leave any spot of pain hidden from His Light, and search your mind carefully for any thoughts you may fear to uncover. For He will heal every little thought you have kept to hurt you and cleanse it of its littleness, restoring it to the magnitude of God.

Beneath all the grandiosity you hold so dear is your real call
for help. For you call for love to your Father as your Father calls
you to Himself. In that place which you have hidden, you will
only to unite with the Father, in loving remembrance of Him.
You will find this place of truth as you see it in your brothers,
for though they may deceive themselves, like you they long
for the grandeur that is in them. And perceiving it you will
welcome it, and it will be yours. For grandeur is the right of
God's Son, and no illusions can satisfy him or save him from
what he is. Only his love is real, and he will be content only
with his reality.[309]

In summary of this section, you feel you have crucified God's Son
and you are in pain seeing what you have apparently done as you
look deeply into your own psyche without denial. But in recognizing
your pain, you understand that you need healing. Your recognition
that you need healing leads you to uncover the call for help, the call
for love, the call for God, which lies beneath the masks of the face
of innocence, the victim, and the ego victimizer. The call for God
leads you to the next deeper level, which is your right mind where
false perceptions can be changed to true perceptions. You can learn to
offer your dark perceptions to the Holy Spirit for healing in the light
and eventually be led from your right mind of true perceptions to the
Christ Mind where you know God and are truly at Home.

The way to find your path Home is to use Christ's vision as a
means of seeing the divine in your brother, which confirms to yourself
your own divine nature. The Holy Spirit enables you to perceive with
Christ's vision, which allows you to distinguish between the real and
the unreal. Christ's vision helps you to look past your brother's body,
which is the symbol of guilt, and instead see Christ in your brother.
By seeing Christ in your brother you realize the true perception that
you also are Christ. Christ's vision shows you that your brother and
you are both sinless.

The holy relationship is a means of learning this lesson allowing
you to be your brother's savior and allowing your brother to be your
savior. By joining in the holy relationship for a common purpose you
invite the Holy Spirit into your relationship and make holiness your
true common goal. Your minds become joined and reflect the joined
nature of your minds in Heaven. The Holy Spirit purifies your joined
minds at the subconscious level, undoing not all, but at least some of
the damage done by the ego. Your ego is still present, of course, but
your ego can no longer totally convince you that you are alone,
because your combined minds joined for a common purpose prove
that you are not alone.

B. PROJECTION AND CORRECTION

Accepting the Course principles will certainly have a strong impact on your practice of Miracle Bhakti Yoga, a specific form of Christian bhakti yoga. This section describes the Course perspective on blocks to the awareness of love, and an upcoming section describes how the Course principles impact Miracle Bhakti Yoga. To practice Miracle Bhakti Yoga of love, you need to understand how to deal with errors, because errors block the awareness of love.

Your response to errors is substantially more important than the errors themselves since your response can eliminate errors or multiply errors. The inappropriate way to deal with your own errors is to not accept responsibility for your errors. The way this non-acceptance of responsibility is accomplished is through *projection*. The mind employs either projection, which involves a seeing of guilt in others, or employs *extension*, which is a sharing of love. Thus, your practice of Miracle Bhakti Yoga will depend on your willingness and ability to let go of projecting guilt and to instead manifest extending love. Extending love is the expression of a universal law of the mind and projection is a distorted application of the same universal law of the mind.

> We have said that without projection there can be no anger, but it is also true that without extension there can be no love. These reflect a fundamental law of the mind, and therefore one that always operates. It is the law by which you create and were created. It is the law that unites the Kingdom, and keeps it in the Mind of God. To the ego, the law is perceived as a means of getting rid of something it does not want. To the Holy Spirit, it is the fundamental law of sharing, by which you give what you value in order to keep it in your mind. To the Holy Spirit it is the law of extension. To the ego it is the law of deprivation. It therefore produces abundance or scarcity, depending on how you choose to apply it. This choice is up to you, but it is not up to you to decide whether or not you will utilize the law. Every mind must project or extend, because that is how it lives, and every mind is life.[310]

Projection is always caused by the ego, which is an erroneous belief about yourself. Overcoming the ego means withdrawing your belief in it. Reinforcing the ego is brought about by not accepting responsibility for your belief in the ego and by projecting your errors onto others. The Course explains the relationship between the ego and projection, as follows:

Do not be afraid of the ego. It depends on your mind, and as you made it by believing in it, so you can dispel it by withdrawing belief from it. Do not project the responsibility for your belief in it onto anyone else, or you will preserve the belief. When you are willing to accept responsibility for the ego's existence you will have laid aside all anger and attack, because they come from an attempt to project responsibility for your own errors. But having accepted the errors as yours, do not keep them. Give them over quickly to the Holy Spirit to be undone completely, so that all their effects will vanish from your mind and from the Sonship as a whole.[311]

Projection is the denial of your own errors and an attempt to get rid of the responsibility for your errors by projecting error outside of yourself. This means projecting errors onto other people. It does not matter whether or not other people actually have within themselves the errors that you see in them. Your premise in projection is that seeing errors in others allows you to get rid of them in yourself. But you cannot break off a piece of your mind and send it outside of yourself. Whatever your mind sends out, it retains in the act of trying to send it out. Because giving and receiving happen simultaneously, whatever you give you keep. By assigning errors to others, you keep the error that you think you have discarded. You must use denial to not see that you are keeping what you seem to be giving away.

You cannot attempt to project an error into another mind without keeping the error in your own mind. All you can really do is falsely perceive an ego-based illusion in another person and strengthen that ego-based illusion in yourself. Your projection of a false perception stays in your mind. But does your false perception travel to the other person who is the object of your perception? No, your false perception does not go to the other person. If the other person appears to be reacting to your false perceptions, it is because the other person is also projecting guilt and false perceptions toward you. By projecting onto you, the other person keeps his own false perceptions. The other person is negatively affected by his own negative projections toward you, not by your projections onto him.

The ego is the false idea of separation, and its activity is attack. Projection is a form of attack that seems to be directed at others. Yet projection is the means for the ego to attack you, while seemingly attacking others. You, as the holy Son of God, cannot be attacked in reality, but the ego can make attack seem real to you. Your own ego, not another person's ego, makes attack seem real to you. When you manifest projection, *you attack yourself*, because "...it is impossible that you be hurt except by your own thoughts."[312] When another person reacts to you negatively because of sensing your projections, he attempts to project guilt onto you. In this act of his own projection, the other person is attacking himself with his own projections, just as you are attacking yourself with your projections.

You know that bodies can attack and cause physical harm, but it may not be clear to you that minds cannot really attack other minds. Two people that argue with each other may appear to be attacking each other, but actually each one is attacking himself. Projection is self-deception fostering the belief that you can send attack thoughts to others without affecting yourself. "Yet projection will always hurt you."[313] You make an attack illusion by your belief in it. You keep it in your mind, and it appears real to you by the same belief with which you made it.[314] Minds can fabricate their own conflict illusions but cannot share them because conflict cannot come to your mind from another mind. Conflict is something you do to yourself, while you imagine it comes from outside yourself. Conflict is always a choice you make, and therefore a choice you can decide not to make.

Because you cannot really send attack thoughts to another mind does not mean that minds cannot receive and send to other minds. In projection, no exchange between minds can occur since the content of attack and guilt cannot be transferred. The foundation of Miracle Bhakti Yoga is *extension* in which love is expressed as minds do, in fact, receive and send to other minds. For example, the miracle is a manifestation of extension in which the mind extends light and love in a real exchange between two minds. If you perform a miracle, light and love will extend from your mind to your brother's mind. Your perception of your brother as the holy Son of God will help him to perceive himself as the holy Son of God. In appreciation, he will in return send light and love to your mind. You will both end up with more love than when you started because all true sharing produces an increase in love and joy as well. In the Course, Jesus speaks of this extension of light from one mind to another when he says:

> You cannot forget the Father because I am with you, and I cannot forget Him. To forget me is to forget yourself and Him Who created you. Our brothers are forgetful. That is why they need your remembrance of me and of Him Who created me. Through this remembrance, you can change their minds about themselves, as I can change yours. Your mind is so powerful a light that you can look into theirs and enlighten them, as I can enlighten yours. I want to share my mind with you because we

are of one Mind, and that Mind is ours. See only this Mind everywhere, because only this is everywhere and everything. It is everything because it encompasses all things within itself. Blessed are you who perceive only this, because you perceive only what is true.

Come therefore unto me, and learn of the truth in you. The mind we share is shared by all our brothers, and as we see them truly they will be healed. Let your mind shine with mine upon their minds, and by our gratitude to them make them aware of the light in them. This light will shine back upon you and on the whole Sonship, because this is your proper gift to God. This is true communion with the Holy Spirit, Who sees the altar of God in everyone, and by bringing it to your appreciation, He calls upon you to love God and His creation.[315]

This kind of real exchange between minds can only occur with the extension of loving thoughts because love is an attribute of the nature of the mind itself. This exchange occurs when you participate in healing your brother in which your brother's perception is corrected and your own perception is corrected in an exchange of love. This exchange of love is always facilitated by the Holy Spirit. In fact, you are sharing the Holy Spirit with your brother in this exchange and the wholeness of the mind is restored through this sharing.[316]

The Holy Spirit is in every mind in this world and keeps these minds joined and in contact with the whole Sonship and with God. When you share the Holy Spirit with a brother, you contact the unity that your mind has with your brother and with every other mind and with God. Loving thoughts can be shared because they belong to every mind and minds were created to share love and thus increase love and joy. However, this sharing between minds cannot occur in the projection of unloving thoughts because unloving thoughts are in opposition to the loving nature of the mind. Minds can truly only communicate love, which produces healing.

Healing is the one ability everyone can develop and must develop if he is to be healed. Healing is the Holy Spirit's form of communication in this world, and the only one He accepts. He recognizes no other, because He does not accept the ego's confusion of the mind and body. Minds can communicate, but they cannot hurt. The body in the service of the ego can hurt other bodies, but this cannot occur unless the body has already been confused with the mind.[317]

The ego does not want to accept that the mind can communicate love and produce healing, so the ego encourages you to think that you are a body because the body is the ego's symbol of separation. The body is the ego's proof that you have attacked God and you are separate from Him. Although this is, of course, not true, your power of belief can make what is untrue seem to be true for you.

I have repeatedly emphasized that the ego does believe it can attack God, and tries to persuade you that you have done this. If the mind cannot attack, the ego proceeds perfectly logically to the belief that you must be a body. By not seeing you as you are, it can see itself as it wants to be. Aware of its weakness the ego wants your allegiance, but not as you really are. The ego therefore wants to engage your mind in its own delusional system, because otherwise the light of your understanding would dispel it. It wants no part of truth, because the ego itself is untrue.[318]

Just as the nature of the mind is love, the nature of the mind is also wholeness. This means that the mind cannot be divided. But the ego convinces you that the mind can be divided so that a piece of the mind can leave the mind and hurt another person in the act of projection. Light can extend from one mind to another and return back to the one giving the light. This is extension that is sharing in which there is no loss of light and no division of the mind. But in projection, no such sharing occurs, but the mistaken idea that there is sharing is the underlying illusion perpetuated by projection.

You cannot perpetuate an illusion about another without perpetuating it about yourself. There is no way out of this, because it is impossible to fragment the mind. To fragment is to break into pieces, and mind cannot attack or be attacked. The belief that it can, an error the ego always makes, underlies the whole use of projection. It does not understand what mind is, and therefore does not understand what *you* are. Yet its very existence is dependent on your mind, because the ego is your belief. The ego is a confusion in identification.[319]

Your mind cannot hurt another mind by projection, but you can harm yourself through your attempt at projection. The mind is whole and cannot be divided in reality, but your belief that your mind can be divided makes projection seem possible to you and negatively affects your mind. You hurt yourself by making your projections of attack illusions seem real to your own mind. If the mind accepts the illusion of attack imagining it to be real, the mind accepts an idea that is foreign to its own nature.

The mind that accepts attack cannot love. That is because it believes it can destroy love, and therefore does not understand what love is. If it does not understand what love is, it cannot perceive itself as loving. This loses the awareness of being, induces feelings of unreality and results in utter confusion. Your thinking has done this because of its power, but your thinking can also save you from this because its power is not of your making.[320]

Projection is an attack on yourself in the sense that it fosters guilt and fear in you. Projection brings about guilt in you because it is a dishonest act of disregarding your brother's true holiness in order to make him seem guilty in your eyes. The guilt you see in your brother becomes your own guilt that you keep by attempting to give it away. In this sense, projection is always a boomerang that becomes an attack on yourself bringing guilt to you.

Projection brings you fear because of the belief that what you have apparently given away through projection will be returned to you and will harm you. Your projection denies the fact that sending out any thought in the mind is the way to retain that thought in the mind. The false belief that any error can be discarded through projection creates the false belief that the discarded error will return to you. The more you invest in projection the more you will be concerned for your safety. Your safety concerns will be caused by your fear that what you have projected will come back and hurt you. Because the mind is conflicted within itself due to illusions about itself, the mind attempts to use projection to get rid of the conflict. The Course states two major errors involved in the projection of this conflict:

First strictly speaking, conflict cannot be projected because it cannot be shared. Any attempt to keep part of it and get rid of another part does not really mean anything.[321]

The second error is the idea that you get rid of something you do not want by giving it away. Giving it is how you *keep* it. The belief that by seeing it outside you have excluded it from within is a complete distortion of extension. That is why those who project are vigilant for their own safety. They are afraid that their projections will return and hurt them. Believing they have blotted out their projections from their minds, they also believe their projections are trying to creep back in. Since the projections have not left their mind, they are forced to engage in constant activity in order not to recognize this.[322]

The psychological description of projection is that it is a defense mechanism in which you have a specific fault in yourself, and you project that fault onto another person. For example, you can manifest projection by first denying your own inner anger and then projecting anger, which lets you see anger in another person. But projection has a much broader origin than this since the separation itself was a manifestation of projection in which you tried to divide your mind and project a part of your mind outside of itself. This is impossible because the mind is whole and cannot be divided in reality, but you were able to produce an illusion of separation. Your projection of an illusion of separation made the physical world. The separation that was the original projection was healed by the Holy Spirit. But the separation still manifests as an illusion for you because you continue to project the idea of separation as an expression of your will.

In your subconscious mind you feel guilty that your separation is an attack on God, and you are in denial about this guilt. You believe you are the ego and the belief in the ego always produces guilt. The ego deceives you by offering to "help" you release your guilt by giving it to others because it knows this is the way to keep guilt. Following the ego results in seeking out opportunities for manifesting more guilt. Guilt appears to be only the effect resulting from attack, but guilt is actually the *unconscious motivation* for attack. If you are tempted to attack, it will be because you think you can obtain something you desire to have. However, you may decide not to attack if you remind yourself that your decision to attack will actually be motivated by an unconscious ego-based desire to obtain more guilt.

In addition to the overall projection of the world and the body, you manifest selective projection at the ego's direction. Thus you attempt to attack your brother, the holy Son of God, who deserves only love. Trying to attack your brother is never justified and can only produce guilt. Just seeing your brother as a body and as an ego is in itself an attempt to attack his true nature and will result in a generalized form of guilt. Seeing your brother as a body and an ego is so much a part of daily life that this kind of projection usually goes unnoticed.

However, projection can become a very intense experience when it becomes applied specifically to particular individuals and events. An example would be when you manifest anger toward a specific brother, since your anger could not occur without projection. You use projection to perceive another person's actions as an attack on you. Then you use your belief that you have been attacked to justify your own anger and your attack in return. Anger is always an attempt to project guilt so someone else will feel guilty instead of you. Anger as a projection of attack and assigning blame to others will be explained in the next section.

Projection requires denial so the giving up of projection requires the giving up of denial. The way to let go of projection is to let go of denial and to acknowledge the truth to yourself. Acknowledging the truth means that you fully accept responsibility for your errors. But accepting full responsibility for your errors can be misinterpreted as meaning you need to blame yourself when you stop blaming others. Accepting full responsibility does not mean accepting guilt and then imposing some sort of self-punishment. God does not want you to blame yourself and feel guilty, which would only be adding another error. As soon as you accept errors as your own responsibility and not someone else's responsibility, you must quickly give your errors to the Holy Spirit without blaming yourself.

The importance of accepting responsibility for your own errors is accepted by most spiritual seekers, but the problem for many seekers is that denial is part of projection. Because of denial, you cannot see when you are not accepting responsibility. One way to overcome this blindness of denial is to look at the results of your errors.[323] If you experience negative emotions, this is an indication that you need to take responsibility for making your own emotions due to some error on your part. If you do not accept responsibility for your negative emotions, you will add to your original error that caused the negative emotions by projecting and blaming others for your emotions.

Another problem for you is learning to accept responsibility for all of your experiences without exception. Many seekers think they can make exceptions that allow them to not accept responsibility for some of their own experiences. The Course maintains that *every* experience without exception comes into your life by your invitation. You may not make the connection between your experience and how you made the invitation. Yet this lack of your awareness does not take away the need for you to fully accept responsibility for your every experience. If experiences could come to you without your invitation, you would be a victim of circumstances that are beyond your influence. The Course says you cannot be a victim of outside circumstances. You can deceive yourself into believing you are a victim by being in denial about your invitation. The Course states in unequivocal terms that you "ask for" every experience, and you need to accept responsibility for the results of your invitation:

Say only this, but mean it with no reservations, for here the power of salvation lies:

*"I **am** responsible for what I see.*
I choose the feelings I experience, and I decide upon the
goal I would achieve.

*And everything that seems to happen to me
I ask for, and receive as I have asked."*

Deceive yourself no longer that you are helpless in the face of what is done to you. Acknowledge but that you have been mistaken, and all effects of your mistakes will disappear.

It is impossible the Son of God be merely driven by events outside of him. It is impossible that happenings that come to him were not his choice. His power of decision is the determiner of every situation in which he seems to find himself by chance or accident.[324]

You may want to accept responsibility for your own errors but also may want to believe that someone else's actions caused a particular response in you. It is not possible for another person to *cause* you to respond in a particular way. You cannot accept responsibility if you believe others can cause your responses. Regardless of someone else's actions, you are responsible for your actions and emotions.

A variation of avoiding accepting responsibility is to accept your responsibility for your part in an experience but only if someone else accepts their responsibility for their part in the experience. Making your acceptance of responsibility contingent on someone else doing the same is a way of disempowering yourself by making yourself a victim of someone else's choices. You accept responsibility because doing so enables you to then let go of the error by giving it to the Holy Spirit. If another person wants to not accept responsibility and thus hold on to his error, this is that other person's choice and not your responsibility. It is also your responsibility to accept your brother as he is without trying to change him, otherwise you will be making the mistake of imposing your will on your brother.

Many believe that totally accepting responsibility for attack is just acknowledging that you have attacked another person. The commonly overlooked aspect of accepting responsibility for your errors is that you always attack yourself first. After you have attacked yourself, you deny that you have attacked yourself. Having denied your attack on yourself, you project your attack onto another person by perceiving that this other person is guilty of attacking you. It is very helpful to acknowledge that every outer attack you make has been started by an attack on yourself because this reveals to you how self-defeating attack really is. The more clearly you see attack as a way of attacking and hurting yourself the less likely you will want to indulge in attack and in projecting guilt. In this sense, the giving up of attack benefits not only your brother but is a form of enlightened self-interest.

A basic premise of the Course is that you can never be a victim of other people or outside circumstances because all the experiences you have are determined by your own choices that have invited these experiences.[325] When you feel you are a victim, you mistakenly imagine that some outside force is the cause of your experiences. By accepting full responsibility for your errors, you are no longer a victim. Since you accept yourself as the cause of your errors produced by your own choices, you can make different choices. You can choose to let go of your errors and have them be corrected by surrendering them to the power of the Holy Spirit.

Fortunately you are not responsible for undoing your errors even though you made them. You are not capable of undoing your own errors. You must not try to assume the function of undoing errors because that function has not been given to you. The function of undoing errors has been given to the Holy Spirit. You will forget to give Him your errors if you attempt to perform His function.[326] When you give your errors to the Holy Spirit, all your errors will be undone along with all the effects of your errors.

This explains how you deal with your own errors, but how can you deal with the errors of others? You may think you are doing a good service by trying to correct the errors of others, but this is not your function.

> To the ego it is kind and right and good to point out errors, and "correct" them. This makes perfect sense to the ego, which is unaware of what errors are and what correction is. Errors are of the ego, and correction of errors lies in the relinquishment of the ego. When you correct a brother, you are telling him that he is wrong. He may be making no sense at the time, and it is certain that, if he is speaking from the ego, he will not be making sense. But your task is still to tell him he is right. You do not tell him this verbally, if he is speaking foolishly. He needs correction at another level, because his error is at another level. He is still right, because he is a Son of God. His ego is always wrong, no matter what it says or does.
>
> If you point out the errors of your brother's ego you must be seeing through yours, because the Holy Spirit does not perceive his errors.[327]

Correcting errors is the function of the Holy Spirit. Errors are a manifestation of the insanity of the ego. The ego itself is insane and teaches an insane doctrine. The ego teaches the insane idea that what you truly are is not your true nature. Yet you cannot help your brother by telling him that he is behaving insanely. But you can help to heal your brother by seeing the sanity in him that is his true nature.

When a brother behaves insanely, you can heal him only by perceiving the sanity in him. If you perceive his errors and accept them, you are accepting yours. If you want to give yours over to the Holy Spirit, you must do this with his. Unless this becomes the one way in which you handle all errors, you cannot understand how all errors are undone.[328]

It is your own ego that would focus on his ego actions. You will be tempted to project your own errors onto your brother, as described above. If you point out your brother's errors to him, you are telling him that he really is an ego, which in turn would be telling yourself you really are an ego also.

You cannot correct yourself. Is it possible, then, for you to correct another? Yet you can see him truly, because it is possible for you to see yourself truly. It is not up to you to change your brother, but merely to accept him as he is. His errors do not come from the truth in him, and only this truth is yours. His errors cannot change this, and can have no effect at all on the truth in you. To perceive errors in anyone, and to react to them as if they are real, is to make them real to you. You will not escape paying the price for this, not because you are being punished for it, but because you are following the wrong guide and will therefore lose your way.

Your brother's errors are not of him, any more than yours are of you. Accept his errors as real, and you have attacked yourself. If you would find your way and keep it, see only truth beside you for you walk together. The Holy Spirit in you forgives all things in you and in your brother. His errors are forgiven with yours.[329]

Instead of projecting your own errors onto your brother, you can see his errors as being unreal in the very beginning. If you see his errors as real, you will react to these errors as if they were real. Even though his errors are not in fact real, these errors will become real to you if you perceive them as being real. "To perceive errors in anyone, and to react to them as if they were real, is to make them real to you."[330] If you make his errors real in your own mind, you will also make your own errors seem real. In making errors appear real, you have attacked yourself. "Accept his errors as real, and you have attacked yourself."[331] If you make errors real, you disregard your brother's true nature and your own true nature and reinforced your allegiance with the ego. Forgiveness allows you to see errors as unreal and overlooking them rather than making them real to your mind.

To forgive is to overlook. Look, then, beyond error and do not let your perception rest upon it, for you will believe what your perception holds. Accept as true only what your brother is, if you would know yourself. Perceive what he is not and you cannot know what you are, because you see him falsely. Remember always that your Identity is shared, and that Its sharing is Its reality.[332]

Seeing errors as being unreal in the beginning means you can immediately give them to the Holy Spirit, who forgives your brother's errors along with your own errors. Unlike the guidance of the Holy Spirit, the ego will guide you to take time to examine your errors in the beginning rather than immediately overlooking them.

The ego's plan is to have you see error clearly first, and then overlook it. Yet how can you overlook what you have made real? By seeing it clearly, you have made it real and *cannot* overlook it.[333]

Following divine guidance allows you to immediately give errors to the Holy Spirit without thoroughly examining these errors. Through reliance on the Holy Spirit and by overlooking errors in the act of forgiveness, you release what had no effect on your brother's reality or your own reality in God. Therefore, you are forgiving only illusions and not reality. This is why you need to see errors as unreal in the beginning. Once you give them reality, you will not be able to see them as illusions and will not be able to let go of them as easily.

Forgiveness through the Holy Spirit lies simply in looking beyond error from the beginning, and thus keeping it unreal for you. Do not let any belief in its realness enter your mind, or you will believe that you must undo what you have made in order to be forgiven. What has no effect does not exist, and to the Holy Spirit the effects of error are nonexistent. By steadily and consistently cancelling out all its effects, everywhere and in all respects, He teaches that the ego does not exist and proves it. Follow the Holy Spirit's teaching in forgiveness, then, because forgiveness is His function and He knows how to fulfill it perfectly.[334]

Forgiving your brother's illusions and forgiving your own illusions about yourself are enabled by accepting the *Atonement*, God's Plan for healing the separation, explained in the next section. Through the Atonement, the Holy Spirit undoes all errors. Accepting the Atonement is an important practice of Miracle Bhakti Yoga. If you accept the Atonement for yourself, you can assist your brother's healing as well as your own healing. The best way to help your brother is to remove all your own illusions about your brother, which will allow you to accept him in his true nature as the holy Son of God. Accepting the Atonement will help you to let go of the projection of guilt and replace it with the extension of love.

In the teacher and student holy relationship, the teacher can help the student correct errors not by focusing on the errors, but by inviting the Holy Spirit to perform the function of correcting error. A teacher of God can assist a student by accepting the Atonement himself to heal his own mind and by extending love and forgiveness to his pupil. A teacher can assist a student to correct his errors by listening to the Holy Spirit and sharing with his pupil the guidance provided by the Holy Spirit.

C. THE MEANING OF THE ATONEMENT

The way of healing guilt is described previously as it applies to you individually, but there is an overall plan for overcoming guilt and bringing about salvation collectively. This plan described in the Course is called the *Atonement*, a return to "at-one-ment" with God. The traditional Christian understanding of how salvation is attained is quite different from the Course version. In traditional Christianity, you, as part of mankind, sinned against God, became unacceptable to God and deserving of punishment. Your punishment for sin was the loss of the perfection and happiness of the Garden of Eden.

In this traditional Christian view, guilt is the result of sin, and since sin is a real mark on the soul, guilt is also real. The only way mankind could become reconciled with God is to express *atonement* by paying the price of a just punishment. Christianity says that Jesus paid the price, not for his sins, but for the sins of all mankind. He paid for mankind's guilt and redeemed mankind by being punished in the form of his crucifixion. In this picture of atonement, the crucifixion is the most significant event of Christianity.

In Christianity, God is divine Love, but His Love requires divine "justice" that includes punishment to produce reconciliation. But this picture of God does not sound like the father of the prodigal son who runs to his son when he is still at a distance and gives him a feast and place of honor. In this parable, the need for justice as a requirement for returning to God is expressed by the attitude of the eldest son who thinks his brother should not be welcomed back by his father with unconditional love.

The Course offers a picture of God and His Atonement in which God is very much like the father of the prodigal son who invites his son home with unconditional love. The Course is based upon the fundamental premise that God created His Son, the Sonship, as part of Himself and therefore the Sonship is forever joined with God. As an analogy, you can consider that it is impossible for a branch of a tree to disconnect from the trunk of that tree and to begin floating in the air. The identity of the branch is in its connection to the trunk and in its relationship to all the other branches that are also joined to the trunk. The identity of the branch is a shared identity, in which the same sap flows through all parts of the whole tree.

Similarly, you have a shared Identity. You are part of the Sonship joined with God and you could never disconnect from God. You are loved by God, and you could never make yourself unacceptable to God and could never separate yourself from God. Consequently, you could not really commit a sin, and you could not really be guilty. But because of free will, you do have the capacity to create an illusion and become tricked by your own illusion into thinking that you have separated yourself from God. Because you can make an illusion of separation appear real to yourself, you can also manufacture guilt about your illusory separation. Then you can punish yourself with the illusory guilt that you have manufactured.

God could not interfere with your choice because to do so would be to violate the unconditional free will He has given you. However, God did respond to the separation by the incredible creation of the Holy Spirit that would allow divine grace to come into your dream world of illusions. Because of the Holy Spirit's activity, divine grace waits patiently until you express your freewill desire to give up your illusions. Then divine grace will provide help in your waking up to your true union with God that was never really lost.

Consequently, reconciliation occurs in relation to God, but it is only a one-sided reconciliation. God does not need to be reconciled with you because God has never left you. You need reconciliation with God only because you imagine that you have separated yourself from God. The Atonement is God's Plan for this reconciliation of the entire Sonship. However, the Atonement will heal only an imaginary separation, not a real separation, explained as follows:

The Holy Spirit uses time, but does not believe in it. Coming from God He uses everything for good, but He does not believe in what is not true. Since the Holy Spirit is in your mind, your mind can also believe only what is true. The Holy Spirit can speak only for this, because He speaks for God. He tells you to return your whole mind to God, because it has never left Him. If it has never left Him, you need only perceive it as it is to be returned. The full awareness of the Atonement, then, is the recognition that *the separation never occurred*. The ego cannot prevail against this because it is an explicit statement that the ego never occurred.

The ego can accept the idea that return is necessary because it can so easily make the idea seem difficult. Yet the Holy Spirit tells you that even return is unnecessary, because what never happened cannot be difficult.[335]

The Atonement, as a one-sided reconciliation, is the realization that the *separation between God and man never really happened.* Separation only happened in your mind in a distorted picture that was not real. Since God *is* Reality, only what is done with God can have reality. Anything else is not real and is neither good nor bad but only meaningless. Your judgment may be that you are a sinner and guilty. But God's judgment is that His Son is holy and guiltless. God created you holy and guiltless. What God creates is changeless and eternal. Consequently, you remain holy and guiltless, just as God created you, no matter what you think of yourself.

From this viewpoint, the Course presents a reinterpretation of the most cherished symbols of Christianity. Jesus dictating the Course says that the crucifixion was not a payment for sins to atone for guilt. It was a demonstration that the body can be put on a cross and crucified, but the Son of God that you are cannot be harmed. For sin to be real, it must produce real negative effects that are the cause for guilt. Jesus showed that sin is not real because the worst attack upon Jesus produced no negative results. The resurrection proved that the crucifixion produced no negative results.

The Course describes the crucifixion as an extreme example of a teaching device that demonstrates four mistaken beliefs in relation to anger and attack. Anger can only occur if you manifest projection of separation between yourself and the person with whom you are angry. Projection of anger includes the four false beliefs, which are in italics below, followed by why these beliefs are irrational, as follows:

1. "... *you believe you have been attacked.*"[336] The Course counters this irrational belief by affirming, "You cannot *be* attacked ..."[337] The crucifixion shows that it is not possible for you to be attacked since the holy Son of God, your true Identity, is invulnerable to attack. Indeed, a body can be attacked and an attack can negatively impact a body, but you are not a body. The crucifixion teaches you to never perceive any apparent attack as an attack on you since your reality cannot be attacked.[338]

2. You believe *"your angry attack is justified in return"* as a response to someone first attacking you.[339] Yet the Course says unequivocally "... attack *has* no justification."[340] The crucifixion demonstrates that there is no justification for anger or attack in return. Your body can be attacked, yet your body is not who you really are. No one could attack you first, because it is not possible to attack your reality.

3. You believe *"that you are in no way responsible for it,"* meaning you do not accept responsibility for your attack or your beliefs about attack.[341] The Course contradicts this irrational conclusion by saying, "...you *are* responsible for what you believe."[342] If you hold false beliefs that you can be attacked and that attack in return is justified, you are indeed responsible for these false beliefs. When you do not accept responsibility for your false beliefs, you manifest projection. Anger itself is always a form of projection in which you attempt to blame others and make them feel guilty. In addition, your anger is an attempt to punish others for your own false beliefs because you do not want to take responsibility for your own guilt.

4. You believe *"your brother is worthy of attack rather than love."*[343] The Course says the false conclusion that others deserve attack not love is reached by believing in the three previous false premises. However, your brother and you are always deserving of only love. The most important message of the crucifixion is that you are love and therefore love needs to be your only teaching. "Teach only love, for that is what you are."[344] When you mistakenly attempt to attack you brother, you are teaching attack by your example, and so you are disavowing your own true nature of love.

The crucifixion is an extreme teaching example of how to manifest love to your brothers. The example of the crucifixion expressed that your brother is only capable of doing either one of two things in his actions: he is expressing love or a call for love. "Every mistake *must* be a call for love."[345] In the apparent attack of the crucifixion, Jesus saw only a mistake that was a call for love. Jesus gave his apparent attackers the love they were calling for. Without judging his attackers and overlooking their error, he expressing only forgiveness.

> Miracle-mindedness forgiveness is *only* correction. It has no element of judgment at all. The statement "Father, forgive them, for they know not what they do" in no way evaluates *what* they do. It is an appeal to God to heal their minds. There is no reference to the outcome of the error. That does not matter.[346]

In the Course, Jesus changes the traditional view of forgiveness. Jesus does not advise you to tell a person that he has hurt you and committed a sin for which he should feel guilty and then tell him that you forgive him anyway. First, as indicated previously, you cannot be hurt, and if you think you can be hurt, you are responsible for that false belief. Second, if you believe that someone has sinned, you mean what was done is real and has real effects. In making his sin real, you tell your brother he is really a sinner, is really guilty, and is worthy of punishment, even though you forgave him. The Course says this is using forgiveness in order to condemn your brother.

True forgiveness relieves your brother of guilt by seeing him as guiltless in the beginning and relieves your own unconscious guilt. You forgive your brother for what was never done to you and had no effects on you. You heal your brother by letting go of your own illusions about him and see his true innocence as a Son of God. People do make mistakes, but these can only hurt you if you choose to believe it is possible for your reality to be hurt. This is why it is important to be responsible for what you believe. The crucifixion was an extreme example showing you that even if someone apparently attacks you in their own mind, you can only feel attacked in your mind if you share their belief that your reality can be attacked.

You will not be required to be crucified, but there are everyday situations in which you can claim to be a victim of what someone else did to you. These are temptations to believe you can be attacked. These are temptations to believe you are an ego. If you chose to react as if you have been attacked, you are expressing a belief in attack. In this case, you become a teacher of attack since you always teach by your example. In the crucifixion, Jesus set the example of how to not be a victim, even if apparently attacked. You will be tempted to show your brother that he hurt you, but you can learn to follow the example of Jesus by showing your brother that he did not hurt you demonstrating that there is no cause for guilt.

The crucifixion is a good teaching example, but the real victory of Jesus is in the resurrection, which is the true starting point of the Atonement that frees you from guilt. You are saved from guilt because sin is not real and produces no results. Your true nature in God, expressed in the resurrection, is a state of union with God in holiness that cannot be defiled, even by an unjust crucifixion.

If the crucifixion was the atonement for sin that would mean that sin is real and guilt is real. But the crucifixion was only a symbol of what the ego wants to do, which is to attack. Crucifixion is also a symbol of the punishment that the ego says your guilt deserves. If the crucifixion is only the symbol of the ego's nature of attack and guilt, why did the crucifixion become the centerpiece of atoning and being reconciled with God in the eyes of traditional Christianity?

When Jesus was asked about the practice of his time instituted by Moses of a man putting away his wife, he was asked why he refuted the established law. Jesus responded that the law of putting a wife away was created because of the hardness of heart of the people. For this reason Jesus said it was appropriate to establish a new Law that would express what God really wanted all along. Thus the hardness of heart in humanity is the reason why the crucifixion became viewed as payment for sin in Christianity. The traditional interpretation of the crucifixion is all that could be expected from humanity that had not yet evolved to the point of being able to come to grips with the illusory nature of the ego and guilt.

The Course offers the higher calling to be aware of the distortions present in the ego, including the false perceptions of sin and guilt. Though the Course uncovers the dark aspects of the ego, the Course does not recommend dwelling on darkness within you. The Course says to merely notice in the beginning any darkness, but only so that you can bring that darkness to the light of the Holy Spirit. If you focus too much on the darkness within you, you could begin to think it is real. Instead, see the darkness as unreal in the beginning and right away give this unreal darkness to the Holy Spirit Who undoes all your errors and all the effects of errors on yourself and others.

D. THE COURSE AND MIRACLE BHAKTI YOGA

Miracle Bhakti Yoga is certainly highly influenced by the Course emphasis on divine Love. The Bible stresses that if you say you love God, but do not love your neighbor, you really do not love God. The Course takes a similar stance saying that love of your brother leads to love of God. Divine Love is often expressed in lofty terms, but the main focus in the Course is on loving your brother in order to reveal that you are not only loveable, but you *are* love because you were made by God's divine Love.

God's Love is infinite oneness beyond fully comprehending, yet His divine Love can be experienced. You are an expression of God's Love. Since love is your true nature, the Course focuses on how to remove the blocks to your awareness of the presence of love. The way to remove blocks in order to reveal love is forgiveness that sees past appearances to see the love and light behind forms.

The Course mostly speaks in a philosophical manner that appeals to the intellect and not in a heartfelt tone, but the ideas themselves are focused on love. For example, miracles as expressions of love are stated in intellectual exactness. Miracles are impersonal in the sense that they are extensions of love that through the Holy Spirit may touch many lives of people you have never met. Yet the actual manifesting of a miracle is a highly personal expression since each miracle boils down to the effect that one heart has on another.

You can, of course, express inner devotion to God as part of your Miracle Bhakti Yoga. In fact, direct devotion to God is the cornerstone of traditional Hindu bhakti yoga. Such valuable inner worship would include devotion to both God and Jesus. A good example of inner devotion is repeating the Name of God. Also, repeating the Name of Jesus, called the Jesus Prayer, is an expression of Miracle Raja Yoga, and an equally important expression of Miracle Bhakti Yoga because of the love aspect of this practice. One of the chief ingredients of Miracle Bhakti Yoga is gratitude, explained as follows:

> Remembering the name of Jesus Christ is to give thanks for all the gifts that God has given you. And gratitude to God becomes the way in which He is remembered, for love cannot be far behind a grateful heart and thankful mind. God enters easily, for these are the true conditions for your homecoming.[347]

Gratitude to Jesus is just as important as gratitude to God. Jesus does not need your love in the form of gratitude for his own sake, but he wants your love for your sake so you may become more receptive to his love and God's Love.

> Jesus has led the way. Why would you not be grateful to him? He has asked for love, but only that he might give it to you. You do not love yourself. But in his eyes your loveliness is so complete and flawless that he sees in it an image of his Father. You become the symbol of his Father here on earth. To you he looks for hope, because in you he sees no limit and no stain to mar your beautiful perfection. In his eyes Christ's vision shines in perfect constancy.[348]

Even when the Course points the way inward to God and Jesus, there is always a reminder that the divine can be seen in the face of your brother. The Holy Spirit sees everyone with Christ's vision and offers the eyes of Christ to you so you too can see the loveliness of your brother and know that this same loveliness is within you. For Miracle Bhakti Yoga based on the Course, outwardly expressing love to others is more important than inner devotion. Expressing love to others is your means of discovering the love of God that is already in you. God has created you by extending His Love into you, and now God's Will is for you to practice extension. Through extension you pass along the love you have received from God to your brothers and sisters. By extending love to others you confirm to yourself the truth of your own love nature.

Your belief system will determine whether you practice extending love or not. The Course offers a thought system based on the belief in love as the basis for your actions and your teaching. You may not think of yourself as a teacher, but your thought system is acted out in the way you live your life, and that is your teaching. Others will be influenced by your example, which is your teaching. The Course advises that love is the only thing you need to teach, but you have to live it to teach it. "Teach only love, for that is what you are."[349] When you look at your brother, how you look at him teaches him who he is and who you are. If you see him as an ego, you will teach him he is an ego and teach yourself that you are an ego. But the Course advises you to see every action of your brother as either an expression of love or a call for love. This reminds you that all your own actions are expressions of love or calls for love.[350]

Every person you meet offers you what the Course calls a "holy encounter." You can find your true Self in this holy encounter, rather than through looking at yourself alone.

> When you meet anyone, remember it is a holy encounter. As you see him you will see yourself. As you treat him you will treat yourself. As you think of him you will think of yourself. Never forget this, for in him you will find yourself or lose yourself. Whenever two Sons of God meet, they are given another chance at salvation. Do not leave anyone without giving salvation to him and receiving it yourself. For I am always with you, in remembrance of *you*.[351]

The word "salvation" has a simplified meaning in the Course, as follows: "Again, how simple is salvation! It is merely a statement of your true Identity."[352] The reason why you can give salvation to your brother and receive salvation from your brother is that every holy encounter offers your brother and you the opportunity to remember your true Identity. Your Identity can be found in your brother because your Identity is in him as his Identity is in you.

> The goal of the curriculum, regardless of the teacher you choose, is "Know thyself." There is nothing else to seek. Everyone is looking for himself and for the power and glory he thinks he has lost. Whenever you are with anyone, you have another opportunity to find them. Your power and glory are

in him because they are yours. The ego tries to find them in yourself alone, because it does not know where to look. The Holy Spirit teaches you that if you look only at yourself you cannot find yourself, because that is not what you are.[353]

There is no such thing as "only yourself," since you are not alone as the ego would define you. Your Identity exists in your relationship not only to God, but also to your brothers. If you can affirm your brother's place in God's Kingdom, you offer him salvation by seeing his Identity. In accepting your brother's place in the Kingdom of God, you can accept your own place in the Kingdom and accept your own salvation and Identity in God. Whether you give salvation to your brother and to yourself or not depends on your decision to follow the ego as your teacher or to follow the Holy Spirit. Your decision will mean imprisonment or release to your brother and you.

> He will be imprisoned or released according to your decision, and so will you. Never forget your responsibility to him, because it is your responsibility to yourself. Give him his place in the Kingdom and you will have yours.
> The Kingdom cannot be found alone, and you who are the Kingdom cannot find yourself alone.[354]

Love is your true nature and Identity in the Kingdom and on earth this is expressed through extension. You learn about your true loving Identity in union with God and with your brothers through extension. If you extend love to your brother, you will discover the love that is within you. The Course advocates manifesting "holy relationships" as a means of extending love. In the holy relationship, you join with another person for a common purpose. Forming holy relationships is considered an exalted expression of love blessed by God.

The holy relationship consists of two people joining for a common purpose, and in that joining the Holy Spirit enters that relationship. This has already been addressed in Chapter 7, but here the specific aspect of *giving* that occurs in the holy relationship will be discussed. Giving expresses love if it is truly giving. Yet, if giving is made in order to get, it becomes a transaction, a bargain. Also, if you feel your gift is a sacrifice, it cannot be giving. Your thought of sacrifice means you think you should be compensated or at least the other person should feel guilty for your sacrifice. This kind of giving is an unloving way of controlling the one who receives the gift.

Unlike giving to get, true giving occurs in the holy relationship in which giving is without hooks. You give to your partner and your savior, whom you love and from whom you need no return. Giving is done for its own sake. In fact, the Course clarifies that giving *is* receiving. In the world of form, if you give something, you lose it. Therefore, you deprive yourself of something, and you have less than before your giving. But this is only a form-related perspective. When you give freely without trading to get a return, you receive love back just as you have given. The Course clarifies that giving is the way to keep and not giving is the way to lose. You are love and by giving love, you keep your awareness of the love that you are. By trying to keep love to yourself, you lose your awareness of love.

Love must share itself to be itself. God must share Himself to be Himself. You must share yourself to be yourself. This is how the holy relationship teaches you who you are through your relationship. As you give love to your partner, you receive all the love you give. You realize in this sharing and in the joy and fulfillment that you feel, that this expression of love frees you to be yourself. This sharing reminds you of the total giving of yourself that you manifested in Heaven as a part of the Sonship in oneness with God.

Giving and receiving occur simultaneously. The giving that is given in a gift on the form level may, of course, not be returned in exactly the same form in which it was given. But giving is actually related to content and therefore has nothing to do with a lost form. Even in giving forms, it is your love itself that you put into the giving of forms. It is your love that you give that is returned to you. Your act of giving, whether it involves form or not, opens you up to the inner joy, peace, and love that are at your core. You also realize the immense value you have in God's eyes as His holy Son. Your true worth is revealed to you with every gift given without any concern for the gift being given. Your holy relationship may not start out with this kind of giving, which is not really a giving of a gift after all, but is a giving of yourself. Your unconditional giving is the direction in which your holy relationship is leading you over time. The best gift you can give your partner is the gift of seeing him as the guiltless holy Son of God, which also confirms your own guiltlessness and your Identity as the holy Son of God. The love as the giving of yourself is the basis for Miracle Bhakti Yoga and this love penetrates all the other aspects of Miracle Yoga.

E. THE COURSE AND MIRACLE KARMA YOGA

If you accept the Course as your thought system and you want to practice Miracle Yoga, this would affect your practice of all its aspects: Miracle Jnana Yoga, Miracle Raja Yoga, Miracle Relationship Yoga, Miracle Bhakti Yoga, and Miracle Karma Yoga. The effect that the

Course thought system will have on your practice of Miracle Jnana Yoga is hopefully apparent by now and will become more evident if you decide to deepen your study of the Text of the Course. Studying the Course concepts with increasing depth will produce changes in perception, and hopefully you will learn to generalize the ideas in the Course to apply to your daily life experiences. You may begin to notice your ability to shine your light into the lives of others bringing miracles into their lives and into your own life.

The expression of miracles may also become apparent in your practice of Miracle Karma Yoga. The emphasis in Miracle Karma Yoga is on the dedication of all your actions to the divine influence. Even though you can give the fruits of your action to Jesus, God, or the Holy Spirit, the Course teaches that you receive everything that you give, and, in fact, giving *is* receiving. The Course encourages you to make no decisions alone because you are not alone and aloneness is not your true nature. The Course recommends that you invite the Holy Spirit into your decisions. This means that even in the smallest of tasks you can dedicate your actions to the divine.

Miracle Bhakti Yoga includes all actions dedicated to the divine, and these expressions would naturally overlap into all of the other aspects of Miracle Yoga and into the practical expression of Course principles. Obviously actions are expressed in the various Miracle Yoga activities of relationships, intellectual pursuits, meditation, work, and loving expressions. When these actions are dedicated to the divine, they become manifestations of Miracle Karma Yoga.

To understand Miracle Karma Yoga, it is helpful to consider the ego's approach to action in contrast to dedicated action, which would be guided by the Holy Spirit. The ego's approach to any situation is that it wants to foster the belief in separation and will have no set positive goal. The ego will allow situations to run their course and produce any outcome. This is like being in a boat without oars and without a sail. You will float in any direction. In this case, situations bring outcomes. Because any outcome, good or bad, is possible, this is a disorganized way of entering situations. You will look back on this kind of disorganized situation after it has occurred and not know how to evaluate what occurred. You will not be able to evaluate since no standard was set for what you wanted to happen.[355]

The Course states that if you are uncertain about any situation, it is best in the very beginning to ask yourself the question, "What is it for?"[356] By asking this question, you direct your mind to practice Miracle Karma Yoga. You are deciding to dedicate your actions not just in a vague general way that is disorganized, but in a specific way. You are encouraged to set a clear positive goal for the purpose of the situation. You may be thinking it would be better to just be spontaneous and respond as the situation unfolds. However, without knowing the goal, how will you know how to respond?

The way you perceive the situation will depend on your having set the goal in advance. The importance of having set the goal is that you see the situation *as a way of accomplishing the goal.* The situation then becomes the means of reaching the goal. How can your perception of the situation as being the means to the goal help you? You will be able to keep the goal in mind as the situation unfolds. Focusing on the goal throughout, you will direct your mind to overlook whatever aspects of the situation that would be blocks to attaining the goal. You will focus your mind instead on those aspects of the situation that would facilitate attaining the goal.

> The value of deciding in advance what you want to happen is simply that you will perceive the situation as a means to *make* it happen. You will therefore make every effort to overlook what interferes with the accomplishment of your objective, and concentrate on everything that helps you meet it. It is quite noticeable that this approach has brought you closer to the Holy Spirit's sorting out of truth and falsity. The true becomes what can be used to meet the goal. The false becomes the useless from this point of view. The situation now has meaning, but only because the goal has made it meaningful.[357]

The Course suggests setting the goal of truth. When you perceive the situation in the light of the goal of truth, you will let go of false perceptions that do not lead you to the goal. You will focus on true perceptions that will achieve the goal. The meaning of the situation rests in this sorting process of the false, which is meaningless, and the truth, which provides meaning. You find meaning by first setting the goal of truth, which then allows you to evaluate the situation properly in terms of accomplishing the goal.

Of course, this form of Miracle Karma Yoga overlaps into an expression of Miracle Jnana Yoga with the emphasis on seeking truth by rejecting false perception and accepting true perceptions. Karma yoga is sometimes seen as dedicated actions only in the physical world. Yet thinking is an action and thinking will determine results in the physical world. The ego wants you to believe that situations will give you experience, but the Holy Spirit wants to show you that you experience a situation in the light of the goal that you set for that situation. Regardless of the outcome of the situation, when you experience the situation, you will actually be experiencing the goal. If you set the goal of truth, then you will experience truth throughout the situation, no matter what the apparent outward outcome of the situation happens to be.[358]

The practice of setting the goal for the situation, discarding false perceptions, and accepting true perceptions may seem like merely a mental exercise without any significant effect on the actual outcome of the situation. Yet when you engage in this practice, you let go of the ego's purpose of separation and accept the Holy Spirit's purpose of truth. Thus you invite the Holy Spirit into the situation. Having set the goal with the Holy Spirit's purpose of truth, a remarkable thing happens: All of the people involved in the situation will come into alignment with the goal and will accomplish the goal.

However, for this to happen requires your faith. When you set the goal of truth, you also have to have faith that, with the help of the Holy Spirit, the goal will be achieved. Having guided you to set the goal of truth, Holy Spirit will help to bring the situation, which is the means, into alignment with the goal for it to be accomplished.

> The goal of truth requires faith. Faith is implicit in the acceptance of the Holy Spirit's purpose, and this faith is all-inclusive. Where the goal of truth is set, there faith must be. The Holy Spirit sees the situation as a whole. The goal establishes the fact that everyone involved in it will play his part in its accomplishment. This is inevitable. No one will fail in anything.[359]

If you choose truth as your goal, the situation will unfold and bring peace. In spite of the apparent result of the situation at a form level, if you perceive the situation in light of the goal of truth, then you will have peace as your experience of the outcome. Your peace confirms your achievement of the goal of truth because peace and truth go together. Being at peace enables you to see past the illusions of false perceptions. Your peace allows you to perceive the outcome correctly and recognize that the goal of truth has been accomplished.

> If the situation is used for truth and sanity, its outcome must be peace. And this is quite apart from what the outcome *is*. If peace is the condition of truth and sanity, and cannot be without them, where peace is they must be. Truth comes of itself. If you experience peace, it is because the truth has come

to you and you will see the outcome truly, for deception cannot prevail against you. You will recognize the outcome *because* you are at peace. Here again you see the opposite of the ego's way of looking, for the ego believes the situation brings the experience. The Holy Spirit knows that the situation is as the goal determines it, and is experienced according to the goal.[360]

You can approach any situation in the manner just described as a standard for practicing Miracle Karma Yoga. The key is dedicating your actions in the very beginning by determining what your action is for and dedicating yourself to the goal you set. This can be applied even to an apparently solitary activity such as meditation.

A superficial examination of what meditation is for will determine that your meditation is for yourself and your relationship with God. But can you really meditate for yourself? You are part of the Sonship and what you do is shared with all the other parts of the Sonship. Even in your apparently separated current condition, every loving thought you have goes out as a blessing to all the other parts of the Sonship. Likewise, every loving thought of any of your brothers in the Sonship comes to you as a blessing.[361]

Because you are part of the Sonship, your relationship with the Sonship needs to be included in your understanding the purpose of meditation. Your meditation is an experience of your relationship and communication with the Sonship and with God facilitated by the Holy Spirit. Your Father created the Holy Spirit and placed Him in your sleeping mind to serve as the connecting link between you and all the parts of the Sonship and God. The awareness of your wholeness in the Sonship and in God is kept safe in your mind by the Holy Spirit. By opening yourself to the Holy Spirit in meditation and contemplation, you increase your awareness of your wholeness. Consequently, you can consciously dedicate your meditation and contemplation to the goal of awakening your awareness of oneness with the Sonship and God through the Holy Spirit.

Because there can be a tendency to think of your meditation as being for yourself, it is helpful to make a dedication in the beginning of your meditation that is a statement of what your meditation is for. In addition to dedicating your meditation to your spiritual ideal, you can dedicate it to the Sonship, to all of your brothers and sisters. All experiences of situations in which the goal is set in advance are experiences of the goal. Therefore, if you set the goal of union with the Sonship and with God through the Holy Spirit, your experience of meditation will become an experience of this goal.

One way of focusing on the Sonship and God is to set the goal of accepting the Atonement, the Plan of salvation, as your purpose for your meditation. You can affirm this goal prior to beginning your meditation practice. You can allow your experience of meditation to be an experience of accepting both the Atonement and the holy instant in which the past is left behind and in which you experience your connection with your brothers and sisters and God.

If you practice meditation to express your individual attainment, you may want to focus more than usual on your connection with others and recognize that seeking God is a joint effort with everyone participating together. Temporarily, you can focus on an affirmation such as, "For All," to indicate your meditation is for everyone and God. You can let your meditation be a conscious expression of giving. You can feel yourself receiving light and love from God and radiating this light and love to all your brothers and sisters. You keep light and love by giving them away, which reinforces the awareness that you are light and love. In meditation, you do not focus on perceptions, but after meditation, you can direct your perceptions toward prayers of gratitude, as well as prayers for the well-being of others.

F. YOUR SPECIAL FUNCTION

Most opportunities for dedicated action in the practice of Miracle Karma Yoga involve your daily experiences in life with other people. In these situations, you can set the goal of truth, but you might be guided to choose a goal other than truth, for example, holiness or love. You can ask the Holy Spirit to choose the goal for you. Indeed, some goals for your life have already been assigned to you by the Holy Spirit, even if you are not yet aware of these goals. The reason for this is that you have an important work to accomplish for God and for your brothers that no one else can do. This work is called your "special function."[362] The Holy Spirit assigns you this function in God's Plan for the awakening of the Sonship. His Plan cannot be completed until your special function is fulfilled.

> To each He gives a special function in salvation he alone can fill; a part for only him. Nor is the plan complete until he finds his special function, and fulfills the part assigned to him, to make himself complete with the world where incompletion rules.[363]

Your special function may include becoming a teacher of God as is explained in the part of the Course called the *Manual for Teachers*.

Teachers of God will form holy relationships with students who are guided to them and will join for the common purpose of the learning. Your special function might include healing, which can also be a function of being a teacher of God. Expressing the function of healing involves accepting the Atonement that is described as the "remedy" that produces the "result" of healing.

> Our emphasis is now on healing. The miracle is the means, the Atonement is the principle, and healing is the result. To speak of a "miracle of healing" is to combine two orders of reality inappropriately. Healing is not a miracle. The Atonement, or the final miracle, is a remedy and any type of healing is a result. The kind of error to which the Atonement is applied is relevant. All healing is essentially the release from fear. To undertake this you cannot be fearful yourself. You do not understand healing because of your own fear.[364]

Accepting the special function of healing involves the willingness to face your own fears and overcome them. You may think that your fears are involuntary so you do not have control over them. Yet you are responsible for your fears because you are responsible for your thoughts that produce fear in your mind. Fear is caused when you are conflicted about what you want. What you want is your choice, so correcting fear involves you changing your choices that produce fear. In the Course Jesus says that He cannot control your fear, but you can control it yourself and ask for His help and the help of the Holy Spirit.

> The correction of fear *is* your responsibility. When you ask for release from fear, you are implying that it is not. You should ask, instead for help in the conditions that have brought the fear about. These conditions always entail a willingness to be separate. At that level you *can* help it. You are much too tolerant of mind wandering, and are passively condoning your mind's miscreations.[365]

When your mind is conflicted about what it wants, fear will be the result, and you can take steps to correct this error. You can accept the Atonement to correct your error. However, you are responsible for taking the steps that would enable you to accept this remedy for error that the Holy Spirit offers to you for your healing.

Only your mind can produce fear. It does so whenever it is conflicted in what it wants, producing inevitable strain because wanting and doing are discordant. This can be corrected only by accepting a unified goal.

The first corrective step in undoing the error is to know first that the conflict is an expression of fear. Say to yourself that you must somehow have chosen not to love, or the fear could not have arisen. Then the whole process of correction becomes nothing more than a series of pragmatic steps in the larger process of accepting the Atonement as the remedy. These steps may be summarized in this way:

> Know first that this is fear.
> Fear arises from the lack of love.
> The only remedy for lack of love is perfect love.
> Perfect love is the Atonement.[366]

The Course states that accepting the Atonement produces healing and performing miracles is the expression of the Atonement. Overall, the Atonement is the principle of coming Home. If you accept the Atonement, you are accepting reconciliation with God. Being God's Plan, the Atonement has already been accomplished. You have never been separated from God, so you are already reconciled with God. But since you are unaware of your reconciliation, you feel you need reconciliation to heal your illusion of separation. When you choose to accept the Atonement, you realize that you are in God's presence now, and the separation never really occurred, except as an illusion in your own mind. When you accept the Atonement, you accept forgiveness that sees through illusions and accepts oneness with God as your own true reality and your brother's true reality.

If you want healing for yourself, all you have to do is to accept the Atonement for yourself. Similar to healing yourself, if you are drawn to becoming a healer for others, which is a miracle worker, you will have only one responsibility required to help you manifest healing:

> The sole responsibility of the miracle worker is to accept the Atonement for himself. This means you recognize that mind is the only creative level, and that its errors are healed by the Atonement. Once you accept this you can only heal.[367]

Healing between you, as a healer, and another person being healed is a temporary holy relationship in which you join with another person for the common purpose of healing. In this holy relationship, you also see the common interest of you both wanting divine assistance. When you accept the Atonement for yourself, you open your own mind to right-mindedness that is healing for you. Because you are joined with your brother, you open his mind to allow healing to happen for him bringing right-mindedness to him.

The sick person does not realize he has made the decision at the subconscious level to invite sickness as a reflection of seeing himself as being separate from God. You may be tempted to sympathize with the one who is sick, but sympathy will give that person the mistaken impression that he really is sick and he really is separate from God. It is your function as a miracle worker to help open his mind to the fact that he is not separate from God and therefore not sick. You weaken your brother's belief in sickness by simply not holding the belief in separation in your own mind.[368] You do not try to verbally convince him to give up his false belief in separation and sickness. As a healer, you are a miracle worker who can express miracles by shining the light of your mind into your brother's mind without even saying a word, unless you are guided to do so.

> The miracle is the act of a Son of God who has laid aside all false gods, and calls on his brothers to do likewise. It is an act of faith, because it is the recognition that his brother can do it. It is a call to the Holy Spirit in his mind, a call that is strengthened by joining. Because the miracle worker has heard God's voice, he strengthens It in a sick brother by weakening his belief in sickness, which he does not share. The power of one mind can shine into another, because all the lamps of God were lit by the same spark. It is everywhere and eternal.[369]

Because you are joined with the sick person in a temporary holy relationship, your minds are joined. It is your function to realize on his behalf in your own mind that the sick person's belief that he is sick and separate from God is simply not true. You forgive him for his illusions about himself by recognizing that he is in reality the holy Son of God that can never be separated from God. By opening your own mind to God's Light and Love, a light shines from your mind into his mind.[370] As part of the healing process, you may choose to include calling on the name of Jesus because Jesus does not see Himself as separate from God.[371]

Having removed all judgment in your mind of this person, you then accept the Atonement for yourself. You only have to accept the Atonement for yourself because in your temporary holy relationship, your mind is joined with your partner's mind. Because minds are joined in a holy relationship, what one mind accepts and experiences, the other mind also accepts and experiences. It takes the invitation of only one mind in a holy relationship to bring healing to both minds. Healing is an all-inclusive experience that includes the acceptance of the Atonement, forgiveness, and a miracle all in one. In accepting the Atonement, you can become open to your oneness with God and connection with your brother in the experience of a holy instant in which the past falls away as you seize the present moment.

Being a teacher and healing can become aspects of your special function, but after discussing in Chapter 7 how specialness is an ego device, it may sound odd to hear that you have a "special" function. The whole idea of being special is to think of yourself as being better than someone else. Yet the Course uses the term "special function" to mean that no one else can perform your unique function, but the specialness of your function does not mean you are special in the sense of being better than anyone else. In fact, your special function cannot be found within yourself alone but can be found in your relationships with others, who are your equals in the Sonship. The long-term holy relationship is your best means of discovering the special function that the Holy Spirit has assigned to you.

There is a very important link between Miracle Relationship Yoga and Miracle Karma Yoga, and these two in turn overlap into every aspect of Miracle Yoga. By reviewing the sequence of events that happens in the long-term holy relationship, the nature of this link becomes apparent, as follows:

1. You and another person join for a common purpose. The common purpose can be a common work project to which you each dedicate yourself. You do so because you both see common interests, rather than each of you joining for separate interests. Just as in Miracle Karma Yoga, you can dedicate your actions together to God, but for your initial joining your common purpose can be mundane and not dedicated to God.

2. When you and your partner join for a common purpose, either mundane or spiritual in nature, your minds become joined in this act. With this joining of minds, the Holy Spirit enters your relationship and brings in holiness. The Holy Spirit cleanses your joined minds and the Christ child is reborn in your holy relationship.

3. You may be only aware of your agreed-upon common purpose, but the Holy Spirit immediately brings in a new overall long-term common purpose. The Holy Spirit establishes the new goal of holiness itself. Your new goal is to come Home together, but in the beginning you have already come Home without realizing it. Your minds are

joined just as your minds are joined in Heaven therefore you are together in Heaven now. It will only take time to realize you have already come Home, but time is only an illusion anyway.

4. A disconcerting period follows in which you and your partner feel that the present format of the way you are relating to each other will not facilitate reaching your goal. You may be only aware of the consciously agreed-upon common purpose, but at some level, you are aware that your relationship is not in alignment with the goal of holiness that has been established by the Holy Spirit. In order to remove the discomfort, you and your partner will have to change the format of your relationship to better fit the goal of holiness.

5. In a lifelong holy relationship, the discomfort may be reduced in the beginning by making significant changes but may still persist for many years. The goal is holiness, which is linked to the goal of love. Miracle Karma Yoga that happens in the holy relationship likewise expresses Miracle Bhakti Yoga because you and your partner are dedicating your actions to the divine purpose of manifesting love. In the Hindu practice of bhakti yoga, one possible way of expressing love is in the relationship of the seeker being the parent and God being the child. In a way, this is happening in your holy relationship because the Christ child has been born into your relationship. Thus you play the role of the parent by keeping the Christ child alive in your relationship through the love that you manifest.

6. To learn how to love, you will need to join together in holy instants, as part of Miracle Raja Yoga. You will need the understanding that comes from Miracle Jnana Yoga to be able to discern between false and true perceptions. Your Miracle Jnana Yoga discernment will help you to be able to overlook mistakes and see the true holiness in your partner. In Miracle Relationship Yoga of the holy relationship, you can see clearly that all five forms of Miracle Yoga come together in a wonderfully integrated way to offer a perfect learning opportunity for you and your partner. In this environment of learning to love, the Christ child grows up.

7. In the mature holy relationship, you and your partner learn over time how to give love to each other unconditionally. By putting away the childish things of the ego in your relationship, the Christ child becomes the adult Christ and is ready to manifest more fully in an outward manner. The direct attention you devoted to your partner taught you to see Christ in him, but the next step is to generalize your experience and see Christ in everyone. Having learned to love one, you can learn to love everyone.

8. In your mature holy relationship, your partner and you will find that your special function will become increasingly clear. You will have a special function, but it will be within the context of your holy relationship that your function will flourish being nurtured by the love of your partner, just as you will nourish your partner's special function. This will likely manifest as a common work that you can together dedicate to God giving Him the fruits of your labors. But it will be a labor of love because the love of your holy relationship could no longer be contained between just the two of you. The love that is expressed in your mature holy relationship must be given away in order to keep it because the nature of love is inclusiveness and extension.

9. Finally, you will realize that when you first joined in a common purpose with your partner, the Holy Spirit's goal was for your minds to be joined and for your minds to overflow with love so your love would become your gift to everyone in the world. Because of your choice to join, Heaven rejoiced that through you many souls who were in darkness would find the light. You and your partner will go into Heaven, and your extension of love will help others to wake up in Heaven along with you. You will all rejoice together.[372]

10. You and your partner will see how gently the Holy Spirit will guide you along and allow your love to blossom and overflow into every aspect of your lives bringing blessings to all those around you. You will be able to fully dedicate all of your actions to extending love and letting the Holy Spirit bring miracles and salvation to all those whom your life touches and even to others whom you have never met. Your special function can be fully completed only by helping others find salvation, just as you have found salvation.

In the holy relationship, you become a savior for your partner and your partner becomes your savior, and then you become saviors for many others. It is helpful for you to seek to find a partner for the holy relationship. However, it is important to place your faith in the Holy Spirit, trusting that He is guiding your life and will guide you to a holy relationship partner or partners.

Holy relationships can ideally occur in the marriage relationship, but can just as well occur between male and female friends or friends of the same sex. In my opinion, partners in a holy relationship are not meeting for the first time, but have repeatedly met in many lifetimes to learn the lesson of how to love and extend that love to others. A significant kind of holy relationship that can help you find your special function is the teacher and student holy relationship, which is elaborated upon in the *Manual for Teachers.*

Hopefully, you will decide to accept the Atonement that is God's Plan of salvation for everyone, and you will want to fulfill your part, your special function, in His Plan. Accepting the Atonement can be renewed on a daily basis to let your errors be undone and to help bring healing. Once you accept the Atonement and also accept your special function in God's Plan as a firm conviction, then the Holy Spirit will accept your special function as your consciously chosen goal. Having this firm conviction gives permission to the Holy Spirit to provide the means to the goal by *arranging everything in your life* to facilitate accomplishing the goal.

> Once you accept His Plan as the one function that you would fulfill, there will be nothing else the Holy Spirit will not arrange for you without your effort. He will go before you making straight your path, and leaving in your way no stones to trip on, and no obstacles to bar your way. Nothing you need will be denied you. Not one seeming difficulty but will melt away before you reach it. You need take thought for nothing, careless of everything except the only purpose that you would fulfill. As that was given you, so will its fulfillment be. God's guarantee will hold against all obstacles, for it rests on certainty and not contingency. It rests on *you.* And what can be more certain than a Son of God?[373]

With your permission, the Holy Spirit will guide you every step of the way in this world as you are being led Home. But you can also call on the help of Jesus and Mary as well. In Christianity the best single example of the holy relationship has occurred in the son and mother relationship of Jesus and Mary. To be a Christian is to follow the example of Jesus, but in Miracle Karma Yoga of dedicated action in the holy relationship, you will be following the path of Jesus *and* Mary. In this patristic society, Jesus is recognized as the Savior, but Mary was her Son's holy relationship savior. Jesus is certainly the Christ, but Mary is no less the Christ than Jesus.

You can follow their example in all things, but you can also reach out to either or both of them personally. Even right now, the holy relationship of Jesus and Mary is still performing the special function of waking up the Sonship. You can form a personal relationship with either Jesus or Mary or both of them and not be disappointed with the divine love that extends to you as they assist you in your journey to your true Home in Heaven.

CHAPTER 10

~ • ~

SPIRITUAL DEVOLUTION AND EVOLUTION

A. THE SEPARATION AND SPIRITUAL DEVOLUTION

Before looking at the spiritual evolution of returning to God and a vision of the future, it is important to look at how humanity *devolved* away from God. What traditional Christianity calls the "Fall," the Course calls the "separation," which has been discussed in previous chapters and will be elaborated upon in this chapter.

To manifest this separation, parts of the Sonship joined together to create a collective dream. Before the separation, these parts of the Sonship were minds in the Christ Mind. These minds were formless and totally abstract, but after the separation, these minds changed their nature and became unnatural. The separation produced a split in the mind. The decision to separate resulted in the giving up of knowledge, which is infinite, whole, complete, and a full expression of the Christ Mind as God created it. Knowledge was lost and was replaced by perception. The splintered mind changed into a perceiver, apparently separate from what is perceived. This splintering of the mind produced "consciousness," which is awareness experienced in the ego condition. Consciousness is awareness within the domain of perception, explained as follows:

Consciousness, the level of perception, was the first split introduced into the mind after the separation, making the mind a perceiver rather than a creator. Consciousness is correctly identified as the domain of the ego. The ego is the wrong-minded attempt to perceive yourself as you wish to be, rather than as you are. Yet you can know yourself only as you are, because that is all you can be sure of. Everything else *is* open to question.

The ego is the questioning aspect of the post-separation self, which was made rather than created. It is capable of asking questions but not of perceiving meaningful answers, because these would involve knowledge and cannot be perceived. The mind is therefore confused, because only One-mindedness can be without confusion. A separated or divided mind *must* be confused. It is necessarily uncertain about what it is. It has to be in conflict because it is out of accord with itself.[374]

It may think you can have idle thoughts that produce no results and in particular produce no form-related result. But the Course states that every time you think your perceptions have the effect of producing form at some level.[375] Knowledge is beyond form and perception can only occur within a form-related context. When the separation occurred, the changing of awareness from knowledge to perception brought form into "existence." The Course makes a clear distinction between "being" and "existence." Your being is in Heaven and is your reality. Only a very small portion of your being is asleep and dreaming. In your dream, your real life, your being, in Heaven appears to you in the dream as your existence. A small portion of your mind in Heaven has made up a dream, but the illusions of the dream appear real. You are a Thought in the mind of God, but in your sleeping state, you have thoughts that are not extended from God. Because you are separated from God in your thinking, your thoughts exist but are not real.

The mind that sees illusions thinks them real. They have existence in that they are thoughts. And yet they are not real, because the mind that thinks these thoughts is separate from God.[376]

How can something exist and not be real? God is Reality. All things that are part of God are real. Your being is real because your being is an extension of God and thus part of God. Your ego-based thoughts are not real because they exist in the dream only but not in God, not in Reality. You traded the reality of being in God for the unreality of existing in your dream. In your existence within the dream, everything will appear real even though it is not real. Your experience in the dream certainly feels real to you so it exists for you although it is not real. However, you, as the sleeping dreamer in Heaven, are real, although the dream is not real.

On page 38, the idea of your dual nature was explained in this way: "Each individual is a part of the one Christ, a part of the Sonship, and each part contains the whole and is one with the whole. Each part exists in communion with every other part. In fact, the very nature of each part is to be in relationship with every other part and with the whole, which is contained within each part."

"You are a combination of individual part-ness in Christ and shared wholeness in Christ. Your ego identity in the world is a distortion of your divine individual part-ness in Christ and is a complete denial of your wholeness in Christ. Your true divine nature is paradoxically a part of the Sonship and yet contains the whole Christ, united with the Father and the Holy Spirit."

Your true individuality is in your being a unique part of Christ. It is only this individual part-ness that became distorted by identification with the ego and concrete forms. The other part of your spiritual nature, which is your being the whole Christ, did not separate and did not lose the awareness of the knowledge of God and oneness with God. In the separation, your mind did not split in reality, but it did split in the awareness of reality. Although your wholeness in Christ continued to have knowledge of God, your part-ness in Christ slept and had dreams. This dreaming part-ness of your mind, which is only a small portion of your total mind, somehow took on form by becoming identified with form. It became "concrete."

> Ego illusions are quite specific, although the mind is naturally abstract. Part of the mind becomes concrete, however, when it splits. The concrete part believes in the ego, because the ego depends on the concrete. The ego is the part of the mind that believes your existence is defined by separation.
>
> Everything the ego perceives is a separate whole, without the relationships that imply being.[377]

This portion of the mind that believes in the ego and becomes concrete "exists" in the dream, but at the same time is not real. For the mind to become concrete would mean that instead of the mind observing the dream, the mind would have to be caught up in the form of the dream. In this sense, the mind which is naturally abstract becomes like water that takes the shape of its container but does not have a shape of its own.

But the mind that had left knowledge and split into a part that is using perception to dream did not instantly go from formless Heaven to a concrete form, including body awareness. The mind becoming concrete was a gradual process that took place over eons of time, with time itself being an illusory division of eternity into an individual sequence of moments, days, and years.[378]

The Course seems to say two contradictory ideas. One idea is that the separation never happened in reality and your mind is still as it always was as an abstract Thought in the Mind of God. The other idea is that the mind fell asleep in Heaven and although it is just dreaming, the mind changed from its natural abstract nature and instead became concrete in the dream. How can the mind be abstract in reality and concrete in the dream at the same time? Perhaps this question cannot be fully answered by someone in the dream, but an analogy may help shed some light on this contradiction.

For this analogy, the mind in the being state with knowledge of God is white light. The dream state is made by a prism that takes the white light of knowledge and breaks it down into separate parts, separate colors of the rainbow spectrum. Using this prism analogy, the spectrum represents knowledge divided into different perceptions. The different perceptions are divided into categories of seven levels of consciousness. The different levels of consciousness express various different experiences of existence in the dream that replace the one all-encompassing being of Heaven.

Using the analogy of the colors of the spectrum, the violet level of consciousness made a dream world reflective of Heaven, but not really Heaven. The indigo, blue, green, yellow, and orange levels of consciousness, which each produced a corresponding dream world. Finally the lowest level, the red level of consciousness, made the dream world of the physical universe. I call this process of moving from higher consciousness to the lower levels of consciousness the *devolution* of the spiritual consciousness.

The making of the physical universe was the collaborative effort of all minds, all the parts of the Sonship, that fell asleep in Heaven. To make the illusion appear real, each individual mind would have to identify itself with being concrete. The mind cannot really be physical, but these individual minds projected their awareness into physical bodies. By believing in the ego, these minds became identified with physical bodies. In Heaven, each soul is part of the whole Sonship. Each part of the Sonship in Heaven is part of the one Christ, and yet paradoxically each part is the whole Christ. Similarly the physical body had to be both part of the levels of consciousness and all the levels of consciousness. So the body needed to become a microcosm of the macrocosm of levels of consciousness in the dream.

Therefore, the body took on the rainbow spectrum with the violet consciousness at the crown of the head. Each color took its place in a downward sequence with the red color at the base of the spine, closest to the earth. These levels of consciousness are not a part of the body but are related to certain body parts. The levels of consciousness are the chakras from the crown chakra down to the sacral chakra with the kundalini coiled at the base of the spine. In this analogy, the prism is the device that enables the white light of the mind to be divided into pieces changing from its natural state of knowledge to the unnatural state of becoming concrete.

The same prism of awareness that allows the mind to be changed from its abstract nature and to identify with being concrete, also allows the oneness and eternity of Heaven to be divided. It is as if the prism could take eternity, symbolized by an endless circle, and lay it out in a line. Then that line is cut it into smaller and smaller pieces to create a linear sequence of seconds and minutes that are called time. Einstein proved time is relative, but it appears to be an absolute within the dream, even though it is just a trick of the dreaming mind.

The Course says that the separation did happen as the slightest instant in eternity. Yet the separation was corrected just as instantly as it occurred, and it produced no change in Reality, so in that sense it never really happened. That tiny instant that is now over appears to be still happening in time. How is this possible? There is no time in Heaven and since Heaven is the only Reality, the illusion of time has ended already in Heaven. Still, how could the illusion keep going even though it is already over?

You can think of this as a homemade movie that you have already seen so the whole movie is already in your mind. Since you saw the movie in the past and have it all in your mind now, your awareness of the whole movie now would correspond to the tiny instant of time in which the separation occurred. Your mind attempted to give up reality in that instant. But instead of looking at the whole movie all at once in your mind and seeing that it has already occurred and is over, you decide to look through the prism. As you look through the prism, you see only each individual frame in the film of the movie, and your mind forgets all the previous frames and all the future frames. So then your experience of the movie becomes your experience of each individual frame rather than the whole movie. This "frame of reference" creates the illusion of time, which requires extensive use of denial to not see that you already know the whole movie.

This is the denial of knowledge and the division of knowledge into separate perceptions. In the analogy of the prism, you can see that the white light of the being of the mind is divided into the spectrum of different levels of consciousness in the dream and also eternity is divided into tiny units of time. The prism that makes these divisions possible is the ego, which is the idea of separation. If the division of knowledge into separate perceptions and the division of eternity into separate units of time were not reversible, the separation would have really occurred, producing real results.

The Course says all real causes must produce real effects. You cannot have a cause without an effect or an effect without a cause. If there is no effect produced, there could not have been a cause either. Without an effect and without a cause, nothing could have really happened. God created the Holy Spirit to correct the separation and reverse the effects of the prism, the ego. By canceling out the effects of the separation and also the effects of the ego, the Holy Spirit proves that the effects do not exist and thus the cause does not exist either. Through this cancellation of effects, the Holy Spirit corrects apparent error and proves that the separation and the ego itself do not exist in reality.[379]

God as He is in Himself, complete and whole, could not enter the divided world of perceptual dreams without totally obliterating the dreams. God created the Holy Spirit to be in Heaven and in the dream world simultaneously. The Holy Spirit has total awareness of knowledge in Heaven and has the partial awareness of perception in the dream world of form. In response to the separation, the Holy Spirit created the real world, which consists of only true perceptions. The real world enables souls to awaken from the dream and realize that they never really left Heaven in the first place.

Having been created by God, the Holy Spirit interceded into the "space-time belief" and built the Atonement, the Plan for awakening the sleeping parts of the Sonship, into this belief.[380] The space-time belief is part of the thought system of the prism, the ego, that built the physical universe. Bringing the Atonement into the space-time belief meant that built into the devolution of consciousness is the evolution and restoration of spiritual consciousness. Indeed, this Atonement has already been accomplished, and the whole Atonement is at the end of time waiting for the sleeping minds of the Sonship to find it. The Atonement undoes errors and saves time through the intercession of miracles, thus shortening the time for the return Home.

> The Atonement is the device by which you can free yourself from the past as you go ahead. It undoes errors, thus making it unnecessary for you to keep retracing your steps without advancing to your return. In this sense the Atonement saves time, but like the miracle it serves, does not abolish it. As long as there is need for Atonement, there is need for time. But the Atonement as a completed plan has a unique relationship to time. Until the Atonement is complete its various phases will proceed in time, but the whole Atonement stands at time's end. At that point the bridge of return has been built.[381]

The Course states that the world was created as an expression of insanity by minds that no longer knew who they were. The mind could only know itself as being whole because it is whole. The mind divided into levels of consciousness could not know itself as parts because its nature is to be whole. The introduction of confusion into the divided resulted in fear, which was not possible in the wholeness of Heaven. The mind could not heal itself from this condition because the mind no longer knew what it was. The sleeping mind made a world that reflected its confusion and fear.

If the dreaming minds that had fallen asleep were left entirely to their own devices, the world with all its current fear, isolation, pain, and death would be an even darker nightmare than it is currently. Just like a mother may clean up her child's messy room, the Holy Spirit corrected the errors made in making the universe. The Holy Spirit built into the universe God's own law adapted to the needs of the dreaming minds of God's children. This correction included an underlying love, unity, harmony, and order, along with the Atonement as a way of coming Home.

The best example of the Atonement being built into the space-time belief is the real world which contains all the loving thoughts of the minds that created the world, but stripped of all the unloving thoughts that were also made. These loving thoughts are saved by the Holy Spirit and only these loving thoughts give the world any sense of reality.[382] Perhaps some forms in the world, such as flowers, express more divine love than other forms, but hidden within every form is the love that manifests in the real world. Within even apparently drab or even ugly forms of the physical world, there is a spark of hidden beauty and love that expresses the perfection of God.[383]

There are two reasons why the prism creating a rainbow spectrum of colors has been used here as an analogy of the ego as a means of bringing about the separation: The first reason is that the world is seen in the colors of the spectrum by the physical eyes. But with Christ's vision, it is possible to change your perception and have the by-product of Light vision. Through Light vision, you can reverse the normal spectrum of color seen by the physical eyes and instead see the white and then golden light of the real world behind every form showing its true loveliness. Of course, this light is not the same as the Light in Heaven since it is a dream symbol of the true loving nature of the sleeping parts of the Sonship that made this world.

The ability to utilize Christ's vision and the by-product of Light vision, in which you can visually experience seeing the light behind all forms, has already been discussed in Chapter 6. Christ's vision can be an awareness of love and forgiveness without the visual experience of Light vision, but the visual component is emphasized here because this experience is a helpful confirmation of the fact that the real world interpenetrates all of the everyday world of appearances.

The second reason the prism creating the rainbow spectrum has been used as an analogy of the ego as a separation device is related to the chakras. The chakras are usually associated with the sequence of colors in the spectrum. The crown chakra is related to the color violet. The brow chakra is associated with indigo. The other five chakras from the throat center with the color blue to the sacral center with the colored red follow the sequence of the spectrum. That does not mean that the prism and spectrum analogy can be taken literally but just makes the analogy particularly appropriate.

Some esoteric philosophies make the crown chakra an exception to following the spectrum. These philosophies associate the crown chakra with the all-inclusive color white (or golden). The crown chakra may be the exception to following the colors of the divided spectrum because the crown chakra represents the real world and is symbolic of the undivided nature of Heaven. In these philosophies, the brow center is associated with the color violet instead of indigo. The other chakras have the same color associations as indicated above.

Now consider again the previous question: how could the mind be abstract in reality and at the same time be concrete in the dream? The key idea of the analogy is that the white light on one side of the prism is the same substance as the separated light of the spectrum on the other side of the prism. Likewise, the being state of mind in Heaven is the same mind that is divided into the seven chakras in the dream. This is similar to steam, water, and ice all being water. Of course, changing physical states is easier to understand because the three states of water are all within the realm of form.

Mind in its natural state maintains the formlessness of being in Heaven. But the Course does say the mind at least subjectively split from its natural condition and became unnatural. Part of the mind became concrete. If you have a prism that breaks down the white light into the divided spectrum, and if you remove the prism, the spectrum disappears leaving only white light again. The white light starts out in oneness, then is divided into the spectrum, and then returns to the oneness of the white light. Similarly, if you have the prism of the ego that makes the mind concrete, and if you remove the prism of the ego, the concrete mind that exists in the dream returns back to the abstract mind of being in Heaven. In this sense, the mind is really the same in substance, but only changes in the way it is being used—first for oneness, then for division, and then back to oneness.

When the abstract mind sleeps in Heaven, it remains in Heaven because Heaven is the only place that is Reality. Heaven is the only place any kind of life can be. Therefore, the entire physical universe is actually within the sleeping mind in Heaven. But paradoxically the sleeping mind becomes concrete by the prism of the ego that divides the natural oneness of the mind into different levels of consciousness like the pattern of a rainbow spectrum. The Course does not explain how the abstract mind can become concrete, but yoga philosophy offers the belief in the chakras. In yoga philosophy, the abstract divine mind, which is naturally infinite, is projected into the seven chakras that are not really physically in the body but are related to parts of the body along the cerebral-spinal axis. These chakras are contact points between spirit and matter that allow the mind to become identified with the physical body.

The seven chakras are primary levels of consciousness, the most distinctive pieces of the concrete mind that can be experienced in the dream before these are further subdivided into more concrete parts of the dream. These seven levels of consciousness in the chakras are levels of perception that are the result of having lost the knowledge of oneness in Heaven. Therefore, the chakras are distortions of the abstract nature of the mind. Nevertheless, they are the closest contact points in the body to the Spirit. Bringing these chakras back together and returning them back to their source in oneness has been the goal of yoga for ages.

In your personal devolution from God, you divided the abstract mind into the concrete mind with seven chakras. As a dreaming mind identified with the ego, you caused your condition. The chakras and the body related to the chakras and the whole universe itself is the effect. But within the frame of reference of the space-time belief, you appear to be the effect because you are identified with the ego. The ego perspective creates the illusion that the outer physical world is the cause that produces an effect on the inner world of your mind in your body. The apparently outer world of form brings forces into your life that appear to be beyond your control. Thus you appear to yourself to be the victim of the outer world when in reality your own mind is just manufacturing an illusion of victimization.

In the illusion of victimization that you have created, you appear to yourself to be lacking. Before the separation, you lacked nothing and therefore you had no needs. After the separation, you divided yourself into the seven levels of consciousness that made for seven levels of needs. These seven levels of needs are only illusory needs based upon fears and the belief that you are lacking in something. However, the only lack you have is a lack of awareness of your true oneness with God.[384]

Ideally you want to return to the awareness of oneness and let go of the perception of all levels of consciousness. The idea is to produce integration and become one, which makes your needs become only the one need for God. With unified needs, you see all your needs being met in the one need for God, and this way you can unify your mind. Nevertheless, this unification cannot be done by ignoring the lower levels of consciousness and only focusing on the seventh chakra alone, which symbolizes oneness.

Conceptual levels of needs, produced by levels of consciousness proceeding from the separation, need to be corrected at each level individually before all levels can be transcended. While you are in your current ego condition, you are functioning on different levels rather than the way you functioned in Heaven where there are no separate levels. Because you are now functioning on different levels, the correction of these levels must be accomplished starting at the bottom and moving vertically upward according to the Course. This vertical orientation of correction of the different levels of functioning is the closest that the Course comes to discussing the existence of the vertical levels of consciousness that are the chakras.

> The idea of orders of need, which follows from the original error that one can be separated from God, requires correction at its own level before the error of perceiving levels at all can be corrected. You cannot behave effectively while you function on different levels. However, while you do, correction must be introduced vertically from the bottom up.[385]

The quotation above apparently refers to the vertical levels of consciousness, but the emphasis is placed upon the necessity for correction at each level in sequence upward. This idea of correcting each individual level "vertically from the bottom up" is consistent with the yoga meditation practice of focusing on the chakras in which the meditator starts at the sacral chakra and moves upward in a step-by-step sequence to the crown chakra.

The Course says the separation into levels was a departure away from the perfection of love in Heaven and a turning in the direction of fear. The ego is described not only as the thought of separation but as a thought of fear.[386] When you fragmented into levels, each of the different levels in sequence became increasingly invested in fear. The bottom level, the sacral chakra associated with the earth, is the most fearful level. The most primal fears are at the sacral chakra level and are related to security, safety, survival, and death.

If you are focused on apparent needs at the sacral level related to fears that make you feel insecure and unsafe, you will not be open to higher levels of consciousness. In addition, if you are in denial about such basic fears, you will also limit your potential for spiritual growth. The basic fears at the lowest level need to be addressed first.

Other emotions and false perceptions also need to be addressed at the level in which they are occurring. Correction must take place by inviting the Holy Spirit into each level of consciousness since the Course maintains that all errors need to be addressed at the level in which they are happening for correction to take place.

A major step in the Atonement plan is to undo error at all levels. Sickness or "not-right-mindedness" is the result of level confusion, because it always entails the belief that what is amiss on one level can adversely affect another. We have referred to miracles as the means of correcting level confusion, for all mistakes must be corrected at the level on which they occur.[387]

The inner blocks at each level are different, yet all these blocks involve fears at every level. In fact, according to the Course letting go of fear is the most essential aspect of the healing that occurs in correction offered by the Holy Spirit. Correction needs to occur at the bottom level and then move upward vertically, yet the process of correction is the same at each level of consciousness. The correction process is always an invitation for the Holy Spirit to come into each level in sequence upward. The Holy Spirit brings in love to replace fear at each level and brings in truth to replace false perceptions.

You are the cause of your experiences in spite of appearances, even though you think you are the effect and victim of what you made. You cannot control the effects of fear in each level of your consciousness, because you are the maker of your fears. You believe what you made has power over you. Your belief in the fear that you made gives it self-imposed power over you.

The real purpose of this world is to use it to correct your unbelief. You can never control the effects of fear yourself, because you made fear, and you believe in what you made. In attitude, then, though not in content, you resemble your Creator, Who has perfect faith in His creation *because* He created them. Belief produces the acceptance of existence. That is why you can believe what no one else thinks is true. It is true for you because it was made by you.

All aspects of fear are untrue because they do not exist at the creative level, and therefore do not exist at all.[388]

By victimizing yourself with what you made, you would perhaps forever remain the apparent victim of your own fears, if it were not for the Holy Spirit Whom God placed in your mind as your Guide helping you to find your way Home. The Holy Spirit reveals to you the real world, which may be considered the home of the Holy Spirit. But in my opinion, the home of the Holy Spirit related to the chakras is the crown chakra symbolizing oneness. Your devolution of spiritual awareness into deeper and deeper sleep was a descent from Heaven and then to the crown chakra and progressively downward through each chakra to the sacral chakra. Your path Home regardless of what religion you adopt is always a journey that reverses the descent and becomes an ascension from the sacral chakra upward through each successive chakra to the crown chakra and then to Heaven.

Full spiritual awakening will involve dissolving of all the chakras from bottom to top. This is the full spectrum of light reversing its path from division back to oneness by the grace of God, the Christ, and the Holy Spirit. Ironically, the typical opportunity for complete spiritual awakening is death. In physical death, under ideal circumstances the kundalini rises full force up through all the chakras and exits out of the top of the head. All the life force exits the body and does not come back to the body. The soul can awaken fully in Heaven or, if attached to the ego, can again reject the Light of Heaven and manifest at lower levels of consciousness and finally reincarnate in another body.

The spiritual awakening that occurs in revelation is an experience very similar to death, but without dying. In revelation, as in death, the kundalini rises with full force upward through all the chakras. The body consciousness is left behind in this experience. The body will stop breathing, but is left unharmed because of divine grace. The life force then is returned from the crown chakra downward through the chakras all the way down to the sacral chakra, and there is a return to body consciousness.

The experience of revelation only temporarily dissolves all levels of consciousness and brings the experience of knowledge. After coming back to body awareness and the world of perception, some attitudes are retained from the experience. Revelation provides a revealing of the end result of your spiritual journey, but you will still have to use the means provided in your daily life for walking each step of the way back to that final destination.[389] After the revelation experience is over, the experience of different levels of consciousness returns. As a result of revelation, these levels of consciousness have been partially purified so there is less fear at each level. Because the purification is only partial, you will still need to continue purification practices that would release inner blocks from the bottom upward.

Under ideal circumstances this purification process from the bottom upward would already have been a part of your daily practice prior to having a revelation experience. In revelation, God is experienced directly beyond time and space. This direct and personal experience of God in revelation is best described by the word "awe."

Awe should be reserved for revelation, to which it is perfectly and correctly applicable. It is not appropriate for miracles because a state of awe is worshipful, implying that one of a lesser order stands before his Creator. You are a perfect creation, and should experience awe only in the presence of the Creator of perfection.[390]

Awe is an appropriate response to your Creator. In this case, awe would consist of an overwhelming sense of wonderment rather than fearfulness. The inexperienced seeker may possibly confuse awe with fear. Because of this possible confusion, preparation and purification are needed prior to this experience so that the experience will be a beatific one. If there is not proper preparation and purification, the awe may be misinterpreted as fear and could possibly be a negative experience rather than an uplifting experience. This is why the Course cautions seekers to use the means recommended in the Course for purification and healing. The Course specifically states that the more direct approaches to God in the latter portions of this book, which provide Workbook lessons in what is basically contemplation, require "careful preparation" and purification first.

Some of the later steps in this course, however, involve a more direct approach to God Himself. It would be unwise to start on these steps without careful preparation, or awe will be confused with fear, and the experience will be more traumatic than beatific.[391]

For purification the Holy Spirit needs to be invited into each level of consciousness starting at the bottom and moving upward vertically. There are different ways of making this invitation depending upon the level of purification that has already occurred previously. As an inner meditative practice, there can be a general invitation through contemplation, which is the typical invitation to the divine presence recommended in the Course. Certainly the Holy Spirit acting through the crown center can release inner blocks in each of the levels of consciousness from the bottom upward. This is the best approach for the more advanced seeker. This is true because the advanced seeker has integrated the mind sufficiently enough to be focused on the one need and one purpose of awakening oneness with God.

Yet less advanced seekers do not have an integrated mind and are thus heavily invested in functioning at different levels with different needs. The less advanced seeker needs a more systematic approach than a general invitation to the Holy Spirit. One systematic invitation is the traditional Hindu yogic practice of focusing on each of the seven chakras. But you can affect all seven chakras systematically without focusing on each individual chakra. Chapter 3 recommends Christian Yoga Meditation as the basic method for inviting the Holy Spirit into each chakra. Christian Yoga Meditation is a combination of the six techniques practiced from the bottom upward. Inviting the Holy Spirit into the navel center in Centering Meditation involves the turning your awareness and energy upward from the bottom two chakras. Heart Meditation inviting the Holy Spirit into the heart center draws energy upward through the third and fourth chakras. Brow Meditation inviting the Holy Spirit into the brow center draws energy upward through the fifth and sixth centers. Inviting the Holy Spirit into the crown center in Crown Meditation involves the final chakra.

Oneness Meditation is a practice of openness to the Holy Spirit integrating all seven chakras. Inner Silence Meditation, which is the final technique of Christian Yoga Meditation leads to contemplation, and symbolizes the completion of the journey of coming Home—the journey from form to formlessness—from techniques to surrender to God. The Holy Spirit works mainly through the crown chakra, but with your invitation enters the other chakras and brings a purifying and unifying effect no matter what method is used.

Inviting the Holy Spirit to manifest through the heart center is particularly important as a balance point between the three lower chakras and three higher chakras in your journey Home. The heart center provides the emphasis on love that balances out the vertical aspects of meditation with the horizontal aspects of extension to your brother. You are not coming Home alone because you are not alone. Holy relationships, forgiveness, Christ's vision, holy instants, miracles and many forms of extension provide the means for you to come Home to Heaven while you hold the hand of your brother.

When the purification process of using Christian Yoga Meditation has been successful for an extended period of time, your meditation practice can become primarily an experience of contemplation. Your general invitation to the Holy Spirit in contemplation can bring about whatever inner changes that need to be made from the bottom up. You may experience an inner feeling of light. This opening to light is significant because it is this light that makes Christ's vision possible both as an inner experience and as an outer visual experience of Light vision. Likewise, for you to accept the Atonement you will need to allow yourself to be open to this inner light because the Atonement is in the light: "The Atonement is entirely unambiguous. It is perfectly clear because it exists in the light."[392] The Atonement is accepted by opening yourself to the inner light: "The Atonement can be accepted within you only by the releasing of the inner light."[393]

Just as Christ's vision is made possible by light and can be used to affirm the truth and release errors, the Atonement similarly is made possible by light and serves as a remedy for error. To "atone" means undo the errors of false perceptions. By accepting the Atonement, you become open to using miracles that produce correction of errors and healing. You will need to have already made progress in releasing doubts and fears using purification practices before your acceptance of the Atonement will result in performing miracles.

The body in itself cannot be a means of obtaining Atonement. The misguided belief that the body can atone for error is the cause of physical sickness. Errors are produced by the ego that attacks and produces guilt. Guilt brings with it the expectation of punishment and the desire to mitigate the expected punishment through some kind of atonement. Because the mind identified with the ego wants to atone for guilt produced by error, the misguided mind makes the body physically sick as a form of punishment, which is a self-imposed atonement. Punishment of the body being misguided atonement for guilt can hardly be useful in regard to the Atonement, which if truly accepted, brings healing, not sickness.

A step in the right direction of perceiving the body correctly is to perceive that the body is a temple. The Course says after seeing the body as a temple, the next step is to realize that the essence of the temple is not in the outer structure of the temple at all. Preoccupation with the form of the body, the outer structure, is a way of avoiding the Atonement out of fear. The real meaning of the temple can only be found in the altar within the temple, rather than in the surrounding structure.[394] The outer form of the temple, the physical body, is really a symbol of fear and separation. Physical vision with the physical eyes will see only the outer form and will make error appear real and therefore appear to be beyond undoing.

Spiritual vision with the eyes of Christ looks past the form of the temple and sees the altar.[395] The altar can only be seen by overlooking all errors, which are not real anyway. The altar is the symbol of God's presence within you where God and His Son can make their Home together. This is such a sacred altar that there is only one gift on this altar. This one gift is the Atonement.[396] When you accept this gift of the Atonement, you in turn give your own willingness to have all your errors undone at all levels and give your willingness to fulfill your part, your special function, in the Atonement.

The outer form of the physical body is the outer structure of the temple, but where is the inner altar? The Course does not say where the inner altar is, but in my opinion, the altar is the crown chakra. The crown chakra, like all the chakras, is not physical but is related to a specific body part. The crown chakra is related to the crown of the head, but some believe also extends to above the body. This chakra represents oneness and therefore is the logical location as the *meeting place* of holiness, which would be the most holy altar within the temple of the body.

This altar, this holy meeting place of the God and His Son, is also the home of the Holy Spirit.[397] The Holy Spirit holds the Atonement in this altar for you, but waits for you to accept the Atonement as your gift to yourself.[398] You can leave the gift on the altar refusing to open it, but the Atonement will remain for you to eventually accept when you chose to do so. Accepting the Atonement unleashes great power to help you undo errors at all levels.[399]

> Merely by being what it is, does truth release you from everything that it is not. The Atonement is so gentle you need but whisper to it, and all its power will rush to your assistance and support. You are not frail with God beside you. Yet without Him you are nothing. The Atonement offers to you God. The gift that you refused is held by Him in you. The Holy Spirit holds it there for you. God has not left His altar, though His worshippers placed other gods upon it. The temple still is holy, for the Presence that dwells within it *is* holiness.[400]

Unfortunately prior to accepting the Atonement, the altar has been defiled by the belief in separation and fear. These are like false gods on your holy altar and must be removed in order to let the holiness of the altar shine. The awakening of Christ's vision makes it clear that the altar is defiled, and therefore requires purification.[401] Christ's vision overlooks the errors of false gods that have defiled the altar and looks for the Atonement as the remedy for all errors.[402] With the acceptance of the Atonement, the altar can be repaired and inner peace can be restored. When you accept the Atonement, you allow your mind to be used in the service of the Holy Spirit.

> For perfect effectiveness the Atonement belongs at the center of the inner altar, where it undoes the separation and restores the wholeness of the mind. Before the separation the mind was invulnerable to fear, because fear did not exist. Both the separation and the fear are miscreations that must be undone for the restoration of the temple, and for the opening of the altar to receive the Atonement. This heals the separation by placing within you the one effective defense against all separation thoughts and making you perfectly invulnerable.
>
> The acceptance of the Atonement by everyone is only a matter of time.[403]

Everyone will eventually accept the Atonement entirely and come Home since that is God's Will. This may appear to be a contradiction of free will, but it is not. Your true will is God's Will. Your Identity is God's Will. "You *are* the Will of God. Do not accept anything else as your will, or you are denying what you are."[404] Your true Identity is unlimited. By denying God's Will, you limit yourself. "You are the Will of God because that is how you were created. Because your Creator creates only like Himself, you are like Him. You are part of Him Who is all power and glory, and are therefore as unlimited as He is."[405] God's Will, which is your true will, brings joy. Your will apart from God's Will brings pain. Exerting your will to resist God's Will of Love will imprison your true will and will bring pain to you. However, the Atonement will eventually be accepted because there are limits on how much pain can be endured.

You can temporize and you are capable of enormous procrastination, but you cannot depart entirely from your Creator, Who set limits on your ability to miscreate. An imprisoned will engenders a situation which, in the extreme, becomes altogether intolerable. Tolerance for pain may be high, but it is not without limit. Eventually everyone begins to recognize, however dimly, that there *must* be a better way. As this recognition becomes more firmly established, it becomes a turning point. This ultimately reawakens spiritual vision, simultaneously weakening the investment in physical sight. The alternating investment in the two levels of perception is usually experienced as conflict, which can become very acute. But the outcome is as certain as God.[406]

The ego-based mind causes your loyalty to be divided between love and fear, between true perceptions and false perceptions. This makes it hard to make a definitive uncompromising commitment to the Atonement, which is perfect love. By accepting the Atonement, you accept your God-given true holiness, which can be denied but not lost. The return of the awareness of your holiness awaits your decision to accept the Atonement, described as follows:

In the temple, holiness waits quietly for the return of them that love it. The Presence knows they will return to purity and grace. The graciousness of God will take them gently in, and cover all their sense of pain and loss with the immortal assurance of their Father's Love. There, fear of death will be replaced with joy of life. For God is Life, and they abide in Life. Life is as holy as the Holiness by Which it was created. The Presence of holiness lives in everything that lives, for holiness created life, and leaves not what it created holy as itself.[407]

The Atonement offers so much holiness that it is difficult at first to accept. Minds that are split because of the ego are accustomed to entertaining thoughts of holiness and love and thoughts of sin and unworthiness. Having a divided mind that fluctuates between love and fear makes it seem to be hard to accept the Atonement, which is perfect love and perfect holiness. The gift that the Atonement presents appears to be too great to be readily accepted all at once. Although you may accept the Atonement during prayer time, the acceptance of the Atonement needs to be continually renewed. Each renewal of your acceptance of the Atonement opens you to greater healing of the divided mind, which is healed by letting go of fear. Renewing your acceptance of the Atonement is your way of healing yourself and becoming a miracle worker, who can bring miracles and resulting healing into the lives of others. One of the best ways of renewing your acceptance of the Atonement is to make this renewal part of your daily meditation practice. As an opening prayer of dedication before meditation or as a closing prayer after meditation, you can again accept the Atonement opening yourself to the service of the Holy Spirit for the benefit of others and yourself.

The acceptance of the Atonement is extremely important for your own return Home. But besides your individual journey Home with your brothers and sisters guided by the Holy Spirit, the Atonement also represents God's Plan for the world as a whole. The remainder of this chapter will look at the spiritual evolution of mankind that has already occurred in history and that is occurring now.

B. THE FIRST TWO STEPS OF SPIRITUAL EVOLUTION

Since the spiritual devolution away from God has been addressed previously, now let's look back at the past in regard to understanding the overall spiritual evolution that has occurred on earth as a whole. Just as each individual elevates his consciousness from the lowest chakra upward in his own body to evolve spiritually, the world is going through a similar process. My theory of spiritual evolution is that the divine impulse began at the gonad level of consciousness in the earth and has been moving upward ever since. At this first stage in evolution, Krishna was incarnated as God manifested as a master of the gonad level, related to the "serpent energy" of the kundalini at the base of the spine. Krishna with his consort, Radha, and his other devoted cow herding girls, called gopis, expressed mastery of the sexual energy associated with the element of the earth. Krishna, along with his disciple, Arjuna, also addressed the issue of death in facing war as is described in the Bhagavad-Gita.

This initial divine expression will be called the *Krishna Impulse* in this book. This will be used here as a symbol for the whole Hindu divine manifestation of yoga as a path to God that originated in India and evolved over many years in different ways. This path included great diversity which would correspond with the diffused nature of the energy of the gonad center itself. In particular, this path represented the creative energy that is a union of the male and female energies and thus included relationships. But the higher understanding was that these energies were inherent within each human vehicle. Sexual union with a partner was only a preliminary for joining the male and female energies within the individual seeker's own body. Joining the male and female energies within the seeker could produce a return to the primordial source of creative energy.

These methods advocated in yoga certainly did work but only the greatest spiritual athletes could transcend this world. There was the passing of spiritual training from guru to disciple in the teacher and student relationship that the Course would call a holy relationship. Freedom was perceived in yoga as the leaving of this world in order to achieve the freedom of returning to God. The idea of leaving this world to become free evolved into the tantric yoga goal of freedom based upon being freed while still living in the earth. The beginning focusing point in tantric yoga is the base of the spine associated with the gonad center and raising energy upward from that point.

A significant aspect of this first step in spiritual evolution is that this Krishna Impulse encapsulated in a seed form all of the spiritual evolution that would follow. It contained the joining of the male and female polarity to bring unity. The joining of sperm and egg produces a living person and all of this person is contained in this initial seed cell. Likewise, the Hindu impulse contained all the forms of union through yoga, such as karma yoga, jnana yoga, bhakti yoga, and raja yoga. The Hindu influence also expressed relationship yoga in the forms of tantric yoga and the teacher and disciple holy relationship exemplified by Krishna and his disciple, Arjuna.

Yet Hinduism taken as a whole did not stand for any one of these, but all of them. The Krishna Impulse was the expression of the seed that contains everything within itself. This seed was a foreshadowing of the full mature manifestation that would occur in the future. The diffusion of Hinduism mirrored the diffusion of the gonad center. The next steps in spiritual evolution were ones that focused on specific paths that had a more central message, a specific kind of yoga.

With the first step of the gonad level of consciousness grounded in the earth as a foundation, the next step of spiritual evolution was focused specifically on the path of meditation, such as raja yoga. This path starts by focusing at the navel level of consciousness. This second step is the *Buddha Impulse,* related to the incarnation of the Buddha. The navel center is the area in the body where the creative energy from the gonad center is redirected from a downward flow of diffused energy to an upward flow of focused energy. This level is associated with meditation itself and in the Zen Buddhist method of sitting meditation called *zazen* the focus of meditation is specifically on the *hara* in the navel area. The navel center is associated with the element of water, often represented by the image of a completely still lake in which the perfect reflection of the moon can be seen. The still lake stands for the still mind that can perfectly reflect the divine origin of the mind.

The Buddha Impulse more than other divine expressions brought the image of total renunciation and desirelessness. Buddha himself was the example of one individual who abandoned this world and its forms and attained perfect enlightenment. The Buddha passed along through the student and teacher holy relationship with the common purpose of benefiting the student's learning. However, there was not the same relationship element of male and female energies as there was in the previous level of consciousness.

Also, there was a missionary element here in which the original impulse was born in India, but in the adulthood of its evolution, it left its native home, moving to other countries to encompass more of the world. India itself over time let go of the Buddha Impulse and returned to its original Krishna Impulse. India retained the original gonad level of consciousness with its inherent diversity of spiritual expression and male/female emphasis. The Buddha Impulse evolved and surpassed the earlier Krishna Impulse in terms of sheer numbers of people who are Buddhist. Moving beyond its foundation in the Krishna Impulse, the Buddhist Impulse retained its unique navel level of consciousness with its focus on seeking Buddha nature.

Today these two initial paths of Hinduism and Buddhism retain their unique differences just as the gonad center and navel center are different, but these two are also bonded together in certain ways. Both paths represent the individual seeking personal transcendence one person at a time. There is no consideration of the idea of group transcendence, yet there is the linear progression of guru to disciple in Hinduism and dharma transmission from the enlightened teacher to the disciple in Buddhism. Spiritual advancement basically depends on personal effort using meditation techniques.

In the most evolved aspect of these two paths, there is a nondual awareness. This nondual awareness can be called a *unitive awareness* that can be attained and in which everyone is already living. It is just a matter of waking up to this unitive awareness that is one's own true nature. This emphasis on unitive awareness is the evolutionary high point of both of these paths that together symbolize the best of what the East has to offer.

Another common aspect of these two paths is that the lack of emphasis on the concept of guilt. With a nondual approach, there is no need to indulge in speculation about who is to blame for the separation from oneness. The goal is set simply for the individual to return back to unitive awareness. Hinduism calls the illusion of this world "divine play" of God. Buddhism affirms the illusory nature of the world but does not call it anything in relation to God because the concept of God is omitted.

This setting aside of guilt is a two-edged sword. The positive side is that the individual seeker is allowed to release guilt as a conscious consideration in his own spiritual seeking. The negative side is that guilt is so much a part of the ego that many spiritual seekers have genuine spiritual experiences, yet retain ego-based thinking, such a guilt. Thus the Eastern approach can often just mask the guilt without really healing underlying guilt in the psyche. From an evolutionary perspective, guilt needed to be addressed directly. Indeed, guilt was addressed directly in the third and fourth steps of spiritual evolution, although not necessarily in a completely healthy manner.

The weakness of the Hindu and Buddhist paths is their emphasis on spiritual attainment being a matter of individual effort and not a collaborative effort. Hinduism contains elements of God's grace, but there is a much greater emphasis on individual effort. Buddhism has no idea of God so there is no idea of God's grace. Though the teacher/disciple relationship is a part of both paths, the importance of relationships in general is not seen as a significant means of spiritual growth, and this oversight is a noticeable shortcoming.

C. THE THIRD IMPULSE OF SPIRITUAL EVOLUTION

The first step of the Krishna Impulse produced a foundation for individual spiritual attainment. The Buddha Impulse, building on that foundation, manifested perfect enlightenment. In this evolutionary step, one man and then others could achieve individual transcendent consciousness, but actually the divine goal is for everyone to become One. The divine Plan then necessitated the next evolutionary step of manifesting a people who could form a "holy people relationship," on the pattern of the holy relationship. This would be a people who would gather for a common purpose and see common interests. This obviously was the Hebrew people, who had the common purpose of offering salvation to the world, even if they saw it as salvation for only their people. Joining for this common purpose invited the holiness of God and the Holy Spirit as it does with all holy relationships.

In all holy relationships, there is a period of discomfort at the time when the means of accomplishing the goal of holiness is out of line with the goal. Prophets who rose up in Israel were themselves in line with the goal of holiness. Yet these prophets had difficulty in bringing the Hebrews as a whole people in line with the goal. Unfortunately, the time of discomfort for the Hebrew people was many, many years. Nevertheless, the new impulse being brought into spiritual evolution was the holy relationship expanded to include all souls who wanted to dedicate their lives to the purpose of holiness and salvation.

In addition to representing relationship yoga, although in a rather imperfect manner, this path also symbolized karma yoga because of the dedication of their lives to God and His Plan. However, here too, this yoga was expressed in a rudimentary manner precisely because bringing an individual in line with the kind of selfless dedication required of karma yoga is much easier than bringing a people as a whole into this alignment. The Hebrew expression of karma yoga was manifested within the limits of the level of understanding that prevailed at that time. For example, the Hebrews relied on an "eye for an eye" as an expression of justice, rather than seeking to express the higher ideal of love manifested as forgiveness.

The Hebrew path can be called the *Elijah Impulse*, symbolized by the prophet Elijah. The Hebrew Elijah Impulse was associated with the adrenal level of consciousness. The adrenal glands, being on the right and left sides of the body, have a dual nature. Yet the adrenal level of consciousness expresses duality between God and man, as well as the duality of human relationships. Associated with fire and purification, the adrenal center is the transition stage between the navel area and the heart area. The adrenal level of consciousness is related to anger and attack issues and the need for purification that is required before being able to evolve to the next level of love. Elijah is singled out here because he called down fire from Heaven to bless his sacrifice and vanquish his enemies. Also, he was described as rising up to Heaven in a chariot of fire. Symbolizing purification by fire, the Elijah Impulse involved facing all the unresolved issues of the ego including guilt. Hebrews felt the sacrifice of burnt offerings was necessary as a representation of atonement for sin and guilt.

Although there are various prophets who could symbolize the Hebrew Impulse, Elijah fits best because he was the natural transition figure to the Messiah. There was a prophecy that Elijah would have to return before the Messiah would come. After being transformed into a light being on Mount Tabor, the disciples asked Jesus about this prophecy and Jesus told them that Elijah had returned in the form of John the Baptist, and this statement by Jesus is interpreted literally by those who believe in reincarnation.[408]

D. THE FOURTH STEP OF SPIRITUAL EVOLUTION

The fourth step of spiritual evolution is related to the heart level of consciousness. The heart level is associated with the element of air, the breath of life. In yoga, the breath is equivalent to prana, the vital life force energy. In Christianity the heart is related to the soul or psyche. The heart center is the meeting place between the three higher centers and the three lower centers of consciousness, and in this meeting place, the Heavenly influence and the earthly influence can meet in an integrated way.

Therefore, the heart level of consciousness played a central role in the spiritual evolution of the earth. Most important of all, the heart level symbolized divine love being born into the earth. Jesus, the Lord of Love, embodied the heart level of consciousness and the perfection of bhakti yoga in particular. In fact, Jesus Christ in his life manifested the fulfillment of all of the previous steps cumulatively. The Krishna Impulse contained all the forms of yoga in a potential seed form. In Jesus this potential is achieved and perfected. As a jnana yogi, his wisdom is unsurpassed in his awareness of his Oneness with God, which is the goal of jnana yoga. The wisdom of Jesus was reflected at the human level in the mental ability of Jesus used to refute his detractors and tell parables that had many levels of meaning.

In the Edgar Cayce readings, there are references to Jesus having gone to the East, perhaps India, in the years before his ministry. If this is true, his visit to India brought him back to the womb of both the Krishna Impulse and Buddha Impulse, which is the foundation of the spiritual evolution of the world. Here in India, he would have been exposed to inward spiritual disciplines leading to unitive awareness. There is no mention of an early enlightenment experience like that of the Buddha, but I believe he was an enlightened and perfect master of raja yoga meditative practice.

As a perfect karma yogi, he dedicated everything, even his blood, to following the Will of God. He elevated the old karmic law of justice into the new law of grace and forgiveness. He lived a life of healing and of giving of himself, denying his ego in all things. Even in the smallest occurrences of daily living, he did not miss any opportunity to provide kindness to others.

Jesus was the perfect bhakti yogi, who manifested divine love in all respects. Jesus in the spiritual evolution of the earth represented the cumulative progression of perfection expressed at the gonad level, the navel level, the adrenal level, and most notably at the heart level of consciousness. In his life, guilt was overcome at the heart level and replaced by forgiveness and totally selfless love.

Finally Jesus was the perfect master of relationship yoga which can be seen throughout His life as an expression of love and the heart level of consciousness. In Chapter 7, there is a description of the holy relationships that assisted in bringing Jesus himself into the world, so it can be said that Jesus was born out of holy relationships. Every holy relationship today allows Christ to be born again with each one reflecting the birth of Jesus into the world.

Jesus established a holy relationship with John the Baptist as a coworker with the common purpose of fulfilling salvation. John the Baptist baptized Jesus and, as in all holy relationships, the Holy Spirit descended into the relationship. Jesus joined in a holy relationship of teacher and disciple with each of his apostles. The twelve apostles, similar to the twelve sons of Jacob who formed the twelve tribes of Israel, symbolized the twelve aspects of human development that are expressed by the twelve signs of the zodiac. With his disciples, Jesus established a holy relationship having the common purpose of raising human consciousness to a transcendent level.

The Holy Spirit entered each relationship with his disciples and produced times of discomfort because the format of each relationship was out of line with the goal. Each disciple had to make changes in his relationship to come into alignment with the goal of holiness. Only Judas could not make his way through this time of discomfort.

A holy relationship can be a temporary encounter in which the Holy Spirit enters the relationship when two join in a short-term common purpose. Jesus did not go up to people uninvited and heal them. People came to Jesus asking for healing and even then he did not immediately heal. He actually asked each one to join with him in a temporary holy relationship so that the Holy Spirit could enter in and produce holiness and healing. A good example of this request for a temporary holy relationship is the healing of the boy possessed. In this encounter, Jesus said:

> "If thou can believe, all things are possible to him who believes."
> At once the father of the boy cried out, and said with tears, "I do believe; help my unbelief."[409]

Jesus typically requested that seekers join with him to be of one mind, to have a common belief and common purpose, which was healing. Jesus could not work miracles in his home town because of disbelief, which meant that there could not be a true mutual joining of minds in the common purpose of healing.

The most important holy relationship Jesus established was with Mary. Their holy relationship started even before he was born. This was a unique situation in which a soul in Heaven in union with God made a holy relationship with a soul in the earth to join in a common purpose initiated by God's Will. The effect of this joining was to literally bring the influence of Heaven into the earth. Mary joined with Jesus, the Holy Spirit, and God for the purpose of manifesting the Immaculate Conception that brought a new *concept* of holiness into the world. Since the Son is a Thought in the Mind of God, this Thought could come into the world in its purest form by entering a vessel of pure holiness. Mary as this holy vessel joined herself with the Thought in the Mind of God for the common purpose of bringing salvation to the world. In that conception, perfect holiness entered the earth as a manifestation of God's Will of Love.

I believe that this is the most important holy relationship in human history since it manifested the birth of the Christ in a perfect manner that would raise human consciousness to a new transcendent level. Starting with this mother and child relationship, the holy relationship of Jesus and Mary went through many stages as their roles changed. With the common purpose of the education of Jesus, Mary took on the teacher role and Jesus the student role. Mary taught Jesus the scriptures she had learned in the Temple. Mary, being a contemplative herself, was the first to teach Him how to pray and contemplate. But Mary's greatest gift was her great love that she gave wholeheartedly to Jesus. Mary taught Jesus by example how to give and receive love. With adulthood, their roles reversed because Jesus became the master and Mary became the disciple.

Yet it was not an ordinary discipleship because Jesus relied on Mary's love throughout his life. Mary Valtorta's visions of the life of Jesus portrayed his divinity, but also his human compassion. Jesus endured many hardships in his ministry yet always found consolation in Mary on those occasions when they were able to be together. In particular, Jesus was troubled by the repeated transgressions of Judas before he entirely betrayed his calling. Jesus rebuked him privately in order to avoid exposing Judas to shame. Repeatedly Jesus forgave Judas, and Judas promised it would never happen again, but it did. Judas was addicted to specialness and to pride so he wanted to be recognized by others. Jesus sent Judas to live with Mary and her love and her prayers converted him so he became a new man. But the conversion did not last. Jesus was greatly distressed in realizing that Judas was his lost sheep who did not want to be found.

Mary's presence consoled Jesus when he was distressed about Judas. He was able to confide in her in ways that he could not with anyone else. It was not only her as his mother that consoled him. He saw in her the holiness of God Himself just as she saw in him the holiness of God Himself. In the mature holy relationship, each partner becomes the savior for the other. Jesus was certainly the savior of the world, but Mary was his savior. When all the disciples except for John, the Beloved, abandoned Jesus, only John and Mary stayed at the foot of the cross. Knowing the human side of his holy relationship with Mary was ending, he gave John to Mary as her new son in order to console her.

However, it was Mary who consoled Jesus in his time of greatest trial. Being in a holy relationship, Mary and Jesus were joined as one mind. Whatever one experienced, the other also experienced. That is why, when Jesus was brought to the Temple for circumcision and presentation to the Lord, Simeon told Mary his predication, recorded in the Bible as follows: "And thy own soul a sword shall pierce, that the thoughts of many hearts may be revealed."[410]

This concept of minds being joined is important because if minds are not joined they cannot have a common purpose. The way Mary helped Jesus is by being the one who was most joined with him when others abandoned him. Maria Valtorta's visions revealed that Mary did not give in to despair in her own torture in seeing Jesus tortured. Mary was the only disciple who actually *believed* that Jesus would rise from the dead. Not even death could sway her trust in Jesus and in God. Jesus on the cross knew that she alone believed in him, and he was consoled by her faith, as well as by her love. This was the great service she extended to Jesus in his time of trial.

In the time of Jesus, women were considered unimportant and so it would have been hard for the people of that time to understand the full impact of Mary's contribution to salvation. Yet Mary by her spiritual attainment produced a change in perception that elevated the status of woman in the eyes of the world. But the contributions of Mary are often overlooked in this present day and perhaps some of this is due to Mary's own nature of stepping back so that Jesus is emphasized. In my opinion Jesus became the perfect Christ, but also Mary became the perfect Christ as well, accomplishing God's Will in all things. As with all holy relationships, partners enter Heaven holding the hand of each other.

The singular accomplishment of the Buddha in attaining perfect enlightenment was surpassed by the resurrection of Jesus, but was also surpassed by the perfect awakening of both Jesus and Mary as a partnership for the benefit of all mankind. Their holy relationship is continuing now in the same common purpose of salvation that originally brought them together. Their example demonstrates the importance of forming holy relationships as a means of assisting in salvation. In each holy relationship each partner can see Christ in the other and bring their own joint salvation and the salvation of the world one step closer to fulfillment.

CHAPTER 11

~ • ~

PROGRESS IN SPIRITUAL EVOLUTION

A. SPIRITUAL EVOLUTION TAKING A STEP FORWARD

This section looks at the spiritual evolution of the earth and why now there is a change in which humanity is ready to let go of the traditional views of sin and guilt and accept the Atonement instead. Jesus in the Course makes it clear that his purpose is to facilitate the Atonement that recognizes you are guiltless and sinless because you are the holy Son of God. The four divine impulses that have been identified in the previous chapter are summarized below:

1. THE KRISHNA IMPULSE represents consciousness at the gonad level and contains the seed of karma yoga, jnana yoga, bhakti yoga, and raja yoga, as well as the relationship yoga of the spiritual teacher and student. The goal is individual unitive awareness.

2. THE BUDDHA IMPULSE represents consciousness at the navel level represents the perfection of raja yoga, the individual returning to unitive awareness.

3. THE ELIJAH IMPULSE represents consciousness at the adrenal level and focuses on relationships and a people seeking salvation as a collective path to God. There is an emphasis on duality, sin, guilt, and the need for atonement, expected to be realized with the coming of the Messiah.

4. THE JESUS IMPULSE represents consciousness at the heart level of consciousness. The emphasis is on bhakti yoga and relationship yoga, but Jesus also embodies jnana yoga, karma yoga, and raja yoga. Jesus symbolizes complete divine integration because Jesus brought the influence of Heaven to the earth in His arrival and manifested the Heavenly transcendence of the earth in his resurrection.

I believe that the spiritual evolution of the world is now in the process of taking the fifth step in this sequence in order to bring mankind closer to salvation. This fifth step is now and will be in the future a manifestation of the throat level of consciousness that has to do with communication and the proper use of the will. Using the will properly means alignment with God's Will and also means having freedom of choice. As you might expect, the throat containing the apparatus of speech relates to the expression of words, but also to the communication of the Word of God and the Will of God.

There is a direct connection between communication and God's Will. In your true nature as an abstract mind in the Mind of God, you are in direct communication with God and all of God's creation in Heaven. The Course says the Will of God is this direct and complete communication between God and all of His creation.[411] There is no difference between communication and creation.[412] Your mind was created by God communicating His Mind to your mind. Thus you became a channel to continually receive His Mind and His Will and to extend your mind to other minds like God communicated His Mind to your mind.[413]

> In contrast, spirit reacts in the same way to everything it knows is true, and does not respond to anything else. Nor does it make any attempt to establish what is true. It knows that what is true is everything that God created. It is in complete and direct communication with every aspect of creation, because it is in complete and direct communication with its Creator. This communication is the Will of God. Creation and communication are synonymous. God created every mind by communicating His Mind to it, thus establishing it forever as a channel for the reception of His Mind and Will. Since only beings of a like order can truly communicate, His creations naturally communicate with Him and like Him. This communication is perfectly abstract, since its quality is universal in application and not subject to any judgment, any exception or any alteration. God created you by this and for this. [414]

Your being in Heaven is in a state of mind in which you are really communicating your mind abstractly to all of creation.[415] In your communication, you give all of yourself to everything that is real and receive as you have given. In Heaven, you have everything and your joy is in this total sharing of yourself.

God, who encompasses all being, created beings who have everything individually, but who want to share it to increase their joy. Nothing real can be increased except by sharing. That is why God created you. Divine Abstraction takes joy in sharing. That is what creation means. "How," "what," and "to whom" are irrelevant, because real creation gives everything, since it can create only like itself. [416]

This sharing of yourself is your extension of love and your reality. Since your being, which is your reality, is the communication of all of yourself to God and His creation, the limiting of your communication limits your awareness of your own reality. [417] The limiting of your communication shifts your experience from being to existence, which is a shift from being in Heaven to existing in the world of form. The difference between existence and being is described as follows:

Existence as well as being rest on communication. Existence, however, is specific in how, what and with whom communication is judged to be worth undertaking. Being is completely without these distinctions. It is a state in which the mind is in communication with everything that is real. To whatever extent you permit this state to be curtailed you are limiting your sense of your own reality, which becomes total only by recognizing all reality in the glorious context of it real relationship to you. This is your reality. Do not desecrate it or recoil from it. It is your real home, your real temple and your real Self. [418]

With your participation in the separation, you closed off most of your communication and therefore reduced your sense of your own reality. Any improvement in communication is therefore an openness to God's Will and an openness to a greater awareness of your own true reality. The fifth step in the spiritual evolution of the earth, which is the new manifestation of the throat level of consciousness, is an expression of increased communication and the expression of the Will of God. God's Will can only be expressed by souls having freedom of choice, so any movements in the direction of freedom will also be a part of this new impulse in the spiritual evolution of the world.

The Holy Spirit and Jesus Christ, representing God's Word and Will, will be the focus of this new manifestation of the throat level of consciousness. This step forward in spiritual evolution will require changes and traditional established ideas will be challenged by these changes. Just as the Elijah Impulse was challenged by the introduction of the Jesus Impulse, so too the new impulse will be challenged by the established Christian order.

This new impulse will not replace the central role of Jesus but will be a greater manifestation of Jesus in some manner. I choose to call this new step the *Second Coming Impulse*. In my opinion, this new step forward will follow the same very gradual unfolding process as the other steps in spiritual evolution. I do not believe Jesus will come back one time only for this Second Coming Impulse. Just like the other steps, there will be a sequence of events that are all part of God's Plan for this new step forward.

The first events of this sequence are already occurring, but not in a dramatic way. The significance of these events in relation to the Second Coming Impulse will not be apparent until more overt or even miraculous manifestations occur. In order to be a step forward this new Second Coming Impulse will have to be a manifestation of greater oneness and spiritual integration, especially in regard to communication and freedom of choice. Signs of the Second Coming Impulse are already occurring and can be seen by looking at the overall elements of increased communication, freedom of choice, and oneness that have happened in recent history.

For example, the ecumenical movement has been a noticeable foreshadowing of the Second Coming Impulse toward greater oneness worldwide. The series of appearances of Mary all over the world in this century with an increase in recent years is part of the sequence of events of the Second Coming Impulse. In this case, Mary is the forerunner of Jesus again assisting in bringing Christ to the earth as she did two thousand years ago.

The Jews being scattered in the Diaspora all over the world was a symbol of a scattering of the Elijah Impulse, a scattering of the impulse dedicated to bringing the Messiah to earth. The suppression of the Jewish people, best symbolized by the Holocaust, has given way to new religious freedom. The Jews coming back to Israel is an important event that symbolizes the reestablishment of the Elijah Impulse dedicated to bringing the Messiah to earth. Many Christian groups see this event as a foreshadowing of the return of Jesus.

In the past two hundred and fifty years, mankind has taken giant leaps forward in the direction of democracy and freedom. America with the establishment of a government that stated "all men are created equal" was the communication of a new idea of freedom at the time. It has taken many years for that seed for freedom to mature into a meaningful American policy of freedom from discrimination based on ethnicity, race, religion, sex, or disability.

This seed of freedom, which for the first time meant total religious freedom, has become established in many other countries since 1776. In recent history, democratic freedom has sprouted as far away in distance and in ideology as the Soviet Union. The conversion of Russia to democracy (before Putin's version of limited democracy) was an event related to the freedom mankind is seeking. Another significant event has been the establishment of the United Nations as a sign of increased world unity, communication, and cooperation. The secular freedom of democracy and the increase of worldwide communication are manifestations of the Second Coming Impulse. This is leading the way toward the ultimate goal of God's plan, which is complete freedom from the limitations of the world and awakening to the true transcendent freedom and limitless communication of Heaven.

Another seemingly secular event is the advent of the first television and then the computer, which ushered in the age of information and communication. Technology has revolutionized communication. The increased communication exemplified by the internet has made a scattered world smaller and more unified. You can be in your home and press a few computer buttons, and you can easily communicate with someone halfway around the world. The Course says the best way to use the body is as a communication device. Technological advances have fostered this best use of the body, facilitating the free flow of sharing that occurs from one mind to another mind. This is a technology-aided fostering of oneness. Increased communication is an important part of the Second Coming Impulse that is a preparation for awakening to unlimited divine communication of Heaven.

There are probably many other events that are happening as the beginning part of the Second Coming Impulse that may go unnoticed for the time being. However, I will focus here on one significant event that is a very important part of the Second Coming Impulse, which is *A Course in Miracles* that will be discussed next.

B. THE COURSE AND THE SECOND COMING IMPULSE

The Second Coming Impulse is a manifestation of God's Plan for salvation that emphasizes communication of God's Word and following God's Will. This manifestation presents a new way of looking at God's Word and a new understanding of how to express God's Will. The better you understand God's Will, the easier it will be to follow God's Will. The Course presents a thought system that claims to express God's Will correctly within the limitations of conceptual thinking.

The Course indicates that it is dictated by Jesus, whom many would call the Word of God. In the Course, Jesus presents no theories.

Jesus, as you would expect, if you believe He is narrating, speaks with certainty. Because Jesus speaks with authority, He turns off some listeners, just as He did two thousand years ago. In addition, Jesus speaks in the Course about the illusion of guilt and the inner workings of the ego. Jesus asks you to look at the darkest corners of the ego in order to bring them to the light. You may find it very challenging to accept that your own psyche contains such dark corners. Reading about guilt may bring up feelings of guilt. While reading about the darkness of the ego, you may continue to read the Course and yet decide to judge against the Course. If you judge against something, you will not see the value in what you have judged against. What you do not value, you will not fully accept. At this point, you may take in the words of the Course without absorbing the meaning.

The Course says about itself that it is either all true or all false. In narrating the Course, Jesus cannot be expected to maintain that some of what He says is true and some is not true. With this in mind, I read the Course and looked for one idea that I was sure was not true, but I could not find a single untrue perception. In spite of this, I still resisted accepting the Course. My resistance was probably due to pride. My ego was offended that all my work of accumulating ideas of truth from different spiritual traditions was being replaced by an all-encompassing theology that contained the best of what the East and West had to offer. Because I had judged against the Course, I could not see the value in what I was reading.

The Course presents a coherent picture of Reality that is different from any other spiritual writings. There can be many different opinions about Reality and everyone has the right to their own opinion. But when explanations contradict each other, only one explanation of Reality can be true. In my case, after about seven years of resistance, I have become convinced that this material in the Course is an entirely accurate thought system and offers the best means for waking up to Reality. Because of my own resistance for so long, I understand why it is hard to accept the Course principles. One obstacle to accepting the Course is one's willingness to accept change without fear.

> Many stand guard over their ideas because they want to protect their thought systems as they are, and learning means change. Change is always fearful to the separated, because they cannot conceive of it as a move towards healing the separation. They always perceive it as a move toward further separation, because the separation was their first experience of change. You believe that if you allow no change to enter into your ego you will find peace.[419]

If your current thought system is based on your identification with the ego and with the body, the acceptance of the Course as a new replacement thought system will be resisted. The ego will guard your current thought system against change promising you that peace can be found by avoiding change. But all promises of the ego are ways of maintaining the status quo of the ego condition. However, moving in the direction of overcoming the ego requires learning of right thinking and learning means change. Learning of right thinking is frightening to the ego because through learning the meaningless of the ego will be revealed. As a result of learning, you will relinquish the ego by seeing that it is not worthy of you.

> Spirit need not be taught, but the ego must be. Learning is ultimately perceived as frightening because it leads to the relinquishment, not the destruction, of the ego to the light of spirit.[420]

> Teaching and learning are your greatest strengths now, because they enable you to change your mind and help others to change their minds.[421]

Letting the ego be the guardian of your thought system cannot be the way to overcome the ego. In the Course, Jesus makes a plea for you to give up the function of guarding your own thought system and instead open your thought system to Jesus himself. In return for opening your thought system to Him, Jesus in coordination with the Holy Spirit promises to gently correct your thought system and guide you back to God.

> You dream of a separated ego and believe in a world that rests upon it. This is very real to you. You cannot undo it by not changing your mind about it. If you are willing to renounce the role of guardian of your thought system and open it to me, I will correct it very gently and lead you back to God.[422]

Hopefully you can keep an open mind and ask for help from Jesus and from the Holy Spirit in your decision-making process in regard to the Course. Exposure to others, who are Course students or teachers, can be very helpful in the process of understanding these principles better and accepting the value and application of Course principles. Since the Second Coming Impulse emphasizes communication, it is not surprising that Jesus himself, as the central figure of the Second Coming Impulse, communicates this new theology presented in the Course. As the narrator of the Course, Jesus has the task of teaching you in your ego-based awareness to believe what seems unbelievable, which is that right now you are the guiltless Son of God. In order to do this, he must teach you that what you think is true now is not true. One way Jesus teaches you is through those who volunteer to be teachers of God. Course teachers learn the Course themselves, and their goal is to transfer all their learning:

> Every good teacher hopes to give his students so much of his own learning that they will one day no longer need him. This is the one true goal of the teacher. It is impossible to convince the ego of this, because it goes against all of its own laws. But remember that laws are set up to protect the continuity of the system in which the lawmaker believes. It is natural for the ego to try to protect itself once you have made it, but it is not natural for you to want to obey its laws unless *you* believe them. The ego cannot make this choice because of the nature of its origin. You can, because of the nature of yours.[423]

Learning something new is relatively easy, but learning to unlearn what you think you know is more difficult. The ego can be offended that so many of its strongly held perceptions are being challenged. The ego will tell you that everything you have learned in the past is valuable and that this past frame of reference tells you who you are. The Holy Spirit wants to teach you how to let go of what you have taught yourself in the past by revealing to you what you are now.[424] In fact, the Holy Spirit wants to assist you not only in letting go of past learning, but also wants to show you how to undo the past and experience the present moment.

The Course says that if you use your past learning as your guide to determine the value of what you do not yet know, you will not know how to respond to what the Holy Spirit would give to you now. If you abandon your reliance on your own guidance based on past learning, you can allow the Holy Spirit to guide your mind and open you to new perceptions. The ego will resist the process of unlearning that is required to accept new perceptions because that learning will naturally lead to an undoing of the ego itself, which is based on false perceptions. Consequently, learning to value the Course requires your willingness to be open-minded and to not allow your understanding to be affected by your ego.

Modern psychology has made great strides in understanding the ego. But the great thinkers in the field of psychology had their own egos that limited the potential of their understanding. Because Jesus no longer has an ego, he was able to clearly examine the true inner workings of the ego and describe how to transcend the ego and return

Home. The Course is mainly a theology with a one-year program of practical application, plus guidelines for becoming a teacher of God. The Course appeals mostly to intellectually oriented seekers and thus is not for everyone nor does it claim to be for everyone.

Nevertheless, the Course is an integral part of the Second Coming Impulse because its thought system represents the *jnana yoga* aspect of the Second Coming Impulse, explaining its theology. The Krishna Impulse had the Bhagavad-Gita and Vedanta. The Buddha Impulse had Buddhist sutras. The Elijah Impulse had the Old Testament. The Jesus Impulse had the New Testament. In the future, the Course might be acknowledged as the scripture of the Second Coming Impulse. Yet there will probably be additional inspired writings during the Second Coming Impulse that might be less intellectually oriented and more geared toward practical application.

The New Testament of the Jesus Impulse focuses on love and offers a significant reinterpretation of the Old Testament of the Elijah Impulse that emphasized "an eye for an eye." Similarly, the Course of the Second Coming Impulse provides a significant reinterpretation of the New Testament. The Course view of the crucifixion is a good illustration of this reinterpretation, which is radically different from the traditional Christian interpretation.

In summary of what has already been addressed previously, the crucifixion is not the punishment required in order to atone for sin and guilt by a God demanding justice. Instead, the crucifixion is an extreme teaching example used by Jesus to demonstrate that sin and guilt are not real and have no real results. Jesus showed that his real nature could not be harmed. He forgave his brothers not for what harm they did to Him, but for what they had *not* done to Him. Jesus saw through the illusion of an apparent attack and saw only *a call for love.* Those who attack do so because they feel deprived of love and do not know that they have deprived themselves of the awareness of love that is their own true nature. Their attacks call for love from outside themselves because they do not know they have love that is already within themselves. Jesus gave his apparent attackers the love that they called for. The resurrection proved that the crucifixion had no effects on the true nature of Jesus.

As you can see from the examples given of the meaning of the crucifixion and forgiveness, the thought system of the Course sets very high standards. It takes time and effort to understand the thought system of the Course, and even more time and effort to apply the Course principles to your daily life and relationships. For example, it may be difficult initially to perceive that your brother cannot attack you because you are the holy Son of God. It may be hard to see that when your brother seems to be outwardly attacking you, he is only self-abusively attacking himself, and he is at the same time calling for love from you. Your ego may be offended, and you may be unwilling to give your brother the love he is calling for from you. Even if you attempt to forgive your brother, you may still feel hurt at times and feel you are forgiving attacks that really had negative effects on you. You may not want to accept full responsibility for experiencing your own negative reactions because of your own beliefs that make attack seem possible in your mind. But learning to first understand and then apply the Course principles to your daily life is a gradual process.

As the narrator of the Course and the leader of the Second Coming Impulse, Jesus raises the standards of this new age, just as he raised the standards two thousand years ago by asking his disciples to love their enemies. Yet it would be inappropriate to say this or that idea in the Course is what Jesus was trying to teach long ago. For instance, all the Course emphasis on the nature of the ego and the inner workings of the subconscious mind would have meant nothing to the Hebrews and Romans of two thousand years ago.

It was the advent of modern psychology that prepared the way for the concepts presented in the Course regarding the workings of the psyche. A sign of the importance of psychology in the Course is the fact that the Course is the result of the efforts of two psychologists. They joined in a holy relationship to improve how they related with each other and within their psychology department environment. The Course does not just incorporate traditional psychology. It goes further than any modern psychologist would dare to go because it describes an extremely detailed version of the inner dynamics of the ego. Of course, psychotherapists have patients go below the surface to bring up underlying emotions. Yet traditional psychology does not go deep enough to uncover what is really happening in the mind. Traditional psychotherapy does not integrate spiritual concepts with psychology, with the exception of transpersonal psychology.

The Course is more than just a reinterpretation of Christianity that includes deep psychological understandings. As part of the Second Coming Impulse, the Course presents a new way of approaching spiritual growth that builds on the already established foundation of the Jesus Impulse and the other three previous impulses. The Jesus Impulse incorporated some aspects of all the previous impulses in spiritual evolution creating an integration that is embodied in Jesus himself. Consequently, Jesus lived a human life that was a balance of meditation, dedicated action, knowledge, love, and relationships. Thus Jesus became the perfect model of manifesting Christian raja yoga,

Christian karma yoga, Christian jnana yoga, Christian bhakti yoga, and Christian relationship yoga.

The Second Coming Impulse does not replace this Jesus model but does bring this model to a new level by creating a more complete synthesis of all the previous impulses. The Jesus Impulse redefined the Elijah Impulse keeping some elements and discarding others. But the Jesus Impulse did not truly fully synthesize with the Krishna Impulse or the Buddha Impulse, except to incorporate some of the raja yoga influences. Today all four of the prior impulses are concentrated in separate parts of the world and ecumenical initiatives are focused on interacting but maintaining separate spiritual identities.

Since spiritual evolution is a growth worldwide toward oneness, I believe the Second Coming Impulse will incorporate the truest aspects of each impulse into a new synthesis and leave out those aspects that are not in alignment with oneness. An example of this synthesis may occur if Jesus manifests in some dramatic way in a Second Coming manner. The Hindu portion of the world might embrace Jesus as a "new" avatar for this age. The Buddhist part of the world may see Jesus as the predicted return of the new Buddha that is expected for this age. The Jewish part of the world may see Jesus in His return as the coming of the Messiah. There is certainly potential for this kind of universal joining to bring the fragmented pieces of the world together rallying around the Second Coming Impulse. But the barrier to this kind of joining would be the disparity of theologies. A new universal theology would be needed to facilitate this unification of the separate parts of the world.

The Second Coming Impulse is already offering this new unifying theology through the Course, which incorporates theological elements from all four previous impulses. For simplicity, the four impulses can be reduced to just two basic impulses. The Krishna Impulse and the Buddha Impulse that both came from India can be combined into one basic impulse: the *Unitive Impulse* of the East. The Elijah Impulse and the Jesus Impulse that came from Israel can be combined into one basic impulse: the *Relationship Impulse* of the West.

The Unitive Impulse is like a giant jigsaw puzzle that is being put together in time as part of the spiritual evolution of the East. This impulse represents the highest nondual aspirations of Hinduism and Buddhism, as well as Taoism. The Unitive Impulse also represents the individual seeker, who believes in nondualism, seeking oneness as an individual attainment. This impulse expresses the desire for *unitive awareness*: the direct vertical union of the seeker with God. Because of this vertical emphasis, there is less emphasis on relationships.

The Relationship Impulse can also be seen as another giant jigsaw puzzle being put together in time as part of the spiritual evolution of the West. This impulse manifests the desire for *relationship awareness*: the horizontal union of the seeker with his brothers as an expression of divine seeking. In the West, relationship awareness manifests through relationships as a means of unfolding the divine plan in the earth, as exemplified in Judaism and Christianity, as well as Islam. There is an emphasis on bringing the divine into the earth horizontally and less emphasis on the unitive awareness consisting of the vertical direct contact with the divine, such as through meditation.

The Unitive Impulse of the East and Relationship Impulse of the West each have what the other needs for completion. The Second Coming Impulse represents the coming together of the jigsaw puzzle of the East and the jigsaw puzzle of the West. The gradual stages of the Second Coming Impulse that have been happening are also like pieces of a jigsaw puzzle that reveal connecting links between the jigsaw puzzles of the East and West. Eventually the Second Coming Impulse will reveal that the two separate jigsaw puzzles of the East and West fit together and make one whole unified jigsaw puzzle. The wholeness of this one all-inclusive jigsaw puzzle will reveal a synergy in which the whole is greater than the sum of its parts. This new wholeness, which is a union of the Unitive Impulse and Relationship Impulse, will bring mankind closer to collectively coming Home, which either of these impulses could not accomplish in isolation from each other.

The Course is one example of this synthesis of the East and West as part of the Second Coming Impulse. The Course is a theological and practical expression of the Second Coming Impulse but does not describe itself as a new religion. The Course was created as a result of a holy relationship between two people, yet as an analogy, you can also think of the Course as a result of a holy relationship between two theologies, instead of between two people.

You can use your imagination to think of the Unitive Impulse of Eastern theology and the Relationship Impulse of Western theology as two separate entities coming together in the hopes of forming a "holy relationship." Because both impulses are part of the spiritual evolution of the earth and since both impulses have the same goal of coming Home, it becomes apparent that these two separate entities have common interests. Then these entities mutually decide to form a "holy relationship" in which the two different aspects of the spiritual evolution join for the common purpose of bringing holiness into the relationship and coming Home. Imagine that the current forms of this relationship are like bodies based upon false perceptions that cannot join, but they can join at the level of the mind that is based on true perceptions. This joining manifested the Course as an expression of holiness. This allowed the Christ Child to be reborn and embodied in the Course, expressing the Second Coming Impulse.

This holiness would contain the true perceptions of both halves, where minds can join, and leave out the false perceptions of both, where there can be no true joining. The East offers the strength of true perceptions related to unitive awareness—the individual direct union of the seeker with God. The West accentuates the strength of true perceptions related to relationship awareness—the individual united to his brothers in divine seeking involving relationships. Although these strengths emphasize true perception, they have some false theological perceptions. The Holy Spirit comes into the relationship to remove these false perceptions leaving only the true perceptions.

The East tends to foster the false perception that seeking the divine is mainly an individual effort rather than a collaborative venture. The West teaches false perceptions based on dualism that God and man are separate and sin and guilt are real. The Course replaces these false perceptions with true perceptions that emphasize seeking the divine through holy relationships, Christ's vision, miracles, and forgiveness. The purpose is to highlight the guiltlessness of God's Son, who is still joined with God while dreaming of this world of separation.

In addition to including the strengths of the East and West, the Holy Spirit includes many true perceptions that are a unique evolutionary step forward that expresses the Second Coming Impulse. Examples of these innovations are introducing Christ's vision and acknowledging the real world as the bridge from this world to Heaven. The central theme of the Course is forgiveness producing healing through giving up illusions of sin and guilt. There is a focus on expressing miracles as an exchange of love that benefits both the giver and receiver equally. Also, there is an emphasis on holy relationships and the acceptance of the Atonement as a realization that the separation never occurred in reality but is only as an illusion.

The Christ Child that has been reborn in the world with the advent of the Course will grow up to become the mature Christ who will bring forth an even greater manifestation of the Second Coming Impulse. These new principles of the Course will prepare seekers to be receptive to the other manifestations of the Second Coming Impulse that will be manifesting in the future. However, these new concepts may be difficult to initially understand and apply. Just reading the Text and practicing the workbook as a self-study course may not be enough. It can be very helpful to study with others and to also find a teacher to whom the Holy Spirit guides you.

C. FACING DEATH

The Course describes the Second Coming of Christ not as a one-time historical event but as the relinquishment of the ego, which means the healing of the split mind.

> The First Coming of Christ is merely another name for the creation, for Christ is the Son of God. The Second Coming of Christ means nothing more than the end of the ego's rule and the healing of the mind. I was created like you in the first, and I have called you to join me in the second.[425]

The Second Coming Impulse facilitates unifying the split mind that was caused by the separation, and the unified mind prepares you to awaken in Heaven. The separation happened in the past and was immediately corrected by the Holy Spirit by removing all of its effects. With its effects eliminated, the separation never happened in reality so never happened at all. Because the event of the separation never happened, why are you experiencing the separation now? Although the separation is gone, the separation exists for you because you are still maintaining the separation as a belief in your own mind now. The separation would cease to exist for you if you let go of your belief in the separation in the present moment.

The belief in death is the single strongest symbol that the ego uses to keep you believing in the separation. The Second Coming Impulse is intended to assist souls in accelerating the process of waking up, and this includes facing and overcoming death. Thus this section will address the issue of waking up in relation to death.

There is no way of tellin g how many souls wake up when their bodies cease to function. However, if the number of souls that are awakened while still living here is any indication, the current process of mankind waking up as a whole seems to be very inefficient, at least by outer appearances. My mother, Elizabeth, was a living saint in my life teaching me by example how to love and live a life of service. She lived to age ninety-five and by then her memory had faltered. One of the last times I visited her, I commented about Jesus, and she asked me who he was. I was very emotionally moved in telling her about the life, death, and resurrection of Jesus as she listened with childlike wonder at the story. Then I talked about Dad being in Heaven and that she would join him there one day and she liked that idea. But will she wake up and be able to accept her place as a bright shining star in the Sonship?

My heart wants to believe she will wake up, but my mind tells me that she may have to wait. You may believe there will only be two choices when you die: Heaven or hell. If that is your belief, you may feel that you or your loved one do not deserve hell. In that case, you will most likely believe that you or your loved one will go to Heaven. This can be a comforting thought, but is it true?

Addressing the issue of hell, a God of Love could not create a hell for his children where they would suffer for eternity. Imagine that you are an eternal being filled with only love, peace, and joy, and you could take a peek at this world, in which there is pain and death. You might conclude that this world *is* hell, and you would be right. But you would also see that this world is an illusion in which there is only dream pain and dream death. What is death? Previously, the ego has been defined as the thought of separation. Death is a symbol of the ego. Death, like the ego, is also the idea that separation from God is possible.

Death is the thought that you are separate from your Creator.[426]

You think that death is of the body. Yet it is but an idea, irrelevant to what is seen as physical.[427]

And death is the result of the thought we call the ego, as surely as life is the result of the Thought of God.[428]

In this world where death is considered the ultimate reality, the truth is that death has no reality at all. Death is merely a thought in your mind that you can choose to believe so it seems real to you. You believe in this thought because you made it, but only God and what God created has reality. Since God did not create death, it could not possibly have reality. Nevertheless, you can still believe in the reality of death and allow the illusion of death to appear real to you. Death is a decision you made when you decided to turn against God in the original separation. Decisions stay in effect until you change them. Since death was a decision you made to fall asleep in Heaven and to use dreams to forget your Father, you need to make a new decision. Your new decision will reverse the decision to forget God and will express your desire to fully remember God and wake up. All of spiritual growth has the purpose of helping you to become fully committed to making this new decision. Consequently, the purpose of the Course and of Miracle Yoga is to help you become dedicated to making a definitive new decision to awaken.

The Course maintains that the original separation did not happen in reality so it is a failed attempt to find an alternative place to exist outside of Heaven. But there is no place outside of Heaven that is real so you could only pretend to live in a illusory world where sin, guilt, pain, and death could appear real. You adopted the ego as your new identity in order to make your illusion seem real to you.

Heaven has remained the only place where life exists. Life itself is an extension of God and all life is in God. Subconsciously, you believe that you have attacked God who is Life, have sinned, and deserve punishment for your guilt. You also subconsciously believe this world is your prison with death as your just sentence for your crimes. The Course bluntly says that the ego wants your death as proof that you can be separated from God. Since death is the opposite of life, the ego sees death as its final victory over God who is Life. But God does not exist in duality and cannot have an opposite.[429] Since death is not real, it can only be nothing and produce no changes.

When your body and your ego and your dreams are gone, you will know that you will last forever. Perhaps you think this is accomplished through death, but nothing is accomplished through death, because death is nothing. Everything is accomplished through life, and life is of the mind and in the mind. The body neither lives nor dies, because it cannot contain you who are life. If we share the same mind, you can overcome death because I did. Death is an attempt to resolve conflict by not deciding at all. Like any other impossible solution the ego attempts, *it will not work*.

God did not make the body, because it is destructible, and therefore not of the Kingdom. The body is the symbol of what you think you are. It is clearly a separation device, and therefore does not exist. The Holy Spirit, as always, takes what you have made and translates it into a learning device.[430]

Bodies on the earth appear to have life and then stop moving and appear dead. But bodies were never alive in the first place. You are in Heaven now and dreaming of being a body that is alive. When you die, you will be dreaming of a body that you think is you, and you will think you are dying when the body dies. You are alive eternally because you share God's Life that He gave to you as the Son of God. But your life is always in Heaven where you are now, not here on the earth. No real death exists here on earth because no real life exists here.

If death is real for anything, there is no life. Death denies life. But if there is reality in life, death is denied. No compromise in this is possible. There is either a god of fear or One of Love. The world attempts a thousand compromises, and will attempt a thousand more. Not one can be acceptable to God. He did not make death because He did not make fear. Both are equally meaningless to Him.

The "reality" of death is firmly rooted in the belief that God's Son is a body. And if God created bodies, death would indeed be real. But God would not be loving. There is no point at which the contrast between the perception of the real world and that of the world of illusions becomes more sharply evident. Death is indeed the death of God, if He is Love.[431]

Death is not real, but you can believe in death because it is only a perception that you can think is true. But you cannot assert that your belief in death is the truth and at the same time assert a belief that God is the God of Life and Love. Either you believe in death or life. Either you believe in a god of death or a God of Life. You cannot believe in both simultaneously because each denies the other. Most people are in denial about issues related to death. This is quite understandable because the ego stands for death and wants you to die.

The death penalty is the ego's ultimate goal, for it fully believes you are a criminal, as deserving of death as God knows you are deserving of life. The death penalty never leaves the ego's mind, for that is what it always reserves for you in the end. Wanting to kill you as the final expression of its feeling for you, it lets you live but to await death. It will torment you while you live, but its hatred is not satisfied until you die. For your destruction is the one end toward which it works, and the only end with which it will be satisfied.[432]

Your identification with the ego makes the ego's idea of death an extremely dark corner of the psyche that you would naturally want to hide from your conscious awareness. The revealing of this dark hiding place is what happens in the depths of the dark night of the soul. These statements about the ego and death are the kind of challenging ideas that may be a stumbling block for you in regard to accepting the principles of the Course. You will naturally not want to believe that the ego is so vicious that it wants your death, preferring to believe in

the goodness of your own ego. The bad news from the Course is that
this is simply denial, but the good news from the Course is that the
ego is not you. The ego is motivated by the fear of its own extinction,
and so it insanely wants your extinction. But the ego itself is neither
good nor bad, but merely without meaning. It gains meaning only
by your belief in it. Similarly death has a negative meaning for you
because of your belief that death is the end of life. Part of the illusion
of death is to think that with death you are escaping from the problems
of life, but the following passage contradicts the idea of death as an
end and as a release:

> You see in death escape from what you made. But this you
> do not see; that you made death, and it is but illusion of an
> end. Death cannot be escape, because it is not life in which
> the problem lies. Life has no opposite, for it is God. Life and
> death seem to be opposites because you have decided death
> ends life. Forgive the world, and you will understand that
> everything that God created cannot have an end, and nothing
> He did not create is real. In this one sentence is our course
> explained.[433]

Instead of accepting death as a fact, and consequently denying
the belief in life, you can reverse this illusory thinking. The Course
says that instead of avoiding the thought of death, you can face the
thought of death as an illusory belief in your mind. This requires true
forgiveness. For the initial step in your forgiveness, you can take
responsibility for wanting to separate from God and for your choice for
death in the past. You can accept responsibility with accepting guilt
about the past because you realize now that God does not require or
want you to invest in guilt. You can also take responsibility for recent
false beliefs in the reality of death.

After you accept responsibility for your false thinking, you can
take the second step in your forgiveness. You can decide that your
choice to separate from God in the past can be your reminder that
separation is not what you want now. Because your former choice
for separation meant a belief in death, you can now choose to change
your belief and choose to believe in life.

For the third step of forgiveness, you can allow yourself to be
open to Christ's vision that allows you to discern the light from the
darkness, the real from the unreal, and the true from the false. When
you see sights of death with forgiving eyes, you can practice looking
through this illusion of form and instead affirm the light, reality, and
truth that are hidden behind form.

In the past your denial was used in service of the ego to hide your thoughts about death. Denied thoughts cannot be shared with the Holy so they cannot be corrected. But there is a positive way of using denial. You can use denial for the correction of false thoughts, rather than for hiding them. You can use denial positively by denying the false belief in death. You do not deny that the body can stop moving, but you can deny the former meaning you had attributed to death and affirm that life is eternal. The resurrection of Jesus is the proof that He chose to believe in life and not death. You can make the same choice He made, and He will help you with Christ's vision to enable you to do so. If you are tempted to give in to the desire to believe in the reality of death, you can remember that Jesus did not yield to this temptation.

> When you are tempted to yield to the desire for death, *remember that I did not die.* You will realize that this is true when you look within and *see* me. Would I have overcome death for myself alone? And would eternal life have been given me of the Father unless He had also given it to you?[434]

If death is not real, what happens when your body stops moving? Because death is not real, nothing happens. There is no real change. If your mind is at peace, it will remain at peace. If your mind is not at peace, it will still not be at peace. Your mind is not in this world; this world is in your mind. So when you supposedly leave this world, you are still possessing your mind and the world is still in your mind just as it was before.

> Mind reaches to itself. It does not go out. Within itself it has no limits, and there is nothing outside it. It encompasses you entirely; you within it and it within you. There is nothing else, anywhere or ever.[435]

> The world is not left by death but by truth, and truth can be known by all those for whom the Kingdom was created, and for whom it waits.[436]

The world is an illusion so leaving the world can be achieved only by finding the truth beyond illusions. But believing in death, another illusion, cannot release you from the illusion of the world. Yet facing the passing of body awareness called death can be an opportunity to wake up? However, this depends on your frame of mind at the time of transition. If your mind is focused mostly on true perceptions of the real world and if you decided with all your heart that Heaven is the only thing you want, you certainly can wake up by divine grace. But unfortunately, if you die with your mind being a fluctuating mixture of false and true perceptions, as most minds are, you will probably not fully awaken. If you die thinking you are an ego, you will want to be an ego again. You will be afraid of accepting your true nature of pure light and love. You would react traumatically to Heaven because of the great contrast between the nightmares of this world from which you apparently have come and the bliss of Heaven. Since you would be afraid of Heaven, you would seek something else.

Heaven is typically interpreted to mean complete union with God, but Jesus spoke in the Bible of "many mansions" in the afterlife. There is speculation that there are other levels of existence between Heaven and earthly existence. But these levels in between are illusory, just as earthly existence is illusory. Only your full awakening will satisfy your yearning for truly coming Home. For this reason, I believe souls keep coming back to incarnate in new bodies over many lifetimes to learn the lessons needed to come Home.

The Course acknowledges some value in the idea of reincarnation. The idea of reincarnation can be helpful if it reminds you that you are eternal. Yet the Course does not want the teaching of reincarnation to be included as part of its curriculum because the idea of reincarnation is not helpful. It can lend itself to misuse. Possibly you can become egotistical about your past incarnations. You may invest in the idea of your past incarnations being real and forget your current incarnation is unreal, and therefore every former incarnation was also an illusion. Investing in past incarnations may divert you from transcending your current incarnation in the present moment.[437]

Although death of the body is not a change and leaves the mind as it was before death, this can be an opportunity to truly enter Heaven since the body is a limitation on who you really are. You can respond to losing your physical body in either one of two ways after the body stops moving. The first way is to remain attached to the idea that you are an ego and that you therefore need a body. Out of fear that you need a body to exist so you will be attracted to some form of bodily experience. This means you will find the illusion of a body on another level between Heaven and earth or means you will again be attracted to incarnating in a physical body on earth.

The second way of responding to losing your physical body is to realize that you are not an ego, and you do not need a body to exist. You will probably not be able to have this realization in the afterlife unless you have first lived a life on earth in which you were already investing in the idea that you are not an ego and you are not a body. Also, you would probably have had to previously cleared out most of the hidden false perceptions in your conscious mind and subconscious mind. In your life on earth, it is not enough to resist false perceptions and invest in true perceptions as a mental discipline only. In addition, your true perceptions need to be manifested in the way you live your life as an expression of love. It is only by embodying true perceptions as an expression of love and true forgiveness that you will be able to identify with love being your own true nature.

The physical body provides the illusion that your communication is limited. When you give up the body at death, this illusion of limited communication can also be given up. If you chose to deny the belief in death as an end, you can see it as a beginning. Death cannot be an end of you, but it can possibly be an end of the ego if you allow it to be such. Death can be a beginning in the sense of being your birthday into Heaven, which is your birthday into full communication with God and the Sonship. This is an opportunity to release concrete ideas about yourself and fully accept yourself as an abstract Thought in the Christ Mind. This can be your moment of truth in a real sense in which you accept your true nature. All your expressions of love and in particular your holy instants in your earthly life are a preparation for this great challenge. In this moment of truth, you can look at the ego and in your mind laugh at the thought that such a meaningless idea could have attracted your attention. In your mental laughter, the ego will dissolve into nothingness, while the whole Sonship will laugh with you in celebration of your coming Home.

I believe that in this moment of truth, you will have the opportunity to see the entire face of Christ as a blazing circle of light expanding infinitely. As mentioned in Chapter 6, "*The face of Christ* has to be seen before the memory of God can return."[438] This is the opportunity to see the perfect symbol of Christ that can best remind you of your own true nature in God. Nevertheless, you will have to decide that you *want* this experience of overpowering light and that you *deserve* it. Without having prepared yourself to see this light and fully wake up in the divine grace of this light, you will reject that face of Christ and not fully enter everlasting Heaven. Instead, you will be attracted to one of the other "many mansions" offered in the afterlife. This afterlife experience may be very wonderful for a time, but the end result will be your eventual reincarnation in order to grow spiritually in preparation for your eventual entrance into your eternal home of Heaven. After each lifetime of failing to embrace the face of Christ, you will be reincarnated and come back again and again to this "holy place of resurrection." Eventually, you will decide to embrace the face of Christ, and you will experience redemption when you awaken to your true Self as the Christ in Heaven. "Here is the holy place of resurrection, to which we come again; to which we will return until redemption is accomplished and received."[439]

D. SPECULATION ON THE SECOND COMING

In my opinion, the Second Coming Impulse will be expressed as a series of events, similar to the series of events that occurred in the first four divine impulses. But each of the four former impulses had dramatic events that stand out as focal points for the whole impulse. Consequently, I do believe there will be dramatic events in the Second Coming Impulse. There is a lot of speculation in Christianity about what might happen in the "Second Coming," portrayed in the Bible as a dramatic event.

What will specifically happen in this Second Coming? I do not know, but I have some general ideas about what will happen during this new era of awakening. The Second Coming Impulse has already ushered in an era of increased communication. The dramatic Second Coming events will reveal in a startling way the combined messages of the Unitive Impulse and the Relationship Impulse. Regarding the Unitive Impulse, the message that will be communicated is that at this time there is a great opportunity for awakening to direct union with God and with the Sonship. Regarding the Relationship Impulse, the message that will be communicated is that joining with others in holy relationships to learn how to love is an effective way to prepare to receive the gift of awakening to divine union.

An increased number of individuals will believe in the possibility of transformation, and hopefully an unprecedented spiritual conversion will occur all over the world. This new era of awakening will need a theological foundation that will require a reinterpretation of traditional Christianity. The Course will help with this new Christian theology that will facilitate spiritual transformation. The exclusive aspects of different Christian dogmas will have to give way to a more universal approach to spirituality, which can be found in the Course.

Holy relationships will become increasingly recognized as the daily life training ground for Heaven. Holy relationships of all kinds will be important. However, the teacher and student holy relationship will gain greater significance in this new era. Learning the principles in the Course that teach how to love will prepare souls for their spiritual awakening. Miracles, the holy instant, forgiveness, and Christ's vision will be better understood and more commonly practiced as various means of expressing love.

The Course encourages you to make a decision that you want to go to Heaven and to realize that Heaven is all you really want.[440] But a mind that holds on to false perceptions will be afraid of Heaven. Consequently, there is the necessity to let go of false perceptions and to invest in true perceptions. By replacing false perceptions with true perceptions, you are replacing the nightmares of this world with the happy dreams of the real world. Focusing on the true perceptions of the real world is a preparation for making the transition beyond all perceptions to the total awareness of knowledge of Heaven. When the mind is filled with the true perceptions of love, it becomes so much like the love of Heaven that the transfer from true perceptions to knowledge becomes possible. At this point, divine intervention can take place and through God's grace produce true awakening to the knowledge of Heaven.

> Every child of God is one in Christ, for his being is in Christ as Christ's is in God. Christ's Love for you is His Love for His Father, which He knows because He knows His Father's Love for Him. When the Holy Spirit has at last led you to Christ at the altar to His Father, perception fuses into knowledge because perception has become so holy that its transfer to holiness is merely its natural extension. Love transfers to love without any interference, for the two are one.[441]

The process of changing from false perceptions to true perceptions to prepare for Heaven seems like only an interesting theory to some. But in the new era, this theory will become widely accepted as a very practical means of preparing for Heaven. The motivation for learning to love and coming Home will increase for many souls, who had previously not been interested in spiritual growth.

Much of this Second Coming vision has been explained in Course terms, yet the Course is definitely not for everyone now and will not be for everyone in this new era either. The Course is primarily a jnana yoga expression that will mostly appeal to the intellectual side of human nature that needs rational explanations of divine realities. This new era will most likely bring forth new ways of awakening for souls who are not intellectually inclined. Other inspired writings will emerge, and these will become scriptures for the new era that will appeal to those who are heart-centered, contemplative, or practically minded, as well as to intellectually oriented souls.

Those who are not drawn to the Course during this new era may still be attracted to Christian yoga. Christian yoga holds the ideal of balancing some jnana yoga of the intellect, with the meditation of raja yoga, the dedicated action of karma yoga, the love of bhakti yoga, and the loving relationships of relationship yoga. This balance will still be relevant in the new era so Christian yoga will flourish during this time. But the specific format of these kinds of Christian yoga, as described in this manual, will probably change with the new times bringing new expressions of how to reflect the divine. Yet the current goal in Christian yoga of union with your brothers in Christ and with God through the Holy Spirit will remain the same.

As an outgrowth of the Second Coming events, a new model for society will emerge in the future in which traditional Christianity will no longer be the model that will bring spirituality into every aspect of daily life. The goal of spiritual awakening will not be associated with becoming an extraordinary spiritual athlete. Ordinary people will learn how to increasingly manifest love and have faith in God, and they will become open to awakening and will be transformed. The process of spiritual awakening will not be a solitary task. Rather, awakening will be a matter of seekers helping each other to wake up.

This is my idealized vision of the future, but it is only my best guess. You probably have your own ideas about how the Second Coming will manifest, and your guess is as good as mine. It is not important to be able to figure out how the future will play out on a form level. The truth is that no one can know exactly how God's Plan will unfold and be accomplished. Indulging in speculation about the future salvation of mankind is not harmful in itself as long as there is no attempt to substitute a speculative plan for God's Plan. Therefore, there needs to be a willingness to quickly set aside speculative ideas about the future and instead accept whatever is revealed in the present moment about God's Plan. You can be sure that God's Will cannot fail to be fulfilled, and you will certainly be wonderfully surprised beyond anything you could possibly imagine.

God has a Plan for the salvation of mankind as a whole, but His Plan also includes your individual salvation. One potential danger of focusing on speculation regarding the salvation of mankind is that you may think that your own individual salvation must automatically wait for some future event to occur. This would be a contradiction of the Course's perspective that emphasizes the idea that your salvation is awaiting only your desire to accept it in the present moment. If you seek salvation in the past or in the future because doing so would ensure that salvation would never actually be found. Salvation can only be found *now*, and thus your primary focus needs to be on the present moment. You bring yourself one step closer to salvation every time you enter into the holy instant in which you let go of the past and future. Your experience of the holy instant brings you into direct communication with the Sonship in Christ, with the Father, and with the Holy Spirit where salvation can truly be found. The truth is that your life has never actually been separated from its divine Source. Consequently, your divine life is here and now, awaiting only your recognition of its presence.

CHAPTER 12

~ ○ ~

UNIFYING THE MIND

A. THE ONE DIMENSION

Because God can be experienced as the Void, a divine darkness, emptiness, and nothingness, and He can also be experienced as divine Light, this raises theological questions concerning God's true nature. It is very healthy, normal, and necessary to have theological ideas about God, even though God defies all definitions. I have my own ideas about how God can paradoxically be experienced as both the Void of darkness and a divine Light. These ideas are expressed in my theory of dimensions, as follows:

Our three-dimensional world appears to be larger than the second dimension that has only the dimensions of length and width and no depth, so it appears that the three-dimensional world must be larger than the two-dimensional world. Then a logical conclusion is that the One-dimensional world must be the smallest dimension of all, probably an infinitely small dot.

This may be logical, but I believe it is untrue. However, it is true that the One-dimensional world may interface with the second and third dimensions through the connecting point of an infinitely small dot. Even though the One-dimensional world may intercede and manifest in the second and third dimensions in the appearance of a dot, this does not mean that the One-dimensional world itself *is* a dot.

The One-dimensional world has no length, no width, and no depth. It is not an infinitely small dot because any dot would need to have some size, at least some length and width. Applying "size concepts" to the One-dimensional world is not reasonable because size has no real meaning in this *dimensionless dimension*. The One-dimensional world transcends and thus includes and encompasses all other dimensions because it is beyond any ideas of size, form, time, or space. Being a world that has no limitations, the One-dimensional world is an abstract world of pure universal awareness only.

The One-dimensional world is a world in which the Oneness of God encompasses everything we call "Heaven." This One-dimensional world is God Himself, Who is the whole of the dimension. God is usually associated with Light and rightly so since God *is* Light. This is not a light that must obey physical laws because it is a supernatural Light beyond the physical world. This One Dimension of Light is the unmanifested ground of Being from which all other dimensions and life forms have manifested.

The unmanifested Being of God, as the First Cause, is sometimes called the "Void." The Void is described as a divine nothingness and divine darkness. How can this Void of nothingness and darkness be reconciled with the Light of God? The One Dimension of Light is a dimension of nothingness only in the sense that it contains "no thing" in particular. Yet it is more than everything, including and transcending all things and all kinds of consciousness. But the One Dimension is not a divine darkness though it may appear to be.

Within the reality of the One dimension, there is only the Light of God, but outside this awareness, the One Dimension can appear as being the Void. The Void of darkness does not describe the reality of God. The Void is a valid way of describing only how God appears to perceptual awareness from the typical viewpoint of the ego. In the dark night of the soul, God is perceived as the Void of darkness. If you are not aware of God as divine light, you will experience God as divine darkness. You will have to rely on finding God in the darkness of faith. However, because the Void is a perception of the ego, the Void itself is an illusion. The Void is a picture of God seen from not knowing who *you* are. If you are identified with the darkness, God will appear as a divine darkness. However, if you become identified with the light that you are, you will first picture God perceptually as light and eventually experience God increasingly as His Light in which you exist. The unmanifested Being of God the Father is the Light that is the basis of all manifested existence. Even though all multiplicity comes from this One dimension, this dimension remains unchanged and undivided in itself. It is all One, undivided and whole. It is the One that is the source of all oneness.

This idea of the One Dimension is supported by a strange source: science. Science always seeks to discover the true nature of matter. At first it was discovered that the structure of matter consists of energy and empty space, with the assumption that empty space is nothing. But the most recent discoveries in quantum physics have revealed that empty space is not truly empty. Dr. Edgar Mitchell, the scientist and astronaut turned metaphysical thinker, explains,

> But science has finally probed deeply enough into the structure of matter to discover only two things: empty space and energy.

And even the empty space is now believed to possess an energy —vacuum energy, or what is also referred to as the zero-point field. The zero-point field is defined as the field of quantum fluctuations that exists at the temperature of absolute zero. More recently, however, it has been interpreted as that field of energy that underlies all matter. This is the basic, infinite unstructured quantum potential from which the Big Bang arose. Everything we know (and everything we don't) arose from the zero-point field of energy.[442]

Yet science now believes the vacuum of empty space is not nothing after all, but rather an all-pervasive energy field that science would call the quantum potential of matter. This energy field is the invisible ground-state of all forms of matter—the blank canvas upon which all of matter has been painted. This vacuum energy of empty space appears to be nothingness. But it contains all things, all matter, within itself as its source. Vacuum energy sounds very much like the Void that appears to be nothingness but is the ground of all that exists. Dr. Mitchell says matter was not created out of nothing ("ex nihilo"):

> Zero-point energy is also interpreted as an infinite sea of unstructured energy potential from which the universe arose, a sea that pervades all space in the universe (and probably outside as well). In this sense the universe did not arise ex nihilo but rather arose, was created, or "intended" from this underlying quantum potential.[443]

If it is true that this energy field is the source of the Big Bang, the question arises, "Can this zero-point field not only be the source of all matter, but also the source of all life—of all existence?" Dr. Mitchell believes that there is a connection between this underlying energy field that is the source of matter and the highest state of spiritual experience. In yoga philosophy, the highest state is *nirvikalpa samadhi*, which is a state of being in awareness of Awareness Itself. Dr. Mitchell describes this correlation between the awareness of Awareness and the energy from which all matter originates, as follows:

> If we postulate that the experience of nirvikalpa samadhi state is the experience of resonance with the ground-state of all matter, this would tie the Great Chain of Being to its roots in the quantum potential of matter. The modern term for this energy field is called *zero-point energy* or *vacuum energy*. Vacuum energy is the presumed energy field that is in continuous dynamic exchange with matter that sustains the form and existence of matter at the quantum level. To be aware of the zero-point is tantamount to being aware only of awareness itself.[444]

From this scientific viewpoint, the following is what Dr. Mitchell says about this vacuum energy in relation to dimensions:

> The zero-point field approach is particularly more appealing because variables such as time, mass, spatial dimensions, velocity, and momentum apparently have no meaning there.[445]

Dr. Mitchell specifically calls the zero-point field "a zero-dimension realm"[446] that has "no spatial dimensionality."[447] Time, space, matter, velocity, and momentum that have no meaning in the zero-point field. These same variables also have no meaning in the One-dimensional world that is whole and indivisible with no parts. In my opinion, what Dr. Mitchell calls the "zero-dimension realm" where the vacuum energy exists is actually the One-dimensional world that possess no spatial dimensions and is therefore devoid of all things.

The One-dimensional world of Light is more than just the Home of the Father, it is the Home of God's Son. God created His Son, the Christ, as an extension of Himself. God as the Light extended Light into His Son making His Son part of Himself. Christ, perfectly one with the Father, exists infinitely in the limitless One-dimensional world. The children of God are all part of the one Christ in the Sonship and are perfectly one in the wholeness of the One Dimension.

The children of God who initiated the Fall lost their awareness of Heaven, which the Course maintains is the only Reality. Another name for Heaven is the One Dimension that is the only Reality. All other dimensions are illusions. The fallen children of God could not leave the only true Reality, but they did fall asleep and dreamed of illusions they could mistakenly believe were their reality. The sleeping children of God identified with their illusion of the third dimension. As God's Answer to the Fall, the Holy Spirit was created by the Father. God the Father could only function as Himself in the One Dimension of Heaven. But the Holy Spirit was created by God to function both in the One Dimension and in the second dimension. Both the third dimension and the second dimension are illusions. Yet Holy Spirit could encourage the sleeping Sons of God to use the illusion of the second dimension as a stepping stone to release the illusion of the third dimension and awaken again to the One Dimension.

My theory is that the Holy Spirit, as He was created by God, was extended from the first dimension into the second dimension as an infinitely small dot of light. From that dot, the Holy Spirit extended His Light into a perfect two-dimensional circle of light. That perfect circle of light is expanding infinitely. Yet the expanding circle retains its center in the indivisible point of light from which it originated and from which it continues to originate in Holy Spirit in union with God the Father. This circle of light with a dot of light in the center is the "vision of the Son of God" in union with the Father.

B. THE REAL WORLD IS THE SECOND DIMENSION

This circle of light is not the same light that is experienced in the three-dimensional world of the physical universe. It is also not the supernatural Light of the One Dimension. This expanding light is the second dimension and is a perfect *reflection* of the Light of Heaven that permeates the One-dimensional world. This second-dimensional world is what the Course calls the "real world" that has many levels of consciousness. The very lowest level of the real world can be glimpsed through Christ's vision by seeing outlines of light around people or objects. The deepest level of the real world is the *face of Christ* that is the best reflection of Heaven.

This face of Christ is not actually Christ Himself in Heaven, but it is the vision of the Son of God. It is the beacon for coming Home. This is the light that can be perceived by the spiritual seeker as the doorway to Heaven. This circle of light has length and width but not the same thickness of forms in the third dimension. The second dimension is often thought of as a flat plane that intersects the third dimension of the universe. Belief in this flat plane gives the impression that the second dimension is smaller than the third dimension and encompassed by the third dimension. This is a mistaken perception seemingly justified by applying three-dimensional thinking to another dimension. The One Dimension encompasses all other dimensions, including the second dimension. In turn, the second dimension encompasses the entire third dimension.

The second dimension is the link between the One Dimension and third dimension. For the second dimension to be this link, it possesses qualities of both the first dimension and the third dimension. The second dimension has the qualities of length and width that the third dimension has. All the forms of the three-dimensional world have corresponding two-dimensional forms in the second dimension. Unlike the solid objects of this world, these corresponding two-dimensional "objects" are made of the light of the real world and appear with Christ's vision to be flat with only length and width.

Is it possible for there to be some kind of thickness and depth, in the second dimension? It could be argued there is no thickness, no depth, in the second dimension. However, I have an alternative theory of how thickness does exist in the second dimension: I believe the forms of the second dimension that have length and width also have a thickness that is unlike the finite thickness of three-dimensional objects. This thickness of the second dimension is an *infinite thickness*. If my theory is correct, every two-dimensional object in the second dimension has an infinite thickness that gives the second dimension an aspect of the infinite nature of the One Dimension. It is this infinite thickness of the second dimension that allows this dimension to encompass the third dimension that is more limited in nature. Thus the second dimension is actually a *hybrid dimension,* having the infinite nature of the first dimension and having two of the three finite dimensions of the third dimension.

Chapter 6 explains the "real world" may be experienced by you by being open to Christ's vision. The forms of this three-dimensional world will at first appear to have a glow of light around them indicating an openness to the very lowest level of awareness of the real world in the second dimension. Going to a deeper level of awareness requires the ability to let go of using the physical eyes to perceive three-dimensional forms. This requires your willingness to allow the Holy Spirit to affect your mind so you can perceive what the physical eyes alone cannot perceive. Your invitation to the Holy Spirit allows Christ's vision to manifest, which bringing the awareness to perceive the light of the real world as a reflection of the light of Heaven.

After seeing the edges of light around objects, entire objects can be perceived through Christ's vision as being entirely filled with light. The three-dimensional forms begin to be perceived as flattening out and appearing as two-dimensional forms, which supports the premise that the real world is actually the second dimension. By continued reliance on Christ's vision, your whole panorama of vision can be perceived as a "veil" of light, consisting of two-dimensional forms shimmering with light. These flat forms are seen as two-dimensional shapes outlined or filled with shades of light, some brighter than others. But behind this flat veil of light, there is a much deeper level of the real world that is not easily accessed. One way of finding this deeper level of the real world is to use your Christ's vision to look on your brother. Only this thin veil separates you from seeing the Christ in your brother. Through Christ's vision, you can perhaps allow the veil of light to be lifted to reveal the deepest level of the real world, which is the face of Christ.

> *You* are the means for God; not separate, nor with a life apart from His. His Life is manifested in you who are His Son. Each aspect of Himself is framed in holiness and perfect purity, in love celestial and so complete it wishes only that it may release all that it looks upon unto itself. Its radiance shines through each body that it looks upon, and brushes all its darkness into light merely by looking past it *to* the light. The veil is lifted through its gentleness, and nothing hides the face of Christ from its beholders. You and your brother stand before Him now, to let Him draw aside the veil that seems to keep you separate and apart.[448]

Lifting the veil to see the Christ in your brother lets you recognize your own Christ nature. Yoga has its own unique method for revealing the face of Christ. This method is a yoga meditation that focuses on the experience of what is called the *bindu*, an infinitely small dot of light. It is interesting to note that the literal translation of the Sanskrit word "bindu" is not only "dot" but also "zero," calling to mind the previously mentioned scientific term "zero-point energy." This yoga technique of focusing on the bindu involves looking at a *mandala* during meditation. The mandala is always characterized by its circular shape with the dot of the bindu in the middle, symbolizing undifferentiated consciousness. The mandala may include divine images or geometric shapes. It may be symmetrical all the way around. One kind of mandala a *yantra*, which is symmetrical on the right and left sides so it could be folded in half along its central vertical axis. This vertical axis is symbolic of the cerebral-sacral axis of the body along which the kundalini rises in the *susumna*, central spiritual channel associated with the spinal column. The yantra contains triangles placed symmetrically along the vertical axis symbolizing the balance between the male and female principles. The meditative goal is the union of the male and female energies to encourage inner oneness and the rising of the kundalini.

The mandala as a whole always symbolizes both the cosmos and the individual seeker. Through visualizing the mandala, the meditator moves his awareness from the outer circle inwardly to deeper levels of consciousness. It may take years of practicing mandala meditation to produce a progressive refinement of consciousness. The seeker may be able to gradually bring the awareness to a state of oneness with the dot in the center of the mandala. The dot in the center of the circle of the mandala is only a physical symbol of the bindu, which is in reality a nonphysical, indivisible point of light that is the undifferentiated oneness of consciousness. The goal is to become one with the undifferentiated consciousness that is the reality of the bindu. In yoga philosophy, when the meditator experiences the true nature of the bindu, this indivisible point of light becomes an infinitely expanding circle while paradoxically retaining its central point of light.[449] This is the spiritual illumination of awakening to one's true Self in God.

Mandala meditation is just one of many ways of progressing toward awakening the inner light. Similar to the experience of the bindu of light expanding to reveal an infinite light, St. Symeon the New Theologian describes his own experience of a tiny light expanding to become a disc of light of immeasurable size, as follows:

> What is this great marvel that I consider in my interior and which I do not understand, and which remains hidden to me? As a star indeed, I see it which rises in the distance, then it becomes like a large sun which has not, in it greatness, either measure or weight or limit; its ray rises small and then makes itself be seen

as a flame in the center of my heart and of my bowels, turning
without stopping and illuminating all the interior of my entrails
and rendering them light.[450]

Here in this description a tiny light is seen as a star in the distance,
which would correspond to the tiny bindu of light. Just as the bindu of
mandala meditation expands into an infinite circle of light, this tiny
star becomes like a sun of limitless size. St. Symeon specifically says it
has no "weight," which would indicate a disc of light like a circle rather
than a ball of light. However, this vision by St. Symeon is not merely
an observation of something apart from himself. Rather the light that
he sees becomes a flame in the center of himself transforming him into
light. Yet St. Symeon's transformation is not a one-time experience of
expanding light, but rather an ongoing encounter with an expanding
and contracting light that alternates back and forth from a point of
light to an immense sun of light. St. Symeon's describes this:

> At first, I may be aware of certain contrasts: between phases of
> expansion and contraction of the light, between descent of the fire
> from above and ascent of the flame within, between its presence
> in my head and its descent into my heart. As I rise and descend
> along the path of light within, I may find that at times the light
> from what is like a solar disc, contracts to a point like a star,
> and then expands once again.[451]

St. Symeon's experience of alternating expanding and contracting
light culminates in a stabilization and interiorization of the light. This
interiorization produces St. Symeon's extraordinary condition of living
in time while being constantly aware of the eternal divine light as a
preliminary experience of Heaven, described this way:

> As I advance, the alternating phases and contrasting moments
> which take me out of myself will gradually cease, and I will begin
> to find my center. The light which first came to focus in my head
> will then be seen in my heart. The expansion of the inner sun
> will become a perfect interiorization.....the flaming light will fill
> me wholly and will become the constant reality of my existence,
> illuminating my every thought and action.
> Likewise the apparent conflict between grace and effort will
> disappear; the inner light will be a second nature. The various
> centers of consciousness in the body [the navel, the heart, the
> head] and all its members will become equally luminous; having
> seen the light of God in part, I now see it in the whole.[452]

In addition to the correlation between the bindu of light becoming an infinite circle of light and the small star of St. Symeon becoming a blazing sun disc, there is a similar correlation in the Course. This Course version of a small light becoming a greater light is identified by the terms tiny "spark" and "Great Rays." In the same way that focusing on the bindu of the mandala and on the star of St. Symeon lead to a greater light, the Course advocates turning the awareness toward the tiny spark that will lead to the awareness of the Great Rays.

> The power of one mind can shine into another, because all the lamps of God were lit by the same spark. It is everywhere and it is eternal.
>
> In many only the spark remains, for the Great Rays are obscured. Yet God has kept the spark alive so that the Rays can never be completely forgotten. If you but see the little spark you will learn of the greater light, for the Rays are there unseen. Perceiving the spark will heal, but knowing the light will create. Yet in the returning the little light must be acknowledged first, for the separation was a descent from magnitude to littleness. But the spark is still as pure as the great light, because it is the remaining call of creation. Put all your faith in it, and God Himself will answer you.[453]

The above quotation indicates that the spark is everywhere. It is everywhere because it is in the One dimension, which transcends space and time. This indivisible point of light is the contact point between the One Dimension and the other two dimensions—the second and third dimensions. Though only an infinitely small point, this point transcends all other dimensions. In the Hindu tradition, Gopi Krishna experienced the rising of the kundalini. He described his experienced of "a luminous circle around the head, which was now constant in me, and an extended consciousness."[454] This ever-present radiant circle of light was constantly expanding and then contracting, bringing a fluctuating level of higher consciousness. With his expanded consciousness, he experienced a single point of awareness as ironically the source of his experience of the expansiveness of the universe, as follows:

> My body, the chair I was sitting on, the table in front of me, the room enclosed by walls, the lawn outside and the space beyond including the earth and sky appeared to be most amazingly mere phantoms in this real, interpenetrating and all-pervasive ocean of existence which, to explain the most incredible part of it as best I can, seemed to be simultaneously unbounded, stretching out immeasurably in all directions, and yet no bigger than an infinitely small point. From this marvelous point the entire existence, of

which my body and its surroundings were a part, poured out like radiation, as if a reflection as vast as my conception of the cosmos were thrown out upon infinity by a projector no bigger than a pinpoint, the entire intensely active and gigantic world picture dependent on the beams issuing from it. The shoreless ocean of consciousness in which I was now immersed appeared infinitely large and infinitely small at the same time, large when considered in relation to the world picture floating in it and small when considered in itself, measureless, without form or size, nothing and yet everything.[455]

Since this point of awareness or spark of light is everywhere, seeking this spark cannot be limited to looking within one spot within the body. However, there are certain parts of the body that facilitate opening to higher consciousness. Zen Buddhists focus on the navel area. Some Hindu seekers focus on the forehead area or the top of the head. Christian monks of Mt. Athos in Greece have for centuries practiced the Jesus Prayer of the Heart and focused on the location of the physical heart. St. Symeon emphasized awareness of the light in various parts of the body, most noticeably in the head and the heart. The method recommended in this book is Christian Yoga Meditation, which includes focusing on several focusing areas in sequence: the navel area, the heart area, the forehead area, and then the top of the head.

Of these focusing areas, the most important is the heart area since focusing here helps especially to awaken the awareness of both inner love and inner light. Even though the spark is not limited to any one part of the body, I believe it is easiest to contact this spark by focusing on what may be called the "flame in the heart." The seeker can focus on a flame of light in the location of the physical heart and also focus an expanding light in the heart center, in the center of the chest, in order to contact the divine spark. The Course itself does not recommend focusing on a particular part of the body but does recommend looking within to find the light of the spark to help you awaken.

Turn toward the light, for the little spark in you is a part of a Light so great that it can sweep you out of all darkness forever. For your Father *is* your Creator and you *are* like Him.[456]

Finding the spark is important because it represents who you really are since you are "the Son of God, who was created *of* light and *in* light."[457] Clearly the little spark in you is crucial to the awakening of your true nature. You are a Thought in the Mind of God, and God has created you by extending His Great Light to you. You have the power to diminish your awareness of the light that you are, but you cannot extinguish the tiny spark of light that is eternally yours. You have power at any time to allow the little spark to expand into the Great Light. Just as God created you by the extension of His Light into you, you can extend your light to remove darkness. Only your ego condition blocks your awareness, however you can allow the little spark to bring light into the darkness of your ego condition, as follows:

> You make by projection, but God creates by extension. The cornerstone of God's creation is you, for His thought system is light. Remember the Rays that are there unseen. The more you approach the center of His thought system, the clearer the light becomes. The closer you come to the ego's thought system, the darker and more obscure becomes the way. Yet even the little spark in your mind is enough to lighten it. Bring this light fearlessly with you, and bravely hold it up to the foundation of the ego's thought system. Be willing to judge it with perfect honesty. Open the dark cornerstone of terror on which it rests, and bring it out into the light. There you will see that it rested on meaninglessness, and that everything of which you have been afraid was based on nothing.[458]

The spark is little because it is only a point of indivisible light in the One Dimension where size has no meaning thus the spark cannot be measured by three-dimensional standards. The spark may appear little, but it contains *within it* the immenseness of the infinite Great Rays. At first, the contact point of the little spark can be found within the body, and as the light expands, you can still be aware of the body. However, when your awareness of the light expands, the awareness of the body changes so the body is seen differently, explained as follows:

> For a time the body is still seen, but not exclusively, as it is seen here. The little spark that holds the Great Rays within it is also visible, and this spark cannot be limited long to littleness.[459]

What happens to the awareness of the body when the littleness of the spark is expanded into the unlimited awareness of the Great Rays? Egos rely on body awareness and form special relationships based on body awareness. Overcoming body awareness and overcoming special relationships based on body awareness is necessary in order to make the transition from the three-dimensional world to the One-dimensional divine world. Most people see only three-dimensional physical objects because that is the world that is valued. The Great Rays can help you to value the world beyond physical form. The revealing of the vision of the Great Rays enables you to let go of body awareness:

The Great Rays would establish the total lack of value of the special relationship, if they are seen. For in seeing them the body would disappear, because its value would be lost. And so your whole investment in seeing it would be withdrawn from it.[460]

In order to understand how the Great Rays assist in making the transition from three-dimensional awareness to other dimensions, it is helpful to understand how the Holy Spirit fits into the dimensions. The Holy Spirit is the communication link of Light and Love between God and the sleeping parts of the Sonship. The Holy Spirit's function is to awaken the children of God. In order to fulfill His function, the Holy Spirit has the unique quality of being at home in both the first and the second dimensions. The Holy Spirit is not "in" the third dimension, but He is very actively involved with helping the sleeping Sons of God to awaken by guiding them through the third dimension.

The specific purpose of the Holy Spirit is to lead you from the third dimension to the One Dimension of Heaven. The way Home is through the second dimension, which is the real world. The One dimension of Heaven transcends all perception, but the second dimension is within perceptual awareness. The Holy Spirit wants you to use perceptions to lead you beyond perceptions to the *knowledge* of Heaven. The Holy Spirit is guiding you to perceive the face of Christ, which is the vision of the Son of God as the circle of light expanding infinitely. First this vision is perceived at a distance with you apart from the vision of what you see. But then by seeing this vision from a distance, you can be drawn into the center of the circle that is the doorway to Heaven. Being drawn into the center of the circle, you can decide to embrace the Light and awaken in Heaven to your rightful place in the Sonship.

The Course does not really address the issue of dimensions. Thus the idea that the One-dimensional world is Heaven and the real world is the second dimension can only be a theory and not a stated Course principle. Nevertheless, the Course does talk repeatedly about a specific two-dimensional form: the circle. In the Course, this repeated emphasis on the circle is related to many lofty ideas. I believe these repeated references to the circle indirectly refer to the second dimension. After all, if there is a two-dimensional world, it is reasonable to assume that the circle would be the most perfect expression of that world. It should not then be surprising for the Course to describe the real world as being a place beyond three-dimensional form and specifically refer to the real world as a "circle." "This world of light, this circle of brightness is the real world, where guilt meets with forgiveness."[461]

The Course describes the vision of the Son of God as the vision of a circle of light—"a great and shining circle,"[462] which is expanding infinitely. This two-dimensional description of the vision of the Son of God corresponds exactly to the yoga description of inner realization in which the bindu, the infinitely small point of light, suddenly enlarges into a vision of a circumference of light expanding without limit. The transformation of a small light into a greater light is also similar to St. Symeon's experience of a tiny star that becomes an immense shining solar disc. Yoga mandala meditation that focuses on the bindu in order to awaken the vision of the infinitely expanding circle of light is one means of facilitating an inner encounter with the divine light. Likewise, St. Symeon's experience with the contracting and expanding light is a description of an inner encounter with the divine light. In each of these examples, divine light is uncovered only after deep and focused inward seeking. Nevertheless, it would be a mistake to think that access to the divine light can be found only by an inner process.

The Course way of finding divine light includes an emphasis on looking within but is not limited to only an inner approach. The Course recommends both looking within and looking outside. It is important to seek the help of the Holy Spirit, and specifically the help of Jesus in this inner and outer journey. In the Course, Jesus says:

> And you will see me as you look within, and we will look upon the real world together. Through the eyes of Christ, only the real world exists and only the real world can be seen. As you decide so will you see. And all that you see but witnesses to your decision.
>
> When you look within and see me, it will be because you have decided to manifest truth. And as you manifest it you will see it both within and without. And you will see it without *because* you saw it first within. Everything you behold without is a judgment of what you beheld within.[463]

The Course advocates looking within first and then looking outside. Looking within and allowing Jesus and/or the Holy Spirit to guide you is important as the first step because this decision to seek this guidance will affect your ability to see outwardly. What you see outwardly will be a reflection of your guidance, which is referred to as a "witness" to the guidance you have sought within, expressed as follows:

> I said before that what you project or extend is up to you, but you must do one or the other, for that is a law of the mind, and you must look in before you look out. As you look in, you choose the guide for seeing. And then you look out and behold his witnesses.[464]

The Course places an equal emphasis on first looking within and then looking outside to see the witnesses to what has been sought within. Ideally, you can see the light within and then see the light outwardly, but the Course says you must see the light within before you can see it outwardly. The previous quotations say you need to seek the truth and inner guidance, and then what you see outside will be witnesses to what you have chosen. Even if you are not able to perceive the divine light of your own true nature when you look within, you still have the ability to extend light from your mind to other minds. It is the nature of the mind to either project, which involves wrong perception, or to extend, which involves right perception. When you replace mental projection with the extension of light, you discover the light must be in you. You cannot give light unless there is light in you to begin with. When you give light to the mind of your brother, your brother returns the light to you. This light that returns to you from your brother is your witness to the light that you extended and that is within you. The light that you may not perceive inwardly can be perceived indirectly by its witnesses, expressed as follows:

> Child of light, you know not that the light is in you. Yet you will find it through its witnesses, for having given light to them they will return it. Each one you see in the light brings your light closer to your awareness.[465]

Your giving of light to others and receiving of light from others is what the Course calls a "miracle." You can give light to your brother by seeing him in the light. For some this can be a visual experience of Christ's vision, but it can also be done simply by seeing your brother as guiltless, just as God created him and you. Your giving of light to your brother is the giving of love to him as well. Both light and love are returned to you from your brother to witness your gift of giving. This giving and receiving of light helps you transcend the three-dimensional world of appearances, described as follows:

> There is a light that this world cannot give. Yet you can give it, as it was given you. And as you give it, it shines forth to call you from the world to follow it. For this light will attract you as nothing in this world can do. And you will lay aside the world and find another. This other world is bright with love which you have given it. And here will everything remind you of your Father and His holy Son. Light is unlimited, and spreads across this world in quiet joy. All those you brought with you will shine on you, and you will shine on them in gratitude because they brought you here. Your light will join with theirs in power so compelling, that it will draw the others out of darkness as you look on them.[466]

Even though the light can be found by looking within, the Course emphasizes in the quotation above that the light reminds you of your loving relationship with your brothers. Brotherly relationships in the light become your means of awakening each other. The Course idea of relationships becoming a means of divine awakening can be confusing if relationships are mistakenly perceived as consisting of the interaction between one finite body and another finite body. Relationships are not limited to physical bodies. The Course maintains that two people can participate in a holy instant together in which they can temporarily let go of all the uses that the ego has for the body. In this holy instant, these two people can join, transcend body awareness, and experience an elevation of consciousness, described as follows:

> In the holy instant, where the Great Rays replace the body in awareness, the recognition of relationships without limits is given you. But in order to see this, it is necessary to give up every use the ego had for the body, and to accept the fact that the ego has no purpose you would share with it. [467]

The term "Great Rays" refers to an opening to higher awareness. I believe this term is another way to describe the infinite circle of light, which is the vision of the Son of God, also called the face of Christ. In this vision, the edges of the expanding circle of light become blurred, and this sounds like a description of the Great Rays:

> And all the circle fills with light before your eyes. The edges of the circle disappear, and what is in it is no longer contained at all. The light expands and covers everything, extending to infinity forever shining and with no break or limit anywhere. Within it everything is joined in perfect continuity. Nor is it possible to imagine that anything could be outside, for there is nowhere that this light is not. [468]

This light expanding from the circle contains everything so it would shine light on the holy relationship. This same idea is expressed in the above quote that says the Great Rays displace body awareness and reveal unlimited relationships. The connection between the expanding circle of light and the holy relationship is described, as follows:

> Beyond the bodies that you interposed between you and your brother, and shining in the golden light that reaches it from the bright, endless circle that extends forever, is your holy relationship, beloved of God Himself. [469]

According to the Course, "Christ is reborn" in the holy relationship in which you manifest forgiveness of your brother by overlooking all his illusions and perceive Christ in Him.

Every illusion brought to its [the holy relationship's] forgiveness is gently overlooked and disappears. For at its center Christ has been reborn, to light His home with vision that overlooks the world. Would you not have this holy home be yours as well? No misery is here, but only joy.[470]

Thus the holy relationship, as Christ's home, can be your home as well, where you can dwell with Christ. The only requirement is that you see with His vision, explained as follows:

All you need to dwell in quiet here with Christ is share His vision. Quickly and gladly is His vision given anyone who is but willing to see his brother sinless. And no one can remain beyond this willingness, if you would be released entirely from all effects of sin. Would you have partial forgiveness for yourself? Can you reach Heaven while a single sin still tempts you to remain in misery? Heaven is the home of perfect purity, and God created it for you. Look on your holy brother, sinless as yourself, and let him lead you there.[471]

The Course states that the memory of the vision of the Son of God, the expanding circle of light, lies within you and within your brother waiting to be awakened. Your special function in your holy relationship is to awaken the awareness of Christ within and to use Christ's vision to see guiltlessness in your brother:

Consider once again your special function. One is given you to see in him this perfect sinlessness. And you will ask no sacrifice of him because you could not will he suffer loss. The miracle of justice you call forth will rest on you as surely as on him. Nor will the Holy Spirit be content until it is received by everyone. For what you give to Him is everyone's, and by your giving it can He ensure that everyone receives it equally.[472]

By fulfilling your special function of seeing guiltlessness in one brother, you do so on behalf of all your brothers, and you find your own Atonement, as follows:

When you accept a brother's guiltlessness you will see the Atonement in him. For by proclaiming it in him you make it yours, and you will see what you sought. You will not see the symbol of your brother's guiltlessness shining within him while you still believe it is not there. His guiltlessness is *your* Atonement.[473]

The Course uses the word "circle" to describe the Atonement, the real world, the vision of the Son of God, and the face of Christ. My interpretation is that these are not separate circles but rather one and the same circle: an infinitely expanding circle in the second dimension. In describing the Atonement, the Course says:

> The circle of Atonement has no end. And you will find ever-increasing confidence in your safe inclusion in the circle with everyone you bring within its safety and its perfect peace.[474]

> Within its holy circle is everyone whom God created as His Son.[475]

Each one you see you place within the holy circle of Atonement or leave outside, judging him fit for crucifixion or for redemption. If you bring him into the circle of purity, you will rest there with him. If you leave him without, you join him there. Judge not except in quietness which is not of you. Refuse to accept anyone as without the blessing of Atonement, and bring him into it by blessing him. Holiness must be shared, for therein lies everything that makes it holy. Come gladly to the holy circle, and look out in peace on all who think they are outside.[476]

Jesus describes himself as being within the circle, and he calls you to join him within this holy circle. You and all your brothers are already within this circle, but you perceive yourself as being outside the circle because of your investment in seeing guilt in your brother and in your brother. Perceiving guiltlessness in your brother will return your awareness of your own guiltlessness.

Your means of overcoming guilt, provided by the Holy Spirit, is Christ's vision that enables you to see through the three-dimensional forms of this world and to perceive the real world. The real world is a world of only true perceptions of right thinking, which sounds totally abstract, except for the following fact: "There *are* no idle thoughts. All thinking produces form at some level."[477]

False perceptions based on fear and guilt mixed with some true perceptions produce all the forms of this three-dimensional world. The true perceptions of the real world produce a world of light, and this light also takes form. The most perfect expression of true perception in the real world is the vision of the Son of God. This vision, which is also the face of Christ, is manifested as the most perfect expression of two-dimensional form, which is the circle—in this case, a circle of light expanding infinitely in the second dimension.

All perceptions, even the true perceptions of the real world, are illusions since they are partial awareness in contrast to full awareness of *knowledge* in Heaven. Even though the real world is ultimately illusory, it is the place where all illusions come to be dissolved in the infinitely expanding circle of light that is the vision of the Son of God. The real world is the second dimension, although not described as such by the Course. Because the second dimension is the border between the third dimension and the One dimension, the Course does describe the real world as a "borderline," as follows:

> There is a borderline of thought that stands between this world and Heaven. It is not a place, and when you reach it is apart from time. Here is the meeting place where thoughts are brought together; where conflicting values meet and all illusions are laid down beside the truth, where they are judged to be untrue. This borderline is just beyond the gate of Heaven. Here is every thought made pure and wholly simple. Here is sin denied, and everything that *is* received instead.
>
> This is the journey's end. We have referred to it as the real world.[478]

It appears in the three-dimensional world of everyday living that there are many choices to be made, and these choices seem to be very complicated. However, these choices are illusory. Choices in this world involve a preference for one illusion over another illusion. Since all illusions are meaningless, choosing between illusions must also be meaningless. The real world provides a two-dimensional bridge between the third dimension and the One Dimension. When the complicated and meaningless choices of illusions are brought to the real world, choosing becomes simplified and meaningful.

> Nothing the Son of God believes can be destroyed. But what is truth to him must be brought to the last comparison that he will ever make; the last evaluation that will be possible, the final judgment upon this world. It is the judgment of the truth upon illusion, of knowledge on perception: "It has no meaning, and does not exist." This is not your decision. It is but a simple statement of a simple fact. But in this world there are no simple facts, because what is the same and what is different remain unclear. The one essential thing to make a choice at all is this distinction. And herein lies the difference between the worlds. In this one, choice is made impossible. In the real world is choosing simplified.[479]

Rather than making meaningless choices between illusions, the real world provides a basis for making a meaningful choice. First you learn to choose between the illusion of false perception and the illusion of true perception. Then in the real world, you choose between all illusions and reality, between perceptual awareness itself and knowledge. In the real world all the illusions of the third dimension are seen as being one illusion and as being untrue and meaningless.

All illusions are but one. And in the recognition this is so lies the ability to give up all attempts to choose between them, and to make them different.[480]

All illusions of the third dimension are dissolved in the vision of the Son of God, in the circle of light expanding infinitely. With the dissolving of the various illusions of the three-dimensional world, there is no longer a need to choose between illusions, which appear to have different forms, but have the same meaningless content. Experiencing the face of Christ in the real world presents a meaningful choice between what is untrue and what is true. However, even this choice is an illusion because your only real option is the truth. The face of Christ is the ultimate illusion but is the last illusion seen before fully accepting the knowledge of Heaven. The truth for you is forever the same, and it is a fact whether you acknowledge it or not. If you choose what is untrue, you can trick yourself into thinking this is a real choice, and for a time you can live in this illusion. You can make the illusion appear real to you, but you cannot make the illusion into an actual reality, since only God can establish reality as it is. You cannot choose what reality is, but you can choose to blind yourself to reality and pretend that the unreal and untrue is real and true for you.

C. THE PURPOSE OF UNIFYING THE MIND

Possibly you have various short-term goals and some long-term goals. Whether you realize it or not, you and every individual on this planet have only one *ultimate goal*. Your final goal is to wake up in Heaven, regaining the full awareness of what has been hidden but was never really lost. It is your destiny to awaken, but it must be your choice to want to awaken sooner rather than later. When you do awaken, you will fully accept your rightful place in the Sonship and accept your oneness with your Father.

Closely aligned with your ultimate goal is your *ultimate purpose*. Your purpose is all about the overall direction you take that motivates you to accomplish all of your goals, including your ultimate goal.

What is your ultimate purpose? Although you may not consciously realize it, your ultimate purpose is oneness focused on unifying your mind. If you grow increasingly in the direction of unifying your mind, you will eventually experience your full awakening to your acceptance of the wholeness and oneness of your Christ Mind.

Section C. "Facing Death" in the prior chapter explained that the passing away of the body will be your best opportunity to awaken in Heaven and not be reincarnated. Here is the key idea expressed previously: "If your mind is focused mostly on true perceptions of the real world and if you decided with all your heart that Heaven is the only thing you want, you certainly can wake up by divine grace." You can prepare your mind to be mostly focused on true perceptions and to express your wholehearted decision to awaken by practicing Miracle Yoga in order to learn how to unify your mind.

Miracle Yoga is a way to consciously accept your true purpose of growing in the direction of unifying the mind. As the thought system of Miracle Yoga, the Course says that unifying your mind is needed as a prerequisite for achieving your ultimate goal of divine union. This final chapter describes the ways you can increasingly unify the mind. This first section of this chapter is an excerpt from my book *Christian Meditation Inspired by Yoga and "A Course in Miracles": Opening to Divine Love in Contemplation*. This specific excerpt below is likewise quoted on my website: www.miracleyoga.org :

My form of spirituality before studying the Course was a blending of yoga and seeking Christ within, emphasizing meditation. Yoga means "union." I felt meditation was my best way to join with the Holy Spirit to facilitate unification. But the Course emphasizes joining with the Holy Spirit's perception and using Christ's vision to see with Him.

> Joining with Him in seeing is the way in which you learn to share with Him the interpretation of perception that leads to knowledge.... Seeing with Him will show you that all meaning, including yours, comes not from double vision, but from the gentle fusing of everything into *one* meaning, *one* emotion and *one* purpose. God has one purpose which He shares with you.[481]

Yes, union with the Holy Spirit happens in meditation, but prior to studying the Course, I had no understanding of the value of perception and how to use it for my spiritual growth. I know that in meditation I reduced my scattered perceptions by focusing on one perception. I knew that I could let go of even that single perception and enter the restful state of contemplation. But I thought that the limit to perception was its unification into one perception during meditation, and I was convinced that the best use of perception was to let go of it altogether. It did not occur to me that what I had learned about perception in meditation could be generalized into my daily life. I thought my outer experience of the world was so filled with scattered perceptions that I could not possibly unify them as I could in meditation. From the Course I would learn how to focus on what the previous quotation describes as the "*one* meaning, *one* emotion, *one* purpose," which is the one purpose God shares with me. It is the purpose of oneness itself—which in a practical sense means the unification of perceptions that seem to be separate. The oneness of my meaning, emotion, and purpose and indeed my oneness with God Himself is in my mind now. I realized that to find the oneness in my mind, I needed to learn how to unify my thought system, meaning to unify what appeared to be my totally disorganized perceptions. The Course describes many different ways of changing false perceptions into true perceptions, as follows:

The Shift from False Perceptions to True Perceptions

From self-will to God's Will
From illusions of the past to the awareness of now
From private thoughts to thinking with the Holy Spirit
From perceiving separation to perceiving oneness
From unloving perceptions to loving perceptions
From illusions of nightmares to happy dreams
From projecting guilt to accepting innocence
From holding grievances to giving forgiveness
From attack thoughts to miracles
From illusions of special love to extending love to everyone
From mistakes to corrected perception
From seeing with the body's eyes to seeing with Christ's eyes

UNIFYING THE MIND LEADS TO DIVINE UNION

These previously mentioned ways to change perceptions may seem to be different. However, they have the common element of unifying perceptions by directing new perceptions toward the one goal of divine union with God. Having a background in Christian yoga, I decided to use the term "Miracle Yoga" to describe my understanding of the Course. The goal of the Course is to unify perceptions. The five aspects of Miracle Yoga emphasize a single approach to unifying perceptions. Miracle Raja Yoga produces the unification of perception by focusing meditation on *one thought*. Miracle Bhakti Yoga offers the unification of perception by using *one emotion*, which is love. Miracle Karma Yoga brings about the unification of perception through the active expression of *one function*. Miracle Relationship Yoga achieves the unification of perception with *one relationship*. Miracle Jnana Yoga facilitates the unification of perception by seeking *one truth*.

D. MIRACLE JNANA YOGA TO UNIFY THE MIND

Yoga means union, and consequently Miracle Yoga is a means of growing toward unifying the mind in preparation for union with God. All five paths of Miracle Yoga are based on the Course as the philosophical basis for the understanding and practice of spiritual principles. But the path of Miracle Jnana Yoga is the most directly focused on the study and practice of the Course. Described in Chapter 3 starting on page 94, Miracle Jnana Yoga emphasizes discernment between the real and the unreal. This yoga also includes living a life focused on forgiveness, as described in the Course. Miracle Jnana Yoga is practiced by changing ego-based perceptions into perceptions based upon the Truth. Miracle Jnana Yoga requires studying the Course Text and Manual, as well as completing the one year of daily Workbook Lessons.

Since Miracle Jnana Yoga is an intellectual approach to spiritual growth, the focus is on transforming the mind directly. The mind in its ego condition is split. Part of the mind is devoted to the ego condition and this part must be unified with the rest of the mind. The complete reunification of the split mind is what the Course calls "salvation." This section focuses on this reunification process. The ego-based sense of separation from God is what needs to be corrected. However, this correction cannot be made at all levels at once. The greatest sense of separation must be healed first, and the least sense of separation must be healed last. Thus correction must be made from the "bottom up." Dictating the Course, Jesus states that with his guidance, he can help you release false perceptions and accept true perceptions, and he can assist you to provide correction from the bottom up:

> I was a man who remembered spirit and its knowledge. As a man I did not attempt to counteract error with knowledge, but to correct error from the bottom up. I demonstrated both the powerlessness of the body and the power of the mind. By uniting my will with that of my Creator, I naturally remembered spirit and its real purpose. I cannot unite your will with God's for you, but I can erase all misperceptions from your mind if you will bring it under my guidance. Only your misperceptions stand in your way. Without them your choice is certain. Sane perception induces sane choosing. I cannot choose for you, but I can help you make your own right choice.[482]

The only misperception that needs to be corrected is your sense of separation from God. Yet the original and fundamental misperception of separation from God led to more misperceptions so that the result now is that you perceive yourself as having different needs at different levels. Perceiving yourself at different levels is an illusion, yet, "...all mistakes must be corrected at the level on which they occur."[483] Also, correction of misperceptions needs to start at the bottom level where perception is most distorted, and then correction can proceed upward to less distorted levels of misperceptions.

The Course maintains, "Spirit has no levels..."[484] but does not state by name the different levels of perception that must be corrected from the bottom up in order to give up the belief in levels altogether. In the absence of that detailed information, I believe there are seven levels that need correction, corresponding to the seven chakras in the body. In Eastern philosophy, the chakras are related to nerve plexuses along spine and related to the forehead and crown of the head. Yet the chakras themselves are nonphysical levels of consciousness, meaning levels of perceptual awareness. Opening chakras is often described as the "untying of knots" in order to overcome fears and other blocks. The lower centers offer the greatest challenges. Therefore, the knots of the chakras must be untied in succession from the bottom upward to the crown chakra leading to transcendental Oneness.

But because the Course does not spell out the number or kinds of levels where mistakes must be corrected from the bottom up, there is no way to define these levels within Course terminology. However, in a very general sense, there seems to me to be three levels that must be corrected from the bottom up. I simply call these the "bottom level," the "middle level," and the "top level" of consciousness. All three levels of consciousness are illusions so they could be rightly called "levels of misperception." All three levels are related to misperceptions and confusion about identity that must be corrected in order to accept your true Identity as the holy Son of God, the Christ in God.

> The mind is therefore confused, because only One-mindedness can be without confusion. A separated or divided mind *must* be confused. It is necessarily uncertain about what it is. It has to be in conflict because it is out of accord with itself. This makes its aspects strangers to each other, and this is the essence of the fear-prone condition, in which attack is always possible. You have every reason to feel afraid as you perceive yourself.[485]

The bottom level of misperception has the most identification with the body and with the physical three-dimensional world. This level is where there is the most confusion, fear, and darkness, and so it must be corrected first. The middle level of misperception is the level where there is less identification with the body and physical awareness and more identification with the mind. Here there is less confusion, fear, and darkness and more light. The top level of misperception is where there is very little or no identification with the body and only identification with the perceptual mind. Here there is the least confusion, fear, and darkness, and the most light. This is still a level of misperception since even the most subtle forms of perception need healing to remove all confusion, fear, and darkness. "Perception is based on a separate state, so that anyone who perceives at all needs healing."[486] When the top level of misperception is healed, there is no longer any identification with any level because there is no longer any perception. Perception has been transcended and replaced by the knowledge of Heaven. "It is obvious, then, that inducing the mind to give up its miscreations [misperceptions] is the only application of creative ability that is truly meaningful,"[487] because it leads ultimately to awakening the awareness of divine Oneness and accepting one's true Self in God.

Let's consider three stages of unifying the mind that correspond to correcting the three levels of misperceived identification. Correcting the bottom level of misperception is the beginning stage of unifying the mind. Correcting the middle level of misperception is the middle stage of unifying the mind. Correcting the top level of misperception is the final stage of unifying the mind. The section will elaborate on the five different ways of unifying the mind as a prerequisite for awakening to divine union. These are unification through:

1. seeking the truth in the expression of Miracle Jnana Yoga
2. opening to love associated with Miracle Bhakti Yoga
3. dedicated action expressed in Miracle Karma Yoga
4. meditation in the practice of Miracle Raja Yoga
5. relationships in Miracle Relationship Yoga.

These will be described separately, but please bear in mind these are not actually distinctly separate means of unifying the mind. In practice, the mind will become increasingly unified by combining these five practices, which certainly overlap each other.

First we will discuss Miracle Jnana Yoga related to the three stages of unifying the mind that correspond to three phases of letting go of illusions. Miracle Jnana Yoga is the unification of the mind through seeking one Truth. Miracle Jnana Yoga is not just discriminating between the real and unreal. The first phase starts with discriminating between false perceptions and true perceptions. This bottom phase is learning how to let go of the illusions of the three-dimensional world, by refraining from combining false perceptions and true perceptions.

This beginning phase is a very temporary entering of the real world of only true perceptions. The middle phase is a time of more consistently entering the real world and becoming established in the ability to let go of illusions of false perceptions. The real world is a reflection of the truth of Heaven, but still consists of illusions because these true perceptions of the real world are not reality. Consequently, the top phase of letting go of illusions is the letting go of even the true perceptions of the real world. In the top phase of letting go of all illusions, you can give your complete willingness to fully awaken to the one Truth of Reality Itself. In this final phase, all perception is replaced by the knowledge of Heaven, and this can be called "truth unification." Bear in mind that all perception can only be replaced with knowledge by divine grace. The self-effort of Miracle Jnana Yoga expresses your permission to receive the divine grace of awakening.

Now we will discuss Miracle Bhakti Yoga related to the three stages of unifying the mind that correspond to three phases of letting go of illusions. Miracle Bhakti Yoga is the unification of the mind through seeking divine Love. First you seek love as you navigate through this world of dreams and eventually seek divine Love that transcends this world. In the bottom phase of releasing all illusions, you learn to let go of the unloving thoughts of the world and learn to accept only the loving thoughts of the real world. You learn to give thoughts of fear, anger, and guilt to the Holy Spirit and allow them to be corrected and replaced by the perfect love of the Atonement. The middle phase is a time of establishing a loving state of mind by consistently accepting the Atonement. The top phase is letting go of illusions altogether. If you cling to only the loving thoughts of the real world, your mind is still divided because you still believe you are separate from what you see and what you experience. In the top phase, the loving thoughts of the real world are replaced by the Love of God. Seen from the perspective of separation, loving perceptions are reflections of divine Love experienced in union. The combination of these three phases of conceptual focusing brings about the unification of the mind based on moving from many thoughts of love to one experience of divine Love so this process can be called "love unification." The self-effort of Miracle Bhakti Yoga expresses your desire to replace the partial awareness of perception with the total awareness of knowledge. Thus you are giving your permission to receive the divine grace of awakening.

Next we will discuss Miracle Karma Yoga related to the three stages of unifying the mind that include the three phases of releasing illusions. Miracle Karma Yoga is the unification of the mind by expressing the Will of God actively. Miracle Karma Yoga uses the means of dedicating all actions to bring about unification of the mind through a movement from a divided will to one true Will. Every action can be traced to a desire. The will is directed toward obtaining what is desired. The ideal of Miracle Karma Yoga is to desire only God's Will as the motivation for action rather than desiring what would satisfy the will of the ego. The bottom phase of unifying the mind is the beginning of the process of focusing the mind in the direction of dedicating actions to God and accepting His Will. The middle phase is characterized by the ability to consistently hold in the mind the desire to do God's Will in carrying out all actions. The top stage is the awareness of one desire and one will. This is the full recognition that one's true will is in fact God's Will, thus there is only One Will. Once this third phase of focusing on one Will is achieved, the result is a totally unified perceptual mind. In this final phase, the separate will of the ego is replaced by the Will of God as one's own true will. I call this "will unification." Miracle Bhakti Yoga expresses your willingness to unify your mind and gives your permission to receive the divine grace of awakening.

Next we will discuss Miracle Raja Yoga related to the three stages of unifying the mind that correspond to three phases of letting go of illusions. Miracle Raja Yoga is the unification of the mind by focusing on one Thought. Miracle Raja Yoga uses the means of meditation to facilitate the unification of the mind through a movement from many thoughts to one thought. This is similar to Hindu raja yoga meditation, which seeks to reduce the fluctuations of the thought waves with the goal of holding only one thought wave in the mind. This holding of one thought leads to the transcendent experience of samadhi. In Miracle Raja Yoga, the bottom phase starts the process of focusing the mind in the direction of true perceptions, which is the beginning stage of any meditation process. The middle phase is characterized by the ability to hold a few true perceptions in the mind consistently, such as an experienced meditator can do. The top phase is called "total perception" or "single perception," focusing continuously on one thought, which is the same as what occurs in the deepest levels of meditation. Once this final phase of focusing on a single thought is reached, the end result is a totally unified perceptual mind. This then leads to transcending the perceptual mind itself. The single thought of the third stage is replaced by the Thought of God. The single perception is replaced by the higher awareness of the knowledge of Heaven accomplished by God's grace. This can be called "meditation unification." The self-effort of Miracle Raja Yoga expresses your desire to unify your mind through meditation thus giving your permission to receive the grace of awakening.

Finally let's consider Miracle Relationship related to the three stages of unifying the mind that include the three phases of releasing illusions. Miracle Relationship Yoga is the unification of the mind through holy relationships. Miracle Relationship Yoga uses the means of the holy relationship to bring about the unification of the mind by joining for a common purpose and by ultimately perceiving holiness inwardly and outwardly. The bottom phase is the initial joining with the other person in which you recognize common interests and a common purpose. In this joining, the Holy Spirit enters the relationship as the third partner and adds the higher purpose of perceiving holiness in each other. The middle phase is characterized by each partner having fully accepted the Holy Spirit's purpose of seeing holiness in his or her partner. This stage also includes generalizing this purpose to allow the seeing of holiness in others. The top stage is the complete acceptance of the one purpose of seeing holiness in every person and in one's self. This is the recognition that holiness has been given by God in everyone's creation as an extension of His Holiness. In this final phase of fully accepting God's gift of holiness, the result of a totally unified mind is achieved and the union with God and the Sonship is restored. I call this "relationship unification." Using Miracle Relationship Yoga to manifest holy relationships expresses your desire to unify your mind by perceiving holiness in everyone. Your desire gives your free-will permission to receive the divine grace of awakening to your divine relationships with God and your brothers in the Sonship.

Different ways of unifying the mind have been discussed, but the end result is always the same one-pointed state of mind achieved by divine grace. The practices of Miracle Yoga are one way, but not the only way to prepare for completing the third and final stage of oneness of mind. Because God does not impose Himself upon you, awakening requires your permission. When your perceptual mind is prepared and willing to awaken, you will accept the truth about yourself and join with God Himself. Only God Himself could facilitate this final step of transformation. God takes the initiative to transform true perception into knowledge and raises you into Heaven to accept your rightful place in the Sonship. The following quotation describes what it will feel like when you finally let go of all illusions and fully accept the truth:

Can you imagine what a state of mind without illusions is? How it would feel? Try to remember when there was a time,— perhaps a minute, maybe even less—when nothing came to interrupt your peace; when you were certain you were loved and safe. Then try to picture what it would be like to have that moment be extended to the end of time and to eternity. Then let the sense of quiet that you felt be multiplied a hundred times, and then be multiplied another hundred more.

And now you have a hint, not more than just the faintest intimation of the state your mind will rest in when the truth has come. Without illusions there could be no fear, no doubt and no attack. When truth has come all pain is over, for there is no room for transitory thoughts and dead ideas to linger in your mind. Truth occupies your mind completely, liberating you from all beliefs in the ephemeral. They have no place because the truth has come, and they are nowhere. They can not be found, for truth is everywhere forever, now.[488]

E. UNIFYING THE MIND THROUGH CHRIST'S VISION

In summary, the mind can become unified by following the paths of Miracle Jnana Yoga, Miracle Bhakti Yoga, Miracle Karma Yoga, Miracle Raja Yoga, and Miracle Relationship Yoga. These have been described as separate ways of unifying the mind through seeking the truth, extending love, desiring to do God's Will with dedicated action, practicing meditation, and having holy relationships with a common purpose. But, as was mentioned previously, these overlap in practical application. For Miracle Yoga, I recommend a synthesis of these paths, although each person's personality will determine which aspects will receive greater or lesser emphasis. I make this recommendation because in practical application unifying the mind requires a very well-rounded approach to spiritual growth that represents your free-will invitation to receive the divine grace of awakening.

Christ's vision and forgiveness are the central themes of the Course therefore the primary means of practicing Miracle Jnana Yoga. They provide the means of discriminating between the real and the unreal, between true perception and false perception. However, these practices which lead to unifying the mind are so universal that they cannot be pinned down to just one of the five alternative paths of Miracle Yoga. The unification of the mind may also be called the "correction of the mind." Regardless of what practices of the five paths of Miracle Yoga you choose to emphasize in your preparation for unifying the mind, the Holy Spirit brings divine grace that facilitates the correction of the mind.

> A Voice [the Holy Spirit] will answer every question you ask, and a vision will correct the perception of everything you see. For what you have made invisible [the real world] is the only truth, and what you have not heard is the only Answer [the Holy Spirit].[489]

The Holy Spirit is the Voice for God, and therefore one form of correction involves listening to this Word of God to guide the mind in its unification process. This includes accepting the perfect love of the Atonement as the means of transformation. The other form of correction involves seeing a vision provided through the Holy Spirit, expressed in the previous quotation in this way: "a vision will correct the perception of everything you see." In this quote, "vision" can refer to Christ's vision, which involves accepting the Holy Spirit. Likewise, the word "vision" can refer to the vision of seeing the face of Christ, which can be seen only by using Christ's vision. As a means of inner transformation, Christ's vision can be employed to unify the mind by directing the mind toward light. Therefore, I call this "light unification." The bottom, middle, and top stages of light unification are similar to the other means of unification with the significant difference being the use of vision as the means of bringing the mind to one-pointedness. These three stages of using vision also correspond to seeing the face of Christ with increasing depth and understanding along with seeing more and more of the light in that reflection of Heaven.

In regard to vision, the bottom stage of unifying the mind is the beginning of using Christ's vision, which is the initial mental perceiving of the meaning of holiness in objects or people. Some seekers may experience Light vision by the seeing of light visually in objects and people, but most seekers will not have this visual experience. You may possibly see "little edges of light around the same familiar objects which you see now. That is the beginning of real vision. You can be certain that real vision will come quickly when this has occurred."[490] At this first stage, you can experience Christ's vision of mentally perceiving holiness in others without the visual experience of Light vision. Yet you cannot experience Light vision without it being accompanied by Christ's vision. In other words, the seeing of light visually in Light vision cannot occur unless the mental aspect of seeing the meaning of holiness is simultaneously present. If Light vision does occur, the light is seen while the physical eyes are open, but the body's eyes are not the source of this vision. Rather, the source of Light vision is activity of the Holy Spirit that brings the gift of seeing with the eyes of Christ. "The wish to see calls down the grace of God upon your [physical] eyes, and brings the gift of light that makes sight possible."[491]

The middle stage of real vision is a time of being firmly established and increasingly consistent in practicing Christ's vision. This stage is the plateau of self-acceptance. After becoming proficient at practicing Christ's vision in order to see the meaning of holiness at this middle stage, some seekers may have the experience of Light vision, but most will not. The top stage of unification is accepting the highest meaning of holiness by seeing a formless and blazing light that is a reflection of Heaven, which is the entire face of Christ. This is unification of the mind focused on the single perception of the vision of light, which is in fact the same place of single perception found in the other means of unification. This state of single perception is the prerequisite for the transition by divine grace from perceptual awareness itself to the total awareness of transcendental knowledge of Heaven. The end result is the state of mind devoid of illusions described previously.

All three of these stages of unifying the mind through vision involve seeing light. There are a great many Course references to vision, but the word "vision" may refer to vision in two different ways. When the Course refers to "the vision of the Son of God," this phrase is referring to the face of Christ as an expanding circle of Light that is the doorway of Heaven in the real world. It may be mistakenly assumed that "the vision of the Son of God" means the same as "the vision of Christ." Yet Course specifically and exclusively refers to "the vision of Christ," as meaning *the vision possessed by Christ* and as having the same meaning as the term "Christ's vision." Thus "the vision of Christ" and "Christ's vision" refer to the same ability to see the light of the face of Christ, to see the light of the vision of the Son of God, to see the light of the real world, and to see the light of Christ in your brother. The terms "the vision of Christ" and "Christ's vision" are also called "real vision," "the savior's vision" and "the Holy Spirit's vision." The important thing to remember is that Christ's vision can be your vision if you open your mind to the guidance of the Holy Spirit and you choose to perceive with the "eyes of Christ" within you. The following quotations are examples of how the terms "Christ's vision" and "the vision of Christ" both refer to the same ability to see the light beyond the three-dimensional world:

> Christ's vision has one law.... It beholds a light beyond the body... And it looks on everyone, on every circumstance, all happenings and all events, without the slightest fading of the light it sees.[492]

> For light must come into the darkened world to make Christ's vision possible even here. Help Him to give His gift of light to all who think they wander in darkness, and let Him gather them into His quiet sight that makes them one.[493]

> Perception can reach everywhere under His [Holy Spirit's] guidance, for the vision of Christ beholds everything in light.[494]

> Vision depends on light. You cannot see in darkness.... Beyond this darkness, yet still within you is, the vision of Christ Who looks on all in light.[495]

> And in this single vision [Christ's vision, the vision of the Son of God] does he see the face of Christ, and understands he looks on everyone as he beholds this one. For there is light where darkness was before, and now the veil is lifted from his sight.[496]

This is the savior's vision; that he see his innocence in all he looks upon, and sees his own salvation everywhere. He holds no concept of himself between his calm and open eyes and what he sees. He brings the light to what he looks upon, that he may see it as it really is.[497]

Similar quotations are scattered throughout the Course leaving the distinct impression that Jesus dictating the Course wants to convey the importance of seeking the light in a literal sense. Of Course, the most important focus in the Course is on forgiveness, which requires the perceiving of holiness. The Course maintains, "Salvation is the Holy Spirit's goal. The means is vision."[498] Vision is the means of finding salvation, yet simultaneously the Course advocates that forgiveness is the means of finding salvation. Can both vision and forgiveness be the means for salvation? Yes, there is no contradiction here because there is a direct connection between vision and forgiveness. Forgiveness is the practice of seeing holiness in your brothers, and vision enables you to see that holiness, making forgiveness possible.

All three stages of unifying the mind through Christ's vision manifest forgiveness. These stages are experiences of perceiving different levels of the face of Christ, which itself "is the great symbol of forgiveness."[499] The bottom stage of unifying the mind is the beginning of manifesting forgiveness by mentally being aware of the meaning of holiness behind every outer form. It is perceiving only the *meaning* of the face of Christ without any visual component. Although the full blazing light of the face of Christ is hard to see now in the world, one thing you can do is to focus on the holiness of the face of Christ. This requires your belief, understanding, and faith that the holiness of the face of Christ can be perceived in *every* form of the world. Feel free to call on the help of the Holy Spirit to perceive this holiness.

The middle stage of unification through Christ's vision is a time of being firmly established in the practice of forgiveness. This stage may include experiencing Light vision for those who are visually oriented. This is a visual seeing of a portion of the face of Christ, which includes the nonvisual awareness of holiness. Yet I do not want to overemphasize Light vision because it is certainly not necessary for everyone and is a helpful option for only a minority of seekers.

The top stage of unification using Christ's vision is the least practical means of forgiveness in this world. This is because it is unrealistic to expect to see the full blazing light that is the direct seeing of the entire face of Christ. However, ironically everyone is destined to see this blazing light because, "*The face of Christ* has to be seen before the memory of God can return,"[500] which Chapter 6 emphasized. "Sight of Christ is all there is to see."[501] This sight of Christ is everyone's destiny because everyone is destined to wake up in Heaven, and the face of Christ is the one doorway for access to Heaven. As was explained previously, the best opportunity you will have for directly seeing the entire face of Christ will happen as you let go of the physical body at the end of this earthly lifetime. Yet you need to be prepared to embrace the face of Christ. Otherwise, you will be reincarnated repeatedly until you make that final embrace and awaken.

Just as all three stages of unifying the mind are experiences of forgiveness and experiences of various levels of the face of Christ, all three are miracles. "Miracles are natural signs of forgiveness. Through miracles you accept God's forgiveness by extending it to others."[502] Miracles and vision are inseparable:

> It is important to remember that miracles and vision necessarily go together. This needs repeating, and frequent repeating. It is a central idea in your new thought system, and the perception that it produces. The miracle is always there. Its presence is not caused by your vision; its absence is not the result of your failure to see. It is only your awareness of miracles that is affected. You will see them in the light; you will not see them in the dark.
>
> To you, then, light is crucial. While you remain in darkness, the miracle remains unseen. Thus you are convinced it is not there. This follows from the premises from which darkness comes. Denial of light leads to failure to perceive it. Failure to perceive light is to perceive darkness. The light is useless to you then, even though it is there. You cannot use it because its presence is unknown to you. And the seeming reality of the darkness makes the idea of light meaningless.
>
> To be told that what you do not see is there sounds like insanity. It is very difficult to become convinced that it is insanity not to see what is there, and to see what is not there instead. You do not doubt that the body's eyes can see. Your faith lies in darkness, not the light.[503]

This quotation encourages you to take your faith and belief away from darkness and to place your faith and belief in the light. Light unification is made possible by having faith and belief in the light. You cannot expect to have the visual experience of actually seeing light and seeing the entire face of Christ while having faith in and believing that the darkness and illusions of the world are real. But your faith and belief in light are needed not only in the middle stage that may include Light vision and top stage of unifying the mind that ultimately leads to the doorway to Heaven and the awakening experience of Light. You also need faith and belief in the light in the bottom stage of Christ's vision unification in which the meaning of holiness is perceived without a visual component. What does having faith and belief in light have to do with all three stages of unifying the mind? One answer is that all three stages involve an invitation to receive the Holy Spirit, which is also an invitation to receive the light. "The Holy Spirit is the Light in which Christ stands revealed. And all who would behold Him can see Him, for they have asked for light."[504] All three stages of light unification are each an expression of light and of "seeing" the Holy Spirit.

> He [Holy Spirit] knows because He is part of God; He perceives because He was sent to save humanity. He is the great correction principle; the bringer of true perception, the inherent power of the vision of Christ. He is the light in which the forgiven world is perceived; in which the face of Christ alone is seen.[505]

The Course describes the Holy Spirit as the Maker of the real world. Because the face of Christ "is the symbol of the real world,"[506] the Holy Spirit must also be the Maker of the face of Christ, which is a form that reflects formlessness. Only the Holy Spirit could make this because of having a dual nature of manifesting perfect perception of truth and retaining the knowledge of Truth and Oneness in Heaven. Just as God created His Son by extension, I believe the Holy Spirit made the face of Christ by extending Himself. The Holy Spirit is "the Voice for God, and has therefore taken form. This form is not His reality, which God alone knows along with Christ, His real Son, Who is part of Him."[507] Similar to taking a form that can be heard as the Voice for God, the Holy Spirit took a form that can be seen by the making of the face of Christ as an explosion of infinite light reflecting the Light of Heaven.

The terms "truth unification," "love unification," "will unification," "meditation unification," "relationship unification," and "light unification" are merely different labels I have given to identifying the process of unifying the mind with three similar stages. The parallel between love unification and light unification is particularly strong. When you accept the perfect love of the Atonement, you are accepting the Holy Spirit's correction of all your wrong perceptions and thus healing your mind. But you are also simultaneously accepting light since, "The Atonement is entirely unambiguous. It is perfectly clear because it exists in the light."[508] Without opening to your inner light, the perfect love of the Atonement cannot be accepted since, "The Atonement can be accepted within you only by the releasing of the inner light."[509] Each stage of unifying the mind is a means of accepting the Atonement because it enables you to see holiness beyond outer appearances. "Spiritual vision literally cannot see error, and merely looks for the Atonement."[510]

The circle of Atonement and circle of blazing light that is the face of Christ are one and the same circle of light. They are both made of the light of the Holy Spirit and share the same purpose. "What shares a common purpose is the same."[511] When you accept the Atonement, you are accepting the face of Christ and the light of the Holy Spirit. Just as a shower cleans the body, the shower of light radiating from the face of Christ will clean your mind of all your mistakes and their effects. In the second dimension, the face of Christ is the perfect image that expresses the Atonement, serving as the means of your transition from the third dimension to the One Dimension of Heaven.

F. REASON AS THE BASIS FOR MIRACLE JNANA YOGA

Most seekers do not have the personal experience Light vision in which light is seen visually, while also perceiving holiness. Thus it may be difficult to understand why light is important to the salvation, the process of awakening in Heaven. However, this is easier to understand if you can accept that your mind *is* light. "God has lit your mind Himself, and keeps your mind lit by His Light because His Light is what your mind is."[512] When you see your brother as holy and as part of yourself, you are indirectly experiencing the light of your own mind that you share with your brother. "Your right mind sees only brothers, because it sees only in its own light."[513]

The Course persistently talks about "seeing" in relation to Christ's vision, which is seeing the meaning of holiness because you can literally *see meaning*. You can see "reason," explained as follows:

> The introduction of reason into the ego's thought system is the beginning of its undoing, for reason and the ego are contradictory. Nor is it possible for them to coexist in your awareness. For reason's goal is to make plain, and therefore obvious. You can *see* reason. This is not a play on words, for here is the beginning of a vision that has meaning. Vision is sense quite literally. If it is not the body's sight, it *must* be understood.[514]

I am struck by the idea above that reason can be seen and "is the beginning of a vision that has meaning." What is the nature of this reason that is the beginning of vision with meaning? Reason does not fluctuate between what is true and what is false.

> Faith and perception and belief can be misplaced, and serve the great deceiver's [ego's] needs as well as truth. But reason has no place at all in madness, nor can it be adjusted to fit its end. Faith and belief are strong in madness, guiding perception toward what the mind has valued. But reason enters not at all in this. For perception would fall away, if reason were applied.

There is no reason in insanity, for it depends entirely on reason's absence. The ego never uses it, because it does not realize that it exists. The partially insane have access to it, and only they have need of it. Knowledge does not depend on it, and madness keeps it out.

The part of the mind where reason lies was dedicated, by your will in union with your Father's, to the undoing of insanity. Here was the Holy Spirit's purpose accepted and accomplished, both at once. Reason is alien to insanity, and those who use it have gained a means which cannot be applied to sin. Knowledge is far beyond attainment of any kind. But reason can serve to open doors you closed against it....

Faith and belief, upheld by reason, cannot fail to lead to changed perception. And in this change is room made way for vision. Vision extends beyond itself, as does the purpose that it serves, and all the means for its accomplishment.[515]

From this quotation, it seems that reason is not typical perception, but through reason, faith and belief can manifest changed perception that facilitates vision. Reason is not knowledge, the awareness existing in Heaven, but reason can lead in that direction. If reason is not typical perception and not knowledge, what is it? Reason is the intellect of the mind that does not rely on perception as it is usually understood. Usually perception consists of discursive thinking involving analytical comparisons of differences. What happens if this normal perception of rational thinking becomes so unified that it no longer sees differences but is only aware of wholeness? This state of unified mind is called in the Course "redeemed perception" or "total perception."[516] Redeemed perception is the result of the healing of the divisions present in normal perception. This unification of the mind is a preparation for making the transition to the knowledge of Heaven. "Redeemed perception is easily translated to knowledge..."[517] This state of mind that is perfectly unified is so alien to normal perception that a different word is needed to identify it. The word used in the Course to identify this "redeemed perception" of a unified mind is "reason." Reason is a higher function of the mind in which the mind is unified and not touched by the ego. The Course says, "Vision is sense quite literally,"[518] because vision depends on sensing reason that comes from the part of the mind beyond the ego condition where normal perception rules.

The first time I remember being aware of reason was when I solved a Chinese puzzle. I did not call it reason, but I was aware that there was a higher aspect of my mind. It could only have been that higher part of my mind that solved the Chinese puzzle, because my normal perceptual mind could not have figured the puzzle out. Yet I did not understand what this higher mind was, and here is why:

You do not realize the whole extent to which the idea of separation has interfered with reason. Reason lies in the other Self you have cut off from your awareness. And nothing you have allowed to stay in your awareness is capable of reason. How can the segment of the mind devoid of reason understand what reason is, or grasp the information it would give?[519]

The thinking of the ego involves mixing false and true perceptions. Logic is thinking in alignment with a basic premise. The ego starts with the false initial premise of separation, so the ego's logic leads to false conclusions that do not reflect reality. Thus the ego is "perfectly logical, though clearly insane."[520] Reason consists of only true perceptions of wholeness based on reality without any false perceptions of separation. Reason also uses logic, but its logic is built on only true premises so its conclusions are always true and clearly reflect reality. Using reason, "The Holy Spirit judges against the reality of the ego's thought system merely because He knows its foundation is not true. Therefore, nothing that arises from it means anything."[521]

Because the ego's thinking includes false perceptions, reason is foreign to the ego. When you identify with the perceptions of the ego, you cannot open your mind to reason. Reason is a higher aspect of the mind so reason has the function of bringing crystal clarity. The way to access reason is to let go of ego identification. Jnana yoga consists of discerning the real from the unreal that involves opening to the inner divine spirit and releasing investment in the outer illusory form of the body. Sometimes jnana yoga is mistakenly thought of as merely using scholarly perception to study spiritual principles. Actually jnana yoga is the path of insight that relies on reason in order to illuminate understanding. This higher understanding of reason is explained by Georg Feuerstein in his book, *Sacred Paths*:

The scriptures of Vedanta distinguish between a higher knowledge, called *jnana*, and a lower knowledge, called vijnana. The former pertains to the organ of wisdom, or *buddhi*. The latter is a product of the brain-dependent "mind," which functions as a processing plant for the input from the senses. The "lower" mind is known in Sanskrit language as *manas*, the instrument of thought.

Buddhi is that aspect of our being which is natively like a limpid pool—still and clear—and therefore capable of reflecting the light of the Self, the esoteric "sun." The *atman* [the Self, Christ, the Son of God] is described as being self-luminous, whereas all finite objects, including *buddhi*, depend for their visibility on the transcendental "light."[522]

The work of yoga is to be attracted to the light shining from the *buddhi*, which is like a crystal clear mirror that perfectly reflects the Divine Light that is its source. The challenge of the seeker practicing yoga is to gain increasing access to the reflected light of buddhi and to eventually go beyond just seeing the light as apart from himself. The final goal of yoga is for the seeker to directly experience that he *is* the Divine Light that is the source of the reflected light. The seeker in this realization discovers all of the visible and invisible universe is contained within this Divine Light that he is. "You are and will forever be exactly as you were created. Light and joy and peace abide in you because God put them there."[523]

Just as a ray of sunlight has the dual nature of carrying both light and heat, buddhi has a dual nature of being both light and mind that reflects the Light and Mind of Heaven. Buddhi with its dual "light-insight" quality is what the Course calls "reason." From your normal perception that divides concepts seeing them as separate, it is hard to understand how buddhi, known as reason, can have a dual nature as both light and insight with the single inner meaning of oneness. Buddhi or reason is a state of mind so filled with light that it cannot conceive of darkness. Buddhi or reason is filled with what the Course calls "true light," making Christ's vision possible. The connection between true light and the mind is described, as follows:

> And what is light except the resolution, born of peace, of all your conflicts and mistaken thoughts into one concept which is wholly true? Even that one will disappear, because the Thought behind it [one true concept] will appear instead to take its place. And now you are at peace forever, for the dream is over then.
>
> True light that makes true vision possible is not the light the body's eyes behold. It is a state of mind that has become so unified that darkness cannot be perceived at all. And thus what is the same is seen as one, while what is not the same remains unnoticed, for it is not there.
>
> This is the light that shows no opposites, and vision, being healed, has power to heal. This is the light that brings your peace of mind to other minds, to share it and be glad that they are one with you and with themselves. This is the light that heals because it brings single perception, based upon one frame of reference, from which one meaning comes. [524]

Buddhi or reason is "redeemed perception," "total perception," or "single perception." The true light of buddhi or reason is a state of unified mind in which all concepts come together into the one concept of single perception. This single perception is the combination of one true light and one true meaning. This single perception of one light and one meaning gives way to the Oneness of the knowledge of Heaven as "the Thought behind it will appear instead to take its place."[525]

What does buddhi or reason with its dual light and insight nature sound like that has been already discussed? Many different ways of unifying the mind have been discussed, and the third and top stage is the same for every means of Miracle Yoga. This final stage is always the same one-pointed state of mind and this is indeed buddhi or reason. The last stage of light unification using Christ's vision is seeing the entire face of Christ, the vision of the Son of God. But what are you seeing? You are *seeing* buddhi or reason. Here vision and meaning meet. When you see the blazing light of the entire face of Christ, you will be seeing the single light and the single meaning of buddhi or reason. Buddhi or reason *is* the face of Christ, the vision of the Son of God, which has the dual nature of light and mind containing the single meaning of holiness. This is not the Light of Christ Itself but is the reflection of that Light. Many characteristics of the face of Christ have been identified previously, yet none of these captures the complete picture of this mirror of Heaven as well as saying the light and insight nature of the face of Christ consists of buddhi or reason. This understanding explains the following passage quoted previously: "You can *see* reason. This is not a play on words, for here is the beginning of a vision that has meaning. Vision is sense quite literally. If it is not the body's sight, it *must* be understood."[526]

Just as you can see the face of Christ and grasp its single meaning, you can see reason that is contained in that brilliant light and grasp its same single meaning. With reason, "All things are seen in light, and in the light their purpose is transformed and understood."[527] I have said previously that the face of Christ, the circle of blazing light, is the same as the circle of Atonement. The obvious and correct conclusion is that Atonement, which is "perfectly clear because it exists in the light,"[528] also has that same light-insight quality, which is buddhi or reason. Reason reveals the meaning of wholeness and sameness hidden in the parts that perception sees as distinctly separate. In contrast to reason, normal perception sees everything by analyzing it, dividing it into parts and comparing the parts. When Jesus dictated the Course, He spoke from reason, which sees the wholeness, oneness, and sameness of all things. Yet to speak to your limited perception that divides concepts, Jesus in the Course explained different ideas as though they were separate as an accommodation to the limited ego condition. It requires reason itself to take these ideas back to their source in reason and see how Atonement, the face of Christ, and the blazing light of the vision of the Son of God come together in the sacred meeting place where the Holy Spirit and reason itself also reside. This sacred place is also the place where God's Plan for salvation was established and completed with your consent, described as follows:

God's plan for your salvation could not have been established without your will and your consent. It must have been accepted by the Son of God, for what God wills for him he must receive. For God wills not apart from him, nor does the Will of God wait upon time to be accomplished. Therefore, what joined the Will of God must be in you now, being eternal. You must have set aside a place in which the Holy Spirit can abide, and where He is. He must have been there since the need for Him arose, and was fulfilled in the same instant. Such would your reason tell you, if you listened. Yet such is clearly not the ego's reasoning. Your reason's alien nature to the ego is proof you will not find the answer there. Yet if it exists for you, and has your freedom as the purpose given it, you must be free to find it.

God's plan is simple; never circular and never self-defeating. He has no Thoughts except the Self-extending, and in this your will must be included. Thus, there must be a part of you that knows His Will and shares it. It is not meaningful to ask if what must be is so. But it is meaningful to ask why you are unaware of what is so, for this must have an answer if the plan of God for your salvation is complete. And it must be complete, because its Source knows not of incompletion.[529]

God's Will for you is to wake up in Heaven and realize you have never left your union of Love with Him. God's Plan of salvation has been established by God and already accomplished with your consent because God's Will is your own true will. The prior quotation states, "Thus, there must be a part of you that knows His Will and shares it." How do you contact this part of yourself that would reveal God's Will to you that is your own true will? You invite both the Holy Spirit and reason to lead you out of the insanity of the ego condition.

Reason assures you Heaven is what you want, and all you want. Listen to Him [the Holy Spirit] Who speaks with reason, and brings your reason into line with His. Be willing to let reason be the means by which He would direct you how to leave insanity behind.[530]

The purpose of reason is your freedom, as is God's Plan for your return that is the Atonement. When you accept the perfect love of the Atonement, you are also accepting reason. Consider that, "Reason cannot see sin but can see errors, and leads to their correction. It does not value *them*, but their correction."[531] Reason is the means used by the Atonement and the Holy Spirit to achieve the purpose of undoing the ego because it corrects mistakes through its clarity:

The ego's whole continuance depends on its belief you cannot learn this course. Share this belief, and reason will be unable to see your errors and make way for their correction. For reason sees through errors, telling you what you thought was real is not. Reason can see the difference between sin and mistakes, because it wants correction. Therefore, it tells you what you thought was uncorrectable can be corrected, and thus it must have been an error. The ego's opposition to correction leads to its fixed belief in sin and disregard of errors. It looks on nothing that can be corrected. Thus does the ego damn, and reason save.

Reason is not salvation in itself, but it makes way of peace and brings you to a state of mind in which salvation can be given you.[532]

The light-insight aspect of reason is the means used by the Holy Spirit to facilitate all three levels of Christ's vision. You think mistakes are what you do incorrectly, yet in a broader view everything your physical eyes see is a mistake in perception. "Everything the body's eyes can see is a mistake, an error in perception, a distorted fragment of the whole without the meaning that the whole would give."[533] Reason allows you to see past the outer form, which is all the body's eyes can see, and enables you to see the wholeness and meaning hidden by the outer form. Along with your faith and belief, reason facilitates vision allowing you to see past the outer forms to the meaning of holiness in them, as stated in the above quotation and repeated here:

Faith and belief, upheld by reason, cannot fail to lead to changed perception. And in this change is room made way for vision. Vision extends beyond itself, as does the purpose that it serves, and all the means for its accomplishment.[534]

Reason is a unified state of mind centered on oneness that is there already in your awareness waiting for you to uncover it. Having this unified mind is the goal of spiritual seeking, which in turn leads from one-mindedness to the One-mindedness of Heaven. Spiritual growth is a transition from complexity of mind to simplicity, from multiplicity to oneness. Reason, as a mental state focused on oneness, is more than just the goal of spiritual seeking. Reason is also a higher faculty of the mind that can serve as the means needed to reach that goal.

Joining with Him [the Holy Spirit] in seeing is the way in which you learn to share with Him the interpretation of perception that leads to knowledge. You cannot see alone. Sharing perception with Him Whom God has given you teaches you how to recognize what you see. It is the recognition that nothing you see means anything alone. Seeing with Him will show you that all meaning, including yours, comes not from double vision, but from the gentle fusing of everything into *one* meaning, *one* emotion, and *one* purpose. God has one Purpose which He shares with you. The single vision which the Holy Spirit offers you will bring this oneness to your mind with clarity and brightness so intense you could not wish, for all the world, not to accept what God would have you have. Behold your will, accepting it as His, with all His Love as yours. All honor to you through Him, and through Him unto God. [535]

Reason focused on oneness facilitates all levels of Christ's vision and brings spiritually guided discrimination. Inviting the Holy Spirit and reason into the ego condition of your mind lets you discriminate between reality and illusion. Forms are perceptions of illusions, blinding you to reality. Reality is constant, unchanging, and eternal. Anything that changes must be an illusion, not reality.

Nothing so blinding as perception of form. For sight of form means understanding has been obscured.

Only mistakes have different forms, so they can deceive. You can change form *because* it is not true. It could not be reality *because* it can be changed. Reason will tell you that if form is not reality it must be an illusion, and is not there to see. And if you see it you must be mistaken, for you are seeing what can *not* be real as if it were. What cannot see beyond what is not there must be distorted perception, and must perceive illusions as the truth.[536]

G. ACCEPTING THE HOLY INSTANT

Reality is changeless. Because you live in a world of changing form, how can you contact what is eternally changeless? You need to accept that you have denied the Truth about yourself and must want to uncover what God has already given to you eternally. Then you can open yourself to accept the "holy instant," and receive flashes of the Truth you have denied about your relationship of holiness and eternal union with God and with your brothers and sisters.

What is the holy instant but God's appeal to you to recognize what He has given you? Here is the great appeal to reason; the awareness of what is always there to see, the happiness that could be always yours. Here is the constant peace you could experience forever. Here is what denial has denied revealed to you..... Here is the future *now*, for time is powerless because of your desire for what will never change. For you have asked that nothing stand between the holiness of your relationship and your *awareness* of its holiness.[537]

The holy instant is a time given to timelessness by your choice to place the Holy Spirit in charge temporarily. "And so I choose this instant as the one to offer to the Holy Spirit..."[538] You may think that when you forgive and see holiness in your brother through Christ's vision, you are seeing something temporal, but that is not the case. To forgive, meaning to see holiness, is to see eternity. Your brother's holiness is in eternity, and your own holiness is in eternity. It is this holiness in eternity that can be seen in the holy instant, which is the "eternal instant" that the Holy Spirit can reveal to you.

> He [the Holy Spirit] Who transcends time for you understands what time is for. Holiness lies not in time, but in eternity. There never was an instant in which God's Son could lose his purity. His changeless state is beyond time, for his purity remains forever beyond attack and without variability. Time stands still in his holiness, and changes not. And so it is no longer time at all. For caught in the single instant of the eternal sanctity of God's creation, it is transformed into forever. Give the eternal instant, that eternity may be remembered for you, in that shining instant of perfect release.[539]

The holy instant can be invited to give you the answer to problems. If your mind is confused, the holy instant can raise your consciousness to the higher mental awareness of reason where the mind is at peace. In that higher consciousness, the solution to the problem has already been given by God and is waiting there for your recognition.

> Therefore, God must have given you a way of reaching to another state of mind in which the answer is already there. Such is the holy instant. It is here that your problems should be brought and left. Here they belong, for here their answer is..... Attempt to solve no problems but within the holy instant's surety. For there the problem *will* be answered and resolved. [540]

As an expression of love, the holy instant is a miracle. "Offer the miracle of the holy instant through the Holy Spirit, and leave His giving it to you to Him."[541] The holy instant being a miracle is an example of the Course principle that giving and receiving are one since whatever you give away you keep. The love you receive in the miracle of the holy instant is kept by you because the Holy Spirit gives it to others on your behalf. Your active focus is necessary only in the receiving. This is why the Course states, "The sole responsibility of the miracle worker is to accept the Atonement for himself,"[542] which is the receiving of perfect love in the miracle of the holy instant. At your invitation, the Holy Spirit enables you to set aside your sense of judgment and experience the miracle of divine love that is always within you. This is the internal half of the miracle, which is experienced in the holy instant that you invite, but you do not have to direct the external half of the miracle, which is extension. When you receive the miracle in the holy instant, the Holy Spirit instantaneously extends the love that you experienced to others without your conscious assistance. This is how you become a vehicle of spirit bringing healing and experiences of love into the lives of others through the Holy Spirit. Those who receive the love you experienced in the holy instant will send their love back to you. Thus you will often see the love you have helped convey in the response of others, but the Holy Spirit may send love to those whom you do not know so you will not directly see those effects. The giving and receiving that occurs in the holy instant is expressed as follows:

> The holy instant is a time in which you receive and give communication. This means, however, that it is a time in which your mind is open, both to receive and give. It is the recognition that all minds are in communication. It therefore seeks to change nothing, but merely to accept everything.[543]

The miracle of the holy instant is waiting for you in eternity. "You can claim the holy instant any time and anywhere you want it," if you want it and ask for it.[544] I doubt if anyone could go through life without experiencing a holy instant of transcending separation. The holy instant can be experienced spontaneously without any structure, but hopefully you can learn to have holy instants by inviting them.

> You can practice the mechanics of the holy instant, and will learn much from doing so. Yet its shining and glittering brilliance, which will literally blind you to this world by its vision, you cannot supply. And here it is, all in this instant, complete, accomplished, and given wholly.... To learn to separate out this single second, and to experience it as timeless, is to begin to experience yourself as not separate.[545]

Although you can invite the holy instant at any time, setting aside times each day for meditation can be very helpful since a holy instant can be a quiet time of resting in the Arms of the Father. The Course Workbook offers many options for attunement, which include wordless contemplation, visualization, repeating the Name of God, and even directly seeking to see the blazing light. My meditation book, *Christian Meditation Inspired by Yoga and "A Course in Miracles,"* addresses how to make the transition from focusing on one thought in meditation to resting in God's presence during wordless contemplation. I encourage meditators to be open to experiencing inner feelings, such as the feeling of oneness, heightened awareness, the divine presence, inner peace, and happiness. These are felt through intuition during meditation, and the most important experience of inner feelings is the inner sensing of love. By experiencing the inner feeling of love, you can identify with love and learn you are love. I recommend that you consider experiencing *God's Love Meditation* described at the end of the next section.

The most unusual intuition is the inner feeling of light since light is normally thought of as something that can only be seen not sensed. Nevertheless, through experiencing the inner feeling of light, you can identify with light and learn that you are light. Light can be felt within you during meditation. This experience helps to build a very solid foundation of faith and belief in the divine Light. Below is an e-mail that my friend Stuart Dean sent me in which he describes his friend's meditation experience of light:

> Sometimes the person I live near invites me in as he does a breathing meditation. He then holds me in mind, or compresses me, or whatever idea he's playing with. This has been going on for some time.

> Recently though, my neighbor had the surprising idea that perhaps h*e is the light* he has breathed in, rather than the body or self. When he breathes in now, he shifts his sense of identity to being the light and has discovered something remarkable: When he is truly feeling he is the light, he feels that all the radiating light wants to do is to bring joy to whatever it touches, beginning with the inside of his body. He has learned that the light is somehow alive, with a childlike intention to bring joy to everything it touches. And he is beginning now to think it may really be true that his nature is light, and not what he thought he was. For the first time in his life, he knows what it feels like to be without the least trace of heaviness. For the first time, he knows the feeling of wanting only to bring goodness to others. It has also crossed his mind that a greater way of living would be to *act like the light*, and joyfully bring joy to whoever or whatever is around him, simply by shining, simply by being the light he is now identifying with. My neighbor repeats to himself, "I do good work. I am light. I bring joy."

Stuart's email to me ended by describing his own meditation: "By the next morning's meditation, I could identify with the light extending without limit, reminding me of 'the face of Christ' in *A Course in Miracles*."

H. FROM SEPARATE PERCEPTIONS TO WHOLENESS

Below is an expanded variation of a famous Hindu story:

There is an elephant inside a completely dark room. Also, in the dark room, there are men who cannot see the elephant, and who have never seen an elephant and have never heard that such an animal exists. One man only touches the elephant's tail, a second man touches one of the elephant's ears, a third man touches the elephant's trunk, and a fourth man touches one of the elephant's legs. Later, when they are outside, the four men disagree on what was inside the dark room since each one touched only a small part of the elephant, and no one was able to grasp what the elephant actually looked like.

Another man appeared who told the four men he saw the room when it was filled with light and saw there was an animal inside the room called an "elephant" that was almost as big as the whole room. He added, "I am an elephant teacher." The man who touched the elephant's tail said, "There wasn't any large animal in there. If it was an animal, it was small, maybe the size of a snake." Then he walked away. The man who touched the trunk said, "If it was a snake, it was a very large snake. You must be mistaken because no animal could be almost the size of that room." The third man who touched the elephant's leg and the fourth man who touched the elephant's side said maybe it was a large animal so they asked to hear more about this large animal. Next the elephant teacher verbally described the various parts of the elephant. When the third man said, "No, you must be kidding. It sounds like you are describing a dinosaur. No animal could look like that." Then he walked away.

However, the fourth man said, "I believe you. I haven't seen an elephant myself, but you have seen an elephant so I trust you. Tell me more about the elephant." And so the man became the student of the elephant teacher. The elephant teacher first taught his student about the various parts of the elephant that the four men had individually touched. Later he explained that the wholeness of the elephant is much greater than the separate parts that the four men have touched. The elephant teacher made a small drawing of the elephant so his student could see what the elephant looked like in its wholeness. Later the elephant teacher painted a full-size two-dimensional image of the elephant on a gigantic door on one side of the building where the elephant is inside. The elephant teacher told his student to meditate on this image on the door, and he promised that eventually the door with the image on it would open. Finally, one day, the door to the building did open. And in the light of day, the student experienced directly seeing the elephant for himself.

In this Hindu story, the elephant is a symbol for God, Who can be known only partially until we awaken in Heaven. The variation I added to this story is the "elephant teacher," who in my version symbolizes the Holy Spirit, Who is our Teacher of God. The Holy Spirit has the direct knowledge of the Oneness and Wholeness of God. But He also has perfect right-minded perception so He can bring His awareness of God's Wholeness into our perceptual world of fragmentation, where we identify with the ego that itself is the idea of separation. "The ego is the part of the mind that believes your existence is defined by separation."[546]

Just as the elephant teacher offers a drawing of the elephant to his student, Jesus, guided by the Holy Spirit, offers us a "drawing" of God in the words of *A Course in Miracles*. But in the Course, this divine "drawing" is shown to us in parts. Similar to the way the elephant teacher talks about the separate parts of the elephant, many terms in the Course are described as though they are separate as a concession to our limited perception that focuses on differences. For example, consider the terms listed below that at first glance seem to provide different names to identify different ideas:

Face of Christ	World of brightness
Christ's face	Holy instant
Vision of the Son of God	Happy dream
Circle of Atonement	Holy meeting place
Bridge	God's altar
Real world	Holy place of resurrection
World of Light	Great and shining circle

What do all these seemingly different terms have in common? They are all different ways of describing the same one door to Heaven. The Course refers to this door in these ways: "the door the Christ holds open," "the open door of Heaven," "The door to freedom from the world," "The door beyond which lies the end of dreams," and "the ancient door that leads beyond the world." In the Hindu story, the elephant teacher paints an image of the elephant on a gigantic door on one side of the building where the elephant is inside. Likewise, the Holy Spirit has given you "the face of Christ," which is not the Christ, but it is the image of Christ, similar to the image of the elephant. Because Christ's face is an image, it is also an illusion, but it is the one illusion made by the Holy Spirit that transcends all the illusions that you and I have made. When you bring all your illusions that you have made to the Holy Spirit for release, the last illusion you will see before awakening is the face of Christ.

The Holy Spirit reaches from the Christ in you to all your dreams, and bids them [illusions] come to Him, to be translated into truth. He will exchange them for the final dream [the image of the face of Christ] which God appointed as the end of dreams. For when forgiveness rests upon the world and peace has come to every Son of God, what could there be to keep things separate, for what remains to see except Christ's face?[547]

A face is only an outer façade, but the face of Christ is more than just an ordinary image since the Holy Spirit made it for His purpose of awakening. Because this illusory image is a perfect reflection of Christ, it leads to awakening in the reality of Heaven. Similar to the story's painting of an image of the elephant on the door to where the real elephant resides, the image of the face of Christ is the "painting" on the doorway to Heaven where the real Christ resides. This one image of the face of Christ is described in many different Course terms, each one indicating a different aspect of the one "open door to Heaven." When you see this "vision of the Son of God," your mind will shift from perceptions of separation to the one-mindedness of knowledge as you remember your Father and remember your Self as His Son, the Christ. "The face of Christ is looked upon before the Father is remembered."[548] This image of Christ is such a perfect reflection of your true nature that you will see your own Self in it.

Let's discuss the previously mentioned three levels of unifying the mind in relation to Christ's vision, which involves seeing the face of Christ with increasing depth: The first and lowest level is seeing Christ's face in one brother's face and then eventually in every brother's face because you manifest forgiveness that perceives the content of holiness rather than outer forms of separation. "If you see glimpses of the face of Christ behind the veil... you will behold your brother's face and recognize it."[549] Forgiveness will allow you to see the face of Christ in your brother. "Christ's face is seen in every living thing, and nothing is held in darkness, apart from the light of forgiveness."[550]

This first level of seeing the face of Christ in your brother is healing for your mind and brings healing to the mind of your brother. The Course uses the term "magic" to describe the attempt to heal symptoms of sickness without healing the false identification with the ego and with guilt that caused the sickness. "All material means that you accept as remedies for bodily ills are restatements of magic principles."[551] The teacher of God heals the cause of sickness by accepting the Atonement for himself. Thus he identifies with Christ within himself and within every brother. "He overlooks [forgives] the mind *and* body, seeing only the face of Christ shining in front of him, correcting all mistakes and healing all perception. Healing is the result of the recognition, by

God's teacher, [of Christ in himself and others] of Who it is that is in need of healing."[552]

The second level of this vision is a brief transcendent experience of seeing of the deepest level of the face of Christ. This is direct seeing of the blazing light of Christ's face. Then you return to ordinary worldly awareness, but retain the memory of your profound experience. "Once it is seen, this light can never be forgotten."[553] In the story, the elephant teacher saw an elephant himself and became a teacher of what he had seen. Likewise, those who have a temporary experience of seeing the blazing light of the face of Christ can speak to others and teach them of what they experienced. From that frame of reference, I have become a writer of Course books to bear witness to my own personal experience of seeing the face of Christ, described in the following excerpt from my autobiography titled *Memory Walk in the Light*[554] :

Then I got up hurriedly and walked as fast as I could toward the front doorway, but without going so fast as to draw attention to myself. I didn't know where I was going or why I was in such a hurry. I quickly pulled open the screen door and sped down the steps of the front porch. At the bottom of the steps, I moved forward and turned my body toward the left and looked directly up at the sun. As I looked upward, I spontaneously threw both arms over my head. In yoga this body position is the first part of what is called the Sun Salutation. As soon as I threw my arms overhead and saw the sun, I was instantly and completely overcome by a brilliant, blazing white Light. I must have literally jumped out of my body because I no longer had any awareness of it.

There was no up and no down, no right and no left, no front and no back, and no inside and no outside. I was nowhere and everywhere. I was in a state of awe and amazement at the Light, which had struck me with full overwhelming force. The Light was all-powerful, without limit or form. The Light had a center and simultaneously was expanding in all directions at once. *I was that Light*. Since I had no body awareness, in a sense the Light itself was my "formless body." By a crude analogy, it was as though I was in the center of the sun itself and my arms and legs were the rays of the sun expanding infinitely. But the Light was not a physical light like the light of the sun. It was the Light of pure consciousness, and *I was that pure consciousness—that Light*. It was a state of indescribable ecstasy and freedom.

Somehow at the beginning of this experience, I clearly heard my mother's voice [from inside the house] saying the words, "The lights went out!" At the time I was not able to analyze what these words meant or to see the irony in them, because the Light had gathered all of my attention, and indeed my entire being was absorbed into the Light. This Light was not something that I could simply observe as a spectator apart from what is observed. The Light and I were one. My whole being and consciousness were totally immersed in this white Light, which was overpowering. My mind was in a state of total, all-consuming wonderment, unable to comprehend fully what was happening in a conceptual sense. Even now....I cannot describe it to you and do justice to what this Light was like.

This experience occurred in 1969 before the Course was published so I did not know I had seen the face of Christ and been at the door to Heaven. I considered it an enlightenment experience of the Reality of God, which the Course calls "revelation." Though I embraced the Light initially, I could not leave the world behind because I was not prepared to release body awareness as is explained in this excerpt:

I was in complete fascination with the Light for an indeterminate amount of time. Then the thought came to me, *Where is my body?* I had no answer to this question and felt fear at the idea of not having a body. This tiny thought and the emotion of fear attending it were enough to bring about a change in the experience. My sense of ecstasy and expansive freedom evaporated. Within the infinitely expanding Light, I suddenly felt it contracting. Since I identified with the Light, I felt I was contracting along with it, and with this contraction the full steady force changed to pulsations.

After the Light stopped entirely and I returned to body awareness, my father came outside because the electricity had gone out in our cottage at the beach in Westbrook, Connecticut. The excerpt continues, as follows:

He asked, "Donald, would you mind going to the store and ask Baxter if he is having trouble with his electricity? Our electricity has blacked out in the house, and I want to see if it's just our house or if it's a general power failure."

I agreed and walked to the store, located at the beginning of our dead-end street. As I walked, I still felt disoriented, as if I was moving in slow motion. I then remembered having earlier heard my mother's voice coming from inside the house saying, "The lights went out!" However, it seemed odd that the lights would go out in the house precisely when the Light was overpowering me. When I reached the store, Baxter, the store owner, said that the store had lost all its electrical power. Other people had come in and said that their cottages were also blacked out.

As I was walking back to the house and reaching the patio, it occurred to me for the first time that I had actually received enlightenment. It might sound strange that it took me so long to come to this conclusion, but that is how disorienting the experience was. There was also a second, very important, simultaneous realization. I understood that everyone already exists in this Light that I experienced, so everyone is perfectly equal in the Light. In other words, I had experienced what already was there before I found it. The Light is where we all really live and have our being eternally, whether we are consciously aware of that Light or not.

I went inside and told my parents about the general power failure and went to my room to rest. I realized that what had happened was more than a subjective internal experience because the power of the Light had affected the objective external world by blowing out the electricity in the area. This is surprising if you believe the external world is the foundation of reality. But... the external world is an illusion, which only appears to be real because of the ego. The Light that I saw is the real underlying Reality. This Light is the ground of Being, like an artist's white canvas which is then overlaid with layers of colored shapes that prevent the canvas itself from being seen. Just as there can be no painting without a canvas, there is no world without the canvas of Light that supports its appearance.

After returning to the cottage, I rested for a while attempting to use my mental perceptions to better understand this disorienting experience that fully transcended my perceptual mind. This final autobiographic excerpt explains what happened next:

Then I walked outside again, and looked up at the sun, and threw up my arms over my head, but without the spontaneity expressed earlier. I knew that this wouldn't make the experience happen again, though I faintly hoped that it would. However, I felt that this gesture was necessary as a way of expressing that... I was willing to experience it again. At the time it was also my way of asking the question, "Why couldn't I stay in the Light and why did I have to come back to the body at all?" I wondered what would have happened if I hadn't asked the fear-producing question, "Where is my body?" which triggered the return to body awareness.

Before this experience that I now call seeing the face of Christ, I can say that I was indeed a soul completely lost in illusions. The context of my autobiography explains just how lost I was. But if anyone has an experience similar to this seeing the face of Christ, it will probably be the most important experience and the turning point of that lifetime as it was for me. Following this experience, I did not have a thought system that could adequately explain in perceptual terms what had occurred until I accepted the Course in 1988. It is easy for me now to resonate with the words, "I am not a body. I am free. For I am still as God created me," which is repeated twenty times in the Course for emphasis. But will I remember these words and be able to completely embrace the face of Christ the next time I have the opportunity to fully awaken in Heaven? Will I be able to give up the world of illusions, ending the cycle of birth, death, and reincarnation? I hope so.

The temporary experience of seeing Christ's face may happen as part of a meditation or may happen spontaneously at any time. This temporary seeing of the face of Christ is a profound experience of a holy "instant which transcends all vision."

> Into Christ's Presence will we enter now, serenely unaware of everything except His shining face and perfect Love. The vision of His face will stay with you, but there will be an instant which transcends all vision, even this, the holiest. This you will never teach, for you attained it not through learning. Yet the vision speaks of your remembrance of what you knew that instant, and will surely know again."[555]

Yet is it a realistic goal for you to seek to experience this second stage of temporarily seeing the face of Christ and then return to normal body awareness? No, I am not recommending that you set the goal of temporary divine union because the Course says it is not a realistic goal.

> Sometimes a teacher of God may have a brief experience of direct union with God. In this world, it is almost impossible that this endure. It can, perhaps, be won after much devotion and dedication, and then be maintained for much of the time on earth. But this is so rare that it cannot be considered a realistic goal. If it happens, so be it. If it does not happen, so be it as well. All worldly states must be illusory. [556]

The goal is not the second level of temporarily seeing the face of Christ. Instead, the ultimate goal is to succeed at the third level of seeing the face of Christ, which is the opportunity to awaken permanently. When you see the image of Christ's face, you are not only seeing a reflection of Christ. You are also seeing a reflection of your true Self because you are the Christ in your true Identity. "And you will see Christ's face upon it [the holy instant described as a mirror], in reflection of your own [Christ Self]."[557] Since you are seeing a reflection of your true Self, this experience has the power to bring about your awakening to your own Christ nature. Thus the face of Christ becomes your open door to Heaven. When your body is set aside on earth, you will see the vision of the Son of God and have the opportunity to embrace the light and awaken in Heaven. Or you will fear the blazing light of Christ's face and be reincarnated in order to learn all over again how to embrace the light of divine love.

And how long will this holy face be seen, when it is but the symbol that the time for learning now is over, and the goal of the Atonement has been reached at last? So therefore let us seek to find Christ's face and look on nothing else. As we behold His glory, will we know we have no need of learning or perception or of time, or anything except the holy Self, the Christ Whom God created as His Son.[558]

The world stands like a block before Christ's face. But true perception looks on it as nothing more than just a fragile veil, so easily dispelled that it can last no longer than an instant. It is seen at last for only what it is. And now it cannot fail to disappear, for now there is an empty place made clean and ready. Where destruction was perceived the face of Christ appears, and in that instant is the world forgot, with time forever ended as the world spins into nothingness from where it came.[559]

These things await us all, but we are not prepared as yet to welcome them with joy. As long as any mind remains possessed of evil dreams, the thought of hell is real. God's teachers have the goal of wakening the minds of those asleep, and seeing there the vision of Christ's face to take the place of what they dream. The thought of murder is replaced with blessing. Judgment is laid by, and given Him Whose function judgment is. And in His Final Judgment is restored the truth about the holy Son of God. He is redeemed, for he has heard God's Word and understood its meaning. He is free because he let God's Voice proclaim the truth. And all he sought before to crucify are resurrected with him, by his side, as he prepares with them to meet his God.[560]

All of spiritual growth in the Course and even in every spiritual path is designed to help you make the choice to embrace the face of Christ and pass through this doorway to Heaven. But what is the last obstacle that you need to overcome in order to embrace the blazing light of the face of Christ? The last obstacle is the fear of God, which "hangs like a heavy veil before the face of Christ."[561] This dark veil representing the fear of God "seems to make the face of Christ

Himself like to a leper's, and the bright Rays of His Father's Love that light His face with glory appear as streams of blood..."[562] But this dark veil "fades in the blazing light beyond it when"[563] when you can release fear, especially the fear of God. You have forgotten God in what the Course calls, "...the great amnesia in which the memory of God seems quite forgotten..."[564] You have forgotten God's Love and instead become afraid of your Father because you imagined you had attacked Him by leaving behind your awareness of your Home in Heaven. Seeing the face of Christ brings back your memory of your Father and His Love. But you can only remember your Father, if you can "let the fear of God be lifted, so you could look upon the face of Christ and join Him in His Father."[565]

The Course section titled, "The Journey's End," refers to the end of endless reincarnation, which requires a two-part process in order to bring about your awakening. The first part of this process is looking upon your fear of God and letting go of that last frightening obstacle. The second part is seeing the face of Christ that was hidden by the fear of God. This process is not optional. "This is the place to which everyone must come when he is ready."[566] However, you do have the option of delaying the journey's end and being reincarnated over and over again. With each lifetime, reincarnation offers you another opportunity to overcome the fear of God and accept God's Love by embracing the face of Christ.

> Here, with the journey's end before you, you *see* its purpose. And it is here you choose whether to look upon it [the fear of God and then the face of Christ] or wander on, only to return and make the choice again.[567]

But do you really want to keep delaying your homecoming to Heaven? The Course is designed to encourage you to make your current lifetime the one that brings your journey to the happy result of coming home to your Father and to accept your rightful place in the Sonship. If you dedicate yourself to awakening in this lifetime, you have to prepare yourself to confront your fear of God and then see the face of Christ. "To look upon the fear of God does need some preparation."[568]

You may not even be consciously aware of your fear of God since He does not manifest outwardly as God Himself. However, you can see God in your brother, and in your fear of your brother, you can find your fear of God being made manifest. "You are afraid of God *because* you fear your brother."[569] Consequently, you can prepare to confront your fear of God by healing your fear of your brother. Thus forgiveness is your major means of preparing for the journey's end since forgiveness, if manifested completely to everyone, will release your fear of your brother, indirectly releasing your fear of God. "Those you do not forgive you fear. And no one reaches love with fear beside him."[570] You cannot reach the journey's end unless your brother is your savior, and you are his savior. You are prepared and ready to look past the fear of God and embrace the face of Christ once you have completely forgiven your brother, who in turn forgives you to become your savior as you become his savior.

> Beside you is one who offers you the chalice of Atonement, for the Holy Spirit is in him. Would you hold his sins against him, or accept his gift to you? Is this giver of salvation your friend or enemy? Choose which he is, remembering that you will receive of him according to your choice. He has in him the power to forgive your sin, as you for him. Neither can give it to himself alone. And yet your savior stands beside each one. Let him be what he is, and seek not to make of love an enemy.[571]

You will fear God as long as you perceive your brothers are guilty. But if you forgive all your brothers entirely, you will remember God's Love for them and for you. "The fear of God results as surely from the lesson that His Son is guilty as God's Love must be remembered when he learns his innocence."[572] In the Course, forgiveness of your brother is your main means of preparing for the journey's end. Yet in addition to the horizontal approach of connecting to your brothers, there is also the vertical approach to releasing the fear of God by restoring your natural awareness of your oneness with your Father. A major step forward in preparing yourself for seeing the face of Christ and awakening is deciding to focus on investing in God's Love for you, which will automatically help you set aside the fear of God resulting from the separation.

> Love cannot judge. As it is one itself, it looks on all as one. Its meaning lies in oneness. And it must elude the mind that thinks of it as partial or in part. There is no love but God's, and all of love is His. There is no other principle that rules where love is not. Love is a law without an opposite. Its wholeness is the power holding everything as one, the link between the Father and the Son which holds Them both forever as the same.[573]

God's Love is your strength. Why would you not call upon it? I encourage you to practice *God's Love Meditation.* This is the form of meditation I have chosen for myself in order to overcome my fear of God and remember God's ever-present Love. This meditation is best practiced while sitting but occasionally can be used while lying down.

It can be a supplement to using Christian Yoga Meditation as your main method of attunement. For most seekers, an advantage of sitting meditation is that it is easier to prevent drowsiness that sometimes happens during lying-down meditation. In my meditation experience, the first method I used was Zen meditation, and I lived at a Zen center. Then later I used yoga meditation and lived at a yoga ashram. Still later, I focused on Christian methods of meditation. All my adult life, I have used sitting meditation because it helps to raise the kundalini energy. Yet, in addition to sitting meditation, I recently added God's Love Meditation as a daily half-hour lying-down attunement. In this method of meditation, you wholeheartedly focus on God's Love for you personally. You focus on whatever reminds you of receiving God's Love, such as saying to yourself, "I accept God's Love. I accept the Atonement. I accept perfect love. I accept healing." Also, you let go of words, and just focus on the feeling of God loving you. In addition, when you feel God's Love for you intensely, you make sure to let His Love flow through you by sending forgiveness to everyone. After all, "God is the Love in which I forgive."[574]

The greatest benefit from this heart-based method of meditation comes from faith in God Himself. I have an experience of persistent joy in these times of opening my heart to the grace of God's Love, and I find myself automatically smiling after each meditation. I cannot convey the depth of my joy to you, but I want you to know about it because I want to encourage you to have this joy, too. We are fish in the Ocean of God's Love, and yet we keep questioning, "Where is the water of God's Love?" Ironically, we live in that Love, whether lost in dreams or awake in Heaven. We can experience that Love when we stop questioning and simply have faith in His Love. And if we don't have faith we can say to God, as in the Bible, "I believe. Help my unbelief!" After all, faith itself is just another gift of God's grace, but we must ask for this gift in order to give our consent to receive it because God does not impose anything upon us. Happiness is your reward for placing your faith in God's Love.

> Do not interpret against God's Love, for you have many witnesses that speak of it so clearly that only the blind and deaf could fail to see and hear them... His Voice has spoken clearly, and yet you have so little faith in what you heard, because you have preferred to place still greater faith in the disaster you have made. Today, let us resolve together to accept the joyful tidings that disaster is not real and that reality is not disaster. Reality is safe and sure, and wholly kind to everyone and everything. There is no greater love than to accept this and be glad. For love asks only that you be happy, and will give you everything that makes for happiness.[575]

I. DECIDING WHAT TO DO NEXT

Assuming you started at the beginning of this book, I congratulate you for coming all this way in your reading as an expression of your desire for God. If you eat a big meal, it takes time to digest it. A lot of information has been ingested by you in reading this book, and it may take time to digest it all.

You have an individualized spiritual curriculum that the Holy Spirit is revealing to you with loving care. The Holy Spirit has the function and responsibility to guide you every step of the way on your path and to answer any questions you may have along the way. However, it is entirely your responsibility to ask Him your questions. You do not really have to make a lot of decisions if you make the one decision to make no decisions alone. You can refer all your decisions to the Holy Spirit Who will "decide for God for you." The Holy Spirit is your real Teacher who will show you the way Home.

No accident nor chance is possible within the universe as God created it, outside of which is nothing. Suffer, and you decided sin was your goal. Be happy, and you gave the power of decision to Him Who must decide for God for you. This is the little gift you offer to the Holy Spirit, and even this He gives to you to give yourself. For by this gift is given you the power to release your savior, that he may give salvation unto you.[576]

Everything is an illusion except your true mind that rests in the Mind of Christ, which is your true Self. The Holy Spirit speaks to you from your holy mind reminding you of your true Identity until you finally look upon the face of Christ and see your own face reflected in that blazing light. Thus the dreams of this world will fade away, and you will awaken to your true Self as the Christ. "Yet will these dreams be given unto Christ, to fade before His glory and reveal your holy Self, the Christ, to you at last.[577]

This is the purpose of the face of Christ. It is the gift of God to save His Son. But look on this and you have been forgiven.

How lovely does the world become in just that single instant when you see the truth about yourself reflected there. Now you are sinless and behold your sinlessness. Now you are holy and perceive it so. And now the mind returns to its Creator; the joining of the Father and the Son, the Unity of unities that stands behind all joining but beyond them all. God is not seen but only understood. His Son is not attacked but recognized [as your true Self, the Christ].[578]

FINAL THOUGHTS

A helpful way to prepare yourself for awakening is to remind yourself many times during the day that you are loved by God. To express gratitude for God's Love, every morning I start my day by repeating the prayer below that has grown over time to be a long one. At first, my prayer of gratitude was just the first two sentences, which summarize the idea that God's Love must be acknowledged within and then extended to everyone. I am not asking you to repeat my prayer, but I do suggest that you formulate your own short prayer in your own words. The words you choose are not as important as your sense of gratitude and willingness to open your heart and mind to the divine within and without.

Father, thank You for loving me. Let Your love flow through me to bless all my brothers and sisters everywhere. They are the holy Son of God Who deserve to wake up in Heaven. They are Christ. They are the light. They are love. I am the holy Son of God Who deserves to wake up in Heaven. I am Christ. I am light. I am love. I am just as holy now as when You created me without guilt in my eternal Home in Heaven. With Jesus beside me on my journey of awakening, Holy Spirit, guide my mind, decide for God for me, and be in charge of my meditation experience of the holy instant. Holy Spirit and Jesus, with your help, I forgive all my brothers and sisters and I forgive myself because we deserve only love and not the illusions of guilt we have fabricated to unfairly punish ourselves. I am free of all my mistakes and their effects because I gratefully accept the perfect love and healing of the Atonement that corrects all errors. I am not a body. I am free for I am still as You created me. I am still a spirit created in Your Thought and in likeness to Your character. Help me to appreciate and manifest the things of spirit: peace, kindness, love, patience, faith, hope, charity and humility. Help me to let go of the things of the ego and attachments to the body, such as fear, anger, pain, guilt, shame, pride, specialness, and judgment. Father, help me to do Your Will and understand that Your will is my true will, which is all the loving expressions I would create if I were fully aware of all the love You are giving me right now. Help me to love everyone. Father, let Your Light and Love flow through me to bless (names of those in need of prayer).

ACKNOWLEDGMENTS

In bringing this book to publication, I very much appreciate the encouragement and proofreading help of David Luma, Cindy Elliman, Rachel Korponay, Cynthia Fawcett, and Jean Ford.

ABOUT THE AUTHOR

Don Giacobbe was employed for sixteen years as a case manager serving developmentally disabled clients. The professional nature of his work limited his ability to express his spiritual motivations overtly, so out of necessity, he served as an "undercover agent" for God.

A more direct approach to spirituality was facilitated by living with Zen Buddhist seekers and then living in a yoga community. Later he was the director of the Aquarian Age Yoga Center in Virginia Beach, VA. He served as an instructor of meditation and yoga, teaching college courses and appearing on television. He specialized in providing yoga teacher training certification courses and leading meditation workshops and retreats. Don has attempted in his teaching of meditation to strip away the rituals of Zen Buddhism and yoga practices and transpose only the bare essence into a Christian context. Methods of meditation inspired by Eastern sources open the mind to the influence of the Holy Spirit and enhance the use of traditional Christian practices, such as the "Jesus Prayer" and Christian contemplation. These techniques can be found in Don's book *Christian Meditation Inspired by Yoga and "A Course in Miracles": Opening to Divine Love in Contemplation.*

Don's goal is to do God's Will, be receptive to the Holy Spirit, and find Christ within the temple of his own heart. He is not affiliated with any religious group. Formerly Don used the term "Christian yoga" to describe his path that combines following Christ with yoga disciplines. In recent years he has adopted the term "Miracle Yoga" to describe his type of Christian yoga. This spiritual path combines yoga and the philosophy of *A Course in Miracles* that encourages seeing with "forgiving eyes" and perceiving Christ in everyone. Don seeks to maintain a balance between opening to divine love inwardly and allowing love to be extended outwardly to others. Don recorded his life story in his autobiography, *Memory Walk in the Light*. You may contact Don at miracleyoga@gmail.com or at these websites:

www.miracleyoga.org — www.christianyoga.org
www.christianmeditation.org — www.acimgame.com

1. *A Course in Miracles*: The Course is in public domain, so there is no copyright. The former copyright holder, before the copyright was revoked, was the Foundation For Inner Peace,   P. O. Box 598, Mill Valley, CA 94942. The ideas represented herein are the personal interpretation and understanding of the author of this book. Course quotes are from *A   Course in Miracles* second edition published in 1985 by the Foundation For Inner Peace.

2. W-pI.r.VI.In.3:2

3. T-18.VI.11:1-11

4. Luke 17:21

5. T-26.III.7:2-3

6. C-5.5:1-2

7. C-5.3:1-5

8. T-1.II.3:10-13

9. C-2.1:4-7

10. M-10.2:9

11. Pravrajika Vrajaprana, *Regaining the Lost Kingdom*, an article included in *Purity of Heart and Contemplation: A Monastic Dialogue between Christian and Asian Traditions*, edited by Bruno Barnhart and Joseph Wong, (New York, New York: Continuum, 2001) pp. 23-24

12. Luke 17:21

13. Cyprian Consiglio, O.S.B. Cam., *The Space in the Lotus of the Heart*, an article included in *Purity of Heart and Contemplation: A Monastic Dialogue between Christian and Asian Traditions*, edited by Bruno Barnhart and Joseph Wong, (New York, New York: Continuum, 2001) p. 57

14. Ibid., p. 58

15. Ibid., p. 60

16. Ibid., p. 60

17. Ibid., p. 61

18. Thomas Matus, *Yoga and the Jesus Prayer Tradition* (Mahwah, New Jersey: Paulist Press, 1984), (currently published by Asian Trading, Bangalore, India; distributed by Hermitage Books, New Camaldoli, 62475 Coast Highway One, Big Sur, CA 93920), pp. 123-124

19. *Chandogya Upanishad*, VIII. 1. 1., p.191, in *The Upanishads*, translation Eknath Easwaren (Petaluma, CA: Nilgiri Press, 1987).

20. Matthew 20:1-16

21. Matthew 20:1

22. Georg Feuerstein, *Sacred Paths: Essays on Wisdom, Love, and Mystical Realization*, (Burden, New York: published for the Paul Brunton Philosophical Foundation by Larson Publications, 1991), p. 103

23. Ibid., p. 103

24. Pravrajika Vrajaprana, *Regaining the Lost Kingdom*, an article included in *Purity of Heart and Contemplation: A Monastic Dialogue between Christian and Asian Traditions*, edited by Bruno Barnhart and Joseph Wong, (New York, New York: Continuum, 2001) pp. 30-31

25. Ibid., pp. 35-38

26. Georg Feuerstein, *Sacred Paths: Essays on Wisdom, Love, and Mystical Realization*, (Burden, New York: published for the Paul Brunton Philosophical Foundation by Larson Publications, 1991), pp. 76-77

27. Ibid., p. 68

28. Ibid., p. 91

29. Ibid., p. 69

30. Ibid., p. 72

31. Ibid., p. 72

32. Ibid., p. 72

33. Ibid., p. 69

34. Ibid., p. 74

35. Ibid., p. 76

36. Pravrajika Vrajaprana, *Regaining the Lost Kingdom*, an article included in *Purity of Heart and Contemplation: A Monastic Dialogue between Christian and Asian*

Traditions, edited by Bruno Barnhart and Joseph Wong, (New York, New York: Continuum, 2001) p. 37

37. Ibid., p 37

38. Ibid., p. 37

39. Ibid, p. 37

40. Haridas Chaudhuri, *Integral Yoga*, (Wheaton, Illinois; Madras, India; London, England: The Theosophical Publishing House, 1981), p. 55

41. The Sivananda Yoga Center, Foreword by Swami Vishnu, *The Sivananda Companion to Yoga*, (New York, London, Sidney, Singapore: A Fireside Book; Simon and Schuster, 2000), p. 19

42. Swami Vishnu-devananda, *The Complete Illustrated Book of Yoga*, (New York, New York: Bell Publishing Company, Inc., a division of Crown Publishing, Inc.), Copyright 1960, by the Julian Press, Inc., p. 309

43. Gopi Krishna, *Kundalini: Evolutionary Energy in Man*, (Boulder, Colorado and London, England: Shambhala, 1971), p. 108

44. Thomas Matus, *Yoga and the Jesus Prayer Tradition* (Mahwah, New Jersey: Paulist Press, 1984), (currently published by Asian Trading, Bangalore, India; distributed by Hermitage Books, New Camaldoli, 62475 Coast Highway One, Big Sur, CA 93920), pp. 144-145

45. Ibid., p. 117

46. Ibid., p. 18

47. St. Symeon the New Theologian, *Hymns of Divine Love*, translated by George A. Maloney, S. J., (Denville, New Jersey: Dimension Books), Hymn 17, lines 323-325, p.67

48. Thomas Matus, *Yoga and the Jesus Prayer Tradition* (Mahwah, New Jersey: Paulist Press, 1984), (currently published by Asian Trading, Bangalore, India; distributed by Hermitage Books, New Camaldoli, 62475 Coast Highway One, Big Sur, CA 93920), pp. 106-107

49. T-28.I.1:8

50. T-20.IV.2:9-10, 3:1

51. T-26.VII.13:1

52. W-19.1:4

53. W-138.12:5-6

54. T-2.VI.9:8

55. T-2.VI.9:13-14

56. W-132.1:1-7

57. W-132.2:1-4

58. W-126.7:5

59. W-196.8:3-5

60. T-13.V.3:5

61. T-31.VIII.3:1

62. T-2.VII.1:1-4.

63. T-4.V.6:7-11

64. T-31.VIII.3:2

65. T-31.VIII.3:3-5

66. T-4.VII.5:1

67. T-31.VIII.3:6

68. The entire article by Robert Perry can be found on the Circle of Atonement website at www.cirlceofa.org by entering the word "karma" in the search function. Among several articles on the subject of karma, Robert's response is the one simply titled "Karma."

69. *The Revised Standard Version of the Bible*, (New York, New York: American Bible Society, 1952.) All Bible quotes hereafter in this manual are taken from this version of the Bible and will not be footnoted. Matthew 6:33

70 Brother Lawrence, *The Practice of the Presence*, (Springdale, Pennsylvania: Whitaker House, 1982), pp. 20-21

71. Galatians 5:22-23, Ibid., p. 215

72. Maria Valtorta, *The Poem of the Man-God*, Volumes 1-5, Translated from Italian by Nicandro Picozzi, Revised by Patrick McLaughlin, (reprinted by Grafiche Dipro, 31056 Roncade TV, Italy for copyright holder Centro Editoriale Valtortiano sri, 03036 Isola de

Liri (Fr), Italy. Can be purchased from Editions Paulines, 250, boul. Saint-Francois Nord, Sherbrooke, QC, J1E 2B9—Canada.

73. *A Course in Miracles*, now in the public domain, but formerly copyrighted—Copyright 1975, 1995, 1992 by the Foundation For Inner Peace, P.O. Box 598, Mill Valley, CA 94942.

74 St. John of the Cross, *Ascent of Mount Carmel*, edited by E. Allison Peers (New York, New York: Image Books, Doubleday and Co., Inc., 1958), p. 304. This book was published by arrangement with the copyright holder and original publisher, Newman Press, which has been absorbed by Paulist Press, Mahwah, New Jersey.

75. Luke 23:34

76. Luke 23:46

77. Harold J. Reilly and Ruth Hagy Brod, *The Edgar Cayce Handbook for Health through Drugless Therapy*, (Virginia Beach, VA: A.R.E. Press, Copyright 1975), p. 116

78. Swami Rama, Rudolph Ballentine, M.D., Alan Hymes, M.D., *The Science of Breath*, (Honesdale, Pennsylvania: The Himalayan International Institute of Yoga Science and Philosophy, 1979) pp. 126-127

79. Harold J. Reilly and Ruth Hagy Brod, *The Edgar Cayce Handbook for Health through Drugless Therapy*, (Virginia Beach, VA: A.R.E. Press, Copyright 1975), p. 113 (#3549-1 of the Edgar Cayce readings)

80. Reading #3549-1, Edgar Cayce Readings © 1971, 1993-2005 by the Edgar Cayce Foundation. Used by Permission, All Rights Reserved.

81. Ibid., pp. 113-114, (#2823-2 and #555-8 of the Edgar Cayce readings)

82. Ibid., p. 113, (#288-11 of the Edgar Cayce readings)

83. Ibid., p. 113, (#288-11 of the Edgar Cayce readings)

84. Yogiraj Sri Swami Satchidananda, *Integral Yoga Hatha*, (New York, Chicago, San Francisco: Holt, Rinehart and Winston, 1970-1974), p. 142

85. Michael Reed Gach with Carolyn Marco, *Acu-Yoga: Self Help Techniques to Relieve Tension*, (Tokyo and New York: Japan Publications, Inc.,1981-1994), p. 37

86. Richard Rosen, *The Yoga of Breath*, (Boston and London: Shambhala, 2002), pp. 227-229

87. Yogiraj Sri Swami Satchidananda, *Integral Yoga Hatha*, (New York, Chicago, San Francisco: Holt, Rinehart and Winston, 1970-1974), p. 143

88. James Hewitt, *The Complete Yoga*, (New York, New York: Schochen Books, 1978), pp. 96-100

89. Lilian Silburn, *Kundalini: The Energy of the Depths*, translated by Jacques Gontier, (Albany, New York: State University of New York Press, 1988), p. 124

90. Swami Vishnu-devananda, *The Complete Illustrated Book of Yoga*, (New York, New York: Bell Publishing Company, Inc., a division of Crown Publishing, Inc.), Copyright 1960, by the Julian Press, Inc., p. 233

91. Swami Vivekananda, *Raja Yoga*, quoted by M.S.S. Gurucharan Singh Khalsa (with Yogi Bhajan), *Exploring the Myths and Misconceptions of Kundalini*, article written in the book *Kundalini, Evolution and Enlightenment*, edited by John White, (Garden City, New York: Anchor Press/Doubleday and Company, 1979), p. 137

92. Michael Reed Gach with Carolyn Marco, *Acu-Yoga: Self Help Techniques To Relieve Tension*, (Tokyo and New York: Japan Publications, Inc.,1981-1994), pp. 39-40

93. B.K.S Iyengar, *Light on Yoga*, (New York, New York: Schocken Books, 1979), pp. 436-440

94. Ibid., pp. 436-440

95. Ibid., pp. 436-440

96. Guru Dharam S. Khalsa and Darryl O'Keefe, *The Kundalini Yoga Experience*, (New York, London, Toronto, Sydney, Singapore: A Fireside Book published by Simon & Schuster, 2002), p. 135

97. Ibid., p. 135

98. M.S.S. Gurucharan Singh Khalsa (with Yogi Bhajan), *Exploring the Myths and Misconceptions of Kundalini*, article written in the book *Kundalini, Evolution and Enlightenment*, edited by John White, (Garden City, New York: Anchor Press/Doubleday and Company, 1979), p. 143

99. The Sivananda Yoga Center, Foreword by Swami Vishnu, *The Sivananda Companion to Yoga*, (New York, London, Sidney, Singapore: A Fireside Book; Simon and Schuster, 2000), p. 75

100. Robert Svoboda, *Aghora II: Kundalini*, (Albuquerque, New Mexico: Brotherhood of Life Publishing, in 1998 co-published by Sadhana Publications of Bellingham, Washington), p. 58
101. Haridas Chaudhuri, *Integral Yoga*, (Wheaton, Illinois; Madras, India; London, England: The Theosophical Publishing House, 1981), pp. 130-132
102. Swami Sivananda Radha, *Kundalini, An Overview*, article written in the book *Kundalini, Evolution and Enlightenment*, edited by John White, (Garden City, New York: Anchor Press/Doubleday and Company, 1979), p. 50
103. Lee Sannella, Kundalini: *Classical and Clinical*, article written in the book *Kundalini, Evolution and Enlightenment*, edited by John White, (Garden City, New York: Anchor Press/Doubleday and Company, 1979), p. 306
104. Swami Rama, *The Awakening of the Kundalini*, article written in the book *Kundalini, Evolution and Enlightenment*, edited by John White, (Garden City, New York: Anchor Press/Doubleday and Company, 1979), pp. 41-42
105. Christopher Hills, *Is Kundalini Real?*, article written in the book *Kundalini, Evolution and Enlightenment*, edited by John White, (Garden City, New York: Anchor Press/Doubleday and Company, 1979), p. 116
106. John Scudder, *A Psychic Healer Experiences Kundalini*, article written in the book *Kundalini, Evolution and Enlightenment*, edited by John White, (Garden City, New York: Anchor Press/Doubleday and Company, 1979), pp. 189-197
107. Lee Sannella, Kundalini: *Classical and Clinical*, article written in the book *Kundalini, Evolution and Enlightenment*, edited by John White, (Garden City, New York: Anchor Press/Doubleday and Company, 1979), p. 307
108. Matthew 3:11-120
109. Hebrew's 12:29
110. Joseph Campbell, *The Power of Myth*, (New York, New York: Doubleday and Company, 1988), as quoted by Jager, Willigis, *Search for the Meaning of Life*, (Liguori, Missouri: Liguori/Triumph, 1995), p. 169
111. Roy Eugene Davis, *Kundalini in Action*, article written in the book *Kundalini, Evolution and Enlightenment*, edited by John White, (Garden City, New York: Anchor Press/Doubleday and Company, 1979) p. 460
112. Alice A. Bailey, *Ordered Meditation and Loving Service*, article written in the book *Kundalini, Evolution and Enlightenment*, edited by John White, (Garden City, New York: Anchor Press/Doubleday and Company, 1979), pp. 455-456
113. John White, *Some Possibilities for further Kundalini Research*, article written in the book *Kundalini, Evolution and Enlightenment*, edited by John White, (Garden City, New York: Anchor Press/Doubleday and Company, 1979), p. 354
114. M.S.S. Gurucharan Singh Khalsa (with Yogi Bhajan), *Exploring the Myths and Misconceptions of Kundalini*, article written in the book *Kundalini, Evolution and Enlightenment*, edited by John White, (Garden City, New York: Anchor Press/Doubleday and Company, 1979), p. 147
115. Swami Muktananda, *Sensual Excitement*, article written in the book *Kundalini, Evolution and Enlightenment*, edited by John White, (Garden City, New York: Anchor Press/Doubleday and Company, 1979), pp. 157-171
116. Sri Chinmoy, *The Two Paths to Kundalini*, article written in the book *Kundalini, Evolution and Enlightenment*, edited by John White, (Garden City, New York: Anchor Press/Doubleday and Company, 1979), pp. 453-454
117. M.S.S. Gurucharan Singh Khalsa (with Yogi Bhajan), *Exploring the Myths and Misconceptions of Kundalini*, article written in the book *Kundalini, Evolution and Enlightenment*, edited by John White, (Garden City, New York: Anchor Press/Doubleday and Company, 1979), p. 140
118. Lilian Silburn, *Kundalini: The Energy of the Depths*, translated by Jacques Gontier, (Albany, New York: State University of New York Press, 1988), p. 124
119. Ibid., pp. 39-40
120. The "Integral Yoga" of Aurobindo is not to be confused with the "Integral Yoga" of Haridas Chaudhuri or the "Integral Yoga" of Yogiraj Sri Swami Satchidananda
121. Sri Aurobindo, *Letters on Yoga,* (Pondicherry, India: Sri Aurobindo Birth Centenary Library, Sri Aurobindo Ashram, 1972), Part I, Vol. 22, p. 73
122. Ibid., p. 74

123. Vasant V. Merchant, *Sri Aurobindo, The Tantra and Kundalini*, article written in the book *Kundalini, Evolution and Enlightenment*, edited by John White, (Garden City, New York: Anchor Press/Doubleday and Company, 1979), p. 87

124. Yogi Bhajan, quoted by M.S.S. Gurucharan Singh Khalsa (with Yogi Bhajan), *Exploring the Myths and Misconceptions Of Kundalini*, article written in the book *Kundalini, Evolution and Enlightenment*, edited by John White, (Garden City, New York: Anchor Press/Doubleday and Company, 1979), pp. 144-145

125. Itzhak Bentov, *Micromotion of the Body as a Factor in the Development of the Nervous System*, article written in the book *Kundalini, Evolution and Enlightenment*, edited by John White, (Garden City, New York: Anchor Press/Doubleday and Company, 1979), p. 316

126. Shakti Parwha Kaur Khalsa, *Kundalini Yoga: The Flow of Eternal Power*, (New York, New York: A Perigee Book, published by the Berkley Publishing Group, a division of Penguin Putnam, Inc., 1998), p. 49

127. Ibid., p. 55

128. The Sivananda Yoga Center, Foreword by Swami Vishnu, *The Sivananda Companion to Yoga*, (New York, London, Sidney, Singapore: A Fireside Book; Simon and Schuster, 2000), p. 75

129. Swami Yogeshwaranand Saraswati, translated by Bala Brahmachari Dr. Ram Pyari Shastri, Ph. D., English translation revised by Swami Muktanand Saraswati, *The First Steps to Higher Yoga*, (Bharat, India: Yoga Niketan Trust), p. 319

130. Yogiraj Sri Swami Satchidananda, *Integral Yoga Hatha*, (New York, Chicago, San Francisco: Holt, Rinehart and Winston, 1970-1974), p. 148

131. Swami Yogeshwaranand Sarasati, translated by Bala Brahmachari Dr. Ram Pyari Shastri, Ph. D., English translation revised by Swami Muktanand Saraswati, *The First Steps to Higher Yoga*, (Bharat, India: Yoga Niketan Trust), p. 305

132. Ibid, p. 329

133. Harold J. Reilly and Ruth Hagy Brod, *The Edgar Cayce Handbook for Health through Drugless Therapy*, (Virginia Beach, VA: A.R.E. Press, Copyright 1975), p.113 (#3549-1 of the Edgar Cayce readings)

134. Richard Rosen, *The Yoga of Breath*, (Boston and London: Shambhala, 2002),   pp. 227-229

135. https://www.nationaljewish.org/conditions/medications/asthma-medications/alternative/nasal-wash-treatment

136. Bo Stapler, MD, "The Saline Solution to Covid-19?" June 26, 2020 https://medium.com/illumination/the-saline-solution-to-covid-19-bad3eca3626c

137. https://www.nationaljewish.org/conditions/medications/asthma-medications/alternative/nasal-wash-treatment

138. Bo Stapler, MD, article "The Saline Solution to Covid-19?" June 26, 2020 https://medium.com/illumination/the-saline-solution-to-covid-19-bad3eca3626c

139. Mirai, Published online 6-30-2020 "Covid-19: What if saltwater could protect us from serious forms of the disease?"

140. Scientific Reports, Published online January 31, 2019, "A pilot, open labelled, randomised controlled trial of hypertonic saline nasal irrigation and gargling for the common cold," https://www.ncbi.nlm.nih.gov/pmc/articles/PMC6355924/

141. Harold J. Reilly and Ruth Hagy Brod, *The Edgar Cayce Handbook for Health through Drugless Therapy*, (A.R.E. Press, 67th Street, Virginia Beach, VA23451, Copyright 1975), p.116 (#2475-1 of the Edgar Cayce readings Copyright 1971 by the Edgar Cayce Foundation. All rights reserved.)

142. Ray Stanford, *Spirit unto the Churches*, (Virginia Beach, Virginia: Inner Vision Publishing Company, 1987) p. xi

143. Ibid., p. xii

144. *A Course in Miracles*: The Course is in public domain, so there is no copyright. The former copyright holder, before the copyright was revoked, was Foundation For Inner Peace, P.O. Box 598, Mill Valley, CA 94942. The ideas represented herein are the personal interpretation and understanding of the author of this meditation manual.

145. T-3.V.9:1

146. T-13.III.10:2-5

147. T-3.VII.4:1-7
148. T-18.V.1-7
149. T-12.VI.1-7
150. Matthew 16:24-26
151. C-1.1:1-2, 6:3
152. T-3.IV.4:1-2
153. T-3.IV.4:3
154. T-13.VII.1-16
155. T-1.I.1-50
156. T-20.VIII.5:7-9
157. T-3.III.1-7; T-13.VIII.1-10
158. T-1.II. 1-6
159. T-3.III.1-7
160. C-1.1:1
161. W-pI.XV.2:2
162. T-17.II.6:1-3
163. W-pI.rIV.159.5:3
164. W-pI.44.2:1-4
165. T-25.VI.3:1
166. W-pI.rIV.161.9:3
167. T-31.VII.3:3-6
168. T-18.IX.5:1-4
169. T-2.VI.9:14
170. T-14.VII.7:1-8
171. T-12.VI.4:1-8
172. T-31.VII.10:6, 11:1, 15:7
173. C-3.4:1-12
174. T-18.IX.9:1
175. T-2.VI.9:13
176. T-18.IX.9:1
177. T-21.I.8:1-6, 9:1
178. T-12.VI.6:1-4
179. T-12.VI.7:1-3
180. T-11.III.3:3-5
181. T-11.III.4:6-7
182. T-4.VII.7:1-5, 8:1
183. T-4.VII.8:7-8
184. T-1.I.3:1-3
185. T-1.I.6:1-2
186. T-1.I.24:2-4
187. T-1.I.33:1-4
188. T-1.I.36:1
189. T-1.I.40:1-2
190. T-1.I.18:1-3
191. T-1.I.9:1-2
192. T-1.I.9:1-3
193. T-1.I.16:1-2
194. T-1.I.15:1-4
195. T-1.I.13:1-3
196. T-1.I.47:1-2
197. T-1.I.48:1-2
198. T-1.I.19:1-3
199. T-2.V.11:1-3
200. T-1.I.32:1-4
201. T-1.I.27:1-2
202. T-1.I.38:1
203. T-1.I.39:1-2
204. W-pI.rIV.159.4:1-6
205. T-7.XI.5:1-6

206. T-1.I.7:1
207. T-1.I.14:1-2
208. T-1.I.43:1
209. T-2.V.3:3-5
210. T-3.V.9:1
211. T-29.III.3:2-7
212. T-29.III.3:12-13, 4:1-4, 5:1-7
213. W-pI.rIV.158.8:3-4, 9:1-6, 10:1-5
214. T-25.II.7:3
215. C-In.1:4
216. T-31.V.4:1
217. T-4.I.2:8-14, 3:1-2
218. T-5.V3:7, p. 77
219. T-13.III.1:11, 2:1-3
220. T-13.III.2:8-9, 3:1-3
221. T-13.III.4:3-5, 5:1
222. W-pI.25.5:1-2
223. W-pI.93.5:1-9, 6:1-7
224. T-11.IV.5-1-6
225. T-16.V.6:5
226. T-13.X.11:1-6
227. T-16.V.3:7-8, 4:1-4
228. T-15.VII.1:1-7
229. T-17.III.4:5-8
230. W-pI.rII.105.1:4-8, 2:1-3
231. T-22.In.2:5-8
232. T-20.VI.8:1-5
233. T-1.III.1-10; T-2.I-IX; T-9.I-VIII
234. Kenneth Wapnick, *Absence From Felicity*, Copyright 1991 by the Foundation for *A Course In Miracles*, R.R. Box 71, Roscoe, N.Y. 12776-9506, pp. 93-94
235. T-4.II.8:1-4
236. T-23.IV.7:4
237. T-27.II.4:1-7
238. T-27.II.7:1-5
239. T-23.II.2:1
240. T-18.VIII.13:1-3, T-20.III.9
241. T-18.IX.13:1
242. T-22.II.12:1-3
243. T-22.II.12:7-8
244. Maria Valtorta, *The Poem Of The Man-God*, Volumes 1-5, Translated from Italian by Nicandro Picozzi, Revised by Patrick McLaughlin, Volume 1, pp. 17-18 (reprinted by Grafiche Dipro, 31056 Roncade TV, Italy for copyright holder Centro Editoriale Valtortiano sri, 03036 Isola de Liri (Fr), Italy.) Can be purchased from Editions Paulines, 250, boul. Saint-Francois Nord, Sherbrooke, QC, J1E 2B9—Canada.
245. T-17,VII.9:5
246. T-20.VII.2:1
247. T-20.VIII.9:1-2
248. Maria Valtorta, *The Poem Of The Man-God*, Volumes 1-5, Translated from Italian by Nicandro Picozzi, Revised by Patrick McLaughlin, Volume 1, pp. 65-66 (reprinted by Grafiche Dipro, 31056 Roncade TV, Italy for copyright holder Centro Editoriale Valtortiano sri, 03036 Isola de Liri (Fr), Italy.)
249. Ibid, p. 82
250. T-20.V.3:1-5
251. T-17.VI.4:1-6
252. T-20.VI.5:1
253. T-20.VI.5:6-7, 6:1
254. T-22.VI.14:1-7
255. T-18.V.6:1-7
256. T-14.X.9:4-7

257. T-22.VI.5:1-5
258. T-22.IV.4:1-7, 5:1-2
259. The experience Light vision with a partner, called "Blessing Meditation" is described in my meditation manual, *Christian Meditation Inspired by Yoga and "A Course in Miracles"*
260. T-22.In.3:2-9
261. T-8.IV.2:13, 3:1-11
262. T-8.V.2:3-12, 3:1-4
263. T-8.V.5:1-4
264. T-8.IV.4:6-11, 5:1
265. T-8.IV.6:3-5
266. T-8.IV.2:13
267. T-8.IV.7:5-6
268. T-8.IV.2:4-7
269. T-8.V.4:1-4
270. T-8.V.5:5-9
271. T-8.V.6:6-10
272. T-1.II.3:4-13
273. T-1.II.4:1-7
274. T-1.I.35:1
275. T-1.I.42:1-2
276. M-16.4-5
277. The path of darkness and the path of light are described in detail in my meditation manual, entitled *Christian Meditation Inspired by Yoga and "A Course in Miracles"*
278. Kenneth Wapnick, *Absence From Felicity*, Copyright 1991 by the Foundation for *A Course In Miracles*, R.R. Box 71, Roscoe, N.Y. 12776-9506, p. 287
279. Ibid, p. 287, altered version of this quotation in T-4.VI.8, p. 63
280. T-4.VI.8:2-3
281. W-pII.In.10:2-4
282. W-pI.rV.183.1-12
283. Inner Silence Meditation and contemplation are elaborated upon in my meditation manual, entitled *Christian Meditation Inspired by Yoga and "A Course in Miracles"*
284. W-pI.41.5:3
285. T-15.IV.1-9
286. T-18,VII.4:6-10
287. T-18.VII.5:6
288. T-11.In.3:2
289. T-3.V.10:5-8
290. T-15.VI.4:5
291. T-15.VI.6:5-8
292. T-15.VI.7:7
293. T-15.V.10:8-10, 11:1-6
294. T-15.IX.1:1-2
295. W-pI.41.7:2
296. T-8.VII.1:1-5
297. T-8.VII.13:7
298. T-8.VII.3:2-5
299. W-pI.44.8:1
300. W-pI.41.5:3
301. M-23.2:6-8, 3:1-2
302. M-23.4:1-4
303. T-5.V.2:8-11, 3:1-9
304. T-12.VII.13:2-6
305. T-12.VII.14:1-6
306. T-13.II.5:1
307. T-13.III.8:1-2
308. T-5.II.2:1-2; 10:7-8; 12:5
309. T-13.III.7:1-6, 8:1-7

310. T-7.VIII.1:1-11
311. T-7.VIII.1-6
312. W-196.8:3
313. T-6.II.3:1
314. T-7.VI.5:5
315. T-7.V.10:1-12, 11:1-6
316. T-7.II.2:1-2
317. T-7.V.3:1-5
318. T-7.VI.8:1-6
319. T-7.VIII.4:1-7
320. T-7.VI.2:1-5
321. T-7.VIII.3:2-3
322. T-7.VIII.3:6-12
323. M-17.2:1
324. T-21.II.2:2-7, 3:1-3
325. T-10.In.1:3
326. T-9.III.8:2
327. T-9.III.2:1-10, 3:1
328. T-9.III.5:1-4
329. T-9.III.6:1-8, 7:15
330. T-9.III.6:7
331. T-9.III.7:2
332. T-9.IV.1:2-6
333. T-9.IV.4:4-5
334. T-9.IV.5:3-6, 6:1
335. T-6.II.10:1-8, 11:1-2
336. T-6.In.1:3
337. T-6.In.1:7
338. T-6.I.4:6
339. T-6.In.1:3
340. T-6.In.1:7
341. T-6.In.1:3
342. T-6.In.1:7
343. T-6.In.1:4
344. T-6.I.13:2
345. T-19.III.4:7
346. T-2.V.15(6):1-6, Luke 23:34
347. M-23.4:5-7
348. M-23.5:1-8
349. T-6.I.13:1
350. T-14.X.7:1-2
351. T-8.III.4:1-8
352. W-pI.77.1:4-5
353. T-8.III.5:1-7
354. T-8.III.5:10-12, 6:1
355. T-17.VI.2-3
356. T-17.VI.6:1-7
357. T-17.VI.4:1-6
358. T-17.VI.5:2-3
359. T-17.VI.6:1-7
360. T-17.VI.7
361. T-5.I.3:1
362. T-25.VI.4:2-3
363. T-25.VI.4:2-3
364. T-2.IV.1:1-9
365. T-2.VI.4:1-6
366. T-2.VI.6:7-9, 7:1-8
367. T-2.V.5:1-3
368. T-10.IV.7:4

369. T-10.IV.7:1-6
370. T-10.IV.7:5
371. M-23.III.2:8
372. T-18.V.3:1-3
373. T-20.IV.8:4-12
374. T-3.IV.2:1-5, 3:1-6
375. T-2.VII.9:12-13
376. W-pI.99.3:2-4
377. T-4.VII.1:2-5 2:1
378. T-2.VIII.2.5
379. T-9.IV.5:5-6
380. T-2.II.5:1
381. T-2.II.6:4-10
382. T-11.VII.4:9
383. T-17.II.6:1-3
384. T-1.VI.2:1
385. T-1.VI.3:1-3
386. T-5.V.3:7
387. T-2.IV.2:1-3
388. T-1.VII.4:1-6, 5:1
389. T-1.VIII.5:11
390. T-1.II.3:1-3
391. T-1.VIII.5:7-11
392. T-3.I.6:5-6
393. T-2.III.1:1
394. T-3.III.1:7-9
395. T-3.III.1:9-12
396. T-3.III.5:4-5
397. T-14.VIII.2:10-13
398. T-14.IX.3:5-7
399. T-14.IX.3:2
400. T-14.IX.3:1-9
401. T-2.III.4:3
402. T-2.III.4:1
403. T-3.III.2:1-4, 3:1
404. T-7.VII.10:1-2
405. T-8.II.7:5-7
406. T-3.III.3:3-10
407. T-14.IX.4:1-7
408. Matthew 17:9-13
409. Mark 9:22-23
410. Luke 2:35
411. T-4.VII.3:4-5
412. T-4.VII.3:6
413. T-4.VII.3:7
414. T-4.VII.3:1-10
415. T-4.VII.4:4
416. T-4.VII.5:1-6
417. T-4.VII.4:5-6
418. T-4.VII.4:1-7
419. T- 4.I.2:1-4
420. T-4.I.3:1-2
421. T-4.I.4:1
422. T-4.I.4:4-7
423. T-4.I.5:1-7
424. T-14.XI.3:1
425. T-4.IV.10:1-3
426. W-pI.167.4:1
427. W-pI.167.3:1-2

428. T-19.IV(C)2:15
429. W-pI.167.1:5
430. T-6.V(A).1:1-7, 2:1-4
431. M-27.4:2-10, 5:1-5
432. T-12.VII.13:2-6
433. M-20.5:2-8
434. T-12.VII.15:1-4
435. T-18.VI.8:5-11
436. T-3.VII.6:11
437. M-24.1:4-11
438. C-3.4:1
439. T-19.IV.D.16. H
440. W-pI.rIII.138.10:1
441. T-12.VI.6.:1-4
442. The Way of the Explorer, Dr. Edgar Mitchell, G. P. Putnam's, (New York, New York: 1996) p. 133-134.
443. Ibid., p.157
444. Ibid., p.157
445. Ibid., p. 175
446. Ibid., p. 175
447. Ibid., p. 175
448. T-25.I.4:1-6
449. Thomas Matus, *Yoga and the Jesus Prayer Tradition* (Mahwah, New Jersey: Paulist Press, 1984), p. 141 (currently published by Asian Trading, Bangalore, India; distributed by Hermitage Books, New Camaldoli, 62475 Coast Highway One, Big Sur, CA 93920)
450. St. Symeon, the New Theologian, *Hymns of Divine Love*, translated by George A. Maloney, S.J., Dimension Books, (Denville, New Jersey), Hymn 22, lines 3-11, p. 107
451. Thomas Matus, *Yoga and the Jesus Prayer Tradition* (Mahwah, New Jersey: Paulist Press, 1984), p. 126-127 (published by Asian Trading, Bangalore, India; distributed by Hermitage Books, New Camaldoli, 62475 Coast Highway One, Big Sur, CA 93920)
452. Ibid., p. 127
453. T-10.IV.7:5-6, 8:1-7
454. Gopi Krishna, *Kundalini: Evolutionary Energy in Man*, (Boulder, Colorado and London, England: Shambhala, 1971), p. 138
455. Ibid., p. 207
456. T-11.III.5:6
457. T-11.III.4:6
458. T-11.In.3:1-10
459. T-16.VI.6:2-3
460. T-16.VI.4:5-6
461. T-18.IX.9:1
462. T-21.I.8:1
463. T-12.VII.11:6-9, 12:1-4
464. T-12.VII.7:1-3
465. T-13.VI.10:1-3
466. T-13.VI.11:1-10
467. T-15.IX.3:1-2
468. T-21.I.8:2-6
469. T-22.II.12:1
470. T-22.II.12:7-10
471. T-22.II.13:1-7
472. T-26.II.6:5-10
473. T-14.IV.1:1-4
474. T-14.V.7:6-7
475. T-14.8:3
476. T-14.V.11:1-7
477. T-2.VI.9:13-14

478. T-26.III.2:1-6, 3:1
479. T-26.III.4:1-10
480. T-26.III.7:2-3
480. T-14.VII.7:1, 5-6
482. T-3.IV.7:3-11
483. T-2.IV.2:3
484. T-3.IV.1:6
485. T-3.IV.3:3-8
486. T-3.V.10:3
487. T-2.V.1:11
488. W-pI.107.2:1-5, 3:1-6
489. T-12.VIII.4:3-4
490. W-15.2:2-4
491. T-25.VI.3:1
492. W-158.pI.7:1, 3, 5
493. T-13.VIII.5:5
494. T-13.VIII.2:7
495. T-13.V.8:1-2, 9:2
496. T-31.VII.8:6-7
497. T-31.VII.11:5-7
498. T-20.VII.9:4-5
499. C-3.4:5
500. C-3.4:1
501. T-24.V.7:7
502. T-1.I.21:1-2
503. W-pI.91.1:1-7, 2:1-9, 3:1-5
504. T-13.V.11:1-2
505. C-6.3:3-6
506. C-3.4:7
507. C-6.1:4-5
508. T-3.I.6:5
509. T-2.III.1:1
510. T-2.III.4:1
511. T-27.VI.1:5
512. T-7.III.5:1
513. T-7.III.4:10
514. T-22.III.1:1-7
515. T-21.V.8:1-9, 9:1-5, 10:4-6
516. T-12.VIII.8:3
517. T-12.VIII.8:6
518. T-22.III.1:1-7
519. T-22.V.1-4
520. T-7.V.3:4
521. T-9.VII.7:6
522. Georg Feuerstein, *Sacred Paths:Essays on Wisdom, Love, and Mystical Realization*, (Burden, New York: published for the Paul Brunton Philosophical Foundation by Larson Publications, 1991), p. 72
523. W-93.7:6-7
524. W-pI.108.1:3-5, 2:1-3, 3:1-3
525. W-pI.108.1:4
526. T-22.III.1:4-7
527. M-28.4:6
528. T-3.I.6:5
529. T-21.V.5:1-11, 6:1-6
530. T-21.VII.8:5-7
531. T-21.VI.1:1
532. T-22.III.2:1-7, 3:1
533. T-22.III.4:3
534. T-21.V.10:5-6

535. T-14.VII.7:1-9
536. T-22.III.6:7-8, 7:1-6
537. T-21.VIII.5:1-4, 6-7
538. T-18.V.7:6
539. T-15.I.15:3-10
540. T-27.IV.2:3-6, 3:1-2.
541. T-15.I.15:11
542. T-2.V.5:1
543. T-15.IV.6:5-8
544. T-15.IV.4:4
545. T-15.II.5:4-6, 6:3
546. T-4.VII.1:5
547. W-pII.6:1-3
548. T-30.V.7:5
549. T-20.I.4:3
550. M-28.2:6
551. T-2.IV.4:1
552. M-22.4:5-6
553. T-26.V.11:10
554. Donald James Giacobbe, *Memory Walk in the Light: My Christian Yoga Life as A Course in Miracles* (Cottonwood, Arizona: Miracle Yoga Services, 2010) pp. 612-616
555. W-157.9:1-4
556. M-26.3:1-7
557. W-124.9:5
558. W-pII.6.5:1-3
559. C-4.4:2-5
560. M-28.6:1-9
561. T-19.IV.D.2:1
562. T-19.IV.D.2:3
563. T-19.IV.D.2:3
564. T-19.IV.D.3:4
565. T-19.IV.D.4:6
566. T-19.IV.D.10:2
567. T-19.IV.D.10:7-8
568. T-19.IV.D.11:1
569. T-19.IV.D.11:5
570. T-19.IV.D.11:6-7
571. T-19.IV.D.13:1-8
572. T-31.I.10:1
573. W-127.3:1-8.
574. W-60.1.1(46)
575. T-16.II.8:1, 4-8
576. T-21.II.3:4-8
577. W-pII.6.3:4
578. C-3.7:6-8, 3:8-1-5